PHAENOMENOLOGICA

SERIES FOUNDED BY H.L. VAN BREDA AND PUBLISHED
UNDER THE AUSPICES OF THE HUSSERL-ARCHIVES

155

RUDI VISKER

TRUTH AND SINGULARITY

Taking Foucault into Phenomenology

RUDI VISKER

TRUTH AND SINGULARITY

Taking Foucault into Phenomenology

KLUWER ACADEMIC PUBLISHERS

DORDRECHT / BOSTON / LONDON

A C.I.P. Catalogue record for this book is available from the Library of Congress.

ISBN 0-7923-5985-2 (HB)
ISBN 0-7923-6397-3 (PB)

Published by Kluwer Academic Publishers,
P.O. Box 17, 3300 AA Dordrecht, The Netherlands.

Sold and distributed in North, Central and South America
by Kluwer Academic Publishers,
101 Philip Drive, Norwell, MA 02061, U.S.A.

In all other countries, sold and distributed
by Kluwer Academic Publishers,
P.O. Box 322, 3300 AH Dordrecht, The Netherlands.

Printed on acid-free paper

Printed in the Netherlands.

"Waarachtig, 't is hier gezellig"

Voor André
van Nescio's *Uitvreter*

TABLE OF CONTENTS

ABBREVIATIONS

The following is a list of cross-chapter abbreviations for Heidegger, Foucault, Merleau-Ponty and Levinas. Further abbreviations for these or other authors which are restricted to a chapter or a section thereof will be introduced in the notes. When appropriate the English pagination will be followed, after the solidus, by the pagination of the original.

Throughout this book all italics, unless otherwise indicated, will be my own. Whether or not a reference is given, double quotation marks, even around single words, always indicate that I am using a term by the author I discuss. Single quotation marks will be used for all other cases.

Heidegger:

BT   *Being and Time* (transl. J. Macquarrie & E. Robinson), Oxford, Basil Blackwell, 1988; *Sein und Zeit*, Tübingen, Max Niemeyer, 1979 (15th edition).

GA   followed by the number corresponding to Heidegger's *Gesamtausgabe*, Frankfurt a.M., Vittorio Klostermann. Details are given when first introduced.

Foucault:

AK   *The Archaeology of Knowledge* (transl. A.M. Sheridan-Smith), London, Tavistock, 1974.

ODis   *The Order of Discourse*, in R. Young (ed.), *Untying the Text: A Post-Structuralist Reader*, Boston/London and Henley, Routledge, 1981.

OT   *The Order of Things. An Archaeology of the Human Sciences* (transl. anon.), London, Tavistock, 1977.

Merleau-Ponty:

PP   *Phenomenology of Perception* (transl. C. Smith), London and Henley/New Jersey, Routledge & Kegan Paul/The Humanities Press, 1981; *Phénoménologie de la perception*, Paris, Gallimard (Collection TEL), 1945.

PrP   *The Primacy of Perception and Other Essays on Phenomenological Psychology, the Philosophy of Art, History and Politics* (transl. J.M. Edie), Northwestern U.P., Evanston Ill., 1964.

PW   *The Prose of the World* (transl. J. O'Neill), Northwestern U.P., Evanston Ill., 1973; *La prose du monde*, Paris, Gallimard (nrf), 1969.

S   *Signs* (transl. R.C. McCleary), Evanston Ill., Northwestern U.P., 1964; *Signes*, Paris, Gallimard (nrf), 1960.

SO   *Merleau-Ponty à la Sorbonne - résumé de cours* 1949-1952, Grenoble, Cynara, 1988.

TLC   *Themes from the Lectures at the Collège de France 1952-1960* (transl. J. O'Neill), Northwestern U.P., Evanston Ill., 1970; *Résumés de cours. Collège de France 1952-1960*, Paris, Gallimard (Collection TEL), 1968.

VI   *The Visible and the Invisible. Followed by Working Notes* (transl. A. Lingis), Northwestern U.P., Evanston Ill., 1970; *Le Visible et l'Invisible suivi de notes de travail*, Paris, Gallimard (Collection TEL), 1964.

Levinas:

CPP   *Collected Philosophical Papers* (transl. A. Lingis), Dordrecht/Boston/Lancaster, Martinus Nijhoff/Kluwer, 1987.

DF   *Difficult Freedom: Essays on Judaism* (transl. S. Hand), London, The Athlone Press, 1990; *Difficile Liberté. Essais sur le judaïsme* (3rd edition), Paris, Albin Michel (biblio essais), 1976 (1963[1]).

EE   *Existence and Existents* (transl. A. Lingis), Martinus Nijhoff, The Hague, 1978; *De l'existence à l'existent* (2nd edition), Paris, Vrin, 1990 (1947[1]).

TI   *Totality and Infinity. An Essay on Exteriority* (transl. A. Lingis), Dordrecht/Boston/London, Kluwer, 1991; *Totalité et Infini. Essai sur l'extériorité* (4th edition), The Hague/Boston/Lancaster, Martinus Nijhoff/Kluwer, 1984 (1961[1]).

TO   *Time and the Other (and additional essays)* (transl. R.A. Cohen), Duquesne U.P., Pittsburgh, 1987; *Le temps et l'autre* (2nd edition), Paris, Quadrige/P.U.F., 1985 (1948[1]).

OB   *Otherwise than Being or Beyond Essence* (transl. A. Lingis), Dordrecht/Boston/London, Kluwer, 1991; *Autrement qu'être ou au-delà de l'essence*, Dordrecht/Boston/London, Kluwer, 1988 (1974[1]).

One does not write solely for oneself,
or solely for truth, but not simply for others either.
One writes.

M. Merleau-Ponty

INTRODUCTION

THE PART OF THE SUBJECT

At the origin of these essays, an increasing weariness produced by all those attempts to oppose what came to be known as Foucault's 'post-structuralism' to phenomenology – as if the two were incompatible and as if one could only proceed with thought after having chosen sides. And an equal reluctance to join those who pretended they could carry on as they had before since, quite obviously, there were no sides to choose, 'Foucault' being but the latest example of a relativism that one could easily ignore since it had, like all relativism, already refuted itself by daring to speak. And, finally, behind that weariness and that reluctance, a suspicion that what these two reactions to 'Foucault' had in common was a refusal to go 'toward the things themselves' and thus a refusal to approach the texts that we refer to by that proper name as we would approach other phenomena: not as the body-object of a thought that we would have to locate as coming either 'before' or 'after' phenomenology, but as a series of statements that appear to us in a certain way and whose appearing reveals to us something about our own, finite being. I am thinking, for example, of those passages in *The Order of Things* in which Foucault tried to show how what we thought to be discontinuous, opposing positions, really belonged to a same 'archaeological' soil and how what we considered to be in continuity (like Natural History and biology) was in fact marked by the harsh caesura that separated two such 'epistemes'. The bewilderment with which one read these statements was not, I think, caused by the immense erudition displayed in them. It was rather, I am inclined to believe, the expression of a certain unease with which we discovered that from a certain point of view all those magnificent fortresses which people – and not the least important – had erected in order to gain immortality in that great and ongoing battle for the truth, were no more than ripples on the surface of what Foucault called knowledge (*le savoir*), or, at best, positions whose effort to win that fight suddenly strikes us as grotesque once the archaeologist has taught us to recognize in them the "tines" of a fork which provides them with their common 'ground': "If we question Classical thought at the level of what, archaeologically, made it possible, we perceive that the dissociation of the sign and resemblance in the early seventeenth century caused these new forms – probability, analysis, combination, and universal language system –

to emerge, not as successive themes engendering one another or driving one another out, but as a single network of necessities. And it was this network that made possible the individuals we term Hobbes, Berkeley, Hume, or Condillac" (OT 63).

'The individuals we term ...', – it is this depersonalizing syntax and the long list of names to which it gives rise, that betrays what was really at stake in *The Order of Things* : not a history of ideas or a history of opinions, but a dispassionate attempt to unearth the "general system of thought" (OT 75) which made possible the interplay of simultaneous and apparently irreconcilable opinions. But an attempt that had the strange force to make *us* feel insecure: what if there would be a similar network which made *us* possible? What if one day *we* would be part of a similar list?

Anti-relativism could point as much as it liked to the underlying performative self-contradiction in which this 'relativism' seemed to trap itself as soon as it was brought down to the level of its theses[1], it could not prevent Foucault from playing foul and giving, instead of a thesis that would summarize his position, example upon example that managed to both *fascinate* and *irritate* his readers. Irritation of course with the iconoclasm with which the archaeologist seems to want to toss our history books into the paper shredder; irritation also with the air of superiority with which he dismissed as a "tempest in a teapot"[2] what until then had seemed of highest importance. Fascination with that gaze which seemed to come from without, with that knowledge that seemed fundamental and representative of a deeper wisdom because it appeared to have tapped the very source of knowledge itself. But also irritation in the fascination since Foucault, not wanting to place that source in our subjectivity, deliberately made it inaccessible: "it is not possible for us to describe our own archive, since it is from within these rules that we speak" (AK 130). Irritating was not so much Foucault's idea that our knowledge had to be emancipated from the sovereignty of 'the' subject and that it could only be understood when we shifted its source to "an anonymous field whose configuration defines the possible position of speaking subjects" (AK 122). For we might have been

---

1. E.g. H. SIEGEL, *Relativism Refuted. A Critique of Contemporary Epistemological Relativism*, Dordrecht, D. Reidel, 1987; H. PUTNAM, *Reason, Truth and History*, Cambridge U.P., 1981, esp. pp.150-73 on Foucault's (self-defeating) relativism. I have found David CARR's 'Welt, Weltbild, Lebenswelt. Husserl und die Vertreter des Begriffsrelativismus' a great help in trying to approach the return of relativism in contemporary thought somewhat differently (in E. STRÖKER (ed.), *Lebenswelt und Wissenschaft in der Philosophie Edmund Husserls*, Frankfurt a.M., Vittorio Klostermann, 1979, pp. 32-44).

2. Cf. OT 262: "Their controversies may have stirred up a few waves and caused a few surface ripples; but they are no more than storms in a children's paddling pool." Foucault is speaking here, in the heady days of Althusserianism, about Ricardo and ... Marx!

prepared to give up our sovereignty had someone only told us what our submission consisted in, what form that anonymous field had, and what position we occupied in it. What disturbed us was that Foucault refused to become that someone who would finally reveal to us the outside of our thought and thus the significance of our significance, the meaning of our meaning. Unwilling to take the role of the new high priest of our existence, Foucault infuriated us because he confronted us with our fascination with what he refused to reveal and because he understood and dared to name that fascination: "they cannot bear (and one cannot but sympathize) to hear someone saying: 'Discourse is not life: its time is not your time; in it, you will not be reconciled to death' " (AK 211).

Instead of declaring the death of the subject, as our histories of philosophy would have us believe, it would seem that Foucault's archaeology was involved in a much more intricate attempt to 'de-centre' the subject: in pulling the subject out of the centre which it traditionally occupied, it was also suggesting that we should perhaps reconceive what we mean by 'death', 'mortality' and 'finitude'. For the decentred subject is a subject that is not only dependent on a law which lays down "what can be said" (AK 129 – Foucault's most succinct definition of an "archive"), but above all a subject that would either like to find access to that law (and thus to take up its place in the centre again) or, if that proves to be impossible, to simply consider itself and its own speech as a mere effect of a discourse that it doesn't control. But Foucault, as we have seen, frustrates both these ambitions: if 'discourse' does not reconcile the subject to death, it is not because discourse stands for the death of the subject, for that strangely anonymous structure into which it would disappear, but because it confronts the subject with the conditions of its appearance and with its desire to have access to these conditions. In frustrating that desire, in denying the subject access to its own 'archive', *Foucault is redefining the subject as that instance that would like to, but cannot disappear*. Discourse does not speak or think for us, it is not an anonymous subject that takes over the burden of subjectivity for us. Discourse, to the contrary, is what provides that burden with its weight since it puts the subject in a position in which it is neither fully constituting, nor fully constituted. A subject that would 'disappear' completely in its de-centredness, that would be completely absorbed in something else of which it is only the dependent effect, would not suffer from that burden, for the simple reason that it would no longer be there to feel its weight. A discursive objectivism would be but the other side of the sort of subjectivism that 'Foucault' rightfully attacked[3]. Indeed, nothing would be gained if 'discourse' would simply have moved us, so to speak, from a subject that knows of no death to a death that no longer has a subject. The expression 'the death of the subject' only makes sense if it refers to a subject which, in being expelled from its traditional place in the centre, also finds itself bereft of the comfort of a decentred 'en-soi' where its speech would no longer have anything to do with it, since it would be spoken in its stead. Far from being itself an anonymous subject, 'discourse' is simply making *our own* subjectivity more anonymous, and less in our control than we had hoped it to be. And it thereby changes the meaning of our 'death'. 'Death' loses some of its terror, since it comes to stand for that situation where we will be finally relieved of the burden of having to speak a speech the meaning of which does not simply originate in us. But 'death', while drawing nearer to us, also becomes more elusive, since henceforth the meaning of our finitude and our mortality lies not in us preparing for that black hole into which, at the 'end' of our existence, we will disappear, but in our not being permitted to disappear. We may not be the ones who decide about "the difference between what can be said and what actually is said", there may be something called discourse which is establishing that difference for us and thus offering us "the positions and the functions that we could come to occupy", it is nonetheless we who speak and who have always already occupied such positions.

It is that originary delay, that de-centredness which we have with respect to our own discourse or our own archive, which explains why we find ourselves so troubled by Foucault's message. What we discover when we read *The Order of Things* is not that for each and every epoch, there is a hidden causality (called 'archive', *'savoir'*, 'discourse' or *'episteme'*) that had pre-programmed whatever statements people had uttered or written down. We discover that there are a vast number of things which had been said in other epochs, which we could no longer say and which nevertheless, as Foucault shows, somehow made sense for them. And we start to suspect that similarly our own effort to make statements that our contemporaries could

3. My reason for 'bracketing' Foucault's name here, is that, as I said before, one should strive to distinguish between the way his texts appear to us and the way they appeared to him. Indeed, the historical Foucault was perhaps more on the side of a discursive objectivism (the 'subject' is dead, everything of man lies outward) than I am suggesting here (for details cf. my *Michel Foucault. Genealogy as Critique*, London/New York, Verso, 1995). The point to remember here is that such 'anti-humanist' enthusiasm for *The Order of Things* by Foucault and others, was but the flip-side of humanist 'subject-centred' rejections of it. These historical reactions divide between camps the mixture of fascination and irritation with which we today still 'respond' to that book's 'message'.

take seriously, secretly obeys a hidden order that would make no more sense to them as theirs to us.

*

As I try to show in the essays contained in the first section of this book ('Truth and Finitude'), the sort of picture that begins to emerge once one concentrates on the effects Foucault's archaeological texts seem to have on us, is not all that different from the one phenomenologists like Heidegger and Merleau-Ponty are offering us in their reflections on truth, finitude and death. Not that all these authors are saying the same thing, but the thought of each one touching on that of the others leaves room for an alliance which they might not have liked, but from which we could be the ones to profit, as long as we do not take the parallels that are thus drawn to be the pillars of a bridge on which we could stand and hover over the history of our most recent past so that we could 'make up' our minds and leave the scenery thus displayed, richer and wiser than we were before. My concern is not doxographical, I do not wish to 'compare' in these essays Foucault 'to' Heidegger or 'to' Merleau-Ponty. Here and elsewhere in this volume, I am, to the contrary, trying to break out of a history of ideas less interested in the thought of a thinker than in the fact that he is the one who owns it. Thought is not a matter of possession and one should not flatter oneself for having made the thought of a philosopher accessible, when all one has in fact done is to have restored his property rights. Proper names, I should hasten to add, are important, perhaps more so in so-called Continental Philosophy than elsewhere; but they do not refer to the thought of a thinker who fully controls it, they merely indicate that point where a certain 'unthought' (Heidegger), in attaching itself to a thought, has rendered it to a certain extent *inaccessible* and *unrepeatable* for those who come 'after' it. One can, to be sure, share everything with an author – except his way of being dispossessed by that which, in withdrawing, allows him to think. If we wish to take seriously a notion like *das Ungedachte*[4], we should stop congratulating ourselves for having made the thought of someone else accessible and try to reach for that point where, although we no longer have the feeling that we fail to understand what the other says or fail to see what he is trying to show us, the distance between him and us is greater than it was before, simply because in trying to understand him we also had to take into account what he had to leave out of the picture in order to draw at all.

4. Cf. S. IJSSELING, 'Das Ungedachte im Denken und das Ungedachte im Sagen', in H. KIMMERLE (ed.), *Das Andere und das Denken der Verschiedenheit*, Amsterdam, B.R. Grüner, 1987, pp. 151-7.

There is, then, an asymmetry between an author and his readers, which, due to a false humility on their part, is all too often forgotten. Or repressed. For there is something utterly disturbing and highly unpleasant in having to admit that, notwithstanding our best efforts, in the end (but when have we reached it? – for we should never rule out that we did not read well enough), communication between him and us is interrupted because the unthought for him is what he did not have to think in order to formulate his thought, whereas it is what we should try to think at all costs, if we are to avoid merely becoming disciples who mistake the thought of an other for a thought of their own.

One would misunderstand the ethos of reading that I am trying to convey here, were one to simply read in these last lines the covert expression of an ambition to think for oneself. The point is rather that in allowing Foucault, Heidegger, Merleau-Ponty and so many others in this volume to have what would no doubt be considered illicit contacts from the point of view of a history of ideas obsessed with rendering thought accessible, I am trying to find out what it means that we, today, are not exempted from the task of thinking. If there is any ambition in the pages that follow, it is not to generously offer the reader new insights, but to leave him with the impression that this book – these 'essays' – has made him poorer than he was before and that there is something which has not been thought for 'us'.

*

One need not, then, make one's way back to Protagoras (as our textbooks present him) or to Pirandello (as the French translated him[5]) to suspect that 'truth' and 'singularity' might be more intimately connected than the brutal

---

5. 'Chacun sa vérité' is the title of the French translation of Pirandello's wonderfully complex 'parable in three acts' *Così è (se vi pare)* (literally: 'it is such (if it appears to you)'). One need only read this play in order to see that it suggests a reading that goes beyond the vulgar 'to each his own truth'. For example in its last lines:

> *The prefect*: Ah! But no! For yourself, madam, you must be the one or the other! *Ms. Ponza*: No, sirs. For me, I am the one that one believes me to be! (She throws a proud look *through her veil* on the whole company and *withdraws*. A silence). *Laudisi*: You see, ladies and gentlemen, how the truth speaks! (A defying ironic glance). Are you satisfied? (Bursts out in laughter). Ah! ah! ah! ah! (Curtain).

My italics indicate the Heideggerian reading. But there is, in the whole play, a sort of 'raw being' to Ms. Ponza who seems to demand from us 'creation for there to be adequation' (Merleau-Ponty). Whereas Laudisi, the sophist, seems to have just read Foucault's *Discipline and Punish*: his point is that there is an 'inquisitory' moment to the sort of truth the prefect and the rest of the crowd are looking for. He is the only who realizes that the veil of Ms. Ponza is not just an obstacle between us and the truth...

oxymoron of a true singularity or a singular truth ('chacun sa vérité') would suggest. As always, the difficulty comes with the smallest word, but philosophy as I have just suggested would not be the practice it is, had it not already assumed that difficulty. If it were only about 'truth', then argument would prevail, and it could, like science, forget about its past. But whereas to argue with a painting or a religion is merely to display one's lack of education, one would be equally mistaken to locate philosophy entirely within a sphere of 'meaning' that some, like Habermas (but in a different context), like to oppose to 'validity'. Perhaps more than anything else, philosophy should come to mind as a prime example of a practice that escapes or undermines such neat oppositions. One does not fully understand it if one restricts it to a quest for a truth that is the opposite of falsehood. There is, to be sure, that sort of truth in philosophy. There are 'validity claims' and they should be taken seriously. But, as we all know, the difficulty is precisely that before we can debate these claims, we must be able to hear them and that before these claims can claim anything, they need quite literally to be understood. And to understand them is to take them on their own terms, which demands not just that we learn each time a new language, but that we allow it to transport us into a world to which it is at once the key, and the door and all that lies behind it. Validity does not come apart from meaning. It is to their interconnection that we refer when we speak of the world of Plato or Novalis, as we speak of that of Henry James or Arthur Miller. But since we are not worldless beings, it would seem to be unduly optimistic to rule out in principle that we should experience difficulties living in all these worlds at once, or even consecutively. It is our own inscription in a world that sometimes can block our access to the world of another philosopher and that explains the fact that although we might be able to reconstruct internally what he has to say, we nonetheless feel unable to share the passion with which he states his case. We might be able to teach his work in our class, but we cannot make use of his ideas for our own thought. They leave us indifferent, not because we judge them to be without value, but because we find ourselves unable to pass judgement in these terms. We may, of course, be wrong in this and find that what we took to be a sign of our finitude was but an excuse for our laziness. But what this shows is that the connection between 'meaning' and 'validity' or between 'singularity' and 'truth' may be such that the finitude of the subject which follows from that connection includes its inability to know at what point exactly these dimensions cross. But it does not show that they do not cross at all and it would thus be equally unwise to suspect behind every inability to judge an unwillingness to do so. A subject that would always be able to judge the claims of another would not be decentred. But a subject that could identify, and put to its own use its inability, would have appropriated its own decentrement and it would not be finite either. What this means is that the so-called 'transcendence' of truth cannot simply be played off against the 'particularism' of those who are accused of 'immanentizing' truth into a finite, particular context. What is overlooked in this discussion between the so-called defenders of 'modernity' and those of 'postmodernity' is that the very 'finitude of truth' – if there is any sense to this expression – is not opposed to its transcendence. Even the 'finite' subject of a 'finite' truth is exposed to truth's transcendent claims, but this 'transcendence' does not just come from a validity which breaks all contexts of 'meaning' asunder. It is equally situated on the side of a 'meaning' which may or may not be in play when a subject finds itself unable to draw the line between what is true and what is not.

As these last lines suggest, it is not just the desire to account for the complexities of philosophy as a practice of truth, which has prompted me to let the whole of my first section rest on the distinction between a 'truth' which is opposed to falsehood and a Truth which is not. As I try to show there, what Foucault calls 'discourse' and Heidegger, in his later work, 'aletheia', seems to touch on something that one misses if one thinks that to understand an utterance one needs to be able to bring to mind the reasons with which the one who uttered it would defend its validity, and then to assess these reasons on one's own account. Not that these reasons as such would be inaccessible – as I pointed out before, The Order of Things is precisely a book that attempts to show how what strikes us as primitive or unreasonable in the thought of someone like Cardan or Paracelsus, starts to make more sense and can even be considered highly sophisticated once one realizes how these authors, in formulating what they said, were conforming to a different distribution of the sayable and the unsayable than we are. We need not know what our own 'discourse' consists in, in order to experience a certain incapacity to respond "in the performative attitude of the participant" (Habermas) with either a 'yes' or a 'no' to the 'validity claims' of the other. As I learned from Ian Hacking's efforts to make what is at stake here respectable to an audience that would otherwise dismiss it as 'relativism'[6], the basic intuition behind notions such as 'discourse' is that

---

6. My debts to Hacking are immense: see especially his 'The Accumulation of Styles of Scientific Reasoning', in D. HENRICH (ed.), Kant oder Hegel? Über Formen der Begründung in der Philosophie, Stuttgart, Klett-Cotta, 1983, pp. 453-65 and his 'Language, truth and reason', in S. LUKES and M. HOLLIS (eds.), Rationality and Relativism, Oxford, Blackwell, 1982, pp. 48-66. But I would probably have missed the importance of his work, had I not already been influenced by a number of essays by Bernard Waldenfels (quoted below) which seem to point in the same direction.

before we can judge about the truth or the falsehood of a proposition, we have first to take it seriously as a candidate for a truth value. And we cannot exclude that the foreignness of the other may be due to him and us not sharing the same class of sentences that have a possible truth value. What is on offer as true or false may vary among us, due to the interference of something that Foucault calls 'discourse', Heidegger 'aletheia' and Hacking 'styles of reasoning' or even, defying Davidson's celebrated critique of the term[7], 'conceptual schemes' (consisting not, as in Quine, of sets of sentences held for true, but of sets of sentences that are candidates for truth or falsehood, and thus escaping Davidson's argument). What non-philosophers call the scandal of philosophy (its lack of progress, etc.), may very well be due to the fact that every philosophy worthy of the name consists of such a conceptual scheme – the unthought consisting of the class of sentences that, within that style of reasoning we call 'Plato', 'Levinas', etc., does not (can not, need not) have a possible truth value. What Hacking says about Paracelsus and other manufacturers of 'hermetic lore' is perhaps a more common experience than he seems to suggest: "What we have to learn is not what (the others) took for true, but what they took for true-or-false"[8]. And, as I suggested before, once we have learned that, we have thought what for them remained (could remain, had to remain...) unthought, we have opened an 'archive' that they could not open themselves, and we are more – or differently – alone than we were before.

*

Relativism may not be the best of terms to refer to what is at stake in this loneliness in which, as the title of my second section ('A silence which escapes intersubjectivity') suggests, something returns that does not let itself be consumed by the intersubjective. But neither does it simply originate in the subject. What I call 'silence' there and elsewhere in this volume, is neither voluntary nor imposed and if it escapes the intersubjective, it is because it also escapes the subjective. Something that does not have its source in the subject, silences it, as it were, from within and somehow isolates it from the others, even if it would give whatever it takes to be with them. To be sure, this something (which, as one has understood, is not a thing) points to a passivity at the heart of the subject, but it is a passivity that renders 'impassive', it is an 'impassibility' that is not the denial of a prior 'passibility', and if it leaves the subject 'indifferent' to the appeal of the

7. D. DAVIDSON, 'On the Very Idea of a Conceptual Scheme', *Proceedings and Addresses of the American Philosophical Association*, 1974 (47), pp. 5-20.
8. 'Language, truth and reason', p. 60.

Other, this indifference itself cannot be qualified by that appeal, it does not secretly have to recognize it before turning it down. As those who know Levinas will have recognized, what I am trying to formulate here, in terms which closely resemble his own, is precisely what he has anathematized. But at what a cost! Man is put before the choice of being either a tree in a forest or fully without roots, he is either for himself or he is for the other, and once the appeal of the Other has put us before that alternative, everything in us that does not respond to that appeal is but the accomplice of the violence with which we resist leaving our 'self'[9]. The only passivity that Levinas allows for is what one could call an interpassivity: a passivity which from time immemorial has "tied" and "vowed" the subject to the Other, *before it was tied or vowed to itself.* To deny that 'tie', that prior 'attachment' would be to put oneself at one's own origin, to play off the 'principle' against the 'an-archical', and to prefer the war of Being to the peace of the Otherwise than Being. I do not want to turn Levinas into a caricature and as I hope to prove to those who feel that I am doing him an injustice in portraying him the way I just did, there is perhaps no author in this volume whom I have read with more patience and respect. But my impression stands as strong as before that Levinas's impatience with what he calls 'interiority' ("we must denounce," he says somewhere and it is not a *hapax*, "all that constructs itself as interior world, as interiority") follows from the prior and unjustified 'decision' – but it is a decision he never had to 'take', it is the 'unthought' that took him and rendered him his thought – that singularity is nothing if not ethical.

As the rest of the essays in this second section make regrettably clear, one does not turn against Levinas without being forced to give up on some of those in whose companionship one would have hoped to remain forever. I should never have expected to feel the need to leave the climate of Merleau-Ponty's philosophy, whose texts had inspired me with the idea of an attached, decentred subject tied to something of which it was neither the source nor the mere effect – and thus with the sort of subject that would fit my way of introducing 'Foucault' into phenomenology. But there comes a point where one has to wonder whether one is not simply reading one's own thoughts into the work of those that supposedly inspire us. I would not have included 'The Untouchable' (chapter 7), had I thought I were the only one to have stretched that extraordinary phrase ("what I cannot touch in the other, he cannot touch either") well beyond what was intended by it. But

---

9. To put this more fashionably, one would need to patiently 'deconstruct' Levinas's texts every time they bring up the animal or the plant and the tree to make a point about the human. It is to such a 'deconstruction' that the chapters on Levinas in this volume aim to contribute.

The Visible and the Invisible is an extremely complex text and one does not compensate for its sadly having been neglected for too long a time by now reducing it to a handful of fashionable quotes ("the originary explodes" ...) that make Merleau-Ponty look like a cross-breed of Derrida and Lacan. As I argue in 'A Western Problem', the problem with this new 'endo-ontology' of the 'flesh' and with the "wholly new concept of subjectivity" that it tries to forge, is not, as one has often thought, that in the end it moves in the direction of an asubjective phenomenology ("it is not I who sees, nor the other, but an anonymous visibility inhabiting both of us") but that, not unlike Levinas but in a totally different context, it is redefining the subject in such a way that it fully fits into intersubjectivity ("what is private to each is public to all"). No privacy! – the battle-cry with which Levinas mounts his attack on ontology and interiority – is rendered strangely superfluous by an ontology which, while refusing to think the subject as what is equiprimordially open and closed, now folds it in such a way that what closes it is the same as what opens it. The subject of endo-ontology is, to be sure, "attached" but there is nothing in it that attaches it, as it were, from within to this attachment – it is "attached" to a Being which links it to others.

My reason for no longer being satisfied with what this endo-ontology has to offer us, is not that in the end it lets compossibility triumph over incompossibility and Eros over Eris, or that there is no place for rupture, discord, radical dissensus, death or whatever in what looks like a philosophical reappropriation of the idea of a mystical body (chapter 8). Instead of a strange predeliction for linking subjectivity to pain, or a crypto-romantic coquetry with the lonely and the gloomy sides of existence, it is quite simply the wish to do justice to some of the phenomena that embarrass all of us today (racism, multiculturalism, Eurocentrism, nationalism, ethnocentrism, etc.) that makes me distrust any philosophy which leaves us without the means to understand the dynamics behind these particularisms. Instead of taking this upsurge of particularism at face value and then, depending on one's politics or ethics, choosing either for or against it, I think that we would be better advised to interpret what is happening here at the level of collective subjectivities as an attempt to solve a tension we are already familiar with from our analysis of individual subjectivities. Nationalism, for example, however factitious the 'imagined communities' it puts on offer may be, would not have the sort of success it sadly has, if it did not appeal to a certain longing in the subjects that it addresses. The longing, that is, to rid themselves of what we called earlier the 'burden of subjectivity'. As I see it, there are two sides to this burden and neither nationalism nor its critics are able to accept that the two together constitute the condition of a decentred subjectivity. Nationalism has no problem in affirming that we are attached to something that we cannot get away from (the first moment of decentrement), but it denies that we cannot get access to that 'something' (the second moment). Indeed, one of the first and basic moves of nationalism is to define what the nation consists in and who belongs to it. But to define that nation is to define its proper name, and thus to substitute the latter by what one could call with analytic philosophy a uniquely determining description. With the result that the proper name of that people, instead of being at best a kind of silent monument which reminds them that they have forgotten – or that they had perhaps never known – what it was that made them differ from others, now suddenly gives away its secret and starts telling them what they need to do in order to bear it with honour[10]. To put this slightly differently, one could say that nationalism constitutes one of the two obvious responses to the problem that something like the proper name seems to be posing to standard forms of particularism or universalism: the name, as it were, always leaves its job half done, it suggests that there is something proper to its bearer, but there is never 'enough' of the name to know what that something consists in, and yet always 'too much' to simply ignore what it thus singles out. Particularism compensates for this insufficiency of the proper name by adding on to it, whereas universalism always seems tempted to subtract from it[11]. But both react to the sort of decentrement to which the name testifies by its very insufficiency – particularism tries to appropriate the proper name by eliminating everything in it that seems 'outward', whereas universalism tries to get rid of it by treating it as a merely outward label with no ties whatsoever to what it serves to indicate. One could say that particularism tries to 'be' the name – thus ignoring that the proper name is never proper enough for the subject to fall together with it (it remains after all a signifier) – whereas universalism would like the name to be merely something that one 'has', and thus not more revealing about what 'belonging' means for us than any of our other belongings. Particularism thus forces an access to our attachment (and, as a result, does away with decentrement by placing itself in the centre again), whereas universalism in its more subtle forms typically

10. Nationalism's *proton pseudos* is not just that it is always inventing a past of its own, but that in making up such a fictive history, it inserts it within a time-structure in which the past is essentially a past *present*, and never a past which has never been present. In excluding the 'original past' and the 'immemorial' from that time-structure, nationalism can plead for a restoration of contact with an Origin that in being lost, has never left us and is still sending out its calls.

11. Here in particular (but also more generally), my debt to Lyotard's later work is undeniable: see his 'Le nom et l'exception', in H. NAGL-DOCEKAL and H. VETTER (eds.), *Tod des Subjekts?*, Wien / München, R. Oldenbourg Verlag, 1987, pp. 43-53.

will consider the idea that we find ourselves attached to something that we cannot get rid of, nor find access to, altogether suspicious and unrewarding and needing replacement by such ties as will allow us to be at once singular and universal.

These scant remarks on 'the name and the exception' do not, of course, aim to contribute to a political philosophy of nationalism or to a theory of proper names. They merely suggest that, if one wishes to come to grips with the massive return to roots in our contemporary world, it might not be the best strategy to bluntly identify such roots with a particularism that closes off a prior and more fundamental openness in us. As I try to argue repeatedly in some of the chapters in this second section, the sort of crisis that Europe is going through at the moment cannot be situated correctly if one keeps approaching it in the terms of this alternative. As is shown both by the rather artificial attempt to establish a European identity and by the embarrassment of those who can only see in that attempt an unwillingness to draw the right conclusions from their own analyses of 'Eurocentrism', the European problem is not just economic or political, but deeply philosophical. In the end, both Europe's defenders and its detractors, and even those whom it leaves profoundly indifferent, will have taken a position on the line which divides or unites 'Europe and its others' and they will have dealt in their own way with the difficulty of not letting in the expression 'European humanity' one of the terms absorb the other.

Whether they be European or otherwise, 'roots', as an expression for particularism, is something of a misnomer. It wrongly suggests that there is a part of man which is vegetative and which ties him to nature; and that there is another part in him which lifts him above it, and gives him the chance of cutting through those ties and becoming a member of a full-fledged humanity. What is forgotten when one, on the basis of this crudest of 'metaphysical' divisions[12], puts man before the choice of either being a plant (and thus nature) or letting himself be uprooted (and thus humanized), is that the problem for us humans is that we are not plants or trees: we have 'not enough' roots to be like them. But this need not mean that, *qua* humans, we have no roots at all. It could mean that roots do not belong to the 'facts' of human life, but to what one could call with Heidegger its 'facticity'. They do not determine us, nor do we simply have it in our power to determine what they mean for us. They confront us with

---

12. Although I think that there is indeed such an unpolished core at the heart of Levinas's *impressively subtle* metaphysics, I should like to add, as Heidegger once did with regard to Nietzsche, "but Levinas can pull it off!" (cf. *Die Grundbegriffe der Metaphysik. Welt–Endlichkeit–Einsamkeit* (Freiburg Lectures, winter semester 1929/30), GA 29/30, p. 111: "Aber Nietzsche kann sich das leisten. *Und doch ist das kein Freibrief*").

the difficulty of bearing what in us is neither simply universal nor charmingly singular. They confront us, that is, with an attachment that prevents us from becoming simply absorbed into the universal – and which thus lies at the source of our dignity since it makes us non-substitutable with others – but at the same time they place that dignity in a dimension where we are neither at home with ourselves nor fully out in the open and which thus afflicts us with a metaphysical unrest that at times can dissociate us from the others since at all times it dissociates us from – or rather: within ourselves[13].

*

Having said this, it should be clear that the sort of loneliness I refer to in the title of my third section ('The loneliness of a subject unable to disappear') is neither directly social, nor psychological. It is the loneliness of a being whose being consists in being decentred and its proper status is thus ontological. But this ontological solitude does not just derive, as Levinas suggests in an early text, from the fact that my existing constitutes an "absolutely intransitive element" since "to be is to be isolated by existing" and since "one can exchange everything between beings except existing" (TO 42). It is true, of course, that to be is to be separated and one would underestimate the complexities of Levinas's early work were one to forget that to be separated does not just mean for him that one *is* one's being, but that one is attached to it, and that this attachment also means that one suffers under the weight of a being to which one sticks like to a double one would like to but cannot get rid of. To be, Levinas stresses, is not just to be alone. It is to be alone with one's being, and thus in a sense not to be alone, since as soon as one is, one is with oneself, and since it is this 'with' which follows us as a shadow, which turns what looks like our privacy into an overcrowded place where we perpetually stumble over ourselves. It is no doubt these dramatic tones with which Levinas early on decided to make his own certain Heideggerian notions like 'mineness', 'thrownness' and 'facticity', which explains why everything in his work could come to depend on there being in the subject a desire to escape being. One need not doubt that there could be such a desire in order to have reservations about the sort of architecture Levinas is constructing for it, in his later 'ethical' work. As I suggested before, Levinas has an understandable tendency to claim that ethical responsibility singularizes us in a way that nothing else does. Only

---

13. Dissociation is not just a deficient mode of our being-with-others. It is, as I shall argue in the conclusion to this volume, the condition of a being in whose being something refuses to give way to its ek-sistence.

in ethics can the subject be disconnected from the self which haunts it as long as it is alone with its being, and still remain a self. But as I try to show in the opening chapters of this third section, this move toward an ethical redemption of the subject's desire to escape being, depends at least in part on the sort of picture one has of this desire. And Levinas's picture is both exceedingly gloomy and overoptimistic. Once more man is portrayed as a citizen of two worlds, and the dark glow that hangs over the first where he raises questions but gets no answers (for "Being does not respond to us", EE 23) would make the effort of life unbearable – even if life has its brighter zones, where living is enjoyable – were it not that man also encounters in himself an answer that was not preceded by a question. Responsibility gives life a meaning and an orientation which it lacks by itself. It makes it human by bringing a moment of peace in the constant struggle with the impersonal elements which are not just a threat to the joy of living, but to its very independence. This is the gloomy part of the story: ontology may allow man a being of his own, but this privacy necessary for the personality of the person is under a permanent pressure from the anonymous and impersonal element from which it arose. What Levinas calls the *il y a*, the Being without beings, relentlessly pursues its own course and although there must be times – for there are, after all, beings; we exist – where it graciously opens itself "to leave room for a private domain" (EE 99), it subsequently, by mere forgetfulness or sheer malice, endeavours to tear down the walls it had just erected. As if the life of the subject, before it is released by the Other, would be that delicate balance in which it had managed a *grand écart* on the ever widening banks of a swamp into which it can, and in its less "virile" moments (TO 72), will disappear. Such are the moments when we break down and realize that what we called 'meaning' was but the thin veil with which we tried to brighten up the cold indifference of a darkness in us – the very Being of our being! – that no amount of light could ever hope to thaw.

It is not to this indifference – it is not to this despair – that I ultimately give in, when after going in great detail through the other part of Levinas's story (a part that is of such an astonishing complexity, of such intricacy in its minutest detail, that one would wish admiration could drain that source of wonderment from which philosophy fatally drank), I nonetheless tentatively suggest that man is a being that has to reckon with something that does not reckon with him. This is not a pessimistic, nor a tragic view of man. It does not put the personal at the mercy of an impersonal that does not care about its failure or secretly enjoys it. Instead of opposing the personal to the impersonal, it tries to redefine them such that, as in our earlier example of the proper name, what seems at first sight not personal enough, can only do its job because of this apparent insufficiency. To be,

that is, is not just a transitive verb (one is one's being) or a reflexive one (one
is oneself, *on s'est*), it hovers between the transitive and the intransitive,
because in the moment of its transition it stumbles on something that
cannot be fully reflected in it: to be is to be one's attachments and these are
more intimate than the objects of other transitive verbs, and differently
exterior than that double to which, according to Levinas, my being chains
myself. As I try to illustrate with another example (the colour of our skin),
man's being is not so much intimate as that it is, if I may put this expression
of Lacan to my own use, ex-timate. And this ex-timacy which is not quite
inside nor quite outside, somehow seems to bring into disorder that nice
partition between the visible and the invisible which one finds, albeit in
different forms, in the phenomenology of Merleau-Ponty, Sartre or Levinas.
It is not just another 'in'visible which puts itself forward here, but it also
brings with it a new role for the 'visible'. Instead of merely being portrayed
as that realm where the Other gets 'reduced' to the same, the visibility of the
visible also deserves appreciation for offering both the Other and the same
protection from what is other in them. As I argue in the last chapter of this
section, Arendt's idea that man's freedom depends on there being a realm
in which he can *appear* and meet others whom it allows a visibility of their
own, becomes even more important once one realizes that the attachments
to which we owe (part of) our singularity are differently invisible for us than
they are for the others. There is no way of telling them or of making them
see why these attachments are important to us, because their very
singularizing force depends, as I have shown, on them escaping us. It is, for
example, because we do not know the meaning of that colour to which we
find ourselves attached, that we not only resent others who want to reduce
us to what in that colour is visible for them (and this is how I will define
racism), but also those who tend to think that they can share that invisibility
with us (and this is perhaps the saddest form of a well-meaning anti-
racism). Man's dignity is taken away from him when one robs him of what
remains invisible for him. And yet, as I find myself claiming against Rorty's
liberal idea that people wish to be left alone with "their own thing", our
reason for turning to others is precisely because that "own" thing which we
do not own and which rather owns us, is not something that we could bear
to be left alone with. What I called earlier our metaphysical unrest is what
makes us turn to others and what gives inter-subjectivity a place and a role.
But a role it isn't quite up to, since its capacity for 'psychological' comfort
is highly limited by the ontological discomfort which lies at its origin.
Which is why its place cannot be restricted to that – if it could, our lives with
others would be of a permanent disappointment – and why there is a deep
wisdom in its anonymous aspects (*das Man*) in which it unknowingly

repeats or incarnates those rules or structures which society has invented to protect its members from the embarrassment of losing face. *Larvatus prodeo*[14] – this does not mean that I hide from others what I keep for myself; it means that the symbolic structures of society allow me to dress in a cloak of visibility which protects me from what in me remains private – invisible – to me.

*

This is not, of course, to hand over subjectivity to Reason. But it is to affirm that there is more meaning in Being than that total lack of orientation which Levinas sees in it, but also more drama than Merleau-Ponty seems to have allowed in it. Indeed, I cannot help thinking that all the struggles for recognition of a group-specific particularity, or all the hopes of being recognized in some aspect or other of our facticity, would somehow lose their point, if, at bottom, in our "last reality" (as Levinas says), we would be tied to the Other before we are tied to ourselves, or if what ties us to ourselves at the same time ties us to others (as Merleau-Ponty seems to think). Man's uprootedness, as we have seen, does not leave him without 'roots': there is always both something too much and not enough of that something to fully come to rest. The particularisms I am trying to analyse in some of the chapters below forget, repress or try to make up for that 'not enough'. One does not satisfactorily reply to them by mirroring their blindness and forgetting the 'too much'. Man is 'not without' roots, his decentredness ties him to some 'thing' to which he neither has access (the 'not enough') and from which he cannot simply detach himself (the 'too much') since that attachment of which he is neither the source nor the mere effect somehow cannot be undone without undoing his singularity. The subject, as I shall argue again in the conclusion to this volume, is singularized by some 'thing' that refuses to become part of the order of meaning (signification). This some 'thing' which is not a thing does not 'appear' – like Levinas's face, it is not a phenomenon, it does not give itself, but it seems to indicate a different intrigue than the one Levinas has opposed to Being.

I shall leave it to the reader's curiosity to discover what the true name of that other intrigue is (I should add for those who insist on immediate gratification that my 'conclusion' is rather open-ended and that it gives little more than a clue). But there is an astonishing passage in *Otherwise than*

---

14. The expression is from Descartes. On his "masked do I proceed", Jean-Luc NANCY's excellent 'Larvatus Pro Deo' (sic), in ID., *Ego Sum*, Paris, Aubier-Flammarion, 1979, pp. 61-94.

Being that points at least in the direction we ought to be looking. It comes right at the beginning of the fifth chapter in a section whose title leaves nothing to imagine about Levinas's intentions ('The Subject absorbed by Being'). I should like to quote it in full, if only because it restores the context to the title I have given to this introduction: "Being's *esse*, through which an entity is an entity, is a matter of thought, gives something to thought, stands from the first in the open. In that there is indeed a kind of indigence in being, constrained to an other than itself, to a subject called upon to welcome the manifestation. (...) (It) follows that, outside of *the part subjectivity plays* in the disclosure of being, every game that consciousness would play for its own account would be but a veiling or an obscuring of being's *esse*, a lie or an ideology, whose status is difficult to establish without ambiguity" (OB 132). What makes this passage so crucial, both for Levinas and for us, is that it illustrates how his conviction that the subjectivity of the subject 'disappears' before Being drives him to an ethics that lies beyond Being in order to find a part which the subject can play for its own account. But it is perhaps no accident that this attempt to save the subjectivity of the subject through ethical responsibility strangely has to fall back on the same gesture which Levinas has just related to the indigence in Being. It is indeed striking that Levinas's ethical subject is *opened up* by the appeal of the Other and that, *formally* homologous to what Heidegger calls *Entschlossenheit* in *Being and Time*, the part that responsibility reserves for it is to hold open that openness (that *Erschlossenheit*) of which it is not the origin. The least one can say then, is that if Being is indigent, the Good seems similarly indigent, such that – at least on the reading of Levinas I am giving in this volume – outside of the part subjectivity plays in the Revelation of the Good or of God, every game that it would play for its own account is immediately unmasked as the result of an intoxication, as "illusion", "drunkenness" and a flight for the "irremissibility" of responsibility (OB 192 n21). Irresponsibility is not due to what does not respond in us, but to us trying to block off what always already responds. All silence is voluntary, not to respond is already to respond, and what fails to register in this *Antwortregister* is but an adult playing the role of the in-fant. The subject, that is, is defined by a saying that cannot, without violence, be absorbed into a said. Hence Levinas's strange sympathy for those skeptics[15] who were not in the least bothered by their critics blaming them for their inability or their unwillingness to synchronize the level of what they *said*, with that of them *saying* it. Against a long tradition that had treated skepticism as it had treated relativism, by

---

15. See Robert BERNASCONI's thoughtful 'Skepticism in the Face of Philosophy', in R. BERNASCONI and S. CRITCHLEY (eds.), *Re-reading Levinas*, Bloomington / Indianapolis, Indiana U.P., 1991, pp. 149-61.

catching it on the horns of a dilemma on which it would in either case bleed to death, Levinas remarkably suggests a way out for the skeptic. Far from being that irresponsible or sick subject that lacks either the willingness or the force to synthesize the time of his saying and the time of his said, the skeptic, instead of suffering from a transcendental pathology, would reveal the extent to which those who wanted to cure him are themselves ill. Skepticism, that eternal shadow of philosophy, would be its repressed other whose persistent return ought to be read as a symptom of what is lacking in philosophy's fixation on Being. Unwittingly, the skeptic would stand for the very subjectivity of the subject, his illness – the rift between his saying and his said – would, properly understood, point to the subject's only possible redemption: the part reserved for it in the ethico-religious intrigue of the infinite.

I hesitate to conclude, but there seems little room for concluding otherwise, that the remarkable immunity which we have seen a 'relativism' like Foucault's develop against the argument of self-refutation, points to another 'other' of philosophy, repressed in its turn by Levinas's Otherwise than Being. What 'returns' in relativism is not, I believe, a saying looking for a redemption it cannot find on the level of the said. Everything seems to indicate that the part of a subject, for whom a said that came too early to be ever absorbed into its saying, is the source of both its dignity and its misery, can only be written if one breaks with the old habit of staging a play for two characters: there is not only Being and Otherwise than Being, there is that mysterious *lèthè* of which Heidegger spoke and in which, if there is any logic in the essays that follow, one cannot but see the trace of a still otherwise than otherwise than being. Hence no doubt the philosophical importance of Lacan, too present in these pages to be cited frequently.

*

*   *

A volume of essays is not a book. It is what one could call a longer lie and, this introduction notwithstanding, one should thus expect it to get caught at some point or another in the web which it had itself spun. But this loss of control over a synthesis that one has failed to provide oneself (as the German kindly reminds us when it refers to collections like this one as 'Buchbindersynthesen') is perhaps the very point of ageing in which phenomenology, not without reason, has recognized what it calls a 'synthesis of transition'. Speaking for myself, I do not think that I would have been able at least to take some pride in it, were it not for the support and encouragement Rudolf Bernet has given this project from its earliest beginnings. I should like to thank him not only for his generous invitation to publish in this series and for the time he put into reading and critically commenting on a first draft of this book, but also for his willingness to accept that one cannot, without the risk of a total collapse, change a baroque construction like my own into the fine classicist structure which he would no doubt have preferred.

The dedication of this volume is to André Van de Putte who tolerated (in the classical sense of the word) my gradual usurpation of the office where all of these pages have been written.

I

Truth and Finitude

CHAPTER ONE

HEIDEGGER'S CAVE
BEING AND TIME ON DISAPPEARING EXISTENTIALS

The philosopher, Heidegger says somewhere, is "the friend of Being"[1] and he then goes on to explain that precisely because of this friendship the philosopher will have to die.

This death, however, need not be a physical death, it need not happen in some forlorn corner of the cave where the poor light of the hearthfire will not betray the cold dagger's steel. Philosophers today are no longer invited to drink the liquor from the poisoned chalice, they do not as a rule have to choose between either committing their books or their bodies to the flames. Such a death, violent as it may be, could in principle be prevented: Amnesty International could be alerted, or one could try to influence public opinion in the cave by collecting signatures and handing over petitions, and, as we all found out during the Gulf War, in the last resort the United Nations could send in their armies to restore the philosopher's right to the freedom of speech. But however effective such interventions might be, they would not restore Heidegger's peace of mind. For what if the poisoning happened in a less spectacular way? What if it had to do with the fact "that those living in the cave get interested in the philosopher? That they tell one another that one should have read this philosophy; that the cave decides to give awards and bestow honorary titles to the philosopher; that they even print his name on the frontpages of their journals and magazines? In short, that they start to admire him?" (GA 34: 84). If that is how the poisoning works – not by ostracizing philosophy but by giving it pride of place – the prospects of our interventions could be less bright than they may have seemed at first sight. Then the war to free philosophy from its bonds threatens to be without end. For it is no longer a matter of restoring the freedom of philosophical speech, since it is precisely speech itself which, for all its freedom, condemns the philosopher to be buried alive in a cave from which he may not escape, provided he does not misunderstand both himself and his task.

Such then is the death which, according to Heidegger, no true philos-

---

1. M. HEIDEGGER, *Vom Wesen der Wahrheit. Zu Platons Höhlengleichnis und Theätet* (Freiburg lectures, winter semester 1931/32), GA 34, p. 82.

opher ever sought to escape. And this death, Heidegger stresses, is not what supposedly happened to Socrates at the end of his life when he, as Plato tells us, was forced to drink from the chalice. For the poison that killed Socrates was not in the chalice: it was there all along and what Socrates had to "endure" was the permanent confrontation with death during his *Dasein* – with death not as something happening to his body, but as the undermining of the strength and power of his *Wesen*, of his ess*a*nce[2]. That philosophy will always die in the cave, that it will remain powerless in the ruling domain of the self-evident, only testifies, for Heidegger, to the fact that philosophy is, for essential reasons, a lonely enterprise (GA 34: 86). It should not try to engage in a discussion with idle talk, but neither can it disengage itself and seek refuge in some ironic feeling of superiority (GA 34: 85). At most it can hope to violently grab one or two from the mob and to force them out of the cave to which they will eventually have to return and die (GA 34:86).

I did not start off with this section from Heidegger's 1931 lecture course on the ess*a*nce of truth, to recall how lonely we have been or should have been, since we made friendship with Being and chose philosophy as our 'subject'. Nor did I simply summarize this passage in order to point to the 'obvious' link between what is being said here about the fate of the philosopher and what happened to Heidegger in 1933. What worries me is precisely that on the one hand this link seems so obvious, and that on the other hand, in one way or another – we will have to come back to that – right here and now, we might ourselves be exposed to the very risk Heidegger warned us about and then fatally succumbed to. What worries me is precisely the possibility that while we are on our way to attack or to defend Heidegger's assessment of the relation between philosophy and the public sphere, we might be ourselves falling prey to just the kind of popularity Heidegger took to be a symptom of the perhaps unavoidable crisis of philosophy. The recent 'Farias-affair' is there to remind us that we will not make this crisis any more avoidable by laughing away Heidegger's supposedly doting praise of loneliness; or by dismissing his reservations about the power of the "they", and by seeing in his concern about the fate of philosophy a mere expression of his lack of concern for the public sphere, his lack of *amor mundi*, of "love of the world". In saying this, I am not suggesting however that Heidegger got it all right, but I want to defend, at least for the time being, the legitimacy of his worries about the fate of a tradition that would be merely repeated, without any concern for the

2. Following Levinas I will write "ess*a*nce" to refer to the verbal character of Heidegger's "Wesen".

"original experience" (BT 266/SZ 224)[3] behind it, without any attempt at appropriation (*Zueignung*). And if I want to focus on these worries, if I refuse to discard them right away, it is not only because, given the situation we are in, it would be preposterous to do so, but also because they take us – indeed, they have already taken us – into the heart of our subject here, into the heart, that is, of *the* subject.

In fact, the whole of the Heideggerian discourse on the subject or on what ontologically precedes it but ontically does not seek to distinguish itself from it first of all and most of the time (*zunächst und zumeist*), – everything *Being and Time* has to tell us on Dasein before or after the subject, rests on the semantic chain of the 'proper', the 'appropriation', the 'authentic' and the 'own'. Heidegger's worries about the fate of philosophy and of tradition cannot be understood without investigating this chain which leads us from the symptomatological description of a possible, perhaps inevitable, "crisis" (the lack of *Zueignung*, of appropriation) to an aetiological level (*eigen, selbst, Man-selbst*) and further on to what looks at first sight like a therapeutic discourse on *Eigentlichkeit* and *Uneigentlichkeit*. And this discourse, which was perhaps too quickly dismissed as "the jargon of authenticity", is itself crossed as it were by another semantic chain around such terms as *Zerstreuung* (dispersion), *Verfallen*, *Abfallen* and *Zerfallen* (falling, dropping from..., decaying), *Schweben* (floating), *Bodenlosigkeit* (groundlessness), *leicht* and *schwer* (light/easy and heavy) and many others. The intertwining between these two semantic chains is, of course, no coincidence, since Heidegger's programme in *Being and Time* involves an analytic of Dasein in terms of a fundamental drive or a tendency or a mobility which characterizes Dasein's structure of being and since, as will become clear later on, the reason why Heidegger is worried about the dispersion (*Zerstreuung*) to which the ambiguity of idle talk exposes philosophical and any other truth, has to do precisely with this analysis of Dasein in terms of the ontological kinetics which characterizes it. In order to understand this strange movement which links Heidegger's crisis-symptomatology to a description of its causes in terms of an ontological kinesiology and to a – notoriously difficult and more often than not "mis"understood – therapy, let us first turn to those pages in which Heidegger starts to develop, from § 25 onwards, his well-known analysis of the "they" (*das Man*).

---

3. In this chapter I will parenthetically quote from BT/SZ in that order without repeating each time the corresponding abbreviations.

I. An interpreting liberation

At first sight, what is at stake here is a phenomenological description of Dasein in its everydayness, of the way Dasein maintains itself in its Being first of all and most of the time. Dasein, Heidegger tells us, is first and foremost fascinated with (*benommen von*) or absorbed into its world. Dasein is busy. It is constantly occupied, always short of time, hustling around (222/177) and understanding itself in terms of that with which it is customarily concerned. As Heidegger puts it: " 'One *is*' what one does" (283/239). And what one does, is done in the way others do it: "we read, see and judge about literature and art as *they* [*man*] see and judge [or as 'one' sees and judges]; likewise we shrink back from the 'great mass' as *they* shrink back; we find 'shocking' what *they* find shocking" (164/126-7). In everydayness no one is himself. "What one is and how one is, is a no one", and this no one "by whom we are lived in everyday life" Heidegger calls *das Man*, the They, the "One"[4]. This anonymous experience is a positive phenomenon (69, 220/43, 176). Its description is part of an ontology of everyday life and Heidegger stresses that it should not be mistaken for a moralizing critique of everyday Dasein (211/167). And yet De Waelhens[5] is surely not the only interpreter who leaves it to the reader to decide whether this holds true for Heidegger's descriptions of, for example, "curiosity, for which nothing is closed off, and idle talk, for which there is nothing that is not understood" (217/173). Indeed, today, due to the influence of Hannah Arendt[6], these descriptions are generally considered to be the somewhat embarrassing sign of Heidegger's failure to understand the public sphere, and the sarcastic tone in which he sometimes sketches some of its features[7] is taken to be but the reverse side of the elitist *existential* solipsism allegedly advocated in the remainder of *Being and Time*. In all its eagerness to argue its case, this Arendtian reading has of course to neglect important passages where Heidegger stresses the ontological

---

4. M. HEIDEGGER, *Der Begriff der Zeit. Vortrag vor der Marburger Theologenschaft. Juli 1924*, Max Niemeyer, Tübingen, 1989, p. 13.

5. A. DE WAELHENS, *La philosophie de Martin Heidegger*, Louvain/Paris, Nauwelaerts - Béatrice Nauwelaerts, 1971, p. 115.

6. See especially her 'Was ist Existenz-Philosophie?', in H. ARENDT, *Sechs Essays*, Heidelberg, Lambert Schneider, 1948, p. 73 and Jacques TAMINIAUX's interesting remarks in his 'Arendt, disciple de Heidegger?', *Études Phenomenologiques*, 1985 (nr. 2), pp. 111-36, now extended in his *La fille de Thrace et le penseur professionnel. Arendt et Heidegger*, Paris, Payot, 1992.

7. E.g. BT 218/174: "In the end, idle talk is even indignant that what it has surmised and constantly demanded now *actually* happens. In that case, indeed, the opportunity to keep on surmising has been snatched away [*Ist ihm ja doch damit die Gelegenheit entrissen weiter zu ahnen*]".

impossibility of getting rid of the "they", and keeps repeating that proper or authentic (*eigentlich*) existence "is not something which floats above falling everydayness" (224/179 and *passim*), just as this reading, which is the dominant one today, has to neglect that *Being and Time* in more than one passage suggests that although everydayness is first and foremost under the sway of the "they", it need not be: "(...) Dasein comports itself towards its Being in the mode of average everydayness, even if this is only *in* the mode of fleeing in the face of it and forgetfulness thereof " (69/44 – Macquarrie and Robinson drop the 'in' which I italicized) or more explicitly: "Everydayness is determinative for Dasein *even when* it has not chosen the 'they' for its 'hero' " (422/371). Yet, as these quotes make clear, there can be no doubt that Heidegger considers everydayness *in so far as* it has been taken over by the "they", to be inauthentic. Or perhaps one should better say: to be im-proper, while not leaving open the possibility for a proper-ness, an own-ness. "As they-self [*Man-selbst*], the particular Dasein has been dispersed [*zerstreut*] into the 'they' " (167/129).

Commenting on this 'dispersion', Heidegger finds himself using such terms as "temptation" (*Versuchung*), "entanglement" (*Verfängnis*) and even "alienation" (*Entfremdung*) (221 ff./177 ff.). He suggests that this dispersion should be seen as a "flight" into "the illusions of the 'they' " (311/266) and even seems to recommend "weaning from the conventionalities of the 'they' " (444/391). The use of the "*Entwöhnung*" in this last quote – a word which also refers to a detoxification process – leaves no doubt that although Heidegger does not underestimate the power of the seducement of the "they", he at the same time thinks its spell can be broken in principle. It should not come as a great surprise to find him characterizing *Being and Time* as an "interpreting liberation of Dasein for its utmost possibility of existence" (*interpretierende Befreiung des Daseins für seine äußerste Existenzmöglichkeit*) (350/303). Or maybe it should. For what exactly is meant by an "interpreting liberation"? Does this mean that Heidegger is preparing some kind of deep – or even 'very deep' – hermeneutics which, once implemented, will end up with having liberated Dasein? Sadly perhaps, matters are more complicated than our nostalgia may have hoped them to be.

The briefest glance at *Being and Time* will suffice to liberate us from any illusions we might have concerning the ease of such a liberation. The book's strength is precisely that it aims at an *interpreting* liberation. Unlike other theories that operate with the concept of 'alienation' and more often than not fail to explain – or even consider as a problem – the fact that alienation *has* success, that indeed people *can be* effectively alienated, that they are willing to bite the bait of what is – all too rapidly perhaps – labelled as 'ideology', that the falseness of consciousness apparently does not seem to stand in the way of the *success* of false consciousness, unlike all such theories Heidegger in *Being and Time* is acutely aware of the difficulties involved in the concept of alienation, a concept he himself regularly uses. He knows that the interpreting part of his analysis, the part which is to explain what there is about the Being of Dasein which lets Dasein first and foremost (*zunächst und zumeist*) alienate from itself – from its self – could end up with showing that in fact there is no alienation at all, that the reason why alienation is so successful is precisely because there is nothing else than that, because, in short, alienation would be original, a supplement to some frailty in Dasein's Being, a suit of armour without which it could not survive. And yet, *Being and Time*, as we have seen, is also a liberation programme, and as such it depends on the viability of concepts like 'alienation'. Or so would it seem. For on the one hand, Heidegger tries to show that if Dasein gets 'alienated', this is due to the constitution of its Being (*Seinsverfassung*) and has its roots in the fact that this Being is ultimately without grounds, that Dasein's essence lies in its existence, that it is that being which has to be its Being. And this is what turns Dasein's Being "into a burden", and this "burdensome character of Dasein" (*Lastcharakter des Daseins*) (173/134), this unbearable heaviness of its Being, lies behind Dasein's tendency "*zum Leichtnehmen und Leichtmachen*", to take things easily (lightly) and make them easy (light) (165/128). Hence it seeks refuge from the un-homeliness of its Being into the warm and cosy corners of the "they" (233/188). But having said this, it should on the other hand not be forgotten that Heidegger, for all his understanding of the fact that Dasein, as he expresses himself in an earlier text, "is bowed under its own burden"[8], is not willing to consider the "tranquillized familiarity" Dasein gets here as something else than a "flight into the 'at-home' of publicness", a flight which makes Dasein turn its back to its "*Unheimlichkeit*", to the 'not-at-home' which is its proper home. But how can Heidegger reverse things the way he does, calling what we consider to be our home, a hiding-place (*Versteck*) (317/273), and hence not a proper home at all? How can Heidegger still appeal to the 'proper', if not by basing this appeal merely on his personal preference for some ideal of existence, or on an elitist tendency that Rorty[9] and other 'post-modern bourgeois liberals' are certainly not willing to share? This is, in a nutshell, the problem of *Being and Time*, a problem of which – to a certain extent – its author was

---

8. M. HEIDEGGER, 'Phänomenologische Interpretationen zu Aristoteles (Anzeige der hermeneutischen Situation)' (1922), *Dilthey-Jahrbuch*, 1989 (6), p. 238.

9. See his paper on 'Moral Identity and Private Autonomy' published in the second volume of his *Philosophical Papers: Essays on Heidegger and Others*, Cambridge U.P., 1991, pp. 193 ff.

acutely aware (358, 360, 361/310, 312, 313 and *passim*).

It is a problem, moreover, which is central to the project: to prepare for the question of Being by questioning the Being of Dasein. For the problem is of course that Being is not what occupies Dasein 'first and foremost'. On the contrary, Dasein tends to live in what Eugen Fink called "ontological indifference"[10]. This indifference obfuscates both Being as such and Dasein's Being. It prevents it from realizing that Being is what Dasein is already pre-ontologically familiar with and it is this indifference which is ultimately responsible for the fact that the metaphysics it develops, instead of opening up the question of Being, in fact drops it altogether. If *Being and Time* is to be a phenomenology and if Being is *the* phenomenon par excellence, then of course the covering up of this phenomenon by Dasein and its metaphysics has to be understood and interpreted. If "covered-upness is the counter-concept to 'phenomenon' " (60/36), one will have to analyse Dasein's tendency to cover-up, in order to get '*zu den Sachen selbst*', i.e. to Being as such. And here the subject – our subject – comes in.

For Heidegger, what lies at the basis of this covering-up by Dasein of the ontological difference, of the fact that it is – to quote Fink again – "only open for things but not for the openness of things"[11], is nothing else than Dasein's 'Being-in-the-world' itself. In its Being Dasein is, as it were, not closed in upon itself, it is not to be characterized as primarily consciousness and does not face the task of throwing a bridge to the world. Rather, the Being of Dasein is such that Dasein is always already out of itself: with the world (*au monde* as Merleau-Ponty translates), with things and with others. This Being-already-alongside-the-world is not "a fixed staring at something that is purely present-at-hand" (88/61), it is a practical familiarity with the world, with things and with others, which engages or absorbs Dasein to such an extent that it tends not to think of itself as a distinct self, but rather understands itself "in terms of that which it encounters in the environment and that with which it is circumspectively concerned" (439/387). Dasein does the things it does the way 'one' has always been doing it and the way in which the others – any other – are still doing it now. In other words, Dasein is released from the burden (*entlastet*) of having to go through the painstaking process of having to find out everything for itself (165, 312/127, 268). In falling back upon the world in which it is and in interpreting itself in terms of that world, Dasein simultaneously "falls prey" – the German text which I am paraphrasing, reads "*verfällt*" – to the tradition of which it has more or less explicitly taken hold. This tradition, Heidegger adds, "keeps it

10. 'Philosophie als Überwindung der "Naivität"', in E. FINK, *Nähe und Distanz. Phänomenologische Vorträge und Aufsätze*, Freiburg/München, Alber, 1976, p. 116.
11. *Ibid.*

from providing its *own* [*eigen*] guidance", "nimmt ihn die *eigene* Führung, das Fragen und Wählen ab" (42-3/21). Due to this 'falling' into a tradition, Dasein can now repeat what others repeated before it, and still others before them. It can become irresponsible in that it lets others respond for it or by responding as others would – in short others are always involved and this is how Dasein gets deprived by the "they" of its own responsibility: "*Das Man (...) nimmt dem jeweiligen Dasein die Verantwortlichkeit ab*" (165/127). And thus, as we will see in more detail later, Dasein can forget about truth, and can even become severed, cut off from truth altogether. It can think of truth as correspondence and forget about the fact that at the root of truth there lies a more original truth which is Dasein's own '*entdeckend sein*', its Being-uncovering (BT § 44).

It is this possibility of a repetition without explicit appropriation which will force *Being and Time* to pick Dasein's ears. For there is something ambiguous about these ears. They are both too powerful and not powerful enough. Helpful, indispensable even as they may seem in any process of appropriation, they have at the same time a tendency to undermine the need for such an appropriation by making their bearer forget his true task and by leading him to believe that mere repetition will do. Untrustworthy allies, then, these ears. And that is why they need fine-tuning. For without such fine-tuning, repetition will inevitably end up in ambiguity. And ambiguity is what Heidegger fears most.

II. Fine-tuning Dasein's ears

Ambiguity, then, is what Heidegger fears most. It is the sign of a crisis, and it is also for Heidegger, as it was for Husserl – though not in exactly the same way – the crisis of the sign, of the signifying moment. But whereas Heidegger agrees with Husserl on the symptom of the crisis, his existential analysis of Dasein forbids him to share Husserl's optimistic faith in the (teleological) possibility of coping with it. If the crisis for Husserl was due to a loss of contact with the originary and originating experience, and if for Husserl this loss in turn was due, as Derrida reminds us, to "a short-coming, rather than to a defeat"[12], then for Heidegger the roots of this ambiguity seem to lie deeper. To be sure, these roots do not reach so deeply that ambiguity becomes unavoidable and incurable. Heidegger still opposes on an ontic existentiell level the possibility that Dasein either takes hold (*ergreifen*) of its existence or neglects (*versäumen*) it (e.g. 32/12). But from an ontologico-existential point of view, this neglect "is not accidental, not an

12. J. DERRIDA, 'Introduction', in E. HUSSERL, *L'origine de la géometrie*, Paris, P.U.F., 1974, p. 98.

oversight which it would be simple to correct [*kein Versehen, das einfach nachzuholen wäre*], but [one that is] grounded in a kind of Being [*Seinsart*] which belongs essentially [*wesenhaft*] to Dasein itself" (133/100). The "shortcoming" then – for shortcoming there is – seems for Heidegger to be an original element of Dasein's structure of Being. It is a weakness, certainly, but a weakness without which it would be difficult to define Dasein's Being. It is not a weakness of the will and it cannot be overcome by simply willing to overcome it[13]. This is not to say of course that Heidegger thinks this weakness, which is a basic tendency in Dasein, cannot be overcome at all: the fact that it is both embedded in Dasein's structure of Being and that it can *and should* be overcome is precisely the problem with which *Being and Time* struggles. At first sight, Heidegger's solution seems both simple and attractive. All that is needed is a certain puncture through "the thin wall by which the 'they' [and Dasein itself as a they-self] is separated, as it were, from the uncanniness of its Being" (323/278). All that is needed to unblock the road toward ontology and the question of Being, is a simple ontological operation[14], a small puncture through Dasein's ears so that it could for a moment at least escape the deafening sounds of the "they" drowning out the question of (its) Being. All that is needed to allow Dasein to let itself be called back from "its lostness in the 'they' " (e.g. 312, 333/268, 287) and to "modify [its] they-self so that it becomes authentic [or proper – *eigentlich*] Being-one's-self [*Selbstsein*]" (312/268) and finally hears the question of (its) Being, all that is needed to let Dasein grab itself together and turn it into a whole (348ff/301ff), is a hole, a small puncture. And yet, given Heidegger's views on language and on Dasein's structure of Being, nothing could be more difficult and more risky than unblocking or piercing Dasein's ear. For if Dasein overhears the voice which calls it back to itself, it is ultimately because its ear is directed toward others, because, as

13. Although it should be noted that *Being and Time* at times engages in a discourse on the will that should be analysed carefully with respect to its position in the economy of Heidegger's argument (e.g. 237/193 where 'to comport oneself *unwillingly* [*unwillentlich*] towards one's possiblities' is equated with the inauthentic (*uneigentlich*); also, of course 316/271 'The call reaches him who *wants* to be brought back' and 334/288 (*Gewissen-haben-wollen*)).

14. I owe this play on ontology/otology to J. DERRIDA's *Otobiographies. L'enseignement de Nietzsche et la politique du nom propre*, Paris, Galilée, 1984. At the time of writing this paper I was not yet familiar with Derrida's own analysis of "Heidegger's ear" (now published as 'L'oreille de Heidegger. Philopolémologie (*Geschlecht IV*)', in J. DERRIDA, *Politiques de l'amitié*, Paris, Galilée, 1994, pp. 341-419). But I may have been influenced by Derrida since I heard (if 'heard' is the correct term for what happens to one's ears during a four and a half hour conference) the 1989 lecture at the University of Loyola (Chicago) which formed the basis of what he published now.

Heidegger says, Dasein existentially "as a Being-with which understands can listen to others" (*[weil] Dasein als verstehendes Mitsein auf Andere hören kann*) (315/270-1). Being able to lose itself in the publicness (*Öffentlichkeit*) and the idle talk (*Gerede*) of the "they", Dasein – because its ontological structure necessarily involves *mitsein* – "fails to hear (*überhört*) its own (*eigen*) self in listening to the [or its] they-self " (*ibid.*). The overhearing, the absence of a true or proper hearing (333/287: *das rechte Hören*), the success of idle talk is first of all rooted in the fact that Dasein, as we have seen, is primarily not a proper self, but an im-proper *Man-selbst*. In other words, what happened in the cave has to be understood against the background of Dasein's existential rootedness in community, in *Mitsein*. And Heidegger realizes of course, that if the cave is what it is, philosophers will always have to swallow its poison. Unless the cave could be changed. Unless those who are in the cave would, instead of sacrificing others, come to terms with their own death. Unless they would become Being-toward-death themselves, by not flying away from death as their "ownmost, non-relational, certain and as such indefinite, not to be outstripped possibility" (303/258-9). Unless, like Tolstoi's Ivan Ilyitch, they would learn to die and become mortals. But again, according to Heidegger, nothing is more difficult than dying, truly dying in the cave. For the cave is the resort of the "they", and as such it is the condition of impossibility for coming to terms with death as "the possibility of impossibility" (307/262). *Mitsein* in the cave cannot be but inauthentic as long as it is ruled by the "they", and yet what makes (or should make) *Being and Time* such an interesting book for political philosophers, is that it is not clear whether it is willing to give up the cave and to render it to the "they".

What the analytic of Dasein shows to be its prime characteristic – *Jemeinigkeit* or mineness – must be shown (*gezeigt*) to Dasein in its possible authenticity (68, 313/42-3, 268). If Dasein is to find itself, the crust by which it covers up its Being-toward-death and under which it seeks refuge in the warm cosy-corner of the "they", must be pierced. That which shows Dasein the possibility of being its 'own' or 'proper' self, cannot of course undo the structure of its *Mitsein*. But it should be able to go against the existentiell solidification of this structure. And death cannot do this by itself, on its own. For "they" have always already turned death into something which overcomes others. Like Ivan Ilyitch, "they" agree that "since Kaj is a human being, and human beings are mortal, Kaj must be mortal", but just like him, "they" know that "they" are not Kaj, nor *a* human being in general, and hence conclude that the syllogism only concerns Kaj, or for that matter all other human beings, but not "them". In short, "they" have turned death into something ambiguous, that might, and then again might not, end one's life. And this is why Heidegger has to come up with something stronger than this ambiguity, something as unambiguous as possible, a voice perhaps, or perhaps not even a voice. In any case, something that could make the "they" "collapse" (*zusammensinken*) (317/273). Such is the power of "the voice of the friend whom each Dasein carries with it" (*Stimme des Freundes, den jedes Dasein bei sich trägt*) (206/163). Or at least, such is the power Heidegger expects it to have.

III. A-PHONIC VOICES AND
SILENTLY RINGING TELEPHONE-CALLS

Heidegger first mentions this voice in §34 where he introduces language (*Sprache*) into the existential analysis. Nothing much is said here about this voice, in fact Heidegger tells us nothing more than the one-line remark I have quoted, and he does not say who this friend "whom every Dasein carries with it" is, nor does he tell us why he is a *friend*. However, in his analysis of conscience (§ 54 ff.), Heidegger speaks once more about a voice, and although this voice might not be identical to the voice of the 'friend' – the one could be an instance of the other – we might do well to have a closer look at what is being said here about the voice of conscience.

First of all, this voice says nothing. It tells Dasein nothing at all. It only interrupts idle talk, like the insistent ringing of an urgent telephone call which takes one out of a party or a conference. This telephone call interrupts and the function of this interruption is to make the otherwise inconspicuous (*unauffällig*) at least for a moment (*Augenblick*) conspicuous. I will later on come back to this conspicuousness when I will link the function of this telephone call to Rudolf Bernet's analysis of the phenomenological reduction in Heidegger. But for the moment, let us concentrate on the call itself. In a way the image of the telephone that keeps ringing is not entirely accurate. For a telephone is the more insistent the louder it rings. But loudness is a qualification Heidegger exclusively reserves for the "they". Since the "they" are always noisy, and always shouting the latest rumours into each others ears, the call of conscience, however loud it may be, would only add to the overall racket. Hence, it has to call in silence, it can only *silently* interrupt idle talk, it has to be – if one wants to keep the image – an *inner* telephone call[15]. It does not need, as Heidegger says, vocal utterance (*Verlautbarung*), it does not need, as a more literal translation would say, to be put into sound (316, 318, 322/271, 273, 277).

The *presence* of this voice which does not need *vocalisation* – let us agree

---

15. Cf. J. DERRIDA, *Ulysse gramophone. Deux mots pour Joyce*, Paris, Galilée, 1987, p. 89 ("*téléphone intérieur*").

to translate *Verlautbarung* by this neologism – could not be more
disconcerting. And not only because, as Heidegger tells us, it interrupts idle
talk, but also because in a way its presence interrupts *Being and Time* and
catches it by surprise. The strange thing about this voice is of course not that
it is *inner* – we might well be willing to agree with Heidegger's phenomenological description, itself backed up by a whole tradition which tells us
precisely that the voice of conscience is an inner voice. It is *not* the
inner/outer distinction *as such* which should arouse our suspicion, but the
fact that this distinction is crossed by another one, or even by two other ones:
first, by that between *presence or absence of vocalization* and second, by that
between *ambiguity or lack of ambiguity*. The inner voice is precisely able to
interrupt idle talk because it is unambiguous, and it is unambiguous because it does not need vocalization. This voice which is ontologically prior
to the *phonè*, this a-phonic voice called upon by Heidegger to ensure that
Dasein is called back from its "alienation" in the "they" and is thrown back
upon its *proper* self, can only succeed in its task by borrowing nothing from
anything outside itself, "in the world or in 'reality', not a single
supplementary signifier, not a single substance of expression" that would
break its intimacy[16]. As one can expect, the unambiguousness of this a-
phonic inner voice is the linchpin which holds together the analysis of *Being
and Time* and lets it at the same time dangerously balance on the top of the
thin wall which at once both separates *Being and Time* from and connects
it with the *phono*logocentric forgetting of Being in metaphysics. I will leave
it there for the moment, in its precarious balance, as a monument to remind
the generations to come of what Derrida called "the ambiguity of the
Heideggerian situation (*situation*) with regard to the metaphysics of
presence and logocentrism"[17]. Let me refrain from the foolish urge to push
it over, for the stakes are much too high and our time here is limited. Let us
have a look at the consequences of this Heideggerian defiance of the forces
of gravity and concentrate on what it does not *with* but *to* the place of
language (*Sprache*).

Heidegger explicitly introduces 'language' into his analysis in § 34, on
"*Dasein und Rede. Die Sprache*", translated for lack of a better English
equivalent as "Being-there and *Discourse*. Language". This translation
which renders *Rede* as 'discourse' is not without its problems. It is, in fact,
very misleading. *Rede*, as Heidegger immediately points out, is not to be
confused with language (*Sprache*). It is the ontological condition of
possibility for the latter (203/160). *Rede* – Heidegger's translation for the

16. J. DERRIDA, *De la grammatologie*, Paris, Minuit, 1967, p. 33. Dasein, as one will
remember, is both what calls and what is called in the voice of conscience (320/275).
17. *Ibid.*, p. 36.

Greek *logos* (208/165) – is what provides for linguistic articulability, but it is not linguistic articulation itself. *Rede* can, but need not give rise to a process of vocalization, to a *phonè*. Just as the voice of conscience was an inner a-phonic voice, vocal utterance is not essential for *Rede* (208, 316/165, 271). It is not *as such* dependent on it. On the contrary, *Sprache* is but its mundane component, its " 'worldly' Being" (*'weltliches' Sein*) (204/161) and is itself existentially grounded in *Rede* (203/160). It is because *Rede* already articulates Dasein's practical familiarity with the world at a pre-linguistic level, because there is already a "totality-of-significations" (*Bedeutungsganze*) for Dasein, because Dasein's world is not without significations (*Bedeutungen*) that there can be *linguistic* articulation (204/161). But as Heidegger remarks, this ontological order of priority between *Rede* and *Sprache* does not entail a relapse into a philosophy of interiority: "(...) Dasein *expresses itself* [*spricht sich aus*] not because it has, in the first instance, been encapsulated as something 'internal' over against something outside, but because as Being-in-the-world it is already 'outside' when it understands [*verstehend*]" (205/162). This *Aussprechen* however is not to be mistaken for a simple expression in the context of a naive instrumental view on language. Heidegger stresses that it would be wrong to describe what happens in the transition from *Rede* to *Sprache* as a process in which word-things (*Wörterdinge*) get supplied with significations (204/161). Instead "to significations words accrue" (*den Bedeutungen wachsen Worte zu*) (*ibid.*). But if it is clear what this "coming-to-word" (*zu Wort kommen*) of an already constituted "totality-of-signification" (204/161) does not mean, it is less clear what exactly is meant by it. For example, does this '*zu Wort kommen*', this '*sich aussprechen*' add anything to the already articulated (*gegliedert*) totality-of-signification, except its 'worldly Being'? But the possibility of it being shared with others? Is its only role that of the indispensable linguistic flesh which has to make its master's *Rede* accessible and attractive? Is it no more than a cloth or a sober gown, destined to remain *einstimmig* (326/281), in unison with its master's silent voice, but secretly speculating on the eyes and the ears of the others to deform its unambiguous song? Secretly fostering hopes that it will catch "their" attention and one day become more important than the master himself, free and finally rewarded for the long years during which – to use Husserlian terms – it laboured to set free the master's ideality of meaning by tying it to and receiving it into its flesh[18]? Why doesn't Heidegger, instead of holding that "to significations words accrue", take the opposite view that to words significations accrue? Why can't it be the practical familiarity with a language, into which each Dasein finds itself

18. For Husserl's views on linguistic incarnation and its role for the constitution of ideality, see DERRIDA's 'Introduction' to Husserl's 'Origin of geometry' (*l.c.*, pp. 86-7).

thrown (*geworfen*), that gives rise to significations? For, after all, Heidegger himself points out that language as an entity within-the-world, as the "worldly Being" of *Rede* "becomes something which we may come across as a ready-to-hand (*Zuhandenes*)" (204/161). If language has indeed this characteristic of being ready-to-hand, just like equipment (*Zeug*), if the Being of language is at least in some respect "readiness-to-hand" (*Zeuglichkeit*)[19], wouldn't one then be justified in expecting Heidegger to say that it is to *words* that significations accrue? Just as equipment only gets its practical meaning within a totality of equipment (*Zeugganzes*) (97/68), so words would derive theirs from a *Wortganzheit* (204/161), from a totality of words. Just as, ontologically speaking, "there 'is' no such thing as *an* equipment" (97/68), there would be no such thing as *a* word in isolation, and hence there would be no ontological sense indeed to the idea Heidegger himself dismisses, that word-things get supplied with significations (204/161). In other words, why didn't Heidegger in order to refute a naive instrumental view on language, appeal to the far more subtle instrumental theory of language he himself prepared by introducing readiness-to-hand and equipmentality (*Zeuglichkeit*) into ontological discourse? Why didn't he reckon with language as an always already pregiven symbolic order that is part and parcel of Dasein's facticity (*Faktizität*)? Why didn't Heidegger draw this consequence from his own remarks on the readiness-to-hand of language? Why did he insist on ontologically deriving it from *Rede*? It is clear that part of the answer at least has to do with what Heidegger fears most, with ambiguity.

IV. THE RISK OF LANGUAGE

Just as the voice of conscience is not ambiguous because it is not a *phonè* (316, 318/271, 274), so *Rede* which is not dependent on vocalization, cannot be ambiguous. Ambiguity only comes in with language. And with language untruth comes in[20]. Untruth not only in the special sense of a forgetting of a more primordial truth, of a forgetting of Dasein's *entdeckend-sein* (Being-

---

19. As is well known, Heidegger left this question unanswered in *Being and Time*: "Is [language] a kind of equipment ready-to-hand within-the-world, or has it Dasein's kind of Being, or is it neither of these? What kind of Being does language have, if there can be such a thing as a 'dead' language?" (209/166).

20. A full analysis of the problem of (un-)truth in *Being and Time* would have to confront the remarks one finds in § 44, where untruth seems clearly linked to the vocalisation of *Rede* (e.g. 262, 264/219, 222), with earlier passages where it was suggested that truth and falsity already characterize *Rede* before it is expressed. I still hope to come back on these issues on a different occasion.

uncovering) (BT § 44), but also in the narrow sense of *Verdeckung*, covered-up-ness. In fact, as will become clear in a moment, both occur together. Untruth arises as a result of *nachreden*, merely repeating what the others say. And since the possibility of this repetition is inherently inscribed in language, *Rede*, once vocalized, is always under the threat to become *Gerede*, idle talk, and to fall prey to the "they" and become dominated "by the way things are publicly interpreted" (by the *öffentliche Ausgelegtheit*) (264/222). In such repetition, that which is linguistically expressed as such (*das Ausgesprochene als solches*) takes over Dasein's Being-towards those entities which have been uncovered in the original assertion (*Aussage*) (267/224). To be sure, Being towards entities has not been extinguished, but it has been uprooted (*entwurzelt*) by the "they". Entities have not been completely hidden, Heidegger says, but they have been uncovered and disguised at the same time: "the entity shows itself, *but in the mode of semblance*" ([*das Seiende] zeigt sich – aber im Modus des Scheins*) (264/222). *Schein*, semblance is the effect of *Gerede*, idle talk; and as such it is what constitutes the realm of the "they", i.e. *doxa*, life in the cave. *Semblance* is due to Dasein's losing hold of *itself* (its Self) and becoming absorbed and lost in *das Man*. Semblance is a disease *Rede* becomes exposed to by trusting *phonè*, its (un-)faithful servant. But is this disease a fatality, attached to language as such? Would it be wrong to suggest, as De Waelhens did[21], that language in *Being and Time* resorts under the inauthentic?

At first sight, it seems it would. For Heidegger seems to consider the transition from *Rede* to idle talk (*Gerede*) not as a fall *into* language, but as a fall *within* language. He does state that "*Rede* which is communicated [and hence vocalized, R.V.] *can* be understood to a considerable extent, *without* the hearer bringing himself into such a kind of Being towards what *Rede* is about as to have a *primordial* [*ursprünglich*] understanding of it" (212/168), but he does not say that this is what necessarily happens. Or again, we read that "Dasein *need not* [*braucht nicht*] bring itself face to face with entities themselves in an 'original' experience [in '*originärer*' *Erfahrung*]" and that "it nevertheless remains in a Being-towards these entities" (266/224). Ample evidence, it would seem, for the fact that it is not language as such which is inauthentic but only a way of being in language (first quote), although even that lack of 'original' experience might not, as the second quote seems to suggest, be sufficient to call it inauthentic. But matters are more complicated than that.

Immediately after having said that Dasein does not need to have an 'original experience', Heidegger goes on to explain that this fact about Dasein's relation to language is what gives rise to the "they": "In a large

21. *La philosophie de Martin Heidegger, o.c.*, p. 194 n4.

measure uncoveredness gets appropriated not only by one's own uncovering, but rather by hearsay of something that has been said. Absorption in something that has been said belongs to the kind of Being characteristic for the 'they' " (266-7/224). On second sight then, Heidegger's use of verbs like "need not" and "can" in the foregoing quotes was plainly descriptive, and the quotes should be read as an attempt to find an answer to the following question: "what is the Being of *Rede* which is expressed and what does this tell us in principle about Dasein's everyday kind of Being?" (211/168). And what Heidegger is telling us, is that Dasein's everyday absorption into the "they" has something to do with the vocalization of *Rede*, with language. If there is a fall *within* language, this fall is due first of all to a fall *into* language. For the fall of *Rede* into language is always a fall into the risk of losing contact with the 'original' experience. But if language involves such a risk, how involved exactly is language into this risk?

Heidegger tells us that "what is expressed becomes as it were, something ready-to-hand within-the-world (*innerweltlich Zuhandenes*) which can be taken up and spoken again (*weitergesprochen*)" (266/224). And he also tells us, in analysing equipment (*Zeug*) as an example of readiness-to-hand, that "the peculiarity of what is proximally ready-to-hand is that, in its readiness-to-hand, it must, as it were, withdraw in order to be properly ready-to-hand" (99/69). In dealing with equipment, e.g. in using a hammer, *Dasein* is not confronted with the Being of equipment as such. Equipmentality or readiness-to-hand only shows itself as such when the hammer gets lost or is broken or is lying in the way, etc.; only then is Dasein's attention drawn to the Being of its equipments, to the fact that they belong in a wider network of equipment (*Zeugzusammenhang*), and only then can this network reveal to Dasein something about the difference between the innerworldliness of equipment and its own Being-in-the-world (BT § 16). Dasein's natural attitude is, as it were, corrected by a phenomenological reduction that overcomes it, and takes it by surprise. As Rudolf Bernet stresses, it is precisely this feature of Heidegger's use of the reduction – the fact that it "is the result of an event that imposes itself upon Dasein unexpectedly"[22], which separates him from Husserl. And as we will see in a moment, this is not a minor feature. For if this reduction is no longer the result of a jump (*Sprung*) which, as Bernet says, is willed and risked by a responsible subject that wants to know all about it, if it not only comes to Dasein as a surprise, but as a bad surprise, not as something which it enjoys, but as something which it resents, then one can expect Heidegger to have great difficulties in

22. 'Phenomenological Reduction and the Double Life of the Subject', in Th. KISIEL - J. VAN BUREN (eds.), *Reading Heidegger from the Start. Essays in his Earliest Thought*, Albany, SUNY, 1994, p. 259.

not losing together with the Husserlian subject the possibility of responsibility and authenticity as such. And the least one can say is that Heidegger is not making it easy for himself. Instead of condemning Dasein's clinging to the natural attitude, he seems to defend it: "the self *must* forget itself if, 'lost' in the world of equipment, it is to be able 'actually' to go to work and manipulate something" (405/354). But it is clear of course that this defense cannot be unambiguous, if Heidegger does not want to see the tables turned against his own analysis. For if vocalization turns *Rede* into something ready-to-hand, and if the world of equipment *necessitates* a forgetting of the Self, then language as the 'worldly Being' of *Rede* not only involves the risk of a certain forgetting *of*, or of a loss of contact *with* an originary and proper-ly (*eigen*tlich) appropriated experience, but is built on it. Language is so much involved in the risk it involves, that it presupposes it: 'lost' in the world of language the Self in some way *must* forget itself if it is actually 'to go to speech'. And maybe this 'forgetting' is not really a forgetting, maybe this risk is not literally a risk. For does not Heidegger himself stress that "when we are explicitly hearing another's *Rede*, we proximally [*zunächst*] understand what is said, or – *to put it more exactly* – we are already with him, in advance, alongside the entity which the *Rede* is about" (207/164)? And how could we be, if not because language itself not only articulates an already articulated world, but intertwines with it and opens up a world itself? But this "Heidegger" in *Being and Time* cannot concede. For it would mean conceding not only, as "Heidegger" is willing to do, that "*idle talk* (...) is the kind of Being which belongs to Dasein's understanding *when that understanding has been uprooted [entwurzelt]*" (214/170), but also that this uprootedness which characterizes both the mode of Being of the "they" and of *Gerede*, might not be just the result of a fall (*Verfallen*) out of which Dasein can and must free itself, and might not be just the sign of Dasein's alienation or its being-lost in the "they". What prevents Heidegger from following the train of his own thought here is not the concept of authenticity *as such*. It is, as I will try to show, a certain pre-conception of authenticity, a certain pre-conception of the self, and of the way they relate to in-authenticity and not-self, which *imposes* on *Being and Time* a decision that is to a certain extent arbitrary.

V. HEIDEGGER'S DECISION

We have seen how language and equipment, in order to function properly, presuppose a certain forgetting and how the anonymous existence of the "they" thrives on the structure of this inconspicuousness (*Unauffälligkeit*). If the "they" can provide Dasein with an improper self, it is precisely because Dasein, in dealing with equipment and language, "must forget" its proper self (220, 405/176, 354). Put paradoxically, what Heidegger's first reduction shows is that the *proper* functioning of the realm of language and equipment is dependent on the functioning of an *im-proper* (*uneigentlich*) realm of the "they". If this realm is to give way to a proper (*eigentlich*) realm, if the inauthentic (*uneigentlich*) is to be modified into the authentic (*eigentlich*), then a new attempt is needed to make what remains inconspicuous (*unauffällig*) conspicuous (*auffällig*). What has to be made conspicuous is, of course, Dasein's proper self and, as is well known, in order to do that, Heidegger will be looking for a way to tear Dasein's death away from "the inconspicuousness" in which it remains first and foremost – an inconspicuousness, as he reminds us, "characteristic of what is encountered in an everyday fashion" (*die für das alltäglich begegnende charakteristische Unauffälligkeit*) (297/253). In other words, what the analysis of *Angst* and of the voice of conscience, which Heidegger is (re-)introducing here in order to show the existential-ontological and the existentiell possibility of an authentic potentiality-for Being-a-whole (*eigentliches Ganzseinkönnen*) for Dasein, what these analyses will have to do, is to undo the inconspicuousness (*Unauffälligkeit*) characteristic for everydayness. In anxiety, Heidegger says, "everyday familiarity collapses" (233/189) or again, the voice of conscience, he tells us, can – by its lack of ambiguity – "make the 'they' collapse" (317/273). The call is to rob (*rauben*) the self of its lodgement (*Unterkunft*) and its hiding-place (*Versteck*) in the "they", by only appealing to the Self of the they-self and passing-over the "they" (*ibid.*).

In fact, this discourse on the "they" is closely linked to what Heidegger has to say on "truth" in § 44 of *Being and Time*. Let me just recall here that at the end of this long, circuitous and extremely difficult analysis, Heidegger resorts once more to a robbery. After having linked untruth, idle talk, ambiguity (and hence, as we have seen: language), and the "they", Heidegger concludes that truth as *a-letheia* is "a kind of robbery" (*Raub*) and that the *alpha privativum* refers to the fact that "Dasein should explicitly appropriate (*zueignen*) what has already been uncovered, defend it *against* semblance (*Schein*) and disguise, and assure itself of its uncoveredness *again and again*" (265/222). Given our preceding analysis of this semblance (*Schein*) and of the way it is linked to a falling (*Verfallen*) that gives rise both to the "they" and to language, it won't take us much effort to show, first that Heidegger's discourse on the "they" is a discourse on truth and second, that this discourse on truth will get *Being and Time* into trouble.

What § 44 suggests is that truth has time and again to be robbed away from untruth. And since truth and untruth, as Heidegger explains, ultimately relate to Dasein's more original truth and untruth, to its disclosedness (*Erschlossenheit*) and to its closedness (*Verschlossenheit*), and since this *Verschlossenheit* is due to Dasein's tendency to fall into the power of the "they", the fate of truth ultimately depends on Dasein's authenticity, on its "authentic disclosedness" (*eigentliche Erschlossenheit*), on the truth of its existence (*Wahrheit der Existenz*) (264-5/221-2). And so does the fate of untruth, the fate of the "they", the fate of *doxa*, the fate of the cave. And here we have a problem, for what follows is that, because of its conception of truth as robbery, as a-letheia, *Being and Time* seems forced to give up on the cave. Now authenticity itself becomes a robbery, something we have to gain again and again, a perpetual task of appropriating untruth proper-ly (*eigentlich zueignen*) (345/299) in what Heidegger calls resoluteness (*Entschlossenheit*), i.e. the proper truth of Dasein, its disclosedness in its proper or authentic mode (cf. 264, 343ff./221, 297ff.). And although Heidegger tells us that "even resolution (*Entschluß*) remains dependent upon the 'they' and its world" or that resoluteness notwithstanding "the irresoluteness (*Unentschlossenheit*) of the 'they' remains in power (*bleibt in Herrschaft*), but [that] it cannot impugn resolute [authentic] existence" (345-6/299), it is anything but clear that what is at stake here, could be regarded as a true rehabilitation of *doxa*. For whereas Heidegger tells us that "Dasein is always already (*je schon*) in irresoluteness, and soon, perhaps, will be in it again" (345/299), he does not show us how everydayness itself, how *doxa* itself could be modified and how *doxa*, on the basis of this modification, not only does, but should remain in power. On the one hand Heidegger is at pains to deny that the authentic Being-one's-self should be regarded as "an exceptional condition of the subject", and he stresses that such authenticity is not "detached from the 'they' " since the "they" remain in power, and since truth is but the result of a robbery (168/130 and the quotes above). But on the other hand he does seem to conceive of authenticity as a momentary escape from inauthenticity and as a robbery which will have to start all over again. First and foremost Dasein is inauthentic, but sometimes it can 'escape' the cave. But even when it 'escapes' the cave, when "the irresoluteness of the 'they' " no longer is able "to impugn [its] resolute existence" (345/299, quoted above), the cave itself, *doxa*, the "they" "remain in power" (*ibid.*). Dasein lives, as it were, both in and out of the cave. Better still: the cave turns into a place where an authentic and an inauthentic self are *Living Apart Together*. Authentic Dasein "remains dependent upon the 'they' and its world" but is no longer "impugned" by it (345-6/299, quoted above). The reason why this *L.A.T. model* is so disappointing is because its interpretation of the existentiell modification of the "they" seems only able to correct Dasein's everydayness by letting Dasein temporarily step out of it. Conceived of in this way, the modification would leave the "they", everydayness or *doxa* as they were. On this reading, then, the philosopher who has to 'return' to the cave could not be but an eccentric, whose sad duty it is to live in a place that goes against the habits of his heart. He will have to die, but not 'after' his own heart. If his resolution is to remain dependent on the "they" and its world (345-6/299), if "the understanding of this is one of the things [his] resolution discloses, in as much as resoluteness is what first gives authentic transparency to [the philosopher's] Dasein" (*ibid.*), then *Being and Time* cannot but lead to the apocalypse Arendt and others have associated with it. Then we will have to give up our hopes to get a new 'political' philosophy from Heidegger, for *doxa*'s inauthenticity will always remain at odds with the philosopher's authenticity and the rehabilitation of a public sphere where they could meet will prove to be an impossible project.

VI. GENTLY FALLING… INTO HEIDEGGER'S CAVE

Is there no way then for *Being and Time* to keep to the promise of its opening pages where it was suggested that everydayness need not be inauthentic (see above section I)? What elements in *Being and Time* are responsible for its apparent failure to stick to this promise, for the fact that throughout the book more often than not everydayness is simply equated with the inauthentic? What if ultimately the responsibility lies with the way Heidegger here conceives of *a-letheia* as a simple opposition between truth and untruth, an opposition in the wake of which all the other oppositions, e.g. that between *Eindeutigkeit / Zweideutigkeit* (lack of ambiguity/ ambiguity) follow, an opposition moreover which he spent the rest of his life to correct? What would happen if we were to introduce into *Being and Time* the idea that truth is not simply opposed to untruth, that there is an untruth in the heart of truth, that there is a *lèthè* which no *aletheia* can finally over-come[23]? Would this 'result' of Heidegger's "Turning" turn us away from the analytic of Dasein? Or would it only do away with a *decision* a certain 'Heidegger' imposed on this analytic, *but not with the analytic as such*? A *decision* which, as I suggested, results from a preconception of truth, and of language, and of the relation between truth and language? A *decision* finally, which rests on a certain conception of the Self and the way it is related to the they-self, on a certain conception of the authentic and the way it is related to the inauthentic, on a certain conception of Being and the way it is related to covered-upness (*Verdeckung*) as its counter-concept (60/36)?

Being for the Heidegger of *Being and Time* has to be robbed, as it were,

23. M. HEIDEGGER, 'The End of Philosophy and the Task of Thinking', in ID., *Basic Writings*, New York, Harper & Row, 1977, p. 390.

of its *Unauffälligkeit*, its inconspicuousness, and therefore, first of all, Dasein's proper self has to be made conspicuous. But whereas Heidegger's first reduction showed that in "the conspicuousness of the unusable", readiness-to-hand "shows itself a last time" and then "takes its farewell" (104/74), his second reduction through anxiety and the voice of conscience[24] seems to forget the disruptive effects of the first one. Instead of realizing that what the first reduction shows is that Being in some way has to be forgotten, or has to remain inconspicuous, or again, instead of realizing that what it shows is that, in the words of the later Heidegger, "*aletheia* (...) has to be overlooked"[25], the second reduction tries to invert this relationship between the conspicuous and the inconspicuous, and to *adjust* it to the concept of truth of § 44. In making death conspicuous, it is the "they", the untruth, which now "shows itself a last time" and then – remember – "collapses" (*das Man sinkt in sich zusammen*; 317/273) in taking its farewell. In doing away with the inconspicuous, what is disrupted is only the inauthentic, and what remains is the authentic, the Self which, as it were, shows itself for the first time. In other words, whereas the first reduction seemed to lead to a defense of the natural attitude – the Self *must* be forgotten – the second reduction attacks it all the more heavily. But this self which is now made conspicuous, can it do without an inconspicuousness? Is it doomed to succumb again to the inauthentic from which it first managed to set itself free? Can it not fall in an authentic mode? Does falling (*Verfallen*) have to lead to inauthenticity?

Although Heidegger in one place suggests that falling (*Verfallen*) can be either authentic or inauthentic (401/350)[26], *Being and Time* in general considers *Verfallen* to be that essential structure of Dasein's Being which explains why Dasein's Being is first and foremost (*zunächst und zumeist*) inauthentic at an existentiell level. What this means is that, strictly speaking, the existential character of falling is due to its being a structural *possibility* inherent in Dasein's Being (it explains for the fact that there *can* be inauthenticity), and not to its being a structure *as such*. Although Dasein is always exposed to its tendency to fall, it does not always give in to this tendency. It is not always falling. In other words, as opposed to other existentials as, for example, Being-in-the-world, falling and the existentials related with it, such as the "they", are in a way *existentials that can*

---

24. I owe the distinction between a first and a second reduction to R. Bernet (see note 22).

25. M. HEIDEGGER, *Grundfragen der Philosophie. Ausgewählte "Probleme" der "Logik"* (Freiburg Lectures, winter semester, 1937/38), GA 45, p. 147.

26. My attention was drawn to this passage by a footnote in E. TUGENDHAT's *Der Wahrheitsbegriff bei Husserl und Heidegger*, Berlin, W. de Gruyter, 1970, p. 316.

'disappear'. For example, the "they" is an existential in so far as it refers to a *tendency* which belongs to Dasein's Being, the tendency, that is, to take things easily (*es sich leichtnehmen und leichtmachen*) given the unbearable heaviness of Dasein's Being. Because the "they" only constitutes an existential *structure of possibility*, and not, as Being-in-the-world does, an existential *structure*, it can but need not put itself through to the existentiell level: Dasein can but need not be inauthentic. In other words, the inauthentic is to be linked to fallenness (*Verfallenheit*), whereas the authentic only arises when Dasein manages to free itself from its tendency toward *Verfallen*. If falling would be like the other existentials, it would allow not only for an inauthentic, but also for an authentic mode; it would be a structure characteristic of Dasein's Being as such, and not merely a structural possibility.

In pointing out this special status of falling and the existentials related to it, in showing some surprise about the fact that we seem to be dealing here with existentials that can disappear, my aim is not of course to contest that there is a difference between existentials and categorials, and to suggest that the first should be considered in terms of the second, namely as *'vorhanden'* properties of the substance of Dasein. Rather, I wonder if part of the violence we have seen at work in *Being and Time*, should not be related to the special status falling seems to get within the framework of Heidegger's existential-analysis, especially since it is this status which will allow him to put the proper (authentic) in an either/or relation to the improper (inauthentic). But is this either/or relationship the only way to think the authentic and the inauthentic? Or does it simply follow from a *decision* 'Heidegger' imposed on his existential analysis? A *decision* concerning the status of falling, a decision motivated by a *parti pris* with regard to the meaning of authenticity and inauthenticity and the way they relate to each other? What if the analysis of anxiety reveals not that "Dasein is authentically itself (*ist eigentlich selbst*) in the primordial individualization of the reticent resoluteness which exacts anxiety of itself" (369/322), but only – and here I quote a very different passage – "*the Being-free for* one's ownmost potentiality-for-Being, and therewith for *the possibility of authenticity and inauthenticity*" (236/191)? What if the analysis of death reveals that death – authentic, proper death – is precisely what happens to the philosopher *in the cave*, namely the "permanent con-fron-tation" with the "Nichtig- und Machtloswerdens des eigenen Wesens" (nullification and becoming powerless of his own ess*a*nce) (GA 34: 84) and thus gives a final twist to Plato's story and robs it of its dramatic overtones[27]? And what if the

27. Let me stress that, as I have shown in the introduction to this chapter, this is not at all the line that Heidegger himself takes on Plato's story in this volume.

analysis of *Rede* and the voice of conscience does *not* reveal a falling into an ambiguity and an inauthenticity that would be due to vocalization itself and from which the voice of the friend would help Dasein recover? What if, since, as Heidegger stresses, "hearing is constitutive for *Rede*" (206/163), and since one can hear either the voice of the others or the voice of the friend, it reveals instead that *Rede* itself is therefore, even *before* vocalization, already *in itself* exposed to the risk of ambiguity? And what if this risk were not really a risk? What if the voice of the friend which comes, as Heidegger says, "from within me and yet from beyond me" (*aus mir und doch über mich*) (320/275), is the voice of the law which cannot be heard without a certain noise? What if a law that would be without noise, perfectly *einstimmig* (326/281), would no longer be a law? To be sure, Heidegger might be right to stress that the voice of conscience tells Dasein nothing at all. But is this 'nothing at all' without ambiguity? Is it not ambiguity itself? Is it not the ambiguity of the 'do not read me' that turns the law into law and makes my responsibility a responsibility? What if the law would have to be as ambiguous as this: 'Read me, but do not just read me, it is not sufficient to read me to know what you have to do and how far your responsibility goes'?

And yet, whereas this essential ambiguity of the law seems to put a limit on all attempts to turn the voice of conscience into something unambiguous, Heidegger, as we have seen, keeps dreaming of a little hole through which all that legal noise could escape, he keeps looking for a way to produce a low-noise, a-phonic voice of conscience, and he is quite prepared to use the violence of his ontological puncture, if it can help him to unblock ontology. But in thus turning his back on ambiguity, does Heidegger not at the same time turn his back to death and to true friendship with Being? For what if this friendship cannot do without a certain ambiguity, and what if it is finally this to which the tension between Heidegger's two reductions should draw our attention? Authenticity then would not be that rare state-of-mind (*Befindlichkeit*) in which the self or Being is no longer forgotten, and in which truth has momentarily appropriated untruth. To the contrary, only in falling *from* anxiety, *from* 'death', *from* silence into ambiguity, only in the moment of losing its self to the "they"-self, would Dasein be able to experience its self and to find access to an authentic, proper mood (*Befindlichkeit*). Just as the writer, only by losing his thread, discovers he has one, just as Sheherazade discovers her 'own' life in watching it disappear in the 'ear of the other', Dasein might only experience its proper self when it discovers that its steadiness and steadfastness (*Selbständigkeit*) is not what it gains, by bringing, *as Heidegger suggests*, the "movement" (*Bewegtheit*) by which it is thrown to a "stop", but by joining this movement and becoming aware of its powerlessness to escape its dispersion (*Zerstreuung*)

(369,400/322,348). This 'falling' need not make Dasein fall back into the inauthentic again; to the contrary it is only by way of such 'falling' that Dasein can reach a state-of-mind or a mood in which it can be authentic.

Anxiety, then, is not what makes the cave collapse (*zusammensinken*) so that it becomes inaccessible forever; *anxiety only disrupts life in the cave in order to show its inevitability*. Never really succesful in its attempt to graft the conspicuous onto the inconspicuous, the phenomenological reduction which overcomes life in the cave will not live to see its unknown buds blossom, and seems doomed to remain the barren trace of a wound on a stem. And yet, in opening up something which has immediately to be closed again, by showing something which has immediately to be forgotten again, this wound, according to Heidegger, has healing power. Indeed the reduction's most important lesson may not only be that it cannot be fully carried through (Merleau-Ponty), but that it must "fail" in order to "succeed" or that its success lies in its failure. Both a failure and a success, the reduction becomes the inevitable chalice by which we experience "das Nichtig- und Machtloswerden" of our own essance. And maybe we should not decline to drink this poison. For it could be a medicine: "das Nichtig- und Machtloswerden" of our *Wesen*, this loss of strength and power of our own Being, is that not the only experience of death we (can) have? If we had more time, I could try to show that such is the experience of a finitude we can only be *finitely* related to, and that this experience has a different structure from the one Heidegger was later to describe as 'releasement' (*Gelassenheit*). But let us leave that for another occasion. It is time for us to return to the cave. Such was, after all, our agreement. But we need not worry. We will have to die, but "they" won't kill us. Not if we 'change the subject'.

CHAPTER TWO

FROM FOUCAULT TO HEIDEGGER
A ONE-WAY TICKET?

Dasein, Heidegger says, stands in the truth. And not only that: it stands equi-primordially both in the truth and the untruth. Or in a later formulation on which the 'Turning' has already stamped its seal: the untruth is 'older' or 'more primordial' than the truth itself, Dasein must be in the untruth in order to be in the truth[1]. Mendel, on the other hand, as we read in Foucault, lies outside the truth: what he says gets lost in the tumultuous space of a "wild exteriority," where those are referred whose speech does not conform to the rules which the "discursive police" of their discipline set down[2].

Mendel produced, if we are to believe Foucault, "true statements, but he wasn't involved 'within the true' of the biological discourse of his time" (ODis 61). Because Mendel lies outside of the truth, what he says can only take monstrous and grotesque forms and this deformation makes it impossible for his speech to warm itself at the hearth of the biological discourse of his time. Mendel lies in the untruth, and that means that he – for a time, at least – irrevocably falls outside the truth. Dasein, on the other hand, cannot do without the untruth if it wants to see or have something to say in the light of the truth. Like Mendel, it cannot separate itself from the untruth, but unlike Mendel, it can only be related to the truth because it is already related to the untruth.

As one can see, we have barely begun and already we find ourselves confused by the truth. In the truth but also in the untruth; in the untruth and just because of that also in the truth; in the untruth and therefore not in the truth – imagine the mess which the convergence of two Heidegger quotations and a page from Foucault could cause for the conclusions by an author of a comparative study on the truth in Heidegger and Foucault. If our author is not already totally put out of joint by 'the truth' or discouraged

1. See the introduction by A. De Waelhens en W. Biemel to their translation of *Vom Wesen der Wahrheit* (M. HEIDEGGER, *De l'essence de la vérité*, Louvain/Paris,Nauwelaerts/Vrin, 1948, pp. 44-5). For the difference with *Being and Time*, see BT § 44b.
2. For Foucault's discussion of Mendel see his 'The Order of Discourse' (ODis, pp. 60-1).

by this surplus of truth, he would probably find himself admitting that Heidegger and Foucault, although clearly related to each other, finally are not speaking about the same thing. Naturally, he would hasten to add that this does not prevent them from having had their say and, that therefore both of them seem to have part of the truth on their side. But if someone would find the truth of Heidegger more attractive because it digs deeper and thus seems to be able to incorporate certain thoughts of Foucault, he should not forget the fact that this mixing and matching has a price and is only partial. And the same warning holds for those who remark very subtly that the communication distortion, which broke off this posthumous dialogue, seems to indicate that it is Foucault's position which is the most reasonable because, as our author's extensive comparative study itself has shown, both Heidegger and Foucault find themselves – not unlike Mendel – outside the order of truth to which the other belongs. But here our imaginary author would strongly object, he is not prepared to give up rationality itself – imagine that – and he refers to further investigations which are necessary to solve the problems that arise here. Investigations, for example, concerning the relation between Foucault and Nietzsche; for, after all, Foucault himself in one of his last interviews pointed out, did he not, that the whole of his philosophical development was defined by Heidegger, but that Nietzsche took the upper hand[3]?

I should apologize for having let myself go and not having been able to resist the temptation of making a caricature of a genre which is still practised with much zeal, in my discipline at least. But it is understood, of course, that my sarcasm in this had a ritual and exorcising function: I wanted to prevent a discourse from forcing itself upon me which, with the fatality I sketched, would stray into some superficial parallels and meaningless conclusions on the so-called Heideggerian background of Foucault. I wanted to avoid, in the midst of a movement from Heidegger to Foucault, being touched on the shoulder by a connective word which would ask me to slow down my speed and would demand more objectivity. Therefore, I will not devote this chapter to Heidegger 'and' Foucault. Let us leave the connectives to those who lack the imagination to come up with better titles and less boring subjects. Let us leave the 'and's' and the 'or's' to those who still mix up philosophy with the history of ideas and whose doxographic bias prevents them from seeing that the name of an author is always hanging between invisible quotation marks which indicate that this name only represents a field of problems in texts which resist domestication by any uniting instance whatsoever. In other words, let us not look for parallels between Foucault *and* Heidegger, but let us concentrate instead on the hesitations

---

3. 'Le retour de la morale', *Les Nouvelles Littéraires*, 28/6 - 5/7 1984, p. 40.

and the rifts in their texts, and let us listen with a third ear as it were to the oppressed moments in those texts, moments which (for some reason or other, and it is important to know which one) were not accessible to the biographical individuals who put their signatures on them. Instead of searching, in the tradition of a comparative study, for parallels between Foucault and Heidegger, I would rather establish where those texts already deconstruct themselves, in the hope of finding, where those cracks do not fit together, the entrance to the secret tunnel which will allow us to sneak out from the Foucaultian orders of truth and to make our way to the alethic machinery Heidegger was constructing from the waters of the river *Lèthè*.

I. 'FOUCAULT': THE ORDER OF TRUTH

When it was mentioned earlier that Mendel fell outside the order of truth, yet made true statements, one of the central theoretical or quasi-theoretical concepts of Foucault was introduced – the notion of order – as well as the embarrassment in which Foucault found himself precisely on the basis of this notion. Strictly speaking, the definition which Foucault gives to the order of truth does not allow him to call Mendel a "true monster" or to assert that it is always possible that one speaks the truth in the space of a "wild exteriority" (ODis 61) that lies outside the ruling order of truth. Mendel was a monster – and not a *true* monster – because he spoke about objects, used methods, and worked within a theoretical horizon none of which were reconcilable with the biology of his time. What Mendel had to say was neither true nor false, because it did not primarily find itself 'within the true' or within the order of truth. Every scientific discourse lays down such an order of truth, acknowledges within those limits true or false statements and in doing so excludes in the same movement a whole teratology of knowledge outside its limits. Discourse is not something other than this order of truth, something that only in a second time proceeds with fixing that order. Discourse is this order itself, it is "the difference between what can be said correctly (...) and what is effectively said"[4]. That not everything "that can be said correctly in a certain period according to the laws of logic or grammar is effectively said"[5], shows that an active instance is at work here, which is of another nature than a logical or linguistic one. Consider Aldrovandi, for example, who in the middle of the 17th Century , in his *Historia serpentum et draconum*, in all earnestness, not only extensively covers the anatomy, nature and habits, coitus and generation, movements and diet of the serpent, but with no less detail situates that animal in mythology, fables, allegories

4. M. FOUCAULT, 'Réponse à une question', *Esprit*, 1968 (36:5), p. 863.
5. *Ibid.* and AK, pp. 44-5, 118-9.

and mysteries, covers the proverbs and historical facts about it, and further-more gives descriptions of the gods to which it is dedicated, of its use in medicine and human diet, of the different meanings of the name itself, of its synonyms and etymologies. All of this may sound strange to us but it was in strict accordance with the discursive regime of the Renaissance, which involved among other things a certain conception of language which deter-mined what could and should be said, how it had to happen, in which order, and what it was to be about[6]. For the same sort of reasons, what is at first sight the unreasonable refusal of eighteenth century anatomical pathology to use microscopes or other optical techniques becomes understandable only if one remembers that the type of visibility that was accepted at that time and imposed upon those who wanted to participate in this discipline was modeled after everyday perception: "a *de iure* visibility (...) and not (...) a natural invisibility that is forced, for a certain time, by a technique of an artificially multiplied gaze"[7]. From examples of this kind, which could be supported by many others, Foucault does not conclude that the discursive regimes of which we speak suffer from a nearsightedness due to artificial limitations which they impose on themselves. On the contrary, these restrictions seem more like positive conditions of possibility that enabled something to happen in the Renaissance or in the classical period which was different from what could be said, done, or happen, in other periods. Discourse is not only incomplete and limited, it is an essentially incomplete and limited space[8]. It is no accident that speech is subject to a rarefaction by discourse. It has to be subject to it, in order not to fall into chaos. Chaos that not only arises by lack of ordering principles, but also, as one can already read in Merleau-Ponty, by a surplus of ordering rules: *Endlichkeit*, human finitude shows itself in man's dependency on a *Verend-lichung* (de-finition); and when this finite ordering falls away or is multiplied, the only thing which remains for man is the panic with which, for example, the victim of colour amnesia who carefully sorted out all of the blue ribbons, throws the whole stack into disorder when he comes upon a pale blue variation and then goes for the pale 'greens'[9]. The astonishment at first, the vexation finally, with which one spontaneously looks upon this spectacle that endures for hours is not different from the involuntary smile on our faces when listening to Aldrovandi's enumerations. They testify to a certain blindness to the fact that the question: How is that possible there?

6. On the episteme of the Renaissance: OT, pp. 17-45; p. 39 on Aldrovandi.

7. M. FOUCAULT, *Naissance de la clinique. Une archéologie du regard médical*, Paris, P.U.F., 1983, p. 171.

8. AK, pp. 67, 110 and 'Réponse à une question', *l.c.*, p. 861.

9. M. MERLEAU-PONTY, PP, p. 176 and the allusion to this passage in OT, p. XVIII.

properly contains the answer in itself. 'That there' is possible in the same way as the 'this here' that makes us pose the question: it is possible on the basis of the fact that "speaking consists of doing something which is something different than giving expression to what one thinks or translating what one already knows, and is also something different than letting the structure of a language function" (AK 209). Speaking is an instance of a discourse, that is to say, of a practice which does not allow itself to be reduced to a function of referral or expression. Such a discourse, for example, does something more and something different than documenting the originality of thinking subjects; it binds them to a set of rules which enables their thought and originality. Discourse is not – and this is well known – the effect of a subject, but – and this is less well known – it doesn't dismiss the subject that participates in it, and to a certain extent is formed by it, from his subjectivity[10]. The kind of speech that Foucault talks about, the speech of the truth, is painful and laborious, it is not at all an automatism that is regulated discursively. It is not because one finds oneself 'inside the truth' that one speaks the truth, but one can only pronounce something which can be judged in terms of true-false when one finds oneself 'inside the true' and submits one's propositions to "certain conditions which are stricter and more complex than [what one usually understands by] the pure and simple truth" (ODis 60). There is no truth which is that pure that it would not be discursively defined. Hence, the definition Foucault gives of 'truth' – and he places 'truth' between quotation marks: "by 'truth' I do not mean the ensemble of truths which are to be discovered and accepted but rather the ensemble of rules according to which the true and the false are separated"[11]. There is no truth outside discourse. Discourse is 'truth' itself. Or again: for Foucault 'truth' is discourse.

Or at least: it seems so or it could have been this way. And problems start here. More precisely: they started here a long time ago. What I have sketched so far, could be called Foucault's problematic, that is to say, a systematic field of problems which is at stake in his work. Foucault's text, however, does not solely consist in an articulation of the problems which become possible through that problematic. This problematic is never purely present – not even in the short text about *The Order of the Discourse* which I commented on a moment ago – but it is always in some way concealed or

---

10. AK, p. 209: "These positivities are not so much limitations imposed on the initiative of the subjects as the field in which that initiative is articulated (without however, constituting its centre)...".

11. M. FOUCAULT, 'Truth and Power' (1977), in ID., *Power / Knowledge. Selected Interviews and Other Writings (1972-1977)*, (ed. C. Gordon), New York, Pantheon Books, 1980, p. 132.

weakened by the resistance Foucault exerts against it as an inner author, by the direction that he wants to take with it, by the problems he has with it[12]. So it is not quite correct, for example, to state that 'truth' and 'discourse' are the same for Foucault. This applies only to those discourses which already lend themselves to the truth, those which let themselves be led by the distinction true-false. Discourses are not only 'dependent' upon a set of internal ordering rules which give colour in a certain manner to the distinction true-false and fill it in with the palette of a certain discursive regime. They also involve an ordering rule which itself imposes the distinction true-false – a distinction which, according to Foucault, is not at all evident, but has the status of an exclusion mechanism which in principle does not differ from the exclusion mechanism which defines our normality and makes us put the madmen in asylums (ODis 53ff). In this exclusion mechanism, Foucault sees the expression of a "will to know" or a "will to truth" which he finds suspect, because it can only assert itself on the basis of "a first and continually repeated *forgery* which poses the distinction between true and false"[13]. Foucault seems to think that resisting this 'truth' is a political business – what's more: it is *the* political business – it is always connected with power, one can never separate truth from politics, but one can form different alliances, and one has to do so, if one does not want to succumb to that 'truth' which has installed itself today. The internal as well as the external rules which establish an order of truth are arbitrary and therefore revisable, albeit in a sea of blood – blood other than that to which they owe their appearance. Every 'truth' consists in a colonization and pacification which can give way at any moment to the dead anger of the silent war which it temporarily manages to suppress[14].

As one can see: it is Nietzsche – a certain Nietzsche – who holds the

---

12. For this notion of an 'inner author' cf. my 'Can Genealogy Be Critical? A Somewhat Unromantic Look at Nietzsche and Foucault', *Man and World*, 1990(23), pp. 441-52, esp. the second section: 'Where is the author?'. I there define the 'internal author' as "that instance in a text which closes a problematic that tries to break through" (p. 445). My *Michel Foucault. Genealogy as Critique* (London/New York, Verso, 1995) consequently locates the inner author 'Foucault' in the quotation marks he puts around 'sciences' or around words like 'soul'. I sometimes tend to stress this difference between the inner author and his problematic, be it Foucault or someone else, by putting his name between quotation marks (as I already did when speaking of *'Heidegger's' decision* in the previous chapter).

13. M. FOUCAULT, *Résumé des cours. 1970-1982*, Paris, Gallimard, 1989, p. 14.

14. See the lectures of the 21st and 28th of January 1976, published in German as *Vom Licht des Krieges zur Geburt des Geschichte*, Berlin, Merve, 1986 and now also available in the recently published full lecture course *"Il faut défendre la société". Cours au Collège de France (1975-1976)* (ed. by M. Bertani and A. Fontana), Paris, Gallimard/Seuil, 1997.

upper hand here[15]. But at what price? Let us concentrate for a moment on the structure of the decision that Foucault imposes here on his problematic. In what sense is the truth "the effect of a *forgery* which carries the name of an opposition between true and false"[16]? Is this forgery avoidable? What exactly is counterfeited here? And in the name of what should we resist this? And if a falsification in an improper sense is involved here, if what is meant here is the idea that every "interpretation is at the same time a disclosure and a concealment,"[17] do we have to resist? If there is no order without forgery, without mechanisms of exclusion, if the conditions of possibility for an order are at the same time necessarily the conditions of impossibility which exclude certain things, events, and so forth, from that order, why should we resist? In the name of whom or what, using which comparative principle? What power does Foucault talk about when he connects truth with power, when he says that there is no truth without power? What kind of power is it which is contained in exclusion mechanisms which at the same time make something possible? A power that is both contingent and necessary? Doesn't Foucault extend the political terrain inaccessibly far by turning every determination – even up to the episteme itself – into a political affair[18]?

The manner in which I have formulated my questions already suggests the answer I would give to them: it is different from the answers one could find in Foucault himself. Foucault has always adopted an ambiguous attitude toward the fact that for an order to be an order, it has to rely on a number of selection and exclusion mechanisms which cannot be left out if an ordering is to establish itself. Without selection and exclusion there is no order – exclusion is, therefore, constitutive and necessary – but every factually realized order is merely the arbitrary fulfilment of these necessary mechanisms: this particular exclusion is, therefore, something contingent and capable of being abolished. But a critique of an order which has to support itself on something which is irrevocably given with this and every

15. 'Truth and Power', *loc. cit.*, p. 133: "It's not a matter of emancipating truth from every system of power (which would be a chimera, for truth is already power), but of detaching the power of truth from the forms of hegemony, social, economic and cultural, within which it operates at the present time. The political question, to sum up, is not error, illusion, alienated consciousness or ideology; it is truth itself. Hence the importance of Nietzsche".

16. *Résumé des cours, o.c.*, p. 14.

17. S. IJSSELING, 'Nietzsche en de Rhetorica', *Tijdschrift voor Filosofie*, 1973 (35:4), p. 798.

18. For such a critique see P. DEWS, 'The *Nouvelle Philosophie* and Foucault', in M. GANE (ed.), *Towards a Critique of Foucault*, London/New York, Routledge & Kegan Paul, 1986, p. 82.

other order – the exclusion of other possible orders – has something arbitrary and unsatisfactory about it. One does not get further than the insight that "what is, could also be otherwise"[19], and one could always expect the answer that, precisely because of that, one has to cling to "what is". All orders are equally good or equally bad, because they all exclude, and we lack a criterion to weigh these exclusions against each other: one can no longer judge, in terms of the truth, the rules which establish the distinction between the true and the false, or give colour to it in a certain way. At the same time, in the work of Foucault, there seems to be a sort of resistance to allowing the critical pathos that is so characteristic of his work to depend merely upon a political decisionism that acknowledges the mere partiality of the critique it proclaims. This resistance brings 'Foucault' at certain moments to the point of abandoning the notion of order: Every ordering now becomes unlawful because it violates a sort of primordial self-sufficiency, a "happy limbo of non-identity"[20] before the rise of orders, of partiality, of identity. Behind the critique on discipline, which is an ordering of the body, but which in the process nevertheless oppresses "the body itself," there appears the dream of a sort of primordial spontaneity of a body which does not have to be bridled by any order – a dream which at the same time and with the same vigour was always denied and criticized by Foucault[21]. This game in which one hand erases what the other has written, in which the one hand puts down quotation marks around 'subject', 'science', 'soul' on the basis of arguments which are deleted by the other hand, the whole of this to and fro, which as I have tried to show in *Genealogy as Critique*, continually deconstructs Foucault's texts, all of this is characteristic of a situation in which a relativism of conditions of validity (and notions like 'order' or 'discourse' do not express anything else) finds itself, from the moment that one tries like Foucault or Lyotard, but unlike Rorty or the later Wittgenstein, to escape from the 'conservative' implications which are included in the starting-point[22]. Foucault works himself into difficulties, not on the basis of the notion of order, but on the basis of the critique which he attaches to it. Universalistic positions attempt

19. Paul Veyne uses this expression in his sympathetic description of Foucault's project: 'Foucault révolutionne l'histoire', in P. VEYNE, *Comment on écrit l'histoire*, Paris, Seuil, 1978, p. 204.

20. M. FOUCAULT, 'Introduction', in *Herculine Barbin: Being the Recently Discovered Memoirs of a Nineteenth-Century French Hermaphrodite*, New York, Pantheon Books, 1980, p. XIII.

21. For expressions such as "the body in itself" which one can find in *Surveiller et Punir* (*Discipline and Punish*) and *La volonté de savoir* (*The History of Sexuality. Volume I*) (though not in the English translations!) see my *Genealogy as Critique*, pp. 122 ff.

22. The qualification 'conservative' is not meant to have a political connotation here.

to exempt the critique from arbitrariness by abandoning the notion of order itself and directing themselves to a common ground that precedes orders or to an all-encompassing horizon which binds the phenomenal orders by installing itself in the high altitudes of formal universality. Now, the interesting point with Heidegger is that he does not belong to such 'modernists', nor to the 'post-modernists'. Heidegger does not abandon the notion of order, but deepens it and gives the process of ordering a name which, after everything that has been said about Mendel, cannot come as a great surprise: A-letheia.

II. 'HEIDEGGER': THE ORDERING OF TRUTH

Aletheia, as is well-known, is the groundword for Heidegger, a word which fascinated him from the beginning and that gradually demanded all of his attention; like idea in Plato, aletheia, in Heidegger, is a kind of condensation of all philosophical questions which pre-occupy him, something which keeps these questions open and gives them direction by remaining itself a question[23]. Aletheia thus confronts us with a question here, not with an answer, and surely not with the kind of answer which could be decided on the basis of a purely etymological discussion (this does not mean that this discussion has no relevance – I will return to this). Heidegger is not first and foremost concerned with making sure that from now on aletheia is no longer translated as 'the truth' but by 'the unconcealed' or 'the undisguised' or 'the undistortedness' and that one merely adopts one of those translations. The whole discussion of the translation of a single – albeit important – Greek word only makes sense in so much as the traditional conception of truth which is the basis of the usual translation (aletheia = truth of judgement) is questioned. The conclusion of this discussion is not dependent on Heidegger being right to discern an alpha-privativum in the word a-letheia, but on his being able to show that the primary locus of the truth is not, as it is generally accepted, the judgement and that the presence of the truth still presupposes something other than agreement, correspondence, or homoiosis between a proposition and that with which it deals.

Heidegger's argument concerning the derivation of the truth of judgement is in itself very simple. Something must already be, in one way or another, discovered or disclosed if a proposition is to be made about it. In Being and Time, as we have seen in the preceding chapter, this 'being-discovered' refers to Dasein, which can discover beings because it is a being-in-the-world and not a consciousness enclosed upon itself which has still to

23. Cf. M. HEIDEGGER, Vom Wesen der Wahrheit. Zu Platons Höhlengleichnis und Theätet (Freiburg Lectures, winter semester 1931/32), GA 34, pp. 172-3.

build a bridge to the world. However, because Dasein is not solely discovering (*entdeckend*), but is also prone to having itself guided by what "One" says or talks about, beings about which a statement is made do not always appear the way they are, but only the way they appear to be (BT § 44b). In the latter case, Heidegger sees the conditions of possibility for an untrue statement. True statements, on the contrary, presuppose that Dasein does not allow itself to be guided by the ruling opinions, but is now in its *own* authentic way discovering, and not fleeing from the openness (*Erschlossenheit*) which belongs to the structure of its Being. Dasein has always to incorporate what has been discovered, against the appearances and distortions into which it is tempted by the "they". Dasein has to assure itself of its "own" discoveries and of its "own" discovering power. Thus, *a-letheia* is "a robbery" which temporarily dismisses the concealment and triumphs over the appearance (BT 265/222). The beings, time and again, have to be protected against the false appearance of concealment, against the *lethe* which covers up the original intuitions of truth and leaves it in the realm of idle talk. The way in which Heidegger reads the *alpha-privativum* here makes clear the price which *Being and Time* has to pay to ground the truth of judgement on a transcendental (Dasein's)truth: the ontological status of appearance can only be related to the fallenness of Dasein[24]. Later on, Heidegger will continually try to acknowledge in the appearance more than merely a 'false appearance,' and connect it with the happening of Being. From this attempt, in which Heidegger's so-called "Turning" is executed, there slowly results a different reading of the hyphen in *a-letheia*: the *lethe*, concealing or concealment, now belongs to the core of *aletheia* and can never be fully abolished from it. It is not only that disclosure never manages to dispense with concealment, but also that it needs it – *phusis kruptesthai philei*: Being can only let its Being and beings come to unconcealment on the basis of a fundamental relation to the concealment[25]. Formulated more simply: if there is to be something to be seen, something to be said, or to occur, then that which brings about this possibility and starts us on this way[26] has to withdraw with humility instead of attracting attention to itself. Being 'is' this withdrawal, it establishes a kind of openness in which beings

---

24. I follow here J.-Fr. COURTINE, 'Phénoménologie et vérité', in F. VOLPI e.a., *Heidegger et l'idée de la phénoménologie* (Phaenomenologica 108), Dordrecht/Boston/London, Kluwer, 1988, pp. 81-106.

25. Cf. 'Aletheia (Heraclitus, Fragment B16)', in ID., *Early Greek Thinking. The Dawn of Western Philosophy*, San Francisco, Harper & Row, 1984, pp. 113 ff. and GA 34, pp. 92-3.

26. 'auf einem Weg des Entbergens bringen' is an expression Heidegger frequently uses in his essay on 'The Question Concerning Technology' (in *Basic Writings*, New York, Harper & Row, 1977).

can appear, by remaining in the background. The 'essance'[27] of Being 'is' a *withdrawal*, a *Seinsentzug*.

This is not the place to go into the complex structure of the 'Turning'. This could only be the object of a slow and patient dissection of Heidegger's texts, and an analysis of the role which the hyphen plays in them, starting with *Being and Time*, which, as I have suggested, finds itself shipwrecked on this very hyphen, for reasons which I partly tried to address in the preceding chapter. Let me attempt instead to highlight the risk of the 'Turning' by looking at its effect and at the same time protect the terminology of the later Heidegger from a possible misunderstanding.

To speak about 'Being that withdraws', does that not signify that Heidegger finally turns Being into a substantive again and that he overlooks the ontological difference in a *temporalized philosophy of origins* (Habermas)[28] which displaces the initiative from Dasein to Being and opens the floodgates to irrationality? Not at all. On the contrary, Heidegger tries to understand history and gain insight into the fact that reason and truth appear to have a history. For the later Heidegger the existence of Newton's laws is not solely dependent upon the fact that there is Dasein which allows them by its sheer existence to be 'true'in a meaningful way (BT § 44c). Newton's laws also presuppose that beings have already appeared in a certain way or in a certain light, that they are explained in a certain way – bound up with a certain mathematical conception of nature which differs, for example, from the Aristotelian conception and on the basis of which Newtonian science can only see and observe the beings as such. Before the 'Turning' Heidegger brings the truth of judgement back to a more original discovery of beings and connects this discovery to an even more original disclosure which comes from Dasein. After the 'Turning', aletheia points not only in the direction of the unconcealment of beings but also to an openness ('*Offenheit*') of a different kind, a finite frame in which beings can be set free. Such a frame still presupposes the freedom of Dasein, but it is not dependent upon it. On the contrary, it is allotted to Dasein: "*es ist das ihm Zugeschickte*"[29], that within which it must keep itself or that to which it has to relate itself: "*viewed as Dasein (i.e., with respect to his ec-static condition), man [can] only [be], by reaching outwards out of himself to that which is totally other than he himself, namely, the clearing of Being*"[30]. Dasein

27. As in the previous chapter, the 'a' in "ess*a*nce" refers to the verbal character of Heidegger's "Wesen".

28. *The Philosophical Discourse of Modernity. Twelve Lectures*, Cambridge, Polity Press, 1987, p. 153.

29. *Vier Seminare*, Frankfurt a. M., Vittorio Klostermann, 1977, p. 125 (= GA 15: 387).

30. *Ibid.*, p. 124 (= GA 15: 386).

is no longer itself the 'clearing' (*Lichtung*), but lies *in* a clearing which no longer refers to the light of a *'lumen naturale'*, but to an openness or a leeway in which light can play its game with its shadows[31]. Dasein not only dis-covers beings, it is also the one to which the Being of beings reveals itself.

One will have noticed how, after a long detour, we arrive again at some of Foucault's basic insights, but also how we have progressed to a position which can no longer become entangled in 'Foucault's' problems. To be sure there is no truth without Dasein; but that 'there is' truth is not solely a matter of Dasein. "There is" an order of truth, an *'openness'* (*Offenheit*) or a *'clearing'* that is not simply limited or delimited by something which remains hidden – but by something which hides and withdraws itself. 'Truth' refers not simply to an *order* of truth (*Unverborgenes*), but also to an *ordering* of truth (*Entbergung*). The essance of truth is not a concept, but a happening: "Truth 'is' ['essances'], it is (...) the constituting force for all the true and the false, which are searched for, which are fought and suffered for"[32]. Against Foucault, who merely concludes that orders of truth exist and that truth has a history, Heidegger tries to introduce a terminology which enables us to think the *order* of truth (the *'Gelichtete'*) out of its *ordering* (the *'Lichtung'*), to conceive of the history of truth by way of the "happening", the "essancing" of truth. Like Foucault, Heidegger speaks of a 'decision' which establishes what is to be considered as true and also what can be rejected and thrown aside as untrue[33]. But while Foucault concludes that the truth is what "we struggle for" and relates this "to the power we attempt to make our own" (ODis 53), Heidegger relates this decision to a battle which occurs in the heart of truth itself, insofar as the unconcealment is fundamentally related to a concealment and a concealing it can never simply leave behind. But the sound of this struggle goes unheard in the fury of the battle which people fight for the truth. For Heidegger, the *"struggle between those who are in power and those who want to come to power"*[34] brings the human being into a position which turns him away from the Being of truth

---

31. Cf. 'The End of Philosophy and the Task of Thinking': "*The lumen naturale*, the light of reason, (...), does concern the clearing, but so little does it form it that it needs it in order to be able to illuminate what is present in the clearing" (*Basic Writings*, o.c., p. 386 – transl. modified).

32. *Grundfragen der Philosophie. Ausgewählte "Probleme" der "Logik"* (Freiburg Lectures, winter semester 1937/38), GA 45, p. 44.

33. 'Plato's Doctrine of Truth', in W. BARRETT and H. D. ACKEN (eds.), *Philosophy in the Twentieth Century. An Anthology. Vol. II*, New York, Random House, 1962, p. 269 (transl. modified).

34. 'Overcoming Metaphysics', in M. HEIDEGGER, *The End of Philosophy*, Norwich, Souvenir Press, 1975, p. 102.

and alienates (*Entfremdung* (!)) man vis-a-vis the *Open*[35]. To turn truth into a political situation like Foucault wants to do, means for Heidegger to give in to the *Will to Will* and to prepare for the triumph of nihilism. Against the background of this threat, Heidegger's interest in the 'question of truth' becomes understandable: he wants to prepare a *"re-volution of the whole of human Being"* by showing that man's Being is dependent upon the ruling conception of the Being of truth, a conception which, as is well known, Heidegger wanted to fundamentally question[36]. For Heidegger, what is at stake in the problem of truth is, therefore, not something logical or epistemological, but ethical: what he is questioning is the 'ethos' which must correspond to a "relativism of conditions of validity."

But let us not be misguided. It would be too beautiful if all or even part of Heidegger's writings would now suddenly appear to be an attempt to answer the problem which we have been discussing here, if they would consist of nothing more than one massive and solid answer to our questions. Let us not forget that the work of Heidegger consists of a multitude of layers and that it involves a whole series of parallelograms of forces which, like the blades of a propeller, are put into a certain angle to one another by the internal author known to us as 'Heidegger'. But if this is true, there is nothing here which forbids us to change the angles if necessary. And, indeed, we will see that such a change might be necessary. I will briefly mention three problems which are important for our problematic because in these problems the parallelism until now suggested between 'Foucault' and 'Heidegger' breaks down. The first two problems form obstacles, the third is the springboard which will prepare us for the jump from 'Foucault' to 'Heidegger'.

---

35. *Parmenides* (Freiburg Lectures, winter semester 1942/43), GA 54, p. 225: "weil im Offenen des Seins allein auch das Unverborgene des Seienden erscheinen kann und erscheint, hält sich der Mensch zunächst, und unversehens dann ständig, nur an das Seiende. Er vergißt das Sein und lernt in solchem Vergessen nur das eine: die Verkennung des Seins und die Entfremdung gegen das Offene".

36. Cf. GA 34, pp. 323-4: "Unser Fragen nach dem Wesen der Wahrheit ist kein überflüssiger Nachtrag, sondern das Vortragen unseres Wollens und Daseins in ganz andere Bahnen und Bezirke. Dieser Wandel des Wesens der Wahrheit ist aber nicht die bloße Abänderung einer Begriffsbestimmung (...), sondern dieser Wandel des Wesens der Wahrheit is die *Umwälzung des ganzen menschlichen Seins*, an deren Beginn wir stehen" (text from 1931-2); and GA 45, p. 214: "In der hier gestellten Wahrheitsfrage gilt es nicht nur eine Abänderung des bisherigen Begriffes der Wahrheit, nicht eine Ergänzung der geläufigen Vorstellung, es gilt eine *Verwandelung des Menschseins* selbst (...) die Verrückung des Menschseins aus seinem bisherigen Standort – oder besser seiner Standortlosigheit – in den Grund seines Wesens, *der Gründer und Wahrer der Wahrheit des Seyns zu werden* (...)" (text from 1937-8).

First problem. Until now I have silently presupposed that Heideggerian *aletheia*, like Foucaultian 'Truth', forms a condition of possibility for truth in the usual sense, a kind of frame which allows us to speak in a certain manner in terms of truth and falsehood. But is this so? What is, in fact, the relation between *aletheia* and *adaequatio* (truth of judgement)? If a simple deepening of the problem of truth was concerned here, if *aletheia* would be a more original 'truth' which makes possible the truth of judgement, then where are we to place the *pathos* with which Heidegger calls '*correctness*' (*Richtigkeit*) an error (*Irrtum*) (cf. GA 45: 31 and *passim*) and presents the history of truth as a genealogy of these errors in terms of a history of "decay"[37]? What prevents us from holding on to the conception of *adaequatio* and ground it in *aletheia*? Why does Heidegger have this remarkable sympathy (I did not say nostalgia) for the Greeks to whom the original locus of truth was not the truth of judgement but the beings themselves? Does this sympathy have something to do with the fact that the Greeks recognized, along with the truth of judgement, truth as the unconcealment of what is? And might the decline (since the Greeks) have something to do with the fact that this duality of truth gave way exclusively to the correspondence theory? Where does this 'decline' originate? Here Heidegger hesitates; and one can say, without exaggeration, that the work of Heidegger is this hesitation[38]. Many passages seem to point to the fact that the Greek *homoiosis* is itself the root of the decline: metaphysics starts here (Plato and Aristotle), or at least – first hesitation – it can start from this point. The possibility for the decline, where the *homoiosis* becomes independent, is already inscribed in the origin. But – second hesitation – that origin is itself already in a certain decline because it is corruptible and impure. Behind this origin lies yet another origin, the pre-Platonic start of Greek philosophy, where truth was conceived of as *aletheia*, unconcealment, and *homoiosis* had not yet made its appearance. But even this origin – and this is a third hesitation, to which I will return later – was not totally 'in order' because the Greek experience of *aletheia* here is not quite the experience it should be or could be.

The problem, therefore, is the relation between *aletheia* and *adaequatio*. For Heidegger, this relation was surely not one of a simple condition of possibility. To the contrary, *aletheia* and correctness are sometimes (I do not say always), presented as competing conceptions of truth: *aletheia* or

---

37. Heidegger himself uses the word 'decay' (*Verfall*), e.g. in GA 34, p. 181: "auf dem Wege eines Verfallens (ist) der Begriff des 'Denkens' und der 'ratio' entstanden", and *passim* in GA 45, GA 54. I will return to the difficulties and peculiarities which characterize Heidegger's use of this expression.

38. In what follows I comment GA 45, pp. 100-12 and *passim*.

orthotes[39]. This problem has an interesting corollary in the fact that its formulation is dependent on Heidegger's analysis of the different positions that human beings took or had to take on the grounds of the different essances of the truth, and it has also something to do with the whole discourse on the essance or 'ethos' of the human being. For Heidegger, the Greeks were receptive[40], their apprehension is an allowing-to-bring-forth (*Hervorbringen-lassen*) of something which already arises by itself (*antikeimenon, ob-icere*) from concealment and looks upon the human being. The Greeks were not representing subjects who acknowledge objects only on the basis of representations which allow them to appear. They did not present themselves as a 'scene' where beings have to (re)present themselves, and where they have to be pictures[41]. All of this is well known. But do we have to follow Heidegger here? To be honest, I do not know what to think about it. Does not the word 'scene' by itself already point to Heidegger's resistance to mimesis, and to his mistrust or suspicion of every form of displacement of appearance to a place other than its original one[42]? The whole discussion that arises here on the essance of the human being should be analysed with the utmost care. Does not Heidegger become the victim of a sort of subject-phobia that turns itself not only against the (re)presenting subject, but also against every form of subjectivity which is something more than or different from a perceiving (but not responsive) receptivity? To be sure, the Heideggerian apprehension (*Vernehmen*) is not a passivity; it is a *Hervorbringen-lassen*, an *Entsprechen*, co-respondence[43]. But it is the sort of *Entsprechen* that can and must do full justice to that to which

39. Compare, for example, what is said on GA 45, p. 99 with the remark on the next page where Heidegger evokes an age "in which the conception of truth as correctness was still foreign to the Greeks; in which rather the original experience of truth as unconcealedness held its sway". It seems as if the introduction of *homoiosis* not only has been possible *on the basis of* this original experience of truth, but that it also *corrupted* this experience. With *homoiosis* we have the beginning of a series of *de iure* superfluous supplements to an original experience of truth that (*de iure* again) also could have existed without these supplements and indeed have. At the same time, however, Heidegger seems to be trying to link this corruption of the origin to its "corruptibility" (see my comments in the preceding paragraph).

40. GA 45, p. 139 and 'The Age of the World Picture', in M. HEIDEGGER, *The Question Concerning Technology and Other Essays*, New York, Harper & Row, 1977, p. 131.

41. 'The Age of the World Picture', p. 132.

42. For this characterisation of mimesis as 'appearance in another place': S. IJSSELING, *Mimesis. On Appearing and Being* (transl. H. IJsseling - J. Bloechl), Kampen (The Netherlands), Kok Pharos, 1997, which includes an essay on 'Heidegger and Mimesis' (pp. 59-77).

43. Cf. *Der Satz vom Grund*, Pfullingen, Neske, 1986, p. 88: 'Unser Vernehmen ist in sich ein Entsprechen'.

it *directs* itself (implicit *homoiosis*, but not in the sense of representation). It is a kind of answer which fully absorbs the question; it is a kind of *Entsprechen* that allows that which already arises out of itself to express itself – better still: to impress itself on the wax receptacle it proposes; it is a *legein* in the sense of a bringing together that takes over and publishes something which is already ordered itself, a bringing together that ex-presses without imposing itself on what it ex-presses. In short, what we have here seems to be a receptivity without response which, as Michel Haar formulates it, turns man into a "man without qualities"[44] – pure *da* or pure *ex*, pure ek-sistence. And one can and has to question whether some of the qualities which fall away here – a certain closing or being closed, a kind of impurity – are not ascribed too quickly by Heidegger to the inauthentic. All of the problems which surround this topic in *Being and Time*, specifically in section 44, return here and should be analysed. But instead of simply repeating here the analysis of our previous chapter, it might be helpful to formulate the caution or reservation that I express here in another manner, by approaching this problem in yet another way which will confront us again with Heidegger's resistance to *mimesis*.

Second Problem. *Alethes kai on*[45]: the idea that what is true or what is disclosed are beings themselves, repeatedly makes Heidegger translate *aletheia* by *un-distortedness* (*Un-verstelltheit*): beings are true (*apseudes*) if they can appear as they really are, namely *un-ver-stellt*, un-distorted and un-displaced. But what is the relation between this 'ontic' truth or *aletheia* – the *Unverstelltheit* of *beings* to which Heidegger affords long and painstaking analyses (see e.g. GA 54) – and the 'ontological' truth of *aletheia* as *Lichtung inmitten des Seienden* (GA 45: 190), a "clearing" which, as we have seen, is not a being itself, is not dependent upon it, but, on the contrary, allows beings to appear. Can one say that the clearing, like Foucault's 'order' "does violence to things" (ODis 67)[46], by only allowing them to appear in a certain way, or is the "clearing" itself characterized by a sort of receptivity with a structure analogous to the one of *apprehension* (*Vernehmen*)? Of course, Heidegger warns us that we should not understand the clearing as a simple *"throwing-light-on"* (*belichten*) but as an *"allowing to be present"* (*Anwesenlassen*) – but what is the structure of this *allowing*? At first sight the notion of '*undistortedness*' might seem appropriate to characterize the ontic *aletheia*.

---

44. 'La pauvreté de l'*Homo humanus* ou l'homme sans facultés' is the title of the second part of M. Haar's brilliant book on *Heidegger et l'essence de l'homme*, Grenoble, Millon, 1990.

45. GA 45, p. 118 where Heidegger explains that the Greek 'kai' should be taken here in an explicative sense: "im Sinne von 'und das will sagen'".

46. For what is at stake in such 'violence', see chapter 4 below.

But since this *aletheia* never stands apart from the *clearing*, the use of this notion becomes somewhat problematic to say the least, as it seems to suggest that there is *a* ontic truth, *a* way of appearing for beings *as they are*, regardless of the clearing involved. But if this is to be the case, then the ontological truth threatens to be regulated by the ontic truth[47]. We touch here upon an important and anything but abstract problem – we even find traces of it in a certain obscurity or over-determination of the Heideggerian analysis of the En-framing (*Ge-stell*). Is saying that the Rhine, once guided through the gates of a hydro-electric plant, does not appear as a river anymore, only dependent upon Heidegger's analysis of the "challenging-forth" character of the En-framing[48]? And what can we say about the door that one can no longer open with a doorknob, but that opens with an electric eye? Should we say that it is like an airplane, only a part of the standing reserve (*Bestand*)? Why do we stumble here on such a remarkable neglect of the concrete phenomenological analysis of the technical object; on this hardly repressed depreciation of certain technical media (movies as 'experience' (*Erlebnis*) – surely not a complement[49])? Whence the strange paradigmatics of the examples which Heidegger chooses (the field, the windmill, the wooden bridge), whence this anti-productionism which only wishes to acknowledge a pro-duction (the *Hervorbringen-lassen*)? Can we, for example, refer to a pro-duction in order to clarify the 'relation' (in the above mentioned sense) between 'homosexuality' and the *clearing* which allows it to exist[50]?

The perplexity in which these questions leave us should not be taken as a sign of our superiority, for we do not yet know the answers to these questions and we would not even be able to pose them were it not for Heidegger. In addition, the questions we cannot but raise here, are precisely those questions which keep Heidegger's texts themselves in motion – texts which we have hardly begun to analyse here. But as always, it is far better to have some unanswered questions than to have plenty of unquestioned answers. And we should keep to these questions if we care to understand in some way the role and the status of the problem of 'Greece' in Heidegger's work. That a nostalgia was never present in it, but at most a sympathy – that

47. This seems to be the problem Philippe Lacoue-Labarthe discusses in 'Typographie' (in ID., *Mimesis des articulations*, s.l., Aubier Flammarion, 1975, pp. 165-270).

48. 'The Question Concerning Technology', in *Basic Writings*, *o.c.*, pp. 297 ff.

49. E.g. 'Memorial Address', in *Discourse on Thinking*, New York, Harper & Row, 1966, p. 48: "Week after week the movies carry them off into uncommon, but often merely common, realms of the imagination, and give *the illusion of a world that is no world*".

50. For Foucault the 'appearance' of homosexuality cannot be viewed as a 'pro-duction' but as a production (see my analysis in *Genealogy as Critique*, chapter 3).

Heidegger in the same pages in which he sketches the 'decline' which started with Plato, time and time again qualifies that he sees no fault in this decline, but a certain necessity – all of this indicates how intricate the problem remains as long as Heidegger clings to a certain explanation of the Greek experience on the basis of (but not *exclusively* on the basis of) a questionable etymology. Not that these problems are simplified when Heidegger abandons this explanation – and now thinks that *aletheia*, unconcealment "was originally [this means already with the Greeks] experienced only as *orthotès*, as the correctness of representations and statements" (which means among other things that "the assertion about the essential transformation of truth, that is from unconcealment to correctness, is also untenable")[51]. With this third problem, which as I said, is no longer an obstacle to us, the whole balance of forces changes and it becomes possible to relate the problem of *ethos* to that of *aletheia*.

III. GAMING... IN THE A-LETHEIA

Let us return to the structure of our discussion. I have shown how Foucault saw himself confronted with the choice of either turning every order into an authentic order by accepting exclusion as being constitutive, or condemning every order to inauthenticity by appealing to a pre-ordinal self-sufficiency and interpreting the exclusion as a mere effect of power. In the first case, a convincing critique of any given order seems to be impossible; the only thing that can be said is that "everything could also have been otherwise." In the second case, every order becomes alienating and again one has no reason to adhere to Foucault's critique of orders. In both cases, Foucault does not succeed in doing what he claims to do: to give a critique of a distinct order which is specific enough to prevent it from becoming trivial by being just as applicable to every other order. The only way out for Foucault would have consisted in developing a critique that does not question the being-of-an-order because of what it left unrealized (other possible orders), or because of the violence it did to the things it had to order (a pure pre-ordinality, the wild spontaneity of the body or insanity "itself") in order to be an order. How would such a critique look if it were to question not the ordinality as such, but a specific ordinality? A possible answer could run as follows: it could try to show that certain orders tend to forget, or veil, the fact that they are an order, and on this basis claim an authority which does not properly belong to them. But why should an order not forget or fail to recognize that it is an order? With such questions we have already placed ourselves beyond the boundaries of what for the sake of

51. 'The End of Philosophy', *l.c.*, p. 390.

convenience we referred to as 'Foucault'. With such questions we already find ourselves in 'Heidegger'. And we might as well profit from our new position and rephrase our problem in the terms of 'Heidegger'. A Heideggerian reformulation of our problem would run as follows: What is the 'relation' between an order and the occurrence of the order itself? In terms of the example which we have concentrated on: between the order of truth and the being or becoming of truth? In other words, what call do we get from the occurrence of the truth? Which comportment or 'attitude' is expected of us? Until now, I have only tried to make it acceptable that formulating this question in Heideggerian terms makes sense, and that the answer to this question could clarify a problem that could, in a legitimate way, be transposed from 'Foucault' to 'Heidegger'. Now I shall try to indicate concisely the shape of a possible answer on the basis of 'Heidegger', although it should be clear from the discussion of the first two problems that such an answer cannot unequivocally be found in the texts of Heidegger themselves, even less so when a third problem, as we shall see in a moment, is going to add itself to all of the difficulties I have just mentioned.

That Heidegger's sympathy for Greece never led to a call for a *retour à la Grèce* has something to do with the fact that the Greeks had experienced *aletheia*, were philosophically busy with it, but were busy with it in such a way that they never questioned *aletheia* as such. The Greeks, Heidegger says time and again, never thought *aletheia*. Not that he thought ill of them for that. That they never got further than the insight that what 'is' is the 'un-concealed', that they never questioned unconcealedness itself is not their shortcoming, but perhaps their greatness. It was the destiny of the Greeks to focus on beings as they are, on beings in their unconcealedness and by doing so begin philosophy; if they had questioned further they would have "abandoned their proper task" (GA 45: 137). Nevertheless, for a long time, Heidegger saw in this *not-questioning-further* the reason for the decay in the history of truth as it moved from *aletheia* to correctness. It therefore seemed necessary for him to write a genealogy of the truth in order to get in touch with the 'new element' in the Greek 'beginning', an element that carries with it the possibility of another 'beginning'. Hegel is never mentioned here, but without his influence, which Heidegger would obviously want to defend himself against, it is difficult to understand what could be meant here by the 'hidden law of the beginning' (*verborgenes Gesetz des Anfangs*) or 'inner law of the beginning' (*inneres Gesetz des Anfangs*) and so forth[52]. Whatever there is of this – and the problems that arise here are certainly not unimportant,

---

52. For these expressions: GA 45, pp. 37, 48 and *passim*. For Hegel / Heidegger: M. HAAR, *Le chant de la terre. Heidegger et les assises de l'histoire de l'être*, Paris, Editions de l'Herne, 1985, pp. 141-60.

if only because they will annoy those of our contemporaries who think that they can escape Hegel's long shadow by retiring to the artificial light of their Heidegger library – since the Greeks in their time did not think *aletheia* through to the end, Heidegger is convinced that he can only turn around the history of truth and prepare for a 'complete reversal of human Being' (*Umwälzung des ganzen menschlichen Seins* – see note 36), by now attempting to do what they did not do before and did not have to do: to question the *aletheia* as such.

But if the Greeks, standing in the midst of *aletheia*, were satisfied by this without questioning its status, then why will we have to do something more and something different? The question seems all the more valid since Heidegger himself, in order to show that the Greeks in no way failed, pointed out that the Greek experience of truth was, in a certain sense, dependent upon a forgetting of the occurrence of truth itself. In order to bring to light what lies within a '*clearing*', this '*clearing*' has first to shine forth itself and then shine upon what lies within it; but it can not and may not become that which keeps our attention. "The clearing, the *aletheia* must in a certain sense be overlooked" (GA 45: 147).

Now it is no longer difficult to understand that it became less and less important for Heidegger to hold on to the thesis of the appearance and the immediate disappearance of the truth (*aletheia*) in Greece. One understands why he no longer wanted to make a point of this etymological question. For is not what has just been said about the Greeks valid for every experience? Does not every experience find its possibility in something which is concealed and which precisely conceals itself at the same moment when we, lingering in the 'clearing' which opens up the beings for us and makes them accessible, lose ourselves in these beings? Is it not precisely the case that we must 'lose ourselves' with the beings and occupy ourselves with them if we want to see what is offered to us by this '*clearing*'? Does not the Being of truth (verbally) have to escape from us, if we are to be capable of formulating our truths? Does not *aletheia* always, for essential reasons, "have to be overlooked"? In other words, the Being of truth would not extract itself only factually and according to the 'law' of the 'beginning' from Greek experience; it could not do otherwise than extract itself from this and *every other experience*. *Aletheia* is not something which might appear in an age and attract all the attention of this age, it is that which allows an age to happen, it is 'epochality' itself [53]. That which is experienced or thought is that which is present, not presence as such. That which is present claims our attention, not the presence and the '*clearing*' or *aletheia* that allows it to be

53. Cf. also J. CAPUTO, 'Demythologizing Heidegger: *Aletheia* and the History of Being', *Review of Metaphysics*, 1988 (41), pp. 519-46.

present[54]. The ordering of truth or the occurrence of truth retreats so that truth can occur and appear in an ordered way. In Heidegger's terms: "With regard to beings, Being is that which shows and makes visible without showing or becoming visible itself"[55]. That Being 'is' finite in a transitive sense[56], that it always and necessarily retreats, also entails that there is never a 'clearing of presence' as such but always a clearing of presence concealing itself[57].

Does this mean that we can do nothing more than forget Being, than forget the ordering of truth – and that we can just leave it at that? Has all the pathos with which Heidegger spoke of an "Overcoming" of metaphysics then been in vain? Misplaced perhaps? Not at all. But the situation becomes considerably more complicated, or to be more exact – since a train of thought is in consideration here which could not at every moment measure its own pace – it now becomes possible to get a clear sense of the complexity which has always been there and to gain insight into its difficulties.

The later Heidegger's discussion with metaphysics was never merely about metaphysics' forgetting of Being, but about the fact that metaphysics showed itself unable to think Being in such a way that this forgetting became an essential part of it. The 'overcoming of metaphysics' does not mean leaving metaphysics behind, but abandoning the metaphysical explanation of metaphysics. The "awakening from the oblivion of Being" which the "step back" is to prepare for does not aim, according to Heidegger, at "an extinguishing of the oblivion of Being", but at placing oneself in it and standing within it[58]. What is at stake here is not an escape from the oblivion of Being, but an attempt to make this forgetfulness accessible to experience. What could this mean?

As we have seen, in a certain sense one cannot but forget Being. And this oblivion is not a human affair, something which one can do or not do. Man can only see and act on the basis of a blind spot; he can only deal with beings by not dealing with Being as such, he can only live off the gift of the 'There is' (*Es gibt*) by overlooking the giving itself[59]; almost like someone who can only be captivated by the blue of the sky by forgetting the 'blue-ing' (*das Blauen*) of that sky (GA 34: 187). Being is, therefore, nothing more than

54. 'Time and Being', in M. HEIDEGGER, *On Time and Being*, New York, Harper & Row, 1972, pp. 12-3.

55. 'Summary of a Seminar on the Lecture "Time and Being"', in *On Time and Being*, p. 36.

56. *Identity and Difference*, New York, Harper & Row, 1974, p. 64.

57. 'The End of Philosophy', *l.c.*, p. 391.

58. 'Summary of a Seminar on the Lecture "Time and Being"', p. 30.

59. 'Time and Being', *l.c.*, p. 8 and *Vier Seminare*, p. 102 (GA 15: 364).

the forgetting of Being itself. It is because Being merely "is", "works", "occurs", by keeping itself in the background, because it can merely let beings be by retreating that it is itself forgotten. It is the default of Being (*Ausbleiben des Seins*) that makes possible the omission of the default of Being (*Auslassen des Ausbleibens des Seins*)[60]. But things are even more complicated. That Being withdraws itself seems, for Heidegger, not only connected with the fact that the "clearing" has to step back in favour of what can blossom in that openness, but also with the fact that the "clearing" is finite itself; that it is dependent on a lack of openness or a darkness from which it gains its openness: there never is or can be a total *a-letheia*, but only a *lethe* or concealment which, in a certain sense, is older than the disclosure which arises out of the opposition. And it is this 'concealment' which, because of the structure of disclosure itself, is hidden again. In *On the Essence of Truth*, one of Heidegger's most difficult texts, he calls this concealing of the concealed the "mystery"[61]. Man has to relate himself to this "mystery", or to be more exact, since he is always already related to it, he has to relate to it in a certain way, according to a certain *ethos*. And here we have finally localized the problem which has occupied us for all of this time: What is the structure of this *ethos*?

The essence of truth is an unconcealment which at the same time conceals itself. And because this unconcealment has necessarily to fall back upon a concealment which is concealed along with the concealing of the unconcealment, truth has something to do with a "secret"[62]. "Truth", in the sense of *aletheia*, is therefore, as it were, an occurrence which digs holes which we can only attempt to fill in with our little truths. From these small truths, man borrows measures which give him a direction. But in this he forgets the basis for this measure-taking itself and the essence or occurrence from where the possibility of this measure-taking is handed to him. He forgets the *Mass-gabe* and starts to posit himself as the measure-giver. He insists upon what is accessible for him and thinks that he is the one who made it accessible. Man shuts himself off from the "mystery", he "errs", he goes astray. But, Heidegger says, man always goes astray, this is his condition, and not something which can be left behind. And yet, man may not shut himself off from the "mystery". Therein lies the paradox: on the

60. I follow here *Die Seinsgeschichtliche Bestimmung des Nihilismus (1944/6)*, in *Nietzsche Bd. II*, Pfullingen, 1961, pp. 335-98 (English transl. in: *Nietzsche Vol. IV*, San Francisco, Harper & Row, 1982, pp. 197-250, in particular p. 246).

61. 'On the Essence of Truth, in *Basic Writings, o.c.*, pp. 132 ff.

62. Cf. J.-L. CHRÉTIEN, 'La réserve de l'être', in *Cahier de l'Herne. Heidegger*, Paris, L'Herne (Biblio/Essais), 1983, pp. 233-60. In what follows I comment on §§ 6 and 7 of *Of the Essence of Truth*.

basis of its existential condition, Dasein forgets (cannot but forget) the essence of the truth, loses itself (cannot but lose itself) in its truths, and, nonetheless, Heidegger still expects from such Dasein an *"openness to the mystery"*[63]. Can Heidegger still think something like that? Can Heidegger think an "openness" that does not undo the "closedness" which leads one astray? An "openness" which does not have anything to do with being put on the right track again, because there is no "right" track (how could the "clearing" which makes "correctness" possible be "right" or "correct" itself?), but an "openness" which would have to deal with the experience of erring *as* erring, with a going astray which knows that it is doing so, but cannot help but do so? What could such an openness still mean – if not precisely a certain comportment, an *ethos*? But what, then, is the structure of the *ethos* which Heidegger wants to articulate here against the limits of his own thinking?

"Openness for the mystery" – the question is unclear, but it can gain clarity *ex negativo*. What does this *not* mean? In any case, not that man has to become the pure *Da* of *Sein*, pure ek-sistence. For man is also in-sistence, he insists in the "erring"; and this "fallenness", says Heidegger, is a "natural condition of Dasein"[64] that cannot be tamed or domesticated by any culture. We are of course familiar with Heidegger's thesis of the existentiality of the "fallenness" from our reading of *Being and Time* in the preceding chapter, but it seems that only on the basis of his changed conception of truth – truth that can never expel the untruth, the *lethe*; truth which is essentially finite and historical – that Heidegger can take it seriously (or should have to be able to do so, because it is not at all clear that he has done this – I will return to that). *Being and Time* still held on, as we have seen, to a strict opposition between truth and untruth or appearance. The possibility of a pure truth was grounded in the existential possibility of an authentic openness – *Erschlossenheit im Modus der Eigentlichkeit* – against which an inauthentic disclosure remains stuck in appearances, remains "closedness". This existentiell alternative disrupted or went against the grain of the results of the existential analysis which made the "fallenness" into a structure of the Being of Dasein, or at least imposed a certain reading of it by seeing in it a kind of *in principle* removable "conformism"[65]. Dasein may lie equiprimordially in the truth and the untruth, it can only be 'closed' because it was first 'open' – and thus because it stands (ontologically) 'first' in the truth.

This conflict between the requirements of an existentiell analysis and the

63. 'Memorial Address', *l.c.*, p. 55.
64. *Vier Seminare*, *o.c.*, p. 100 (GA 15:362).
65. R. BERNET, *l.c.*, p. 262.

results of the existential analysis could not or should not arise in the later Heidegger. Dasein does not stand first in the truth, but in the untruth. It "errs" and has always turned its back upon Being. Even more: it has to turn its back upon Being to be able to stand in the truth Being founds.

This experience of having to turn our backs to 'something' that in its turn turns (and in a sense: *has* to turn) its back to us, this double chiasm of faith and unfaithfulness is not a comfortable position. It is the structure of finitude itself. A finitude which leaves one without the comfort of a rule or a law which tells us how to cope with it. One should not deny this finitude, but at the same time one would still be denying it by affirming it triumphantly. The experience of this finitude – of our being in the "erring" – is an 'experience' which in a certain sense always 'forgets' what it has 'learned' but a moment ago. It is the *experience* of a not-being-able (to be pure ek-sistence) and of a not-being-able-to-do-otherwise (than lose oneself in in-sistence) *at the same time*; an *experience* which never allows for the acquiescence that finitude is what it is (e.g., 'since we are all insistent ...'), an experience one has to cope with, or 'to bear' without hope of an "overcoming". One has to *relate* oneself *to* a finitude that one cannot escape. And this relation itself is marked by finitude; it never allows for a tenured position, but at best sends us off with an unclear, merely readable assignment.

Twice Heidegger tried to read this assignment and to translate it. The first time he spoke of a releasement (*Gelassenheit*) and (among other things) meant by it a simultaneous yes and no to the technical world. This attitude, Heidegger says, has to "save the essance of the human being", an essance which is under the threat of being captivated, bewitched, dazzled, beguiled, warped, confused and laid waste by the oncoming technological revolution in the atomic age[66]. But this spell can be broken. "We can use technical devices and yet at the same time, when we use them in a responsible way, keep ourselves so free from them that we can let go of them at any moment. But we can leave these instruments for what they are, as something that has nothing to do with our innermost and most proper core" (MA 54 – transl. modified).

Something that has nothing to do with our innermost and most proper core – this central presupposition at the same time makes it difficult to understand why and how Heidegger can claim in the same breath that technical, calculating thinking has its own legitimate place alongside contemplative thinking (MA 46). How can something which has nothing to do with our essential Being have its own legitimate place? And if it has its place, is it not then because the "innermost essance" of the human being

---

66. 'Memorial Address', *l.c.*, pp. 56 and 54 (henceforth MA).

does not have the purity which Heidegger wanted it to have? Rather, isn't this essance ambivalent, in the way in which Heidegger himself taught us: related to being, "taken into account by a sense, which man did not invent or make" but nevertheless incapable of enduring the impeccable purity of this relation? Is it not precisely this duality which prevents humanity from jumping from the familiar ground of beings to that which has no bottom, to the bottomlessness of Being (GA 54:223)? If Being is bottomless, a permanently shifting bottom full of holes, a bottom which never supports, and if beings are and can only be "a supporting bottom" by forgetting Being (*ibid.*), then can man ever have a relation to the abysmal ground of Being without "representing" this ground to himself? If representational thinking is legitimate because something in the essance of human beings keeps them from the purity of ek-sisting, something that brings them to the point of still wanting to ground the groundless ground that Being is, can one then still leave these technical objects for what they are, as something which has nothing to do with our innermost and most proper core? And, if not, can one still follow Heidegger when he tries for the second time to read the inscription which occupies us here as a "without why"[67]? Can man, like the Rose of Silesius, play without why? "Being", Heidegger says, "as what grounds has no ground itself; it plays the game as the abyss, which delivers to us Being and ground as a destiny"[68]. And he adds a further question to this, although I am not sure whether he formulated it in the same spirit with which we did and with the uncertainty that befalls us here: "the question remains whether and how we, hearing the movements of this play, play along and accommodate ourselves to the play"[69]. What would it mean if this human game were out of joint? What does it mean for man to "play", and is there something in the essance of technology, in the search for grounds, which distorts the structure of human games? With these questions which in a way are still and at the same time no longer questions of Heidegger I would like to end this journey between the continent 'Foucault' and the continent 'Heidegger' without knowing quite where we arrived. But I have the impression that this was not a single journey nor an *aller-retour*, but that it was a ride on the carousel of thought, the core of which displaced itself after some agitation. For is not the question which moved us along in these last questions the same one with which we began? What keeps us from

67. *Der Satz vom Grund*, p. 101 and *passim*.

68. *Ibid.*, p. 188 (my transl.).

69. In rendering "Sätze", which is, of course, strictly untranslatable (it could among other things also mean "bounces"), by "movements" (in the musical sense of the term) – I follow R. Lilly in his translation of *The Principle of Reason* (Bloomington/Indianapolis, Indiana U.P., 1991, p. 113).

Being is not an exclusion which we can avoid, but neither is it something which we can resign ourselves to. Man is finite and he cannot do without the 'violence' which tears him from his ec-stasy, he has to walk the erring path which is allotted to him without despairing and without irony, at the most with the "silent smile"[70] of someone who, by gaming perhaps, has learned that this violence cannot be avoided, and that he has to endure its inescapabilility. Man can at most incorporate this violence into an *ethos* that in some way detaches him from himself, but that at the same time remains fragile, always receptive to the seduction of whatever promises to free him from this fragility, of whatever tempts him into fully ek-sisting or into fully in-sisting. And this could be the reason why technology is dangerous, and even as Heidegger says the "supreme danger"[71]: it tempts us to give up this fragile tension between an existence we are incapable of and an insistence we cannot but give in to. Technology takes the place of the ontotheological God, who keeps recovering from a death which was announced to us a long time ago. And in the shadow of this ever-returning God Zarathustra's last man finds himself standing on a firm technological ground. For does he not know how to cope with his finitude? Did he not invent one technique after another to apply to himself? To perfect himself? To bear what is 'otherwise than self'? This is the man – and the God – Nietzsche warned us about, and this man, I would wager, is not as moribund as he seemed when we first saw his "face drawn in the sand at the edge of the sea" (OT 387) and mistook it for a sign of his imminent death. For "man" is yet to die and, as we can by now suspect, the validity of what some insist on calling 'the philosophical discourse of modernity' will depend on the meaning of this death.

---

70. I borrow this image from my colleague H. DE DIJN, 'Spinoza: rationalist én mysticus?', *De Uil van Minerva*, 1989-90 (6 :1), p. 42.

71. 'The Question Concerning Technology', *l.c.*, p. 308.

CHAPTER THREE

MEANING AND VALIDITY
HABERMAS ON HEIDEGGER AND FOUCAULT

Meaning, Habermas warns us, should not be allowed to consume validity[1]. For once we let meaning exhaust validity, the further exhaustion of the project of modernity and the loss of its normative content are bound to follow, as becomes clear from the writings of those Habermas calls "the theorists of the counter-enlightment", – an epithet wide enough to include authors as diverse as Heidegger, Nietzsche and Foucault. One way or another these philosophers are all undoing the intrinsic connection between meaning and validity and, we are told, the political *mésalliance* of some of them only goes to show how catastrophic indeed the replacement of critical theory's commitment to "the philosophical discourse of modernity" by some blend of post-modernism and post-structuralism is bound to be. For, according to Habermas, only a theory that respects the internal relation between meaning and validity, without at the same time eliminating the difference between the two, only such a theory can be entrusted with the delicate task of defending the legacy of modernity, whilst retaining a critical perspective on the way it is materialized in society. And Habermas is sufficiently confident in the results of his *Theory of Communicative Action* to claim the title for his own theory and to counterpose it to a host of other attempts which are, successively, shown to be mistaken or to have missed the opportunity of taking "the alternative paths" (PDM 295) implicit in their own problematics.

Such was the programme and the underlying intention of the famous series of lectures Habermas gave on the philosophical discourse of modernity: a series of criticisms in the first ten lectures, followed by an attempt to show that the "alternative way out of the philosophy of the subject" (title of Lecture XI) lies in his own focus on a communicative reason that remains faithful to "the normative content of modernity" (title of lecture XII). Ironically perhaps, the book succeeded in doing exactly the

---

1. J. HABERMAS, *The Philosophical Discourse of Modernity. Twelve Lectures*, Cambridge, Polity, 1987, p. 320 (transl. altered); originally published as *Der philosophische Diskurs der Moderne. Zwölf Vorlesungen*, Frankfurt a.M., Suhrkamp, 1985. With PDM I refer to the English translation.

reverse: far from demonstrating the superiority of his own conceptual apparatus and preparing for a power-free exchange among responsible intellectuals, Habermas seems to have estranged himself from his audience to the point where his opponents accused him not only of *seriously* misunderstanding them, but of not having read them at all, as the following quotes from Derrida attest: "It is *always* in the name of ethics, of an allegedly democratic ethic of discussion, it is always in the name of a transparant communication and of 'consensus', that the most violent infractions on the elementary rules of discussion are produced. It is *always* the moralistic discourse of consensus – or at least that discourse that pretends to sincerely appeal to consensus – that produces in fact the indecent transgression of the classical norms of reason and democracy. Not to mention of elementary philology. (...) The most prominent example (...) of this is Habermas (...)"[2]; "With a stupefying tranquillity, here is the philosopher of consensus, of dialogue and of discussion, the philosopher who claims to distinguish between science and literary fiction, between philosophy and literary criticism, daring not only to criticize without citing or giving a reference for twenty-five pages, but, even worse, justifying his nonreading and his atmospheric or hemispheric choices by this incredible alibi: 'Since Derrida does not belong to those *philosophers who like to argue [argumentationsfreudigen Philosophen*, my emphasis! (J. D.)] it is expedient [*ratsam*] to take a closer look at his disciples in literary criticism within the Anglo-Saxon climate of argument in order to see whether this thesis really can be held' (p. 193)"[3].

Far from opening up a dialogue, Habermas seems almost to have lost – at least in the eyes of some – his right to be a partner in any further exchange. Instead of taking sides here, we might do better to analyse what went wrong. For that something went wrong seems beyond doubt: not only Derrida, but almost every other author discussed by Habermas found himself forced into a kind of philosophical Procrustean-bed, which left him speechless before the critical questions addressed to him[4]. No one can claim,

2. J. DERRIDA, *Mémoires pour Paul de Man*, Paris, Galilée, 1988, p. 225 (my transl.).

3. J. DERRIDA, *Limited Inc.*, Evanston Ill., Northwestern U.P., 1988, p. 157 (Derrida is quoting from PDM, the italics are his own).

4. See, *inter alia*, the excellent commentary by B. FLYNN in the fifth chapter of his *Political Philosophy at the Closure of Metaphysics*, London/New Jersey, Humanities Press, 1992; and J. M. BERNSTEIN's insightful discussion of Habermas's failure "to recognize the philosophical discourses of modernity [Foucault, Adorno, Derrida] as the philosophical expression of artistic modernism" ('Frankfurter and French fries: between modernity and modernism' (review of PDM), *Art History*, 1988 (11:4), pp. 586-90, quotation at p. 588). And as a third example, J. RAJCHMAN's lucid review ('Habermas's Complaint') in the Fall 1988 issue of *New German Critique* (nr. 45).

of course, to have a definite reading of an author – not even the author could seriously claim this privilege – and it would be pointless to criticize Habermas merely because his readings of Benjamin or Nietzsche, of Derrida, Adorno or Heidegger are somehow flawed or not particularly interesting. To supply a different reading of some of these authors merely for the sake of contradicting Habermas seems an uninteresting enterprise. But what if what is at stake is not only a misunderstanding, but a *systematic* misunderstanding? What if the 'system' of this misunderstanding is directed by a theoretical position which is both crucial to Habermas's own theory and contentious? What if the whole problem turns out to be focused on the relation between a 'validity' and a 'meaning' which, according to a theory that itself seems to be 'consuming' its opponents, should not be allowed to 'consume' such validity? Could it be that what we witness in Habermas's reading of Heidegger and Foucault is the effect of a theoretical position which, instead of offering validity on the altar of meaning, as Heidegger and Foucault allegedly do, now undoes the internal connection between the two conversely: a theory of validity that in its turn consumes meaning?

I

When Habermas tells us that meaning and validity are intrinsically or inter-nally connected, he seems to be thinking of a reciprocal causality between meaning and validity, of "a dialectical relationship between the world-view structures that make intramundane practice possible by means of a prior understanding of meaning, on the one hand, and, on the other, learning processes deposited in the transformation of world-view structures" (PDM 320). In other words, "the concrete a priori of world-disclosing language systems is exposed (...) to an indirect revision in the light of our dealings with the intramundane" (PDM 321). Less technically formulated, and more to the centre of our concerns here: even if we were to adopt some kind of framework-relativism (and I will later try to explain in what special sense Foucault and Heidegger can be regarded as framework-relativists), our discovery of horizons of meaning (e.g. *epistemes*, paradigms) is still not going to provide us with criteria for the validity of the statements or actions we undertake on the basis of such frameworks. On the contrary, the problem remains of how to discover whether specific validity-claims (claims to truth, rightness, sincerity) can be redeemed; and in the light of whatever such 'valid' experiences we may have, our framework will have to change.

Accommodating as this theory may seem to some weak version of framework-relativism – it allows for changes in the horizon of meaning – it is important to point out that such may not be its ultimate intention. In fact, a similar argument is already present in the early Habermas's assessment of Nietzsche, where he remarks that for all the Nietzschean pathos about our truth being only an extra-moral lie, this 'fictional' status of truth could still be sublated, as it were, in the context of a transcendental-logical pragmatism which points to the fact that some fictions are more serviceable than others in helping the species survive. There are "gattungsgeschichtlich 'bewährte' Fiktionen"[5], and these are the only ones we should care about and be willing to promote. And if Nietzsche, some twenty years later, is still considered by Habermas to be the "turning point" for the mistaken entry into postmodernity (PDM, title of Lecture IV), it is because postmodernity for Habermas consists in the mistaken belief that the fictional character of truth could be used as an argument against truth itself. Indeed, Habermas's disappointment with both Heidegger and Foucault lies in the fact that, instead of taking the alternative road of a "communicatively revised" transcendentalism left open by Nietzsche in his writings, they wander into some kind of relativism which conflates meaning and validity and can therefore be criticized by means of the same transcendental-logical pragmatics. Heidegger, he tells us, "jumped to conclusions in identifying the disclosure of meaning-horizons with the truth [i.e. the validity] of meaningful utterances" (PDM 320). Heidegger allegedly overlooked that this "changed understanding of meaning has to prove itself in experience and in dealing with what can come up within its horizon" (*ibid.*) – an argument that recalls the young Habermas's pragmatist critique of Nietzsche.

Similarly, Foucault, according to Habermas, simply reversed "power's truth-dependency into a power-dependency of truth" (PDM 274). Instead of finding in knowledge the guarantee for power (Bacon), power for Foucault is said to become the true face of knowledge. As with Heidegger, here too Habermas is convinced that such monstrous statements derive from a conflation between meaning and validity. Repeatedly, he points out that Foucault's ideas about an internal link between power and knowledge fall prey to a simple genetic fallacy by seeking to draw conclusions about the validity of knowledge (e.g. that of the human sciences) from an investigation into the conditions under which such knowledge arises (e.g. the link between criminology and the prison in *Discipline and Punish*), or is applied (e.g. PDM 272-3, 415-6 n7, n10). Hence what Foucault considers to be an internal link between knowledge and power is, according to Habermas, no such thing: his genealogical findings have no relevance to the validity of the disciplines whose history he attempts to unearth. As with Heidegger, what is overlooked by Foucault is the fact that "it is only the *conditions* for the

5. J. HABERMAS, 'Nachwort', in Fr. NIETZSCHE, *Erkenntnistheoretische Schriften*, Frankfurt a.M., Suhrkamp, 1968, p. 257.

validity of utterances that change with the horizon of meaning" (PDM 320; Habermas's italics) and that such changes do not affect the problem of validity.

The obvious question is: Is this true? Were Heidegger and Foucault indeed doing what Habermas says they were? Were they simply brushing aside the difference between meaning and validity as such, relying on the existence of frameworks that are nothing more than "protuberances of power"[6] or the effect of some *"ursprungs"*-philosophical "background-occurrence" named Being (e.g. PDM 295 and Lecture VI, *passim*)? Or are they, contrary to what Habermas believes, engaged not in undoing the internal connection between meaning and validity, but in articulating it differently? And if they could be shown to be engaged in the latter enterprise, does not the real question concern at what cost Habermas himself succeeds in preserving an *internal* connection between meaning and validity? And could it be, in the light of the cost, that the connection he seems to be pleading for turns out once again to be an *external* one?

II

Habermas never tires of telling us that we can only understand the meaning of any given speech act when we *know* the conditions under which it can be accepted as valid (e.g. PDM 312-3, 319-21)[7]. Validity, then, is a matter of *knowing* the conditions for validity. For example, truth is a matter of *knowing* the conditions under which a proposition can be confirmed as true. And in order to know such conditions, one has to refer to the horizon of meaning dominant at the time. When this horizon changes, the conditions for the validity of utterances change in their turn. But that is all that happens, as Habermas stresses by introducing an adverb whose significance should not be underestimated: *"only* the conditions for the validity of utterances" change (PDM 320). This adverb is important for two reasons. First, because it suggests that Habermas believes theorists such as Foucault and Heidegger do not see this. Secondly, because one may wonder whether the 'internal' link between meaning and validity, even granting that it holds for the whole reservoir of meaning and for the entire spectrum of validity (not only for truth, but also for rightness and sincerity) (PDM 321), is not still conceived of in terms of knowing, of *theoria*. Changed conditions of meaning, different concrete a priori's of world-disclosing language systems,

---

6. The expression was omitted in the English translation (PDM 275-6 – see the German original p. 326).

7. For a systematic exposition on 'Meaning and validity' see J. HABERMAS, *The Theory of Communicative Action*, vol. 1, Boston, Beacon Press, 1984, pp. 295 ff.

different *epistemes*, different frameworks for Habermas *only* necessitate a different grasp of the conditions under which any given speech act can be accepted as valid. Man's relation to truth for example, would basically involve *knowing* the conditions that render a constative speech act acceptable and then presumably living up to them (but not to complicate matters further[8], I will leave this aside). And the same would hold for man's relation to other dimensions of validity (sincerity, rightness). Any change of horizons of meaning, the very fact that there can be – as Habermas himself seems willing to admit – a change in such horizons, is only deemed to be important in so far as it changes conditions of *validity*. To be sure, such changed conditions of validity will give rise to learning processes which will in turn transform world-view structures, and thus at first sight the 'reciprocal causality' between meaning and validity seems to hold in both directions (though clearly under the aegis of validity itself). But does the role Habermas accords "validity" here – the fact that, in conceiving of horizons of meaning in terms of conditions of validity, the stress for Habermas is on *validity* and not on *conditions* – does this *theoreticist* bias in approaching the problem of meaning, this link between validity and the *knowledge* of its conditions, not endanger Habermas's claim to exclusive possession of a theory which intrinsically connects both terms *without eliminating the difference between them*? Is there not something missing, something Habermas might have picked up from such authors as Heidegger and Foucault, had he been less convinced of the need to conduct a rearguard action on behalf of the legacy of Enlightenment? Are not Heidegger and Foucault, in their different ways, questioning a move Habermas seems to take for granted: the assumption that man's relation to horizons of meaning, and to a validity that gets its conditions from such horizons, can be exclusively seen in terms of knowing, of *theoria*? For what, after all, does it mean for man to be in the truth, or to speak the truth? Could it not be that Habermas, Heidegger and Foucault have been giving different answers to the same question?

Let me first try to show how the need for a *non-theoretical* relation to truth arises just where Habermas would least expect it: in the fact that "the conditions for the validity of utterances change with the horizon of meaning" (PDM 320), a fact that, *pace* Habermas, neither Foucault nor Heidegger overlooked, but that was at the centre of the framework-relativism they were defending.

---

8. See e.g. PDM, pp. 346-7: "as a participant in discourses, *the individual, with his irreplacable yes or no*, is only *fully on his own* under the presupposition that he remains bound to a *universal* community by way of a cooperative *quest* for truth". For the role the alternative 'yes or no' is forced to play in Habermas's universal pragmatics, see the opening section of chapter 5 below.

III

Discourse, limitation and exclusion: such were the terms with which Foucault initially tried to account for the fact that truth (or falsity) can only occur within an *order of truth*. Certain conditions are to be fulfilled, certain models deployed, certain metaphors or concepts given preference over others, before a statement can be considered in its validity. Or better still: before a statement can be judged as either true or false, before it can be considered as a candidate for truth or falsity, it has to fulfil certain conditions which are more complex than those governing truth or falsity in the strict sense. In order to be true or false, a statement first of all has to be taken seriously by the court that is to judge its merits, its validity. A statement has to be 'in the true'; it has to comply with the rules laid down by a 'regime of truth', in order to be either true or false. Not everything can be said in any given discourse; not all statements will be listened to in any given age; and therefore the realm of the truth can not but be finite. If there is to be truth (or falsity), if there are to be claims to validity, there must be first of all a 'regime of truth' that prescribes a principle – or set of principles – of relevance. And that is why Foucault should not be taken as simply attacking or denying truth, not even when he insists that there is a link between truth and power, and that it is senseless to oppose power in the name of truth, because truth itself is already a kind of power[9].

Naturally, if one follows Habermas here in taking such assertions at face value[10], one will be unable to see in this 'politics of truth' anything other than an attempt to "scornfully" reduce "relationships of validity to the powers that triumph behind their back" (PDM 324). Rather than acknowledging power's truth-dependency, Foucault's insistence on the link between truth and power would once more conduct us into the cul-de-sac where Nietzsche allegedly left us: it would leave us with an analysis that "strips the history of discourse-constitutive rules of any authority based on validity and treats the transformation of transcendentally powerful discourse formations just as conventional historiography treats the ups and downs of political regimes" (PDM 255). Truth would no longer be truth were it the mere expression of "power strategies [that] intersect one another, succeed one another; [that] are distinguished according to the type of their discourse

---

9. M. FOUCAULT, 'Truth and Power', in ID, *Power/Knowledge. Selected Interviews and Other Writings (1972-77)*, New York, Pantheon, 1980, pp. 109-33.

10. I cannot repeat here the attempt to show to what an extent the traditional Foucault-reception has been misled by the 'face-value' of his texts (see my *Michel Foucault. Genealogy as Critique*, London/New York, Verso, 1995).

formation and the degree of their intensity; but [that] cannot be *judged* under the aspect of their validity" (PDM 127 – Habermas's italics). All we would be left with, would be "a concept of power [that] does not free the genealogist from [the] contradictory self-thematizations" (PDM 295) familiar from all attempts to claim validity for a *radical* critique of validity.

But the question is of course, whether Habermas is not merely reading this aporetic self-refutation of a *radical* critique of reason that still wants to be reasonable (e.g. PDM 126-7, 341) into the works of authors such as Foucault, who, far from wanting to abandon reason or truth, may simply be trying to shift the meaning of such concepts in a direction which is not at all that of a self-proclaimed irrationality but that of a reason or a truth seeking to come to terms with its own conditions of possibility. For as I already pointed out, *Foucault is not interested in denying truth. Like Heidegger before him, the question he raises is what makes the truth true.* If that which provides for the possibility of truth or falsity is a certain regime involving selections and exclusions – a limited principle of communication – then what follows is not that there is ultimately neither truth nor falsity – or no communication at all – but that a certain 'self-evident', 'natural' way of thinking about these concepts has to be revised. And we not only need a revision of these concepts but a theory which could explain why it is that these concepts have been conceived the way they were.

Such was Heidegger's programme: to understand how it came about that *aletheia* had only been understood as correspondence and *adaequatio*; and why it was that, in speaking the truth, man forgot its ess*a*nce (where the 'a' stresses the verbal sense of *Wesen*) and its conditions of possibility. In raising such questions, Heidegger was also pointing to the fact that truth for man is not only a matter of taking validity claims seriously. Truth, to put it another way, is not only a matter of truth or falsity, but goes to the heart of man's Being. Or again: man, in having to speak the truth, does *not only* have to comport himself as a responsible claimant to validity. What the truth demands of man, is that apart from operating within a realm of the true and the false, he also relates himself to the fact that he is related to such a realm, that "there is" such a realm and that his dependence on this "there is" (*es gibt*) says something about his own Being. In other words, Heidegger realized that what is at stake in the history of truth is not only truth itself but man's own essance (*Wesen*). And this is why his attempt to think that history in terms of a forgetting of *aletheia*, of the essance of truth or of that what makes the truth true, was always linked with the attempt to restore man to his own Being by preparing a "revolution [*Umwälzung*] of human Being" (GA 34:324).

IV

This fairly straightforward summary of the thrust of Heidegger's writings on truth, and the way they link up with Foucault's programme, aims to show that what is at stake here might not simply be the attempt on Heidegger's and Foucault's part to let meaning 'consume' validity, but to think their interrelation in a different way. In fact, as Habermas's criticism of both Foucault and Heidegger makes clear, his contention is not merely that meaning and validity are *internally* related, but that this interconnection also involves a *symmetrical* or 'dialectical' relation. If Habermas's criticism of Foucault was simply that Foucault has severed the internal connection between meaning and validity by reducing truth to power – a criticism which, as we have seen, is certainly part of the argument – then it would suffice to repeat that Foucault does allow for truth, that he even seeks to *defend* truth by investigating discourse as its condition of possibility, and that his use of such terms as 'power', 'regime' or 'politics' vis-à-vis truth cannot be taken to suggest what Habermas reads into it. As soon as one realizes that there is no real opposition in Foucault between, on the one hand, the idea that truth is linked to power in the sense of a limitation, and, on the other hand, an emphasis upon the productive character of power; as soon as one realizes *that power, in order to be productive, has to be selective and exclusive*, one has already seen through what Habermas calls Foucault's "systematically ambiguous" use of the concept of power – a concept Foucault is said to have forged by amalgamating "the idealist idea of transcendental synthesis with the presuppositions of an empiricist ontology" (PDM 270, 274).

In Habermas's reading of Foucault, the fact that "genealogical historiography is supposed to be both at once – functionalist social science and at the same time historical research into constitutive conditions" (PDM 274) points to the "irritating double role" (PDM 273) Foucault preserved for the category of power: "on the one hand, it retains the innocence of a concept used descriptively and serves the empirical analysis of power technologies (...) [whereas] on the other hand, [it] preserves from its covert historical sources the meaning of a basic concept within a theory of constitution as well" (PDM 270). The same genealogy that descriptively lays bare power relationships as conditions for the rise of scientific knowledge and as its social effects is, according to Habermas simultaneously forced to play "the transcendental role of an analysis of technologies of power that are meant to explain how scientific discourse about man is possible at all" (PDM 274). Whereas Habermas may be right in detecting a certain ambivalence in the way concepts such as power/knowledge come to function in Foucault's texts[11], he may be too quick to conclude that it is only this ambivalence which can lend "the empirical analysis of technologies of power their significance as a critique of reason and secures for genealogical historiography its unmasking effect" (PDM 270). For it is only because Habermas already seems to know what power is about, that he is able to dismiss the relevance of such concepts such as power/knowledge. Because Habermas is convinced that Foucault is attempting the impossible in ascribing transcendental capacities to the kind of empirical power strategies we all are already familiar with, he cannot see that Foucault is (or should be taken as) questioning this very familiarity by investigating the empirical bearings of an unfamiliar "power": a "power" which possesses a *constitutive* function. What Foucault really discovers behind – or, rather, in – the empirical power-strategies his genealogy is trying to unearth, is a necessary limitation, a "power" that does not merely have a negative function: a "power" that produces because it limits[12]. For example, without some limits on the true, there would be no truth at all: if anything can be said, there is no longer an order of truth, but chaos. Far from making validity impossible, "power" *in the sense of* a necessary, constitutive limitation, is what, according to Foucault, allows for the possibility of validity as such. Meaning – the realm of a limited discourse, the regime of truth – and validity are connected internally: only within such a realm can there be statements that can be taken seriously as validity claims. Only because in some way the number of candidates for truth or falsity is restricted in terms of conditions of "well-formedness" can there exist truth or falsity.

Discourse, then, is a set of rules that imposes a basic homogeneity upon candidates for truth and falsity. It can only allow for the true and the false by first imposing on them the realm of the "true". Clearly, this version of *framework-relativism*, which does not let the truth of statements depend on a framework, but only their truth *or falsity*, their *possible* truth, cannot be taken to exclude objectivity. For there must be some objectivity if one is to decide *within* the framework between those statements that are true and those that are false. As D.C. Hoy put it: "the way the world is may determine what is true or false, but that will still not explain what is actually said, or comes up for counting as true or false"[13]. And here we have probably

---

11. See my *Genealogy as Critique*, esp. chapters 2.2 and 3.

12. Since the term "power" assumes a specific meaning here, the ultimate mistake would be to oppose *power*-strategies *because* they involve "power". The problem is of course to look for a model of critique that does not mix up the constitutive and the contingent (as a certain 'Foucault' – this much should be admitted – found himself doing).

13. D. C. HOY, 'Taking History Seriously: Foucault, Gadamer, Habermas', *Union Seminary Quarterly Review*, 1979 (34: 2), p. 87.

come to the heart of Habermas's objection. For even were he willing to grant that there is an *internal* connection between meaning and validity in Foucault, he would still be unwilling to accept its terms. According to Habermas, Foucault refuses to let the meaning of his frameworks be judged by the "innerworldly success of the practice [they] make possible" (PDM 154). In other words, what Habermas really opposes is the idea that the conditions for truth and falsity cannot be themselves judged in terms of truth and falsity (e.g. PDM 255). Only conceptions of a meaning-horizon allowing for practices which will ultimately be able to determine the validity of such a horizon can do justice to the internal *and symmetrical* relationship Habermas posits between meaning and validity. And since neither Heidegger nor Foucault seem to be willing to promote such a conception, Habermas tends to suggest that their theories *not only* deny the *symmetrical* relation meaning/validity, *but any connection whatsoever*. Validity is consumed by meaning as soon as one neglects the fact that "whether the validity conditions are in fact satisfied to such an extent that the sentences can also function *is not a matter of the world-disclosing power of language*, but of the innerworldly success of the practice it makes possible" (PDM 154).

According to Habermas, this is precisely what is forgotten by Foucault and Heidegger when they reserve "the title of truth for [something] which *no longer* has anything to do with a validity claim transcending space and time" (PDM 154; compare 255). Instead of seeing that language has "to prove itself" through praxis (PDM 335 and compare 154), these authors are said to let "the 'truth' of semantic world-disclosure *found* the propositional truth of statements [and] *prejudice* the validity of linguistic utterances" (PDM 331). They "hypostatize" the "luminous force of world-disclosing language" and no longer feel the need to let it "prove itself by its capacity to throw light on beings in the world" (PDM 154). Heidegger, for example, allegedly "supposes that beings can be opened up in their Being with equal ease by any given approach" (*ibid.*) and hence finds himself defending a "*superfoundationalism* of a history of Being abstracted from all concrete history" (PDM 104). In fact, for Habermas, this 'abstraction from all concrete history' – extravagant as this claim may be concerning a philosopher who devoted all his efforts to think history – once more seems to have to concern the alleged denial in Heidegger (or Foucault) that the "accumulation of knowledge could affect the previous interpretation of the world and burst a given totality of meaning" (PDM 331), i.e. with the 'dialectical' feed-back between meaning and validity: "As a result, intramundane praxis cannot get learning processes going" (*ibid.*).

Since it is ultimately the possibility of such learning processes, and the way to conceive them, that are in question, one would expect Habermas to do more than implicitly refer the reader to the incorporation in his earlier work of a notion borrowed, *inter alia*, from Piaget's "reconstructive science". Suffice it to point out that Habermas seems to think that learning processes, since they also concern the *truth* of frameworks, not only operate *within* frameworks, but also allow one to proceed from one framework to another in such a way that the gains of learning compensate the dis-learning process involved. The truth of the next framework somehow has to encompass, or be on a higher 'developmental level' than, the truth of the foregoing one (e.g. PDM 84). Otherwise, one would once more be surrendering to what he calls "the imperative force of an illumination compelling one to one's knees" (PDM 255). Since, as far as I can see, one cannot find a *compelling* reason in Habermas's published writings to adopt this Piagetian theory and to pre-serve it in the face of its critics, including those sympathetic to the project[14], and since, on the other hand, a discussion of the role and the position of the 'reconstructive sciences' in Habermas's work by far extends the scope of this chapter and would ultimately involve a full deconstruction of the whole Habermasian project, I will have to restrict myself to a few remarks that return us to the relation between meaning and validity.

The central question in the debate over meaning and validity seems to be whether what is claimed here (and elsewhere in Habermas's work) in the name of a *symmetrical* relationship between meaning and validity, is not doing the converse: letting validity consume meaning by making meaning ultimately *depend* on validity. It should be clear by now that one cannot even begin to investigate this problem if one lets oneself be 'blackmailed' by the implicit presuppositions in Habermas's criticism of Heidegger and Foucault. Given that Habermas's own analysis of the 'symmetrical' relation between meaning and validity does not prevent him from placing it under the aegis of validity, the fact that Heidegger and Foucault seem to be defending a 'non-symmetrical' relation under the aegis of meaning cannot constitute grounds for simply dismissing their attempt. Nor can it be taken as a reason to conclude in their favour. As long as the discussion is couched in the terms Habermas imposed on his adversaries, the only thing which would permit us to choose, would be proof that, at all times and as a matter of principle, crucial experiments for the assessment of regimes of truth are

---

14. Th. MCCARTHY, 'Rationality and Relativism: Habermas's 'overcoming' of Her-meneutics', in J.B. THOMPSON & D. HELD (eds.), *Habermas. Critical Debates*, London/ Basingstoke, MacMillan, 1982, pp. 57-78; B. WALDENFELS, *In Den Netzen der Lebenswelt*, Frankfurt a.M., Suhrkamp, 1985, pp. 110-7; K. MEYER-DRAWE, 'Zähmung eines wilden Denkens? Piaget und Merleau-Ponty zur Entwicklung von Rationalität', in A. METRAUX & B. WALDENFELS (eds.), *Leibhaftige Vernunft. Spuren von Merleau-Ponty's Denken*, München, Fink, 1986, pp. 258-75.

possible; i.e. that it is always possible to asses the conditions for candidacy to truth and falsity laid down by such regimes in such a way that what are considered to be 'relevant' statements in a given regime could somehow be shown to be inferior/superior to what is the case in another regime[15].

But why should the discussion be couched in these terms? What is really at stake when Habermas decides that the transition between such regimes cannot merely be a matter of 'conversion' (Kuhn) to another regime or to another 'style' of scientific reasoning (Hacking); that it has to involve knowing, or being able to show, *ex post factum*, that what one learns in such a conversion compensates for what one dis-learns in abandoning another 'style' or 'regime'? Why can't we simply say that what is deemed relevant, has changed: Foucault's happy positivism? And why can't we add, with Heidegger, that history is precisely the name for the experience that we cannot account for everything in terms of beings or of a highest Being, but are ultimately exposed to the sending of a destiny (*Geschick*) which is *given* to us and never *fully* in our control[16]? In other words: what hidden anxiety has been setting the stage for this debate?

15. No weaker version of a decisive test could do here, since, as suggested above, authors like Heidegger and Foucault are framework-relativists *in the sense that they think that what changes between frameworks is not simply the stock of attainable truths (in which case comparisons of scope would suffice) but also what it means to attain truth (Heidegger) or to be "in the true" (Foucault)*. The strange thing about Paracelsus, for example, is not simply that he was serious about a lot of things we cannot possibly be serious about, but that what it meant for him to be serious about 'truth', seems to be something different from what it means to us. This is why a counterargument to the kind of incommensurability that is at stake here (Hacking's second type discussed as 'dissociation' in his *Representing and Intervening*, Cambridge U.P., 1990, pp. 69-72) cannot rest with the attempt to show that all or part of a framework's empirical propositions have some bearing on its 'core propositions', and that there is therefore room for a 'dialectical feedback' between the two (cognitive pressure feedbacking in such a way that the framework itself would change). Rather, since a framework is not primarily defined by a set of core propositions but by a 'style of reasoning' (Hacking), including a certain view on what it means to know, to argue seriously, to be relevant, to be "in the true", the attempt to refute this position should include a way of showing that from one 'framework' to another, there is not simply progress in knowing, but also in what it means to know, to be "in the true", etc. Habermas, of course, is well aware that he needs to come up with some kind of solution to this Hegelian problem and that is why he has been trying to use (and extend) the results of a Kohlberg-Piaget type of research to build in a diachronical moment into the framework of his universal pragmatics.

16. E.g. M. HEIDEGGER, 'The Question Concerning Technology', in ID., *Basic Writings*, New York, Harper & Row, 1977, p. 299: "Man can, indeed, conceive, fashion, and carry through this or that in one way or another. But man does not have control over unconcealment itself, in which at any given time the real shows itself or withdraws".

V

As we have seen, the crux of Habermas's debate with Heidegger and Foucault – indeed, his motivation in taking it up – resides in his fear that these philosophers will deprive us of "the transcendent moment of universal validity [that] bursts every provinciality [including the provinciality of a framework, R.V.] asunder" (PDM 322). This seems to suggest that, although truth for Habermas may be dependent on cultural practices, it can never be immanent in such practices. Although a truth-claim will always be made from within a provinciality, it can never satisfy itself solely with immanence. Of necessity, truth has a transcendent moment: "though never divorced from social practices of justification, from the rules and warrants of this or that culture [discourse, etc.], truth cannot be *reduced* to any particular set thereof"[17].

But the question is, of course, whether the transcendent character one intuitively associates with truth – embedded as it seems to be in our practices of telling the truth – allows us to infer that comparisons between "frameworks" along Habermas's transcendental-pragmatist lines must *eo ipso* be possible. Might it not be that truth's transcendent character is something one *only* experiences *within* a regime of truth, *within* a provinciality? Something that points to the paradoxical intertwinement of truth as an infinite task and "truth" or discourse or *aletheia* as a finite realm within which the necessity of such a task will be experienced always anew, but that cannot itself be judged in terms of true or false? Can we not take truth as an infinite task seriously, without knowing that which allows for the true to be itself true? Are Heidegger and Foucault indeed undermining the very possibility of truth by claiming that the realm within which truth/falsity becomes possible involves limitations which are neither true nor false since they are what allows for truth and falsity? Can truth still be the task it is once we admit that the situation-transcending import of truth-claims does not by itself point to the possibility (or, indeed, the necessity) of transcending, in the name of truth, that which allows for the truth? Do we need the transcendental-logical pragmatist reassurance that some orders of discourse, some regimes of truth, some "truths" are more true than others, in order to take truth seriously? Can't we speak the truth, all while

---

17. Th. MCCARTHY, 'Private Irony and Public Decency: Richard Rorty's New Pragmatism', *Critical Inquiry*, 1990 (16), pp. 369-70 and compare PDM, p. 323. This argument of McCarthy also constitutes the backbone of his significantly titled *Ideals and Illusions. On Reconstruction and Deconstruction in Contemporary Critical Theory*, Cambridge Mass./London, M.I.T., 1991, in which this essay on Rorty was reprinted in a revised form.

accepting that ultimately "truth" is finite, and that we will never have a more than finite relation to the truth?

If "truth", *aletheia*, as Heidegger contends, always involves some "untruth"; if a *lethe* is ineradicably present at the heart of *aletheia*; or if, as Foucault suggests, in order to speak the truth, man has to come to terms with the fact that there are necessary limitations on the realm he will enter; in short, if truth is itself finite and yet at the same time an infinite task, then taking this infinite task seriously only seems possible when we take our own finitude seriously: what we have is an infinite task, but never a non-finite truth. Indeed, what makes the task *a task*, is precisely the fact that, in order to have truth, there will always and of necessity be something which escapes it: e.g., what Foucault points to when he differentiates between the "truth" (as the regime of the true/false) and the truth.

Viewed from this angle, Habermas's suggestion that we must at least be able to decide in retrospect about the truth of a regime of truth, about the validity of a given horizon of meaning, that we must at least have the possibility of a non-finite truth, may well be another way of seeking to deny man's finitude, yet another way of thinking that finitude is something we can easily come to terms with, if only by the assurance that we are making progress toward the non-finite, gradually throwing light on the *lethe* that obscures *aletheia's* heart. For what is revealed by this Habermasian desire for the truth to be fully true, so true that it even encompasses the truth of its own conditions of possibility? What is revealed by this desire informing Habermas's debate with poststructuralism, if not that truth cannot simply be related to some *uncomplicated* desire for the truth? What complicates this desire for the truth is not, as Habermas seems to fear, that the link between truth and desire would in and of itself threaten the truth. Rather, if there seems to be something threatening about the truth itself, if there seems to be something about the truth which man finds hard to bear, this is because the truth, *qua* intertwinement between a finite "truth" and an infinite task, confronts man with his own finitude and with his desire to escape this finitude. That is why for Heidegger, the fact that, like truth, man is finite, turns finitude itself into a *task* demanding a certain *comportment* of man. And that is why, as suggested earlier, what is at stake in this debate between Habermas and Heidegger must ultimately be related to the question of what it means for man to speak the truth. This question is all the more important since Habermas's insistence on the symmetrical relation between meaning and validity seems to obstruct his access to the kind of ethics he really needs: an ethics that not only explains the possibility of dialogue, but which can also account for the possibility of its absence[18]. Paradoxically, it seems to be the Heideggerian concern with an ethics of finitude which is simultaneously an ethics of truth, that could help us out here.

Let me briefly try to clarify this by taking issue with the Habermasian claim that it is only the context-transcendent character of our notion of truth "that keeps us from being locked into what we happen to agree on at any particular time and place, that opens us up to the alternative possibilities lodged in otherness and difference that have been so effectively invoked by post-structuralist thinkers" (McCarthy, 370 and PDM 322 ff.). That is, the claim that the truth of "poststructuralism" presupposes the truth of universal pragmatics – a claim which, as the title of Habermas's penultimate chapter indicates (PDM 294 ff: "An Alternative Way out of the Philosophy of the Subject: Communicative versus Subject-Centered Reason"), explicitly organizes the argumentative architecture of *The Philosophical Discourse of Modernity*.

VI

For Habermas, Foucault's and Heidegger's refusal to turn the relation between meaning and validity into a symmetrical one, where meaning would ultimately be subjected to a proof of its validity, not only constitutes a threat to the meaningfulness of the project of truth, but also to the very possibility of dialogue and critique. Dialogue can only be what it is, can only find its motive and potential, in the transcendent character of the truth-claims we make. As McCarthy observes, "without that idealizing moment, there would be no foothold in our accepted beliefs and practices for the critical shocks to consensus that force us to expand our horizons and learn to see things in different ways" (McCarthy, 370).

Is this so? Does the possibility of dialogue depend on the link McCarthy/Habermas are making here between their views on truth-transcendence, on meaning and validity, and on universality? Do we have to look for a non-finite truth that encompasses all finite orders of truth in order to save a concept of universality, and, with it, the *possibility* of dialogue? What if we followed Merleau-Ponty in substituting for such a "universality from above" a universality that would have to be conceived in a "lateral"

18. Whereas Habermas tries to ground the possibility of dialogue in an *ethics* of language, he accounts for the absence of dialogue not in ethical but in *political* terms (systematically distorted communication). I suspect that ultimately this dissymmetry in his analysis will prevent him from taking such distortions seriously.

way[19]? What if it were *this* kind of universality that makes true dialogue possible – not the transcendence of truth that breaks all provinciality asunder and opens me up for the other by also breaking his provinciality asunder, but the experience that, for all its transcendence, my truth-claim seems to be as inextricably bound up with my provinciality (order or regime of truth; *aletheia*), as the truth-claim of the other is with his? In other words, what opens us up to "the alternative possibilities lodged in otherness and difference" mentioned by McCarthy (370), might not be the situation-transcending character of the truth-claims *as such*, but the fact that this transcendence is tied to an immanence that at first sight closes us off from, estranges us from the other. In the light of a certain *ethics* of truth – the kind of ethics at the centre of Heidegger's concern with the truth – it is not the experience of a possible common identity (universality from above), but the experience of my own identity which I cannot share with the other, that can throw a bridge between us (lateral universality). In other words, what we may be in need of is not, as Habermas thinks, "an alternative way *out of* the philosophy of the subject" (PDM, title of Lecture XI and 301), but an *alternative* way *into* it. For, after all, would we need a dialogue, or an ethics of dialogue, if we were simply decentred, always already – *de jure*, if not *de facto* – intersubjective?

Ironically perhaps, the philosophy that feels obliged to protest against those who are sacrificing validity on the altar of meaning may well find itself sacrificing subjectivity on the altar of intersubjectivity, oblivious of the fact that it thereby hollows out both concepts. Refusing to let meaning be consumed by validity, Heidegger, on the other hand, seems to be in a far better position to take Habermas's problem seriously and to ground the possibility of dialogue in an *ethics* of "truth". For Heidegger the subject of truth is not decentred because it has no centre but the one it shares with others; it is decentred because it has *a* centre that is not that of the other. That is why finitude confronts us with the difficult *task* of discovering that at the centre of one's own relation to truth there lies a *non*-universalizable core, a moment of *non*-universality, from which we cannot and should not seek to escape, and which makes both truth and dialogue the infinite task we know they are. Having a centre *which it may neither abandon, nor comfortably nestle itself into*, the subject of truth which makes this finitude his own

---

19. Merleau-Ponty introduces the counter-concept of a "lateral universality" (as against an "overarching universality") in the course of his essay 'From Mauss to Claude Lévi-Strauss', the problem being precisely "how [to] understand the other without sacrificing him to our logic or it to him" – see *Signs*, Evanston Ill., Northwestern U.P., 1964, pp. 115 (quote) and 120 ("a second way to the universal"). I give a closer reading of Merleau-Ponty's essay in chapter 8 below.

bursts open towards the other by discovering the wound with which its 'truth' had always already afflicted it. At that moment tolerance is born, as we all are: in a cry of pain. No longer a marginal virtue, but "the point at which recognition of our human condition can begin"[20], it will have to carry the weight of an ontological function.

---

20. E. LACLAU, *New Reflections on the Revolution of Our Time*, London/New York, Verso, 1990, p. XIV.

CHAPTER FOUR

RAW BEING AND VIOLENT DISCOURSE
FOUCAULT, MERLEAU-PONTY
AND THE (DIS-)ORDER OF THINGS

Phenomenology has been too pacifying, Deleuze tells us, and he suggests that we leave Heidegger and Merleau-Ponty for what they are and turn to Foucault in order to discover a more profound Heracliticism[1]. Genealogy is too much a war-machine, others like Habermas respond, and they recommend different remedies. There is nothing extraordinary about this situation. We are, in fact, all too familiar with it. We have come across it in different philosophical settings, with different parties engaging one another and with different choices to be made. We all know from our own experience – and lest we forget, there will always be a flourishing para-philosophical literature to remind us – that this "originating" miracle we know as the philosophical tradition has been "breaking up" (cf. VI 124).

And, now as always, the question is not whether we will be able to live with it, but how we will do so, how we will "accompany this break-up, (...) this differentiation" (*ibid.*). Hence, perhaps, my hesitation and the uneasiness which haunted me at the thought of having to enter in this arena crowded by all those choices that, like the war, "have taken place"[2] for or against "the" subject, for or against universality, for or against the origin of truth. *Either* Foucault *or* Merleau-Ponty, *either* discourse *or* existence – no doubt such apparently clear-cut choices confront us with questions ranging far beyond method. For does not the standard academic response against the kind of pseudo-politicization of philosophy which I have been evoking, suffer from the ills it is supposed to cure? Is there really such a difference between those who bid us to take sides and "merge" with one of the "existing" positions (VI 127) and those who, in refusing to do so, nestle themselves in the comfortable *teichoscopic* position from which they can observe the heroes at the foot of the wall (*Iliad*, III, 121-244) and report in

1. G. DELEUZE, *Foucault*, Paris, Minuit, 1986, p. 120 ("la phénoménologie est trop pacifiante, elle a béni trop de choses") and *passim*.
2. I am alluding to the title of chapter 10 in MERLEAU-PONTY's *Sense and Non-Sense*, Evanston Ill., Northwestern U.P., 1964.

a detached manner on the choices that others found themselves making?
Did not Merleau-Ponty himself commit the best of his efforts to showing
that both the attempt to retain an infinite distance and the attempt to
replace it with an absolute proximity express – as a soaring over (*survol*) or
as fusion – the same positivistic relationship to philosophy itself (e.g. VI 127)?
Is it not the belief that the world of philosophy is an objective world, where
the meditating subject is in no way implicated in that upon which it reflects,
is it not paradoxically this same basic creed in the presence of a set of already
available philosophical positions which underlies both the error of those
who urge us to side with one of them, and the error of those who end up
distorting philosophy's internal structure by trying to look at it from above
(*survoler*) and to think it from no point of view (PP 62,204)?

As one can see, these questions are not merely methodological. Rather,
what they reveal is that the whole of Merleau-Ponty's philosophy is already
implied in any attempt to approach it and that such an approach is always
open to the risk of already belying by its very way of proceeding, the position
which it tries to articulate. But since we have already shown ourselves that
our topic here ('raw being *and* violent discourse'; 'Merleau-Ponty *and*
Foucault'; 'existence *and* discourse') can only exist for those who are under
the spell of a positivistic illusion, should we not by the same token accept
that it is, in fact, perfectly superfluous once one has witnessed the issue itself
become but another illustration of that web of problems Merleau-Ponty was
referring to under the item 'raw being' and, in particular, of the fact that a
certain kind of violence will be involved in each and every attempt to express
it? In other words, shouldn't we drop the reference to Foucault altogether
and devote our efforts to bringing into the philosophy of reflection a
moment of hyperreflection which would break the positivist's curse by
stumbling upon that unreflected given which "dispossesses" us (e.g. VI 266),
since we can neither coincide with it nor constitute it? But it is precisely this
conclusion which Merleau-Ponty drew from positivism's failure, which
should arouse our interest in Foucault's "happy positivism" (AK 125).

For Foucault the problem of the *kosmotheoros* (VI 15) whose prejudice of
the objective world makes him forget his own implication in it, derives not
from the fact that he is too positivistic, but from the fact that he is not
positivistic enough. Instead of wishing, like Merleau-Ponty, to bring
positivism back to earth, Foucault tried to follow it way up into the sky, to
those austere heights from which the archaeologist could detect, instead of
a single continuous philosophical tradition, the cracks and the fissures
which explode it from within and which let the space of global history drift
apart into different epistemic "tables" on which things will be ordered ever
anew, until it dawns on us "that we are difference, that our reason is the

difference of discourses, our history the difference of times, our selves the difference of masks" (AK 131). Once more then, we find ourselves confronted with another, not altogether similar, 'dispossession' which reminds us that in our very way of proceeding we already stumble upon the crux of the problem we had hoped to approach in a more gradual and controlled manner. For now we have learned that the only legitimate way to inquire into the relation between the philosophy of Merleau-Ponty and that of Foucault does not consist in overcoming positivism but in deepening it until we discover the epistemic rift which demarcates the set of 'statements'[3] referred to as 'raw being' from that referred to as 'violent discourse'. Unmistakably, then, we find ourselves back to where we started and it appears that we must choose if we want to avoid being chosen. But since such choice amounts to either absorbing Foucault into Merleau-Ponty or Merleau-Ponty into Foucault, would not the best bet be simply to remain silent?

And yet, as Merleau-Ponty reminds us, the philosopher speaks, and if this speech is more than an "inexplicable weakness" in him, if there is more to it than a simple breach of silence (VI 125), it is perhaps because he never finds himself in the clear-cut situation we have been assuming, where the metaphilosophical problems raised by such and such a philosophical architecture forever darken the windows of the building it had been raising in the hope of reaching out to others. If there is any light in there, it is because, as we all know, inevitably the architect falls into the pits of his own drawing and suddenly finds himself in a backroom where he is no longer the only one doing the talking and where none of those present could even in principle decide at any given moment just what question or what answer belongs to each (S 159). Such, then, might be our issue (in both senses of the word): to grow (into) such a room by outrunning those signifiers ('Foucault', 'Merleau-Ponty') between which we were supposed to choose, until their shadows leave their bearers and mingle with the echo of voices it would be pointless to try to identify.

Let us warm up for the first run: "violent discourse".

I

Paradoxically, the book that established Foucault's fame overnight, was not about words, nor about things, nor even about that point where "an obscure web of things" intersects with "a manifest, visible, coloured chain of words" (AK 48). Neither that evanescent surface of contact between a reality and a

---

3. On this notion of 'statement' (*énoncé*) and its function in Foucault's archaeology see AK, part III.

language, nor the intrication of a lexicon and an experience, discourse should rather be compared to a "table", or to a grid of identities, similitudes and analogies according to which every culture sorts out so many different and similar things (OT XIX; AK 48). Neither the effect of "an *a priori* and necessary concatenation", nor simply deriving from "immediately perceptible contents" (OT XIX), this primary "coherence" constitutes a kind of "middle region" which forever loosens "the apparently so tight embrace of words and things" (AK 49). In short, what we are confronted with here is not an order *in* things, but an order *of* things, not a group of signs that refer to already constituted objects eagerly awaiting the moment when they finally will be discovered (e.g. AK 42-3, 45), but a set of "practices that systematically form the objects of which they speak" (AK 49).

From this, one can easily understand why Foucault thinks that discourse is violent and that it cannot be but violent. For if discourse were not "a practice which we impose on things" (ODis 67), but simply that smooth surface on which they can patiently inscribe themselves; if it were not that moment where communication finally becomes possible by a "rarefaction" imposed on our language and by a difference established between the things that could be said and those that in fact are said[4], but simply that inexplicable void due to the speaker's finitude, his inattention or to a defective synthetic act; if it were not that anonymous field the configuration of which defines the possible place for speaking subjects (AK 122), if it were not that "transcendental field where the conditions of subjectivity appear"[5], but merely "the verbal translation of a synthesis established elsewhere" (AK 55), in short, if we were to think of discourse as meek rather than "violent" (ODis 67), and if we were to try to elide its reality by referring it back to the themes of originary experience, universal mediation, or constituting subject (ODis 65ff.), we would rob ourselves of the means to understand the bare fact that "there is order" (OT XX).

The striking thing about this argument is that it seems, both in its aim and its structure, in perfect solidarity with what Merleau-Ponty had already

4. In 'Réponse à une question' (*Esprit*, 1968 (36: 5)) Foucault defined discourse as that which is "constituted by the difference between what could be correctly said in a given epoch (according to the rules of grammar and of logic) and what is effectively said" (p. 863, – my transl.).

5. Foucault who was Hyppolite's student and successor at the *Collège de France*, may have taken this expression from the latter's intervention at the famous 1957 Royaumont-colloquium on Husserl (*Husserl* (Cahier de Royaumont. Philosophie n° III), Paris, Minuit, 1959, p. 323): "*J. Hyppolite*: (...) is the notion of a transcendental field in which the conditions of subjectivity would appear, and where the subject would be constituted out of (*à partir du*) this transcendental field, is such a situation possible? — *Rev. Van Breda*: For Husserl, this solution is inconceivable." (my transl.).

set at stake from the *Phenomenology of Perception* onwards. In its aim: to remain faithful to a certain phenomenal field, to accord a positive significance to the voids it may contain (PP 11; AK Part III, ch. 4); to look for its conditions of reality, and to ground the possible in the real, rather than the other way round (e.g. PP 439; AK 127); to see in it the birth of a norm rather than a birth according to a norm (PP 61); to think of reason as that which becomes possible through a moment of facticity, rather than as that which is threatened by it (*ibid.*). And in its structure: neither subjugate discourse to the constitutive powers of transcendental immanence, nor let it be absorbed into the world of objects; neither try to derive it from that ideal point where it is constituted, nor regard it as the effect of a series of events in 'reality'; neither reduce it from above, nor from below. In other words, just as Merleau-Ponty had argued that perception cannot be conceived in empiricist or intellectualist terms, so Foucault tries to think of discourse as that *tertium quid* which cannot be accounted for by empiricism or intellectualism. Since this parallel is so striking, let us freeze the picture here for a while and concentrate on that strange overlap of the shadows of two authors whose names already by themselves are commonly taken to refer to a radical break in the history of French philosophy.

One of the most interesting features of Merleau-Ponty's treatment of empiricism and intellectualism[6] is that he regards their disagreement over the ontological status of the world ('realism' versus 'idealism') as but the flip-side of their agreement as to which world should be given an ontological status. Since both positions suffer from what he calls "a dogmatic belief in the 'world'" (a reality in itself for the empiricist; an immanent term of knowledge for the intellectualist) (PP 29), neither of them manages to account for "the peculiar way in which perceptual consciousness constitutes its object" (PP 26). Whereas empiricists rely on the explanatory powers of a third-person process and intellectualists refer us to an epistemological subject bringing about the synthesis (e.g. PP 232), Merleau-Ponty tries to conceive of such a constitution as something more akin to a co-constitution, a "knowing" in the biblical sense, a marriage or a communion between our lived body – "the fabric into which all objects are woven" (PP 235) and hence only in a weak sense the "subject" of perception – and a perceptual *field* which is "already pregnant with an irreducible meaning" (PP 21-2). Unable to free themselves from subject-object thinking and to grasp the rootedness of their "objective world" in a lived world to which "consciousness", i.e. the lived body, is open and in

6. For a lucid account see Russell KEAT's 'The Critique of Objective Thought' which is the fifth chapter of the jointly written *Understanding Phenomenology* (M. HAMMOND, J. HOWARTH, R. KEAT), Oxford, Basil Blackwell, 1991.

which it finds itself "as the heart in an organism" (PP 203) "breathing life into it and sustaining it inwardly, and with it forming a system" (*ibid.*), empiricism typically ends up with having absorbed the subject into the world (realism), whereas intellectualism, in its eagerness to correct empiricism, veers off into an idealism which absorbs the world into the subject. But behind the intellectualist world which has become "the correlative of a thought of the world and which has thus come to exist only for a constituting agent", there still lurks the "ready-made world" of the empiricist, to which is simply added the indication 'consciousness of...' and we seem to have gained nothing with this reversal from the "natured" into the "naturing" (PP 208). A state of consciousness simply becomes the consciousness of a state and perception, like discourse, is left with the poor choice of being reduced either from below or from above. Or to fully spell out the parallel: just as Foucault tried to save discourse from the grip of empiricism or intellectualism, so Merleau-Ponty tries to conceive of "a perceptual element (*milieu*) which is not yet the objective world [of the empiricist or the intellectualist], a perceptual being which is not yet determinate being" (PP 47). Just as Foucault tries to account for a "there is order" (OT XX) by introducing discourse, so Merleau-Ponty tries to conceive of a "consciousness" which would not be "too poor" (as in empiricism: PP 26) to *account for* a "there is meaning" (PP 296; PrP 23), nor already containing everything in itself and hence too rich to *accept* a meaning already intimating itself before its constitution (as in intellectualism: PP 28ff.).

This parallel is not too beautiful to be true, but, like consumption art, its beauty and its truth derive from the fact that once erected, it crumbles down. Discourse, for example, may not be the mere "translation of a synthesis established elsewhere" (AK 55), but isn't it itself the operator of a similarly conceived synthesis? In other words, Foucault may have been aware of the danger of an idealist reduction of discourse, but has he been able to prevent discourse itself from behaving like some idealist super-subject, absorbing its objects into it? Granted, it would be "a mistake to try to discover what could have been said of madness at a particular time by interrogating the being of madness itself" (AK 32), but to conclude from this that "mental illness was *constituted by all that was said in all the statements that named it*" (*ibid.*) is to verge dangerously close to the brink of discursive idealism unless one clarifies how exactly these statements which constitute mental illness by naming it "give *it* speech by articulating, *in its name*, discourses that were *to be taken as its own*" (*ibid.*); unless, that is, one answers just those questions Foucault, the archaeologist, decided to exclude. What is this 'it' to which speech is being given and in the name of which discourses are articulated? What is this 'own' to which such discourses were taken to (or mistaken to, as the

French text suggests) remain faithful? What is this intrication between a discourse and its referent, where do they and how can they meet? How can they meet beyond intellectualism and empiricism?

Should it surprise us that once the archaeology which refused to go into a history of the referent (AK Part II, ch. 3) has given way to the genealogy which seems to aim at nothing else, this same question of a meeting – or in Merleau-Ponty's language: a mating – beyond intellectualism and empiricism will now draw the genealogist into the abyss of the latter position, in spite of his effort to jump over it? To be sure, Foucault wants to break away from a conception where the operations of power would be comparable to those of "a searchlight (which) illuminates objects pre-existing in the darkness" (PP 26): power would not be merely pro-ductive in the etymological sense, it would inscribe itself in whatever gets caught in its beams of light, it would be productive in the *industrial* sense of creating new objects[7]. In other words, the operation of power would have to be compared to the operation of that *creative* act of attention which the *Phenomenology of Perception* tries to set off against empiricist and intellectualist misconceptions which refuse to see it as an "efficient cause of the ideas which it arouses" (PP 26) and insist on treating it as an empty "light which does not change its character with the various objects which it shines upon" (PP 28). But once more, the parallel breaks for we witness Foucault literally put between quotation marks all those supposedly *new* objects produced by power, like the soul, the sexualized body or the disciplined body in general[8], and we cannot but wonder whether this problem of a production which is not a true production after all, does not derive directly from Foucault's failure to provide what Merleau-Ponty already found lacking in empiricism, namely some "internal connection" between (power's) attention and that which awakens it, a connection which could show how attention is awakened and then how it develops and enriches that which awakened it, how, in short, its result would not have to be found in its beginning (PP 26-7, 31). Unable to resolve or to highlight what Merleau-Ponty considers to be "literally a question of creation" (PP 29), the genealogical approach to discourse fails both to convincingly set itself off against empiricism and to correct for archaeology's tendency to collapse into discursive idealism. Hence, this discourse which seemed so similar in its aim and structure to that *tertium quid* Merleau-Ponty was looking for between the legs of empiricism and intellectualism, in fact remains caught in an ambiguity which is even worse than the one into which, according to some commentators, the *Phenomenology of Perception* found itself trapped in

7. On this shift see my *Michel Foucault. Genealogy as Critique*, pp. 66 ff.
8. *Ibid.*, chapters 2 and 3.

having been unable to come up with the ontology for that "communion" or that "coition (*accouplement*) of our body with things" to which it so often referred (e.g. PP 320). In other words, and to put it bluntly, though not without the piety and the sober earnestness such reflections command: the question for which both Merleau-Ponty and Foucault needed an answer, the question that as much triggered the former's so called 'turning' as it hindered the latter's attempt to make a truly new start, is this: what is the ontological status of copulation, what ontology is going to make it possible, or, at least, is not going to make it impossible, and how, if not as a simple midwife, are we to conceive of a father who, upon entering the stage, is confronted with "a whole *already* pregnant with an irreducible meaning" (PP 21-2)? What is the ontological status of this immaculate conception and how can there still be the need for a "putting into form" of a "matter *pregnant* with its form" (PrP 12, 15)? An Augustinianism for the late twentieth century? *Rationes seminales* which we did not put there, yet somehow create by breathing life into them? How to conceive of this communion with a text which although already present, nonetheless is not simply copied, but constituted (e.g. PP 9)? How to conceive – and how to live – a creation which is not simply *ex subjecto*?

At the heart of his writings, and yet not fully his own, these could be the questions that we might have wished Merleau-Ponty to have addressed to Foucault. But since, as the *Working Notes* tell us, "the others' words make me speak and think because they create within me an other than myself" (VI 224) we might expect them to turn back on him and to have already provided us with a "grillwork" (*ibid.*) through which we can see his texts dislocating themselves and diverging from what we thought them to be. It is time, then, for a second run which will bring us right back to the Renaissance.

II

Merleau-Ponty does not seem to have liked the Renaissance. Its paintings tended to be too adult, too prosaic and not spontaneous enough. Or at least, that is what they would have been, had Renaissance painters done exactly what their artbooks told them to do (SO 519). The ideal of painting was to represent, even to replace nature. The canvas was not yet, as it will be from Manet onwards, that silent witness of a momentary and always dated contact between the painter and the world. It was to be an object out of time that bore no trace of the hand that drew it and that could have been the work of anyone and in fact was more often than not the work of several who came and went without endangering the end-product, for all they had to do was to carry out an exact construction based on the techniques that were described by the theoreticians of the *"perspectiva artificialis"*[9]. But these theoreticians, Merleau-Ponty tells us, were "not without bad faith" (PrP 174): they left out the inconvenient parts from their translations of Euclid, disrespectfully referred to the angular perspective of preceding periods as but a common or natural, i.e. mistaken, perspective and pretended to have found a way to produce a copy of the world, whereas all they did was give man one more way "for projecting the perceived world before him" (S 48).

Perspective, then, was not what it pretended to be. Far from being that "secret technique for imitating a reality given as such to all man" (S 50), it was the attempt to domesticate "things disputing for my glance" (S 49), to impose a false harmony on this "incompossibility" (VI 216), to install "a space without transcendence" (VI 210) by imposing a (pseudo-)Euclidian mask on savage perception (VI 213), and letting a polymorphous perception "orient itself by the system" (VI 212), – to summarize: it was the attempt to *order things* by introducing "a notation of the world that would be valid for everyone" (PW 149). But such two-dimensional perspective "does not give me a human view of the world" (*ibid.*), it is "monocular" and in order to represent what is thus perceived, it has to "congeal lived perspective" and transport me into the position of "a god who does not get caught in finitude" (PW 149-50). In short, perspective is "the invention of a world which is dominated and possessed through and through in an instantaneous synthesis which is at best roughed out by our glance when it vainly tries to hold together all these things seeking individually to monopolize it" (S 50).

Foucault would not have understood this anathema on Renaissance perspective. He would have remarked that it was not "bad faith", but a different discourse that expurgated Euclid and to underscore his view that the VIIIth Theorem of the *Oros* at a certain moment literally became unreadable, he might have reminded Merleau-Ponty of the fascinating pages where Panofsky shows how the Renaissance attempt to make sense of this theorem, which was already slightly modified by the Arab translation on which the Medievals had to rely, gradually led them – in all good faith – from one translation to another to turn it into a *demonstratio per*

---

9. Merleau-Ponty's view that classical Italian painting "lacked any idea of the subjectivity of the painting" (SO 518) should perhaps be qualified somewhat in the light of recent research pointing to "an increasingly articulate sense of the artists' individuality" in the course of the 15th century Italian Renaissance, which was, however, primarily based on differences in skill (e.g. the mixing of colours, the drawing of faces, etc.) and does not yet seem to imply the notion of subjectivity Merleau-Ponty seemed to have had in mind (M. BAXANDALL, *Painting and Experience in Fifteenth Century Italy*, Oxford/New York, Oxford U.P., 1991, pp. 20 ff.)

demonstrandum[10]. Or he might have quoted the famous lines from the *Phenomenology of Perception* where Merleau-Ponty himself had referred to the "alleged transparency of Euclidean geometry" as an illustration of the fact that "there is not one truth of reason which does not retain its coefficient of facticity" (PP 394). Whatever arguments he might have come up with, Foucault, no doubt, would have been unable to appreciate the critical role which Merleau-Ponty's many remarks on wild or brute perception and on raw or vertical being seemed to play in his assessment of the 'age of the world-picture'. He would have taken this conclusion to be biased since the case itself merely seemed but another confirmation of his thesis that every culture can be expected to emancipate itself "from its linguistic, perceptual and practical grids" by superimposing on them "another kind of grid which neutralized them" and "both revealed and excluded them at the same time, so that the culture, by this very process, comes face to face with *a raw being of order*", "*anterior* to (the) words, perceptions and gestures" that are "more or less happy expressions of it" (OT X-XI). Has Foucault been reading too quickly? Would he have been mistaken in assuming that it was simply the theme of an originary experience (e.g. ODis 65; AK 47 and *passim*) which prevented Merleau-Ponty from accepting Renaissance-discourse, or better still: Renaissance *as* discourse? What lies at the basis of these diverging positions? What difference does Merleau-Pontian "raw being" make to the 'order of things'? What exactly could be the place of this "savage" and "baroque" world where "things are no longer there simply according to their projective appearances and the requirements of the panorama, as in Renaissance perspective, but on the contrary upright, insistent, flaying our glance with their edges (and) claiming an absolute presence" (S 181)? What is the place of raw being? And does it have *a* place?

Interestingly, raw being for Merleau-Ponty, just as for Foucault, is what motivates him to undertake an archaeology. But for him that archaeology is not the attempt to unearth an archive containing the rules and the basic operations that together form that primary coherence Foucault called discourse and which he thought, as we have seen, to be anterior to lived experience. To the contrary, it has to be an archaeology of the lived or the perceived world and its goal seems to be just the opposite of Foucault's: "to regain possession of that wild region in (us) which is *not* incorporated in (our own) culture" (S 120). Hence for example the questions that occupied him so much while studying Renaissance perspective: "how can one *return* from this perception fashioned by culture to the 'brute' or 'wild' perception?

---

10. E. PANOFSKY, *La perspective comme forme symbolique et autres essais*, Paris, Minuit, 1975, pp. 63-6. Merleau-Ponty quotes repeatedly from Panofsky's famous 1924 piece on 'perspective as symbolic form' in *Eye and Mind* (PrP, 174-5).

What does the informing [i.e. in-forming, – R. V.] consist in? By what act does one *undo* it (*return* to the phenomenal, to the "vertical" world, *to lived experience*)?" (VI 212). These questions are less unambiguous than they might seem at first sight, since they could be taken to suggest that Merleau-Ponty thinks of raw being as some sort of archaeological layer, whereas he explicitly denies this in more than one passage and stresses the fact that his ontology should not be confused with the attempt to return to "precomprehension or prescience" (VI 182) or to "a 'first layer' of experience" (VI 158). The *"mistrust* with regard to lived experience" would be of the essence of philosophy and philosophy would have "nothing to do with the privilege of the *Erlebnisse*" (VI 181-2). But since we were told before and elsewhere that the philosopher is in search of contact with raw being (S 22 and VI 102, 212 quoted above) and since raw being is explicitly identified with the perceived world (or the "lived", silent, prelinguistic world: e.g. VI 170), it may seem, of course, as it has seemed to many a commentator, that here at best we have come across an unresolved tension, if not an alternative within his conception of raw being and, to be sure, there might be some truth there, though not the truth we are in need of. For example, after having explained that we should not, like Piaget and Luquet, try to reduce the child's experience to our own and regard his drawing as but an imperfect approximation of our own due to his inattentiveness (empiricism) or synthetic incapacity (intellectualism) "as if perspectival drawing were already there before the child's eyes and the whole problem were to explain why he was not motivated by it" (PW 149), after having made it clear that to consider it in that way would be once more to resort to an empiricist or intellectualist concept of attention instead of seeing in it a creative "power to restructure" (SO 516) that transforms the object and allows us to conceive the passage from child to adult drawings as "a different structuration", involving different norms for drawing, a different relation to the object, in short, a different world, a different order, Merleau-Ponty all of a sudden goes on to tell us that the child's drawing is not only different from, but "richer than" (SO 517) perspectival perception which leads to "an impoverishment of the perceived" and produces a "reduced vision" which "translates" rather than "expresses" (*ibid.*). But then Renaissance perspective and adult drawing are not merely "different conceptions of painting" (SO 519), and the adult's "polymorphous contact with the world when it ends with representations" (SO 524) does not merely seem to have "a different structure" (*ibid.*) from the one of the child. Rather, this contact now seems farther off, if not lost altogether, and in the very moment one begins to see what might be at stake in Merleau-Ponty's attempt "to restore the world as a meaning of Being absolutely different from the represented" (VI 253), one is left without a clue as to how he can enchain "that is, as the vertical Being which *none* of the 'representations' exhaust *and which they all reach*, the wild Being" (*ibid.* – same sentence ctd.). Isn't Merleau-Ponty implying here that both adult and child drawing, both Renaissance perspective and a-perspectival art are all "reaching" wild Being without exhausting it and that hence there would be no reason to speak of "reduced vision" since vision is reductive anyhow and since there is a moment of violence in every perception, as the *Phenomenology* had already told us (PP 239-40, 361, 382)?

If we were to read Merleau-Ponty in this way, we would have drawn him very close to Foucault and both could be taken to represent an interesting continental variant of what Putnam dubbed "internal realism"[11], i.e. the idea that "there is more than one 'true' theory or description of the world" (Putnam, 49) and that "'objects' do not exist independently of conceptual schemes" but that we "cut up the world into objects when we introduce one or another scheme of description" (Putnam, 52). Being would then be "what requires creation of us for us to experience it" and such creation would at the same time be "an adequation, the only way to obtain an adequation" (VI 197) (Putnam's cut-ups which somehow 'fit' – Putnam, 55, 64). There would be "an inexhaustible reserve of being" (VI 169), a "perpetual resource" "which contains no mode of expression and which nonetheless calls them forth and requires all of them" (VI 170). For example, this "polymorphous" (VI 170, 270 and *passim*) or "amorphous" (*ibid.*) Being would somehow "justify all (metric systems) without being fully expressed by any" (PrP 174) and Renaissance perspective would be but "a particular case, a date, a moment in a poetic information of the world which continues after it" (PrP 175). But whereas this reading would not make it impossible for Merleau-Ponty to make some sense of Foucault's notion of discourse, it is not far from letting them both, like Putnam, simply historicize Kant (culturally different cut-up's rather than one set of categories) and from putting them into a corner which they were each keen to avoid[12]. Shall we revert then to our first reading and simply equate raw being with the perceived and the lived world, a pre-linguistic and pre-cultural layer of originary experience which somehow would be reduced, if not forgotten, impoverished, if not betrayed,

---

11. For a brief exposition see H. PUTNAM., *Reason, Truth and History*, Cambridge U.P., 1981, esp. chapter 3.

12. As can be inferred from Merleau-Ponty's discussion with Kant throughout PP and in the opening chapter of VI or from Foucault's explicit disclaimers in AK 126ff. (on 'conditions of reality') and in the 1973 interview 'An Historian of Culture' (in *Foucault Live (Interviews, 1966-84)*, New York, Semiotext(e), 1989): "What I called *episteme* in *The Order of Things* has nothing to do with historical categories, that is with those categories created in a particular historical moment" (p. 75).

but in any case: incompletely expressed by that aboriginal sin we call culture?

Equating raw being with an archaeological first stratum would not only turn Merleau-Ponty's archaeology into the most extreme counter-position to Foucault, it would also seem to counter a great many of the benefits Foucault's readers seem to expect from adopting something like 'discourse'. Whereas Foucault wanted to shock us by pointing to that 'dissociation' existing between 'our' order of things and that of other epistemic formations, hoping that we would lose some of our narcissism and come to realize "that we are difference" (AK 131, quoted in full above), the kind of Merleau-Ponty this reading provides us with would be more like a soothing old bore who tells us that at the heart of this experience of difference, e.g. in our contact with other cultures, we "gain possession" (S 120) of that raw or vertical Being "by which we pass into one another" (VI 204). Communication between cultures would pass through that wild region where they all were born (VI 115) and it would be from that layer, from that "sensible world which forms our bond with the other" (VI 214), that we could derive, all appearances to the contrary notwithstanding, our basic trust ultimately to share the "same world" (e.g. VI 110 and *passim*). But this cannot be what is meant by "lateral universality" (S 120), it rather looks like a universality *from below* which is now taking the place of an overarching universality from above, were it not for the fact that it cannot even be the universality it pretends to be since as the opening pages of the *Phenomenology* remind us "if we set ourselves to see as things the intervals between them, (...) there would not be simply the same elements differently related (...), the same text charged with a different sense, the same matter in another form, but *in truth another world*" (PP 16). Perception itself is already an expression, it stylizes, as we read elsewhere (PW 59-60/83-4), and since there is no reason to assume that we would all – as cultures, or even as individuals within a culture – be bearers of the same style, since style, to the contrary, is for Merleau-Ponty *the* moment of singularity, we are left with the question of "how one can communicate without the help of a pre-established Nature" and "how we are all grafted to the universal by that which is most our own" (S 52). But to that question we, in fact, already have all the elements of an answer.

What has blinded us hitherto is the search for a place, a *topos* at which to locate raw being. Either it would be that pre-linguistic, pre-cultural moment we thought to be an originary experience in all of us, or we tended to look at it as a "radical alterity"[13], an inexhaustible reserve which we never

13. Raw being seen as an 'inaccessible radical exteriority' makes Jean-Pierre Le Goff, in an otherwise interesting article, interpret Merleau-Ponty's last writings as an attempt to turn philosophical reflexion into "an intellectual mysticism" ('Le paradoxe du language et l'être

managed to fully represent. But in the first case we turned raw being into nature and we forgot that even "our perception is cultural-historical" (VI 253); whereas in the second case we were led to believe that we are all culture and we forgot that "everything in us is natural" as well, and that "*even* the cultural rests on the polymorphism of the wild Being" (*ibid.*). The trick, of course, is not to regard raw Being as a being (small b) which can be localized somewhere, but as radically *a-topic* and hence a dimension, instead of a first layer of experience. The trick is to realize that raw Being is not merely another name for our perceptual contact with the world, but that it is precisely there where it is revealed in an exemplary way. The trick is to realize that if Merleau-Ponty equates raw Being with the 'perceived world', the stress is not on perceived but on *world*, since it is there that in an exemplary – though not in an exclusive – way I come to realize that world is not something with which I would be in a subject-object relation (VI 222). "Sensing" (*le sentir*; 'sense experience') precisely is not "the intellectual possession of 'what' is felt, but a *dispossession* of ourselves in favour of it, an *opening* toward that which we do not have to think in order that we may recognize it" (TLC 130/179 – transl. corrected), and "the sensible is precisely that medium in which there can be *being* without it having to be posited" (VI 214). Here Being can manifest itself without becoming positivity, without ceasing to be ambiguous *and transcendent* (*ibid.*) and it is precisely this "silent transcendence" (VI 213) which robs "the sensible *world*" of its alleged positivity and, in making it "ungraspable" for me (VI 214) and yet something from which I cannot detach myself, confronts me with that "paradox of transcendence and immanence" (e.g. PrP 16) which made Merleau-Ponty compare perception to a communion or to a copulation (see above and VI, *passim*). For isn't a copulation precisely that experience of almost losing myself in the other and yet at the brink of fusion losing hold of him in the uncontrolled movement of my spasms? Immanent *and* transcendent this "indivision of sensing", this "initial yes", this "primordial unconscious" which would be a "letting be" rather than a "positing" of the perceived world (TLC 131; VI 102), would at the same time be a division which is not yet that of the no (VI 216) or of the Sartrean cut between the For Itself and the In Itself (VI 215) but that of a chiasm where "every relation with being is *simultaneously* a taking and a being taken, where the hold is held (...) and inscribed in the same being that it takes hold of" (VI 266). This inscription is *not* a fusion but rather the indicator of its impossibility: hence Merleau-Ponty's reservations against any metaphysics that, like Bergson's, resorts to coincidence and tends to forget that the fact that I am "of the world" means

brut', *Les Cahiers de Philosophie (nr. 7: Actualités de Merleau-Ponty)*, 1989 (spring), pp. 69-84, esp. pp. 76 ff.).

at the same time that I am not it (VI 127). But it *is* an inscription and hence of course his attempt to push Husserl out of idealism and to conceive of the reduction not in terms of transcendental immanence, not as a reduction *of* the natural world, but as a reduction *to* it, as that successful failure which in its attempt to break away from it reveals our ineradicable attachment to it, in short as a reduction which is necessary to reveal a tension, but uninhabitable as such[14]. Ineffaceably inscribing me into the world to which I am open (*Offenheit*, e.g. VI 251), the sensible is both "the being which I reach in its raw or untamed state", but also "the being which reaches me in my most secret parts" (S 171) and confronts me with the 'mineness' (*Jemeinigkeit*) of my singularity.

But how, then, could I forget it? How could I "not see what makes me see, my tie (*attache*) to Being" (VI 248/301)[15]? What other dramas am I to expect if my perception is "of itself ignorance of itself as wild perception, imperception" that "forgets itself" as "being at" (VI 213), as com-munion? What sort of conscience is this which "as a matter of principle disregards Being and prefers the object to it" (VI 248/302, transl. corrected)? And can I even hope to reduce it now that I learned that its immanence is forever postponed, never to be washed of this "original stain" (*souillure originelle*, VI 45/69) which prevents our philosophy from becoming "total and active grasp, intellectual possession, since what there is to be grasped is a dispossession" (VI 266)?

Before we let these questions take us on a third run, we would do well to recapitulate, since we have come a long way and by now may be gasping for breath.

III

As one will remember, first we were taken from a series of *prima facie* epistemological problems (the impossibility of understanding discourse or perception in either intellectualist or empiricist terms) to the brink of a metaphysical problem concerning a creation which is not *ex subjecto* and yet more than a mere reproduction of already pre-existing givens. Though in the subsequent discussion of the various possible readings of the notion of 'raw being' we did come up in passing with a Merleau-Pontian variant of internal realism as a means of coping with the epistemological problem that

14. In his intervention at Royaumont Merleau-Ponty stressed that "the transcendental attitude is not an attitude where one can stay (*se tenir*) or install oneself (*s'installer*)" (*Husserl*, *o.c.*, p. 159 – my transl.)

15. Depending on the context, I shall throughout this volume sometimes alternatively translate *attache* as 'attachment'.

first aroused our curiosity, the focus of our attention imperceptibly shifted to the strange status of that new ontology that, far from pretending to make us *understand* the metaphysics of creation by providing us with its conditions of possibility, seemed to have set itself the no less radical aim of teaching us how to *live* this creation by confronting us with the conditions of reality for the communion that we are. This ontology, then, cannot be neutral. It is not positivistic. Rather, its aim seems to be to intervene in "our state of non-philosophy" since "never has the crisis been so radical" (VI 165). The pathos of such passages notwithstanding, one may wonder whether the crisis to which Merleau-Ponty is referring may not be yet one more crisis but, rather, a moment endemic to the 'human condition', a moment the criticality of which ultimately derives from the fact that, once its ontological structure is revealed, it becomes apparent that it might not be easy to inhabit this condition or to dwell in it in an authentic sense of 'dwelling'. In order to introduce or to 'express' (in the Merleau-Pontian sense – see below) this Heideggerian moment to which I alluded before, let us join our relay-race at the point we left it.

What really emerged during our second run, though it might have gone unnoticed, is that the originary (*l'originaire*)[16] has "broken up" (VI 124/165). For two reasons. First, we have seen that raw Being is not to be located *in* an originary experience. Instead of an *origin*-al (e.g. prelinguistic) layer, it is that *dimension* (VI 182) revealed to us by sensing (*le sentir*), since on that level at least we are confronted both with an indivision and a division and find ourselves unable to either coincide or to detach ourselves, unable even to coincide with our attachment since it is precisely what exposes us (e.g. VI 35 ff.). But what has been said about sensing need not be restricted to that domain. To the contrary, it has an exemplary status. Raw Being as a dimension is the *atopos* in every *topos* and not just in that layer known to us as perceptual experience. Perception is simply the "archetype of an originary encounter" the *paradox* of which one finds "imitated and renewed" (VI 158) on all other levels which Merleau-Ponty insists on seeing related to it by what he calls 'expression'. Just as pre-linguistic perception itself had to be considered against empiricism and intellectualism as a process that is neither a mere reproduction, nor a creation out of the void, but a communion, i.e. a *creation* "which is *at the same time* an adequation" (VI 197), now everything which relates to the perceived world as that primal

---

16. At the cost of introducing a gallicism, I have tried to accomodate for the double meaning of the French *originaire* (both 'original' (i.e. 'first', 'primitive') and 'originating') by simply transcribing it as 'originary' in order to remain faithful to the semantic resonances of Merleau-Ponty's text (Lingis's translation which opts for the sole 'originating' (VI 124) seems to lose an essential ambiguity).

"source of meaning for us" (VI 157) is shown by Merleau-Ponty to have exactly the same structure: the structure of an expression which does not simply copy or reproduce already pre-existing data[17]. Far from letting such givens leave their imprint on a perfectly flexible mould, the expressive medium (e.g. language) itself seems to have a logic of its own which makes it impress itself on that which it was at first naively supposed to simply express and make readable. Far from being that unproductive pro-duction, that perfectly colourless medium of which, as Derrida has shown[18], Husserl was dreaming, language or expression in general (e.g. painting) has its own power of refraction, which is why it betrays as much as it translates. But it still translates (i.e. *trans*lates) and the difficulty is precisely to come up with a theory of expression that does not have the consequence of annihilating the experience that is expressed, and that at the same time does not make the expression itself superfluous[19] by turning it into 'a voice which would have to remain silent' (Derrida). In other words, the problem is to avoid turning language (expression) into an absolute or to find such an absolute in experience[20]. And the solution is Derridian *avant la lettre*: expression is an "original" supplement and it is the supplement to an origin that has broken up. It is not in spite of the fact that the origin has been shattered, but rather because of it, that there can and must be expression and that upon interrogating our experience "in order to know how it opens us to what is not ourselves" we come across this strange "movement toward what could not in any event be present to us in the original and whose irremediable absence would thus count among our originary experiences" (VI 159/211, transl. altered). Expression, in short, is a translation which produces its own original[21]: it translates an experience "that only becomes text by the word that it inspires" (TLC 26). In other words, there is an original, but precisely because it has broken up, there is this never ending attempt to translate that which one in fact produces. And yet this attempt is still an attempt to express

---

17. On this "transition from the mute world to the speaking world" (VI 154/202) which was already a major theme in PP, see J. TAMINIAUX, 'Experience, expression and form in Merleau-Ponty's itinerary', in ID., *Dialectic and Difference: Finitude in Modern Thought*, New Jersey, Humanities Press, 1985, pp. 133-54 and Y. THIERRY, *Du corps parlant. Le langage chez Merleau-Ponty*, Brussels, Ousia, 1987.

18. Most succinctly in 'Form and Meaning: A Note on the Phenomenology of Language', in J. DERRIDA, *Margins of Philosophy*, Chicago, The University of Chicago Press, 1982, pp. 155-73.

19. M. RAINVILLE, *L'Expérience et l'expression. Essai sur la pensée de Maurice Merleau-Ponty*, Montréal, Editions Bellarmin, 1988, p. 119.

20. Cl. LEFORT, 'Editor's Foreword', in VI, p. XXX.

21. B. WALDENFELS, 'Vérité à Faire. Merleau-Ponty's Question Concerning Truth', *Philosophy Today*, 1991 (35: 2), p. 189.

an irremediable absence, which is why it does not end in sheer whimsicality, in mere dissemination, in total creation. Philosophy for example is caught in this virtuous circle of being both more and less than a mere translation (VI 36), and this is why we can and must always call it into question without having – or needing – the hope of arriving at an ultimate expression. Indeed this hope itself can only be the hope of those who are unable to accept and to dwell in the "paradox of expression" (VI 144) and who seek to console themselves by dreaming the sweet dream of a fusion or a soaring-over (*survol*). Philosophy cannot coincide with what it expresses, nor can it have a bird's-eye-view of it.

The important thing to realize here is that for Merleau-Ponty precisely because of the way he conceives of the relation of expression, not only is the original (in the first and naive sense of *l'expérience originaire, le vécu*) going to further disappear, but also the 'original stain' (*souillure originelle*) (VI 45/69) of my attachment (*attache*) is going to colour all attempts to express it. In doing philosophy I belong to it and yet I am not it, my attachment (*j'en suis*) is such that it constantly seems to draw me away from universality and always brings me back to a position within that wider field we call the philosophical tradition. And this is why, since we have here its prime example, we need to reconceive our notion of universality and to understand how we can be grafted onto it by our own singularity. And because this grafting is a difficult operation, we need to come up with an ethics, in the sense of an *ethos* which tells us how to live our attachment since the mere fact that one is 'in' philosophy (or 'in' any other world) does not automatically mean that one's dwelling there is as it should be, – the reverse, as we all know, is more often the case. And this is why finally Merleau-Ponty came up with "a wholly new idea of subjectivity" (VI 269) to account for, as I will show in a moment, the *alethic* structure of a truth that in its singularity is not cut off from universality.

One last step then. If raw Being is that which demands creation of us and if this creation or expression is "the only way to obtain an adaequation" (VI 197), then the kind of truth that is at stake here of necessity involves a certain kind of violence which is not yet ethical. If I am to come up with an answer that gives form to those raw or "poorly posed questions" (PP 214; TLC 34; VI e.g. 39) with which I am confronted, and if my answer is only one among many, all of them reaching and none of them exhausting raw Being (e.g. VI 170), if it is but one possible way to give form to those questions or to those demands of experience, then the fact that of necessity it will always fall short and betray cannot by itself have an ethical significance. And yet it may not be without some bearing on the ethical problem. For how can I avoid becoming totally absorbed in the particularity of my response which, like discourse (and here Foucault comes in again), is of necessity selective and exclusive and, by that constitutive limitation, produces an excess or a moment of alterity to which it at the same time seems blinded? Should I, and why should I, be concerned about this excess that I cannot account for but also am in no need of accounting for? Whereas it is clear that we would have to pay an incredibly high price for failing to come up with an answer to these questions and that we would simply become one more victim of the 'law of the heart' which is, as is well known, not a law at all (hence its terror), the bare fact is that it seems difficult to avoid paying that price. To be sure, it may be the case that "with every demand one meets in experience, something comes up that produces selective and exclusive formations" that in their turn are unable to fully absorb it[22], but the problem is precisely that that which confronts us here is too wild to be an interlocutor and that once it gets tamed by our finite domestication it seems in danger of losing its alterity. "Things", Merleau-Ponty tells us, are *"no* interlocutors", "like madmen or animals they are *quasi*-companions" (VI 180), which is why this moment of transcendence in raw Being, the fact that being "is not only *what it is*" and is inflated "with the possible" (*ibid.*) is not going to solve our riddle. For why should we care about this transcendence, why should we follow Ponge in his *'parti pris pour les choses'*[23], why should we be worried about the fact that our rationality is both responsive and finite in its response, unless we reintroduce some kind of metaphysics of plenitude[24] from which to generate a teleology that, contrary to Merleau-Ponty's advice, would not have "to be written and thought about in brackets" (S 181)? And yet, were there not some kind of "desire" driving expression beyond itself (VI 144) and confronting it with the limits of its factical vision (*ibid.*), we would find ourselves in the crudest of culturalisms or solipsisms. Hence we will have to generate this desire from within. We will have to derive it *not from that which exceeds a response which always falls short, but from the structure of*

22. B. WALDENFELS, *Ordnung im Zwielicht*, Frankfurt a.M., Suhrkamp, 1987: "Mit jedem Anspruch, der in der Erfahrung auftritt, tritt etwas auf, das selektive und exklusive Formungen produziert, aber in diesen nicht aufgeht", (p. 178). Waldenfels's attempt to generate from this insight a notion of a 'responsive rationality' is further documented in some of his essays in the two companion volumes to *Ordnung im Zwielicht*: *In den Netzen der Lebenswelt*, Frankfurt a.M., Suhrkamp, 1985 and *Der Stachel des Fremden*, Frankfurt a.M., Suhrkamp, 1990. Cf. also, more recently, his *Antwortregister*, Frankfurt a.M., Suhrkamp, 1994.

23. As is suggested in B. WALDENFELS, 'Das Zerspringen des Seins. Ontologische Auslegung der Erfahrung am Leitfaden der Malerei', in A. MÉTRAUX - B. WALDENFELS (eds.), *Leibhaftige Vernunft. Spuren von Merleau-Ponty's Denken*, München, Fink, 1986, p. 185.

24. A solution which, it should be noted, is explicitly rejected in 'Das Zerspringen des Seins', p. 159.

response itself which, as one will remember, always involves a moment of attachment (*attache, adhérence*), of singularity. And this is precisely what Merleau-Ponty hoped the reduction could do: not as a guarantee for authentic dwelling, but as a possible revealment of the need for it.

At first sight the chances for such a reduction seem almost nil. Expression tends to regard itself as mere ex-pression, perception doesn't perceive what makes it perceive (VI 213), consciousness inevitably is mystified (VI 248), and language finally is more often than not a merely spoken speech (*parole parlée*) that makes us forget the instituting moment of speaking speech (*parole parlante*) and, like a worn metaphor, seems to consist merely of a set of signs on which an already constituted thought can depend in order to make itself communicable[25]. And yet all these mystifications are precisely what is going to save us. For if language or expression would immediately confront us with our attachment, they would lose their attraction. It is precisely because the Being of language withdraws, that I can trust those heavily trodden tracks that seem there to guarantee that my alleged self-presence will not get frustrated. It is precisely because spoken speech presents itself as that highly reliable realm into which I can be absorbed or disappear without running the risk of getting so tangled up in it that I might be altered by it myself, it is precisely because it seems to provide me with this possibility of a fusion in which I will not be losing myself, that I am attracted by it and see in it the means to accommodate that "patient and silent labor of desire" (VI 144) with which expression starts. This desire may be none other than that for an origin the breaking up of which has been covered over – which is, as Merleau-Ponty reminds us, a paradox of Being as well as of man (VI 122). Hence, for example, the fanaticism with which I start to read the texts of the other and try to translate them into my own thoughts without altering them. For at first I do not want to read these texts to find out what might be wrong with them, I want to know what is in them and instead of being vigilant I treat them as signs governed by a code I will be able to break if only I pay enough attention. Hence my frustration at my lack of success and the renewed attempt to manipulate that key to the reality that seems to lie beyond those texts, and to lose myself in them – in that respect I am not unlike the painter who starts by copying the old masters (VI 211). And yet it is precisely because of this *desire to disappear* that I *can* be confronted with my subjectivity. It is precisely at that moment when the painter discovers his own hand or when I fail to lose myself in the other

25. One will find this theme of a 'retreat of language' differently developed from PP, through PW to VI. For a good overall account of Merleau-Ponty's views on language see e.g. J. SCHMIDT, *Maurice Merleau-Ponty. Between Phenomenology and Structuralism*, London/Basingstoke, MacMillan, 1985, chapter 4 (with literature).

or to absorb him in me, that I *can* become attentive to that "diaphragm" in me (VI 99) to which Merleau-Ponty so often seems to refer (e.g. VI 201, 246) and from which the *Working Notes* try to generate a new concept of subjectivity which would not be identity with oneself, but non-difference with oneself (VI 204) or, if one insists: an identity that would be "difference of difference" (VI 264), a same which would be "the other than the other" (*ibid.*), in other words: "separation" (*écart*) (VI 216/270). And this gap (*écart*) which "forms meaning" should not be conceived of as "a *no* I affect myself with, a lack which I constitute as a lack by the upsurge of an end which I give myself" but as "a natural negativity, a first institution, *always already there*" (VI 216). It is this separation which prevents my communion from becoming mere indivision, mere fusion. It is this primordial 'no' constituting the singularity of my 'attachment' that explains why Merleau-Ponty can understand something Foucault at best could only postulate – a subjectivity which is both dependent and indeclinable (cf. PP 400)[26] – and why we do not have to choose between both of them. For what is this primordial 'no' if not the moment where existence escapes discourse, but in such a way that it does not make discourse impossible? What is this 'no', this 'relief' (VI 269) which I bring into language, if not the point at which a difference between what is said and what could be said[27], is established? To be sure, what is at stake here is not the attempt to reduce discourse to existence, or existence to discourse, but to find in their mutual intrication some indication of what it could mean for us to be those subjects who take up positions we did not ourselves generate. And also, it is the attempt to turn discourse into something less spectacular that calls for solutions with which we are – or could be – already familiar. For here I am, I am the voice of truth, with this text here I am in the truth of my expression, and although I did not choose to be there, although I did everything possible to be out there with the others in the truth of their texts, at this moment when I would have wished them to be here, I no longer care about their absence. For while their presence would make my truth less solitary, "they are not gods" that would make it more true, and their absence doesn't make it less true[28]. And in this moment in which I am confronted with an attachment

26. In Foucault this problem becomes most apparent in his later 'genealogy' which tries to understand the 'subject' as the 'subjected' (on the double sense of 'subjectivation' (*assujettissement*) and its theoretical aporia: *Genealogy as Critique*, pp.82 ff.), but it is already present in AK: "I wanted not to exclude the problem of the subject, but to define the positions and functions that the subject could occupy in the diversity of discourse" (AK 200).

27. See note 3.

28. I am, of course, putting a twist upon the famous passage from Merleau-Ponty's *In Praise of Philosophy*: "Our relationship to the true passes through others. Either we go towards the true with them, or it is not towards the true that we are going. But the real

to something in me which is more me than me, in this moment where I am at the crossroads of a truth I did not choose and a singularity I cannot control, in this face to face with the *alethic* structure of my truth I can only burst into the laughter of the adult who, unlike the infant that cries in order not to disappear in its hunger, is betaken with fits of laughter for having, no matter how hard he tried, failed to disappear into the other. This laughter is not self-complacent. It is, in Kundera's terms, both angelic and diabolic since it reacts to a truth which is both too full and too void of meaning[29]. In this laughter I realize that there is this something around which all my thoughts circle and without which I would not make the effort toward truth, and that this something is not that of the other. In this laughter, I realize that my consciousness is but "a figure against a background" (VI 191/245, transl. altered) and that what is figure for me may be background for another. It is as if for a moment I see the *Gestalt* that I am and that no matter how hard I try, I remain unable to make the picture switch. And in that moment in which I am confronted with the full shape of my own shadow, just before he and I will walk the same road again, a certain "dehiscence" (e.g. VI 123) is produced which is not large enough to make me lose him and yet not small enough to prevent me from becoming grafted to the universal by that which is my own. In other words, I become appealable by the other not in spite of the fact that I have a centre different from his, but precisely because of my awareness that I will have to dwell in my own shadow and stop treating it as simply "the actual absence of future light" (S 178). But perhaps the problem with this suggestion is that, like the other essays in this section, for all its willingness to embrace man's finitude, it nonetheless attempts to leave out what is unpleasantly finite about that finitude. As we shall see in our next sections, there may be grounds to suspect that the move from one finite subject to another may not be as smooth as that.

---

difficulty is that, if the true is not an idol, the others in their turn *are not gods*. There is no truth without them, but it does not suffice to attain to the truth to be with them" (Evanston Ill., Northwestern U.P., 1970, p. 31). Moreover, the necessity of this twist, which follows from our reading of Merleau-Ponty, is but another illustration of the point I am making here.

29. M. KUNDERA, *The Book of Laughter and Forgetting*, London, Penguin Books, 1983, pp. 61 ff. ('On Two Kinds of Laughter').

II

A Silence Which Escapes
Intersubjectivity

CHAPTER FIVE

DIS-POSSESSED
HOW TO REMAIN SILENT 'AFTER' LEVINAS

As we look back today to that obscure but for none of us insignificant period of (post)structuralism, it would seem that none of the slogans which at that time were intended to sweeten its message can still claim any credibility. Far from being dead and buried, like some purloined letter, the 'author' seems to have been with us all along, barely hidden by the folds of those quotations marks from where he was laughing behind our backs[1]. And far from taking over the place of the subject, 'structure' has, so to speak, only displaced it: much to our surprise, the 'eccentric' subject is still a subject – it is precisely its dependence on something which it did not itself institute or constitute that has prevented it from dying a peaceful death. Forcing the subject to abdicate from the centre did not entail the subject's destruction[2]. Quite to the contrary, this decentring has managed to revitalize the subject, and the unexpected result of its rejuvenation is simply that its accusers are now themselves accused: relieved of the heavy burden of a centre where it stood constantly accused of falling short in its every endeavor, the subject seems to be thoroughly enjoying its new freedom to linger wherever it pleases, as long as it is not in the centre, and to exploit its elusiveness to harass whoever came in its place with new, apparently insoluble questions and problems. Granted, discourse functions without a meaning-giving subject underlying all knowledge; but then what could it mean that *I* know? And, of course, knowledge evolves according to rules I have not made, and which continually escape me; but why would I not attempt to break into that archive and show the complex genealogy by which those rules came to be? To be sure, I go through life with a certain name – the name of my

1. This is an ironical reference to my earlier analysis of Foucault's use of quotation marks (cf. chapter 2 n12). On Heidegger's quotation marks, see: J. DERRIDA, *De l'esprit: Heidegger et la question*, Paris, Galilée, 1987.
2. Cf. J. Lacan's intervention in the discussion following Foucault's 'What is an Author?': "structuralism or not, it seems to me it is nowhere a question, in the field vaguely determined by that label, of the negation of the subject. It is a question of the dependence of the subject, which is quite different ..." (*Bulletin de la Société française de Philosophie*, 1969(64), p. 104, my transl.).

father, the name of my people – which precedes me and which obligates me; but isn't it normal for me to try and know what this obligation asks of me and, failing to get an answer, can I be blamed for myself attempting to determine what this debt consists in?

Instead of sounding the death knell of the subject, decentring seems to have resulted in a new and different kind of subject: one that would like to know why it was not allowed to die and what the nature of its debt could be; a subject that must try to find its own way, having been denied a centre that would provide all the answers. An explosive situation no doubt, for what could be more dangerous than a debt that is determined by the debtor himself? Is it not the echo of such explosions that recently gave cause for alarm: one need only think of the recent upsurge of nationalism? The difficulty seems to be that the subject is far from content with the ambivalent situation in which it finds itself after being decentred: what it cannot tolerate is not so much that it is excluded from the centre, but that it cannot do away with that centre, to which it is nonetheless denied access. Now that it has given up its claims, it fails to understand why it cannot die in peace. It fails to understand that whatever dispossessed it after all still obligates it. It thought it could disappear – we all remember: "a face in the sand ..." – but now that it has sobered up, it discovers that the scenario for its voluntary retirement was really just an excuse to make it work even harder. In its old age the subject finds itself forced into discharging a debt it has nothing to do with, a debt to a centre that it thought it had turned its back on and left behind...

Decentring the subject, then, aimed at more than a mere change of position: at stake was an asymmetry in which the subject is obligated by "something"[3] without ever having given its consent and without even being consulted in the matter. The position from which it finds itself being put under obligation is not a position that it could possibly occupy in its turn. The addressor and the addressee of 'obligation' belong to non-substitutable and non-simultaneous positions: the reason why the subject cannot disappear – and perhaps one must define the subject today as a "not-able-to-disappear" – is to be found precisely in its decentring. The subject did not just happen to arrive too late to take up its place in the centre; it is itself the effect of this originary delay. It is that which cannot be where it would like to be. It is not without a centre, but caught in the unbreakable spell of

3. An expression which comes up regularly in Lyotard's more recent work (cf. the references in my: 'Dissensus Communis: How to Remain Silent after Lyotard', in Ph. VAN HAUTE - P. BIRMINGHAM (eds.), *Dissensus Communis: Between Ethics and Politics*, Kampen (The Netherlands), Kok Pharos, 1995, pp. 7-30. The considerations about 'silence' that follow are intended as a provisional development of the problematic presented there).

something from which it derives its singularity. Accordingly, what is most 'proper' to the subject, what lies at the basis of its irreplaceability, of its non-interchangeable singularity – in short of its being "itself" – has nothing to do with some secret property or some hidden capacity, but results from a lack of resources on its part, from its ineliminable poverty, its incapacity: the subject is something that has missed an appointment, and it would never have even existed without that break, rent or gap through which it gains, rather than loses, its intimacy, or without that non-simultaneousness or that 'retardation' *vis-à-vis* itself through which, if we are to believe Levinas, it can fall into time and be related to the Other without being absorbed into them. Even before it is able, the subject is a 'not-able', and whatever it can do, it can only do on the basis of and within the horizon opened by the 'not-able'.

No doubt this is why, instead of seeing in the subject an active principle, contemporary philosophy prefers to emphasize the receptivity that must precede this activity. The subject is no longer thought as an auto-affection, but as an affectedness by the other. And contemporary thought seems to expect a kind of salvation from this passivity or passibility (Lyotard) which, as the expression goes, precedes all opposition between activity and passivity. The anaesthesia of a completely technical world in which there is a system that controls not only its own output but also its own input[4], this nightmare which, since Heidegger, has emerged on our horizon, could only have its inexorable advance arrested by a renewed attention for this affectedness or this "aesthesia" which involves the subject in a past that is absolute and irrevocable: a past that has never been present nor ever will be present; a past which, precisely by withdrawing, leaves behind a being who must find salvation in his helplessness.

One might wonder if such commonplaces bring us any further. They are, no doubt, too suggestive to be precise. But perhaps for that very reason they are able to invoke something of our strange climate of thought which might best be defined by a certain impatience with all those (supposed) attempts to eliminate the subject, and by the desire to know how things stand with it and what will come after it, assuming its place has been vacated. Questions that seem of utmost importance, and that have led – or misled, as some would argue – such a notable philosopher as Habermas to the conclusion that what is at stake in the attempt to find a way out of the philosophy of the subject is the heritage of modernity itself. But the paradigm shift that Habermas represents – a turning from subjectivity to

---

4. J.-Fr. LYOTARD, "Grundlagenkrise", *Neue Hefte für Philosophie*, 1986, pp. 1-33.

intersubjectivity[5] – has, to put it mildly, not been greeted with universal enthusiasm. And since the opposition that is marshalled in the name of a certain postmodernity seems to be concerned precisely with this emphasis on the receptivity of a subject who finds himself in an irrevocably asymmetric position, I thought it not unwise to drop anchor for a moment in these murky waters to which the pilots of modernity and postmodernity have towed the Kantian ship. Or into which, Levinas will suggest, that ship has towed them. This suggestion seems to me to merit consideration: it ought to allow us to appreciate the uncompromising position that Levinas occupies in the contemporary crisis of post-Kantian ethics. This is more or less the programme for my first half: an attempt, let us say, to not underestimate the 'opponent'. And what an opponent! For how could one even begin to think about the problems under consideration here without first having spent some time – and perhaps a very long time – wandering through the incredibly rich heritage Levinas has bequeathed us? Wasn't he one of the first to have insisted on the absoluteness of a past that is too much past to ever become present, and to have linked this absoluteness with all of those themes so dear to us, and for which we use his own words: asymmetry, hetero-affection, passivity older than every opposition between activity and passivity? Wasn't it Levinas who taught us to define the subject as something that does not have the choice of disappearing, and who related the subject to an outside that is so much outside that it can allow itself to go to the very heart of the subject without running the risk of becoming a part of it or being absorbed by it? Are we not quoting Levinas when we speak of the 'other in the self', and do we not share his *own* suspicion when we attempt to think the subject on the basis of a "dispossession" that would be more originary than every form of possession? All of this is undoubtedly true and we ought to be grateful. But Levinas, whose entire philosophy attempts to dispel even the tiniest hint of ek-stasis, would surely agree that gratitude should be cool-headed, and should maintain an awareness of the distance separating the one who teaches from the one who is taught. Keeping this distance is the programme for my second half: as we shall see, it is a matter of a single, but not insignificant, word. It is, for Levinas, the first word, a word that passes our lips, nowadays, none too easily, a word that we tend to mention rather than use. Which is why the significance and function of this word in Levinas fascinate me, and why I would like to know what happens when this word is dropped, or rather – since it is a word that we have

5. Cf. the title of the penultimate chapter of his controversial *The Philosophical Discourse of Modernity: Twelve Lectures*, Cambridge, Polity, 1987: "An Alternative Way out of the Philosophy of the Subject: Communicative versus Subject-Centred Reason", and chapter 3 above.

wanted for a long time to drop – I would be interested to know how much damage resulted from leaving this word behind. Perhaps I ought to apologize for such curiosity. It will take up much of our time, but that is just the time needed in order to answer the question that this chapter was meant to address: the question whether "subjectivity implies a certain closedness that seems difficult to reconcile with the desire for openness and receptivity so prevalent these days"[6]. There is, in my opinion, nothing to be said about this closedness so long as one avoids confronting this first word of Levinas. I have not yet said *what* word, but it will not keep us waiting long – for it is only by introducing the word 'God'[7] that Levinas can avoid being drawn into the maelstrom where Habermas and Lyotard attempt to keep their boats afloat. But not to panic: we will maintain, as mentioned already, a safe distance.

Levinas in the crisis of post-Kantian ethics

I

It is well known that, for Kant, practical reason is both legislation and efficient causality. In order to bring autonomy into ethics, Kant had to show that reason contains within itself both a *principium diiudicationis bonitatis* and a *principium executionis bonitatis*[8]. Reason should be capable of showing us what has to be done, without having recourse to any considerations other than those that follow from the structure of reason itself (first principle). Yet reason should also have the power to execute the actions that are proposed because they comply with reason (second principle). The first principle led Kant to the discovery of the categorical imperative, while the second led – much later – to what became known as the doctrine of the "fact of reason". Only by bringing these two principles together could Kant reach the conclusion that the law is obligatory *because* it is universal, where, as Lyotard has shown[9], the "because" operates like an "iff". Accordingly, Kant's first formulation of the categorical imperative lends itself to a double

---

6. I am citing the brochure for the symposium, "Interpretaties van subjectiviteit" (= "Interpretations of Subjectivity"), where this chapter was first presented (University of Amsterdam, April 1995).

7. Levinas calls the word "God" the "first word" in, among other places, 'Language and Proximity', in CPP, pp. 125-126.

8. On this distinction, cf. Dieter Henrich's brilliant piece: 'Ethik der Autonomie', in ID., *Selbstverhältnisse*, Stuttgart, Philip Reclam Jun., 1982, p. 14 and *passim*.

9. J.-Fr. LYOTARD, "Levinas's Logic", in ID., *The Lyotard Reader* (ed. A. Benjamin), Oxford, Blackwell, 1989, p. 297.

reading: not only "if the norm of such-and-such an action is a universally obligatory norm, then you must perform this action", but also "if you must accomplish such-and-such an action, then the maxim of your will is a universally obligatory norm". Both "if p then q" (if reason then will), and "if q then p" (if will then reason, i.e. universality); in other words, "p iff q".

In support of his claim that the underlying transformation of an obligation into a norm is valid, Kant had to introduce an extremely elaborate conceptual architectonics. Since it is precisely this architectonics that was so vigorously assailed by Kant's immediate followers[10], it should come as no surprise that it is on this exact point that contemporary Continental philosophy appears to have become deadlocked. Take, for instance, Habermas's attempt to reformulate the categorical imperative, giving it the intersubjective spin of a discursive ethics organized around the so-called "D-principle": "only those norms may claim to be valid that could meet with the consent of all affected in their role as participants in a practical discourse"[11]. As a consequence, the categorical imperative would be freed from its bondage to a "monologic" reason and readapted to function as a rule of argumentation in practical discourses: "for a norm to be valid, the consequences and side effects of its general observance for the satisfaction of each person's particular interests must be acceptable to all" (*ibid.*). But Habermas's critics reply that this only holds for the logic of norms and, moreover, already presupposes what is to be shown: that the transition from obligations to norms is unproblematic. Thus Lyotard's objection that the whole question of the lawfulness of the law – of its obligatory character – is not even raised here. Lyotard insists that one cannot understand why an ethical law holds if one remains caught in this alternative: either *convincing* (hence reasonable) or else *constraining* (hence unreasonable)[12]. For a law does not hold because it convinces, nor because it constrains, but because it *obligates*. It takes the form of a prescription that places the addressee in the asymmetric position of a "Thou" to whom the prescription is directed. Such a prescription obligates whether or not the addressee is convinced of its correctness. Its prescriptive force does not depend on such a deliberation; indeed, to make it so depend would mean abandoning the logic of obligation and transforming the law into a commentary on the law, thus replacing *prescription* with *description*. And of

---

10. For a perspicuous overview, cf. D. HENRICH, *l.c.*

11. J. HABERMAS, 'Morality and Ethical Life', in ID., *Moral Consciousness and Communicative Action*, Cambridge, Polity, 1990, p. 197 and cf. p. 66.

12. J.-Fr. LYOTARD, *The Differend: Phrases in Dispute*, Manchester U.P., 1988, nr. 176 (I will henceforth refer to this work as "D", followed by the number of the paragraph being cited). Habermas is not mentioned in this passage, but he is clearly the target.

course, for Lyotard, who has made it his task to "testify to the Differend", this is an unjustified move. The prescriptive clause 'it is an order that p' is transformed into the descriptive clause 'someone has said that p must be done (by me)'. And it is precisely this transformation that Habermas carries out in order to determine what "valid norms" are: the maxim which says that p must be done will only be a valid norm if, in Habermas's formulation, it can count on the agreement of all those concerned. But this whole procedure necessarily presupposes that instead of remaining in the asymmetric position of one who is obligated by a prescription, each participant in such a practical discourse can freely occupy the position from which the prescription is addressed. A norm is valid only if the addressees of the prescription could "at the same time" regard themselves, without coercion, as its addressors. Which is to say that a norm is valid only if it could *convince* all those concerned. But of course, like Kant, Habermas also wants to make the reverse claim: if one is convinced by a (moral) validity claim, then one is committed to defending it, and the result of such a defence must be such that it satisfies the conditions for a valid norm[13]. Just as with Kant, "p if and only if q".

Both Lyotard and Levinas would protest here, though not for the same reasons. I will come back to this point later. For the moment, let us concentrate on their rather curious alliance against humanism, or at least against a certain version of humanism[14]. For both Lyotard and Levinas, it is a humanism that still believes in the possibility of doing away with an *Unmündigkeit* (the famous "immaturity" in Kant's "What is Enlightenment?") that one owes only to oneself. And yet, Lyotard wonders[15], might there not be a different *Unmündigkeit* than the one Habermas has in mind, and is this *Unmündigkeit* not excluded *a priori* whenever one substitutes the logic of norms ("either convincing or else constraining") for the logic of obligation? Is there not in obligation another, more deeply buried *Unmündigkeit*, an inability to speak and – *a fortiori* – to argue, an "in-fantia" that one cannot and should not render communicatively transparent, for to do so would

13. J. HABERMAS, *o.c.*, pp. 197-8. Habermas sees here a possibility of working Kant's *Faktum der Vernunft* into communicative theory – clearly this implies a distancing from Kant that does not contradict the symmetry noted here, but qualifies it to a significant extent.

14. Cf. the title of Levinas's collection *Humanisme de l'autre homme* (=*Humanism of the Other Man*), s.l., Fata Morgana, 1972; cf. also OB 128 (ordinary humanism is "not human enough"). For his part, Lyotard discusses humanism in *The Inhuman: Reflections on Time*, Cambridge, Polity, 1991.

15. Besides the work just mentioned, cf. especially *Lectures d'enfance*, Paris, Galilée, 1991 (specifically the exordium on the idea of "infancy"), and *Moralités postmodernes*, Paris, Galilée, 1993.

mean destroying 'something' (something which Lyotard calls "the inhuman") that belongs to the very condition of our humanity? An 'inhuman' that, far from being a simple denial of our humanity, constitutes its very tissue, to the point that Lyotard can even refer to it as our "soul": that other in me to whom I owe a vague debt, but which is precisely *in*human because it left me this debt without telling me what I must do in order to pay it off. The result of this emphasis on the passivity (or "passibility") of the subject is that the human subject's humanity is tied to a "mancipium"[16] from which it cannot e-mancipate itself. There is some "Thing" that obligates it without it ever being able to abandon the position it is forced to take as a result of this (quasi) obligation. The subject is de-centred, not because it lacks a centre but because, in its singularity, it gravitates around a centre it can neither have access to nor simply leave behind. Given this position, one can well imagine why Lyotard remains skeptical about the hopes that Habermas has invested in the operative power of practical discourse. For in terms of the above discussion, it seems that the Habermasian transformation of values into valid norms would require participants who not only argue *from* a centre that has them in its grasp (the values 'have' them), but who also have managed to break *into* that centre and exercise argumentative control over it (they 'have' the values). Failing such ideal participants, practical discourse could not consist only of those reactions to validity claims allowed by Habermas's model: affirmation ('yes'), negation ('no'), or suspension (a future 'yes' or 'no')[17]. If one of the participants were to say, for example, "and yet these are my values; I have them simply because I have them", then *according to this model* the discussion would only come to a temporary end, since the reason given is actually not a reason at all. There is only an incapacity for argument, an "in-fantia" which, for Habermas, is only the temporary absence of something

16. J.-Fr. LYOTARD, "The Grip", in ID., *Political Writings*, Minneapolis, University of Minnesota Press, 1993, pp. 148-58. Lyotard refers here to the etymological origin of "mancipium": "*Manceps* is the person who takes hold, in the sense of possession or appropriation. And *mancipium* refers to this gesture of taking hold ... we are held by the grasp of others since childhood, yet our childhood does not cease to exercise its *mancipium* even when we imagine ourselves to be emancipated ... we are born before we are born to ourselves. And thus we are born of others, but also born to others ... subjected to their *mancipium* which they themselves do not comprehend. For they are themselves children ..." (pp. 148-49 *partim*).

17. In considering suspension as the actual absence of a *de iure* possible 'yes' or 'no', Habermas is taking the sting out of finitude: see my remarks in the introduction to this volume and my attempt to explore some of the consequences of this Habermasian position for multiculturalism in my 'Transcultural Vibrations', *Ethical Perspectives*, 1994(1:2), pp. 89-100, esp. 94-95.

still to come (or which should already have come). Such a subject – in opposition to Lyotard and Levinas – is only temporarily *unmündig*. Its lack of *Mündigkeit* would not point to its de-centring but would need to be seen as deriving from its being only stalled halfway in its attempt to break into a centre to which it already had right of access, and the ensuing dissociation between the participants would need to be regarded as a *dissensus* that emerges against the background of a possible *consensus*. Not that Habermas would go so far as to say that one could (or should) in principle reach a consensus; his point is only that, if one enters into argument, then one is already committed to a possible 'yes' or 'no', and the 'no' which claims that things are like this simply because things are like this is not really a 'no'. It is rather a kind of silence that derives its status from the order from which it has withdrawn. That it could derive this status from an order opposed to the argumentative order that Habermas has in mind; that it could point to an obligation that obligates without the addressee knowing the reasons for the obligation; that it could be a silence which concerns something more and something other than simply the factual absence of future speech; the silence of a dissensus that cannot be forced into an argumentative 'yes' or 'no' – this possibility is ruled out from the start by the assumptions from which Habermas explicitly begins: there is no 'silence' that does not already point to an imminent 'yes' or 'no'. In the end, 'validity' will rule over 'meaning'. Consequently, the dispute over the possibility of what Lyotard calls the "differend" is itself at the root of the "differend" separating Habermas and Lyotard[18]. The hiatus between prescription ('you must') and description ('something obligates me to do this or that') cannot be traversed by argument, for that would presuppose that one has access to the 'something' that obligates, and that one could assent to its reasons for obligating – which means that the hiatus must already have been bridged before it can be bridged.

But, of course, if one denies Kant or his followers the transition from prescription to description, then one replaces autonomy with heteronomy. As a consequence, the law is no longer obligatory because (iff) it is universal; it is now obligatory because it is obligatory[19] . In doing this, however, one would seem to have thrown away Kant's first principle (*diiudicatio bonitatis*) and thus to have surrendered ethics to what Lyotard calls "the anxiety of

---

18. For Lyotard, a differend is a dispute between two parties that cannot be settled for lack of a common idiom or, I would add in light of Lyotard's recent writings, for lack of any idiom *at all* – a lack of which the assertion "it is like this because it is like this" seems to be a symptom.

19. J.-Fr. LYOTARD, 'Levinas's Logic', *l.c.*, p. 307.

idiolect"[20]. For if it is only the fact of obligation that allows me to recognize the ethical law, and if I am the only one who finds himself in the asymmetric position of the law's addressee (hence *idio*-lect), and if there is no possibility of trading or even comparing my responsibility with that of others (cf. is my maxim universalizable?'), then how can I ever know if the appeal that obligates me is an *ethical* one? How will I even know that there is an appeal? Both Abraham and President Schreber heard the voice of God, and they each heard a voice that spoke only to them (i.e., *idiolect*). Did they *both* hear the voice of God? And did they both hear the voice *of God*? Can a voice that commands me to kill my own son be the voice of God? Did I not just imagine hearing a voice, when in fact it was only my own infanticidal urges? Does it even really matter which voice I heard, as long as there is obligation? Instead of trying to escape these problems, Lyotard seems satisfied with simply acknowledging them. Suggesting a *rapprochement* with Levinas, he seems content to summarize them in the statement that "obligation should be described as a scandal for the one who is obligated" (D nr. 170). And on this point the alliance falls apart. Levinas's position may not be modern, but neither is it postmodern[21]. As we shall see, it is – and I use the term in a neutral sense – anti-modern[22].

20. D, nr. 206 (cf. nrs. 144, 145, 162, 164...).

21. The characterization of Levinas's ethics as 'postmodern', introduced by Marc-Alain Ouaknin in his rather facile *Méditations Erotiques. Essai sur Emmanuel Levinas*, (Paris, Balland, 1992) and taken over by Z. Bauman in his *Postmodern Ethics* (Oxford, Blackwell, 1995, e.g. p. 84) is, I believe, profoundly misleading. Surely one is doing an injustice by painting black perhaps the only cow that stands out in the night of our present time.

22. Levinas would have no problem with this qualification – cf. for instance TI 210: "In positing the relation with the Other as ethical, one surmounts a difficulty that would be inevitable if, *contrary to Descartes*, philosophy started from a *cogito* that would posit itself absolutely independently of the Other. For the Cartesian *cogito* is discovered, at the end of the Third Meditation, to be supported on the certitude of the divine existence qua *infinite, by relation to which the finitude of the cogito, or the doubt, is posited and conceivable*. This finitude could not be determined without recourse to the infinite, *as is the case in the moderns* ..." Cf. also Derrida: "But by the force of a movement proper to Levinas, he accepts this extreme 'modern' audacity only to redirect it toward an infinitism that this audacity itself must suppose, according to himself; and the form of this infinitism is often quite classical, pre-Kantian rather than Hegelian" (*Writing and Difference*, Chicago, University of Chicago Press, 1978, p. 104.).

II

Although Levinas would side with Lyotard in stressing the importance of the asymmetric position of the one obligated by the ethical law, he would also want to protest against Lyotard's pagan appropriation of some of his major concepts. Their disagreement has to do with the identity of what Lyotard calls the addressor. Contrary to Lyotard, Levinas is not content to characterize the ethical law solely by the fact that whoever is put under obligation finds himself "placed in the position of addressee for a prescription" (D nr. 163) and then to simply call this a scandal. Levinas would like to say a word about the addressor as well. Though he will emphasize that responsibility "precedes freedom" (OB 197 n 27) and that values " 'weigh' on the subject", thus pointing to a fundamental passivity "which cannot assume what it receives, but which, in spite of itself, becomes responsible for it" (OB 198 n28), what he wants to emphasize above all else is that this "antecedence of responsibility to freedom" signifies "the *Goodness of the Good*: the necessity that *the Good* choose me first before I can be in a position to choose, that is, welcome its choice" (OB 122). To be sure, ethics has to do with an absolute appeal, as Lyotard also admits, but this appeal is precisely an *ethical* appeal because its addressor is the Good. Neglecting this difference and mistaking what is only a necessary condition (obligation) for a sufficient one, inevitably leads to the problems that Lyotard has signalled under the heading "anxiety of idiolect". But for Levinas, these problems are only a consequence of the pagan *quid pro quo* that makes values depend on drives, instead of *vice versa*. "From the Good to me there is assignation: a relation that survives the 'death of God'. The death of God perhaps signifies only the possibility to reduce every value arousing an impulse to an impulse arousing a value" (OB 123). Accordingly, Lyotard's brand of postmodernism is for Levinas only the return of the sacred, a return that becomes inevitable when, along with the idea of the Good, the idea of the holy is lost as well. For the holy is not the sacred, but the only thing that can prevent it from overwhelming us.

If one misses this distinction between the sacred and the holy, one will have missed the structure of Levinasian ethics. To be sure, ethics for Levinas is a matter of 'something' that "has chosen me before I have chosen it" (OB 11) and he, too, will consider the ethical subject as carrying an 'other-in-himself' that he will explicitly designate as the "soul" (OB 191 n 3). But what thus "penetrates" the subject "with its rays unbeknownst to itself (*á l'insu*)"[23]

---

23. An expression that crops up regularly in OB and that, interestingly enough, also gives the title to a brief article in Lyotard's *Moralités postmodernes* (chap. 12).

(OB 11) is not simply that inhuman "Thing" around which we gravitate without ever reaching it, as Lyotard thinks in the wake of Lacan. It is not something which attracts us but which we can never reach, since the condition for its "fatal attraction"[24] is that we have always already lost it and that we derive our singularity from this loss since it is only through this loss that we are who we are. To be sure, ethics for Levinas too is about an absolute past and refers back to a trauma that is too great to be taken up. But, unlike for Lacan[25] or Lyotard, the problem for Levinas is not that of a "tragic ethics" which says that we should not "give way on our desire" and at the same time shows us the terrible consequences of not giving way on our desire. The problem is not how we should relate to the "Thing" that makes us non-interchangeable nor how, at the same time, that opaque attachment must be interrupted by another dimension (Lacan's 'law of the signifier', Lyotard's 'norms') so that we can maintain enough distance from that point where we would, as it were, become so singular that we would suffocate in our own singularity. The Good for Levinas is not good because it attracts us, but because it interrupts such an attraction: "The fact that in its goodness the Good *declines the desire it arouses* while *inclining it* toward responsibility for the neighbor, *preserves difference* in the non-indifference of the Good, which chooses me before I welcome it" (OB 123). One does not "gravitate" *around* the Good. The Good is only good because it breaks that sacred spell – that desire to touch what we have always already lost and which, by that very fact, attracts us – and reorients the course of the dynamic thus awakened, inclining it toward the others. This makes all the difference between the heteronomy Lyotard supports and the special kind of

24. Ph. VAN HAUTE, "'Fatal Attraction': Jean Laplanche on Sexuality, Subjectivity and Singularity in the Work of Sigmund Freud", *Radical Philosophy*, 1995 (nr. 73), pp. 5-12. Laplanche's idea of the "enigmatic signifier" seems to me to give support to the ontological base structure that Lyotard is implying in the quote I gave in note 16. Although Levinas never takes account of such a structure (for reasons that will become clear in this chapter and that we will further explore in the third part of this volume), Levinas would surely wonder whether every enigma refers back to the sexual/erotic enigma described by Van Haute, and if there isn't an asymmetry between that register and the register of the Infinite which provokes metaphysical Desire.

25. In this and the following sentence, I refer to a number of ideas from Lacan's important seventh seminar: *L'ethique de la psychanalyse (1959-1960)* (Paris, Seuil, 1986, esp. p. 361 – "tragique" – and *passim*). What Lacan means by *"ne pas céder sur son désir"* is explained, although with other (not insignificant) accents, in: R. BERNET, "Le sujet devant la loi (Lacan et Kant)", and P. MOYAERT, "Sur la sublimation chez Lacan: Quelques remarques", both in S.G. LOFTS & P. MOYAERT (eds.), *La pensée de Jacques Lacan: Questions historiques, Problèmes théoriques*, Louvain/Paris, Peeters, 1994. In this seminar Lacan repeatedly uses words such as *graviter* or *tourner autour de* ("gravitate around") to indicate our (decentred) position with respect to *das Ding* (o.c., pp. 72, 77...).

heteronomy found in Levinas.

The Good would be no different from Lyotard's "inhuman" if it were only to place us in the position of an addressee of a (quasi)obligation, leaving us "disoriented" with regard to that "vague debt" we do not know how to deal with. It would obligate us without itself feeling the least obligation to us, thus surrendering us to the whims of that capricious and opaque "law without law" that Lacan calls "the Thing". There would be "something" in us that would, in Levinas's words, "reign *in its own way*" (OB 194 n2). A classical heteronomy, where the law is given by an authority outside the law, an "*Hors-la-loi*"[26] that also behaves as an out-law. But such is not the heteronomy of Levinas; it is rather the sort of heteronomy one gets when the link between the absolute and the Good is severed, as Lacan and Freud have done[27] – a heritage that, as we have seen, Lyotard has no hesitation in accepting. But Levinas not only refuses to sever that link, he likewise refuses to see the Good as that authority which precedes the law and arrogates to itself the power to make the law, as is the case in an ordinary ethics of heteronomy. For Levinas, there can only be an ethical law because the Good renounces such a power, because it abdicates and *refuses to "reign"* (OB 194 n4): "an-archy" of the Good which "chooses" us, but refuses to subject us, thereby making us free. No one, says Levinas, "is enslaved to the Good" (OB 11). We would have been condemned to slavery had the Good manifested itself to us in its full splendor, for then we would have had no chance to avert our gaze. But because the Good is good – i.e., holy and not sacred, "not numinous" (TI 77) – it has given us that chance. And, as is well-known, Levinas 'deformalizes' this by pointing us to the trace of something that refuses to present itself, the trace of a transcendence that already "effaced" itself before it could be "assembled" (e.g. OB 161; TI 104). This trace is, of course, the face of the Other: an appeal directed to us, but which is defenceless against our refusal, lacking the means to exact what it asks. The face of the Other is not sacred; it is holy. It is not the object of a taboo, not something whose separation attracts me and, despite the prohibition, arouses in me the desire to touch it. The face is holy because it speaks, and speech for Levinas means establishing a distance. Speech is a prohibition of the contact that would bridge the distance thus established.

---

26. For this expression, see Jacob ROGOZINSKI's excellent "Vers une éthique du différend", in H. KUNNEMAN & H. DE VRIES (eds.), *Enlightenments: Encounters between Critical Theory and Contemporary French Thought*, Kampen (The Netherlands), Kok Pharos, 1993, pp. 92-119, esp. p. 102.

27. For a lucid presentation of the way this link is severed in Lacan and Freud: P. MOYAERT, *Ethiek en sublimatie: Over de ethiek van de psychoanalyse van Jacques Lacan*. Nijmegen, SUN, 1993, pp. 92-119.

According to Levinas, the one who speaks to me does not arouse in me the desire to touch him, but accuses me of that desire, transforming it into a desire to serve and give.

Yet the word of the Other would not have this force, were it not the echo of a word that preceded it, were it not the descendant of that first word: "God". The Other can only deflect my urges and escape my attempts at appropriation because he is more than what I see of him. The face is not a phenomenon. In the words of Levinas, "the face breaks through the form that nevertheless delimits it" (TI 198; CPP 96). The Other can only be other because he finds his light in himself, and bears his meaning within. He is, therefore, *kath'auto*: more than what I can know and comprehend – not unknown but unknowable. So the alterity of the Other is ab-solute and this absoluteness comes to me under the form of a prohibition, in the face: "Thou shalt not kill me". To kill the Other is to extinguish his light, to reduce him to his form – in other words, to make of him a phenomenon, to reduce his meaning to what I can see of him. And since the Other is not only face, but also form, not only a speaking *to* me, but also a spoken that I hear, the possibility to "kill" him, to reduce him to what I see and hear of him, will always remain open. Without this possibility, there would be neither ethics nor responsibility. Nor could there be ethics or responsibility if this choice I have to make would be indifferent, if it were not qualified. The Other must be not only outside me, but *above me*. To kill him must signify: his *murder*[28]. To reduce him to his form must signify: to commit an injustice, to rob him of his ethical dignity. *And the Other does not owe this ethical dignity to himself.* The Other is face, a *surplus* over his form; he is a face that is *too large* for his form, and the Other owes this infinity to the fact that he is in the trace of the Infinite. Consequently, the Other for Levinas, *pace* Sartre, is "not simply another freedom: to give me knowledge of injustice, his gaze must come to me from a dimension of the ideal. The Other must be closer to God than I" (CPP 55-56). This elevation of the Other which Levinas calls face would not have been possible without the abdication of the Good that lends his ethics a special sort of heteronomy. By coming in the trace of the Good – or of *the* Infinite, as Levinas so often calls it – the face of the Other is invested with a value that I must and at the same time do not have to respect. The appeal comes from above, but it is an order that implores. I am free to respond to it or not, but whatever I do, I cannot keep *silent*: "I cannot evade *by silence* the discourse which the epiphany that occurs as a face opens, as Thrasymachus, irritated, tries to do, in the first book of the *Republic* (...) Before the hunger of men responsibility is measured only 'objectively'; it is irrecusable. The face opens the primordial

---

28. TI 198: "The Other is the sole being I can wish to kill".

discourse whose *first word* is obligation, *which no 'interiority' permits avoiding.* It is that discourse that obliges the entering into discourse, the commencement of discourse rationalism prays for, a 'force' that convinces even 'the people who do not wish to listen' and thus founds *the true universality of reason"* (TI 201).

Hence the programme for my second half: what to think of a philosophy that tells us that we cannot be silent, that grants us our interiority but then seems to make this interiority fully signifiable through ethics? What to think of an ethics that *precisely for that reason* – as I shall explain – has made sacrifice "the norm and criterion of the approach" of the Infinite?[29] What if it has come too late? What if, apart from this ethical dispossession (TI 172) or decentring that Levinas speaks of, there is still another dispossession that he will not or cannot think, in order to be able to think as he does? At stake then is but a word, but for Levinas it is the "first word": "monotheism, the word of the one and only God, is precisely the word that one cannot help but hear, and cannot help but answer. It is the word that obliges us to enter into discourse. It is because the monotheists have enabled the world to hear the word of the one and only God that Greek universalism can work in humanity and slowly unify that humanity" (DF 178/250, translation corrected). The death of Parmenides?[30] Or ethical henology?

---

29. CPP 72: "To the idea of the infinite only an extravagant response is possible. There has to be a 'thought' that understands more than it understands ... a 'thought' which, in this sense, could go beyond its death ... To go beyond one's death is to sacrifice oneself. The response to the enigma's summons is the generosity of sacrifice outside the known and the unknown, *without calculation, for going on to infinity* ... I approach the infinite *by sacrificing myself. Sacrifice is the norm and the criterion of the approach"* – a train of thought which is rigorously taken up in OB (1974) but, in light of the previous citation, in a way that is not completely foreign to the framework of TI (1961). But the readers of Levinas who see a *caesura* between TI and OB will, of course, disagree. They should, perhaps, reconsider.

30. It is the hesitation before this murder that, for Levinas, has hindered the development of a pluralistic ontology. But killing Parmenides means primarily the overthrow of ontology as *prima philosophia*, and henceforth deriving it from ethics. This is the very project of TI, which thus can be read as "totality *or* infinity": Only the exteriority of infinity can bring a pluralism into being and prevent it from closing into the totality which, for Levinas, it would become if left to the devices of ontology. For this reason, one might use the following adage to describe Levinas's metaphysics: *"bonum et dispersum convertuntur"* (cf. e.g., "The social relation engenders this surplus of the Good over being, multiplicity over the One" (TI 292)).

How to remain silent after Levinas

III

There would be no silence, then, that could evade "the discourse which the epiphany that occurs as a face opens" (TI 201). Of course Levinas is not denying the obvious here, as if, when confronted with the face of the Other, one would not be able to hold one's tongue and refuse to speak. He means that any refusal to respond to the appeal of the face, and thereby to enter "ethical discourse", should be seen as a silence which receives its meaning from that appeal and within that discourse: "silence" is already a falling short of what is demanded. Not only literal silence of course; every attempt to evade the appeal of the Other, every excuse made, is a kind of silence – even if it is announced out loud. For this "true universalism", there is no interiority that can avoid the ethical obligation. We can try to outwit God, like Jonah; we can hide from him, taking refuge in a ship's hold and falling asleep in the midst of a storm. But then we take to sleep the very thing we were trying to avoid[31], thus affirming what we wanted to deny: it may be that there are some responsibilities that we cannot handle, but this does not mean that we do not have them, and once we have them, there can no longer be anything like the sleep of the innocent. *All* sleep is now a lack of wakefulness.

One might find this somewhat exaggerated, but in that case one must ask oneself just what it is about Levinas's ethics that leads to such exaggeration. Better still: one must ask why it is founded upon this exaggeration and cannot get around it. For according to Levinas, ethics begins by "penetrating"[32] the armour of my interiority. It is this interiority that is

---

31. OB 128: "The impossibility of escaping God, the adventure of Jonas [sic], indicates that God is at least here not a value among values (...) The impossibility of escaping God lies in the depths of myself as a self, as an absolute passivity (...) [as] the impossibility of slipping away (...) the birth (...) of a being able to die *subject to sacrifice*". The reader will perhaps recall the quote in note 29.

32. Ethics, for Levinas, is a penetration (OB 49: "one-penetrated-by-the-other") but, according to his recurrent formula, "*before* eros" (e.g. OB 192 n 27). A penetration, then, without the consolation nor even the fantasm of union, whose consequence is that the subject penetrated becomes an ever wider "opening" ("*ouverture*") which can never contain or encompass what is always already inside without being absorbed by it, an opening which seems rather to be a hole through which interiority continually discharges itself: "It is always to empty oneself anew of oneself, to absolve oneself, like in a hemophiliac's hemorrhage" (OB 92) – a "hemorrhage" which already shows that Levinas, as we shall indicate later, is ethicizing the Sartrean universe all the while using Sartre's own concepts and metaphors.

thrown into question by the face: the face does not accuse me of having neglected to do something, nor of doing something which I should not have done. Such is not the responsibility the face confronts me with. Rather, it blames me for something that was out of my hands, for a guilt without fault, or a 'fault' that I am not guilty of, but that I am nonetheless responsible for. This 'fault' is my existence itself: just by 'being there', by taking up a place, by breathing and eating, by all those processes in which I arbitrarily appropriate things, I *inevitably* and unwittingly make a claim on something to which I have no right. And the fact that I have no right to it is not something that Levinas just postulates; he tries to find a phenomenological basis for it in his description of what exactly happens when I am confronted with the appeal of the Other. It is to this description that one must refer if one maintains that Levinas is doing a phenomenological ethics, or an ethical phenomenology – a characterization that should be kept separate from the role played by the notion of the 'face' in this ethics since, as we have seen, the face is not a phenomenon. Indeed, according to Levinas it is precisely because the face is *not* a phenomenon – precisely because it does not *show* itself to me, but rather *addresses* me and *appeals* to me – that it manages to embarrass me. The appeal of the Other does something to me that no phenomenon could ever do: it disconcerts me and gives me a conscience that is primarily and necessarily a *bad* conscience since it questions and casts in doubt something which, until then, I would not have been able to question: "what is most natural becomes the most problematic. Do I have the right to be? Is being in the world not taking the place of someone?"[33]; "Is not my existing, in its quietude and the good conscience of its *conatus*, equivalent to letting the other man die?"[34]. The Other puts my very existence in question: my place on this earth suddenly appears as a usurpation, for which I am ashamed. And this shame forms the phenomenological cornerstone on which Levinas's ethics rests. Place this in question, and one places all the rest in question.

Nevertheless, it is a question that can hardly be avoided. For is it indeed the case that my reaction to the appeal of the Other is one of shame? Do I then suffer the bad conscience of one who realizes that he has no right to his rights nor even to his existence, and for whom that existence, formerly so evident, suddenly appears in all its "detestability"[35], "imperialism" (OB 110,

---

33. E. LEVINAS, *Ethics and Infinity. Conversations with Philippe Némo*, (transl. R.A. Cohen), Pittsburgh, Duquesne U.P., 1985, p. 121.

34. E. LEVINAS, *Of God Who Comes to Mind*, s.l., Stanford U.P., 1998, p. 164.

35. *Ibid.*, p. 165 ("detestable I").

121) and "egoism"[36]? Is it true that in the confrontation with the face of the Other, I not only see my naturalness put into question, but that in the same move I also experience it as something which, for me to keep it, will henceforth require me to make an unnatural (for ethically qualified) move? Levinas seems to think so, and it is perhaps unsurprising that in order to buttress this assertion – or this description – he resorts to a vocabulary deriving from Sartre: the ethical appeal, one reads in *Otherwise Than Being*, turns me into a *pour autrui* (OB (64)/81). I cease to be *pour soi* (OB (52)/67) and become a hostage of the Other without ever coinciding with him; I am "turned inside out", "denucleated", "dispossessed", "uprooted" and, strangely enough, it is this "abdication" that takes place "despite myself"[37], this abandoning of my spontaneous naturalness that, for Levinas, liberates me (TI 88), humanizes me, and summons me to my "final essence" (TI 179). In order to be, to be "there", to be "someone", being – as it were – had to be enclosed within my person, and not by choice but by necessity; the alternative would mean that I as a person would disappear in the anonymous night of what Levinas calls the *il y a*. And yet, it is exactly this *conatus*, this "closedness" (TI 148) in Being that is thrown into "crisis"[38] by the gaze of the Other. A crisis which, for Levinas, summons this interiority "from the outside" (OB 150) and exposes a level deeper than my "closedness" where I am first of all an "openness" (OB 115), an inability to "remain in [my]self" (CPP 149), an "inability to shut myself up" (CPP 150), and yet a 'self' that is not interchangeable with that of others, because it is *this* self that is responsible for those others, and it has this responsibility to thank for the dispossession which singularizes it and makes it a self. It is with regard to this level that Levinas calls ethics a *religion*: *religare* which binds me *with others* (*noué*, OB 76/96) and devotes me to them (*voué*)[39] even before I am bound to myself. And it is from this point of view that henceforth *every* attempt – albeit only momentary – to escape this appeal, the *least* remainder of concern for myself, will be seen as a closure of a pre-existing opening. It will be seen as a refusal of the orientation to which the Good has invited us, without compelling us since, as we have seen, the Good is only good because it does not take possession of us, because it "inspires" (OB 140ff) us without becoming our master. And it is in order to safeguard this distinction between the holiness of the Good that liberates us and the *ecstatic* obsession of the sacred that strips us of our position, our *stasis*, that Levinas must

---

36. 'The Trace of the Other', in M.C. TAYLOR (ed.), *Deconstruction in Context: Literature and Philosophy*, Chicago/London, The University of Chicago Press, 1986, p. 353.

37. These terms are standard vocabulary in OB. They can be found on almost any page.

38. *Of God Who Comes to Mind*, o.c., p. 165.

39. E. LEVINAS, *De Dieu qui vient à l'idée*, Paris, Vrin, 1992, p. 249.

simultaneously recognize and deny the possibility of keeping silent: "The will is free to assume this responsibility in whatever sense it likes; it is not free to refuse this responsibility itself; it is not free to ignore the meaningful world into which the face of the Other has introduced it" (TI 218-219). To be able to keep silent means: to be able to disregard the appeal, to not have to take it up. But, as Levinas will insist, this presupposes that it has already been heard: "The being that expresses itself imposes itself, but does so precisely by appealing to me with its destitution and nudity – its hunger – *without my being able to be deaf to that appeal*" (TI 200). It is from this hearing before one has chosen to listen, from this "unconditioned 'Yes' of submission" (OB 122), that Levinas will derive his "true universality" – a universality that has its origin in an asymmetry *and therefore* in a hierarchy between Good and Evil. For there can be little doubt that what is at stake here, for Levinas, is this hierarchy. From the moment there is an appeal, "silence", interiority and closure have an *ethical* significance: it is the "claim" of *"Evil"* to be "the contemporary, the equal, the twin, of the Good" (CPP 138).

This is a strong thesis, but one which is, for Levinas, unavoidable. It is the idea that my naturalness, my spontaneous and involuntary self-concern cannot *appear* without thereby immediately losing this naturalness and becoming the object of my free choice. Ethics is the *complete* submission of nature to the order of good and evil which breaks into that nature *from without*. This is why Levinas says, and tirelessly repeats, that ethics is a *liberation*. The face of the Other liberates me because it confronts me with the possibility of choosing something which, left to myself, I could never have chosen. One only becomes human when one's existence is no longer *conatus*, no longer something working behind one's back, but choice, in other words, "morality": true humanization comes from the Other, i.e., from the invitation to place above my own existence something else – the existence of the Other. Hence, for Levinas, what defines the humanity of man is his ability to sacrifice. Man is the sort of being who can reject his being, "reverse" his *conatus* (OB 70) and sacrifice himself: "To discover in the I such an orientation is to identify the I and morality"[40].

Such an identification is only possible for Levinas if he can refer to something that would bring into the I, from the outside, this orientation against naturalness, against *conatus essendi*. And this outside which is so much outside that it can enter the I without becoming part of it – and which owes its *orientational power* precisely to this refusal to participate in the I or to let the I participate in it – this outside is the Good, or the idea of the Infinite, whose trace is the face of the Other. By being a trace of this idea,

40. 'The Trace of the Other', *l.c.*, p. 353.

the face of the Other can make an appeal to me that I cannot take possession of (since the face overflows the form lying within my reach) but which *dispossesses* me, because I cannot not hear it and because, from the moment I have heard it, the naturalness of my being shows up only to immediately 'take its leave'. The face effects a phenomenological reduction that does not add a dimension to my being, but takes one away. The feeling of shame with which I react to the gaze of the Other does not concern the fact that, with this gaze, I receive a nature and with the purity of my *pour soi* lose the absoluteness of my freedom. According to Levinas, and contrary to Sartre[41], I am ashamed not so much of the nature that I become, but of the nature that I was. The gaze of the Other does not enslave; it liberates. And it liberates because there is no way for me to transcend it without already submitting to it. Keeping silent is merely a refusal to speak. It is merely the expression of a *im-passibility* that Levinas can only treat as a shortcoming, and hence as "egoism or Evil" (CPP 137) – but this link can only be made if one can rely on a universe which is also an *univers de discours* that has ascribed *all possible* discourse a place within it. And for Levinas, there is such a universe. For there is a word that "one cannot not hear, to which one cannot not answer". It is through the operation of this word – 'God' – that the ethical situation becomes, for Levinas, a religious situation: "a situation where the subject exists in the impossibility of hiding itself", "an exceptional situation where you are always in the face of the Other" and, let us note, "*where there is no privacy*"[42]. I would like for a moment to consider, in concluding, what would happen if one would put this word out of operation. I would even go so far as to start from one place – but it is a central one – where Levinas unexpectedly seems to have put this word out of operation himself, although apparently without realizing it and without drawing the necessary consequences. And it is perhaps not without importance that, at the very moment when he was offered the opportunity to free himself from Sartre, he let it pass.

IV

But why should Levinas have taken such an opportunity? Did he still need it? Have we not just seen that the simple introduction of an ethical factor had enabled Levinas to exorcise the entire Sartrean universe? For if the

41. J.-P. SARTRE, *Being and Nothingness: An Essay on Phenomenological Ontology*, New York, Philosophical Library, s.d., esp. Part 3: "Being-for-Others".

42. E. LEVINAS, 'Transcendence and Height', in A. PEPERZAK, S. CRITCHLEY, R. BERNASCONI (eds.), *Emmanuel Levinas. Basic Philosophical Writings*, Bloomington/Indianapolis, Indiana U.P., 1996, p. 29.

Other is not only outside me, but also above me, then he is not just "another freedom", irreconcilable with mine, who need only look at me to transcend my freedom and make me an object in the world, just as I, in turn, can make him an object in the world by looking at him and transcending his transcendence. This whole endless aporia which turns Sartre's description of intersubjective relations into that hell where 'love' boils down to a choice between sadism (the Other is an object) or masochism (I am an object for the Other) seems to fall apart from the moment one realizes that "the Other is not transcendent because he would be free as I am" (TI 87), but that this transcendence points to a "superiority" (*ibid.*) which makes his gaze "incomparable" (TI 86) to mine, allowing him to give me the "bad conscience" of a freedom that is not just transcended but qualified, a freedom that is ashamed of being still *too much* nature, the freedom of "a tree that grows without regard for everything it suppresses and breaks, grabbing all the nourishment, air and sun" (DF 100). It is shame – shame for the "arbitrariness" and "injustice" of a freedom that was mere *conatus* – which chastens me, turns me into a moral being and, according to Levinas, gives me the possibility of carrying out that *metanoia* which, it is true, Sartre mentioned[43], but conspicuously failed to articulate.

In order for this chastening to occur, there must be a "disproportion"[44] between the Other and me, a disproportion referred to by Levinas when he says that the Other is "closer to God than I": "for me to feel myself to be unjust I must measure myself against the infinite" (CPP 58). But that infinite which provides me with a measure does not, as we know, show itself to me directly. It comes to me in the face of the Other which appeals to me, and it lends that face the force needed for an "*ethical* resistance": to ignore the imperative of that face means, as was pointed out above, to let oneself be judged by it. This is why it is crucial for Levinas to maintain a distinction between the face of the Other and what I can see of the Other. Only if the Other is *more* than this form that I see, only if there is something about him by which he finds his meaning in himself and can thus always question the meaning I give to him, can there be any talk of an ethical resistance and an injustice that I commit against him by reducing his face to its form. And in

---

43. *O.c.,* p. 412n: "These considerations do not exclude the possibility of an ethics of deliverance and salvation. But this can be achieved only after a radical conversion which we cannot discuss here". OB should be read as one long description of this process of conversion whose central – and never argued – premise would not have satisfied Sartre: the idea that the wound which the Other's appeal not so much brands me with, but burns me with again, has a chastening effect.

44. E. LEVINAS, 'Signature', in ID., *Difficile Liberté: Essais sur le judaïsme*, Paris, Albin Michel, 1963[1], p. 326. (This version of "Signature" is not included in DF).

the course of making this crucial distinction, Levinas takes the *further* crucial decision to link that "surplus" of the face over its form – that "something extra" by which the face can break through the form which manifests it – with the idea of the infinite: "The idea of infinity, the infinitely more contained in the less, is concretely produced in the form of a relation with the face. And the idea of infinity alone maintains the exteriority of the other with respect to the same, despite this relation" (TI 196). While, for Levinas, the form is only an exteriority that turns toward me, thereby becoming involved with my interiority, the exteriority of the face is, through the idea of infinity, ab-solute: "a face is the unique openness in which the signifyingness of the trans-cendent does not nullify the tran-scendence and make it enter into an immanent order" (CPP 103). In order to have this status, then, the face must be *completely independent* of form; although it manifests itself in form, this form can in no way affect or "touch" it. Hence the face, even before entering into the form that manifests it, must already have withdrawn from it: a "supreme anachronism" that Levinas calls "trace", yet which he notes is not "simply a word", but "the proximity of God in the face of my neighbor"[45]. Without this proximity of a "God who passed" (CPP 106), i.e., without this "abdication" of the Good that has always already withdrawn from the desire which it awakens and which orients that desire toward my neighbor(s), the face would not be independent of form: "The supreme presence of a face is inseparable from this supreme and irreversible absence" which Levinas calls "God" or "He" or "*illeity* of the third person" (CPP 104). A "face, wholly open, can at the same time be in itself because it is in the trace of illeity" (CPP 106).

Without this independence of the face with respect to form – without this autarky – the otherness of the Other could not be ab-solute. And without this ab-solute foreignness that the face has by virtue of its being in the trace of the illeity of a God who passed, it could not impose its rights on me nor put up any (ethical) resistance against my attempt to brush aside its appeal. But *if the ethical value of the Other is to be situated in the face*, if, in other words, the face is not dependent on the 'form' or the 'context' in order to be what it 'is', if it is "*signification without a context*" (TI 23), manifestation "over and beyond form" (TI 66), "*not disclosure but revelation*" (TI 65-66), then how can Levinas at the same time call this autarky of the face, this "infinity of the Other", a "destitution" (TI 213)? How can something which "is not of the world" (TI 198), and which enters the world without ever becoming a part of it, at the same time *suffer* under "its absence from this world into which it enters" (TI 75)? How can Levinas call this absence from form, which is also

45. E. LEVINAS, 'Un Dieu Homme?', in ID., *Entre Nous: Essais sur le penser-à l'autre*, Paris, Bernard Grasset, 1991, p. 73.

called supreme presence and the condition for the alterity of the Other, an "exiling" (*ibid.*)? How can this strangeness that guarantees the alterity of the Other be, at the same time, "strangeness-destitution", "his condition of being stranger, destitute or proletarian" (*ibid.*)? Why does the nakedness of the face – which is naked because it exceeds form and whose status requires independence from form – why does this *glorious* nakedness extend "into the nakedness of the body that is cold" (*ibid.*)? How can Levinas say that the face is naked because it "breaks into the order of the world", that it is without context because it is "wrested from the context of the world"[46] and, at the same time, call this nakedness "a distress" (CPP 96)? Does this mean that, contrary to what was suggested, the distress of the Other does have some 'relation' to the 'context' or the 'form' from which his face was supposed to be independent? But can we then keep situating the ethical dignity of the Other in his face? Could it be that it is less independent from form than the analysis of the face that Levinas himself has given us might have led us to suspect?

Levinas, of course, could easily make room for this objection by pointing out that it is precisely through form that this ethical dignity is *ethical* – a dignity that *makes an appeal to me* – because it is through form that the Other is vulnerable. In order to *keep* his dignity, the other is dependent on my help; after all, I retain the possibility of reducing his face to its form – I can murder him – and it is this possibility that makes the "ethical resistance" of his face an *ethical*, not a real resistance[47]. The *dignity* of the Other, then, has to do with his face, but because that face cannot circumvent the form, from which it is nevertheless independent, this dignity is, *in concreto*, an *ethical* dignity.

And yet, this answer is hardly satisfying and passes over the problem I want to pose. For if Levinas calls the face "naked" and sees in this nakedness the "destitution" of the Other – in other words, the fact that he is not only "above me" but also "beneath me", that he not only commands but supplicates – he is alluding not only to the fact that the Other, as a concrete person, remains vulnerable in that form from which his face becomes detached in the very moment the form shines forth (CPP 96). For Levinas, this nakedness also alludes to *a lack of form*: "Stripped of its very form, a face is frozen in its nudity. It is a distress" (*ibid.*)[48]. The nakedness Levinas has

---

46. *Ibid.*

47. On the distinction between an ethical and a real resistance: E. LEVINAS, 'Freedom and Command', in CPP, pp. 15-23; and TI e.g. 199; OB 198n2.

48. Here I have altered the English translation which reads "paralyzed" for *"transi dans sa nudité"* (*Humanisme de l'autre homme*, o.c., p. 52). In preferring "frozen" to "paralyzed", I am following Adriaan Peperzak in his annotated Dutch translation of *Humanisme*

in mind *here* is precisely what the word says: a lack of clothing, in other words, a need for 'form' or 'context'. But, once again, how can this face – which for Levinas is "living" because it "undoes the form" which would make it "adequate to the Same" and would "betray" and "alienate" its "exteriority" (TI 66) – how can this face which is a "bareness *without any cultural ornament*" suffer because of the absence of something from which it *already* withdrew, even *before* entering? And yet this is what Levinas suggests when he sees the nakedness of the Other as his destitution, calls the Other "fatherless", "stranger", "uprooted", and contrasts this lack of roots, home and a fatherland with my own situation: "To hear his destitution which cries out for justice is not to represent an image to oneself [to know the 'form' of this destitution – R.V.], but is to posit oneself as responsible, *both as more and as less than the being that presents itself in the face.* Less, for the face ... judges me ... [and] comes from a dimension of height ... More, for my position as *I* consists in being able to respond to this essential destitution of the Other, finding resources for myself. The Other who *dominates* me in his transcendence is thus the stranger ... *to whom I am obligated*" (TI 215). To take up the appeal of that stranger, or even already to receive that appeal (and, as we have seen, one cannot not hear it) means to be ashamed of one's own wealth, to experience one's own existence as a usurpation, to lose one's titles – in short, to be oneself uprooted and *dispossessed* by the appeal of the other who is uprooted, to cease being *pour soi* and to become completely *pour l'autre*, for the "altruism" in question here is "total"[49]. One will no doubt recall: "no privacy". "The I in relationship with the infinite is an impossibility of stopping its forward march ... it is, *literally*, not to have time to turn back. It is to be not able to escape responsibility, to not have a hiding place of interiority where one comes back into oneself, to march forward *without concern for oneself*" (CPP 98). Ethics is "without calculation, *for going on to infinity*" (CPP 72). Sacrifice becomes the norm and criterion for the approach of the Other.

A 'conclusion' that both presupposes and implies that for Levinas the nature and definition of ethics do not *ultimately* depend upon the destitution of the Other, but upon what Levinas calls his "height"(i.e., the infinity of his face). The Other's destitution is infinite, thus asking an infinite sacrifice from me, *since this destitution comes from the face* – a face which Levinas has defined as always already being stripped of a form it has no need of and in which it cannot be at home precisely because of the

(*Humanisme van de andere mens*, Kampen/Kapellen, Kok Agora/DNB-Pelckmans, 1990, p. 78, which paraphrases *"transi"* as "shivering with cold"). The change is not unimportant given the point I shall be making.

49. 'Transcendence and Height', *l.c.*, p. 18.

infinity of being a face. Strange as it may sound, it seems that, by its very definition, there is nothing I can do to prevent such a face from being "frozen" for it lacks and will always lack that clothing or context or form that I apparently possess. Which is why, for Levinas, the essential uprootedness of the Other cannot but have my uprootedness as a consequence. Since the Other (by definition) "lacks" roots, in other words, something which, according to Levinas, I posses, he can never become rooted like me. Rather, I will have to become like he is by giving up in an *infinite* sacrifice the roots he does not have. And in that process, I will asymptotically approach my true humanity, for that ground to which I am attached, that attachment itself is, for Levinas, only a sign of my naturalness. Humanity, after all, "is not a forest" and the individual "is not a tree" (DF 23). Being uprooted is a humanization, a leaving nature behind. True universality: community of the uprooted[50].

But is one a stranger only when one has no roots? Is uprootedness always a 'lack' of roots? – this strange lack which for Levinas, as we have seen, cannot really be a lack since it results from his definition of the face, which is infinite and therefore cannot really be in need of a form that is too small, too finite, to contain it. *But what if what Levinas insists on treating as a 'lack' of roots were really an 'excess'?* Might there not also be an uprootedness that comes from an excess of roots, an excess that is yet *not enough* to be rooted like a tree? Does the difference between a man and a tree lie in the absence or presence of roots, as Levinas suggests, *or in the nature of the rootedness itself*? What is the cold that makes the face freeze? What, finally, is the destitution of the Other?

Let me try to make these questions and this suggestion of an alternative somewhat more concrete by coming back to the opposition which regulates all of Levinas's thought and which, *in the final analysis*, amounts to an

---

50. Note that, according to Levinas, Christianity can for essential reasons only make an incomplete contribution to this universality: "If Europe had been spiritually uprooted by Christianity, as Simone Weil complains, the evil would not be great. And it is not always the idylls that have been destroyed by Europe's penetration of the world ... *but is Europe's misfortune* (malheur) *not due to the fact that Christianity did not sufficiently uproot it?*" (DF 137/195, transl. corr.). Though I hope to have made it clear from which standpoint I am myself arguing – but isn't it a surprising alliance? – in light of this quote (which is in no sense a *hapax*) one can only wonder at the success with which Levinas's ethics has been assimilated in Christian circles (for two noteworthy exceptions: U. DHONDT, 'Ethics, History, Religion: The Limits of the Philosophy of Levinas', in P.J.M. VAN TONGEREN, *et al.* (eds.), *Eros and Eris: Contributions to a Hermeneutical Phenomenology. Liber Amicorum for Adriaan Peperzak*, Dordrecht, Kluwer, 1992, pp. 273-80 and I. VERHACK, 'Over de moralisering van het "verlangen naar de Oneindige" bij Levinas' (= On the moralization of the 'Desire for the Infinite' in Levinas), *Tijdschrift voor Filosofie*, 1999 (61:2), pp. 235-69).

ethicization of Sartre's dualism. Levinas does not deny that the Other has a 'form' by which I can 'perceive' him, nor that I can encounter him in a context where he fulfills a certain role and is situated by this role, the context of a culture for example. What he opposes is that the Other would be reduced to this form, context or culture, for then he would lose his alterity and be swallowed up by something which I can know, which "appears" to me. If the Other is only "in a cultural whole and is illuminated by this whole, as a text by its context", then understanding the Other would be "a hermeneutics and an exegesis" (CPP 95). To avoid this, Levinas wants the Other *also* to have his "own meaning" that would not depend on "this meaning received from the world" (*ibid.*) but that would disrupt it. To avoid what he perceives as the danger of contextualism – be it in the guise of rela- tivism or of culturalism – the worldly (mundane) meaning of the Other must be thrown off balance by "another presence that is abstract (or, more exactly, absolute) and not integrated into the world" (*ibid.*). This other meaning – which, both for Sartre and Levinas, comes from "*au-delà du monde*", and which both call 'infinite' – is for Levinas the face, a face which he calls "ab-stract" because it "disturbs immanence without settling into the horizons of the world" (CPP 102). Because the face is *independent of* world, context and culture, because it comes from an "elsewhere ... into which it already withdraws" (*ibid.*) even before it arrives, Levinas sees in it a guarantee that the Other is more than a "cultural meaning" who approaches me from out of his cultural whole. Ethics, therefore, must *precede* culture: as face, the Other is an "*abstract* man", in the sense of someone "disengaged *from all culture*" (CPP 101).

But doesn't this ethics begin too late? Isn't there something that precedes it, something that it wanted to suppress but that ultimately returns and disrupts its analysis? What seems to be taken for granted in this entire discussion is precisely the opposition between infinite and finite, face and form, transcendent and immanent, uprootedness and rootedness, an opposition that seems to undergo slippage when Levinas states that the face, "stripped of its form", and hence in all its nakedness, is "frozen" (*supra*). Has the shivering of this nakedness, this destitution, really been understood when one forces it into the above oppositions and clings to the alternative: "either swallowed up by context like a thing, or without context, hence a person"? In other words: either *en soi* or *pour soi*, either mundane or transcendent, either visible form or 'invisible' face – oppositions all of which Sartre made already and which, despite all his criticism of Sartre, seem also to govern Levinas's definition of the Other. But does the Other's destitution allow itself to be forced into these oppositions? What if this destitution would consist of the Other being stuck with something that he can neither get free of nor dissolve into? Isn't that, for example, the relation one has with one's 'ground', in its literal or metaphorical sense – the ground, for instance, of one's history, or of one's culture or one's personal life? Wasn't it Levinas himself who said that "the great experiences' of our life have properly speaking never been lived [*vécu*]" (CPP 68), and isn't it exactly this inability to fully live these moments that gives them, for every one of us, a surplus of meaning? Isn't it precisely this inability to work through moments which for others perhaps were insignificant, since they could work through them; isn't it precisely this inability to forget, this recollection *despite ourselves*, that singularizes us? Isn't it this, this unassimilable strangeness, that makes us different from trees and from things, but also from one another?

What I am suggesting, then, is that there is a nakedness that cannot be thought if one adheres to the opposition between face and form, finite and infinite. The nakedness of a being which is attached to 'something' that *it cannot do away with nor even less have access to*[51] . Such a being is naked in the double sense of having not enough 'form' to clothe itself in, and yet too much 'form' not to notice its nakedness. Of course, Levinas is correct when he draws our attention to the violence involved in fully clothing a person with that 'form' that he presents to us, and he deserves praise for warning us of the temptation to let the Other be absorbed and determined by the functional, everyday context in which we meet him. But in averting this danger, he seems to have made an overcorrection, one that consists in fully detaching the person's dignity from this 'form' or context and hence reducing his nakedness to only the first of the two senses mentioned above. To make the dignity of the Other depend on this "visitation" or on this "revelation of the other ... in the gaze of man aiming at a man precisely as abstract man, *disengaged from all culture*" (CPP 101) means perhaps that one ascribes, unwittingly and with the best of intentions, a dignity to the Other

---

51. Cf. the introduction to this chapter, where these two moments were used in defining the concept 'decentring'. As I already pointed out in my introduction to this volume, as soon as one of these moments is relinquished, problems arise. Nationalism, I claimed there, rests on a misrecognition of this *double* structure of 'decentring' in that it claims to *have access to* that 'something' to which a nation is irrevocably 'attached'. In other words, the mistake is that it purports to be able to specify what I called in this chapter's introduction the 'vague' debt. Nationalism pretends to know what 'our' debt to the nation consists in. On the other hand, the stress on the *two* moments in decentring allows one, in principle, to steer away from an extreme cosmopolitan/universalistic correction to the mistake of nationalism/particularism, an overcorrection that consists of the claim that there is no singular attachment as such (and hence gives up decentring, 'in-fantia' as such). In other words, 'decentring' seems to point the way to an alternative position which is neither universalistic nor particularistic in the traditional sense.

that ignores his true destitution, and the full extent of his nakedness. Might it not be that the true nakedness of the Other has less to do with his being disengaged from all culture, all context, all form, and more to do with his being engaged in it in such a way that the engagement never renders its secret to him? Isn't the Other not only an Other to me, but also someone who owes his 'own' alterity to some 'Thing' which remains 'other' to him and yet singularizes him at the same time?

In other words, perhaps the Other is, *like myself*, primarily a "stranger" not because he is without those roots that I possess, but because we are both attached to 'something' which is too close to leave us indifferent, but not close enough to be called our possession. Isn't it this structure that makes us similar to one another at the very moment when it distinguishes us? But the Other would then be decentred *like me*. And yet he would be an Other precisely because that vague debt which he must discharge is still not 'vague' enough to let it coincide with mine. And isn't that the reason he 'bears' a name – in the sense which connotes an *effort* – that is different from mine? Where is the Other more naked than in his name – a name that he does not possess, but has received; a name that he does not coincide with, but which can neither leave him indifferent; a name that summons him to life, but which will also survive him? In other words, what I am suggesting here is that one misconstrues the Other's ethical dignity when one thinks of it in terms of the opposition between a face that is a "living present" and a form that sucks the life out of that present and "congeals" it (TI 66). The dignity and destitution of the Other do not have to be thought on the basis of that face that speaks and in which "the revealer" "coincides" with "the revealed" (TI 67). The destitution of the Other seems rather to reside in the fact that he is neither that presence of the face nor that absence of form, but someone caught in a tension between face and form that must be thought of in such a way that they *precede* this opposition – which, ultimately, is the opposition between exteriority and interiority, infinity and totality.

To work this out would require, among other things, a different ontology than the one with which Levinas is arguing, whose traces, despite all the criticism, he still carries with him. And perhaps the problem of the name could point the way to this new ontology. For a being who bears a name cannot be grasped in the categories of *pour soi*, *en soi* and *pour autrui* that Levinas provides with an ethical meaning. The name to which someone is attached *without the meaning of this attachment ever being clear to the person* might itself be an example of that tension that seems to precede the opposition between face and form. To have a name is to be-in-the-world by being, first and foremost, 'present' to 'something' in the world – a certain sound, a privileged signifier – which is nearby but, at the same time, at a distance. To have a name is, in this way, an example of all those forms of *en soi pour soi* where the subject is already attached to something even before it could have chosen it, and which, for that reason, precedes the opposition between *en soi* and *pour soi*[52]. But this is a privileged example because the name, like the Good for Levinas, is not sacred but holy. There is something about the name which, like the Good, turns me away from itself and directs me toward others. And ethics must be about this turning away, this *metanoia*. Yet there is also something about the name that escapes this turning and cannot be consoled by it: that which escapes discourse, punctuating it with a silence that no word can break. I think it is not only a mistake to try and force that silence by naming it with a word that one cannot not hear and – important qualification – by making that word do ethical work. I think it is also dangerous because one will then run the risk of closing off the only source from which we could draw in an attempt to extinguish the flames of that fire which is slowly but steadily burning away everything in us that points to the possibility of a common humanity that would not need to pay the price of universality in order to avoid the folly of blind particularity.

52. Given that the endo-ontology which Merleau-Ponty was working on in *The Visible and the Invisible* was trying to undercut exactly this opposition, we will deal with it in due course (chapter 7). But we will have to wonder whether it is not insensitive to the problem of singularity which we have indicated in the preceding lines. The thought of the chiasm and of the polymorphism of vertical Being ("*l'être brut*") can explain why we don't live in a *different* world, but seems able to conclude from this only that we live in the *same* world because it turns in the direction of an asubjective phenomenology, for which "the I - other problem is a *Western* problem" (VI 274).

CHAPTER SIX

UNEUROPEAN DESIRES
TOWARD A PROVINCIALISM WITHOUT ROMANTICISM

On the tabletop before me, a woman, half naked, her skin not the same colour as mine, the gaze slightly turned. What strikes me are the hands which support the breasts and, between thumb and index finger, prominently point a nipple in my direction. Does this body refer to a tradition with which it is unfamiliar? The *Caritas Romana* for instance[1], a pictorial motif that returns here in the form of a stereotyped, intercontinental allegory: just as, at that time, Pero kept her old father alive in prison with mother's milk, so would "childlike"[2] Africa offer to Europe what it had lost in the jail-cell of cultivated reason: a wild, unspoiled, yet pure and natural life. *Caritas Africana*. But the anthropologist peering over my shoulder calls my imagination to order and with his finger on the caption – "Femme de Tambo" – lectures me on the Eurocentrism of colonial postcards from the beginning of this century[3]: we view "Timbo women", "Soussou women", "Fulani women", etc. as if, from the standpoint of cultural interest, we were seeing one more ethnic group, and not always another bosom, always another body. Detached from the context of her daily activities, relations, home, poverty, hunger and illness, the anonymous African is here rendered as the object of the masculine colonizer's erotic interest, an interest concealed by captions, no more visible in the photograph than the photographer himself. At most a mere shadow, like the silhouette of a pith helmet in this photo of "a very young girl with

1. Cf. R. ROSENBLUM, 'Caritas Romana after 1760: Some Romantic Lactations', in T.B. HESS and L. NOCHLIN (eds.), *Woman as Sex Object: Studies in Erotic Art, 1730-1970*, London, Allen Lane, 1973, pp. 42-63. The term emerges for the first time in the Renaissance but refers to a legend which can be found in differing versions in Pliny the Elder, Hyginus and Valerius Maximus.
2. Hegel is one among those who have called Africa a "Kinderland" *(Vorlesungen über die Philosophie der Geschichte* (Werke 12, ed. by E. Moldenhauer and K. M. Michel), Frankfurt a.M., Suhrkamp, 1970, p. 120).
3. What follows is a collage of almost literal citations from R. CORBEY, *Wildheid en beschaving. De Europese verbeelding van Afrika [Wildness and Culture: The European Image of Africa]*, Baarn, Ambo, 1989. The postcard to which I refer here is depicted on page 29 of Corbey's study; the one discussed below is on page 36.

just developed breasts" and a "wraparound skirt worn far too low" (Bandziri woman, hairstyle and specimen), the relation between the photographer and his model is panoptic and asymmetric: "to see without being seen". Which is why Africa can actually remain absent here. For the purpose of these photos, as well as those in the numerous handbooks of physical anthropology, was not accommodation but assimilation: they forced African reality into the straitjacket of existing opinions and instead of objectively recording reality, they sought to obtain representations which answered already existing European stereotypes and European, masculine needs. In short, what all those thousands of postcards of naked women, magic rituals or nail figures really show is not Africa, but the "European image of Africa", as Raymond Corbey – whom I am following here – indicates in the subtitle of his book. This Africa was simultaneously represented and misrepresented: one saw what one wanted to see, what one was able to see. And what one saw was a feast for the eyes: an erotic dreamworld, a virgin continent at the disposal of European, masculine aims; shy, wild and untamed, yet as voluptuous as her women, Africa uncovers what is hidden underneath her traditional costumes, throwing open her skirts to be violated by a Europe who, remembering only too well her own adventures on the back of a bull, cannot but be excited by this mirror image of her own desire. This wildness cries out for culture.

Dressed by missionaries, undressed by anthropometrists, exorcised by photographers, this Africa is for Corbey a sad paradigm of the terror brought on by thinking in terms of binary oppositions such as that between wildness and culture. And Corbey is not alone with such an analysis. What he says about Africa, others before him have said about America or the Orient – under nearly identical titles, with the same metaphors, the same arguments, the same proof and the same rhetoric. What this burgeoning library conserves is a discourse in the strict sense of the word[4], a discourse in which rage and melancholy, hope and description attempt with combined forces to burst this binary logic without being bruised by the fragments. But the result is doubtful. For how can one avoid falling into precisely the position that was to be problematized? If there is a link between a semiosis in terms of wildness/culture on the one hand and a colonial attitude on the other, then will this link not be repeated in the ethno-anthropological discourse on the European imagination itself? Is not this imagination now represented as that wild element in ourselves which we must civilize with the support of such an anthropology? And, in so doing, does not anthropology once again become *Kolonialanthropologie*, with the difference

4. For this idea of "discourse" see chapter 2 and 3 above and my commentary in *Michel Foucault. Genealogy as Critique, o.c.*

that now the colony is within Europe and that, with the help of a discipline which we have ourselves invented, we must now tame and subdue, discipline and colonize ourselves?

That anthropology's enlightened protest against colonization seems inevitably to result as a kind of reprise of the "Dialectic of the Enlightenment" – in an auto-colonization; that ethno-anthropology – whose goal was to analyse and neutralize the ethnic preconceptions (Eurocentrism) of our anthropology – could not itself break free of the opposition between wildness and culture, and thus would have to be treated by an ethno-ethno-anthropology; all of this already indicates the difficulty in simply posing the problem of European identity. A difficulty which has everything to do with the fact that this problem of Europe is a European problem, a problem in which almost all the other problems which Europe has posed converge. In the first place, the problem of the relation between reason and imagination as it figured in the debate between Enlightenment and Romanticism, for instance, and finds offshoots still today in all those discussions about modernity and postmodernity, universalism and particularism, relativism and pluralism, alterity and difference. I can hardly open all those files at once to audit and balance their accounts, but I would like to try and show why they should be opened if we are to arrive at any insight into this European problem that seems to me to be the problem par excellence of the relation between *provincialism and uprootedness*.

I. QUOD TANGIT, FRANGIT

European provincialism distinguishes itself from all other forms of provincialism precisely in that it leads *as such* to uprootedness or, in any case, is the expression of such uprootedness instead of – as one might expect from a provincialism – providing its cure. While all around us we witness triumphant new separatisms, particularisms and nationalisms – in short an upgrading of the "provincial" – Europe on the other hand appears to be that province which makes us ashamed. Indeed, Europe's self-shame seems to go directly together with the discovery of her own provinciality. The critique of Eurocentrism was nothing else than a critique of Europe's pretension to be something more and something other than a province. And this critique was successful. Who would still want to adopt Joachim Ritter's description of the Europeanization of the world: "Europeanization is the process in which non-European peoples detach themselves from their deep-rooted forms of life, take on the European forms of social production, education and state institutions, and *spontaneously and actively make all this their own*"[5]? Who could still pronounce Jaspers's famous "Europe's specificity is perhaps that it is the possibility for anything" without being immediately forced to hear that this Europe, which "experienced everything from without not only as opposition, but absorbed it into itself as a component of its own being"[6], was really only interested in interacting with the Other – and I quote a Japanese – so that it could *give itself* recognition, not *be* recognized in turn[7]? From Husserl to Kolakowski, "the ability to bring itself up for discussion, to abandon its own exclusivity, and the wish to see itself through the eyes of others"[8] was still the *insignum* par excellence which distinguished and raised European culture above all others, transforming Europe into a *"geistige Gestalt"*[9], and so more than simply a geographic location ("we feel, Husserl states, that an entelechy is inborn in our European civilization"[10]). Today this same openness, the wish to see oneself through the eyes of others, seems everywhere to be exposed as nothing more than a narcissistic self-satisfaction in which the other is first compelled to see through *our* eyes, so that he can then resettle in this already familiarized other, and gaze admiringly at himself. It is, in Lemaire's words, "the Indian in our consciousness" whom we allow to gaze at us – not the Indian himself, but the Indian "as Europeans presumed him to be, based on reports describing him as he was imagined through the spectacles of our interests and illusions (...) incorporated into the history of our economy"[11]. Europe is not this continent which was driven by curiosity for the other to overstep its borders time and again; – it just wanted more of the same, it wanted to meet itself *in* the other. Columbus, who according to Todorov discovered America but not the Americans, is in this sense the perfect emblem for a Europe which never discovered without covering up, which never

5. 'Europäisierung als europäisches Problem', in J. RITTER, *Metaphysik und Politik. Studien zu Aristoteles und Hegel*, Frankfurt a.M., Suhrkamp, 1969, p. 324, (text from 1956).

6. 'Vom europäischen Geist', in K. JASPERS, *Rechenschaft und Ausblick*, München, R. Piper, 1958, p. 283 (text from 1946).

7. N. SAKAI, 'Modernity and Its Critique: The Problem of Universalism and Particularism', *The South Atlantic Quarterly*, 1988 (87:3 special issue: "Postmodernism and Japan"), p. 477.

8. L. KOLAKOWSKI, 'Op zoek naar de barbaar. De illusies van een cultureel universalisme [In search of the barbarian. The illusions of a cultural universalism]', in *Essays van Leszek Kolakowski*, Utrecht/Antwerpen, Het Spectrum (Aula), 1983, p. 12.

9. E. HUSSERL, 'Philosophy and the Crisis of European Humanity' (= the 'Vienna Lecture' of May, 1935) in ID., *The Crisis of European Sciences and Transcendental Phenomenology*, Evanston Ill., Northwestern U.P., 1970, p. 273.

10. *The Crisis...*, p. 275.

11. T. LEMAIRE, *De Indiaan in ons bewustzijn. De ontmoeting van de Oude met de Nieuwe Wereld [The Indian in our Consciousness. The Encounter of the Old and the New World]*, Baarn, Ambo, 1986, p. 138.

represented without misrepresenting, which broke what it touched, distorted what it reflected, and swallowed up everything it came across[12]. Hence the image – perhaps the only one – that we still have of Europe: the most cannibalistic of all cultures, a pure and unfettered nominalistic violence which subjected and mastered what it named. And the strange thing is that this image preoccupies us, that we cannot get enough of it, that we have invented a discipline which seems well on its way to making even François Mitterand's "Very Big Library" seem small. Whence this fascination and whence the refusal to find, in this capacity for self-criticism and scrupulous self-examination, precisely our own identity? Whence this tendency to no longer recognize ourselves in that which lends the European nations their "particular inner spiritual affinity" of which Husserl still spoke – "a sibling relationship which gives all of us in this sphere the consciousness of homeland"? Why is Europe no longer a "homeland" for us, not even the homeland of that "infinite task" and that "infinite responsibility" which Husserl saw emerging in Greece and which he saw as the basis of a teleology which ultimately concerns all humanity, and which should have become a motive for all particular humanities – the European included – "to Europeanize themselves even in their unbroken will to spiritual self-preservation", that is, to serve "the absolute norm of truth"[13]?

Why has this will been broken? Is Europe simply worn out, as Husserl suggests, and will the pep pills of a phenomenologically renewed "heroism of reason"[14] soon reawaken her and make her equal to her task? Or is Europe sicker than Husserl suspected, so sick that the cure which Husserl had in mind – transcendental phenomenology – not only seems to be ineffective, but even exacerbates the sickness and gives the patient a good push into the abyss? For the last thing a schizophrenic can take is someone who speaks to him in the second person, confronting him in this way with a responsibility which he has to bear: "I could never accept that she [the psychotherapist] addressed me directly: 'You have a nice body, how beautiful you are!' That gave me terrible guilt feelings (...) By saying 'you, your body', she made me responsible, but by speaking in the third person, or rather by personifying my body – 'What a beautiful body, let's wash it with this refreshing soap' – she released me from it"[15]. And is Europe not in the depths of psychosis? A gaze which distorts everything it observes; a hand

12. Tzv. TODOROV, *La conquête de l'Amérique: la question de l'autre*, Paris, Seuil, 1982, p. 54.

13. All preceding quotes from *The Crisis...*, p. 274.

14. *Ibid.*, p. 299.

15. The patient Renée, quoted in M.A. SECHEHAYE, *Dagboek van een schizofreen [Diary of a Schizophrenic]*, Rotterdam, Lemniscaat, 1982, p. 81.

which shatters everything it touches; an anthropology which is said to destroy its object of knowledge in the very act of knowing, which commits "epistemocide" (Scholte) and which, in the words of no one less than Lévi-Strauss, should rather be called an "entropology"[16]; a continent which infected everything it came into contact with – is it any wonder that such a Europe has come to hate itself, that it takes its own body to be the source of all evil, and has radically divested itself of this body which, as Paul Moyaert puts it, "produces nothing good any longer, having become one undifferentiated 'shit factory'"[17]? And is it any wonder that the only discourse on Europe still making the rounds is a third person discourse, namely the scientific discourse, and specifically the discourse of anthropology which, far from having itself provoked this psychotic regression, seems to be a kind of final hope and the only bridge which has not yet been burned?

I am in no way suggesting here that Europe is more than ready for psychoanalysis and that such an analysis, with anthropology's assistance, would succeed where Husserl had failed. For the moment it is far from clear if Husserl really has failed. But what in any case seems quite clear is that facile formulas such as Kolakowski's, which impress upon us that we should be finished once and for all with "the West's doubts about its own cultural identity" and with "the weakening of the will to establish itself as a universal culture", are not much help to us. For there are doubts, Europe doubts itself, and Europe's doubt (Kolakowski's "European self-critique") has become, in Ton Lemaire's words, a doubt *about* Europe[18] which cannot be assuaged by a simple decree. It is time then to clear up an ambiguity which until now has remained unspoken and which, in a certain sense, has regulated my own argument: does Europe's doubt about itself have to do with the realization that we have fallen short of that norm of universality whose validity is not even questioned, or does the doubt reach so far as to touch this norm itself? In the first case the Enlightenment ideal is not itself questioned, but only our inability to fulfill it. In the second case that ideal is questioned and we seem to have to resign ourselves to the usual paradoxes of a neo-Romantic relativism. It seems to me that the problem anthropology

16. Cf. B. SCHOLTE, 'Reason and Culture: The Universal and the Particular Revisited', *American Anthropologist*, 1984(86), p. 965; and also Cl. LÉVI-STRAUSS, *Tristes Tropiques*, s.l., Plon (Terre Humaine/Poche), s.d., p. 496.

17. P. MOYAERT, 'Schizophrénie et paranoïa', in A. VERGOTE/P. MOYAERT (eds.), *Psychanalyse: l'homme et ses destins*, Louvain/Paris, Éditions Peeters, 1993, p. 261.

18. Cf. T. LEMAIRE, *Twijfel aan Europa. Zijn de intellectuelen de vijanden van de Europese cultuur? [Doubt about Europe. Are Intellectuals the Enemies of European Culture?]*, Baarn, Ambo, 1990, p. 12 and *passim*.

has to wrestle with is that it is in no position to make this choice. This does not necessarily mean that it lacked in scientificity, but it does mean – as we shall see – that the place of science in our culture has something to do with the space our culture makes for lack as such.

II. FIAT VERITAS, PEREAT VITA

Until now I have emphasized, somewhat one-sidedly, the critical and self-critical character of anthropology, not in my own name, but in the name of those who – like Lemaire, Corbey, Said[19] and many others – have tried to convince us that there was never any question of a "real confrontation, in the sense of an encounter" between the West and non-Western cultures. What actually took place was "a cannibalistic absorption (...) of what was considered different", a "violent representation", a "violent imagining of others"[20]: "When modern anthropology began to construct its Other in terms of *topoi* implying distance, difference, and opposition, its intent was above all, but at least also, to construct ordered Space and Time – a cosmos – for Western society to inhabit, rather than 'understanding other cultures', its ostensible vocation"[21]. Yet, one might object, hasn't anthropology overcome its childhood illnesses, doesn't its rationality lie precisely in the fact that it has continually struggled to correct these misrepresentations and wean itself of these cannibalistic leanings? Doesn't anthropology's rationality consist precisely in the fact that it has become an anthropology of our rationality, not content to limit itself to an ethnology of other cultures, but also branching out into what Foucault has called an ethnology of our own culture[22]? Isn't anthropology "that European science *par excellence*" "whose historical task was to put (European) universalism to the test", and to decide just to what extent it really applies to the dimension of humanity, or to what extent it is only a projection of (European) provincialism[23]? Has anthropology not been exactly what has taught us to see through the "closed", particular reason of European cultural imperialism, and to exchange it for an "open, critical reason" which recognizes the value of other cultures, mainly by attempting to know these cultures as

---

19. E. W. SAID, *Orientalism: Western Conceptions of the Orient*, Harmondsworth, Penguin Books, (1978[1]) 1991.

20. R. CORBEY, *o.c.*, pp. 161-2.

21. J. FABIAN, *Time and the Other: How Anthropology Makes Its Object*, New York, Columbia U.P., 1983, pp. 111-2, quoted in CORBEY, p. 155.

22. P. CARUSO, 'Gespräch mit Michel Foucault', in M. FOUCAULT, *Von der Subversion des Wissens*, Frankfurt a.M./Berlin/Wien, Ullstein, p. 13.

23. T. LEMAIRE, *Twijfel aan Europa, o.c.*, p. 43.

they are in themselves, free of our prejudices and expectations?

Strangely enough, the authors of the discursive genre which I have presented here are at a loss as to what to do with this objection which they nonetheless regularly invoke against their own position. They complain about European closedness in the name of a European openness which they want to have nothing to do with. "My European identity" – writes Lemaire at the end of a book in which he pleads for an "open, distantiated gaze which is truly interested in the otherness of (the) Others" – "prevents me from identifying with a certain Indian-ness (...) in order to know the Indian outside myself, I must have become an Indian for myself, but this latter is perhaps the distorted image of the former"[24]. At once plaintiff, defendant and counsel, and in no position to build the courthouse in which the trial of "anthropological Reason" could take place, the anthropologist is left with only the drama of an unhappy consciousness that doesn't know what to do with itself. The sorrow of Europe, which the anthropologist makes his own, concerns a crease in our openness, a closure which he cannot open without disappearing irrevocably into the hole he created: "a social form attains full self-realization only when it is already falling into ruin. As long as it believes in itself and identifies with its own dominant values, it must either assimilate other cultures into itself or else turn them into the barbarous, evil Other"[25]. Anthropology appears to fill in one hole with another, and to relieve one guilt with another: it replaces the evil Other with the familiar Other, the ostracized Other with the assimilated Other, leaving us with the hardly attractive choice between the barbarity of anthropoemia and the barbarity of anthropophagy. As the always again failed "*attempt* at redemption", anthropology is that peculiar "symbol of penance" that inscribes the guilt still deeper within us[26]. Lemaire: "anthropology seems to be not only the endeavour to understand non-modern forms of thought, but even more the endeavour to keep them at a distance" by "protecting Western reason against an invasion of 'wild reason'" – an allusion to Lévi-Strauss, "a hyper-rationalist who only rehabilitated other modes of thinking by admitting them to the dignity of rationality". "The *science* of mythology ultimately destroys the religious import of myths"[27]. So anthropology appears here as "a doubtful achievement: made possible through the discovery of a new world, it prevents us from coinciding with ourselves as much as from identifying with anyone else"[28]. Constantly involved in

24. T. LEMAIRE, *De Indiaan...*, *o.c.*, pp. 32, 299.
25. *Ibid.,* p. 248.
26. Cl. LÉVI-STRAUSS, *Tristes Tropiques*, *o.c.*, p. 466.
27. T. LEMAIRE, *Twijfel...*, *o.c.*, respectively pp. 82, 83, 84, 85.
28. T. LEMAIRE, *De Indiaan...*, *o.c.*, pp. 305-6.

wrapping up again what it had just unwrapped, anthropology resembles a compulsive neurotic ritual which is really only established in order to avoid the insight that "unmasking and dejection appear to be the core of the scientific experience"[29].

This conclusion should not surprise us. It is simply the consequence of the ambiguous position which anthropology was forced to occupy from the outset: the position of a science which, at the same time, had to bring us salvation. Simultaneously tied to an epistemological imperative ("objectivity", "realism") and to a soteriological mission (civilizing our distorting imagination), anthropology's "shortcomings" in the one sphere had immediate repercussions in the other. Its scientificity seemed to depend on the success with which it accomplished its mission of salvation, and the success of this mission seemed, in turn, to depend on its success as a science. Subject to two masters whose instructions constantly contradict each other, caught in this double bind, every success was at the same time a loss. Hence the paradox that the better anthropology's success in grounding the equality of all cultures on a cognitive relativism, by "opening oneself to the reason of others rather than opening others to reason"[30], the more anthropology undermines its own position by losing its Enlightenment heritage to Romanticism[31]. For if we must respect diverse societies as so many "patterns of culture" (R. Benedict), what then could be wrong with the pattern of our own culture, specifically with the fact that it misrepresents instead of represents all other cultures? And if there is something wrong with this, then haven't we already admitted *ipso facto* that cognitive relativism is mistaken and thus put the idea of equality at risk? Anthropology must know the other as he is *in himself*, but at the same time it must be able to show, on the basis of this very knowledge, that the other really cannot be known since he is *an other*. And the latter is likewise not a good message, for then my own culture – as Lemaire has said – stands in the way of an encounter with the other culture.

By now it will have become quite clear what a gigantic confusion affecting a number of fundamental concepts is hidden behind this crisis which, it must not be forgotten, manifests itself in real suffering, real sorrow and real shame. Or in a real absence. For Europe's doubt about itself seems to me to be not only a matter for certain "crazed intellectuals", as someone once put it, but also a matter for those who perhaps no longer feel any

---

29. *Ibid.,* p. 305.
30. A. FINKIELKRAUT, *La Défaite de la Pensée*, Paris, Gallimard, 1987, p. 72.
31. On Enlightenment and Romanticism see R. LEGROS, *L'idée d'humanité. Introduction à la phénoménologie*, Paris, Bernard Grasset, 1990, especially the first part: "L'homme comme arrachement et l'homme comme appartenance (Des Lumières au romantisme)".

shame, for whom the entire European problem and the complexity which that problem still had for Husserl's generation can be reduced to the simple statement "I do business, therefore I am ... – in favour of the European common market". Such a discourse on Europe – a discourse, that is, which unfolds over our heads and has turned the European question into a technico-juridical-economic (and, *in that sense*, a political) question which we seem to have lost all touch with – can only prevail and succeed because it could take the place of another discourse which, for one reason or another, was unable to endure. To understand this *underlying* crisis, I would like to turn briefly to the scheme of Nietzsche's well-known question: Is there something like a "use and disadvantage of anthropology for life"? Or formulated differently: how is it that anthropology has apparently not succeeded in finding a way of being useful without also being disadvantageous? Is this due to anthropology or to life?

Nietzsche's considerations on history in the so-called "Second Untimely Meditation" *(On the Use and Abuse of History for Life)*[32] seem to me to be quite relevant in this regard. There is not only a clear structural parallel between the problematics of historicism and exoticism – between the other in his temporal and the other in his spatial distance – the crisis which Nietzsche speaks about looks essentially the same. Nietzsche also describes a time which runs the risk of "being overwhelmed under the overflow of the past and the foreign" (NuN 284) and much of what he says sounds unusually "timely". Nietzsche on a visit to our bookshops: "we moderns have nothing of our own. Only by filling ourselves to overflowing with foreign customs, art forms, philosophies, religions and sciences, do we become something noteworthy, namely wandering encyclopedias" (NuN 233). And then the diagnosis: "the *unrestrained* historical sense, pushed to its logical extreme, uproots the future, because it destroys illusions and *robs existing things of the only atmosphere in which they can live*" (NuN 252). Does there still exist, after the discovery of Eurocentrism, an atmosphere in which Europe can live? Isn't the future of Europe itself radically affected by the profligate exoticism and historicism which overruns us today? Are we not also uprooted and capable at most of an "irony with regard to ourselves" (NuN 237) which is expressed in a "restless cosmopolitanism and an unceasing search for novelty" (NuN 227), for difference and otherness? Do we archivists of the alien, bookkeepers of our own guilt, still possess the strength to "enclose ourselves within a limited horizon" (NuN 281)? Can we still endure a limitation which we do not want to interpret *ipso facto* as a shortcoming and

---

32. Parenthetical references are to the Schlechta edition (Frankfurt a.M./Berlin/Wien, Ullstein, 1979), volume I. For the English text, I have occasionally consulted the translation by A. Collins (Indianapolis/New York, Bobbs-Merrill, 1957).

a guilt?

At first sight Nietzsche seems to suggest that the cause of this modern incapacity, whose self-appointed task is "to be just to everything before it" (NuN 250), is to be found in the misplaced ideal of objectivity for history which has become a science: "*fiat veritas pereat vita*" (NuN 231). But on a closer look, this scientificization of history seems only to reinforce an already existing degeneration or uprootedness. For Nietzsche, we are overcome by a "malady of history" (NuN 281) – and one might add: by a "fever for the exotic" – because we have lost the natural antidotes: the unhistorical and the superhistorical. We are no longer able to forget *(ibid.)*, we have become historical through and through, and our only reaction to the insight which history has given us into the one condition for every event – namely, a certain "blindness and injustice in the soul of the one who acts" (NuN 216) – is an almost catatonic condition of complete apathy. What we have seen takes away all our desire to act because, says Nietzsche, we no longer possess "the power which turns the gaze from the process of becoming to that which gives existence an eternal and stable character" (NuN 281). Are there still any such "powers" that can divert our gaze from that "inexorable, blinding light"[33] which we call the Other? Is there still anything which can temper this light so that we – and I refer here to Europe – are there as the others are there? Is there anything left which could bring to an end these ravings and stop the pain which we would undoubtedly feel after having been exposed for so long to what could be called, following Michel Haar's pointed article on Levinas, "the traumatization by the other"[34]? I make no excuse for the violence of these questions, for it is a pure, non-empirical, pre-ethical and transcendental violence. I wish to deal with Husserl.

III. VIDEMUS PER SPECULUM ...

Let us return to the beginning. We have seen how the conceptual opposition between representation and misrepresentation has led anthropology to a situation in which it can fulfill neither its scientific nor its soteriological mission: a double bind which I suggested was connected in one way or another with the absolute historical novelty of European shame about itself – a shame which could be described as a sort of Midas complex which has not been worked through. It would seem that the core of this complex is a mistaken conception of alterity and that precisely this conception has

33. During her psychotic attacks, Sechehaye's patient found herself in "a land (...) with an inexorable, blinding light, *with no place for shadows*", (p. 29).

34. Cf. M. HAAR, 'L'obsession de l'autre. L'éthique comme traumatisme', in *L'Herne. Emmanuel Levinas*, Paris, 1991, pp. 444-53.

functioned aš the binding element in the fatal conjunction between "anthropology" and "life" which ultimately led – in a relation of mutual paralysis and destruction – to what I have called, somewhat frivolously perhaps, the European psychosis. It remains for us to dissect this cuckoo's egg which we have called, not without self-irony, the "Other", using the transcendental scalpel of Husserl's famous fifth "Cartesian Meditation"[35]. We restrict ourselves to the essential.

One of the lessons of Husserl's transcendental meditation on the ontological significance of the other is that the other is always and necessarily an alter ego. There is only an alter *for* a (transcendental) ego or, as Ricoeur comments, there is only something foreign because there is something my own, not the other way around[36]. Husserl goes even further however: there is no alter except *through* an ego, which means that it is a transcendental *ego* which constitutes the other, and Husserl's whole problem is whether that point of origin does justice to the alterity of the other and does not result in transcendental solipsism – all of which leads to a doctrine known as the analogical appresentation, of which I will consider only the most elementary implications. The constitution of the other is analogical and appresentative because I have no direct access to the other's "own essentiality" *(das Eigenwesentliche)*. If I had such access, if I would be able, to put it simply, to see not only the other but also "the life of the other", then the other would be merely a moment of my "own essence" and he and I would be the same (CM 139). But what I have is precisely an appresentative and not an original access to the other (CM 150) because he, like me, is an origin. The other is precisely an *alter* ego because he is as much the centre of a world as is my (transcendental) ego. Hence he is not a thing of which I only have adumbrations (*Abschattungen*) but which I can always exchange for other adumbrations by, for example, walking around it. The other is infinitely other, that is, in another sense 'other' than a thing. He is in another sense non-totalizable because there is no surplus of adumbrations which can give me access to his lived reality as it is lived *by him, from his perspective*[37]. The other appears, for *me*, as something which

---

35. Parenthetical references are to E. HUSSERL, *Cartesianische Meditationen und Pariser Vorträge* (Husserliana I), Dordrecht/Boston/London, Kluwer, 1991. For the English text, I have occasionally consulted the translation by D. Cairns, *Cartesian Meditations*, The Hague, Nijhoff, 1960.

36. P. RICOEUR, *Husserl. An Analysis of His Phenomenology*, Evanston Ill., Northwestern U.P., 1967, p. 119.

37. For this and some of the following formulations, see Derrida's exemplary commentary on the stakes of the Fifth Meditation: 'Violence and Metaphysics: An Essay on the Thought of Emmanuel Levinas', in J. DERRIDA, *Writing and Difference*, Chicago, University of Chicago Press, 1978, pp. 123 ff.

withdraws in principle from my possibility of being, and were this not the case, then he would either no longer be an *alter* ego and would coincide with mine, or else he would no longer be an alter *ego* and would be fully absorbed by the world instead of being its origin. The appearance of the other, then, implies a necessary and non-phenomenalizable moment which Husserl indicates very precisely by characterizing the problem of the alter ego as "(a) kind of verifiable accessibility of what is not originally accessible"[38]. In other words, the other is not simply accessible, he is accessible *in* his inaccessibility.

Every word is important here. The other is not simply accessible or simply inaccessible, and certainly not accessible "in spite of" his inaccessibility[39]. He is accessible *in* his inaccessibility because his accessibility does not abolish his inaccessibility, but rather lets it appear. To put it another way, the other can only appear as other *for me*, not as he is *in himself*, but as he appears *for me*. Thus there is always a moment of coveredness in the discovery of the other, a non-phenomenality which is the very price of every phenomenality and hence the violence of an elision which is inevitable because the other must expose himself to that violence in order to appear and because I cannot let the other appear *to me* without committing this violence against him. A violence of an unusual sort since it opens the relation with the other; a non-ethicizable and hence pre-ethical violence because there is no ethics without the preceding appearance of the other; a non-empirical "transcendental violence"[40] because it is a misrepresentation which every possible representation implies. A violence which not only cannot but may not be avoided if our well-meaning attempts to "keep the peace" are not to veer into the outrageous cruelty of a self-destruction which annihilates both the dimension of distance and that of proximity, thus exhibiting all the symptoms of what Derrida has called a "transcendental pathology"[41], and what I would call a transcendental

38. "(eine) Art bewährbarer Zugänglichkeit der original Unzugänglichen": E. HUSSERL, *op. cit.*, p. 144. Cf. E. Husserl, *Zur Phänomenologie der Intersubjektivität. Texte aus dem Nachlass. Dritter Teil: 1929-1935* (Husserliana XV), The Hague, Nijhoff, 1973, pp. 627ff. (among others p. 631: "Fremdheit besagt Zugänglichkeit in der eigentlichen Unzugänglichkeit").

39. Cf. B. WALDENFELS, 'Erfahrung des Fremden in Husserls Phänomenologie', *Phänomenologische Forschungen Bd. 22: Profile der Phänomenologie*, 1989, p. 41.

40. The term is Derrida's (*o.c.*, pp. 118ff.: "Of Transcendental Violence").

41. J. DERRIDA, 'Introduction', in E. HUSSERL, *L'Origine de la Géometrie*, Paris, P.U.F., 1974, p. 74.

psychosis[42].

It is understood: where would the Indian be if not "for" my consciousness, and what would still remain of the other if his eyes would not reflect my own before they even looked at me, and if there were not at least the violence of this membrane or this hymen separating me from him as he is "in himself" and preventing me from identifying with him[43]? I am well aware that a transcendental cannibalism is not yet an empirical cannibalism and I would gladly give Lemaire and others the benefit of the doubt were it not for my suspicion that a certain conceptual carelessness and the mixing-up of two meaning registers which should be carefully distinguished have made of Europe's doubt a doubt about Europe, and have led to a terror in which what occurs is precisely the opposite of what was feared: it is in the first place the self that disappears or appears as an obstacle, and with the self the other disappears also. For are there any others left? Didn't the world from pole to equator become European through and through? I am not referring to buildings and supermarket chains, but rather to what makes them possible: an enormous amount of information, boxes and libraries full, which we have gathered about the other in order to establish that it all boils down to this: slightly different mores, other customs, etc. in short, nothing to lose any sleep over – after all, we are all "human beings".

To reduce the other to a content which can be known, to think that alterity is something which I can learn to respect by gathering information about it, to think that that respect increases and the encounter becomes more interesting the more I am able to find out, or even: to think that the other is the one who confronts me with a possibility which is also my possibility, with an alternative from which I can learn by taking it up or by trying it out, or in any case, with which I should relate in a sort of transcultural vibration on pain of a complete loss of respect and indifference with respect to what is interesting about the other whom I must try to interact with at any cost, if I am not to overlook the possibility and desirability of pluralism – it is all this which has turned the world into one large European village and left us with the nasty taste that we are missing something, if we even notice it, for it takes the sensibility of a Leiris to notice

42. Schizophrenic psychosis is precisely the absence of that first Gestalt be it in the form of a mirror image through which proximity *and* distance are simultaneously and for the first time instituted. Cf. A. DE WAELHENS, *Schizophrenia: A Philosophical Reflection on Lacan's Structuralist Interpretation* (transl. W. Ver Eecke), Pittsburgh, Duquesne U.P., 1978.

43. Cf. again T. LEMAIRE, *De Indiaan...*, *o.c.*, p. 299: "In order to know the Indian *outside me*, I must have become an Indian for myself, but the latter is perhaps *the distorted form* of the former" – my italics to indicate the empiricization of a transcendental problematic.

such things: "One does not get closer to people when one gets closer to their customs. They remain, before and after the inquiry, obstinately closed"[44]. But then what is it that closes off the other and, now and then, as Baudrillard says, freezes that gigantic stock exchange which we call alterity or difference[45]? And how is it that we usually do not even notice?

What makes the other other is not his content, not the attributes of his being. Levinas says it himself and he is correct: "The alterity of the Other does not depend on any quality that would distinguish him from me, for a distinction of this nature would precisely imply between us that community of genus which already nullifies alterity" (TI 194). The Other is not "unknown, but unknowable" (TO 75). And this for the reasons which Husserl, *pace* Levinas, indicates. For even and especially in the order of knowledge and truth, Husserl is concerned not with a community of what we share, but with a community of what we do not share. An identity, for example, and even a European identity. Indeed one could transpose, without too much difficulty, the schema of the fifth Cartesian Meditation to the relation among the various "cultural worlds" (*Kulturwelten*) which are, in turn, accessible in their inaccessibility[46]. Admittedly Husserl – wanting to avert relativism as much as he formerly wanted to drive out solipsism – particularly emphasized accessibility and the "one world" of which the "lifeworlds" would be only adumbrations, a gesture which as Held rightly notes amounts to making the world an object and thus not a world at all[47]. But all that is not intrinsic to the order of knowledge, as there is still something in the "alien world" (*Fremdwelt*) which I can, in principle, *not* appropriate, in the sense that it can never be for me what it is for the alien world: different forefathers – in the broadest sense – and hence a different tradition, a different historicity. This inaccessibility is not primarily cognitive – I can learn to know and reconstruct this tradition (Foucault for example did nothing else) – it is primarily existential: an anthropologist who becomes a shaman is and

44. M. LEIRIS, *L'Afrique fantôme*, Paris, Gallimard (TEL), 1981, p. 260 (note from 31-3-1932).

45. J. BAUDRILLARD, *La Transparence du Mal. Essai sur les phénomènes extrêmes*, Paris, Galilée, 1990, pp. 129, 133.

46. Cf. the texts in *Husserliana XV* (cited in note 38) and the announcement of this problematic in CM 159-63 with regard to the so-called "Analytik der höheren intersubjektiven Gemeinschaften". For this transposition see Kl. HELD, 'Heimwelt, Fremdwelt, die eine Welt', *Phänomenologische Forschungen Bd. 24/25: Perspektiven und Probleme der Husserlschen Phänomenologie. Beiträge zur neueren Husserl-Forschung*, 1991, pp. 305-37, which has inspired me for what follows.

47. Kl. HELD, *l.c.*, pp. 327ff.

remains simply that, an anthropologist who has become a shaman[48]. It is not the content which is inaccessible, but the natural evidence, the fact that it is *this* and not, for example, *that* content around which everything in this alien world hinges. What makes Paracelsus strange for us is not the fact that we cannot understand what he was interested in. Our dissociation – the term is Hacking's[49] – has more to do with the fact that we cannot 'understand' *that* he was interested in this. In Husserlian terms: between Paracelsus and us lies a generative gap; we understand perhaps what it could have meant for him to have had these or those forefathers, but our forefathers are different. I say 'could have meant' and not 'did mean' because this latter formulation would presuppose that Paracelsus understood himself better than anyone else and that he had access to the discursive law which allowed him to be interested in those things he was interested in and which made it possible for him to take certain things seriously and not others, just as there is a discourse which prevents us from still taking seriously those things which interested Paracelsus, and this on the basis of a discursive law to which we have just as little access. One has to recognize then, as Baudrillard formulates it, that "real knowledge is knowledge of what we will never understand in the other, of that in the other which insures that he is not himself *(soi-même)*"[50]. It is because there is something in the other (the other culture in this case) thanks to which he stands outside of himself, that the transcendental hymen separating him from me does not prevent me, but precisely allows me to know him. What I cannot touch in the other, Merleau-Ponty says, he cannot touch either: "The untouchable is not a touchable in fact inaccessible (...) The negative here is not a *positive that is elsewhere* (...) It is a true negative, i.e. an *Unverborgenheit* of the *Verborgenheit*, an *Urpräsentation* of the *Nichturpräsentierbar*, in other words, an original of the *elsewhere*" (VI 254, his italics). It is, in other words, a certain Husserl (accessibility of the inaccessible) and a certain Heidegger (*aletheia*) who come together here and show us that there is no real contradiction between the problem of generativity, which can be taken to indicate an existentiell and possibly even an existential relativism, and the problem of a transcendental violence to which Husserl himself on occasion referred as a "transcendental relativism"[51].

48. This example is from B. WALDENFELS, *Der Stachel des Fremden*, Frankfurt a.M., Suhrkamp, 1990, p. 63.

49. I. HACKING, *Representing and Intervening*, Cambridge U.P., 1990, pp. 69-72.

50. J. BAUDRILLARD, *La Transparence du Mal, o.c.*, p. 153.

51. M. Theunissen coined this expression with reference to Husserl's letter to Georg Misch (16-11-1930) where he speaks of a "transcendental relativierenden 'Phän[omenologie]'" (*Der Andere. Studien zur Sozialontologie der Gegenwart*, Berlin, W. de

There remains, of course, a cognitive misrepresentation whenever I look from my *Heimwelt* toward this other world: what Lévi-Strauss saw was the *rationality* of wild thought because that "thought" had to appear to *him* and to *his* culture. Lévi-Strauss did not "keep" wild thought at a distance; it was rather the distance – the generative gap – *between* him and wild thought, as much as the distance *within* wild thought itself which enabled him to know it at all. I say "know" and not "misrecognize", and certainly not: "freely fantasize about". For the first thing which must be done in every crisis, the European crisis included, is the introduction of a certain hygienics. Which presupposes that one begins by removing the parasites from the wound and by recognizing, for example, that it would be an unparalleled stupidity, which illustrates rather than remedies the 'demise of thought', to assert that "an insurmountable contradiction lurks behind the attempt to ground hospitality on rootedness"[52]. It would suffice to realize that *only* if I have become a foreigner for myself can all the others be foreigners also. Not cease to be a foreigner, as Kristeva suggests[53] – a difference both essential and political. For it is my rootedness which makes me a foreigner and – for example – a European. One hears Heidegger approaching.

IV. ... IN ENIGMATE

But it is Lévi-Strauss who has the first word. In a polemic against Caillois as brilliant as it is venomous, Lévi-Strauss notes in passing that the anthropologist is a "resurrected Lazarus" who has "returned from among the dead"[54]. By confronting his traditions and beliefs with social experiences which cannot be reduced to his own, by performing the autopsy of his own society, *"he is truly dead to his world;* and if he manages to return, after having reorganized the disjointed members of his cultural tradition, *he is, all the same, someone resurrected"*. Thus the anthropologist suffers from a

Gruyter, 1965, p. 34). I would not have been so confident in pushing Husserl to this extent, had I, at the time of writing these lines, already been able to read Anthony STEINBOCK's impressive *Home and Beyond. Generative Phenomenology after Husserl*, Evanston Ill., Northwestern U.P., 1995.

52. A. FINKIELKRAUT, *La Défaite de la Pensée, o.c.*, p. 115.

53. J. KRISTEVA, *Strangers To Ourselves*, New York/London/Toronto, Harvester Wheatsheaf, 1991, p. 192 (transl. altered): "The foreign is within me, *hence* we are all foreigners. *If I am a foreigner, there are no foreigners*"; what I have italicized should be read as follows: there are foreigners already, and it appears that the foreign is within me also, so we are all foreigners and there are no foreigners. I challenge both the premise ("there are foreigners already") and the conclusion ("there are no more foreigners") for reasons which are given below (cf. *infra* on the logic of attachment and the illusion of content).

54. Cl. LÉVI-STRAUSS, 'Diogène Couché', *Les Temps Modernes*, 1955 (10:110), p. 1217.

"dislocation", he is the victim of a "chronic uprootedness". "Never again, says Lévi-Strauss, will he feel at home". Elsewhere he speaks in this respect of "an *inner revolution* which truly makes of him *a new man*"[55].

At first sight, this passage recalls Nietzsche's *"fiat veritas pereat vita"* which we initially understood as an adage referring to the inevitable effect of the uprootedness which accompanies the scientificization of life. And yet this does not seem to be the interpretation which does justice to the experience of "metanoia" which Lévi-Strauss describes here. Or at least not the only one.

What overcomes the anthropologist looks very much like what *Being and Time* has analysed under the heading "angst". Heidegger describes there the depressing experience in which Dasein is confronted with its own ontological status: in and through the appearance of the world *as* world and being-in-the-world *as* being-in-the-world, Dasein experiences angst and its being-in-the-world becomes blocked and immobilized: none of the things and concerns which normally address us have any more hold on us. Ontological knowledge, just like anthropological knowledge, looks like a forbidden fruit: what shows itself here, appears for the last time, and then "takes its farewell"[56]. Something disappears which we never saw because we lived too close to it, and from which, now that it has disappeared, we seem to be too far away. We are uprooted. Now, *Eigentlichkeit* – "authenticity" – for Heidegger does not mean that we try as soon as possible to fill in this lack by seizing whatever gives us those roots that we seem to have lost in angst. *Eigentlichkeit* has something to do with the realization that we need not less but more uprootedness. Or even that it is in uprootedness – and only there – that we are truly at home. Or to put it yet another way: our roots lie in an uprootedness, that is, in something which we never coincide with, in something which withdraws from us, something decentred with respect to us but which still retains for us the attraction of a centre. Being at home is not simply proximity, a *hic*, but a proximity within distance, an *illic*, the promise of a here[57]. This is the reason why it is so difficult, for example, to say precisely what keeps 'a Berliner, a Madrileño and us' together, and gives us a European identity. Perhaps what keeps us together should not even be said; perhaps the proper name "Europe" is precisely the expression

---

55. *Anthropologie Structurale*, s.l., Plon, 1958, pp. 409-10, quoted in M. HÉNAFF, *Claude Lévi-Strauss*, Paris, Pierre Belfond, 1991, (p. 32) from which the entire first chapter, 'L'anthropologue, l'Occident et les autres', is relevant here.

56. BT 104/74. On this problematic of the "Unauffälligkeit" and the relation to "Eigentlichkeit", see chapter 1 above.

57. J. DERRIDA, 'Violence and Metaphysics', *l.c.*, p. 145: "The thinking of Being thus is not a pagan cult of the *Site*, because the Site is never a given proximity but a promised one".

of this insight which is threatened whenever one tries to ground this identity by positing it as a sort of firm foundation. Heidegger in *Der Satz vom Grund*: "the unique unleashing of the demand to render reasons threatens everything of humans' being-at-home and robs them of the roots of their subsistence"[58].

I interpret: only a "life" that thinks "subsistence" in terms of a final ground, only a life that turns the epistemological project of science into a soteriological project, only such a life becomes truly uprooted. This is the reason why the anthropologist can in principle escape the "never again being at home anywhere", and why I said earlier that the anthropological discourse can be a kind of final hope, for becoming a "resurrected Lazarus" could also mean that we have learned what "dwelling" means for man. In the words of Verhoeven: "It does not much matter where we live, but we do have to live *somewhere*; and this 'somewhere' is never the entire world (...) The evil of cosmopolitanism is that it ignores the concreteness of this 'somewhere', and the evil form of provincialism makes of this 'somewhere' the whole world"[59]. We always already live somewhere, in Europe for example. The cosmopolitanism which would like to make world citizens of us misunderstands this attachment. Romantic provincialism, to the contrary, makes the mistake of trying to reach for it and appropriate it. Both share with science the illusion of content, so neither one thinks. But when science should not think[60], a life that does not think loses its content. And this is less elitist than it sounds, for life is always on the point of thinking, for example when it travels. Travel today, as Baudrillard tells us, is no longer what it used to be a means of being somewhere else or of being "nowhere": "today it is the only means to experience the sensation of being anywhere"[61] – and I would say: "of having been somewhere", and I also mean: of being at home somewhere. In Europe for example.

In this sense, all of anthropology's so-called failings are, *for us*, so many successes. For what appears in this extreme effort to detach is precisely attachment: our hymen and our *untouchable*, our forefathers. And it is not in the first place a question of contents, but of a formal moment: not the content of our imagination (Corbey) but the fact *that* we are referred to an

58. M. HEIDEGGER, *The Principle of Reason* (transl. R. Lilly), Bloomington/Indianapolis, Indiana U.P., 1991, p. 30.

59. C. VERHOEVEN, 'Wonen en thuis zijn. Aantekeningen bij 'Bouwen Wonen Denken' van Martin Heidegger' [Dwelling and being at home: Notes on Martin Heidegger's 'Building Dwelling Thinking'], in J. DE VISSCHER & R. DE SAEGER (eds.), *Wonen. Architectuur in het denken van Martin Heidegger*, Nijmegen, SUN, 1991, p. 103.

60. M. HEIDEGGER, *Was heißt Denken?*, Tübingen, M. Niemeyer, 1954, p. 4: "die Wissenschaft denkt nicht (...) und zwar zu ihrem Glück".

61. *La Transparence du Mal*, *o.c.*, p. 156.

imagination. The contents only become meaningful on the basis of that formal moment. They only acquire meaning as *our* contents, i.e. as that which concerns us without our ever being able to fully penetrate and recuperate it, because they occupy for us "the place of that which escapes us"[62]. What will serve then as a foundation for tolerance and hospitality is just *this* rootedness which is an *up*rootedness because it decentres us and keeps us at a distance from ourselves at the same time that it links us to a centre. It makes me become a "foreigner in myself", not one *like* all the others but one *beside* all the others. I respect the other's humanity only when I accept that he, like myself, is the bearer of a lack. Not a lack that I can fill up, or that might fill up my lack, and not a lack that is the cause of mine, but a lack that I *let be*. Something unremarkable, the zero degree of all meaning, but still that which generates all meaning for him and for me. The odour of a cuisine, a ritual slaughter, and the core of his belief. And with this I am already asking him to be European. For Europe, as is by now understood, is as much the name of a specific culture as it is the name of a "spiritual shape" which concerns all humanity. Europe is a specific attachment and the appearance of attachment as such. And this is why there should be un-European desires and, at the same time, no un-European desires. For Europe is simultaneously the name for a certain way of dealing with a lack – in humility rather than superiority – and the name of a certain lack. It is that split in the signifier which was at stake if not 'for' then at least 'in' Husserl and from which today, in the name of a relativism or a universalism which misunderstand themselves[63], we would gladly be freed. Which signifies perhaps nothing less than the refusal of a proper name. For as we shall see in our next chapter, if the problem of 'Europe' is more than just a Western problem, it is because in calling 'us Europeans' (?) by our 'own' (?) name, it confronts us with what always still calls in any name. It is that minimum of transcendence in the immanence of the familiar which threatens to become obliterated when one is reducing the problem of Europe or of the West to something one can either be 'for' or 'against'. As I hope to have made clear in this chapter, my distrust of those who are 'against' Europe does not rank me amongst its defenders. What I want to

---

62. *Ibid.*, p. 180.

63. One finds both reactions in the Husserl literature. For an example of the first type: E. HOLENSTEIN, 'Europa und die Menschheit. Zu Husserls kulturphilosophischen Meditationen', in Chr. JAMME - O. PÖGGELER (eds.), *Phänomenologie im Widerstreit. Zum 50. Todestag Edmund Husserls*, Frankfurt a.M., Suhrkamp, 1989, pp. 40-64; for the second type: D. LOHMAR, 'Home-world and foreign ethos: a phenomenological attempt to solve ethical problems of intercultural exchange', *Journal of Indian Council of Philosophical Research*, 1992(9:3), pp. 73-87.

defend is rather what in this name 'Europe', like in any other name, remains unnameable. Hence my interest in Merleau-Ponty's *prima facie* similar notion of the 'untouchable' which is at the heart of his attempt to develop a new ontology. We should give this 'endo-ontology' the attention it deserves (chapter 7), before we ask ourselves whether the unnameable is indeed an instance of his 'untouchable' (chapter 8)[64].

64. Readers who are not familiar with Merleau-Ponty may wish to skip the next chapter (which is a close textual study of *The Visible and the Invisible*) and go on to chapter 8 where I sort of take my farewell from an author in whose element I lived too long a time for me to be able to publish what in the end I hold against him without showing first to what extent *The Visible and the Invisible* is a book one has never finished reading.

CHAPTER SEVEN

THE UNTOUCHABLE
MERLEAU-PONTY'S LAST SUBJECT

Philosophy, as we all know and some of us still like to believe, is not a science. Inevitably, its questions seem to turn back on the philosopher who raises them and end up putting him into question (VI 27). Which is why he would miss the specific 'practice of the self' involved in philosophy if he would try to adopt the position of the scientist for whom in principle "there is no special question about being for which there is not a corresponding yes or no in being which settles it" (PW 17). One cannot find a response in being to the kind of questions philosophy raises. They call for an indirect ontology that would explore what it means that there is no answer to the "question of knowing why there are questions and how there come to be those nonbeings who do not know but would like to know" (*ibid.*). Endo-ontology, then, was to look for 'the origin of truth' and as it became more and more convinced that the point was "to understand that truth itself has no meaning outside of the relation of transcendence" (VI 185) the "archetype" of which it found in perception (VI 158), it seems to have concluded that the origin of truth has "broken up" and that "philosophy must accompany this break-up, this non-coincidence, this differentiation" (VI 124).

Such is the point where Merleau-Ponty left us, before he could spell out the consequences of what he had found. His questions in turn were broken up and then discarded as other and more pressing ones came to claim our attention. Truth for example, was linked to power and for some that was all there was to know: truth did not have an origin, it had *Herkunft*[1]. And so the problem was no longer "why there are questions" and why to that question one cannot find a response in being (PW 17), but why, amongst all the possible questions that could be raised, these and only these were raised during a certain period of time. Discourse overtook existence and one fine morning we woke up, and found ourselves literally unable to further hear or take seriously what had hitherto been said. The late writings of Merleau-Ponty had become inaccessible and were left lying at the edge of our new

1. Cf. M. FOUCAULT, 'Nietzsche, Genealogy, History', in ID., *Language, Counter-Memory, Practice. Selected Essays and Interviews* (ed. D. F. Bouchard), Ithaca (New York), Cornell U.P., 1980, pp. 139-64.

discourse as carrion for the few who took it upon themselves to study the writings of the late Merleau-Ponty, of the Merleau-Ponty who left us too early to finish what he had begun and whose untimely death had cast a dark glow over those pages which he did not finish writing. Unfinished, *The Visible and the Invisible* had itself become, ironically or tragically, an instance of its title. Too much in it had become *invisible in fact* (what could have been seen had the book been finished), and the project as such, as a new 'order of discourse' had been established, had become invisible *by right*, i.e. truly invisible and not just actually invisible but possibly visible for others at another time. Henceforth, truth was to be without origin, since it had shown itself to be already there where one had hoped to find the trace of its first beginning. Foucault for one had no difficulty concluding that order was not announced by things, but by itself, imposing upon them that 'primary falsification' that came to be known as the 'regime of truth'[2]. As we would always and of necessity find ourselves within such a regime, there would always and of necessity be certain things which could not be said, or heard or seen. And thus the son had killed the father by showing his intuition to be both true and superfluous. From now on, archaeology was to take the place of endo-ontology.

In a sense, this murder cannot be undone. And it certainly won't help to use the unfinished state of Merleau-Ponty's writings as an excuse to treat them with the means of an 'objective history of philosophy' which for him was "*a* philosophy, and not what it claims to be: a history of what is" (VI 177). Indeed, to treat him that way would only repeat and aggravate the murder, since it inevitably will put us into the position of someone who thinks he can restrict himself to writing a history of "immanent problems" and hence must allow himself to be absorbed by that immanence; or of someone who thinks he can report on what others thought from the detached point of view of a *kosmotheoros*, which, for Merleau-Ponty, would mean to adopt no point of view, and hence to see nothing, for there is no vision without depth, and there is no depth without a point of view, a tie, an attachment (PW 15, VI 219). Truth is not a matter for soaring-over, nor a question of total or effective coincidence (VI 124). It has to do with transcendence, and that is: with being at a distance (VI 181/234: *être à distance*). Which is why it would be unwise for us to deny that between him and us there is a distance, or to pretend that our difficulty to repeat and take over (*reprise*) that gesture he had barely begun to trace would be due solely to the unfinished character of his late writings. As if we would have been in a better position had not most of what was announced been missing. As if in philosophy, when we take up our own work of the past, or that of others,

2. Cf. chapters 2 and 3 above.

we did not always experience a moment of *unrepeatability* which is but the reverse side of our belonging to a philosophical world which, like the world in general, surrounds us and grants us access only by imposing on us a distance which is "not contrary" to proximity, but in fact "synonymous" (VI 135).

So let us accept without further argument that the murder cannot be un-done and that it would be pointless to simply try to reawaken the stifled body or to indulge in a nostalgic caressing of the picture that reminds us of what it once was. To undo that murder, and to pretend there is no distance between our questions and his, would be to deny that philosophy has a history; but to take that distance as an excuse for not engaging with him would be to reduce philosophy to its history (VI 199). Neither way would bring us "a thought of our own that does not kill him, either by overcoming him, or by copying him" (adapted from VI 198). At best we would find ourselves disappointed with a picture of a phenomenology that was once in movement, but that now has been turned into a body floating in the history of thought "like an alga but not moving *itself*" (PrP 184). Why not instead follow the advice Merleau-Ponty himself had taken from Rodin and try to portray the body of his thought "in an attitude which it never at any instant really held and which imposes fictive linkages between the parts, as if this mutual confrontation of incompossibles could, and could alone" awaken it from that "Zenonian reverie on movement" in which our histories of philosophy have caught it for too long a time (*ibid.*)? Why not try to replace their picture by that of what the *Working Notes* called "a vertical history which has its rights alongside of the 'objective' history of philosophy" (VI 186)?

I. A VERTICAL HISTORY?

Let there be no misunderstanding. My aim in these introductory remarks has not been to join the chorus of those who have been lamenting the lack of interest in Merleau-Ponty's writings and who have not missed an opportunity to throw a quote of his at the feet of whoever they found guilty of not having read him. Nor did I want to fire into the back of those who were already happy if they managed "to define his thought in terms of what he had achieved" and thus to protect it from total neglect, even if that meant ignoring his advice to go on to what was left unthought and to understand "the words which circumscribe and delimit it" "through their lateral implications as much as through their manifest or frontal significance" (TLC 114). For in fact the problem that I wanted to point to, and the question that I addressed myself, is not to be restricted to the limited area of Merleau-

Ponty-studies. It imposes itself upon us every time we pick up a book and begin to read: "can one put to a philosophy questions that it has not put to itself? [...] Descartes, Malebranche. Is it not necessary to distinguish their problems such as they thought them and the problems that really move them, and that *we* formulate. – Does this lead to conclusions that are always relativistic?" (VI 199). Since we cannot avoid these questions, I thought that perhaps the fact that Merleau-Ponty's 'vertical history' was to follow from his "conception of perceptual being" (VI 186), would be of interest to those who had not been persuaded by his earlier work that perception should be at the centre of their attention. And as with every new publication, for each of us, including myself, it seems to become less and less evident what there could be left for us to say (if speaking or writing would mean that we do not simply *repeat* what others said or *report* on it), I thought that perhaps the fact that we increasingly seem to be drawn into just those positions of *fusion* or *soaring over* that the indirect ontology had been meaning to criticize, could be an occasion for us to question its status again and to confront it with a question that seems to have bothered Merleau-Ponty himself, as he addressed it in one of his Working Notes: "I say that the Renaissance perspective is a cultural fact, that perception itself is polymorphic and that if it becomes Euclidean, this is because it allows itself to be oriented by the system. (...) And yet someone like Piaget ignores this absolutely, has totally converted his perception into a cultural-Euclidean perception. *What right have I therefore to call immediate this original that can be forgotten to such an extent?*" (VI 212-3). To understand why the status of Merleau-Ponty's indirect ontology depends on the answer given to this question (§ II-III), and why without that answer and that question one is bound to miss its 'subject' (§ IV-VI), let us first try to restore some context to this quote by showing how the project of a vertical history ties in with what this *Working Note* called "the problem of the 'return to the immediate'".

As we have just seen, vertical history wants to avoid both "a flattening of history into 'my' philosophy" and the contrary, which Merleau-Ponty calls "idolatry" (VI 198). Philosophy would not have a history, if we were not situated in it, and if there would not be for us at least the problem of the possible distinction between "*our* problems" and those of other philosophies belonging to that same history (VI 186). If to neglect that distinction would mean that we risk either letting ourselves be absorbed by them or them by us (cf. VI 159), it seems equally true that to pose it as absolute would mean to break up that history into as many histories as there were philosophies, and thus to turn it into no history at all. Hence Merleau-Ponty's attempt to avoid what he calls 'relativism' (e.g. VI 186) and to show that philosophies cannot be reduced "to one unique plane", nor be dispersed into absolutely different planes, since between them there would be "a perceptual relation or a relation of transcendence" (*ibid.*). That these two relations are equated perhaps should come as no surprise once we recall that perception here, far from being "a simple sensorial function that would explain the others", is a function "interrogated in order to know how it opens us to what is not ourselves", and hence presented as "the archetype of the originary encounter, imitated and renewed" in every other encounter (VI 158-9). For example, our encounter with the past would not be what it is, an *encounter*, if our perception of the past did not involve a moment of transcendence: we do not *relate* to a past if in the act of recalling it we would "really become again" what we were, and it is not a *past* to which we relate if memory would only be "the former present preserved" (VI 122). To be related to a past means instead to be separated from it by a gap (*écart*) which opens us to the past *itself* and, in a sense, "enters its definition", since what such relation will give us is not the past "such as it was in its own time", but "the past such as it was one day *plus* an inexplicable alteration", "a strange distance" (VI 124) which is but the flip-side of that "mysterious tie" (*attache*) (VI 113/152) which turns us into the perceiving beings we are. A distance, then, which does not stand in the way of us perceiving the past, but opens us unto it, by preventing us from becoming it. And a *strange* distance indeed, since in making us span it without nullifying it, it turns out to be what we also call proximity, i.e. *être au monde*, that is being 'of the world' (*j'en suis*), without being it (VI 127/169).

Without this "proximity through distance", without this "divergence" which is a "coinciding from afar" and "something like a good error" (VI 125), there would perhaps not be errors at all, since there would be no history, no past, no things to be perceived and no questions to be asked. If we were "cut off from being" and had distance without proximity, "we would not even have enough of the positive to raise a question", whereas proximity without distance would imply total coincidence where, "already caught up in Being", we would also find ourselves "already beyond every question" (VI 120). But if we find ourselves always already "tied to" or "attached to" Being, how comes it that at times we are prone to forget "the umbilical cord" that "binds" us to it, and act as if we could leave behind "the inalienable horizon with which [we] are already and henceforth circumvented" (VI 107)? And if we find ourselves forever marked by "the pre-possession of a totality which is there before one knows how and why" and which "fulfills a secret expectation within us, since we believe in it tirelessly", how comes it that at times we get tired and seem to have lost that faith (VI 42)? How can we "*forget* this non-knowing of the beginning which is not nothing" (VI 49) and act as if we are on the side of Nothingness and Being is on the other side?

How can we lose familiarity with what had already familiarized itself with us before we could even think of familiarizing ourselves with it? How can we hope to take over and fully possess what had long since possessed us (VI 134)? In short, how can there be bad errors, if it is true that we are constituted by a good one? Whence, for example, this desire to "break" our attachment and to consider language, society, history or, for that matter, philosophy as if one "had never been caught up in it" (PW 15)? Why would one "like to be without a point of view" (*ibid.*), if for us there is only vision precisely thanks to such a point of view, and if it is true that giving it up would not make ideas, for example, "better known" to us, since they would have become "inaccessible" (VI 150)?

What these questions point to is a certain unclarity about the status of the indirect ontology set forth in *The Visible and the Invisible*. It should be clear that unless we understand how that 'good error' could still lead us to bad ones (e.g. to the series of bad ontologies Merleau-Ponty dissects in the body of his text: the philosophies of reflexion, of negativity, of coincidence, of soaring over...), and unless we understand how in their turn these bad errors did not apparently exclude at least one ontologist from piercing through them and attempting to "return to the immediate", we understand nothing at all. And, as I already pointed out, Merleau-Ponty is certainly not unaware of this difficulty – which may not be the same as to say that he mastered it. But at least we have the question and since that question was forced on him precisely by what he took to be an attempt to cut through our "tie" (*attache*) and to impose a perspectival vision on us which would no longer be a human vision but the pale "knowledge that a god who does not get caught in finitude could obtain *about* human vision" (PW 150/207, transl. corr.), it is time perhaps to take up that question in our turn and let its true weight be forced on us.

Perception, remember, was to give us the 'archetype' of every encounter, but now it appears that at least in the case of the Renaissance there has been an "informing of perception by culture" (VI 212) where, as Merleau-Ponty tells us, "the perceived world has disappeared" (S 49) and with it "the idea of transcendence, that is, of a world seen within inherence in this world, by virtue of it", and hence also the idea "of an intra-ontology, of a Being encompassing-encompassed, of a *vertical*, dimensional Being, dimensionality" (VI 227). Instead of "things disputing for my glance" and I being "anchored in one of them" feeling myself at the same time drawn toward the others, instead of this "world of teeming, exclusive things which could be taken in only by means of a temporal cycle in which each gain was at the same time a loss", I have become the proud possessor of an "ordered perspective" where "objects in the foreground lose something of their aggressiveness, order their interior lines according to the common law of the spectacle, and already prepare themselves to become backgrounds as soon as it is necessary" (S 49-50). But this gain too has its losses, and as I start to adopt that 'pure gaze' (VI 107), and stop looking at what is visible from within itself (VI 113), I seem to lose my visibility myself, and by the time that I have 'unlearned' that "secret linkage" (*attache*) of sensible Being, its incompatible and simultaneous sides, and with it, that of time (S 15/22), I have turned into a "spectator without secrets" (VI 111) who no longer seems to be capable of experience since he is above it.

By placing us in the position of a kosmotheoros who remains without "ties" and looks at the world from without (VI 227), the Renaissance for Merleau-Ponty is not simply in danger of impoverishing our experience, but of annihilating its structure. Turning vision into "the intellectual possession" of what is seen, one is reducing the world to a thought of the world, and inverting the order between the *percipere* and the *percipi*. One forgets that our vision is dependent on "a visibility older than [us]" (VI 123), and that sensing in general is not a matter of possession of what is 'felt', but first "a dispossession of ourselves in favour of it, an opening toward that which we do not have to think in order that we may recognize it" (TLC 130). If it is thus true, as Merleau-Ponty believes, that, to put it paradoxically, the Renaissance perspective dispossesses us of that first dispossession, one can understand why he wanted to find out "how one can *return* from this perception fashioned by culture to the 'brute' or 'wild' perception" which was in-formed and covered over by it (VI 252). And one can perhaps begin to feel the enormity of the question which he suggested should come first: "what right have I to call immediate [an] original that can be forgotten to such an extent?" (VI 213). But to what extent exactly? What kind of forgetting is implied here? Before we rush on to his answer, and risk missing the question which, as I announced, is *the* question 'of' indirect ontology, let us speculate.

II. THE INDIRECTEDNESS OF INDIRECT ONTOLOGY

Suppose we take this forgetting to be not a 'paradox of Being', but of 'man'. We could then try to relocate what was announced here as 'indirect ontology', within the framework of *Being and Time* which, as is well known, tried to approach the question of Being indirectly by focussing first on "that entity which already comports itself, in its Being, towards what we are asking about when we ask the question of Being as such" (BT, end of § 4). But, and this is where the eventual parallel might prove to become instructive, since *Dasein* has a tendency to understand its own Being "in terms of that entity towards which it comports itself constantly and proximally – that is, in terms of the 'world' " (BT § 5), we cannot simply rely on this pre-ontological interpretation of its own Being. If the question of Being has to be called back out of its forgetfulness, then that being which is to be interrogated first will itself have to be called back out of its self-forgetfulness and will have to be brought into a condition where it understands its Being in its own terms. And it will have to be shown that such a 'proper' (*eigentlich*) condition is possible, which is why *Being and Time* will have to claim for example that "*only in so far as* Dasein has been disclosed (*erschlossen*) has it also been closed off (*verschlossen*)" (BT 265/222) or that, "temporality (...), no matter how much it may get covered up (*Verdeckung*), has not been *completely* closed off" (BT 478/425). As long as closure and covered-upness are still thought within the horizon of an *in this sense* ontologically more primordial disclosure or uncoveredness, as long as untruth remains dependent, even in its 'equiprimordiality', on truth, there can be no question of relating the forgetting of Being to Being withdrawing itself. The forgetting will not be a paradox of Being, but of "man". With the result perhaps that "man's" facticity might not come to be thought in the proper way. For as we know from *Being and Time*, it will prove to be difficult not to let the distinction between Dasein's 'Eigentlichkeit' and its 'Uneigentlichkeit' be colonized by just the kind of problematic Heidegger had tried to destruct. Before we know it, we may have placed dispersion (*Zerstreuung*) on the side of the improper ('inauthentic'), and thus reduced spatiality to temporality or to a certain temporality that would still allow for a 'possibilization' and a 'totalization' of existence, and in its wake we may have reawakened the 'spirits' of a subjectivity we had hoped to overcome[3]. Before we know it, we may find ourselves trapped into seeing in ambiguity (*Zweideutigkeit*) both the sign of a crisis and the crisis of the sign, and having granted this much to Husserl, we should not be surprised to find ourselves further involved in an attempt to ground language (*Sprache*) in *Rede*, as we are drawn into a discourse on responsibility that will have difficulties avoiding a philosophy of the will, itself linked to a notion of *forgetting* which is considered to be "a short-coming, rather than a defeat"[4] and hence can and must be overcome.

So much for the costs. I know that each of these remarks would call for a long and painstaking analysis of *Being and Time*, but as we were only interested in taking the formal matrix of its indirect ontology as a possible model for the 'endo-ontology' of *The Visible and the Invisible*, I think that

---

3. See above, chapter 1.
4. J. DERRIDA, 'Introduction', in E. HUSSERL, *L'origine de la géométrie*, Paris, P.U.F., 1974, p. 98.

even the vaguest awareness of these costs (which are, after all, well-documented in the Heidegger-literature) will suffice to help us realize what risks we are taking here. But there is perhaps no other way to the benefits, and since nothing I have said should be taken for an argument against the distinction between the 'proper' and the 'improper' *as such*, we had better wait for confirmation of the parallel to see if some of these costs could be avoided. 'In-der-Welt-sein' and 'être au monde' might not be the same after all.

First, let us take a look at Merleau-Ponty's answer. It will turn out to be vague enough to necessitate further speculation. *"The key*, he tells us, *is in this idea that perception qua wild perception is of itself* (de soi) *ignorance of itself* (ignorance de soi), *imperception*, tends of itself to see itself as an *act* and to forget itself as latent intentionality, as being at (*être à*) –" (VI 213/267, I have kept Merleau-Ponty's italics). 'Being at', that is, the 'true' ontological structure of us, perceptual beings, is forgotten. Better still: it forgets *itself*, since Merleau-Ponty is equating 'wild perception' with 'imperception' and since, as we have seen, the structure of wild perception is precisely to *be* opened to what is not it (VI 159), that is: to be *at*. But then what way shall we turn this key? What right does it give us "to call immediate an original" that, as it appears now, not only "can be forgotten", but, as it were, enstages this forgetting or helps it, since 'of itself' it forgets *itself*? "With life, natural perception (with the savage mind)", Merleau-Ponty writes, "is perpetually given to us the wherewithal to put the universe of immanence in its place (*mettre en place*)" (VI 213/266, transl. corrected). But what can be this 'place', if the "key" to the fact that "this universe tends *of itself* to become autonomous, [and] realizes of itself a repression of transcendence", is to be sought in perception's being "*of itself* ignorance of itself" (*ibid.*)? If "with sense experience (*le sentir*)" and "with the phenomenal" the "perceptual in the sense of the non-projective, vertical world" is always given, but prone to forget itself, how can we then still call on "the silent transcendence" (*ibid.*) of a world that "upright before my upright body" (S 20) "surrounds" us (VI 271), and in this sense is vertical and not immanent, since we are opened onto it? How can we call on that transcendence, the moment the world becomes flattened and loses its depth, as Merleau-Ponty thinks was happening with the Euclidean perception at work in Renaissance perspective? Should we, and can we, undo what in perception leads to imperception and to a forgetting of this 'openness' and to the subsequent loss of the experience of transcendence? Is this loss and this forgetting an 'improper' modality of our perceptual being, and if so, can it and how can it be modified into a proper mode?

Before we fully draw out the suggested parallel, let us be sure that we know the stakes. There would, then, be a self-forgetting of perception which backs up the "repression of transcendence" in the "universe of immanence" (VI 213). The reference here is, of course, to the philosophy of reflexion which, as the main text of *The Visible and the Invisible* made sufficiently clear, made the mistake (?) of "closing thought too much in upon itself" (VI 89) and of not seeing that its movement of re-flection itself presupposed an "outside" to this immanence, i.e. something, some level, some dimension upon which it was bending back. An outside, that is, to which this movement itself belonged or into which it was inscribed, and hence not a radical exteriority, but a "fold or hollow of Being having by principle an outside" (VI 227). We will come back to this "fold", but for the moment it should suffice to recall that Merleau-Ponty is making recourse here to this expression in order to avoid the distance between "us" and Being becoming either too great or too small. A vision which puts us outside the world or which makes us coincide with it would not be a human vision, which implies "a world seen within inherence in this world, by virtue of it" (*ibid.*). Too much exteriority will lead to a "world" absorbing us; too much interiority will let us absorb the "world". And if the mediation "between" exteriority and interiority would not be original, but solely a mediation between two already existing poles, we would simply correct the mistake of idealism by going to its other extreme: instead of closing thought too much upon itself, we would have rendered it "too much outside of itself" (VI 89). The "absolutely open" of the philosophy of negativity is without that distance which is not contrary to proximity, and which we need to prevent our "openness upon being" from going to the other extreme by becoming an "illusion" instead of an "a priori" (VI 85). Which is why our "implication in Being" rests on more than the inexplicable folly (VI 215) of a For Itself which is haunted by an imaginary In-Itself-for-Itself (VI 85) or why the *En-soi-pour-soi* must be "more than imaginary" (*ibid.*) since it precedes its poles and is not just the result of an empty nothingness which fills itself. Once one substitutes the idea of "vertical and polymorphous Being" for the "Being without restriction" implied by the "total openness" of the philosophy of negativity (S 20), what one gets is an endo-ontology, "an ontology from within" (VI 237) where it is no longer "always I who forms depth, who hollows it out, who does everything, and who closes from within my prison in upon myself" (*ibid.*). Transcendence will not have to be constructed, since it is first, which means that that divergence (*écart*) which gives me proximity and with it transcendence, should not be seen as "a no I affect myself with, a lack which I constitute as a lack by the upsurge of an end which I give myself" but as "a natural negativity, a first institution, *always already there*" (VI 216).

It may appear that we have gotten sidetracked, but in fact we are right on the mark. For we were trying to understand how perception could of itself – *de soi* – come to ignore itself as "savage perception", "latent intentionality" and "being at". And we were almost convinced that, no matter what the costs, there was a parallel to be drawn here with the way Dasein, through facticity and fallenness, loses itself to its "world" and becomes seduced by the "ontological reflection of its understanding of the world upon its self-interpretation" (*ontologische Rückstrahlung des Weltverständnisses auf die Daseinsauslegung*, BT 37/16) to interpret itself in terms of that world ('*Reluzenz*', BT 42/21). We know from *Being and Time* what the result of this self-forgetting of Dasein would be: it would fall "prey to [a] tradition", which "keeps it from providing its own (*eigen*, i.e. 'proper') guidance" (*ibid.*), and leads to concealment (*Verdeckung*). But in Heidegger this loss of *Dasein* to the world is what overcomes it 'proximally and for the most part' (*zunächst und zumeist*), which means that the possibility for, as it were, a 'second' and 'rarer' overcoming of that self-loss is left open. For, as one will remember, "to be closed off (*Verschlossenheit*) and to be covered up (*Verdecktheit*) belong to Dasein's facticity" (BT 265/222), which is Heidegger's expression for the fact that "Dasein as my Dasein and this Dasein is already in a definite world and alongside a definite range of definite entities within the world" (BT 264/221). It is this *je schon* (in each case already) which explains how "falling (*das Verfallen*) belongs to Dasein's state of Being" (*ibid.*): since it is always already busy, Dasein will only in a 'second movement' as it were, be able to fold back upon itself and discover its 'proper' ontological status, and with it, the meaning of its 'own' guidance. In other words, it seems that for Heidegger, the 'essential facticity' of Dasein's disclosedness (*Erschlossenheit*), the 'always already' (*je schon*) of its thrownness, will allow 'falling', which constitutes a separate moment of Dasein's structure of Being, to exert itself 'proximally and for the most part'. Falling then can existential-ontologically be seen as a *structural tendency* which may be curbed: the existential possibility of 'Eigentlichkeit' as proper disclosedness, that is, 'truth of existence' rests on seeing it that way (rather than as a 'structure')[5]. Which is why, when Heidegger states that "only in so far as Dasein has been disclosed (*erschlossen*) has it also been closed off (*verschlossen*)" (BT 265/222), he may not be pointing to a forgetting which would be similar to the one which makes perception of itself (*de soi*) become imperception (and hence lets our perceptual being 'mis'understand itself as an act rather than as being at). For the difference lies precisely in the meaning given to the 'of itself' (*de soi*). Dasein is not 'of itself' ignorance of itself, or at least not in the same way as perception is: "in so far as entities

5. Cf. chapter 1.

within-the-world have always already (*je schon*) been uncovered along with Dasein, have such entities (...) been covered up (hidden) or disguised. It is *therefore* essential that Dasein should *explicitly appropriate* what has already (*schon*) been uncovered, defend it *against* semblance and disguise, and assure itself of its uncoveredness again and again" (*ibid.*, transl. corrected). Heidegger is operating here with a series of oppositions between 'ausdrücklich' (explicit) and 'unausdrücklich' (implicit), proper and improper, appropriation and loss, which should be placed in the ethico-political context of his "das Man nimmt dem jeweiligen Dasein die Verantwortlichkeit ab" (BT 165/127: "the 'they' deprives Dasein of its answer-ability"). Responsibility, own guidance and truth are carefully and almost inextricably stiched together and clearly point to his conviction that if Dasein is 'proximally and for the most part' ignorant of itself, this is not due to Dasein itself (*de soi*), but to the fact that it has *not yet* recovered its Self, by being *still* absorbed in the "they" and dominated by the way things are publicly interpreted (BT 264/222). It is Dasein's improper self, its 'They-self', its anonymity which lets it forget itself. Dasein's proper self will, then, make the 'They' collapse ("*das Man sinkt in sich zusammen*" (BT 317/273)) and rob them, time and again, of their intoxicating power to make us forget. And, as is well known, this is what the diverse phenomenological reductions in *Being and Time* should help Dasein to accomplish. Although these reductions are not 'willed' by Dasein, but overcome it and take it by surprise (e.g. anxiety)[6], Heidegger never suggests, as Merleau-Ponty does, that their success lies in their failure, or that "the incompleteness of the reduction [...] is the reduction itself" (VI 178)[7]. And as we shall see in a moment, this does make an enormous difference. At stake will be a different subject. A subject defined through a divergence (*écart*) which does not result from self-affection, but rather seems to be something 'always already there', a 'first institution' (VI 216). Although we cannot exclude that this subject will still have to be thought within the horizon of the proper/improper-distinction, we can wager that what will make the proper diverge from the improper cannot be that intimate a fission as the one Heidegger introduces when he lets the voice of conscience, by which Dasein affects itself, call it back from its lostness in the 'they'.

---

6. Cf. R. BERNET, 'Phenomenological Reduction and the Double Life of the Subject', in Th. KISIEL - J. VAN BUREN (eds.), *Reading Heidegger from the Start. Essays in his Earliest Thought*, Albany, SUNY, 1994, pp. 263, 265.

7. This does not contradict the suggestion with which we ended chapter 1 – for what is claimed there, is the result of reading *Being and Time* against the grain.

III. REDUCTIONS

It should be admitted: we have been speculating. But perhaps not without a foot on the ground. For we are still trying to understand what Merleau-Ponty may have meant with 'the return to the immediate'. And as it should be clear that the meaning of 'the immediate' might not be without connection to the meaning of the notion of forgetting which he proposed as a "key" to the solution of "*the problem* of the 'return to the immediate'" (VI 212), we may not yet be adrift altogether. Indeed, we may be right on course, since if this forgetting would only be an improper mode, rather than 'original' (whatever that may mean – we will have to consider it as a second possibility), if it would not involve "a paradox of Being" (VI 122/162) but solely of man, it would become all the more difficult to understand why *The Visible and the Invisible* tells us in one and the same breath that our attempt to return to it is "in vain" (VI 107), whereas the immediate itself is nonetheless "at the horizon" (VI 123). If "it must be thought as such (*à ce titre*)" and if it is "only by remaining at a distance that it remains itself" (*ibid.*) by what strange trickery then do I still find "'in myself', the reference to this originary presence" (VI 65)? How is it that I find myself referred to an origin, if it is that it "has broken up" (VI 124)? And how can that which has broken up be still at the horizon and, from afar, by keeping at that distance of a past which perhaps is older than all my presents, still call upon me to return? In vain, as we are told? How 'immediate' is this 'archetypal encounter' we call 'perception' if it not only opens us up to what is not us, but also is going to draw us into "a movement toward what could not in any event be present to us in the original and whose irremediable absence would thus count among our *originary* experiences" (VI 159)[8]. A paradox of Being, or a paradox of man? It is time to check our speculative mood with some solid work on the text.

The reduction first. For if Merleau-Ponty wants to criticize Renaissance perspective for implying the kosmotheoric vision of 'a spectator without secrets' (VI 111), there must be something in the 'life' of us, perceptual beings, to which he can point in order to reveal to us maybe not *what* our secrets are, but *that* we have them, and *that* we cannot or should not (the proper is always close to the authentic) try to be without them. But there must also be some way to help us understand how notwithstanding the former, we could still end up interpreting ourselves in terms of an ontology which leaves us without secrets. So once more, we will have to understand what it could mean that "perception *of itself* is ignorance of itself" and as we try to read this as a paradox of Being, rather than as a shortcoming of man,

8. See above, chapter 4 n16 for my translation of *originaire* as 'originary'.

we may want to remember that at least in *some* sense this ignorance may have to be read as an improper ontology (or at least seems to have been read as such by Merleau-Ponty). Could it be perhaps that there is more than one ignorance, and more than one forgetting at stake here?

Perceptual being, too, is lost to the world. It does not see "what makes it see" (VI 248). But if it thinks of itself as an "act" and thus "ignores" or "forgets" itself, this is not because it was "first empty" and "only afterward" opened itself to get filled by things which were already there and now overflow it to the point of self-oblivion (VI 131). Its loss to the world is more dramatic, since it is "more" original. Not only can it not be thought of in terms of a *pour soi* inexplicably allowing itself to be caught up by an *en soi*, it is perhaps not even correctly understood if seen as an "improper" (*uneigentlich*) result of a synergy between two moments in its ontological structure. For if its relation to the world is not to be seen as an "openness of nothingness upon being, but as openness simply" (VI 99), that openness in its turn may not allow for a distinction between the openness qua structure and the "always already" of a thrownness which gives it its facticity. To speak of "a compound of the world and ourselves" that precedes its components (VI 102) seems to call for an entirely different register than that of thrownness: "this perceived that we call my body applying itself to the rest of the perceived, i.e. treating itself as a perceived by itself and hence as a perceiving, all this is finally possible and means something only because *there is* Being, not Being in itself, identical to itself, in the night, but the Being that also contains its negation, its *percipi*" (VI 250-1). Or again: "it is by [a Being that is *eminently percipi*] that we can understand the *percipere*" (*ibid.*).

But if "what if first is Being" (*ibid.*), and if there is "no anteriority, but simultaneity and even delay" from the *percipere* to the *percipi* (VI 123), we should not look for a key to "the ignorance of perception by itself" in the self of the *percipere*, but in its delay vis-à-vis the *percipi*. Perhaps this self will not so much find itself thrown into "something", as that it will have to arise from "something". And perhaps the forgetting of this self by itself echoes an older forgetting: "if Being is hidden, this is itself a characteristic of Being (*un trait de l'Etre*), and no disclosure will make us comprehend it" (VI 122). But what does it mean that Being is hidden? And if there is this "delay", this "original" retardation of the *percipere* to the *percipi*, will it then not have to force itself upon us as we are trying to phenomenologically reduce perception?

It already has. For if perception is ignorance of itself *by itself*, this is not due to the fact that it lost itself "to" the world or that it is always already so engaged in it that it tends to understand itself in terms of what reflects back from the world upon it. It is due to the fact that it belongs to it. "By itself" means that perception, in order to be what it is, must be part of the world: it is because my body can *be* seen (*percipi*) that it can see (*percipere*) and not vice versa. If it wouldn't be "of" the world, if there wouldn't be this "coiling over of the visible upon the seeing body, of the tangible upon the touching body" "which makes a vibration of my skin become the sleek and the rough, makes me follow with my eyes the movements and contours of things" (VI 146), there would be nothing for me to be seen or to be touched, but only a "thought of" a vision, of a touching. The universe of immanence, again. But once more: if what disturbs this immanence and has always already disturbed it, is that "fission", that "decompression", that "de-flagration", that "explosion" of Being, which does not lead to "a chaos", since it is the weaving of a texture that "returns to itself and conforms to itself" (*ibid.*), how then could my vision forget that it belongs to "a fold, a central cavity of the visible" (*ibid.*)? How could it come to think of itself as "having the world before it through representation", while it is inversely the things of the world that give birth to *it* "by a sort of concentration or coming to itself of the visible" (PrP 181)?

But these are the terms of the delay! For a vision not to be "a being that is wholly knowing", for it not to be able to "soar over objects", but to see them from in their midst, it has to have its "own inertia, its ties (*attaches*)" (VI 147/193). Without such "ties" there could be no perception, no "sensing". But with them, perception can no longer be understood in terms of a "thought of" the perceived. As the perceiving and the perceived intertwine, "one gets a wholly new idea of subjectivity: there are no longer 'syntheses', [but] a contact with being through its modulations, or its reliefs" (VI 269), one of which "I" am. For indeed, what used to be referred to as "the subject" now becomes, as we will see in more detail later, a "fold" or a "relief" of Being. Which implies at least that it is destituted of that "thought" that was defined as an "invisible contact of self with self" (VI 234). Henceforth it will have to live "outside of this intimacy with oneself" and, as it is no longer "I who makes myself think" (VI 221), "thought" becomes "eccentric" – instead of being "in us" it will happen "in front of us" (VI 234). Instead of pointing to a "thought of the world" in full possession of its self, perception will have its "punctum caecum" (*ibid.*), will "of itself" be imperception, since it won't be able "to see what makes it see", "its tie to Being, its corporeity" (VI 248).

Of course, this does not mean that we will remain unable to see our own bodies. For we see them all the time. But that hand that is holding this pen, although in front of my eyes, is not yet "conspicuous" as what it is. I see it, but as background and not as figure, and it will take an "interruption" imposed on its normal functioning to let it appear as such. But if I hammer on my finger, or awake after having slept on my arm, and am now strangely made aware of it by that curious tingling sensation with which it awakens a bit later than myself, even then the strangeness of what I touch there, that object "X" which seems to have wanted to separate itself from me, and which now I find lying like some alien creature in my bed, is only pointing to a separation, a strangeness and a delay that I have carried with me all along. To understand "reflexivity through the body" (VI 246), through that strange inability by which "I do not entirely succeed in touching myself touching, in seeing myself seeing" (VI 249), is to realize that if "the experience I have of myself perceiving does not go beyond a sort of immanence" (*ibid.*), this is due to the fact that "I" as perceiving subject am not "a *nichtiges Nichts*, but a 'lake of non-being', a certain nothingness sunken into a local and temporal *openness* – vision and feeling *in fact*, and not thought of seeing and of feeling" (VI 201).

It is this facticity of "sensing", this "chiasm" of my relation with being which is "simultaneously a taking and a being taken" (VI 266), that produces the "identity of the retiring into oneself with the leaving of oneself" (VI 124), prevents reflection from becoming "identification" and deflects its result to a "non-difference with oneself" (VI 204). Here too, in this "contact of self with self" there is only proximity because there is distance (VI 255). Here too, without that "fundamental divergence" and that "constitutive dissonance" of an original delay (VI 234), there would not be the "openness to oneself" necessary for "touching oneself, seeing oneself" (VI 249). Without that hymen between the hand that touches and the one that is touched, without that *je ne sais quoi* which makes us "miss" ourselves while "reaching for" ourselves, what we apprehend would be "an ob-ject" and what apprehends would not have to be characterized as "being at", but as an "act" (*ibid.*).

And yet we know that that is precisely how it characterizes itself: as if by some inborn eagerness or haste, consciousness has already put itself at the far end of what we have just learned to be only imminent: "It is inevitable", the *Working Notes* tell us, that "consciousness be mystified, inverted, indirect, in principle it sees things from the other end; in principle it disregards Being and prefers the object to it [...] In it it ignores the non-dissimulation of Being, the *Unverborgenheit* [...] which is not something positive, but a far-off" (VI 248). But why would consciousness be that principle which neglects "for reasons of principle" (*ibid.*) its own principle – that from which it originates, the "pre-reflective zone of the openness upon Being" (VI 52) presupposed in all reflection? We are told that there is "something in us more ourselves than the *cogito*" (VI 69), and that the Self returned to in the *cogito* is still "preceded by an alienated Self or a Self in ec-stasy in Being" (VI 51). But the more we are prepared to admit that it is this ec-stasy which puts consciousness "in front of us", the stranger it becomes that consciousness thinks of itself as being "in us" (VI 234). Why would it deny that it is "not without bonds", but "*invested* in a site which it rejoins by its environs" (VI 222)? If it is true that we cannot say that "it is here", but that we must say that "it is *not there*", why then does it pretend to be everywhere, and to be without that "quasi-locality" that prevents it from closing in upon itself (*ibid.*)? Now that we know of that "*indivision* of being and nothingness" which is but another word for its basic "spatiality" (VI 216) and for "the passivity of its activity" (VI 221), its tendency to repress the transcendence of the world in which it "pushes forth" its "roots" (VI 216) and to install itself in a "universe of immanence" (VI 213) becomes all the more intriguing. For instead of regarding it as just wrong, and hence to be modified by a more proper view, we have learned, but not understood, that it must be a "bad" error the possibility of which is inscribed in the "good error", if not necessitated by it: "it is inevitable that consciousness be mystified..." (VI 248).

But perhaps we have not taken this "error" seriously enough. Perhaps it is not an "error" at all. How can it be, if it is inevitable? Clearly our difficulties themselves result from the fact that, not unlike consciousness, we have been seduced into placing ourselves at the far end of what is only imminent. For we too have looked at this inevitable mystification of consciousness "from the other end" (*ibid.*). Instead of letting the reduction "little by little disclose [...] the wild or vertical world" (VI 177), we have impatiently installed ourselves at the point where it was to arrive, and then could only wonder what took it so long to get where we already were. While we were looking for a "paradox of Being, rather than of man", we were in fact still confronting consciousness or perception with the fact that somehow they had lost the "knowledge" of their true condition. It is time, then, to give up our own kosmotheoric position and to think that "mystification" from within.

IV. FOLDING THE SUBJECT

If "there is *Unwahr* in the *Wahrheit*", as the *Working Notes* repeatedly suggest (e.g. VI 181), perception cannot be simply opposed to imperception. Somehow, they must hang together. And that they do hang together is precisely what is suggested by the book's title which does not read "The Visible *or* the Invisible", but "The Visible *and* the Invisible". "It must not be imagined, Merleau-Ponty notes, that I add to the visible perfectly defined as in Itself a non-visible (which would only be objective absence) (that is, objective presence *elsewhere*, in an *elsewhere* in itself)" (VI 247). The visible and the invisible do not contradict one another, but belong together: "one says invisible as one says immobile – not in reference to something foreign to movement, but to something which stays still" (S21). If the invisible is not an "*être en soi*", but "the degree zero *of visibility*", "the opening of a *dimension of* the visible" (*ibid.*), it must be there "without being an object" (VI 229). As a nothingness *already* in being, it implies that "being (in the Sartrean sense) [...] is not only *what it is*" (VI 181). As "pure transcendence" (VI 229), it is that "decompression that occurs in being" and which allows for "a relation to being" "formed within being" (VI 215). To think that one can localize it *in* the visible and make the invisible visible, is to immanentize it and repeat Sartre's mistake: "every effort to see it there (i.e. in the visible) makes it disappear" (*ibid.*). To restore to the invisible the sense of transcendence is to prevent consciousness from becoming total openness (as in the philosophy of negativity) or absolute closure (as in the universe of immanence). If the invisible is not an object, that which relates to the visible can no longer be a subject: "What I want to do is restore the world as a meaning of Being absolutely different from the 'represented'" (VI 253); "the to-be-conscious itself is to be conceived as transcendence, as to be surpassed by ..." (VI 196-7).

Somehow these quotes must hang together and at this point we already understand them well enough to know that it would be foolish to think that it is an ocularcentrism which does the trick (as some, whose haste betrays their lack of depth, have found it necessary to suggest). For what is said of the *invisible* holds for sensing in general and one could think along similar lines – in fact Merleau-Ponty does – of an untouchable which would not be "a touchable in fact inaccessible" but "*de jure*" inaccessible (e.g. VI 254). Here too the negative is a "true negative" and does not refer to "a positive that is elsewhere" (*ibid.*). What is absent here, is not present "elsewhere", "for someone else". It cannot be made present, since "it is *Verborgenheit* by principle" (VI 251), the "secret counterpart", the "virtual focus" of the visible or the touchable or the sensible in general (VI 245). And yet "its absence counts" (VI 228). It is not just "in-visible" or "not touchable", sheer "*Verborgenheit*". To say that it is a "secret counterpart" "behind" the visible or the touchable does not exclude but presupposes that it counts. Hence Merleau-Ponty's use of formulas such as "the *Nichturpräsentierbar* which is presented to me *as such* within the world" (VI 215). "*Urpräsentiert* as *Nichturpräsentierbar*", it remains "another dimension" (VI 228). Only as a "*true* negative" can it be more than merely absent, *Verborgen*, but possibly present elsewhere, at another time, for another seer. To say that its negativity counts is to say that what we have here is not *Verdeckung* but *entbergendes Bergen*, or with the words Merleau-Ponty himself chooses to borrow from the later Heidegger: an *Unverborgenheit* of the *Verborgenheit* "which consequently does not cease to be hidden" (VI 249 (quote), 254).

It is clear, of course, that it is a different Heidegger to whom we are referred here. "Truth" cannot be *equiprimordial* with "untruth", if there is to be *Unwahr* in the *Wahrheit*. To the contrary, untruth has to be "older" than truth. Whatever truth is, it can only be as it is (in the sense of *Wesen*) if it (or we as "subjects" of truth) respects this delay, without undoing it. And as this parallel with Heidegger's *On the Essence of Truth* suggests, perception's being "of itself" imperception, which was presented to us as the key to "the problem of the 'return to the immediate'", may not be imposing on us a search for means to prevent or stop this "self-forgetfulness" after all. Perhaps we should rather try to put ourselves in it anew, just as we should not try to *undo Seinsvergessenheit*, but *relate* to it in a non-metaphysical way[9]. Which could mean that we look for ways to respect that delay or that secret which makes the invisible more than a non-visible. "Returning to the immediate" would then take on the character of a "late arrival" on a scene already "broken up". And what we believed to be "in vain", would only thus be able to do its work. Perhaps here too the "success" would lie in the "failure" (VI 148,255) which somehow modifies what at first seemed a mere in-capacity into what Merleau-Ponty would call "a positive phenomenon", i.e., instead of the negation of a capacity otherwise available to us, it would become its *Wesen*.

But the question is how. How to repeat this 'modification problem' which we know from *Being and Time*, in the context of a work that, in its own indirect way[10], seems to have turned itself toward the very problematic one can find in the later Heidegger: "language has us and (...) it is not we who have language. (...) it is being that speaks within us and not we who speak of being" (VI 194). But the sentence which immediately follows – "but then how to understand subjectivity?" – seems to announce an unheideggerian turn: "the *Gestalt* holds the key to the problem of spirit (*esprit*); one should not look for spiritual things, there are only structures of the void (*vide*) – But I simply wish to plant this void in the visible Being" (VI 235/289); "the subject as a field, as a hierarchized system of structures opened

---

9. "kein Tilgen der Seinsvergessenheit, sondern das sichstellen in sie" (M. HEIDEGGER, 'Protokoll zu einem Seminar über den Vortrag 'Zeit und Sein'', in ID., *Zur Sache des Denkens*, Tübingen, Niemeyer, 1976, p. 32).

10. Cf. TLC 111-2: "If we call philosophy the quest of Being or of the *Ineinander*, is not philosophy quickly brought to silence – that very silence which from time to time breaks into Heidegger's essays? But does not this come from Heidegger's search for a *direct* expression of what is fundamental at the very moment he is showing its impossibility? Is it not the result of his refusal of all the *mirrors* of Being?". And cf. VI 179: "One cannot make a direct ontology. My 'indirect' method (being in the beings) is alone confirmed with being".

by an inaugural there is (*il y a*)" (VI 239/292); "the decisive step is to recognize [...] that the 'objects' of consciousness themselves are not something positive *in front* of us, but nuclei of signification around which transcendental life pivots, specific voids" (*ibid.*).

Should it surprise us that this "subject" became split (more radically split perhaps than in Heidegger)? "To be conscious (*avoir conscience*) = to have a figure on a ground – one cannot go back any further" (VI 191/245). But here he goes: "one perceives only figures upon levels. And one perceives them only by relation to the level, which therefore is unperceived. The perception of the level: always *between* the objects, it is that around which..." But "that around which" (*ce autour de quoi*) (VI 189/243) is repeatedly defined in the *Working Notes* as "the unconscious". "What is the unconscious? What functions as a *pivot*, an existential, and in this sense, is and is not perceived" (*ibid.*). This unconscious is not "at the bottom of ourselves", "behind our backs", but "in front of us, as articulations of our field" (VI 180). As "that through which objects are possible", it cannot itself be "an object". Since it is "before" representation, it is not "a representation in fact inaccessible" (VI 254). It is – like (?) the invisible, or the untouchable – "an original of the elsewhere" (*ibid.*). And as we read in a marginal note to *The Prose of the World* which we may perhaps situate in the same context: "this nonconstituted rationality of the thing-axis [...] has decentring as the ground of meaning" and calls for a "transtemporality which is not that of the ideal but that of the deepest wound, incurable" (PW 45). It is tempting of course to push Merleau-Ponty a bit here and to equate "the unconscious which functions as a pivot" with this "incurable wound", and to see in that object-wound the "specific void" around which transcendental life pivots. To do so would be to give a nice Lacanian twist[11] to Merleau-Ponty's criticism of Sartre that the *En-soi-pour-soi* is not imaginary (or that the *pour-soi* is not a void, but a specific void – VI 201-2,246). But it would be a twist all the same, and if one pushes, one should do it more gently. Let us see if we can be more discreet.

To see, we have just learned, would "always be to see more than one sees" (VI 247). "All perception is only perception of something by being also relative imperception of a horizon or background, which it implies but does not thematize" (TLC 4). In this sense, *The Visible and the Invisible* states that "perception *is* imperception" (VI 247), and even that "this means: perception *is* unconscious" (VI 189/243, transl. corr.). It is "of itself ignorance of itself" (VI

11. I am thinking here of Lacan's attempt in *The Ethics of Psychoanalysis* to "define the field of the subject insofar as it is not simply the field of the intersubjective subject, the subject subjected to the mediation of the signifier, but what is behind this subject" (*The Seminar of Jacques Lacan. Book VII (1959-60)*, London, Tavistock/Routledge, 1992, p. 103).

213) and "forgets itself as being at" (*ibid.*), because "it does not" – and cannot – "see what makes it see" (VI 248): the divergence (*écart*) in and through which it arises. It does not see (perceive) its own "element", which Merleau-Ponty calls "flesh" and by which he does not mean "matter" or "chaos" but that "third term between the 'subject' and the 'object'" (VI 197) which *is* "the distinction figure/background": *"c'est cet écart-là d'abord qui est le sens perceptif"* (VI 197/250). From this one can understand why according to this "wholly new conception of subjectivity" the "subject" should no longer be seen as an *Erschlossenheit* which may be *verschlossen*, but as a "closure" which is there before all opening. Or better still: to say that it is not a total openness, but a "determinate" one, is to think of it as a "relief" in being (e.g. VI 197) or as a "fold" (e.g. VI 146,264) which can only be what it is if one no longer thinks of it in terms of an opening which can be closed, or a closure which must lead to an opening. It is both at once: the effect of a primary differentiation which precedes its presence and constitutes for it an "original past"[12]. The "institution" of the "fold" belongs to a past which could never have been present for what is instituted there: "I am not (...) the author of that hollow that forms within me (...) it is not I who makes myself think any more than it is I who makes my heart beat" (VI 221). There is, then, a passivity which is not contrary to our activity, but presupposed by it. And it is to this "passivity of our activity" that Merleau-Ponty refers as "body of the spirit" (*ibid.*)[13].

Instead of a spiritualization of the body, what is involved here is a corporization of spirit, which is more than its mere reverse. *Geistige Leibhaftigkeit* is not *leibhaftige Geistigkeit*. What we have here is not a *mixtum compositum* nor a miraculous penetration or osmosis of the one by the other. The incarnation is original, and hence calls for a different miracle: "there is not a creation of a For itself by the body in itself, and there is not a descent into the body of a pre-established soul, it is that the vortex (*le tourbillon*) of the embryogenesis suddenly centres itself upon the interior hollow it was preparing – a certain fundamental divergence, a certain constitutive dissonance emerges" (VI 233-4). Yet, what makes this "mystery" (as the next sentence calls it) even more mysterious is that, as we have just seen, 'spirit' or 'thought' or 'consciousness' which is said to emerge in or through or by this divergence, will be affected by "a sort of blindness" (VI 225), a "blind spot" (VI 248) – it will not see the divergence that makes it see. But then how can it be more than such blindness? If it is "de soi ignorance

---

12. One can already find this idea of "a past which has never been (a) present", usually associated with Levinas or Derrida, in Merleau-Ponty's PP 242.

13. Henceforth I shall translate "corps de l'esprit" as "body of spirit" instead of the more cumbersome "body of *the* spirit".

de soi", how could there ever be a 'soi'? How could there be "a presence to self that is absence of self", "a contact with Self through the divergence with regard to Self" (VI 192/246, transl. corrected!)? What divergence? And what Self? For it is not clear whether the "fold" or the "relief" which we thoughtlessly called a "subject", implies a self. Certainly not a personal one: "I do not perceive any more than I speak – Perception has me as has language" (VI 190); "things have us and it is not we who have the things [...] But then how to understand subjectivity?" (VI 194); "*I* must be there in order to perceive – But in what sense? As *one* (*on*)" (VI 190/244). There is an "anonymous in me that sees" (VI 99), it is not I (*moi*) who sees, but an anonymous visibility which inhabits me (VI 142/187).

Seeing turns out to be a matter of "ce qui se voit en nous" (VI 208/261). "We" (?) seem to be the occupants of a 'fold' which we did not institute (VI 216), and which can unfold without us unfolding it: forgetting, Merleau-Ponty tells us, is a a "disarticulation which makes there be no longer a divergence, a relief". "C'est cela le noir de l'oubli" (VI (197)250). But if we wish to "understand that the 'to be conscious' = to have a figure on a ground" (*ibid*.), perhaps "what is it that, from my side, comes to animate the perceived world?" (VI 190) may not be the best question to ask. Rather than looking for *what* is at my side and risking relapse into the dualism we try to overcome, we should ask what could 'awaken' (VI 204) the divergence that it is to this consciousness which 'of itself' forgets that it is a figure on a ground. For it evidently cannot step outside the figure/ground relationship and watch it from a distance. Nor could it be a solution to point to those experiences where instead of consiousness itself acquiring such distance, this distance is forced upon it, as happens in forgetting or loss of interest, both of which seem to involve a "dedifferentiation" of the figure/ground relationship (cf. VI 197). For as the figure will disappear into the ground, consciousness will lose the differentiation on which we were told it rests and will itself disappear into 'the night of forgetting' (*ibid*.). And we evidently cannot escape the difficulty at hand by arguing that there must remain some 'X' to register the trace of such disappearance, for that would be to put consciousness before consciousness and to viciously dissolve the questions that should truly bother us here: how can consciousness ever be awake, conscious – if by that we mean, as Merleau-Ponty seems to, more than 'what thinks itself in us'? How can there be thought, if I am not "the author" of it (VI 221)? How can there be more than an anonymous "one": "a contact with self through divergence" (VI 192)?

One could, of course, think of these questions as trivially belated. For did we not already mention that 'quasi-reflection' of the touching and the touched which, to be sure, would not result in an "identification with oneself" as 'thought of seeing or of feeling' but in "non-difference with oneself" (VI 204), which is what Merleau-Ponty means by 'contact of self with self' (VI 255)? But it seems that, for such contact to be a contact *of self with self*, i.e. to be personal, something else is already presupposed. A separation which does not precede (as in Levinas) the advent of the 'Other', but results from it. For it is the other who will present to me "what I will never be present to" (VI 82).

To fully grasp this point, one should resist the temptation to simply link this 'Nichturpräsentierbarkeit' to the alterity of the Other himself. For, as will soon become apparent, to do so would be to impoverish the analysis one finds in *The Visible and the Invisible* and to fatally miss some of its more subtler points, such as the one hinted at in the following *Working Note*: "[...] the untouchable. That of the other which I will never touch. But what I will never touch, he does not touch either, no privilege of oneself over the other here, it is therefore not consciousness that is the untouchable [...]" (VI 254). But if this is the case, we evidently can no longer assume – as Merleau-Ponty in an earlier *Working Note* still did – that "the decisive step" would be "to recognize [...] that consciousness itself is an *Urpräsentierbar* for itself which is presented as *Nichturpräsentierbar* for the other" (VI 239) – for that would imply exactly the kind of "privilege of oneself over the other" that we were just told to avoid. And as we have just witnessed this new notion of the 'untouchable' being capable of opening a rift in the body of *The Visible and the Invisible*, it is clear that if we now may feel tempted to push Merleau-Ponty into the "wholly new notion of subjectivity" (VI 269) he announces in one of the following *Working Notes*, we should do so with utmost care. Perhaps the safest way is to return to familiar terrain first, and only then let the more explosive material gradually trickle in.

V. FOR THE "FIRST" TIME

As *The Prose of the World* reminds us in some of its most beautiful pages, the experience of the other is always both that of a 'replica of me' (*réplique de moi*) and of a 'reply to me' (*réplique à moi*) (PW 135/188). The other is like me. He can't be a thing for he is "not in that place which my looks flattens and empties of any 'interior'" (PW 134). Instead of appearing in front of me, "he is this side of me, beside or behind me", – "a wandering double which haunts my surroundings more than it appears in them" (*ibid.*) He is 'another me', but he is not me: "The looks with which I scan the world, like a blind man tapping objects with his cane, are seized by someone at the other end and sent back to touch me in turn. [...] I thought I gave to what I see its meaning as a thing seen, and then one of these things suddenly slips out of this condition. The spectacle begins to furnish itself a spectator who is not I but who is reproduced from me (*copié sur moi*). How is that possible? How can I see something that begins to see?" (PW 134-5).

At first sight this analysis which stresses the necessity of conceiving of the other both as 'another' me and as 'an other' me, seems inclined to repeat the gist of Husserl's *Fifth Cartesian Meditation* and to share its worries. But if one approaches it through the spectacles offered by *The Visible and the Invisible*[14], it becomes instantly clear that Merleau-Ponty's worry is not really about the fate of a transcendental ego which would find itself closed in by solipsism. His worry is that it (or whatever will take its place) would not be an ego at all: "it is necessary that a body perceive bodies *if I am to be able to be not ignorant of myself*" (VI 233). It is not so much the constitution of the other, then, that forms a problem, but that of the ego. The problem of the other is a false problem, since it supposes having solved what according to Merleau-Ponty has been the major difficulty, ever since *The Phenomenology of Perception*: "A thought limited to exist for itself, independently of the constraints of speech and communication, *would no sooner appear than it would sink into the unconscious*, which means that it would not even exist for itself" (PP 177)[15]. But then what can be this 'for itself' the necessity of which Merleau-Ponty has never denied? How is it that the perception of the other enables one to be "not ignorant of myself" (VI 233)? How is it that consciousness or thought is awakened in "a body perceiving bodies" (*ibid.*) and why is such perception necessary to break through its slumbering?

Whatever the answer to these tricky questions, we know enough already to realize that if there is to be a connection between 'dialogue' and 'the perception of the other'[16], it is not to be thought of in terms of a relation between an I, already in full self-possession, and some 'Other' whose alterity demands that he be granted both the status of an *alter* ego and of an alter *ego*. For it seems that for such 'I' to be there in the first place and at least in some sense to exist 'for itself', it will have to grow *out of* 'the perception of the other'. But if we are to avoid a simple inversion of the problem of the

---

14. On the problems involved in approaching an older work (the unfinished manuscript of *The Prose of the World* dates back to the early 1950's) through the lenses of a more recent one, cf. the opening quotes of section I above. In what follows, I will only make some indirect suggestions as to the shift in Merleau-Ponty's thought when he moves from PW to VI.

15. As is well known, in *Speech and Phenomena*, Evanston Ill., Northwestern U.P., 1973, Derrida has turned this argument against Husserl's reduction of the indicative moment of the sign (see, in particular, the opening paragraph of Derrida's sixth chapter, and already its title: "The Voice That Keeps Silence").

16. The quotes at the beginning of this section were drawn from the fifth chapter of PW, which is called 'Dialogue and the Perception of the Other'.

constitution of the other, it seems that such perception can be no more than an 'efficient cause': "the factual presence of other bodies could not produce thought or the idea if its seed were not in my own body" (VI 145). And yet, this may be too easy a way out: to speak of 'my own body' is already to presuppose the lack of "ignorance of myself" which we have just learned to be the 'result' of the perception of other (?) bodies: "Il faut qu'un corps percoive les corps si je dois pouvoir ne pas m'ignorer" (VI 233/287).

If one takes this literally – and perhaps we should – it seems that there can be no self-affection 'before' the other. Thus, although it is true that "there would not be others (...) for me, if I did not have a body and if they had no body through which they slip into my field" (PW 138), the reverse seems to be even more true. How could I have a body and 'identify' it as mine, if this body somehow is not bent back upon itself, and forced into this never-ending process of re-flection which, as we know, leads not to "identification with oneself, but to non-difference with oneself" (VI 204)? But it is only "through other eyes" that "we for ourselves" can become "fully visible": "As soon as we see other seers, we no longer have before us only the look without a pupil, the plate glass of the things with that feeble reflection, that *phantom of ourselves* they evoke by designating a place among themselves whence we see them" (VI 143). For my body to have that "other side" (VI 259) which could give it the distance needed for the kind of proximity I refer to when I speak of 'my' body, my vision (or my touch ...) will need to be pulled out of that centre (VI 234: "eccentric") which it takes itself to be. Which may be what happens when 'I' come across something which is no longer just a 'phantom of myself': "visions other than my own [that] in being realized, bring out the limits of [my] factual vision, and betray [its] solipsistic illusion" (VI 143).

Before we go on to wonder exactly how this illusion (which in a strict sense is neither 'solus' nor 'ipse') can be brought out by visions which only in bringing it out become 'other' than 'my own', let us pause and reconsider. If it is only through the other that I can obtain that contact with myself which Merleau-Ponty calls 'non-difference' (VI 255), then clearly what is at stake in the other presenting to me "what I will never be present to" (VI 82, quoted above), may not only, and perhaps not even in the first place, be his transcendence, but also that minimal transcendence without which I could not be an I. Unsurprisingly so, for as we have seen, in *The Visible and the Invisible* the *Nichturpräsentierbar* for me is not modelled on the alterity of the other, but introduced to clarify the very 'foundation' of my sensing which presupposes that primary differentiation between figure/ground in which Merleau-Ponty recognized not only the basic structure of consciousness, but also what infects it with the 'blind spot' of a radical invisibility that 'counts' since it is more than the mere absence of visibility. Hence a twofold problem to which we have until now tried to find a single answer: 1) how is it that such invisible can count, if on the one hand it is to be seen as that dimension which makes us see and, on the other hand, perception and consciousness 'of themselves' ignore themselves as wild perception or 'esprit sauvage', i.e. ignore by principle 'what makes them see'; 2) not only are they structured in such a way that it is hard to see how what they ignore could *count* for them, but also how they could be more than such ignorance, which may not be a cause of worry for perception, but certainly is for consciousness. "But then how to understand subjectivity?" (VI 194).

What if my vision or my touch, if my sensitive being in general could be awakened to the divergence that it is, without that awakening being able to undo such divergence? For the first time, no doubt, something that normally is covered over would appear, without, however, letting itself be absorbed by the light that uncovers it. For the first time the invisible would count, without however rendering itself to the visible. For the first time, the originary would appear as that which has 'broken up', and in its wake consciousness would appear as what is awakened by a desire to close the wound of an absence that cannot be simply introduced from outside, because the void that seems to result from the invasion of an 'interiority' by an 'exteriority' had in fact been there all along. And this first time, before which there cannot have been time, this *first* time, is the time 'of' the other: "henceforth, *through other eyes* we are for ourselves fully visible [...] for the first time I appear to myself completely turned inside out under my own eyes. For the first time also, my movements no longer proceed unto the things to be seen, to be touched, or unto my own body *occupied in seeing and touching them*, but they address themselves to the body in general and for itself [...]. For the first time, the body no longer couples itself up with the world [...]" (VI 143-4). For the first time, that is, a primary complicity or better still: a fusion 'between' body 'and' world is breaking up and about to change its status as a certain "constitutive" "divergence" or "dissonance" is emerging in the "vortex of embryogenesis" (VI 233-4). Which means, of course, that this 'first' time must be *ontologically* prior to that other 'first time' evoked in *The Prose of the World* when I started to "rely on my body to explore the world [and] knew that this corporeal relation to the world could be generalized, as a shifting distance was established between me and being which reserved the rights of another perception of the same being" (PW 136). As the 'first time' in *The Visible and the Invisible* has become a dimension that without 'other eyes' or hands would have remained inaccessible, it is clear that here at last the "problem of the other", instead of having been always already solved (as *The Prose of the World* still seems to argue), has become finally "transformed" (VI 269): "I do not have to constitute the other in face of the Ego: he is already there, and *the Ego is conquered from him*. Describe the pre-egology, the 'syncretism', indivision or transitivism" (VI 221).

Here is the description: "For the first time, the body no longer couples itself up with the world, it clasps another body, applying [itself to it, – Ed. of VI] carefully with its whole extension, forming tirelessly with its hands the strange statue which in its turn gives everything it receives; the body is *lost outside the world and its goals, fascinated by the unique occupation of floating in Being with another life*, of making itself the outside of its inside and the inside of its outside" (VI 144). At first sight, what this "transitivity from one body to another" (VI 143) seems to bring about is that "in the presence of other seers, my visible is confirmed as an exemplar of a universal visibility" (VI 145). Hence, there can no longer be a "problem of the *alter ego* because it is not I who sees nor he who sees, because an anonymous visibility inhabits both of us, a vision in general": "what I see passes into him, this individual green of the meadow under my eyes invades his vision without quitting my own, I recognize in my green his green" (VI 142). It is undeniable that Merleau-Ponty at times, and even in *The Visible and the Invisible*, has a tendency to see in this "chiastic" line of reasoning the final solution to the problem: "Chiasm, instead of the For the Other (*Pour Autrui*): that means that there is not only a me-other rivalry, but a co-functioning. We function as *one unique body*" (VI 215). The other (*autrui*) would be "a relief as I am, not absolute vertical existence" and hence, instead of being "a rival subject for a subject", would be "caught in a circuit that connects him to the world, as we ourselves are, and consequently also in a circuit that connects him to us" (VI 269). "Proper to the visible" would be that it is "the surface of an inexhaustible depth: this is what makes it able to be open to visions other than our own" (VI 143). More generally, "the perceptible (*le sensible*) is precisely that which can haunt more than one body without budging from its place" (S 15/22-3). With this "intercorporeal being" (VI 143) opened to us, 'relativism' (VI 199) would be finally refuted, since – repeated assertion in *The Visible and the Invisible* – there is "this world [...] *common* to us, [...] intermundane space – And there is transitivism by way of generality" (VI 269, Merleau-Ponty's italics).

But here is another description of what happens at that "first time" when "the body no longer couples itself up with the world, clasps another body [and] is *lost outside the world* and its goals, *fascinated* by the unique occupation of floating in Being with another life" (VI 144): "The whole enigma lies in the perceptible world, in that tele-vision which makes us simultaneous with others, and the world in the most private aspects of our life. What is it like when one of the others turns upon me, meets my gaze, and fastens his own upon my body and my face? [...] *the experience is intolerable*. There is nothing left to look at but a look, seer and seen are exactly interchangeable. Nothing can distract them [...] since *things are abolished* and each no longer has to do with anything but its duplicate. [...] Speech, as we said, would interrupt this *fascination*" (S 16-7). If one puts these two long quotes together and focusses on the parts which I chose to italicize, one may wonder whether the problem of the *alter ego* may not have been characterized as a "*Western* problem" (VI 221, Merleau-Ponty's italics) too soon[17] and whether that "fundamental polymorphism by reason of which I do not have to constitute the other in face of the Ego" (*ibid.*), instead of being the irenic solution as which it is presented, will not further aggravate the problem by giving 'me' all the more reason to treat the other as rival: "he is already there, and the Ego is [to be] conquered from him" (*ibid.*!). Perhaps this experience is "intolerable" (S 16) indeed, and perhaps this is why *The Visible and the Invisible*, immediately after presenting us with its own brief, but beautiful phenomenology of eros (VI 144), will take the suggestion in the *Preface* to *Signs* seriously, and, in an attempt to break this fascination, go on to introduce us to that "ruse" (S 16) or "illusion" (VI 204) of language that *The Prose of the World* had already called a "virtue" (PW e.g. 10). Let us make a last effort to understand how that "virtue" can make happen what we had hoped to happen, but did not happen – for we have all but reached the 'untouchable'. Indeed, it is still missing.

VI. THE UNTOUCHABLE

We can not hide our disappointment: our turn toward the other did not bring us what we had hoped to get. Since perception already presupposes a primary differentiation between figure and ground which is 'older' than it, we had expected that confronting a perception at first unaware of that differentiation with perceptions other than its own could awaken it to the divergence that it is, and thus elucidate how consciousness or thought in the strict sense (as what "appears to me"[18]) could in their turn be seen as resting on that first differentiation ("to be conscious = to have a figure on a ground – one cannot go back any further", VI 191). The other would thus not have been the one to let "the originary explode" since perception already

---

17. A question I pursue in the next chapter.
18. Cf. VI 145/190 (Merleau-Ponty's marginal note): "In what sense we have not yet introduced thinking [...] we were not in it [= thought] in the sense that the thinking we have introduced was there is (*il y a*), and not it appears to me that (*il m'apparaît que*) ..." (to be compared with VI 224).

carries that fission within itself. But still we had hoped that he would have been the one to let that constitutive catastrophe "count". And had our hopes not been disappointed, we would have perhaps better understood how we could carry within ourselves that reference to an originary to which we nonetheless try to return in vain[19]. Indeed, this is what a hasty reading of *The Visible and the Invisible* seems to suggest: after that 'first' appearance of the other, my sensible being would be bent back upon itself and in an indefinitely postponed coincidence (VI 147) "movement, touch, vision, applying themselves to the other and to themselves" would "return toward their source", without ever arriving and "in the patient and silent labor of desire, [would] begin the paradox of expression" (VI 144). A consciousness linked to labor and to desire – what better way would there be to understand how "the factual presence of other bodies" could produce thought, the semen of which is not absent from my body (VI 145)?

And yet, in spite of these good hopes and expectations, we find ourselves back where we started. For instead of explaining how thought or consciousness came to be awakened to the divergence that it is and thus how it was "brought to appear", but not "brought to birth" "directly in the infrastructure of vision" (*ibid.*), we found ourselves describing how the confrontation with "other" visions operated as a kind of phenomenological reduction ("for the first time ...") that far from revealing my perceptive being's singularity, uncovered an "anonymous" dimension in it: "it sees in me" (*ce qui se voit en nous* – VI 208/261). With the result that the other, instead of being first of all a "reply *to* me" and bringing me, as in Levinas, that relation of 'proximity' without which there could be no language[20], finds himself, too, turned into a "phantom of me" (VI 143). Through the "generalized transitivism" of my (?) "intercorporeal relation" with him, the other for me becomes 'another me'[21]: what I cannot see or touch, I see or touch through him, since he is "a relief as I am" (VI 269). As there is but "a single Vision" of which his and mine are only "variants", "deviations" (S 15), what he sees is in principle visible to me, caught in the same "circuit" (VI 269). At best, this opening of the field of vision "to other Narcissus", to an

---

19. Cf. the beginning of Section III, above.

20. E. LEVINAS, 'Language and Proximity', in CPP, pp. 109-26, e.g. p. 119: "This relationship of proximity (...), in which every transmission of messages, *what ever be* those messages, is established, is the *original* language, a language without words or propositions, pure communication. (...) Proximity, beyond intentionality, is the relationship with the neighbor *in the moral sense of the term.*" (my italics – expressing doubt about the originality of this proximity which for Merleau-Ponty would be derived from a situation which is already 'non-intentional' and thus seems to call into question at least part of Levinas's favourite stratagem of setting up hasty oppositions between ontology and ethics ...).

21. Or perhaps more appropriately: this transitivism turns me into '*another other*'.

"intercorporeity" (VI 141) and a "transitivity from one body to another" (VI 143), would be a foolproof, but unattractive way to avoid the 'relativism' that *The Visible and the Invisible* so dreaded[22]. For instead of opening an unbridgeable gap between me and the other, we now seem to be left with no gap at all. And instead of making room for an invisible which would be more than a *factual* invisible, transitivism's *imaginary*[23] circuit seems to reduce the invisible or the untouchable to what can be seen or touched from elsewhere. But then, "the circle of the visible" (or of the touchable) will only have been "enlarged" instead of "definitely passed beyond" (VI 144).

Were it not for this last quote, we would not have been entitled to push Merleau-Ponty as we did. It would have been indecent to pretend that the reading we are giving here could be more than a construction of our own. And it would have been mere whimsicality on our part to suggest that that "first time" we have been tracking down could in any sense have been the time of a denial, where instead of letting it be forced upon me that I am 'of' the world, I let myself be 'of' the other, "fascinated by the unique occupation of floating in Being with another life". Or rather, since at this point I "pass into" (VI 204) the other and cannot be distinguished from him, we would have had to give in to a certain tendency in *The Visible and the Invisible* to see in such a chiasm the corrective to what is just a "Western problem" (VI 221). But can there be a chiasm where both terms merely pass into one another? Can there be a chiasm where the circle of the visible has merely become widened, and isn't turned inside out, like a Möbius strip, by a 'true' invisible? And what, if not a true invisible, or a true untouchable – something I could not in any event be present to – could stop my vision from begrudging the world for having made it discover that it is not it? What, if not something that neither I nor the other could touch or see, could prevent me from enlarging my vision through an other whom I treat as my stand-in and to whom I carelessly cling as a way to compensate for that primary trauma of an attachment which I refuse?

Clearly we need another 'other' to force upon us a new reduction which can outwit the cunnings of transitivism. And, as we have already announced, that 'other' other will presuppose language – a "third party" (S 16) that would "interrupt this fascination" without, however, "suppressing" it (S 17). By "putting it off" and "carrying it on forward" (*ibid.*) language will turn what was hitherto a problem and source of an "intolerable experience"

22. Cf. section I above. As to what could have become of *The Visible and the Invisible* had Merleau-Ponty chosen a more subtle form of 'relativism' (?) as discussion-partner, see chapter 4 above.

23. For this use of the term 'imaginary': J. LACAN, *Ecrits. A Selection*, London, Tavistock/Routledge, 1989, esp. chapters 1-3.

(S 16-7) into a virtue. Transitivism will, then, not just "widen" the circle of the visible, but will become the means without which it could not be definitely "passed beyond" (VI 144).

Although the analysis of *The Visible and the Invisible* breaks off before it can fully develop this point, it is easy to see why Merleau-Ponty has to reintroduce some sort of transitivism at the heart of language. For if one wants to avoid reducing speech to a mere envelope for thought, and to insist instead that it is the word which has meaning (PP 177), one will have to show how there is not just a "relation of reversibility" between my own speech and "what it means to say" (VI 145), but also between my speech and that of the other. How else would I be able to understand the other, how else would he be able to hear what I say, if through our words we would not "pass into" one another, and if in a certain sense "to speak" and "to be spoken to" would not be "the same thing" (PW 142): "when I speak to another person and listen to him, what I understand begins to insert itself in the intervals between my saying things, my speech is intersected laterally by the other's speech, and *I hear myself in him, while he speaks in me*" (*ibid.*). If thus in speaking "I precede my thought in the listener" and in listening "I speak according to what the other is saying" (PW 144), Merleau-Ponty may be right to infer from this *Paarung* (coupling – PW 13))of language that through it the "limit between mine and not-mine" is somehow abolished and that speech, by "transforming us into the other and him into us", is able to realize an "agreement" that would be "impossible" between "two rival totalities" engaging themselves in a struggle for life and death (PW 145). Since language "in a sense", as the last lines of *The Visible and the Invisible* announce, "is the voice of no one" (VI 155), it seems tempting indeed to regard it as the trace of a "common effort more ancient than we" (PW 144) and to endow it with the capacity to "graft us to one another" (*ibid.*) and put a halt to "that alternation which makes a rivalry of the relation between consciousnesses" (PW 143). Through an "endless mediation of the same and the other" (PW 142), speech would finally turn what was at first "a universality for me" into a "recognized universality" (*ibid.*). In the resumption of that "common effort", "all preceding expressions" would "revive and receive their place in the expression of the present" in which they can be "recovered". In short, we would be witness to "the manifestation, the becoming (*devenir*) of truth" (PW 144).

But our problem was not how "the limit between mine and not-mine" could become abolished, but if and how it could be established. Instead of showing how "the Ego" is to be "conquered from" an other "already there" (VI 221), *The Prose of the World* presents us with the bright picture of a language that only spreads its wings to offer exhausted consciousnesses the possibility of entering into one another. But the violence of this war, as we said, is nothing compared to the terror of the transitivism which must have preceded the separation between its armies. For at least they had something to defend and their dispute could be over borders. And in ending that dispute, language could function for them as a chiasm, interconnecting what was separate already. Such however, was not our starting-point and we would gain nothing by pretending that what *The Visible and the Invisible* left unfinished could be found in *The Prose of the World*. If we don't want to miss the untouchable once more, we should give up our attempts to close the rift that we witnessed it open[24].

For example, how could language be "the voice of no one" (VI 155), if "what the other says appears to me to be full of meaning because his *lacunae* are never where mine are" (VI 187)? Of course, as long as his *lacunae* and mine relate in a "perspective multiplicity" (*ibid.*) one can go on to compare the chiasm between me and the other, as *The Visible and the Invisible* at times does, to the reversibility of a glove that is turned inside out (VI 263). But then how to explain, as we read elsewhere, that "the others' words make me speak and think because they create within me an other than myself, a divergence (*écart*) by relation to ... what I see, and thus designate it to myself" (VI 224/277-8)? Clearly, to have such divergence I will first have to pass into the others' words or they will have to pass into me, for otherwise I would be left without that "grillwork through which I see my thought" (*ibid.*). But if I am to see *my* thought, and if these words are to make *me* think by creating a divergence within me, there must be something which stops or disturbs this mutual "intercorporation" (VI 263) at some point, and allows that divergence to be designated to me. There must be something which disturbs that "magic machine for transporting the 'I' that speaks into the other's perspective" to which *The Prose of the World* has likened language (PW 19). And since that magic constitutes the "virtue" and the "perfection" of language, which "hides itself from us, in the way it works" and "triumphs in effacing itself" (PW 10), that 'something' which disturbs this magic should not be looked for in language. Indeed, to locate it in it, would be to disturb that "illusion" (PW 13) by which language allows the other to "come to dwell in my world" (PW 11). To look for something *in* language which exposes its illusion and forces it to show itself, would be to leave it without that "trick whereby [the other], touching on significations already present in us", can "make them yield strange sounds" that we "henceforth adopt as our own" (PW 13). It would be to condemn it to an eternal repetition of the same and hence to silence, for speech would lose its attraction.

24. Cf. end of section IV above.

And if we cannot call language back out of its self-withdrawal without undermining that "anonymous spirit which, in the heart of the language, invents a new mode of expression" (PW 37), then what is it that can interrupt this endless reversibility that may indeed explain how "there is neither me nor the other as positive, as positive subjectivities", but does not explain how there can be "*two* caverns, *two* opennesses, *two* stages where something will take place" (VI 263)? It seems as if Merleau-Ponty in his eagerness to make these two caverns "both belong to the same world" (*ibid.*), runs the risk of losing what distinguishes them. For the one will always catch up so well with the other that he will "pass into him": "when I am reading, there must be a certain moment when the author's intention escapes me, where he withdraws himself. *Then I catch up from behind, fall into step* of [...] a bit later, a *happy* phrase brings me back [...] and I find access to the new signification through one of its '*aspects*' which was *already part of my experience*" (PW 142-3). And yet, there are times when I don't fall into step that easily, for example when in reading an author I went through the process described, and then, in grabbing for my pen, find it difficult, if not impossible, to repeat what through that "illusion" of language I had been "deluded" (PW 13) into considering as mine.

One can wonder whether justice is done to such 'unrepeatability' by trying to force it into the alternative of one world / many worlds, common effort / dissemination, to which the reader of *The Prose of the World* and even of *The Visible and the Invisible* finds himself so often referred (e.g. VI 109-10). Isn't the function of a chiasm precisely to undercut these alternatives? Shouldn't it, instead of showing us that we belong to the same world, tell us instead that "the same is the other than the other" (VI 264) and "identity difference of difference" (*ibid.*)? But if "this 1) does not realize a surpassing, a dialectic in the Hegelian sense; 2) is realized on the spot (*sur place*), by encroachment, thickness, spatiality" (*ibid.*), will we not then have to conceive of such spatiality also in terms of that which *cuts through* "the common tissue of which we are made" (VI 203)? Something so wild that it can't even be at home in that "vertical or wild Being" "by which we pass into one another" (*ibid.*)? And if this something would be not only "what I cannot touch" in the other, but what I cannot touch in me either, since it is "what cannot in any event be present to us in the original" (VI 159), will it then not be *impossible* "to go all the way to thinking it *positively*, unto phenomenology" (VI 203, Merleau-Ponty's italics)[25]?

It would be too fashionable to conclude that, in order to break through and definitely pass beyond the circles of the visible or the touchable, Merleau-Ponty at a certain point would have found it necessary to go

25. Cf. VI 203: "It would be *necessary* to go all the way [etc.]".

'beyond' phenomenology. For it seems more likely that in his turn he would have been trying to point out to us that there can be no such 'beyond' *for us*. If what we cannot repeat in the other would be, like the invisible or the untouchable, "an originary of the elsewhere" (VI 254), it would be meaningless to try to catch it in the nets of our language which like all language can do no more than draw up "the inventory of that original departure whose documents we carry in ourselves" (VI 263-4). But perhaps we should learn that to draw up the inventory of our failed attempts to read those documents may not be as useless as it may seem at first sight. Like the painter (PW 47) we should learn to treasure the net not for what it has brought us, but for what it did not bring us. For in a sense, "language is everything" (VI 155) and there is nothing which cannot be said or touched by it. And yet, it is only by enabling us to touch upon everything there is in the other, that language can bestow upon us a silence which is not its contrary. For there is no 'what' that I cannot touch in the other, or he in himself. The divergence between him and me, or between myself and myself (VI 203) cannot be just a matter of a content I still have to catch up with or that he can catch up with a bit quicker than I[26]. As *The Prose of the World* correctly suggests, in allowing me to "pass into the other", language is also letting me know or touch all there is to know or touch in the other. But is this enough to state that we all belong to the "same" world, to a "common" world? Surely there is more to the world than what in it one can see or touch. As *The Visible and the Invisible* might have reminded us, there is also what allows me to see or touch those contents: that "through which they are possible"[27]. Perhaps it is this "passivity of our activity" which in the end separates me from the other and can explain that *although we do not live in a different world, we do not live in the same world either*. To share a world with someone else, it does not suffice to have access to the same contents; one also needs to share a common passivity, a common 'institution' (TLC 39ff.). Which means that it is not enough to be able to understand what it is around which the other's life "pivots", but that, moreover, one would need to be driven in the same direction. And since it is not "I who makes myself think" (VI 221), such a move may not be entirely at our discretion. Just as there can be something which has touched the other without touching me,

---

26. Consciousness is neither a name for such privileged content, nor what privileges access to such content (cf. VI 254: "(...) it is therefore not consciousness which is the untouchable – 'Consciousness' would be something positive, and with regard to it there would recommence, does recommence, the duality of the reflecting and the reflected, like that of the touching and the touched").

27. Cf. section IV above, where we announced our intention to push Merleau-Ponty more discretely.

there seems also to be something which I cannot touch in myself, since it has touched me first. Without this 'something' which may not be a 'thing', the subject could not be a 'fold' that grows out of a primary differentiation to which it could not in any event have been present to. Older than the subject, and unlike the things it has access to, the untouchable far from being just another touchable, will have to be situated on a different plane. It points to an ontological difference occluded by our language which prefers the *what* over the *that* (like when we say "I cannot *understand what* he has seen in such or such", but really mean – since we see all there is to see – "I have no *understanding* for (the fact) *that* such or such could be of interest to him"). *What* I cannot touch in the other, then, is not so much *what* he cannot touch either, but *that* he cannot touch without having been touched first. What separates us is not a *quid* (what) but a *quod* (that). And yet it 'counts', for "every *that* involves a *what* because the *that* is not nothing, hence is *etwas*, hence *west*" (VI 203, Merleau-Ponty's italics)[28].

Perhaps the true virtue of language is that in withdrawing itself it allows us, for a while at least, to overlook this *Wesen* and to treat the "that" as (no more than) a "what". As if instead of immediately confronting us with the "determined void, empty of this or that" (*ibid.*), which we are, language by first presenting itself to us as "a 'transparent' apparatus that gives the illusion of a pure or empty presence of oneself" (VI 204), wanted to grant us the time necessary to adapt to the thought that as speaking beings, although we are *not* alone, we are *not* quite together either[29].

Instead of seeing in these two negatives "a positive that is elsewhere" (VI 254) and of blaming language for its incapacity to bring about a further synthesis, we should see in them two aspects of the same silence that is not brought about by, nor simply kept in language, but that can appear in it for the first time. For it is this silence in language that gives the 'subject' a chance to appear without being either crushed or forced to lose its dignity. For the first time it can appear without being terrorized by its 'failure' to "pass into" and disappear into the other[30]. For the first time, this failure can

28. 'that' and 'what' in English in the original.

29. Cf. TLC 14 which evokes "an 'exchange', a 'chiasm between two 'destinies' ...' in which there are never quite two of us and yet one is never alone". Note that in reversing the order of this sequence, we have altered its message too, as the reader of VI could expect (VI 33: the route from the Etoile to the Notre-Dame is not the inverse of the route from the Notre-Dame to the Etoile!).

30. In this respect, it seems significant that VI, immediately after acknowledging for the first time the existence of "movements (...) that do not even go find in the other body their resemblance or their archetype", starts to concentrate on "those strange movements of the throat and mouth that form the cry and the voice", which therefore seem to constitute a *privileged* instance among the "many gestures" one could think of here (VI 144).

be a success, for in interrupting the endless reversibility and interchange-ability between him and the other, it makes room for a *réplique* that is more than a *replica*. Which is why, just as it would be a mistake to see in the subject a mere effect of language, it would be a mistake to think that there could be a subject without it. Perhaps the subject is like a figure on a ground: unable to make itself disappear, it cannot appear in it, but only appear on it. One cannot go back any further: "the abyss one thus discovers is not such by *lack of ground*, it is upsurge of a *Hoheit* which supports from above" (VI250, Merleau-Ponty's italics). One cannot, and yet, as we shall see, one must.

CHAPTER EIGHT

A WESTERN PROBLEM?
MERLEAU-PONTY ON INTERSUBJECTIVITY

My title is, as a reader familiar with *The Visible and the Invisible* will have recognized, a quote. It comes at the end of the November 1959 *Working Note* which is entitled "I – the other, an inadequate formula". This formula is inadequate, Merleau-Ponty suggests, because it formulates "a *Western* problem" (VI 221). 'Western' is italicized here, which means that it was underlined in Merleau-Ponty's manuscript. And one of the reasons why I put a question mark behind that quote in my title is because I wonder what that underlining means. What goes through our mind when we hear that a certain problem is a *Western* problem? Since we hear this so often and more and more so, we should reflect on this, especially since it is not sure that the way we – today, almost 40 years later and in a different historical setting – hear such statements is the way in which Merleau-Ponty intended us to hear his italics. It is too soon to make wild guesses about what Merleau-Ponty meant when he underlined 'Western' and we will have to come back to that as we go on unpacking this *Working Note*. But for now, let me just confess that this little word 'Western' doesn't sit easily with me and that I cannot but sense a certain discomfort when reading this or similar passages in *The Visible and the Invisible* and elsewhere. And since I am confessing, I might as well add that it is not just this word 'Western' which makes me feel uneasy and that there are other words, or better: a certain atmosphere which I associate rightly or wrongly with this philosophy, which seems to overdetermine the discomfort which I sensed, a bit to my surprise, as I was rereading these pages which for such a long time had inspired me and taught me so much. I realize that in saying this, I might have made some of my readers feel uneasy, if only because confessions in general make us uneasy unless we occupy one of those positions which the symbolic order of our society has instituted for hearing confession (priests, doctors, therapists) and which protect the individuals who are to occupy them against their discomfort precisely because they are *symbolic* positions which they did not institute themselves. But in philosophy there are no such pre-given positions. And yet this does not mean that it is we who institute the position from which we, that is each one of us for him- or herself, 'develop' our own thought. Hence the discomfort when one of us starts confessing that he no longer belongs to our 'circle'[1], that these pages on which he fed so long now leave him indifferent and that in a sense that same air which he is still breathing no longer fills and sustains his lungs, no longer *makes* him think as it is *making* us think. Suddenly, all these distinctions by which thought tried to secure its independence start to crumble and as a certain 'context of discovery' starts to tinge the 'context of justification', the 'circle' or the horizon or the atmosphere or the discourse or the *Boden* on which thought had to rely or within which it had to move for it to be able to formulate what it had to say, lightens up and appears as it were for the first time, and this appearance, this confrontation with "the passivity" of its own activity (VI 221) makes thought feel insecure.

Whatever the effect of my confession, there seems to be at least something about its structure which brings us back to familiar ground. For after all, what would philosophy be – would it be philosophy – if its activity would be without this passivity? Of course, these words 'activity', 'passivity', somehow will find their meaning altered once they are combined and form a mixture that is more than a putting together of separate ingredients. Just as, I remember thinking a long time ago, and it was a thought like that which *got* me interested in Merleau-Ponty, words like 'power' and 'knowledge' could no longer mean the same once they were hyphenated[2]. More precisely, what attracted me in Merleau-Ponty was that, in his own way, he had already anticipated the problems that those who were to follow him somehow could not afford to see if they were to believe, as they did, that this whole philosophy of ambiguity which he developed was but one more instance of that modern and essentially unstable figure of a man who was forced into the mould of an empirico-transcendental doublet(OT 320-2). How could Foucault lay bare the archaeological soil from which we were supposed to speak, and at the same time proclaim the death of the subject, without giving the impression of stopping halfway to someone familiar with what had been at stake in *The Visible and the Invisible*, a book that at least in its initial phase was still referred to by Merleau-Ponty as "Origine de la vérité" (VI 165/219)? How could the subject be dead, if what in fact Foucault had shown was that for it to speak, it had to meet certain conditions which he called 'the order of discourse'? Before one could judge the truth or falsity of statements, before one could call on others to proffer such judgements about the truth-value of one's own statements, the statements had to be "in

---

1. An early draft of the introduction and the first section of this text was read to the Merleau-Ponty *Circle*'s 22nd Annual International Conference at Seattle University (Sept. '97).

2. I am referring to what I developed in chapter 4 above.

the Truth", that is: they had to be formulated in such a way that they could be heard and taken seriously. To be sure, what was so shocking about Foucault's message was that he implied that it was not us who decided what was to be taken seriously or not – truth, that is, implied a synthesis that was not the result of the synthetic operations of a transcendental-epistemological subject. It escaped its powers of constitution and pointed to a constitution that preceded it and dis-possessed it. But why restrict ourselves to the examples that Foucault gives (and which can always be debated as to their correctness)? If we want to be shocked, why look for the spectacular – other epochs, other cultures? Why not direct our attention as we did a moment ago, to the texture of what is more familiar? Wasn't the "succès de scandale" of post-structuralism already a way to deny or to close that wound which Merleau-Ponty, in his own gentle way, had been inflicting on us when he took philosophy as an example of what he called (for I have been using his words) "the passivity of our activity"? The subject of philosophy too finds itself dis-possessed of its synthetic and constituting capacities, it too must be "attached" to a certain *Boden* for it to be interested at all, and just as it is not the one who can decide about what it can hear and take seriously, for example in the texts of others, it is also not able to prevent that attachment, once it is there, from undoing itself and hence it will have to learn that it doesn't suffice to read and to understand texts for it to be at home in them. To be inspired by a text of another philosopher, one needs to sense a certain depth which promises more than one can momentarily see. Instead of being a flat object on which one can report like one is supposed to do in a certain academic discourse which is content to state what a certain X or Y said, the text that inspires stands upright and develops a depth of its own in which we find ourselves caught. It relates to us as that world of which Merleau-Ponty keeps repeating that we are "of it". A certain "hollow" is formed (VI 221), a certain "relief" (VI 256) which makes us see. And just as this text can "fold" (VI 146, 264) around us, just as it can bend back upon itself to get rid of its flatness and make us dwell in it, it can also unfold and leave us out there in the cold, with the feeling that we are not welcome, unable to enter it since it is without any crack or relief. With this unfolding, as *The Visible and the Invisible* says in another context ('forgetting'), a certain "undifferentiation" (VI 197) seems to have occurred – and it is this which makes us sometimes uncomfortable with our own discomfort and with the absence of inspiration when going through texts that had been so telling to us in the past. In Merleau-Ponty's vocabulary one could say that what is so disturbing about this experience is that henceforth and at least for a while we have to go on living like spirits without a body, for we are no longer "of" the world to which we once belonged.

I

If I may continue using for a while the vocabulary of which I said earlier on that I no longer feel comfortable with it, I would like to briefly expand on this idea of a spirit without a body and contrast it to the famous "body of spirit" that Merleau-Ponty opposes to it, not just in *The Visible and the Invisible* (e.g. in *The Working Note* that I was thinking of when trying to show what it could mean for philosophy that, as he says there, "it is not I who makes myself think any more than it is I who makes my heart beat" (VI 221)), but also in the lecture course on *Nature*[3] where Descartes is, once again, criticized for failing to arrive at a "true substantial union of soul and body" (N 39): "This body that I am is never the body that I think", Merleau-Ponty writes in his commentary on Descartes, "it is only for God that they are bodies in the same sense" (N 266). But what this amounts to is that "the metaphysical locus of coherence" is placed somewhere "where I cannot place myself because I am human" (*ibid.*) – and this is exactly what Merleau-Ponty is seeking to avoid: "it is the *nexus* and not the falling into place under the gaze of God that we are looking for", he writes (N 267). And the only way to reach such a *nexus* is by showing that it is not so much the soul or spirit that descends in the body, but the body that "enters the soul" (N 39). Hence the idea of an original incarnation and of a "corps de l'esprit" (VI 221/275) which wouldn't try to reduce the one to the other, nor claim an inexplicable parallel between them, but which rather attempts to point to a "mixture"[4] that is not just more original than its so-called components, but that also makes it impossible to still consider them as separate, positive entities. Hence all these awkward sentences that point to the need for a completely new vocabulary: "The bond between the soul and the body ... is to be understood as the bond between the convex and the concave, between the solid vault and the hollow it forms" (VI 232). Or a bit further: "The soul is *planted* in the body as the stake in the ground, without point by point correspondence between ground and stake – or rather: the soul is the hollow of the body, the body is the distension of the soul" (VI 233). What is needed, then, is not, as in Descartes, "the absolute opacity of an institution that reconnects by the efficacy of [God's] decision two orders each of which would suffice to itself" (VI 232), but "a relation to Being that would form itself *within* Being" (VI 215). And if this Being which Merleau-Ponty, like

---

3. *La Nature. Notes. Cours du Collège de France* (ed. D. Séglard), Paris, Seuil, 1995. Abbreviated as N.

4. M. MERLEAU-PONTY, *Notes de Cours au Collège de France 1958-9 et 1960-61* (ed. St. Ménasé), Paris, Gallimard (nrf), 1996, p. 360. Henceforth abbreviated as NdC.

Heidegger, capitalizes, is to be the name of an institution – of a *Stiftung* –
that, although not transparent, since it precedes us as our *Urstiftung*, is of
less than that *absolute* opacity to which Descartes had to resort, it is because
Merleau-Ponty wants to show that we are "of it" *and that "Nature in us has
some relation to Nature outside of us"*, since the latter is "unveiled (*dévoilée*)
to us by the Nature that we are" (N 267). One would be wrong to read this
as suggesting that everything thus starts with that strange entity that we call
our body and to which Merleau-Ponty refers as "the exemplar sensible" (VI
135), "the universal thing" (VI 260), a "universal measurant" (*ibid.*), "the
thing-standard" (like in: the gold standard) (N 287). For this body is not
"first", it in no way comes to take the position of the transcendental subject
that Merleau-Ponty has just attempted to vacuate (VI 167). If it unveils
Nature outside of us, it is because it carries within itself the trace of "a pact
signed at our birth between it and the world" (PrP 6), or better still, since it
was not present as a signatory to this pact, but results from it: it is that
"miracle" – a word that abounds in Merleau-Ponty's writings[5] – in which
Nature, as it were, unveils itself to itself, or "through which", as Merleau-
Ponty literally states in a passage that shocked Levinas for its "antihumanist
or nonhumanist tendency"[6], "space itself knows itself" (S 167). But one
should not misread passages like this: their anti-humanism rests on more
than a mere reversal of the positions of the constituting and the constituted.
It is not Being that constitutes us instead of us constituting Being, for the
"decompression" (VI 215) that occurs in "Being before *the* Being", in "Being
before representation", is not the result of any finalism (VI 265), it is not a
code-word for what others have called creation, and if space knows itself
through our bodies, if Nature thus reveals itself to itself, this is not the
fulfilment of an intention that it carried within itself without knowing it.
The first and the last word of this metaphysics is, exactly like in Heidegger,
an "es gibt": "there is" (N 303) an "inaugural *there is*" (VI 239), a "relation to
Being within Being" (VI 215), a first "explosion" (VI 265), such that man can
no longer be defined as "a useless passion" which makes him participate in
Being "through a sort of folly" (VI 215), nor as a useful passion on its way to
fulfill a metaphysical destiny. Since the "en soi – pour soi" is original, there
is passion in man, for his "self" is outside itself, it is a "torn self" (N 285), "by
divergence" (VI 249), "alienated or in ec-stasy in Being" (VI 51) and the whole
point is to understand that this "leaving of oneself" is not opposed to
"retiring into oneself" (VI 65,199), and that what others call 'alienation' or

---

5. E.g. N 271,280; PP 354; PW 134,135; S 170; VI 118.
6. E. LEVINAS, 'Intersubjectivity: Notes on Merleau-Ponty', in G.A. JOHNSON - M.B.
SMITH (eds.), *Ontology and Alterity in Merleau-Ponty*, Evanston Ill., Northwestern U.P.,
1990, p. 57.

'estrangement' means in truth that "the one who looks" is "not himself foreign to the world he looks at" (VI 134). To possess, man must be "dispossessed" first (VI 266; N 351, 381), he must find " a weight" (N 351) in himself, the echo of an "initial yes" (N 381), which is the "indivision of sensing" (*ibid.*), this primordial "non-difference" (VI 255, 261) which is not the same as identity or fusion between the sensing and the sensed and the secret of which does not lie in either, but in that "third term" (VI 197) which keeps them together as a "surface of separation and of union" (VI 234). And just as incarnation is not a state, that third term which Merleau-Ponty calls 'flesh', is not a substance, nor perhaps an "element" (VI 147)[7], but a verb: flesh is the working of the chiasm through which the body passes in the soul and the soul in the body, the body in the world and the world in the body, I into the Other and the other into me. All these chiasmic formulas describe the structure of a "field of Being", where Being is not yet domesticated into a noun, but savage, wild, barbaric, a Being where "everything encroaches on everything", a Being "by promiscuity" (VI 234). Not just a Being, but *one* Being: "All verticality comes from the vertical Being" (*ibid.*), there is "*one sole* explosion of Being which is forever" (VI 265), "*one sole* big differentiation of *one sole* Being" (NdC 200)[8].

With this "one sole" we have not just come close to the central intuition behind Merleau-Ponty's metaphysics – an intuition which, by the way, he shares with Heidegger, for whom there is also, as Derrida has always insisted, 'one sole' history of Being – but we have also come close to what I suspect constitutes the kernel of my discomfort, of my impression that, if I may quote an expression from the *Working Notes*, "je n'aime pas cela" ("I don't like that", VI 235). And perhaps the easiest way to give voice to this irritation is to return to the *Working Note* with which we started and to illustrate the bearings of this "one sole" on the problem of intersubjectivity. But let me say something positive first, for my discomfort is too ambiguous to issue in a critique – indeed, it is precisely because it is ambiguous that I call it a discomfort and that I indicated it by a question mark, which is not the sign of a position already taken but of an incapacity to take the position that one is offered by a text that, as I hope to have shown, one more or less understands.

7. Cf. M.C. DILLON's interesting comments on possible misconceptions suggested by the terms 'flesh' and 'element' in his 'Écart. Reply to Claude Lefort's "Flesh and Other-ness" ', in G.A. JOHNSON - M.B. SMITH (eds.), *o.c.*, p. 25: "reversibility must be understood adverbially rather than substantially".

8. I shall persistently translate the French "un(e) seul(e)" as "one sole" (instead of "a single" as in some Merleau-Ponty translations) to make it easier for the reader to recognize the recurrence of this expression. For my translation of 'corps de l'esprit': ch. 7 n13.

Let us return, then, to the italicized "*Western* problem" at the end of that *Working Note*. For I think that by now we know enough to make an informed guess as to what Merleau-Ponty might have had in mind when he underlined 'Western'. Not that this is going to take us on another detour, for as will immediately become apparent, these italics should at least be read as a figure on the background of what we just heard on the "body of spirit" and they will, moreover, immediately lead us into the heart of the problem of intersubjectivity. As one will remember, "body of (the) spirit" or the chiasmic "spirit of the body" (VI 259), points to Merleau-Ponty's attempt to find a connection between two terms that in the tradition were either reduced to one another (reduction of the body to spirit (intellectualism), reduction of spirit to body (materialism)) or put next to one another in some meaningless parallelism. "Corps de l'esprit" then should neither be read as "embodied spirit", nor as "spiritualized body". Rather what is at stake is to show that there is a localization of consciousness which does not mean that consciousness can be located somewhere (materialism), but which is neither reducible to a consciousness of localization: "The mind is neither here, nor here, nor here... And yet it is 'attached', 'bound', it is *not without bonds*" (VI 222). It is this "not without" which provides consciousness with its "punctum caecum" (VI 248,255), with that "original stain" (VI 45) which is also responsible for the fact that there is an "irreducible" or an "unreflected" which resists what Merleau-Ponty considers to be the idealist tendency in Husserl's attempt to reach a complete reduction to transcendental immanence. The existence of the world, he remarks against Husserl's attempt to start from the hypothesis of the "*Nichtigkeit* of the world", "cannot be suspended": "the epoché has the right to be a neutralization only with regard to the world as effective in itself (*comme en soi effectif*), to the pure exteriority: it must leave extant the phenomenon of this effective in itself, of this exteriority" (VI 172/225) – which means that it will have to replace Husserl's 'impartial observer' (*unbeteiligter Zuschauer*)[9] with something essentially and originally 'beteiligt', something that is '*Teil* of ', '*part* of ' the world, something that 'takes part' in it: with an *être au monde*.

9. On Husserl's *Zuschauer* which Merleau-Ponty interprets as another *kosmotheoros*: NdC 368, VI 227. In this context, it is interesting to note that Merleau-Ponty understood Husserl's famous "Philosophie als Wissenschaft, als ernstliche, strenge ja apodiktisch strenge Wissenschaft – der Traum ist ausgeträumt" as an announcement of a *Kehre* away from 'strict' and 'impartial' 'science', whereas it was in fact a cry of despair denouncing precisely the tendency to give up on that project (NdC 382; S 138; cf. E. HUSSERL, *Krisis (Husserliana VI), Beilage XXVIII*, p. 508 esp. lines 32 ff.: "Aber die Zeiten sind vorüber, ist dergleichen *allgemein herrschende* Überzeugung...", – it is precisely against this *doxa* that Husserl offers the therapy of phenomenology as a rigorous science; the *Crisis* is about nothing but that).

With this, Merleau-Ponty voiced the same protest as Heidegger[10] and he drew the same conclusions as to the future tasks of phenomenology. A task which is summarized in the 'not without bonds' that was to prevent phenomenology's attack on materialism ending in a triumph of spiritualism. Consciousness, then, is "attached" and if there is a crisis for Merleau-Ponty it has to do with the fact that a certain *ethos*, which is implied in this attachment, is being threatened with extinction. An example of this can be found in our very own response to expressions like a *"Western* problem". The whole criticism of Occidentalocentrism which is thriving so well today seems paradoxically to rest, as I argued in chapter six, on the strange inference from the detection of something as 'a Western problem' to its disappearance for the one who detects it. What I mean is that the sad effect of a certain cultural criticism, which I believe to be fully legitimate by itself, is that the Western problems which it identifies seem to end up being considered as problems for a province – the West – to which one no longer belongs. With the result that what starts to crumble, is not just a particular configuration of that Western *Boden*, but the *Boden* as such: how else to explain the absence of any significant discourse on, for example, Europe as a cultural idea (l)? The criticism of Eurocentrism or of Occidentalocentrism seems simply to have led to a disinvestment or a de-cathexis of the *cultural* idea of Europe or of the West. With the result that another – no longer cultural – discourse on Europe or on the West could come to occupy the place that thus became vacant: the discourse of something that is not 'not without bonds', but that is *without bonds* altogether – the discourse of capital. Or, if one prefers another vocabulary, the discourse of what Heidegger called technology and the enframing and in which he too sees not so much a triumph of materialism as a triumph of spiritualism[11]. The so-called westernization of the world is perhaps not so much the result of the West's curious tendency to expand and to go everywhere. It is first of all the legacy of a West that is no longer anywhere. A West that is without bonds and without *Boden*. Without attachment, the West has become a wandering spirit without a body.

Of course, this does not mean that for the West to become 'body of spirit' – not again, but perhaps for the first time – one would simply need to

---

10. As I have tried to argue in chapter 7, this does not make Merleau-Ponty into a French version of Heidegger – *in-der-Welt-sein* and *être au monde* are anything but the same.

11. E.g. M. HEIDEGGER, *Über den Humanismus*, Frankfurt a.M., Vittorio Klostermann, 1981 (1949¹), p. 31 on the often misunderstood 'essence of materialism'; ID., *Hölderlins Hymne 'Der Ister'* (Freiburg lectures, summer semester 1942), GA 53, p. 66: "Es ist ein Grundirrtum zu meinen, weil die Maschine selbst aus Metallen und Stoffen bestehe, sei das Maschinenzeitalter 'materialistisch'. Die neuzeitliche Maschinentechnik ist 'Geist' ...".

institute a body in which the spirit could come to rest. For this is exactly what is being done today in Europe, where the whole problem of the absence of Europe as a cultural idea (l) is approached by what one can only identify as a 'Frankensteinian' method: as if the cathexis or investment of that body could be effected by a series of electro-shocks concocted in some EC laboratory – plastic bags with the emblem of the European Community may not be the best of ways to get to a 'corps de l'esprit'. More seriously: as one can learn from Merleau-Ponty, the thing to do with a spirit that is without bonds is not to catch it in a bag and tell it where it should be since it is 'neither here, nor here, nor here'. An artificially enhanced cultural chauvinism and a bureaucratically produced euronationalism are but the latest way in which materialism seeks to become intimate with spirit. It is altogether a poor answer to the idealism that, in the terms of Merleau-Ponty's analysis, may have been ultimately responsible for Husserl's tendency to understand the idea of a 'European humanity' which he was promoting, as an ultimately pleonastic idea. It is not because Europe (or 'the West') is not the name for another province or another particularism that it can easily blend into humanity or have humanity blend into it. There is something in the name 'Europe', like in any other name and to begin with in my own *proper* name, that refuses this easy blend. This is because the Shakespearean question 'what's in a name?' is one of these questions like Claudel's 'where am I?' or 'what time is it?' (cf. VI 103, 121) that would be poorly understood if given a direct answer. But does this mean that it can be given an indirect one? Does it betray "a secret knowledge of interrogation as the ultimate relation to Being and as an ontological organ" (VI 121)? Does this question of the name, instead of announcing "an original way to aim at Being" (NdC 356), not rather point to what in man somehow does not manage to reach Being and infects him with an unrest and a solitude that, as we shall see, are remarkably absent from Merleau-Ponty's analysis of intersubjectivity where both I and the other are "total parts"[12] (VI 217, 218) of "one sole fabric" (PrP 10, 11; VI 110) "open to participation by all" and "given to each" (VI 233)?

---

12. This expression seems to have the status of a root-metaphor in Merleau-Ponty's endology (e.g. VI 118, 134, 217, 218) – although none of these references bears directly on the *ego/alter ego* relation, I think one can nonetheless safely apply the expression 'total parts' to this relation too.

II

One need only probe a little further into the context of these last few quotes to see that Merleau-Ponty somehow did not bend the expression "corps de l'esprit" into the direction we were taking it when suggesting that there might be something in the name 'Europe', as in all these other names to which we find ourselves attached, that refuses to blend into a humanity or an intersubjectivity that transcends us. To the contrary, Merleau-Ponty's insistence on "participation" in a "cohesion that prevails over every momentary discordance" (VI 140) seems to have as its reverse side a sacrifice of everything that a proper name might stand for for those who bear it. What prides itself on being an 'ego' and a 'person', is in fact for Merleau-Ponty 'une personne': a 'nobody' "in the sense of Ulysses" (VI 201/254), a "certain nothingness sunken into a local and temporal *openness*" (*ibid.*) that does not find its origin in man. Before there is 'my' vision, there would be "an anonymous visibility" (VI 142) that makes its way through me and that passes through me, like the sounds that pass through (*personare*) the masks (*personae*) in Greek theatre. That "anonymity innate to Myself" (VI 139) for which "there is no name in traditional philosophy to designate it" (*ibid.*) and to which Merleau-Ponty alternately refers as 'flesh' or 'raw', 'vertical', 'polymorphous' Being, a 'Being in promiscuity' (VI 253) and even "in indivision" (VI 218), seems not only to allow him to do away with all those divisions like 'ego/alter ego' which left 'the West' with its insoluble problems, but also with that one 'undivided' (*in-dividuum*) which it had tried to save under the label of the subject. "If one could open one man", he writes in a section of his course notes entitled 'The magma of men', "one would find all the others like in Russian puppets, or rather: less well ordered, in a state of indivision" (NdC 211), – a "magma" of which he hastens to add that "it is not just disorder, chance, absence of reason (*déraison*)", but "also an excess of meaning" by which human speech and actions find themselves "inhabited" "as if they could not help it" (NdC 212). "Every man" thus becomes "an X where Being comes to itself, lives and relives (*revit*) itself" (NdC 372), as if this excess needed more than one of us to pronounce itself. Being, Merleau-Ponty tells us, "is *what requires creation of us* for us to experience it" (VI 197, Merleau-Ponty's italics), but since it is the "same Being" (e.g. VI 82) which addresses all of us, no matter how divergent or "incompossible" our answers, there will be "a union" at the heart of this incompossibility[13], such that communication between each of us within a given culture, just like the "communication from one constituted culture to another occurs through the wild region wherein they all have originated" (VI 115). Contact between cultures, just like contact between men, presupposes that one breaks with the illusion of immanence, which is for Merleau-Ponty only a "cooled-off transcendence" (*transcendance refroidie*, NdC 190). One need only warm up what has thus become cooled off, and stop thinking of oneself or of one's culture as a "monad" and approach them instead as a "space of open air, a crossroads where all things come to exist for one another" (NdC 371-2), "to *regain possession* [!] of that untamed region of (one)self unincorporated in (one's) own culture" (S 120), or for that matter in one's own name, and "through which (one) communicates with other cultures" (*ibid.*), or quite simply with others. The others, be they other 'subjects' or other cultures, are involved in "one sole task" (S 60), and like me they are "reliefs, deviations, variants of *one sole* Vision in which I too participate" (S 15).

No doubt it is a train of thought like this which made Merleau-Ponty write, at the end of the text in which he proposed his candidature for the *Collège de France*, after mentioning once more that "sole fabric" where "the plurality of monads, the past and the present, nature and culture" would be "reunited", that "to establish this wonder would be metaphysics itself and would at the same time give us the principle of an ethics" (PrP 11). Perception itself – *aisthesis* – seems to show us the way toward an "esthesiological community" where the other is not, as he is in Sartre, "absolute vertical existence" (VI 269), and hence "a rival subject" (*ibid.*) but "caught up in a circuit that connects him to the world, as we ourselves are, and consequently also in a circuit that connects him to us" (*ibid.*). It is Being only which is "vertical", which means that Being is not "flat" (VI 306), that is has a "depth" which is "inexhaustible" and which "makes it able to be open to visions other than our own" (VI 143). This "depth" is not the result of my or the other's 'néantisation', it follows from a "decompression" (VI 215) within Being itself, from that famous explosion of the originary (VI 124) which brings me and the other into the same orbit, or provides us both with a common field of gravitation wherein we can circulate without colliding. The expression "body of spirit" that we encountered earlier, the idea that our spirit or our mind is "not without" attachment, means that there is something about us that is exposed to the *same* gravitational force as the other. Just as there is this sort of *sensus communis* between the organs of

13. One should not forget that 'incompossibility' for Merleau-Ponty is not contrary to 'union' – the "vertical world" that he seeks to uncover is synonymous to "the union of the incompossibles" (VI 228).

my body or between its diverse senses, there is a sort of "cohesion without concept" (VI 152) which makes me and the other "co-function" (VI 215) and which is "ensured by the roots (we) push forth" in an "aesthetic world" which is not "objective-immanent space" but "a space of incompossibilities" (VI 216) that precisely *"forms its unity* across incompossibilities such as that of my world and the world of the other" (VI 215)[14]. Being is thus not just one, nor multiple, or rather: it is the one-within-the-multiple, the one that allows for multiplicity, a "surface of separation and of union" (VI 234) and thus in a sense a good explosion, "that makes us simultaneous with others and the world in the most private aspects of our life" (S 16). It is this "enigma" (*ibid.*) that we are "grafted to the universal by that which is most our own" (S 52) which Merleau-Ponty called flesh and which, far from being a substance common to me and the other or to us and the world, is rather that inner vibration within the sensible that at one point in *Eye and Mind* he compared to a "respiration within Being"[15].

It is difficult to avoid the impression that what this new ethics really amounts to is an attempt to renew with other means the idea of a 'mystical body'[16]. Of course, in a sense, as we have just seen, this 'mystical body' is neither mystical, nor a body. When Merleau-Ponty calls my body and that of the other "organs of one sole intercorporality" (S 168), when he says that we "function as one unique body" (VI 215), he knows full well that "there does not exist some huge animal whose organs our bodies would be, as, for each of our bodies, our hands, our eyes are the organs" (VI 142). And as his

---

14. On this *rapprochement* of Kant and Merleau-Ponty, cf. the perspicacious remarks in R. BONAN's outstanding *Premières Leçons sur l'Esthétique de Merleau-Ponty*, Paris, P.U.F. 1997, pp. 94-101.

15. M. MERLEAU-PONTY, *L'Oeil et l'Esprit*, Paris, Gallimard (Folio Essais), 1964, p. 31 – the English translation in PrP 167 has dropped this clause.

16. For a brief exposition of what this expression meant to the Catholic tradition, cf. J.-L. CHRÉTIEN, 'Le corps mystique dans la théologie catholique', in J.-C. GODDARD - M. LABRUNE, *Le corps*, Paris, Vrin-Intégrale, 1992, pp. 90-106; and M.-D. GASNIER, 'Trouver un corps. Éléments pour une pensée chrétienne du corps', *ibid.*, pp. 71-90. I am, of course, in no way suggesting that Merleau-Ponty had as his secret agenda a sort of crypto-neo-Catholic ontology. But certain notions like 'total parts' or the ever present verb 'participate' (e.g. VI 137) and a number of the expressions that we shall note below, do seem to echo, perhaps unintentionally, the basic structure that was at stake in the notion of a *corpus mysticum*. One need only think of the well-known thesis that each parcel of the Holy Bread contained the whole of Christ, and that in the corresponding ecclesiastical community (which was since the 12th century referred to as 'the Body of Christ') Christ was present in and through each of its members, without of course being reducible to any one of them. In this context, it is worth noting, for example, that Merleau-Ponty calls 'flesh' in a crucial passage "a sort of incarnate principle that brings a style of being *wherever there is a fragment of it*" (VI 139/184, transl. corrected – the last 'it' refers to 'flesh', not to 'being').

discussion with Sartre makes clear, there is nothing mystical about the sort of phenomena that prompted him to forge a new ontology, however arcane some of these notions to which it gave rise (like 'flesh') may sound. But if there is nothing mystical, there is something mysterious about that strange "synergy" (*ibid.*) that seems to exist between my visible and that of the other. It is not just that "they both open upon the same visible world" (VI 216), but also that "the articulation of the (others') body upon the world is lived by me in the articulation of my body on the world where I see them": "just as I touch my touching hand, I perceive the others as perceiving" (N 281). It is this 'Ineinander' which makes Merleau-Ponty reject what he calls "Sartre's formula" ("The other's visible is my invisible; my visible is the other's invisible" (VI 216)) and opt for the "chiasm, instead of the For the Other" (VI 215). The other's vision is not a rival vision, not only because we do not compete for the same object, but more profoundly because without him seeing me, I would not see at all, for I would be without a point of view (N 286) and my seeing – if seeing it still is – would be godlike, not human: "As soon as I see, it is necessary that the vision (as is so well indicated by the double meaning of the word) be doubled with a complementary vision or with another vision: myself seen from without, such as another would see me, installed in the midst of the visible, occupied in considering it from a certain spot" (VI 134). Without the other, that is, I who look "would remain foreign" to the world that I look at (*ibid.*). Merleau-Ponty sees in this "a radical upheaval" which instead of being the alienation that it is for Sartre (my loss of transcendence to the Other), seems rather the cure for what from his point of view would be the inhuman moment of a Sartrean transcendence where the For Itself is driven by a useless passion for an In Itself that remains without any connection with it: "From pre-human, I become human. I am no longer the universal being of space, but a man closed in a bag. ... I am becoming *Raumding*, spatial thing. My body finishes constituting itself. The universe of *Sachen* closes in on me, whereas before I was a tear (*déchirure*) in the world" (N 109). Clearly, one should not read this as me becoming just another thing, but rather as a description of that incarnation which I could not give to myself: only through the other can I become "caught up in the web of carnal things" (*ibid.*) and thus become part of that 'mystical body' which Merleau-Ponty calls flesh. There seems to be here, as it were, a sort of sublimation of a desire which I already found in my body being driven by a senseless and eternally frustrated desire to close itself in upon itself: my hands touching each other, and unable to close the circuit – that immanence eternally "imminent" (VI 147), that, to be sure, opened us to the world, but without that opening being able to drive home its sense to us, now somehow seems to reveal what it was all about:

"extension of the narcissism of the body. *This narcissism is also opening toward generality*: I live as mine the behaviours offered [by the other] and I see them animated by a body image. Here too, it is the flesh that solves the problem ... My body image *projects* itself in the others and *introjects* them, has relations of being with them, seeks identification, *appears to itself as undivided with them, desires them. Desire considered from a transcendental point of view* = common inner framework (*membrure commune*) of my world as carnal and of the world of the other. They both end in one sole *Einfühlung*" (N 288).

It is this passing of the other into me and of me into the other which Merleau-Ponty calls transitivism or syncretism and which prompted him to call the I - other problem "a *Western* problem" since, if one takes his point of view, neither the I nor the other are spheres of immanence, and consequently "I do not have to constitute the other *in face of* the Ego, he is already there" (VI 221). But there is more to this transitivism and it is this more which motivates the expression "transitivism *by way of generality*" (VI 269) and sort of lifts the problem of the other to a metaphysical level: "The chiasm truth of the pre-established harmony – Much more exact than it: for it is between local-individuated facts, and the chiasm binds *as obverse and reverse* ensembles *unified in advance* in process of differentiation [a blank in the ms.] whence in sum a world that is neither one nor two in the objective sense – which is pre-individual, *generality*" (VI 262). Through our vision, both I and the Other "assist from within" to the same "fission of being" (PrP 186) and which is not without leaving its trace in us. One should in this connection reread the whole working note on Leibniz (VI 222-3, and cf. 242-3) where, of course, the monadology is rejected for depending on a divine institution (and hence for similar reasons as we saw Merleau-Ponty reject Descartes), but where at the same time the idea of "the expression of the universe in us" is reinterpreted in terms of raw Being: "certain Leibnizian descriptions – that each of the views of the world is a world apart, that nonetheless 'what is particular to one would be public to all', that the monads would be in a relation of expression between themselves and with the world, that they differ from one another and from it *as perspectives* – are to be maintained entirely, to be taken up again in the brute Being" (VI 222-3).

With this in mind, let us turn again to that strange quote in the essay 'From Mauss to Lévi-Strauss' where Merleau-Ponty was looking for a new way to the universal (S 120) and saw in the "incessant testing" of me by the other and of the other by me a way "to *regain* possession" of that "untamed region" in myself, "unincorporated" in my own culture, and through which I or we "communicate with other cultures" and they with us (*ibid.*). We will have to understand why Merleau-Ponty speaks here both about "*regaining* possession" and about "regaining *possession*", for it would seem that both of these expressions tend to further tip the balance toward the interpretation that we have given in this section of the I - other problem as a "Western" problem, and which clearly differs from the approach we had taken in the first section, where the expression 'body of spirit' allowed us to see the sort of problems that seem to be associated with 'the West' as a result of it forgetting that it is 'not without' its attachments. For if it is a common 'mystical body' that will make us communicate with the other, the problems of the West will not so much follow from its tendency to ignore the specificity of its attachment, which is an attachment to a name which it *does not* share with others, as that it will follow from an incapacity to see how that attachment, however specific it may be, at the same time opens a breach in its proper name, through which it is tied to that 'one sole', 'common fabric' of which it is but one 'member' on a par with its other members. As one can already suspect, what is at stake in these two approaches cannot be simply restricted to the problem of intercultural contact. One way or another, that "untamed region" that we have to "regain possession" of, will also have its repercussions on how we see the relation between the subjective and the intersubjective.

III

Before we move on to the subject's place within intersubjectivity, let us first have a look at the immediate context of the '*From Mauss to Lévi-Strauss*' essay in which Merleau-Ponty, as its title suggests, sings the praises of Lévi-Strauss's anthropology for showing us the way to a "lateral universal" (S 120) that will allow us "to understand someone else without sacrificing him to our logic or it to him" (S 115). This universal would be lateral in the sense that it would not provide a third position between ours and that of the other, that each of us would have to reach and where, once arrived, both us and the other could leave behind the particularities they stem from. To the contrary, it would be a universal that, instead of hovering above such particularities and providing an alternative for them, would leave them as intact as they can be – it could, as Merleau-Ponty approvingly comments on Lévi-Strauss's discovery of a structure underlying its various cultural "incarnations" (cf. S 119), "no more be substituted for the particular than general geometry annuls the local truth of Euclidean spatial relations" (*ibid.*). Indeed, what constitutes for example Lévi-Strauss's breakthrough to what he calls a general mythology is that his approach allows him to disregard the apparently unrelated contents of myths that belong to cultures that are at first sight equally unrelated, and to show how they all seem to work with sets of structural oppositions which in principle allow for an infinite number of different combinations. None of these myths, taken by itself, can exhaust the possibilities that are offered by the structure, yet all of them draw from the same source and are trying to "arbitrate", as Merleau-Ponty echoes Lévi-Strauss, "the same fundamental contradiction" (S 121). Suddenly, it seems possible, for example, to understand the conspicuous correlation between the presence of riddles and the theme of incest that one finds in myths of "people separated by history, geography, language and culture"[17]. For a riddle is "a question to which it is postulated that there will be no answer" (SA 22) and if Oedipus, by solving the riddle, is crudely 'rewarded' by marrying Jocasta, one should perceive a certain "invariant" behind what seems to be an arbitrary narrative move, since "like the solved riddle, incest brings together terms meant to be separate" (SA 23) – joining the son with the mother is as impermissible as giving an answer to a question that was supposed to remain unanswerable. Mankind somehow seems always to have struggled with the problem of separation and union, and although the world of symbolism to which it had recourse in an attempt to 'work through' this problem is, as Lévi-Strauss writes, "infinitely varied in content", the example just given shows that it is "always limited in its laws": "There are many languages, but very few structural laws which are valid for all languages"[18]. But the very presence of these laws – and this is what no doubt aroused Merleau-Ponty's interest – allows Lévi-Strauss "to extend humanism to the measure of humanity" (SA 32), for however diverse the content of men's cultures, they seem to share a common obedience to a common law, which instead of eliminating their diversity, in fact seems to demand it.

What Lévi-Strauss discovers as a structure seems thus to have at least some of the characteristics that we know 'raw Being' has for Merleau-Ponty: it provides a "surface of separation and union", it is an "inexhaustible depth" and it "demands creation for there to be adequation". It is thus not only "unincorporated" in our own or in the other's culture, but "unincorporable" and as such provides us, as Merleau-Ponty comments, with "a ground where we shall both be intelligible without any reduction or rash transposition" (S 122). Henceforth, it would seem that we can leave behind us what one could term 'the illusion of content' – the ethnocentric defence of one's own content and one's own specificity should give way to an attempt "to broaden our reasoning to make it capable of grasping what, in

---

17. Cl. LÉVI-STRAUSS, The Scope of Anthropology, in ID., *Structural Anthropology Volume II*, London, Allen Lane, 1977, p. 22. Henceforth quoted as SA.

18. Cl. LÉVI-STRAUSS, The Effectiveness of Symbols, in ID., *Structural Anthropology [Volume I]*, London, Allen Lane, 1969, p. 203.

ourselves and others, precedes and exceeds reason" (*ibid.*).

This parallel between 'structure' and 'raw Being' should not, however, deceive us. Not so much because one should suspect in it a phenomenological recuperation of structuralist anthropology, but because it is not enough to lead to the sort of ethics that Merleau-Ponty has in mind. Indeed, as much as he may like the ethical recommendations that Lévi-Strauss is drawing from his own discovery, it seems unlikely that he would not have sought in his own endo-ontology a firmer foundation for this anti-colonialist stance. To be sure, anthropology may be that "remarkable method" which "requires us to transform ourselves" "in learning to see what is ours as alien and what was alien as our own" (S 120), but without any further philosophical backing the validity of this requirement would entirely depend on our willingness to read in Lévi-Strauss's results what he suggests we should be reading in them. One could easily read them differently, and it is not sure whether Lévi-Strauss's scientific *hybris* does not turn him into one more offspring of the tragic hero who *by solving the riddle* summons the plague he was supposed to cure. General mythology, to be sure, brings order into the chaos of the innumerable myths of humanity, it provides them with a general grammar and thus in a sense with the question to which they are all answers, but it seems to reason as though peace would result from perceiving a similarity between what hitherto was different, and as though, as Levinas correctly remarked, "incomprehension, war and conquest did not derive just as naturally from the contiguity of the multiple expressions of being"[19]. We discover, for example, with the help of structural anthropology, that what we used to call "primitive thinking" is not primitive at all and that "the kind of logic in mythical thought is as rigorous as that of modern science" (SA 30). But although this discovery makes it impossible any longer to "explain alleged differences between the so-called primitive mind and scientific thought" in terms of "qualitative differences between the working processes of the mind in both cases" (*ibid.*), it does not by itself produce the kind of orientation that Lévi-Strauss assumes it does when he sees in it a step toward a greater mutual respect between those who follow the canons of modern science and those for whom "the same logical processes" (*ibid.*) issue in myth. To the contrary, disclosing what is common to such differences may produce exactly the reverse result. Instead of bringing peace and respect, it might enhance the mutual irritation and lead to war. For now the other is brought closer to us than ever before – but in thus losing his

---

19. I adopt this phrase from an essay in which Levinas is obviously alluding to Merleau-Ponty's Lévi-Strauss essay (E. LEVINAS, 'Meaning and Sense', in CPP, p. 88). My reasons for directing this remark to Lévi-Strauss rather than to Merleau-Ponty will become apparent below.

distance, he may become more of a threat than he used to be: why would we not feel more threatened by the fact that what we thought to be other, is in fact but another "incarnation" of the same logic as ours, another reply to the same fundamental contradiction that is haunting us both? For what this means is that we are not less unique but differently unique than we thought, and it is not sure that we will not secretly or overtly blame the other for thus relativizing to a common ground what we had assumed to be fully our own. If there is indeed an invariant structure to be discovered beneath the multiple symbolisms of mankind, the disenchanting gesture which makes them all push forth their roots in a universal which remains equally inaccessible to each of them, may very well end up by completely uprooting them. Like the sorcerer's apprentice, Lévi-Strauss's inaugural gesture might find itself unable to call back the spirits it set loose in letting us "*gain* possession" of the "wild region" "unincorporated" in our own culture.

Hence, perhaps the importance of the almost imperceptible shift that Merleau-Ponty introduces, all the while reassuring Lévi-Strauss that "his recommendation could not possibly endanger anthropology" (S 123), when interpreting his results as allowing us to *re*gain possession of that wild region. For what this prefix ('re-gain' instead of 'gain') suggests is that the findings of anthropology cannot come as a complete surprise to us – somehow a contact had been lost and if in a certain sense anthropology restores it, this restoration can only impose a *metanoia* on us because far from confronting us with a knowledge that we are unable to bear, it reminds us of a loss with which we were already familiar. "Before being reason, humanity is an other corporeity" (N 269), Merleau-Ponty tells us, and as we know, what is 'other' about this corporeity is that the fact that it never manages to close its circuit is precisely what inserts it in a being which it can share with others. If raw Being is formally homologous to structure, the difference between the philosophical and the scientific concept is that for the former what is unincorporated and unincorporable is not just the mathematically understandable[20] absence of full incorporation, but above all a positive phenomenon. Something withdraws from every 'corporation', but it is precisely because of this loss that human corporeity can take the form it does and that it is *eo ipso* intercorporeity: "the things", Merleau-Ponty writes in *La Nature* – and one might add: "the others" – "are what my body lacks to close its circuit" (N 281). But the point is not just that this lack is not really a lack, but also and more deeply that, if thought to its end, it calls into

---

20. One may wonder whether Merleau-Ponty's protests against the notion of the infinite of the Cartesians who speak of it "as one speaks of some thing, which they *demonstrate* in 'objective philosophy'" (VI 169) could not equally well be directed against Lévi-Strauss's structuralism.

question possessive pronouns such as '*my* body' or '*its* circuit'. The problem with these pronouns is that they seem to approach the 'things' or the 'others' as only an extension of 'my own' circuit – they would be of use to me because they allow me to close a circuit that I somehow could not close on my own. My relation to them would be such that through them I relate to myself, and it would thus not fundamentally differ from the narcissicism with which certain people engage in a conversation that, whatever turn it takes, always seems to touch on what they too experienced – and much more intensely than the other speaker – with the result that all the other voices in the conversation are only there to mark off the originality of their own. The others are needed in this circuit, but only to let it return to itself – they are needed like one needs a mirror because one is unable to see oneself without it. One knows, for example, how tiresome it can be when the paper one has finally managed to write is received so well by one's audience that they cannot wait to declare how the questions it raises reverberate with their own. The little that there might have been of my own in the talk I gave to them suddenly appears not to be what they had been applauding me for and that text which for me was a relief through which I was trying to find my way, now seems to have been only a flat plain where whatever there was to see for me was what they had been seeing too, but from their side of the room. If I feel somewhat lost, and not quite satisfied, it is – perhaps, for narcissism is all around – because I sense that my voice was needed, but only as an occasion for them to hear their own. If I feel deflated, it is – perhaps – because they have flattened that relief in which I gradually got lost, and turned it into a mirror which faithfully reflected what they had expected to see.

But for Merleau-Ponty, like for Lacan, the problem with such narcissism is that it is literally too superficial (the other becoming the flat surface of a mirror) and already presupposes "a second and more profound sense of the narcissism" (VI 139). What the mirror does, is not just to allow one "to see in the outside, as the others see it, the contour of the body one inhabits" (*ibid.*). If the "fundamental narcissism of all vision" could be reduced to the fact that "the seer" who is "caught up in what he sees" would "see himself" in whatever he sees (*ibid.*), there would be no room for the notion of 'flesh'. Instead, my *body* would take over again, and the result would not have removed us much from the philosophy of immanence where the world can only show itself as long as it obeys a set of pre-existent categories. If Merleau-Ponty insists on introducing such strange-sounding phrases as "a relation of the visible with itself that traverses me and constitutes me as a seer" (VI 140), if he sees in this "coiling over of the visible upon the visible" (*ibid.*) the trace of an "anonymity innate to Myself" that he calls 'flesh', it is because he ultimately wanted to oppose to the circle of my own circuit "a circle that I do not form" but "which forms me" (*ibid.*). To the circle of the pre-existent subject *The Visible and the Invisible* opposes the circle of the flesh in which the subject is coming *into* existence, or rather into ek-sistence, for this subject will never be fully 'inside' itself, its 'inside' will always be infected by an outside. What Merleau-Ponty calls the "second sense" of narcissism has to be related to this constitutive "failure" to fully interiorize an outside. Narcissism no longer refers, as its 'first' sense suggests, to a movement from a pre-existent inside which projects itself into the outside and sees in everything its own shadow. Its movement is exactly the reverse: not to see oneself *in* the outside, but "to be seen by the outside" (VI 139) and to be "captivated" (*ibid.*) by it. It is not the subject that is captivated by what it sees, it is "flesh" itself which "lets itself be captivated by one of its fragments" (VI 141) and the result of that captivation is that "one acquires a wholly new idea of the 'subjectivity'" of the subject (VI 269).

'New in what sense?', the reader who has recognized Merleau-Ponty's allusions to Lacan's 'Mirror Stage', will have wondered. Indeed, the use of the word 'captivation' itself is an explicit reference to Lacan's work with which Merleau-Ponty, as we know from "The child's relations with others", was more than familiar (cf. PrP 136 ff.). Lacan, as one will remember, had been using a number of results of child psychology and other disciplines in order to show that what was really at stake in the strange interest that the young child displays for his mirror image, is nothing less than "an ontological structure of the human world"[21]. The sense of triumph ('jubilant activity', E 94/1) with which the child reacts to its Image (which need not be only that of a physical mirror, but could also be another child more or less its age), is not due to its discovering itself in the mirror, but to the formative impact that the image has on it: for what it sees in the mirror is a *Gestalt* that, due to its biological prematuration, it is not yet. This *Gestalt* offers the child a self which is fundamentally different from the more or less fluid and vaguely contoured sort of self implied in its proprioceptive 'self-awareness'. The 'mirror Self' – the *Imago*, says Lacan – is clearly the more attractive of the two: it is not vaguely but sharply contoured, not fluid but rigid (E 97/4). And the child identifies with it, or better: it is that Imago which allows it, for the first time, 'to keep up an image' and to have an identity: "it is in the

---

21. J. LACAN, *Écrits*, Paris, Seuil, 1966, p. 94/2 – henceforth quoted as E followed by the French pagination and after the solidus by the English pagination for essays included in Alan Sheridan's partial translation (*Écrits. A Selection*, London, Routledge, 1989). For a brief but lucid exposition of the 'mirror stage': B. OGILVIE, *Lacan. La formation du concept de sujet (1932-1949)*, Paris, P.U.F., 1987, pp. 96-119; Ph. JULIEN, *Le retour à Freud de Jacques Lacan. L'application au miroir*, Paris, E.P.E.L., 1990, pp. 43 ff.

other [in the outside] that the subject identifies itself (*s'identifie*) and even comes to experience itself [its 'inside'] first of all" (E 181). But this experience, which seems all bliss and joy, the splendour of this mirror which allows us an image 'of' our own beautiful 'self', will soon turn out to be an apple of Discord[22]. As much as I may love that image, I will also hate it, for it both is me (in a transitive sense: it gives rise to me) and it is other, an uneliminable *heteron* that while offering to close my circuit in fact dispossesses me of it. Man's *auto* is the result of a *hetero*-affection through which a 'self' is erected that no longer controls itself. The subject can only come to itself as an other – "Je est un autre" (E 118/23) – by an "essential alienation" (cf. E 187) which it cannot undo without undoing itself: its 'self', Lacan writes, "hangs over the Abyss of a dizzy Assent in which one can perhaps see the very essence of Anxiety"[23]. The "gap separating man from nature"[24] which let him get captivated by an image which seemed to make up for that gap, makes him a captive in his own house where he will never be at ease since it is not Eros but Eris which was its architect: "Thus that *primordial discordance* between the I and being" will become "the fundamental note" that will "resound" throughout the subject's further history (E 187).

When we remarked earlier that Lévi-Strauss's results could very well lead to the opposite consequences than those he was optimistically hoping to contribute to, we were, of course, already alluding to Lacan's idea that it is not just the 'other' other but first and foremost the similar other who can count on my aggression. Or rather, since things are of course more complex than we can suggest here, let us say that we cannot rule that out. The more similar the other gets, the greater the risk that he will find himself drawn into the vortex of that 'primordial Discord' (E 96/4) that "menaces" (E 192) man from within. But if we didn't press Merleau-Ponty by these sort of questions, it was because we were already anticipating the results of the analysis that we just carried through. Not that Merleau-Ponty will make these questions his own. For as we shall see, it is not his allegiance to Lacan, but the way he appropriates his results, which would make him dismiss them as being beside the point.

---

22. Lacan, who knew his mythology, does not miss the opportunity to capitalize 'Discord' (E 95/4, 149).

23. J. LACAN, 'Some Reflections on the Ego', *International Journal of Psychoanalysis*, 1953 (XXXIV), p. 15.

24. *Ibid.*, p. 16.

IV

Something essential has been happening in this at first sight innocent attempt to introduce the results of Lacan's 'reflections on the Ego' into an ontology of the flesh. Indeed, the very premise which Lacan would need in order to point to the aggressiveness that could be triggered by a similar Other has managed to somehow fall out of the picture: the flesh as "a mirror phenomenon" (VI 255) is for Merleau-Ponty, and this is crucial, not at all carrying within itself the seeds of a 'primordial Discord'; quite to the contrary, in so far as both I and the other are "together caught up in one same 'element' [...] this cohesion, this visibility by principle, *prevails over every momentary discordance*" (VI 140). The "concrete vision I have of my body in the mirror" (VI 249) does not seem to have for Merleau-Ponty the paradigmatic status it has for Lacan. Whereas for Lacan the fundamental misrecognition (*méconnaisance*, E 99,109/6,15) implied by the child's 'recognition' of itself in the mirror (*Je est un autre*), seems to introduce a structure of misrecognition into human (including adult) perception as such[25], for Merleau-Ponty the "self-perception" made possible by the mirror "is still a perception" (VI 249) and it obeys the same logic as all perception: "it gives me a *Nicht Urpräsentierbar* (a non-visible, myself), but this it gives me through an *Urpräsentierbar* (my tactile or visual appearance) in transparency (i.e. as latency)" (VI 249-50). This 'Urpräsentierbarkeit' of what is 'nicht urpräsentierbar' is, of course, what gave *The Visible and the Invisible* its title: it is but another word for the very structure of 'flesh' (N 271), and it means, for example, that there is an 'invisible' to the 'visible' – something that is *not*

---

25. Lacan's 'mirror stage' is, in fact, not a stage in the development of the Ego that it leaves behind as it matures. Not only is the Ego an imaginary formation, but the imaginary is an essential and ineliminable part of human experience as such – indeed, Lacan does not shun to speak of a "madness by which man believes himself to be human": "Formule paradoxale qui prend pourtant sa valeur à considerer que l'homme est *bien plus que son corps, tout en ne pouvant rien savoir de plus de son être*. Il y apparaît cette illusion fondamentale dont l'homme est serf ... cette passion d'être un homme ... qui est la passion de l'âme par excellence, le narcissisme, lequel impose sa structure à tous les désirs fût-ce aux plus élevés" (E 188). Merleau-Ponty, who quotes the text this passage is taken from in his 'The child's relations with others' (but under a wrong title: he quotes the title of Lacan's third section instead of the title of the text itself), was among the first to stress the structural character of the mirror 'stage' in Lacan. Yet it would be easy to show how his way of explaining the presence of such a structure, even in adult life, is clearly purifying it of some of its less attractive aspects (basically by distinguishing between normal adult life in which the imaginary seems to fulfil a 'positive' role (e.g. PrP 155: "all relations with others, *if deep enough* [!], bring about a state of insecurity") and pathology where it disrupts life, this in clear contrast to Lacan for whom such a neat distinction normal / pathological seems to be doubtful: the Discord sides at the heart of normality too).

just *de facto* invisible but potentially visible, but also *not absolutely* invisible. It is this invisible *of* the visible which can never be eliminated and which gives Being its depth, its relief and its texture. Without it, flesh would not be an element of Being, or it would not be another word for Being as a verb. If Being is raw, if it 'has' depth, it is because one cannot be 'of it' without being inserted in it and without thus losing the property titles to one's 'own' circuit. This 'loss' is, to be sure, not always the same, *but it always pays back for the wound with which it has inflicted immanence*: "The touching touches itself immediately ('bipolarity' of the *Tastwelt*). Vision *breaks* this immediacy (the visible is at a distance, outside the limits of my body) and *reestablishes the unity by mirror, in the world*" (N 345). What the mirror shows is that there is a union to all separation and that they do not contradict one another: it thus "outlines and amplifies the metaphysical structure of our flesh" (PrP 168). And thus, *whereas the 'mirror' for Lacan points to an ineliminable discord between man and nature, for Merleau-Ponty it simply confirms the metaphysical premise from which he started all along.* Nature in us has a relation to nature outside of us[26], they both 'pass into' one another and it is by drawing attention to the mystery of that transition that the mirror can come to take the emblematic significance it seems to have for Merleau-Ponty. *Eye and Mind* sees in it "the instrument of a universal magic that changes things into a spectacle, spectacles into things, myself into another, and another in myself" (*ibid.*). This magic is more than a cheap trick – it is the "metamorphosis of seeing and seen which defines (...) our flesh" (PrP 169), and in and through which we come to sense something of the immense labouring effort going on in it. "Indivision" of Being is not static – it refers to the mode in which Being 'explodes': "Other consequence: as my images catches (*capte*) my touching, the visual image of the others catches it too: they too are the outside of me. And I am their inside. They alienate me and I incorporate them. I see by the eyes of the others the world. (...) So there is indivision of my body, of my body and the world, of my body and the other bodies, and of the other bodies between them" (N 346). There is no problem of the *alter ego* because the other, like the world, "is already there" (VI 221). "There is" transitivism at all levels and 'nature' seems, for Merleau-Ponty, the name for a principle of transition where there are, like in the old adage, no abrupt leaps (*natura non facit saltus*). "There is" one common fabric, and it somehow always manages to remain *intact*: "In advance every vision or every partial visible that would here definitively come to naught (*échec*) is not nullified (*which would leave a gap in its place*), but, what is better, it is replaced by a more exact vision and a more exact visible, according to the principle of visibility, which, *as though through a sort of abhorrence of*

26. See above, section I.

vacuum, already invokes the true vision and the true visible" (VI 140).

Flesh, clearly, "is an ultimate notion" (*ibid.*). And thus "to regain possession" of the "wild region" in us is to see things and oneself in the light of that ultimacy which pre-possesses (VI 133) us, and puts something like a "pre-established harmony" (*ibid.*)[27] underneath what we may come to live as tensions. For example, underneath those tensions between us and the others. If Lévi-Strauss's other can "require us to transform ourselves" (S 120), it is because somehow these 'selves' seem to have forgotten their origin. But this forgetting is "a paradox of Being" (VI 122/162), not of man: for Being 'works' discreetly, it weaves its texture during the night of men, who in the light of day are too occupied with sensing to be aware of the labour that is needed "so that at the joints of the opaque body and the opaque world there is a ray of generality and of light" (VI 146)[28]. It takes an effort – the effort of a metaphysical *metanoia* – not: to see that ray, for that is impossible, the invisible is not another visible, but to see "according to" it (PrP 164). But if one makes that effort – and here painting, or others, or literature all come to our support – one is like born again. Or rather: like the painter, one becomes witness to "a continued birth" (PrP 168), an "inspiration and expiration of Being" (PrP 167) without which that "pact" that precedes us would but belong to the prehistory of man, instead of being that "initial yes", the "indivision of sensing" (N 381) which "as overlapping and fission,

27. See above note 13 and section II on Leibniz. It cannot be denied that Merleau-Ponty's text is full of images that point in this direction (e.g. VI 133: "two halves of an orange"; 134: "total parts" (see above note 16); VI 139: "commerce"; VI 148: "the zero of pressure between two solids that makes them *adhere* to one another") – all of which basically are to contain the same danger: that of "an ontological void, a non-being" (*ibid.*), in other terms: that of an invisible that would not be an invisible 'of' the visible without being either the *de facto* invisible (e.g. VI 251) or the *absolute* invisible (e.g. VI 266) that Merleau-Ponty tends to see as its alternatives. As our discussion of Lacan made clear, and as I shall be suggesting below, one might wonder whether there is not something which escapes this set of alternatives and refuses to be domesticated by it. For a similar suspicion, cf. Cl. LEFORT, 'Flesh and Otherness', in G.A. JOHNSON - M.B. SMITH (eds.), *o.c.*, pp. 3-13 – although I am sympathetic to Lefort's overall point of view and in particular share his suspicion that "the world that Merleau-Ponty attempted to explore [may have been] an already tamed world rather than that wild experience to which he hoped to give expression" (p. 11), I should like to stress that the argument I am in the course of developing rests on its own and should not be too quickly assimilated with Lefort's even where it touches on points (like the proper name – cf. infra) which he is making too. There is, in fact, a lot to be learned from the replies which follow Lefort's paper in that same volume and I hope to have profited from them.

28. I believe this to be the true context of the rather enigmatic point that Merleau-Ponty is making when saying things like "l'inconscient primordial serait le laisser-être, le oui initial, l'indivision du sentir" (N 381).

identity and difference (...) brings to birth a ray of natural light *that illuminates all flesh and not only my own*" and gives it "that primordial property (...) of radiating *everywhere and forever, being an individual, of being also a dimension and a universal*" (VI 142)[29]. "Regaining possession" is to say 'yes' to that 'yes', it is to return to the mystical body that Merleau-Ponty calls 'flesh'.

The least one can say is that Merleau-Ponty's way of showing that the I - other problem is a '*Western* problem' seems itself, if not an expression of, then at least strangely close to a particular way in which a particular tradition in the West, which itself had not been exactly silent about the mysteries of the flesh, had been approaching that issue. However that may be, and whether one likes it or not, one cannot deny that Merleau-Ponty's notion of 'flesh' seems to bring with it the suggestion that there is no darkness which does not have at its hither side a beam of light. Everything that is opaque in man somehow seems to bear within it that inner glow which is the birthmark which Being left on him. All opacity seems thus transfigured into a good opacity, just as every loss seems "compensated" by the attachment to Being which it makes possible. The "thickness of the flesh" is never "an obstacle", but somehow always a "means of communication" (VI 135). If the self is prey to "confusion", this is because it is "not a self through transparence, like thought, which only thinks its object by assimilating it" (PrP 162-3). The confusion – this *Ineinander* by which I pass into the world or into others, and they in turn into me – seems always a happy one, never a source of pain or panic. If this "self through confusion, narcissism, through inherence of the one who sees in that which he sees" (PrP 163) somehow is confronted with an interruption of this circuit, that interruption itself is only there to prevent this confusion from ending up in what it should not be – confusion is con-fusion, not fusion as such: "Among my movements, there are some *that go nowhere* (...) Those movements end in sounds and I hear them (...) In this (....) I am incomparable, my voice is bound to the mass of my own life *as is the voice of no one else*. But if I am close enough to the other who speaks to hear his breath and feel his effervescence and his fatigue, I almost witness, in him as in myself, the *awesome* birth of vociferation. *As there is a reflexivity of the touch, of sight, and of the touch-vision system, there is a reflexivity of the movements of phonation*

---

29. Again, there seems to be a parallel with the Christian tradition, for which the 'mystical body' of the Church referred to a community that did not found itself, but depended for its constitution on a divine Election (*a first 'yes'*) preceding all initiative of the subjects of that community, and yet calling for a freely given reply to that Appeal on their part (*a second 'yes': a 'yes' to the first 'yes'*) and thus, just like in Merleau-Ponty, for a *metanoia* and a process of conversion on their part.

and of hearing..." (VI 144).

It is unmistakable: the 'unreflected' is only brought up by Merleau-Ponty to contest reflection but it is never allowed to tear apart reflexivity. It darkens and resists the transparency of immanence, belies idealism, cuts a hole in consciousness, but that hole is part of a texture which antedates consciousness and thus is never a total void, but a "determinate" one (VI 204). There is "a presence to self" that in truth is "absence of self" (VI 250/303, transl. altered) but never the absence of the For Itself which mistakes for its own a negativity that properly belongs to Being. "The only 'place' where the negative would really be is the fold, the application of the inside and the outside to one another" (VI 264) and this is why the "awe" with which the English translator makes me "almost witness the birth of vociferation" is a very happy choice for rendering "*l'effrayante* naissance de la vociération" (VI 144/190). For one can only respectfully witness the fold*ing* of a fold which normally goes unnoticed – panic would be out of tune here, since for Merleau-Ponty there is no contradiction between my being "incomparable" and "always at the same side of my body" and my belonging to a common fabric of intercorporeity. 'The same' does not mean 'identical', it refers to my side of a fold which in truth is a Moebius strip where the other's side turns into mine and mine into his...

If one thus loses sight of what side one is on, one gains all the same. At least for Merleau-Ponty who seems to pride himself on having found a way to keep what was good about 'the subject' all the while avoiding its less agreeable sides. Indeed, one would misunderstand his intentions were one to see in that "anonymous visibility" (VI 142) which inhabits both me and the other a prepersonal element which swallows both me and the other and only solves the problem of the *alter ego* because there would be nothing of either of us left. The subject that Merleau-Ponty thought of "rejecting" (VI 239) is only the subject of immanence. But the subject as such is not 'dead' or 'dissolved'. It is rather 'redefined' such as to give rise to a "wholly new" conception of it. And this new conception consists in *redefining the subject in such a way that it fully fits into intersubjectivity*. There is, of course, a cost to this conception, but Merleau-Ponty seems to have no hesitations to pay whatever it takes to prevent the subject's escape from intersubjectivity. All the measures need to be taken to prevent something from coming between the subject and its others. And however strange it may sound, it seems as if such a something could be for Merleau-Ponty a 'proper name' – that is at least what seems to be suggested by that strange phrase in the *Notes de Cours* which echoes a well-known *Working Note* (Ἐγώ and οὔτις, VI 246): the subject would be "as Homer says it brilliantly, nobody (*personne*), οὔτις, the contrary of a monad" (NdC 371). We should perhaps take that suggestion seriously – after all, it might lead us back to the problem of the proper name with which we, as one will remember, began this re-reading of Merleau-Ponty.

V

The suggestion in the quote with which we ended that the subject as a "nobody" is "the contrary of a monad" in a way puts us on the wrong leg. For the word "monad" is not used in a technical sense there. Indeed one only needs to remember our earlier discussion of the *Working Note* on Leibniz to see that what *this retailoring of the subject to the measure of intersubjectivity* is really doing to it, is to turn it into something close to a monad – for as one will remember, "certain Leibnizian descriptions are to be maintained entirely" and in particular that what is private to one "would be public to all" (VI 223). By a totally different way, Merleau-Ponty comes here to formulate a desideratum about the subject that is the same as the one that, as I have tried to show in chapter five, is governing the analysis of Levinas: the only privacy allowed to the subject is what links it to other subjects[30]. Merleau-Ponty's subject may be attached, but this attachment is an attachment to Being, and hence will link it to others. But there may be nothing in the subject that attaches it, as it were from within, to this attachment. There can be nothing that folds back the subject onto itself without that fold being at the same time what connects it to the other. If the subject is a fold, it is a fold which wraps it up in Being – what produces the fold is Being coiling over upon itself and thus ensuring that these folds which think of themselves as subjects, are all subjected to the same Being and all participate in one and the same fabric: "I must no longer think myself *in the world* in the sense of the ob-jective spatiality, which amounts to auto-positing myself and installing myself in the *Ego uninteressiert* (...) what replaces the antagonistic and solidary reflective movement (the immanence of the 'idealists') is the fold or hollow of Being *having by principle* an outside, the architectonics of the configurations. (...) There are fields in intersection, in a field of fields wherein the 'subjectivities' are integrated" (VI 227). Hence what was essential in Leibniz's universe can be saved, but without the *en soi* and without the Divine Architect: "Our soul has no windows: that means *In der Welt sein*" (VI 223)[31]. The folds of Being

---

30. I will return to this point in the Levinas-chapters of my third section.

31. Heidegger, as we now know, would agree: "Das Dasein als Monade braucht keine Fenster (...) weil die Monade, das Dasein, seinem eigenen Sein nach (der Transzendenz nach), schon draußen ist" (*Die Grundprobleme der Phänomenologie* (Marburg Lectures, summer semester 1927), GA 24, p. 427).

"are in a relation of expression between themselves and with the world" (*ibid.*). If they "differ from one another" it is but "as perspectives" upon – or rather: of one and the same raw Being (*ibid.*). And with this, the danger of relativism has been curbed: "not a relativism, a historicism, but inversely the idea that *each present contains everything, is absolute, everything is true and not everything is false*"[32].

Totum simul (VI 219): the truth of what I can formulate, of what I can hear and take seriously from within the limits of my discourse, is as true as what an other standing on a different *Boden* than I do and from that "perspective" which is his and not mine, can come to make of raw Being. If there is between us a tension, a friction, a certain unease, it is due to the fact that we do not see the more general *Boden* beneath the *Boden* specific to each of us. If I feel dissociated from the Other because what he says and does makes sense within his way of being in the Truth, but is meaningless in my own, that *dissociation* is not the sign of a silence or an otherness within each of us that could come between us. It is but a momentary affect, bound to give way to the feeling of awe with which we are soon to discover this 'inter-Being' which is "*between* my perspective and that of the other" (VI 219). In truth these 'truths' do not separate us, for there is no separation without union, and if we do feel separated, it is because we are searching for the universal where it has long since left. It is, in fact, like the God of which Claudel speaks, "not above", but "beneath" us (VI 218) – not "a supra sensible idea, but another ourself *which dwells in and authenticates our darkness*" (S 71)[33].

But what if 'relativism', which since the dawn of philosophy has been accompanying it as its shadow, precisely by permanently returning to it, no matter how often and how decisively it has been refuted, testifies to another darkness? A darkness which escapes philosophy's attempts to "authenticate" it? A darkness that could come to the defence of what escapes that neat transition between the public and the private where "what is particular to one would be public to all" (cf. VI 222-3, quoted before). The darkness which prevents the 'Western *Boden*' from blending with the *Boden* of humanity as

---

32. M. MERLEAU-PONTY, *Notes de Cours sur l'Origine de la Géométrie de Husserl. Suivi de Recherches sur la phénomenologie de Merleau-Ponty* (ed. R. Barbarbas), Paris, P.U.F., 1998, p. 37 (and cf. *ibid.*, pp. 36, 73 for similar dismissals of relativism).

33. The fact that Merleau-Ponty, in the passage just quoted from the *Working Notes*, says of the universal what Claudel in the passage quoted from *Signs*, says of God, again seems to confirm that the parallel we have been suggesting between 'flesh' and the 'mystical body' of the Catholic tradition may not be entirely arbitrary. There seems at least a homology of structure between them, such that the sentence following this passage from *Signs* seems also to describe Merleau-Ponty's own position: "Transcendence no longer hangs over man: he becomes, strangely, its privileged bearer" (S 71).

such, or the darkness which invades the proper name and disturbs the harmonious fit between the subject and its intersubjective element? It is perhaps no coincidence that Merleau-Ponty keeps returning, and with something like a fascination, to Odysseus' reply to the Cyclops: Ἐγώ, οὔτις – as if there is something about the name of the subject that poses a direct threat to the intersubjectivity that Merleau-Ponty wishes to defend. As if he suspected that there could be more in the proper name of the subject than that label where the private is handed over to the public and where the public finds access to the private. Something that would be private perhaps to the subject and yet not "public to all". A point where that surface of union and separation that is at the centre of endo-ontology threatens to become rent and where the Echo of a certain silence at the heart of the subject reminds it of what is "awesome" about the birth of all vociferation, including its own. Had Merleau-Ponty been writing in English he would, no doubt, have had a better sense of the threat that he was trying to contain there – for it suffices that one lets the signifiers regain something of the opacity with which the ancient oracles led astray those who came to consult them, to see that English can sometimes even outbid Greek in philosophical profundity: between "my name is nobody" and "my name is no body" there is but a pause of breath, nothing really that one can hear and yet a silence long enough perhaps to interrupt that 'respiration of Being' from which endo-ontology derives its momentum.

One can, of course, ignore this silence and analyse the name as one more 'mirror' of the flesh: just like the actual mirror of which Merleau-Ponty spoke, the proper name would stand for that in language which gives me and others an 'Urpräsentation' of the 'Nichturpräsentierbar'. The 'proper name' of the subject would then be that signifier through which I qua inaccessible become accessible to others, and in a sense to myself. In being what ties me to myself as less than a transparent subject, my name would be like my "shadow" (cf. VI 255-6) in language, and thus at the same time what ties me to others and prevents me from fusing with them. But is this all that there is to be said about the name? Is there not another shadow hanging over it – one which I will have to bear, alone, and without the others even being aware of it? For them my name is 'a rigid designator' and, as Kripke shows, it can function as such without them being able to substitute a 'uniquely determining description' for it[34]. That it is 'rigid' is to their benefit, for it allows reference to work as it should. But it would seem that in this same rigidity, *in my own inability to replace it by a description which would exhaust its meaning*, something of that primordial Discord of which Lacan spoke has come to reclaim its dues from me: through this name I am

34. S. KRIPKE, *Naming and Necessity*, Oxford, Blackwell, 1981.

decentred, but the meaning of that decentrement escapes me. I can, of course, change it, but this change would not really help, for it would simply mean that another name, no less fitting or unfitting, would have come to take its place. And I would be held captive again, not quite in the same way, of course, as I was by that mirror from which my 'self' originated, for the name is rigid as the *Gestalt* in the mirror, but it is a dark mirror that doesn't allow me to contemplate my 'image' in it. That which I could never subdue in the 'image' – the gap that in being presupposed and denied by that circuit in which I passed into my image and it in me – seems to return to me in my proper name. As if in the 'impropriety' with which my 'proper' name refuses to yield its significance to me, another aspect of my vision is revealed to me and one which, this time, by "going nowhere" (VI 144) except to my 'self', shows that there is something about that self which is *not* 'of' the world. For if the world is Being and generality, as Merleau-Ponty tells us, and if within Being and generality, the many worlds can never be thought of as in opposition with the one world of which they are all expressions, the name of the subject which is no longer immanent, nor simply within Being, seems to safeguard a principle of inexpressibility that one should perhaps oppose to that "expression of the universe in us" which endo-ontology tried to describe. As if there is a 'hollow' in us, through which the sounds of that expression can slip away without them being heard by others or given Voice by some Elsewhere. The one-eyed son of Poseidon may have been referring to that hollow when he told his friends that "nobody had tried to kill him". And as they rightly concluded, if "no body" was behind that pain of his, there was truly nothing they could do about it. For it is not our body (no body) that is causing us trouble, what makes our bodies mortal is not something in them, but something which doesn't let itself be incorporated by them. A primordial Discordance is at the root of our bodies and exacts from us a pound of flesh before they can be called our 'own'. And even then, the trace of that sacrifice forever scars the names to which we resort in order to produce that reference – something about these names will have to remain unreadable, stiff and rigid like the corpse that we once shall be. One could call this something a letter, and oppose to it, as Lacan seems to do when he tells us that "it is the letter that kills us, but we hear it from the letter" (E 848), that Word which was to triumph over both death and the letter, through an Incarnation by which the body became glorified. What is characteristic of Merleau-Ponty's philosophy is perhaps that in trying to speak, it knew that it was no longer backed by such a Word, and that, therefore, it had to do what it could to exorcise the letter. The result is that strange humanism of what is other than man which, in bringing out the happy message that "the other is already there", seems at the same time no longer to have the means to persuade the Ego that "it has to be conquered" (VI 221) from that other[35]. For what would that conquest amount to, whence would it derive its force, once that Ego has given up its attempts to think of itself as a "consciousness" that "cannot but feel itself annihilated (*annulée*) by the absolute other" (NdC 153)? As the subject slowly makes its way back into intersubjectivity and through it into intercorporeity, it discovers that it is – unlike that consciousness – *not* "absolutely guilty, absolutely unjustifiable, responsible, condemned" – but that "it is an existence, i.e. always attached to inertia, to other than me" and that "this generativity absolves it" (*ibid.*). If there is something at stake in endo-ontology, it is, no doubt, this absolution of the subject: the promise that its loss is not final, that it can be recuperated and given ontological dignity. The only problem is that in order to become "cet espace de plein air" (NdC 371) where "all things would come to exist for each other" (*ibid.*), we would first have to give up our proper name. Which means perhaps that we would no longer speak. A *Western* problem?

---

35. I have done what I could to substantiate this assertion in the preceding chapter.

III

The Loneliness of a Subject
Unable to Disappear

CHAPTER NINE

NO PRIVACY?
LEVINAS'S INTRIGUE OF THE INFINITE

As anyone who has tried to find their way through Levinas's texts will remember, these texts are like a moving mine-field. What disconcerts the reader is not just that they proceed "with the infinite insistence of waves on a beach", as Derrida remarked, and therefore would have less of a "treatise" than of a "work of art" in which each returning wave, as it recapitulates itself "also infinitely renews and enriches itself"[1]. The problem is rather that although all of these waves look alike and are often described by Levinas with the same word, they are in fact very different. Overlooking these differences can be fatal; it will inevitably mean that one finds oneself caught up in the midst of the intrigue of what Levinas calls 'the infinite' at the very moment that one thinks one has finally found an exit. Derrida, as we shall see in our next chapter, was perhaps amongst the first to fall prey to this illusion. But he certainly wasn't the last. Indeed, it would seem as if a whole generation of Levinas readers lost their nerve well before he did. These readers think that the plot – which is but another word for 'intrigue' – behind Levinas's philosophy is unnecessarily complex and, in fact, willingly confused. They doubt that Levinas is justified in using the same word – "*l'infini*" – to refer to both God and the Good and they suspect him of smuggling in an "ethico-metaphysical" agenda into his "quasi-phenomenological descriptions of radical alterity"[2]. They think that we can have these descriptions without the "non-human back up"[3] which Levinas

1. J. DERRIDA, 'Violence and Metaphysics. An Essay on the Thought of Emmanuel Levinas', in ID., *Writing and Difference* (transl. A. Bass), Chicago, University of Chicago Press, 1978, p. 312 n7.

2. S. CRITCHLEY, *Very Little ... Almost Nothing. Death, Philosophy, Literature*, London/New York, Routledge, 1997, p. 81 (this quote is taken from a section significantly called 'Holding Levinas's hand to Blanchot's fire'). The present chapter is part of an ongoing friendly dialogue between Simon Critchley and me (cf. *ibid.*, p. 188 n48) which I hope will continue.

3. J.D. CAPUTO, 'To the point of a Possible Confusion: God and il y a', in *Levinas: The Face of the Other. The Fifteenth Annual Symposium of the Simon Silverman Phenomenology Center*, Pittsburgh, Duquesne University, 1998, p. 22.

calls alternately 'the Good' or 'God' or 'illeity'. To suggest, as Levinas does, that the "familiar event of obligation to the other" motivates or requires, as Jack Caputo puts it, "the deep structure of something ... other than the *autrui*", "a 'seal' that God puts on the ethical relationship", is according to these readers "to mystify, or remystify ethics, to conflate it with religion, to absorb religion into it, to supercharge the ethical relation with a metaphysics of infinity" (Caputo 31-2). In short, what these readers suggest is that one can and should 'leave God (or the Good) out of it', for it is precisely "this mystification of the ethical relationship" which has made it "vulnerable to easy dismissal" (Caputo 32). What's more, these readers also suggest that in order to save "what continues to grip" them in Levinas – i.e. in the words of one of them: "the attention to the other, to the other's claim on me and how that claim changes and challenges (one's) self-conception" (Critchley 82) – one should seek support in a more "neutral transcendence" (*ibid.*). In fact, they think that Levinas himself in his more sober moments has been suggesting, albeit a bit begrudgingly, exactly such a move – for example in a famous passage of "God and Philosophy" which I will cite at length, since it goes to the heart of what will also be *our* problem here: "God is not simply 'the first other', the 'other par excellence', or the 'absolutely other', but other than the other, other otherwise, other with an alterity prior to the alterity of the other, prior to the ethical bond with another and different from every neighbor, *transcendent to the point of absence, to the point of a possible confusion with the stirring of the* there is" (CPP 165-6).

I

Whatever reading one is going to give of this passage – and I will not abuse the reader's attention by arguing with the readings of the readers mentioned before – it is clear that something very central is happening here. For the 'there is' which Levinas mentions at the end of this passage is yet another of these waves which move through his texts under the same name of 'the infinite'. The 'intrigue of the infinite' could thus mean either of the following: the intrigue of God (*der Unendliche*), the intrigue of the Good One or the Good (*der oder das Unendliche*), or the intrigue of the 'there is', of that infamous *il y a* of which Levinas has always stressed the inhuman neutrality and anonymity, and which he opposed to the generosity of the Heideggerian 'es gibt'[4]. This *il y a* goes under many names in Levinas's texts, but one of them is indeed 'the infinite' (clearly: *das Unendliche*). But

---

4. See the first paragraph of Levinas's important 1978 preface to the second edition of *De l'existence à la existant* (not included in the English translation; no pagination in the French edition).

in the one passage where Levinas uses the word 'l'infini' to refer to the *il y a*, he takes care to qualify it: it is not called 'the infinite' pure and simple, but 'the bad infinite' (TI 158-9/132: "le mauvais infini"), as if to oppose it to a good infinite, be that 'God' (the Good one) or the Good. Although this distinction between the good and the bad infinite, *literally* occurs, to the best of my knowledge, only once in Levinas's texts, it is so clearly behind all the further distinctions at the heart of Levinas's project that one can wonder how one could come to overlook it[5]. For example, when Levinas tells us at the beginning of *Totality and Infinity* in the very first lines of a central section which is entitled 'The Breach of Totality', that "the metaphysical movement is transcendent" and that "transcendence ... is necessarily a transascendence" (TI 35), he is using a different oppositional pair to refer to the difference between a good and a bad infinite. For what is specific to *transascendence*, and what distinguishes it from the *transdescendent*, is that "the distance" this kind of transcendence "expresses", "enters into the way of existing of the exterior being" (*ibid.*). Without the exteriority of what Levinas calls here 'the metaphysical term' (and *Totality and Infinity*, remember, announced itself as 'An essay on exteriority'), the relation between that term and the metaphysician who is related to it would not be a true movement of transcendence, nor the movement toward a true transcendence. If the distance between the metaphysician and the Other to which he aspires would not enter into the way of being of that Other, there would sooner or later be no Other left (transcendence would collapse in immanence) or – and this is what transdescendence toward a bad infinite would amount to – there would be no metaphysician left. The bad infinite, that is, allows for no relation with it: it is, as Levinas suggests in a later passage, "numinous", it "annihilates" "the I who approaches" it or "transports" it "outside of itself" (TI 77). The good infinite, to the contrary, "does not burn the eyes that are lifted unto him", it "does not have the

---

5. Cf. J. DERRIDA, 'Violence and Metaphysics', *l.c.*, p. 119: "The 'false-infinity', a Hegelian expression which Levinas, it seems to us, never uses, perhaps because it is Hegelian" (transl. corrected). It is true that Derrida continues: "nonetheless haunts numerous gestures of denunciation in *Totality and Infinity*", but his suggestion that while 'the other' for Levinas is "the true infinity" whilst "the same" is "the false-infinity" and the subsequent Hegelian *reductio ad absurdum* ("Levinas would be speaking of the other under the rubric of the same, and of the same under the rubric of the other, etc." (*ibid.*)) mislocates, as we shall see, the "bad infinite" in the economy of Levinas's thought. Indeed, for all its subtlety *Violence and Metaphysics* could, *with the advantage of hindsight*, be held responsible for the picture of Levinas as a philosopher whose well-meaning attempt to play off 'the other' against 'the same' shipwrecks on the contradictory notion of an 'absolute alterity'. But, as we shall see, the other's alterity is, for Levinas, absolute in a different sense and *less or differently* absolute than the absoluteness of the bad infinite.

mythical format that is impossible to confront and that would hold the I in its *invisible* meshes" (*ibid.*). And yet, as we shall see, the good infinite too escapes visibility – which means that the difference between the good and the bad infinite, between the Good / God and the *il y a*, between the transascendent and the transdescendent, will imply, among other things, at least a different economy of the visible and the invisible, and perhaps a different "visibility of the invisible" or, who knows, a different "invisibility of the visible". But let us first explore how all these oppositions relate to the fact that God's transcendence, as we heard Levinas say, should be seen as "transcendent to the point of absence, to the point of a possible confusion with the stirring of the *il y a*". In other words, what we need to understand is how the transascendence of God allows for, or perhaps even necessitates, as Caputo and others think[6], a confusion with the transdescendence of the *il y a*. As we shall see, to understand this is to understand (which is not necessarily to agree with) what the revelation, not of the "divine" (for this is a word that he could never accept, cf. OB 162), but of 'God' means for Levinas.

II

This brief sketch of the difference between the good and the bad infinite, between the transascendent and the transdescendent should already suffice to understand why for Levinas a "revelation of the divine" would be a

---

6. In spite of Levinas's claim that "transcendence is necessarily transascendence" (TI 35/5, just quoted), Hent de Vries finds himself writing that "there is no ethical transcendence without transdescendence, we read in *Totality and Infinity* (TeI 66; TaI 93)". But this is not at all what Levinas says in these pages where he mentions "a movement of *descent* toward an ever more profound abyss which we elsewhere have called *there is*" (TI 93/66) but does not talk about ethical transcendence at all, let alone make the claim that de Vries is attributing to him. ('Adieu, à dieu, a-dieu', in A. PEPERZAK (ed.), *Ethics as First Philosophy. The Significance of Emmanuel Levinas for Philosophy, Literature and Religion*, New York / London, Routledge, 1995, pp. 211-20 (quote: p. 214)). De Vries's article is one of Caputo's sources. It is striking, however, that Caputo lists TO but does not discuss it, and does not mention EE, Levinas's most systematic treatment of the *il y a*. As a result, Caputo seems only to recognize in the *il y a* "the anonymous" (e.g., p. 32), and is entirely oblivious to its depersonalizing character, (e.g. the *rhetoric* of all the questions on pp. 27-8 presupposes this oblivion) on which I shall insist below. The resulting confusion seems to me significant and symptomatic of an unwillingness to engage with Levinas at the level he himself indicated. But we remember with gratitude from this passage that the *il y a* is, for Levinas, linked to *a descent*, which thus authorizes us to see in it a 'transdescendence', a notion that one does not find in Levinas's text(s), where only the antonym is used (transdescendence and transascendence go back to Jean Wahl (to whom TI is dedicated): *Existence Humaine et Transcendance*, Neuchâtel, Éditions de la Baconnière, 1944, pp. 34-56, 113-59).

contradiction in terms. The divine is, as it were, too revealing to allow for a Revelation. It is pure manifestation that *absorbs* into itself the one to whom it is supposed to reveal itself. It enchants and possesses those who come into contact with it. Their ek-stasis is but a sign that they have lost their *stasis* and with it the ability to stand on their own. One does not relate to the divine, one "participates" in it and as a result, one loses one's independence. Such is the "violence of the sacred" (TI 77). But the force with which it overpowers and alienates those that approach it, is also a sign of its weakness: it is *incapable* of a relation with the finite because it is *unable* to control its own infinity. The divine is a bad infinite because it lacks the humility to "contract" itself (TI 104) and to be the source of a manifestation that leaves its addressee the freedom not to take notice of it.

Without that freedom, there can be no Revelation. With it, there may or may not be a Revelation: the one who reveals himself is always at a risk of not being heard – "a lover makes an advance, but the provocative or seductive gesture has, if one likes, not interrupted the decency of the conversation and attitudes; it withdraws as lightly as it had slipped in" (CPP 66). Transcendence does not arrive on its own. If it isn't received, it withdraws without a trace, leaving those it had tried to address as if in the midst of a scene of Ionesco: "we still do not know if, when someone rings the doorbell, there is someone there or not" (*The Bald Soprano*, quoted CPP 61). Hilarious! But deep. This "transcendence to the point of absence" is what Levinas calls "divine comedy" (CPP 166). And we are its characters. Centuries of Bible criticism have immensely increased our knowledge – we are beyond superstition, these texts are man-made, a reflection of their time and culture. In short, they have "reduced to immanence what seemed to be transcendent"[7]. Nothing happened! There was no one on the mountain[8]. God is dead! And Levinas agrees: a certain God, he says repeatedly[9], is certainly dead. But as he would add in the same breath: doesn't this also mean that the one we call God lives dangerously, and that what we call his death, is perhaps his way of life (OB 95)? The voice of transcendence,

---

7. E. LEVINAS in a discussion following his lecture on 'Le Nom de Dieu. D'après quelques textes talmudiques' at the famous Castelli colloquium; reprinted in: E. LEVINAS, *L'Intrigue de l'Infini. Textes réunis et présentés par Marie-Anne Lescourret*, s.l., Flammarion, 1994, p. 230.

8. "A God was revealed on a mountain or in a burning bush, or made himself attested to in Scriptures. And what if there were a storm! And what if the Scriptures came to us from dreamers!" (CPP 66).

9. "You see, I have not at all been reasoning in the abstract; I reason starting from the concrete spiritual situation of our Europe where one says that 'God is dead'. *And a certain God is certainly dead*" (*L'Intrigue de l'Infini*, o.c., p. 230; my transl.), and cf. e.g. OB 5, 95, etc.

Levinas says, the voice of the good Infinite "has to be silent as soon as one listens for its message" (OB 152). For this message is not "a proof" (*ibid.*) and its truth is not "victorious"[10]. It has – and Levinas praises Kierkegaard for having realized this – a different modality: "Persecution, and, by the same token, humility are modalities of the true" (KCR 35). A "persecuted truth" is neither certain nor uncertain. It is not "a truth lacking in certainty" (*ibid.*) for that would reduce transcendence to a "failed immanence"[11]. If the Infinite would only be an idea that is too big for its *ideatum*, it would lose what Levinas calls "its glory" (OB 144 ff.). For this glory would be too glorious, it would be triumphant and remain unaffected by the failure to immanentize it. It would not suffer from this failure, and it would lose the "humility" which is the true name for this glory. Perhaps, Levinas goes on to wonder in a passage where he seems to express his distance from Kierkegaard and Christianity – but that distance is introduced by a 'perhaps'! – "perhaps a Revelation which proclaims its own origin would be incompatible with the essence of transcendent truth, of a truth which can have no authentic manifestation unless it is persecuted. Perhaps the only possible mode of true revelation is the *incognito*, and perhaps a truth which has been spoken must therefore appear as one of which nothing has been said" (KCR 35-6). "Dieu ne prend jamais corps"[12] – a truth too hesitant "to present itself in the Heideggerian 'clearing'", a truth "which does not take the form of un-concealment" (KCR 36). There would be "no genuine exteriority in such an unconcealment": "once being has been unconcealed – even partially or mysteriously – it ceases to be transcendent and becomes immanent" (*ibid.*). There would be "a new philosophical situation" – Levinas knows how to provoke – only once "it becomes possible for something to manifest itself in such a way as to leave us wondering whether the manifestation really took place" (*ibid.*) "First a revelation, then nothing"; "Someone starts to speak: but no – nothing has been said" (*ibid.*) – Levinas thinks that we should contrast this "manifestation without manifestation" not just to the 'lichtendes Bergen' of Heidegger's Being, but to "the indiscreet and victorious appearing of (the) phenomenon" of phenomenology itself (CPP 66). Transcendence would have the discretion of the *enigma* in its Greek sense of an obscure or equivocal word, a riddle, but

---

10. E. LEVINAS, 'Two Comments on Kierkegaard', in J. RÉE - J. CHAMBERLAIN (eds.), *Kierkegaard. A Critical Reader*, Oxford, Blackwell, 1998, p. 35. In the next pages I will refer to this text as KCR.

11. 'Transcendence and Intelligibility', in A. PEPERZAK, S. CRITCHLEY, R. BERNASCONI (eds.), *Emmanuel Levinas. Basic Philosophical Writings*, Bloomington/Indianapolis, Indiana U.P., 1996, p. 158.

12. E. LEVINAS, *Alterité et Transcendance*, s.l., Fata Morgana, 1995, p. 172.

without punishment for the one who does not solve it. God is not a Sphinx. It is even unclear whether He is. His absence does not deny his presence; His presence is not contrary to his absence. He doesn't fit the categories of being, if one equates being – as Levinas seems to do – with appearance. God 'is' either too light or too dark – or better: both at the same time and neither – to be a phenomenon. The relation to Him is not intentional, the non-fulfilment of what is not an intentionality points or does not point to a gift which is not given until it is received and which, *à la rigueur*, may never be given, since it can never be received, if to receive means – as it seems to for Levinas – to fetch and lead into the harbour of a present where one can find the time to unwrap what had stirred one's curiosity. God cannot be unwrapped like a present in the privacy of one's house, once the guests have left. God 'is' the end of all privacy.

III

What a provocation! And what difficulties! One could spend a lifetime pondering what has been said or suggested here, and one could spend another lifetime trying to qualify or correct some of these statements. Are all phenomena victorious and indiscreet? And is there no humility in a Being which discreetly withdraws, is there no sacrifice in a truth, in an *aletheia* "which has to be overlooked"[13]? Could one not risk drawing a bold parallel between Lacan's idea that for there to be a symbolic order one signifier has to remain without a signified and Heidegger's suggestion that for there to be a clearing, an opening of the open, 'something' has to remain satisfied with not being a being but a verb? Should one not also say that Being does "not take" to being[14]? Is Being not, like Levinas's God, inscribed but not incarnated, and thus always at a risk of not being heard? One could, and no doubt one should, make all of these objections and perhaps more. One could accept the provocation at this point. But it is not the point at which I feel myself provoked, at least not directly and it would take too long to lay out all the intermediate steps. What shocks me are the two words in my title and the way they are implied in what we have seen until now. I should like in what follows to make this implication, to which I barely alluded, a bit more explicit by anchoring all these lofty thoughts about the Revelation in what is generally considered, and at least by the readers I mentioned at the beginning of this chapter, to be the more solid ground in Levinas. After all,

13. See above, chapter 2.
14. A literal translation of the passage quoted at note 12 would run as follows: "God *never takes* body. He never becomes, strictly spoken, being. It is that which is his invisibility". Note, in passing, the suggested equation of being with visibility.

this metaphysics is an ethics and isn't ethics all that counts nowadays? I apologize for what may seem sarcasm. It is no sign of disrespect, but the expression of a deep worry. After all, might not Levinas be yet another phenomenologist who by taking the intersubjective turn is purging the subject of everything in it that resists intersubjectivity[15]? Even if this intersubjectivity is a *ménage à trois*, a threesome with God as a "He in the depth of the You" (CPP 165)?

I know that this question sounds foolish and that it must strike readers who know their Levinas as either hopelessly wrong or decidedly misplaced. Isn't responsibility exactly what singularizes the subject and gives it a uniqueness that is beyond that of an individual in a genus? And isn't there still another subject of which Levinas says that it can "forget" (e.g. TI 172, 180, 181) this responsibility which is not a miracle, an instantaneous and once and for all conversion, but a long and enduring process, an "infinite sacrifice" in which there is a subject at war with itself, or better: with its other self, with the part of itself that resists ethics and hence intersubjectivity? Having disqualified my own question as I just did, what else can I do than make the lover's advance and seduce the reader, without interrupting the decency of our conversation, by suggesting that my question for all its foolishness will at least have heuristic value. It may lead us back to phenomenology, and if not, it will at least have led us back to my title.

IV

As one will remember, there are three ways of reading the intrigue of the infinite: as an ethical intrigue around the Good, as a religious one around God, or as a neutral one around the *il y a*. And we are trying to understand how these intrigues interrelate and whether it is possible to disconnect them, as some of Levinas's readers wish. We dealt with the ethical and the religious intrigue under the heading of the transascendent to which we opposed the more neutral one as the transdescendence of the bad infinite. And although it should be clear at this point how Levinas could come to think of a "transcendence to the point of absence", we did not ourselves think through the oppositions which underlie that statement. In short, we were busy defining terminology and did not yet come to philosophy. No wonder, then, that we have not yet understood how there could be, or must be, "a confusion" between the good and the bad infinite. Which is at least surprising once one realizes that this confusion is put by Levinas at the heart of a metaphysical Relation with the transascendent which, as we will soon

15. I am alluding to a point I made with reference to Merleau-Ponty in chapter 8.

find out, can only for Levinas take the form of an ethical relation with the other (autrui) and with the "other than the other" which he calls 'God' (CPP 165). More surprising still, it looks as if without the possibility of this confusion between the good and the bad infinite, another and far worse confusion will come to threaten and disrupt Levinas's "system": the confusion not between the good and the bad, but between Good and Evil!

Evil is not just moral or ethical evil. The problem is that this latter evil seems to have an ontological root. Ethics – the Otherwise than Being – will of necessity and always be at odds, perhaps even at war, with Being because what is inevitable at the level of Being is exactly what constitutes evil at the level of ethics which is 'beyond' Being. The privacy of the private, the interiority without which there would not be the being of *this* being that we call the subject thus gets in the way of or comes into conflict with the 'no privacy' (*pas de privé*) by which, as we shall see, Levinas characterizes the ethical and the religious condition of man (again, ethics and religion are intertwined for reasons we will soon find out)[16]. More complicated still, the same expression – "no privacy" – is also used by Levinas to refer to the inhuman neutrality of the *there is* that threatens or undermines the privacy without which there can be no subject (e.g. EE 62). Let me untangle this step by step.

Privacy means for Levinas first of all: independence, separation, solitude – not in a social or psychological but in an ontological sense: to be a subject means to be *kath'auto*. It means the possibility to withdraw, to be on one's own. It presupposes the interruption of participation where I am the Other, that is, where I am not an I or where I am not *tout court*, because 'I' am absorbed into the Other. One can think of this on an anthropological level, as Lacan does, correctly I think, when he suggests that the first problem for the child, a problem at the root of all further anxiety, is to free itself from the overwhelming and suffocating presence of the Other in which it participates[17]. Separation is for Lacan, just as it is for Levinas, the result of

16. As the readers of chapter 5 will have recognized, the title of the present chapter is a quote: "But it is this exceptional situation, where you are always in the face of the Other (*Autrui*), where there is *no privacy*, that I would call the religious situation" – 'Transcendence and Height', in *Emmanuel Levinas. Basic Philosophical Writings*, *o.c.*, p. 29.

17. J. LACAN, *Anxiety (The Seminar of Jacques Lacan. Book X: 1962-3*, transl. C. Gallagher from unedited French typescripts), unpublished, session of 5/12/62: "anxiety is not the signal of a lack but of something that you must manage to conceive of (...) as being *the absence of this support of the lack*. (...) it is not nostalgia for what is called the maternal womb which engenders anxiety, it is *its imminence*, it is everything that announces to us something which will allow us to glimpse that we are going *to re-enter it*. What provokes anxiety? It is not, contrary to what is said, either the rhythm nor the alternation of the presence-absence of the mother. And what proves it, is that the infant takes pleasure in

an interruption of that participation, an interruption which Lacan calls symbolic castration and which differs from Freudian castration because it introduces a law that does not aim at the child's desire *for* the mother, *le désir de la mère* as an objective genitive, but as a subjective genitive: the overwhelming and suffocating desire of the mother which does not leave place for the desire of the child. The mother's desire is precisely a source of anxiety because it is without limit, irregular, whimsical, unpredictable – Levinas would say: because it stands for the bad infinite, that is – and these are synonyms for Levinas – for the *apeiron*, for what is literally without limits, in-definite and thus undefinable (TI 190-1). If, as we saw, there is no relation with the bad infinite, it is precisely because it is *a-peiron*, that is without *perai*, without borders and thus without any privacy for there is no privacy without a somewhere where one can withdraw and escape total exposure to the Other. The house, for example, will be analysed along these lines by Levinas (TI 152 ff.), for it protects and gives shelter from the elements which are but another avatar of the *il y a*, no less whimsical and unpredictable than Lacan's mother. But before the subject can seek the interiority of the house, it must become, as it were, its own house, it must have its own being to itself and this presupposes that in the limitless plain, in the *apeiron* of being as such, a certain discreteness, (almost) in the mathematical sense of the term, needs to be introduced. Instead of a continuum with a faultless transition, there need to be units. Levinas calls this transition from a being without beings to that being which he calls the subject, hypostasis: being as a verb is as it were frozen or "collected" into a substantive. But hypostasis, Levinas remarks, "is not the apparition of a new grammatical category; it signifies the suspension of the anonymous *there is*, the apparition of a private domain" (EE 82-3). And as he adds in a phrase which might have pleased Hannah Arendt: "By hypostasis anonymous being loses its *there is* character. (...) Someone exists who assumes Being, which henceforth is *his* being" (EE 83). To be born, that is, is to begin and each beginning presupposes a rupture in the fatality of what was – it is a new start. And if one recalls what I said about the mother's desire which is limitless, without a beginning or an end, one understands that *birth for man is not a physiological but an ontological event*. Levinas has just introduced

repeating this game of presence and absence: *this possibility of absence, is what gives presence its security.* What is most anxiety-provoking for the child, is that precisely this relation of lack on which he establishes himself, which makes him desire, this relation is all the more disturbed *when there is no possibility of lack, when the mother is always on his back* [etc.]". Anxiety results from what Lacan calls in this seminar a "lack of lack" and in which Levinas would recognize the imminence of participation, and thus the approach of the *il y a* which knows of no rhythm (EE 66) (cf. also below n30).

natality as a true ontological category! But without that trust and jubilation, without that hope so characteristic for Arendt, since Levinas realizes, as does Lacan, that this victory over the *il y a* is not secure without a law[18]. Indeed, no sooner has "existence in general", Being without beings, "anonymous and inexorable", opened itself "to leave room for a private domain, an inwardness" (EE 99), than it seems, as it were, to change its mind and starts closing in again on the subject as if in an effort to undo that opening. The *there is* is whimsical, it does not seem to know what it wants, it allows for the erection of the hypostasis and then seems to resent what it has brought into being.

This is not the product of an overheated imagination! This is, for Levinas, as deep a reflection as ontology can give about what it means for man to be born and to be 'thrown' into being, as long as this ontology forbids itself to introduce a category that he has tried to invent anew: creation, and more specifically: *creatio ex nihilo*.

V

When Levinas speaks of *creation* he is not attempting to explain how the subject arises in the *il y a*. As he exclaims somewhere "there is no physics in metaphysics" (TO 51) – and one should thus, for example, not expect an *explanation* for the why and the how of the transition from being without beings to *a* being. Metaphysics is not situated at the level of being. It answers to what cannot be answered on that level, since in order for there to be an answer something must appear first and since the problem of the hypostasis is that it had to pay a price – a "ransom", as Levinas says – for its liberation from the anonymity of the *il y a*. In order to be *a* being, a person, the bearer of a "name" (EE 60), the subject, as it were, had to accept one terrible condition: that its own being should never appear to it, except in horror.

One is not, purely and simply – "on n'est pas, on s'est" (EE 28/38); one is

---

18. The opposition that I am all too briefly suggesting here, and hope to elaborate elsewhere, may not be as blunt as I make it look, since in Arendt too one can find this reference to the necessity of a law, which is precisely how she distinguishes human action within the political realm from the structurally identical action (an activity which has its *telos* in itself, hence praxis) in e.g. the performing arts (H. ARENDT, *Between Past and Future. Eight exercises in Political Thought*, Harmondsworth, Penguin Books, p. 154 and *Qu'est-ce que la politique?*, Paris, Seuil, 1995, p. 122 on the opposition between the Greek *nomos* and "the unlimited" (Arendt's name for the *apeiron*)). But in these pages Arendt seems to waver (gracefully, one should admit) between a historical and an ontological argument; a hesitation in which I am tempted to see the reflection of an ontologically insufficient determination of the concept of action.

oneself or with oneself. It is this "inevitable return to itself", the fact that the subject "cannot detach itself from itself" (TO 55), that it is "riveted to itself" or "encumbered by itself" (TO 56), which Levinas calls "the tragedy of solitude" (TO 57), "the misfortune (*malheur*) of hypostasis" (TO 58). This misfortune is like a birthmark left on the subject by the *il y a*, for it seems to introduce the a-peiron, the bad infinity of the being without beings, into the heart of that being which Levinas calls the subject. What we called earlier the solitude of the subject and which we analysed as an interruption of participation in the *il y a*, the introduction of a distance separating the subject from the overwhelming presence of an opaque and whimsical Other, this solitude is now in its turn analysed as a condition in which the subject which finally stands on its own, suffers not from a lack (an absence of others), but from a 'too much'. When one is alone with one's being, Levinas seems to suggest, there is something too much, and this something is precisely one's own self – which Levinas compares to "a double chained to the ego, a viscous, heavy, stupid double, but one that I am with precisely because it is me" (TO 56). To put this differently, one is never at a distance from one's own being, it is always too close and yet it is not close enough for identity to be "an inoffensive relationship with itself", for it not to be "an enchainment" to a self that one has to take care of, that one has to "occupy" oneself with while at the same time being "occupied" by it like by a double over which one stumbles, as in Blanchot's *Aminadab*, and that one cannot get rid of (TO 55). One's own being is present to oneself, but it is a presence that is too present, too close and that produces a feeling of suffocation, of horror. Despite the personal form it takes – it is *my* being – it cannot *appear* to me as mine. When it appears, it appears as impersonal, as an 'it' in the depth of the I and it is this that paralyses me, for example in the face of death. Indeed, as we know from Heidegger, for death to be what reveals the singularity of my existence to me, I need to be able to assume it as my own. But this is precisely what Levinas throws into doubt.

Death, as Levinas famously remarked, is not, as it is in *Sein und Zeit*, the "possibility of impossibility", it is essentially an event that one cannot assume, and thus what Levinas calls the "impossibility of possibility"[19] – the end, that is, of all *posse*, all assumption, of "the virility" or the "heroism" of the subject (TO 72). In dismissing death as what singularizes the subject (no one can take over my death from me) and in suggesting that I cannot

---

19. It is perhaps worth remarking that the original context of Levinas's insisting on this "apparently Byzantine distinction" (TO 70 n) goes back to a discussion with Jean Wahl who made the mistake of attributing to Heidegger the idea that death is the 'impossibility of possibility'. One should never forget Levinas was one of the first to introduce Heidegger in France and to insist that one should read him properly.

assume my own death (which prepares, of course, for the alternative 'no one can take over my responsibility from me'), Levinas is not first and foremost preoccupied with saving 'ethics'. The root of his discussion with Heidegger lies not in the famous 'ethics as first philosophy' thesis, but in a thesis on ontology. It is indeed Levinas's idea of the *il y a* which is not an 'es gibt' which makes him oppose Heidegger on the issue of death. Let me just report what is at stake here *for Levinas* – without choosing sides, for this is an extremely complicated discussion and it would call for a separate chapter.

Just as the *il y a* is not nothing, but not a being either, death would escape the alternative 'to be or not to be'. "In that sleep of death what dreams may come" – Hamlet's "dread of something after death" may come from him realizing that, as Lacan once remarked, it takes faith to die[20]. The faith that it will stop, that one is either alive or dead, and that as Epicurus wrote to Menoeceus "If you are, it is not; if it is, you are not" (quoted TO 71). But Hamlet's fear of death is not dissipated by such wisdom. He thinks that what this ancient adage misses is precisely "our relationship with death" which is, as Levinas remarks, "a unique relationship with the future", or a relationship with a unique, "eternally imminent" future – *ultima latet* (TI 235) – that we can precisely not grasp, assume, or even relate to, because 'death' opens up to the "stirring of the *there is*". Far from being an end, a *finis*, a limit, a *peras*, a horizon that ensures *Ganzheit* to my *Dasein*, the death that Hamlet meditates on has traits of the *apeiron*: it is a nightmarish death, obsessive like a haunting melody where 'it listens' whereas 'I' want to get it out of my head, or insomniac where 'it wakes' while I want to sleep[21]. What if death is not an end, what if after death, we would be neither dead nor alive, but un-dead as it were? What if it is not 'me' who dies, but 'it'? Or rather, what if what announces itself in that horrible imminence of death and escapes all our attempts to appropriate death, to make it our 'own', is that impossible situation where we are aspiring to die but unable to because 'it lives on'? If anxiety is the 'experience' of nothingness, Hamlet might have wanted to point out to Heidegger that "if by death one means nothingness",

---

20.   Lacan in a lecture at the K.U.Leuven (13-10-1972): "La mort est du domaine de la foi. Vous avez bien raison de croire que vous allez mourir, bien sûr. Ça vous soutient. (...) Néanmoins, ce n'est qu'un acte de foi", in *Jacques Lacan parle. Un film de Françoise Wolff*, RTBF productions (Radiotélévision Belge de la communauté française).

21.   Insomnia is one of Levinas's most telling examples of the sort of depersonalization the subject undergoes when the *il y a* approaches (*it* wakes; it is not me who wakes, but something anonymous and threatening). Accordingly, EE will define consciousness not as what wakes but as what is able to interrupt the 'it wakes'. Consciousness is "the breakup of the insomnia of the anonymous being, the possibility to 'suspend'" (EE 65). Consciousness as an *epochè* of the *there is*, is therefore defined by Levinas as interiority, inwardness.

anxiety is "to the contrary ... the fact that it is impossible to die" (TO 51)[22]. Again, at the bottom of this objection, the same point: "Being is evil not because it is finite but because it is without limits" (*ibid.*). Or perhaps not 'evil', but at least 'intolerable'[23]. In other words, Hamlet understands – and this is what takes this beyond the game of guessing what comes 'after' death, and what makes it count as a serious objection to Heidegger, for whom death, of course was not the end-point of life, but for whom it was horizon and peras[24] – what Levinas has been telling us all along: that "the 'not to be' is perhaps impossible" (TO 50). At the heart of man's being, that is, there is the threatening imminence of a radical dispersion (*Zerstreuung*)[25] that no appropriation of that being can collect. Especially not that appropriation that Heidegger expected to become possible when through death man's being would finally appear to him and reveal him his true ontological status and as a consequence allow him to bring to a halt that *Zerstreuung* that characterizes his inauthentic existence. For Levinas, to the contrary, there seems, as it were, to be some *ontological incontinence* inherent in the subject's very being: this being is never entirely the subject's own, it is improper before it is proper, something keeps leaking away in it such that,

---

22. Cf. e.g. *Being and Time*, §65: "The ecstatical character of the primordial future lies precisely in the fact that the future *closes* one's potentiality-for-Being; that is to say, the future is itself *closed* to one, and as such it *makes possible* the resolute existentiell understanding of nullity" (BT 379/330); Levinas is basically calling into question the terms which I italicized.

23. 'Le mal' also connotes what one has to endure during an effort (like in 'on a trop de mal ici'), and "l'être est mal (etc.)" could also be more neutrally translated as "the problem with being is not that it is finite but that it is without limits" – but it is a problem which makes being into a nuisance, turns it into something 'intolerable'.

24. Cf. *Being and Time* §74: "Only an entity which, in its Being, is essentially futural so that it is free for its death and can let itself be thrown back upon its factical 'there' *by shattering itself against death* (etc.)" (BT 437/385). Death in being some sort of wall, is not, however, what "blocks off" *Dasein*. Death seems, to the contrary, an instance of what *The Origin of the Work of Art* called boundary (*peras*) in the Greek sense of bringing to its radiance what is present (*Holzwege*, Frankfurt a.M., Vittorio Klostermann, pp. 68-9).

25. For *Zerstreuung* in BT see above, chapter 1. Also note Heidegger's characteristic opposition of *Zerstreuung* to *Selbst-ständigkeit* (literally: to stand on one's own, i.e. what Levinas ascribed to the hypostasis) in the following passage: "Dieser Modus der Eigentlichkeit der Sorge enthält die ursprüngliche *Selbst-ständigkeit und Ganzheit* des Daseins. Im *unzerstreuten*, existential verstehenden Blick auf sie [etc.]" (BT (370)/323). It is the link between these three terms which Levinas is contesting. Heidegger's insistence that there is to Dasein a "transcendental *Zerstreuung*" as "the binding possibility of its always factical existentiell *Zersplitterung* and *Zerspaltung*" does not seem to us to go in the direction that Levinas is indicating here (*Metaphysische Anfangsgründe der Logik* (Marburg Lectures, summer semester 1928), GA 26, pp. 174 ff.).

if directly confronted with that leak, the subject itself becomes incontinent, loses its control, its cool and its composure and is reduced, says Levinas, to infancy. "To die", he says at the end of an analysis of suffering which makes it clear that when he says 'death', he does not think of that point at which our lives are supposed to end, "to die is to return to (a) state of irresponsibility, to be the infantile shaking of sobbing" (TO 72).

The upshot of all this is, of course, that Levinas contests death the power to be the phenomenological reduction that we know, thanks to the writings of Courtine and Bernet[26], Heidegger had hoped it to be. Death, like the other avatars of the *il y a*, is an *aborted* and even an *aborting* pheno-menological reduction: it paralyses or wipes away the very subject to whom it was to reveal his being. When there is no longer anything between us and 'our' death, what should have been "the supreme responsibility of this extreme assumption turns into supreme irresponsibility, into infancy" (TO 72). Instead of us being-toward-death, that 'toward' which we are supposed to be starts to penetrate us, and as it starts to press together the 'toward' which should have allowed us a distance between 'le moi' et 'le soi', we are suffocated by ourselves. Death, that is, does not bring me the distance between me and myself, between me and my being, necessary to let that being both appear and give rise to a new subject, as the phenomenological reduction is supposed to do. Death, that is, is both too absolute an other (too saturated a phenomenon?)[27], and too much like that other in me, like the birthmark of that other from which it arose, to be the agent of the phenomenological reduction that, as one can by now suspect, Levinas is looking for. Death, that is, is both too absolute (since it crushes me) and not absolute enough (it is too much like what is already other in me)[28]. It is of

26. J.-Fr. COURTINE, *Heidegger et la phénoménologie*, Paris, Vrin, 1990, pp. 207-47; R. BERNET, *l.c.* (cf. chapter 1, note 22).

27. Levinas would thus not agree with the pages in J.-L. MARION's *Etant donné. Essai d'une phénoménologie de la donation* (Paris, PUF, 1997, pp. 84 ff.) where the author under the heading 'Even death' is establishing a 'privilege of donation' (p. 78) to which 'death' would be no exception. But it is not sure whether Marion would accept the expression 'too saturated a phenomenon' (cf. apart from *Etant donné*, his long contribution 'Le phénomène saturé', in J.-L. CHRÉTIEN e.a., *Phénoménologie et Théologie*, Paris, Criterion, 1992, pp. 79-128, e.g. 123 'the possibility of the impossible, the saturated phenomenon' – whereas death, for Levinas, is, as noted before, the 'impossibility of the possible', hence (?): too saturated).

28. One should note, in passing, that it is not sufficient to speak of an 'other in me' in order to undercut the distinction between 'the same' and 'the other' which one finds e.g. in *Totality and Infinity*. Throughout his work (including TI and OB) Levinas has precisely been trying to show how one can conceive of an 'other in me' which still leaves room for such a 'me'. As I have shown elsewhere, his opposition to psychoanalysis seems to derive from his suspicion that the psychoanalytic 'other in me' (the unconscious, the *Es*, the traumatic kernel of the Real, *das Ding*, etc.) is an other which like the *il y a* and its 'messengers' aims

the wrong type of absoluteness: it is an absoluteness that does not allow for an intrigue. For I forgot to mention that 'intrigue' is a technical term for Levinas: it is what "attaches to what detaches itself absolutely, without relativizing it"[29].

VI

We are back at transascendence. And we understand better now, I should think, what is at stake when Levinas claims that the only kind of transcendence is transascendence. For what Levinas wants to do is, as he tells us right at the beginning of *Totality and Infinity*, to save the subjectivity of the subject (TI 26). What the early work on the *il y a* and *transdescendence* shows is that the subject not only needs to, but wants to be saved: it tries to escape the horror at the heart of his being, but cannot do this on his own. Not that it doesn't try to, for as Levinas shows, it precisely engages in the world in order to "loosen the bond between the self (*le soi*) and the ego (*le moi*)" (TO 62/44) which as we have seen, turned solitude into a tragic condition. But its "everyday existence" in which it will eat, enjoy and work, – in which it will encounter what is other than itself, is only a postponement of its return to that self to which it is "riveted" (TO 56). To be sure, the light of the world – the light in which phenomena can come to appearance – will introduce a certain "interval" between the ego and the self, but "the interval of space given by light, is instantaneously absorbed by light": "Light is that through which something is other than myself, but already as if it came from me. The illuminated object is something one encounters, but from the very fact that it is illuminated one encounters it as if it came from us" (TO 64). One understands, if this is the case, why the distance transascendence "expresses", should "*unlike all distances* enter into the way of existing of the

---

at undoing the independence of the self in which it hides and which consequently would be covered by the analysis Levinas has given of the *il y a*. One may disagree with this, but one should not ascribe to Levinas a naivety which he did not have (cf. my 'The Price of Being Dispossessed. Levinas's God and Freud's Trauma', to appear in J. BLOECHL (ed.), *The Face of the Other and the Trace of God: Between Ethics and Religion in the Philosophy of Levinas*, Fordham U.P.).

29. I am here putting together in one formula the following two quotes: "l'intrigue rattache à ce qui se détache, elle attache à l'ab-solu, sans le relativiser" (E. LEVINAS, *Dieu, la Mort et le Temps*, Paris, Bernard Grasset, 1993, p. 227) and OB 147/188: "This plot connects (*rattache*) to what detaches itself absolutely, to the Absolute". Although my translation does not stress it, *rattacher* which also means 'to attach/connect again', is probably used by Levinas to signal the paradoxical movement involved in re-establishing a connection which had never been there, since the Absolute's detachment is original: 'God' has always already withdrawn, He does not 'take body'.

exterior being" (TI 35) and why *Totality and Infinity* had to become, in order to save the subject's subjectivity – and that is: its interiority, its privacy – an essay on an 'exteriority' which would fit that definition of transascendence. Nothing less paradoxical for Levinas than an exteriority which is to save interiority, since on the one hand interiority – privacy – left to its own, would break under "the irremissible attachment of the ego to the self" (TO 64) and since on the other hand, the only exteriority to which it can reach out – which it can *intend* – on its own, will lead to a transcendence "wrapped in immanence" (TO 65). "The object gives itself, but awaits us" (EE 47/73, transl. corrected) – the phenomenon is too discreet, too respectful of the privacy of the subject, to be a cure for what aches at the heart of that privacy: "the exteriority of light does not suffice for the liberation of the ego that is the self's captive" (TO 65).

Given that the subject's need to get out of itself cannot be satisfied by the subject itself, it will need help from the outside. But this help must be such that it does more than simply gratify the subject's *need* for "excendance". For 'need' is a condition the satisfaction of which will inevitably return the subject to itself (*post coitum animal triste* ...). In order to interrupt the fatality of this return, the subject needs to be confronted with an exteriority that retains its exteriority throughout the subject's attempts to immanentize it (and that thus will be different from the exteriority of 'things'), while at the same time allowing the subject to 'connect' with it (and that hence will be differently exterior than death which, as we know, is Levinas's name for the un-relateable – the ab-solute – as such)[30]. As is well-known, Levinas, after some hesitations, comes to the conclusion that only the ethical situation brings with it an exteriority that could satisfy these conditions, which are, of course, the conditions by which he has defined what can count as an 'intrigue'. Ethics will be shown to turn around a notion of otherness that "attaches to what" in this otherness "detaches itself absolutely" and the attachment to this otherness will not, however, "relativize it". The alterity involved in ethics will thus retain its absoluteness not in spite of, but due to the kind of attachment that it calls for. And that there is such an attachment,

---

30. As I stressed before, the un-relateable for Levinas is not so much what escapes any relation, but what crushes and forces into participation the other term of the relation. In participation – a term Levinas takes from Lévy-Bruhl – "the *private* existence of each term, mastered by a subject that is, loses this private character and returns to an undifferentiated background; the existence of the one submerges the other, *and is thus no longer the existence of the one. We recognize here the* there is." (EE 60-1). The Kleinian 'devouring' mother which is in the background of Lacan's concept of anxiety discussed above, would be an anthropological example of what I have italicized in this quote. When Lacan refers to this as 'le *mythe* kleinien de la mère', he may not only be suggesting that this 'mother' has never been 'present', but that her escaping time and presence puts her on the 'side' of the *there is*.

is in its turn not in spite of, but due to the kind of absoluteness that one finds in ethics.

The name for that absoluteness in Levinas is, of course, 'the face of the Other'; and the name for that attachment, 'responsibility'. Although one can assume that this is by now, given Levinas's enormous influence, common knowledge, I should like to focus nonetheless on the sort of argument that Levinas seems to have in mind for claiming that ethics involves a structure that is different from the one that one can find in knowledge (*lato sensu*) or in 'death'. Indeed, we have all the more reason to insist on this argument for the specificity of ethics, since there are those readers of Levinas whom we met in our introduction and who seem to think that in order to describe the ethical relation to the Other, one could dispense with the difference between transascendence (concretized, as we shall see, in the face) and transdescendence (death and the *il y a*). But this, as I shall argue, would be to dispense with Levinas's basic motive for entering the ethical domain: for if there is something in ethics that can help him save the subjectivity of the subject, it is because in ethics the subject not only finds a possibility to occupy itself for the first time with something genuinely other than itself, but primarily, because finding access to that possibility which the appeal by the face of the Other opens for the subject, will necessarily involve a phenomenological reduction which the subject cannot not undergo. And in this at least, as we will see, the sort of transcendence involved in ethics would seem to differ from the "more neutral transcendence" of the *il y a* that some of Levinas's readers are willing to settle for. To see why this may not be the best way out of Levinas's 'intrigue of the Infinite', let us first consider in some detail the difference between the otherness of 'things' and the alterity of the Other.

As we saw at the beginning of this section, 'things' appear in a light which allows in principle for a familiarity between us and them. They are the bearers of a 'weak' alterity – when Levinas says that we encounter them "as if they came from us" he is not, of course, denying their obvious otherness ('knowledge' is not 'fusion'), but merely suggesting that theirs is an otherness unable to call us into question. Even what one calls anomalies would seem to obey this general appreciation of the alterity involved in the 'object' as (ordinary) phenomenon. For an anomaly simply confirms the meaningfulness of my attempt to be *at home* in *the world* – the unexpected and the unfamiliar only strike me as such because they diverge from what I had expected on the basis of a previous familiarity with the world. Such a divergence is simply an invitation to revise these expectations and to think of a pattern where what is at present an anomaly would disappear and slide back into normality again. By contrast, when Levinas speaks of 'the face' of the Other and suggests that this face concerns me, that it is the addressor of an 'appeal' of which I am the addressee, he wants *first of all*[31] to draw attention to the 'fact' that what is genuinely 'other' about this Other is that in a sense I cannot react to his alterity in the same way as I would to the intrusion of an anomaly which confronts me with an alterity for which I *presently* lack concepts. Far from being just a temporary anomaly in the tapestry of my 'normal' experience, there is something about the intrusion of the Other (something that Levinas will refer to by calling that intrusion an 'appeal') that forbids me to 'react' at all and that cuts through my attempts to recover from the shock of that intrusion and to be my 'old self' again. Instead of giving himself, but discreetly awaiting my initiative, as we saw 'things' do, the Other refuses to give himself and resists my attempts to weave his otherness into the web of my normality – a resistance in which Levinas will recognize the ethical moment as such. Whether it speaks or not, the face qua face confronts me with an imperative: 'do not kill me', or: 'help me live'. But in order to understand these well-known formulas, one should first of all realize how they already involve a specification of the otherness of the Other that goes beyond the one that we are focusing on, although it takes its start there.

For if Levinas says that the Other qua Other cannot but confront me with that imperative, this means *first of all* that *his 'resistance' is not optional, and that it follows from the very structure of his Otherness.* And this structure implies *at least* that what makes the Other other and thus different from things, is that he is and cannot but be *kath'auto*. Unlike 'things', the Other is the bearer of his own light. He is not dependent, as they are, on a light which allows them to appear, and that is: to show forth the form (the *morphè*) through which they can find a place in a whole in which we can apperceive their function or their beauty. Qua Other the Other is essentially without such a place: indeed, when Levinas speaks of the 'face' of the Other and opposes it to what we just called the 'form' (that aspect or that face – in a pre-Levinassian sense – which things turn toward us when they appear *for* us), he wants to distinguish an otherness which signifies "before we have projected light upon it" (TI 74), from an otherness which can only signify

---

31. As will become clear in the next section, with this expression ('first of all') I am trying to artificially separate, for the sake of clarity, what in Levinas's description follows from a minimal difference between the alterity of the Other and that of things on the one hand, and Levinas's further suggestion that the Other's alterity is ethical. My purpose here is, for the moment, merely didactical: my aim is simply to show that what might strike one as entirely arbitrary moves on Levinas's part (the sort of 'jumps' that seem an instance of the *latius hos* error) are in fact constituted by a series of highly intricate movements of which one should study the choreography before judging it in the terms of a logic which it always sought to contest.

thanks to what he calls "a borrowed light" (*ibid.*). If to appear means to be dependent on such a loan, the Other does not appear. But this precisely allows him to "turn *to me*" (*ibid.*), – a 'turn' which essentially differs from all that appears *for me* "as if it came *from me*" (TO 64).

One would miss what is at stake in this difference if one would reduce it to the difference between 'things' that are, at most, unknown and 'persons' whose otherness is not just the result of their alien characteristics that may gradually become familiar to me. Levinas's point is not just the rather trivial one that the otherness of the Other belongs to his very essence (TO 88), and that he is thus not so much an 'unknown' but an "unknowable, refractory to all light" (TO 75). The point is the more complicated one that, because of this refraction, light itself and my relation to it, will suddenly appear to me. An appearance of the condition of all hitherto appearance which Levinas characterizes as a "complete surprise" (OB 99, 148) that throws me off balance and that unsettles (or un-saddles) me in a way that fundamentally alters me. It is, of course, this 'alteration' that interests him. To understand the structure of this alteration we will have to understand why Levinas sees in the Other's refraction of the light that I bring with me, an (ethical) "accusation". And why he thinks that this accusation, although it is a "complete surprise" for me, nonetheless touches upon something in me that I cannot deny to be my own.

VII

That the Other's otherness is different from the otherness of things, that his otherness points to an anomaly that is not just an invitation to revise my view of the world, does not prevent me from exerting my grip over him by treating his anomaly as I treat other anomalies. For the Other's resistance to 'light' is not physical, it is, says Levinas, ethical: it confronts me with the weak force of an imperative that would make no sense if it would forbid what is not possible anyway. But I can always 'kill' the Other – even without physically attacking him, for 'to kill' here simply means to ignore what is genuinely other about his Otherness. I can always treat the Other as I treat a thing – I can always impose a light on him that forces him into appearance. But then I miss him *qua* Other. *Qua* Other, the Other refracts whatever light I let shine on him. *Qua* Other, he leaves me without a grip. This being left without a grip is not, however, just a negative phenomenon. *By escaping my grip, the Other also shows me my grip.* But this 'revelation' does not just bear on what is about to happen between the Other and me, it spills over, as it were, on the whole of my existence. What the Other shows is that there is something *typical* about my attempt to re-establish my grip and to remain in control – a *typicality* I was unaware of and could not but be unaware of, for it was the very structure of my life, a structure that could not itself appear since it was the condition of all appearance, of all familiarity and thus of my being at home in the world as such. In being a foreigner to the light of my world, the Other shows me what that light and that world amount to – in other words, he shows me that for me to have been me, was not to be "a being that always remains the same (*le même*), but (a) being whose existing consists in identifying itself, in *recovering* its identity throughout all that happens to it" (TI 36).

What this means is that, *unlike death, the face of the Other manages to operate a phenomenological reduction on me*. Its alterity, that is, is such that it can, as it were, make fluent again what became solidified in the erection of the hypostasis (Levinas's word for the 'subject') where, as we have seen, being as a verb (the being without beings) was 'frozen' into a substantive (*a* being). The face of the Other reveals to me *qua* subject of the hypostasis that what I took to be my substance is in truth a verb: the 'same' of my identity is not a substance, but a movement – and one that I could not not be engaged in, since to be is to be my being, and to be my being is to be at the centre of it, it is to relate everything to me. Whether I like it or not, as soon as I am, I am a centre and everything becomes focused on it. It is this involuntary 'egocentrism' (involuntary since it does not result from my decision, and since it is the precondition of *my* every decision) which the Other's otherness shows me *for the first time*. But this showing is – and this is the transition that we should try to understand – not neutral. It is, says Levinas, an accusation. *To be*, the Other seems to tell me, *is to be at one's defence* – always trying to recover one's identity throughout all that happens to it – *it is to be at war*. But the Other doesn't break through that defence in the way that we saw 'death' do: death was precisely a first figure of the absolute because it consists of an event I *cannot* relate to me (death, as we have seen, is *im-possible*, the end of all *posse*) and that crushes me because it does not allow me to "recover" from its impact. The Other, by contrast, does not break through my defence, but calls my attention to it. But in so doing, he still allows for it. He does not, that is, confront me with the im-possible: instead of crushing my 'I can', he makes me responsible for it[32]. What this

32. For this line of reasoning see e.g. *Totality and Infinity*, section III.7 ('The asymmetry of the Interpersonal') which significantly begins as follows: "The presence of the face coming from beyond the world, but committing me to human fraternity, does not overwhelm me [*ne m'écrase pas*] as a numinous essence arousing fear and trembling" (TI 215/190). Apart from the obvious allusion to Kierkegaard – an allusion which betrays a disagreement on which the next chapter returns – the reader should note that 'écraser' is exactly the term Levinas uses in *Time and the Other* when speaking of *death* and the *il y a*.

means for Levinas is that the Other instead of diminishing my possibilities, promotes them. And again Levinas seems to force us into a transition taking us beyond what is phenomenologically 'given' about the non-givenness of the Other – for when he says that the Other does not diminish my possibilities, he is not satisfied with saying that he makes them visible for me. The Other, we just heard, *promotes* them. Which means for Levinas that the Other puts me before a choice such as I never had before in my existence. But how can he say that? What would that choice consist in, given that the only thing that has been shown until now is that I cannot prevent the Other from having promoted me to the position of the first person singular in which I conjugate the verb 'to be'? Again, let us try to patiently entangle what seems to be for Levinas one movement.

Without the Other, I could not have known about that position: for as we saw, there is nothing in things to draw my attention to the synergy between my involuntary self-centredness and the light in which they appear; and death which switches off that light, could not point to that position, since it entirely consists in taking it over from me (it is not I who dies, *it dies*). With things, my self-centredness was unthematic and involuntary; death puts an end to the self of this self-centredness and is thus unable to make it appear *for me*. Whereas things presuppose and confirm my *stasis*, and death in robbing me of it, is ec-static, the weak resistance of the face of the Other shows or reveals the very 'standing' of my stasis. And Levinas wishes to say that in thus showing it to me, he calls it into question all the while leaving the answer to that question to me. But then what Levinas calls the 'accusation' of the Other can not be an external one. It must be more insidious, it must be, that is, formulated in such a way that it turns me into my own prosecutor.

The Other, one may wish to grant Levinas, has not only put me in a position where I could never have put myself *but he also forces me to realize that I have always been in that position*, even if I ignored it. His 'accusation' thus has in a certain sense already become my affair: it involves the whole of my existence which, like in a *Gestalt switch*, suddenly takes on a new meaning. I had 'forgotten' that the being of my being was not a substance, but a verb – and what is more, I could not but have forgotten it, for as long as I was alone with my being, I could only flee the pain that aches at its centre by seeking the company of things that allowed me to loosen a bit the bond between me and myself so as to be able to forget about the pain of that bondage. The world is a drug, but one that is vital for life. If to be is to be at war and to reduce the other to the same, if thus all light is in that sense violence, the violence of that war is nonetheless to be preferred to the horror at the heart of man's being, against which the distance of that light provides a first protection, but one that life cannot do without. But whereas death laughs at that protection before smashing it, the Other, Levinas seems to suggest, is precisely an *ethical* Other because he silently puts me before the question whether it is worthwhile to live a life that has to engage in a 'war' in which it always wins, in order not to engage in that 'inner' war which it will lose anyway.

It is only because Levinas thinks that the Other has *indeed* the power to bring me before such a question, that he can go on to think (the 'transition', again) that such an Other, by not resisting this war and simply calling it by its name, offers me peace. Not just between him and me, but between me and my existence. But then the Other in offering me peace must do more than reveal a prior state of war of which I was, but also could not help but be, the subject (I was as much the subject *of* it, as I was subject *to* it: *my* existence could only survive by exteriorizing the violence that it suffered from within). Levinas's qualification of the other as an *ethical* Other must also mean that that Other *undermines* the evidence of my prior state of war by *accusing* me of the war that I was *and could not help being*. However counter-intuitive this may seem, it is indeed what Levinas is claiming. Not by mistake, but by conviction – for behind this claim lies a well-reflected view on the origin of *autonomy*: man only becomes truly free when he is accused of not having been free – the accusation needs to be unreasonable, it needs to accuse man of what he could not not have been (he could not help but be that war), for it to awaken in him a sense that his humanity might only begin when a rent has been cut from the outside into the irremissibility of being where the very logic of peace is, as we have seen, still in the interest of the war that goes on underneath it (this peace still bears, like my existence, the stamp of the *il y a*). Ethics takes man *beyond being* because it gives him a freedom that being did not give him: the freedom to be and to continue being that war, i.e., the choice between an egocentrism that is *no longer* involuntary, and a giving up of that position in favour of that other centre which is, precisely, the Other *qua* Other. Whatever decision I take, it will be *my* decision. And it will thus be inscribed in a horizon that is no longer that of Being, but that of a 'beyond Being' to which Levinas, as we know, permits himself to refer with the word 'the Good' and even with the word 'God'.

VIII

One of the reasons why Levinas's readers have such difficulties to understand that he should seek recourse in these words at all, is that they think they can join him in making this last move from an involuntary extra-

or pre-ethical egocentrism to an ethically qualified relation to the Other without obliging themselves to the "ethico-metaphysical agenda" which they believe to be only arbitrarily linked to his "quasi-phenomenological descriptions of radical alterity". And thus, although Levinas quite explicitly speaks of "the necessity for a philosophical meditation" on alterity "to resort to notions such as that of infinity or God" (CPP 100), these readers seem to think that he is simply overstating his case in such passages and that if he is going to bring in religion at all, this should happen, as he himself indicates in other passages, "at the end of (his) analysis" (CPP 93). The question is, of course, whether these readers are correct in assuming that they could then leave Levinas's analysis before it embraces all these words like 'God', 'the Good' and 'creation' which they would prefer to avoid. For example – and it is just one example among many – when we heard Simon Critchley say that what continues to "grip" him in Levinas is "the Other's *claim* on me and how that claim changes *and challenges* my self-conception", one may wonder whether, as my italics indicate, he has not himself unknowingly already adopted one of these words, if not all of them – at least as they function in Levinas. For as should by now have become clear, Levinas's reason for introducing these words, is that the Other he wants to present us with, is an Other who has a much stronger effect on me than an Other whose alterity imposes a phenomenological reduction on me that reminds me that my being is a verb which I conjugate in the first person singular. Although this latter Other, which we met in the last section, could in a sense be said to change and challenge our self-conception (he reminds us of something we weren't aware of), he could not on the sole basis of that analysis be held to have "a claim" on us. Indeed, how could he? Even if one grants that his otherness differs in the way that we explained from that of 'things' or of 'death', and that it forces me to reconceive the whole of my existence, it could not *as such* induce a perspective on that existence which would consist of more than the 'tragic' awareness that that existence, although it did not know it, is and cannot but be 'at war' with its surroundings because it is and cannot but be at war with (something in) itself. That such an Other, in pointing to my egocentrism, is also fundamentally changing it by making it 'voluntary', seems to assume more than we have hitherto shown on the basis of what one could call – in contrast with Critchley's correct, but somewhat obscure usage of the term 'quasi-phenomenological' – a 'strictly' phenomenological analysis. Indeed, it is not because my inevitable self-relatedness becomes thematic that it becomes voluntary, and it is not because it becomes voluntary that it stops being 'egocentric'.

Levinas knows this, and that is why he is not satisfied with presenting the

Other as simply an alternative 'centre' to which I could turn in the hope of thus losing my ego-centrism. For if the Other would simply offer me a possibility to escape myself, if I would use him as a welcome occasion to escape what aches in my being, I would not, of course, have left my egocentrism. The Other's 'misery' would simply have become a function of my happiness – and it would not have helped me 'leave' myself behind. As any economist will tell us, an altruism that is simply an alternative to egoism, changes nothing about the 'form' of the 'utility function' which one may assume operative in the decisions of the 'homo oeconomicus' – it simply changes its 'content' and thus leaves intact its basic assumption which is precisely that of a self-centred being.

For the Other to be able to help me break out of being, he must, as it were, be invested with the power to lay *a claim* on me which I cannot dispute and to which something in me responds before I have the time to consider its credentials and to check how they would fit in my utility-function. It is to such a situation that Levinas refers, when he says that responsibility is "older" than freedom and when he tries to show that just as I am unable not to hear the appeal of the Other, I am not free not to respond *in a certain way*. This last qualification is vital for Levinas, for without it, he would never be able to move beyond the sort of analysis of alterity that we have, somewhat artificially, tried to present throughout the last section before giving it up in its final lines when we mentioned a horizon that would be no longer that of Being, and which would come to qualify whatever decision we take as to the appeal of the Other.

Levinas's reason for linking that horizon to the Good which is 'beyond being' is, as we shall see, that he believes it belongs to the structure of the Good to both *force us to respond* to the appeal of the Other before we can decide to do so, *and to leave us free to respond* to that appeal in accordance with a decision that we are still free to take. It is because the Good is good that it has chosen us before we could choose it (cf. OB 122): it belongs to the semantics of the word 'the Good' that it should not keep its goodness for itself and that it should thus be *"non-indifferent"* (OB 123). But if the Good cannot but make the first step, if it cannot but "love me before I love it" (OB 187 n.8)[33], it would lose its goodness if this love would consume me, if it would "enslave" me "to the Good" (OB 11), if there would be no "difference"

---

33. It is worth quoting this note in full: "The Good invests freedom – it loves me before I love it. Love is love in this antecedence. The Good could not be the term of a need susceptible of being satisfied, it is not the term of an erotic need, a relationship with the seductive which resembles the Good to the point of being indistinguishable from it, but which is not its other, but its imitator. The Good as the infinite has no other, not because it would be the whole, but because it is Good and nothing escapes its goodness."

that preserves me from its "non-indifference" (OB 123). Which is why the Good, for Levinas, can only indirectly approach us and why this approach needs to be such that on the one hand I cannot ignore it while on the other hand retaining the freedom to reject the invitation that it brings me. And since Levinas thinks that the Other has a claim on me, *a claim he would not have were he only an Other whose otherness resists my light*, he believes that it is a plausible move to link this claim whose origin we do not understand, to what we just learned about the formal structure of a word that he is not inventing, but merely picking up in a tradition which had already been using it: instead of attracting us, the Good, through some sort of *ethical clinamen*, is what interrupts its attraction and deflects it to the Other who thus receives a weak force that is nonetheless stronger than the force we could have expected him to have if we only focused on what phenomenologically distinguishes his otherness from that of 'things' or of 'death'.

As I just stressed, this is not an implausible move. For Levinas seems simply to present a richer phenomenological analysis than the one we have given until now: he does not just *claim* that the Other has a claim on me, and thus a force which he derives from the Good, but he presents us with what seems to be a phenomenological attestation of that claim. That the Other does more than reveal to me the structure of my being, that this revelation is *eo ipso* an accusation, seems testified by my 'reaction' to his 'appeal' (a word that itself becomes the proper word to refer to the manifestation of the Other because of this 'reaction'): I feel "guilty" and "ashamed" of what I have just come to discover about the structure of my being. This guilt and this shame are more than the expression of an (at most) tragic awareness with which I discover the inevitable self-relatedness of my being. It is a realization of that being's "imperfection" (TI 84), which means for Levinas that the Other introduces something in me which I could not have on my own: "the idea of the perfect", or "of infinity" (*ibid.*) – an idea which, says Levinas, "is not an idea, but desire: it is the welcoming of the Other, the commencement of moral consciousness, which calls in question my freedom" (*ibid.*).

The point couldn't be more important since 'desire', in contradistinction to 'need', is for Levinas "beyond satisfaction" (TI 34): "it nourishes itself with its hunger" and thus is "deepened", rather than "fulfilled" by what it desires (*ibid.*). If it is indeed desire which characterizes my relation to the Other, then that relation will be such that the return of the subject to itself becomes infinitely postponed. And thus Levinas will have found an exteriority that is sufficiently exterior to loosen that tragic bond that kept the subject riveted to a self from which it tried to, but could not, escape on its own. The distance characteristic for transascendence would thus be located in the Other whose exteriority would not be that of an "obstacle" (TI 84) but what allows him to be "desired in my shame" (*ibid.*). But why would I *desire* an Other who accuses me? Especially if he is, as we have seen, unreasonably accusing me of what I could not not have been? And yet, if it is indeed shame and not, for example, indignation with which I respond to the otherness of the other, then Levinas has a point. For the difference between these two responses is precisely that one could explain the latter by only focusing on what is going on in the present context between me and the Other. Not so with shame – here we deal with an affect which seems to escape that context and which is precisely for that reason so disturbing for the subject who feels itself overcome with shame without understanding why[34]. It is as if something in the subject responds to the Other, before it could decide on how to respond itself. The subject is taken by surprise by its own shame which seems to acknowledge that there is a point to the Other's accusation which has escaped it altogether. My shame *shows* that the Other has, as it were, convinced me of the righteousness of his accusation before I could even come to consider what exactly he is accusing me of.

It is this extreme unlikelihood of our response to the Other which will allow for Levinas's next – and in a sense final – move. For it would appear as if we are somehow 'connected' to the Other, even though we ignored it and only come to discover it through him. And such a connection cannot be a connection within Being where we are, according to Levinas's definition of Being, only connected to our selves. It points, says Levinas, to "another kinship" in man "than that which ties him to being" (OB 177). The Good can thus be supposed to not only have deflected the rays of its goodness onto the Other. Since that Other does not leave me indifferent, since he is able to make me feel ashamed without any reason, it would also seem that these rays are able to move me. But then a more complicated story needs to be told about this 'me' which clearly does not only stand on its own (*kath'auto*). And Levinas, as one can expect, is not going to make up that story on his own. He will use the occasion to revivify two other concepts which he takes from 'our' tradition ('God' and 'creation') and which will allow him to pull all the threads together, including those of the metaphysics of Revelation with which we started. And if we want to understand why it might not suffice to call on the *il y a* to save *ethics* from the clutches of a God who is "transcendent to the point of a possible confusion with the *il y a*", we had better take a look at the full picture that will appear once Levinas has

---

34. I have reason to feel anger or indignation when being unjustly accused. But Levinas's point is that my 'response' to that accusation is shame, and that there is nothing of which I could think that could explain such shame.

completed his fabric. For we might not like what we will thus come to see.

IX

If one recalls our earlier analysis of the erection of the subject out of the *il y a*, it becomes easy to see why Levinas should be so keen on turning 'shame' into the phenomenological cornerstone of his attempt to redeem the subjectivity of the subject. For 'shame' points to a completely different relationship between the 'private' (the subject *qua* interiority) and the 'no privacy' with which we hitherto characterized the *il y a*. The *il y a*, as one will recall, is a *depersonalizing* force that is constantly trying to tear down the walls that constitute the subject's interiority. It wants to undo the *separation* by which the subject's being became its own being and to restore an *impersonal* realm where "the private existence of each term, mastered by a subject that is, loses this private character" (EE 60-61) and where all that remains is being "like a heavy atmosphere belonging to no one" (EE 58) and from which not even death, as Racine's *Phaedra* realizes, could prove to be an escape. Phaedra cannot go on living after doing what she did, but she also cannot die: "Where may I hide? Flee to infernal night. How? There my father holds the urn of doom ..." (Act IV, scene 6). All the exits around her are blocked, life no longer has any meaning and the thought of Minos makes suicide impossible. With death no longer a possibility and the tragic heroine's last refuge being taken away from her, Phaedra is put 'beyond tragedy' "in a full universe in which her existence is bound by an unbreakable commitment, an existence no longer in any way private" (EE 62). Unable to live and unable to die, Phaedra is no longer 'able' as such, she is "exposed" (EE 59) to the "irremissibility" of being (EE 63) which continues its course without caring for her and from which she *cannot* withdraw. No privacy: Phaedra is "held" (EE 65) by a being which is no longer hers, like by a nightmare from which one cannot awake, "held to be" (*ibid.*) by a "corybantic necessity" (*ibid.*) that never "lets up", spell-bound by "the anonymous rustling" of an existence that goes on forever: "Tomorrow, alas! one will still have to live!" (EE 63).

If these were the terms of the choice, who could blame the subject for clinging to its privacy and trying to uphold its mastery over being? Interiority may be, as we know, a cage both for the subject and for whatever it comes into contact with, but isn't it better to hide like Gyges than to be exposed like Phaedra? The ring with which Gyges could make himself invisible, "symbolizes", says Levinas, "separation" (TI 173): it stands for the possibility of withdrawing and interrupting participation. To move without being watched is the precondition for any privacy. Man could not be on his own without the possibility of keeping a secret. Interiority presupposes what one could call an *ontological insincerity*: there would be no 'I think' – there would be no *personal* consciousness – without the possibility of keeping one's thoughts for oneself. The child's first lie does not have the moral significance it has for the adult who punishes it: it is an attempt at discretion where the indiscrete continuum between it and its adult environment *in which it bathed*, becomes disunited so that it can become a term on its own that is *related* with but not absorbed into its Others[35]. Speech can only be called sincere when and after it had the opportunity to experiment with insincerity. As is shown by the case of the child who embarrasses its parents by blurting out in front of a visitor whatever goes through its head, adult language is the language of a speaking *subject* who no longer bathes in language as such and who can celebrate its triumph and its mastery over language as an impersonal element (the 'there is' of language) in poetry where language is able to simulate and to approach its pristine state of independence. Such is aesthetics: it plays with the *il y a*, – it approaches it, but it stops in time. Horror is sublimated into a beauty which consoles. Art is never collective, its aim is to make the secret of interiority bearable. But it knows no shame – which is why Levinas distrusts it[36].

Shame exposes interiority, instead of supporting it, as art does. Shame is what makes Gyges visible: the blush that colours one's cheeks betrays the secret and gives the interiority of the subject an exteriority that it cannot control. Sincerity triumphs over insincerity and it thus shows that there is more to the life of the subject than its struggle with the *il y a*. "Society with the Other", Levinas writes in a striking passage, "marks the end of the absurd rumbling of the *there is*" (TI 261). This passage is all the more striking since Levinas proceeds to describe this end of the *il y a* with exactly the same expressions he used when trying to render its horror. In shame, the subject is not only exposed, but totally exposed, without escape, without the possibility to withdraw in a private domain, even if that be, like it was for Jonah, its sleep. The 'no privacy' which was characteristic of the subject's predicament when the *il y a* had sneaked through its walls (like the *haunting* melody that drives us 'outside of ourselves', precisely because it nestles in what we had hoped to be our inside) – this *'pas de privé'* becomes, in its turn, the main characteristic of the ethical "relation" with the Other, which Levinas, as we know, also calls "the religious condition of man". Of that condition he says and no doubt cannot but say – as we shall see in our next

35. This example (and the following reflection) is my own, although in the spirit of Levinas. But I am, of course, simply pointing to a well-known insight in the psychoanalysis of children.
36. Cf. E. LEVINAS, 'Reality and its shadow', in CPP, pp. 1-13.

two chapters – that there we are "in our truth" (TI 253). A new interiority will be born, "an interiority without secret", "transparency without opaqueness", absolutely "sincere" for no longer in a position "to take a distance", "to close itself in on itself from the inside"[37]. And Levinas will insist that this interiority which is born with delay (*après coup, nachträglich*)[38] is "older" than the one that we had in view until now. And this is an important decision – it is the decision *par excellence* which makes both *Totality* and *Otherwise than Being* a new start, rather than, as I have been suggesting until now, a consistent development of Levinas's early work.

Again, this is not an implausible move. For one should not forget that when Levinas talks about shame, he is not referring to that already intra-ethical affect with which an already ethical subject admits to its having acted against an already established moral rule. Shame, to the contrary, is for Levinas the affect which opens the ethical as such. And not only the ethical, but the intersubjective as such – it is, as we have seen, the subject's response to the alterity of the Other qua Other. Any Other, and not just an Other that the subject has wronged, will be able to trigger off that response in the subject. A response that surprises the subject, for it doesn't fit into the structure of its being which the Other's alterity has just let appear. It would seem that the phenomenological reduction which the Other imposes on me is even more complex than we thought: in letting the structure of my being appear, the Other at once invalidates it and something in me agrees, as it were, that there is more to myself than that movement of interiorization to which my attention has just been drawn. Levinas refers to this other side of myself as a "pre-original not resting on oneself" (OB 75). And he thinks that he needs the word 'creation' – and thus 'God' – in order to understand how a being can both rest on itself – be independent, *kath'auto* – and not rest on itself: "Creation", he writes at the end of a section on 'Separation and Absoluteness', "leaves to the creature a trace of dependence, but it is an unparalleled dependence: the dependent being draws from this exceptional dependence ... its very independence" (TI 104-5).

37.   Respectively: OB 138; 146; 142-5 (145: a sincerity which "breaks the secret of Gyges, of the subject that sees without being seen, without exposing himself, the secret of the inward subject"); OB 112 (141, etc.); and E. LEVINAS, 'The Contemporary Criticism of the Idea of Value and the Prospects for Humanism', in E.A. MAZIARZ (ed.), *Value and Values in Evolution*, New York / London / Paris, Gordon and Breach, 1979, p. 185: "Free man is chained to his neighbor; no one can save himself without other people. The guarded preserve of the soul does not *close in on itself from the inside*. It is 'the Eternal which closed the door of the Arc on Noah', a text of Genesis tells us with wonderful precision".

38.   For an argument that this "delay" involves the double time of a "trauma" which has the same formal structure in Levinas as it has in Freud, see my article quoted above in note 28.

A created being is a being that is independent and that can stand on its own. Creation implies rupture of participation, separation between 'cause' and 'effect' – it is therefore *ex nihilo*. But its true marvel lies elsewhere – the "miracle of creation" is that the created being can "learn that it is created" (TI 89) without thereby discovering that what it took to be its independence was only a semblance: "the marvel of creation" is that "it results in a being capable of receiving a revelation" (*ibid.*) that does not "burn" it. All of Levinas's threads are pulled together here, since, as one will have guessed, ethics is for Levinas the realm in which the created being can learn that it does not rest on itself[39], all the while retaining its power to go on with its life, as if it did rest on itself. The miracle of creation may lie in "creating a moral being" (*ibid.*), but a moral being is a being that "can close itself up in its egoism" and that can "banish the transcendent relation that alone permits the I to shut itself up in itself" (TI 172-3/147-8, transl. corr.). What is *ex nihilo* can always pretend to be without any other links than those that tie it to itself. God cannot impose Himself – He can reveal Himself, but only through the Other, and separation would not be "radical" (*ibid.*) if it were not possible to ignore even that indirect revelation through the face of an Other that calls me into question.

But haven't we been insisting all along that the Other puts us into question before we could allow him to do so? Wasn't shame that response in us for which we did not take the initiative? Didn't we just learn that this exposure is so absolute as to leave us without shelter in ourselves, without the possibility to withdraw in our shell?

It would seem as if Levinas's turn to ethics makes transcendence less discreet than we pictured it to be (section II): for if I hear "the word of God" in the face of the Other, as Levinas now says, and if I cannot not hear the appeal of the Other, then it follows that I cannot not hear 'the word of God'

---

39. That *ethics* should be that realm, has to do with it being, as Levinas explains to Richard Kearney "against nature": "it forbids the murderousness of my natural will to put my own existence first". Kearney then asks a crucial question to which Levinas gives an answer that one should not forget when trying to come to terms with what he calls 'creation': *"Kearney:* Does going towards God always require that we go against nature? – *Levinas:* God cannot appear as the cause or creator of nature. The word of God speaks through the glory of the face and calls for an ethical conversion or reversal of our nature. (...) the moral priority of the other over myself could not come to be if it were not motivated by something beyond nature. (...) In this respect, we could say that God is the other who turns our nature inside out, who calls our ontological will-to-be into question. This ethical call of conscience (...) remains an essentially religious vocation. God does indeed go against nature for He is not of this world. God is other than Being." (in R. KEARNEY, *Dialogues with Contemporary Continental Thinkers. The Phenomenological Heritage*, Manchester U.P., 1984, pp. 60-1).

– all not hearing will be a pretending not to hear, and thus a flight[40]. Blocking one's ears is still possible, but there is, contrary to what we learned earlier about the Revelation's enigma, a price to be paid: one cannot withdraw from the appeal of the Other "without the torsion of a complex, without 'alienation', without fault" (OB 87). Interiority, as a consequence, appears in a totally different light: whereas the ontological story about the *il y a* portrayed the 'privacy' of the subject as a fragile victory over the 'no privacy' of a subjectless Being, now the link between ethics and the metaphysics of creation brings Levinas to a completely different assessment: "we must denounce", he states, "all that constructs itself as interior world, as interiority"[41].

Otherwise than Being is not only the book in which Levinas goes farthest in carrying out this denunciation, it is also the book in which the *il y a* (which had remained somewhat in the background of *Totality and Infinity*) makes a rather spectacular 'return'. Not, however, as an opponent of ethics, but as what would seem to have become its best ally: for without the absurdity of the *il y a*, the denunciation of interiority would remain without effect. As Levinas tells Philippe Nemo who questions him on this 'return of the *il y a*': "the responsibility for the Other, being-for-the-other, seemed to me (...) to stop the anonymous and senseless rumbling of being. (...) But the shadow of the 'there is', and of non-sense, still appeared to me necessary as the very test of dis-inter-estedness"[42]. What this means is that the *il y a* is made to work for ethics – its non-sense must prevent the subject under appeal from making sense of that appeal and thus from returning to itself. Its non-sense, that is, must make it possible for the subject to undergo the effects of a sense which is not its own and which it cannot reduce to itself. "The for-the-other", Levinas writes, "thwarts the subject and affects it in its inwardness (*intimité*) through pain", but this pain would not be enough if the "passivity" involved in it would "revert into an act" (OB 74/93). It must have the power to "core out" (OB 64/81: *dénucléer*) the subject, i.e. to rob it of that 'core' through which it could still 'assume' or take upon itself that pain,

40. Cf. the extremely revealing note in the section on 'proximity and obsession': "It is perhaps by reference to this irremissibility that the strange place of illusion, intoxication, artificial paradises can be understood. The relaxation in intoxication is a semblance of distance and irresponsibility. It is a suppression of fraternity, or a murder of the brother. The possibility of going off measures the distance between dream and wakefulness. Dream and illusion are the play of a consciousness come out of obsession, touching the other without being assigned by him. A play of consciousness is a semblance" (OB 192 n 21).
41. E. LEVINAS, *Dieu, La Mort et le Temps*, Paris, Bernard Grasset, 1993, p. 219. The fourth and fifth chapter of OB are full of this denunciation, e.g. OB 145 (quoted in note 37).
42. E. LEVINAS, *Ethics and Infinity. Conversations with Philippe Némo* (transl. R.A. Cohen), Pittsburgh, Duquesne U.P., 1985, p. 52.

and it can hence only be a meaning-less suffering, a suffering which no longer allows the subject to recognize any meaning in its pain, which can turn it into a for-the-other which has no longer anything left for itself. It is in this "possibility in suffering of suffering for nothing" (OB 74), it is in this *'for nothing'* that Levinas now locates the place and the function (!) of the *il y a within* ethics: "pain, an overflowing of sense by nonsense, *in order for* sense to bypass non-sense; sense, that is the-same-for-the-other" (OB 64/85, my italics indicating what was significantly left out of the English translation!). Without "the restlessness" and the "insomnia" of the *il y a*, there would not be the "non-coinciding of the ego with itself" (*ibid.*) which Levinas needs in order for ethics to attain the dis-inter-estedness of a subject completely for-the-other[43]. As a result, the subject's being-for-itself can become a necessary stage for it to undergo that fundamental conversion which ethics, *with the help of the il y a*, will arrange for it: "Without egoism, complacent in itself, suffering would not have any sense, *just as* it would lose the passivity of patience, if it were not at every moment an overflowing of sense by non-sense" (OB 73-4/93, my italics indicating another elision). The self-complacency of enjoyment – sense in a first sense – through the non-sense of suffering (the *il y a*), suffers quite literally a defeat from which the subject (of enjoyment) cannot recover, but through which it is transformed into a subject no longer for-itself, but for-the-other. There is thus a Meaning at work behind the meaninglessness of the *il y a*; indeed, it is this first Meaning or Sense which seems to be behind the title of the famous fourth section of the fifth chapter of *Otherwise than Being*, in which some of Levinas's readers – as must now seem: against their better knowledge – saw an opening to an ethics 'of the *il y a*', i.e. without 'God'. But it seems extremely doubtful whether that is indeed what this section on 'Sense and *there is*' is saying: "The incessant murmur of the *there is* strikes with absurdity the active transcendental ego, beginning and present. *But the absurdity of the there is, as a modality of the one-for-the-other, signifies*" (OB 164). Signifies! The *il y a*: a *modality of* the one-for-the-other!

There can be no question about it, the *il y a* is ethicized, functionalized for and within ethics. Its nonsense has become the carrier of a Sense that comes before all opposition of sense and nonsense: "To support without compensation, the excessive or disheartening hubbub and encumberment of the *there is is needed*" – for without it "the identity of the chosen one, that

---

43. Notwithstanding the extreme vocabulary, it is not too difficult to think of examples of what Levinas has in mind here. One need only think of the unreasonableness with which children can take one's help or attention for granted, to the point of trying one's patience, or of our being taken aback when a beggar we have just given alms to, returns and asks for more.

is, the assigned one [i.e. the subject of responsibility], *which signifies before being* (avant *d*'être; not: avant l'Être), would get a foothold" (OB 164). The *il y a* can only remove the foothold for 'identity', it cannot attain the singularity of the chosen or assigned one. It remains subservient to a Sense which it, willingly or unwillingly, prepares: "Signification", Levinas can now conclude, "is the ethical *deliverance* of the self through substitution for the other" (*ibid.*). Such is indeed "*the surplus* of nonsense over sense" (*ibid.*) – but it is a surplus the value of which does not return to the negativity that produced it. It is ethics that reaps its benefits. Through that surplus "expiation is possible" but this possibility is no longer a possibility *of* the subject, it no longer belongs to the 'I can' which Levinas had portrayed as the heart of its 'interiority'[44]; it is a possibility 'given to' a subject that no longer has an interiority to receive it, and that itself signifies nothing but that expiation (*ibid.*). "Free from the concern 'that existence takes for its very existence'" – freed that is from its *conatus* which the *il y a* has "extirpated" (OB 142), instead of motivated and necessitated (as in Levinas's early work) – this 'subject' "has in its clarity no other shadow, in its rest no other disquietude or insomnia than what comes from the destitution of others" (OB 93). "Its insomnia is but" – and in this 'but' the triumph of ethics over the *il y a* is consecrated – "the absolute impossibility to slip away and distract oneself" (*ibid.*).

Any other distraction will from now on be seen by Levinas as an "intoxication" and as lack of "lucidity" (*ibid.*) for which the subject can be blamed. For the shift that this ethicization of the *il y a* has produced in Levinas's work is that he no longer thinks that the subject *must* forget and close itself off from the non-sense that threatens to overflow it. In a world where the appeal of the ethical other derives its dignity from him coming in the trace of an Other "transcendent to the point of absence, to the point of a possible confusion with the stirring of the *there is*" (CPP 166), the subject *can but no longer must forget*. This forgetting "has to be put back into the significance of the whole plot of the ethical or back into the divine comedy without which it could not have arisen" (*ibid.*). But this comedy has the strange *cathartic* effect of sobering up whoever in it made the mistake of getting intoxicated: "in it", Levinas concludes the passage which we have been following throughout this chapter, "the laughter sticks to one's throat when the neighbor approaches – that is, when his face, or his forsakenness, draws near" (*ibid.*). It is then that the *il y a* plays its last trick on the subject. Not to annihilate it, but to "rescue" or to "deliver" (OB 164) it. But that, of course, it cannot tell it. In order to work for the Good, the *il y a* must, like

44. See note 21 above: this 'I can' presupposed in all consciousness is first of all an 'I *can* sleep' (EE 69).

the Good and like God, do its work in silence.

X

One way to summarize the foregoing would be to return to a quote which we met at the beginning of this chapter, when we heard Levinas affirm that "the only true transcendence is transascendence" (TI 35). For, as we have just seen, 'transdescendence' does not really have a part to itself in Levinas. At least not in his later work, where the only role it gets is that of a comedian that makes the divine comedy all the more divine. And no less serious. There seems, then, only one intrigue of the Infinite, and the wish of some of Levinas's readers to leave 'God' or the 'Good' out of this intrigue, which they still wish to be an *ethical* intrigue, seems all the more unreasonable since the *il y a*, if left to itself and trusted to play a part on its own, would clearly send us back to square one: instead of extirpating the subject's *conatus*, it would make it necessary for the subject to cling to it, and it would thus not dis-interest the subject, but to the contrary, make it immune to anything calling into question the interest by which alone it could survive. There is an *il y a* 'of' ethics (subservient to ethics), but no ethics of the *il y a*. At least for Levinas.

And yet, like those readers of Levinas with whom I have tried to let him argue throughout this chapter, I must confess that I too find myself wondering, but not for the same reasons, whether something is not going wrong here, although 'wrong' may not be the correct term. Let me put this differently: is there no way to escape from this intrigue of the Infinite? To be sure, as I already mentioned, even in *Otherwise than Being*, Levinas seems to leave open the possibility that the subject should affirm its own self over that which is deeper and older in that self and which binds and vows it to the other before it is bound and vowed to itself. The subject can "repudiate" (OB 76/95 "renier"), that is, what Levinas calls its "soul". Indeed the possibility of this "forgetting"[45] of what Levinas also calls the subject's "last reality", of its "last essence" – of the fact that as "a creature" (cf. e.g. OB 92) it is "initially for the other" – this possibility is inevitable since it is inscribed in the very "sensibility" of the subject which makes it vulnerable or sensitive to the appeal of the other: "without egoism complacent in itself, suffering

---

45. Let me simply note for the moment that Levinas never affirms the *possibility* of this forgetting without underlining that its success is only apparent since what it aims to achieve is in another sense *impossible*: "The unlimited initial responsibility ... can be forgotten. In this forgetting consciousness is pure egoism. *But egoism is neither first nor last.* The *impossibility* of escaping God [Levinas now significantly mentions 'the adventure of Jonah'] (...) lies in the depths of myself as a self, as an absolute passivity" (OB 128).

[for-the-other] would not have any sense" (OB 73). "Only a subject that eats can be for-the-other, or can signify" (OB 74); "giving has meaning only as a tearing from oneself despite oneself (*malgré soi*) and not only *without* me (*sans moi*)" (*ibid.*). And thus, since there is ethics only "among beings of flesh and blood" (*ibid.*), there of necessity remains what Levinas calls "an insurmountable ambiguity": "the incarnate ego, the ego of flesh and blood (...) can affirm its *conatus* and its joy like an animal"[46] (OB 79). But apart from the fact that one can wonder where the ego would still find the force to affirm its *conatus* once the movement of this *conatus* is revealed to him by the face of the other (especially if such a 'revelation' has the power to 'denunciate' that ego and drag it into the insomniac ethical night), no such affirmation will ever *escape* the intrigue of the infinite. In fact, Levinas suggests that it is doomed to fail: for a *conatus* that has been revealed to itself as the enactment of the very subjectivity of a subject that cannot but relate everything to itself, will through that revelation lose its very innocence. Once the *conatus* is revealed to itself as *conatus*, it is up for choice[47]. And if the subject should still find in itself the force to affirm itself above the other (although, and I repeat, it is not clear how the ethical beleaguerment (ob-session) would still leave room for that), it will still differ from the animal that it would like to be (!), because it will have chosen for itself and because there is, as we have seen, no such choice "without fault" (OB 87). Animality is no true option, when faced with the ethical appeal. It is but a semblance of spontaneity, a result of self-intoxication. It thus presupposes and affirms the shock with which the Other has awakened the subject to its humanity. Drunkenness is but a denial of and a flight from sobriety. It is but another word for Evil's pretention "to be the equal, the contemporary and the twin

46.   One should analyse patiently all the passages in Levinas in which the animal (or the tree, cf. the introduction to this volume) is mentioned as a figure or an emblem for what in the preceding note was described as a strange mixture of possibility and impossibility. Here as always Levinas affirms animality as an impossible possibility for the human – which is not a play on words, since it stands for a flight into the irresponsible which by fleeing already affirms and accepts a Meaning which it cannot make its own (hence: *impossible* possibility). See also above note 40 on intoxication.

47.   The *conatus essendi* being what is natural in man (cf. note 39) should remain unnoticed for it to retain that status. The phenomenological reduction through the appeal of the Other in breaking with the natural attitude thus also breaks with nature in man. The always possible decision by the responsibilized subject to put its conatus above that of the Other, cannot undo what is thus broken once and for all. Nature *choosing for* nature is no longer natural. And if creation is, as we have seen, 'against nature', there is no turning away from this 'against' which does not already affirm it. A subject to whom its creature-status is revealed, can disobey the imperative which has sobered it up, but it cannot *return* to an innocence which that imperative has called into question.

of the Good" (CPP 138).

The central premise which not only seems to allow for this reasoning, but which, if true, even makes it necessary, is Levinas's idea that there is no genuine intrigue of the *il y a*. In fact, although *Otherwise than Being* is often credited for letting the *il y a* 'return', there is even less of an intrigue of the *il y a* in it, than there was in *Totality and Infinity*. For in *Totality and Infinity* Levinas at least had tried to conceive of a subject whose "door to the outside", as he put it there, had to be "at the same time open and closed" (TI 148, 149)[48]. The subject was to be 'closed' since it had to remain independent and separated from its creator who, by granting it that ontological independence, distinguished himself from the numinosity of the sacred. But in so doing, He allowed the subject the privacy by which it distinguished itself from the anonymity of the Being without beings. And it had to be 'open' for that Creator to show the non-indifference which further distinguished Him from the transdescendent – the true marvel of creation, one will remember, was to create a being capable of receiving a 'revelation', albeit only indirectly, through the appeal of the Other. Although this may not have been the wisest of decisions, *Totality and Infinity*, in insisting on a subject "open and closed *at the same time*", still allowed for a subject both linked to itself and to the Other. There were, of course, signs in that book that Levinas could not regard this as a stable solution[49]. After all, how could he, since ethics turned around an asymmetry which could not but mean that it is *better* to be open than to be closed? Be that as it may, the subject under appeal had in *Totality and Infinity* at least the defence of its "apology" to respond to the appeal of the Other (e.g. TI 59). By the time of *Otherwise than Being*, however, Levinas has decided that ethical persecution "disqualifies" all apology (OB 121).

As we shall see in our next chapter, one of the reasons why Levinas can go as far as this, is that by now his reflection on the relationship between 'justice' and 'ethics' allows him to do what we have just seen him do. The depiction of the ethical 'relation' with the Other in just those terms which his earlier work had used for describing the *il y a*, the characterization of ethics as a 'nightmare', an 'obsession', a tearing down of the walls of the subject's interiority – none of this would have been possible had Levinas, via his deepened reflection on the role of 'the third', not found a way of showing that the result need not be, as it was for the *il y a*, a complete desubjecti-

---

48. TI 149: "Interiority must be at the same time closed and open. The *possibility of rising from the animal condition* is assuredly thus described"; the animal seems to be a closure without openness, cf. *ibid.*: "animal complacency in oneself".

49. E.g. TI 84 ("usurper and murderer"), if thought to its end, already leads to OB. See also the frequent – and surprising – use of expressions like "my final reality" (e.g. TI 178).

vization of the subject. For as we shall see, Levinas now tends to conceive of justice (i.e. the relation with the other than the other, with the third that, as he had already stressed in *Totality and Infinity*, "looks at me in the eyes of the Other" (TI 188)) as that which interrupts the ethical nightmare. Ethics becomes a sort of purgatory in which the subject is purged of whatever in it that might have attached it to itself. The subject, that is, through an ethical "paralysis" becomes separated from its *conatus essendi*. After which it can, in a sense, "return", but in a fully new dress. For 'justice' does not undo the effects of ethics: what awakens from that nightmare, is not, as it was in *Existence and Existents*, simply consciousness or interiority, but a consciousness that *in principle* could be that of an interiority *without secret*: with the help of justice the ethical nightmare in which the subject could not keep anything for itself, thus seems to give birth to that interiority without interiority for which Levinas has been looking all along. Finally he has found a way to put a distance between *le Moi* and *le soi*, albeit at the expense of one of them, for what remains is what *Otherwise than Being* calls an accusative without nominative. But this 'without' is for Levinas not a deficit; as he told Jean Wahl: "I am *for* the I, as existence in the first person, to the extent that its ego-ity signifies an infinite responsibility for an Other. Which amounts to saying that it is as if *the substance of the I is made of saintliness*"[50].

What this means is that Levinas now[51] has decided that the subject's door to the Infinite, instead of being "open and closed at the same time", is initially open and that it only awaits the *après coup* of the phenomenological reduction to realize that the true name for the attempt to close it, is violence: "the violent man does not move out of himself" (DF 9). But one wonders whether Levinas, in thus deciding that all closure comes 'after' a *more primordial* opening, has not also decided to erase what I called above the birthmark of the *il y a* on the subject's being. Indeed, it is striking that Levinas's analysis of enjoyment as *conatus essendi* – as the root of that very *conatus* which the appeal of the Other is going to extirpate – never seeks to explore a possibility to which his earlier work seemed to invite: for if there is an "it wakes", an "it listens" or an "it dies", would there then not also be an "it enjoys"? And would the subject's personal enjoyment then not have to be regarded as a way to protect itself from such an impersonal enjoyment where 'it' enjoys whereas 'I' suffer? And in calling me into question, in seeing in whatever closure there is in me a giving in to "Evil's" claim to be the contemporary, the equal, the twin of the Good" (CPP 138, quoted before),

50. 'Transcendence and Height', *l.c.*, p. 23.
51. Levinas's presentation and the discussion at the *Société Française de Philosophie* from which I just quoted are from January 1962 – immediately after TI was published (1961). Which again seems to me to reduce the difference between TI and OB (cf. note 49).

would the appeal of the Other not have to make exception for this attempt to close off something in me that if 'I' had left open, would surely destroy me?[52] Would it not be unreasonable, in a sense that escapes the link we have seen Levinas explicitly making between autonomy and an accusation that escapes my reason, if it would go on to accuse me of what is perhaps a 'closure' without which there could be no *human* enjoyment? Would it not be unjust, in a sense not covered by Levinas, if it would see in that closure my attempt to turn – unsuccessfully – to animality? *And if it should stop here, should it perhaps not also stop elsewhere?* For example, in not accusing me of protecting myself against an "it sees" which in its turn could mean the end of my seeing?

We shall return to these questions later. Suffice it to say here that nothing indicates that they would have made Levinas come back on his decision that in the face of the Good, the ontological root of ethical Evil loosens its independence. The subject's attempt to protect itself by its privacy from what remains private *to it*, i.e. from what it experiences as intolerable (*l'être c'est le mal*: intolerable or evil), is now discovered as being itself evil. "The law of evil", Levinas now says without hesitation, "is the law of being"[53]. Perhaps the lesson to be drawn from this by those who hesitate like me before this ethicization of the subject's subjectivity, is that the singularity of the subject is (also) to be looked for at another level. Singularization, as we shall see in the next chapters, points to a still otherwise than otherwise than being that escapes both ontology and ethics. But first we have to further understand what Levinas was up to when setting up 'Being' against an 'otherwise than Being'. We will thereby, once again, let a contemporary thinker take the lead. Not in order to discredit his efforts, but with the sole aim of understanding what it would take to be a contemporary of Levinas, or what it means that he is perhaps – and why should this plead against him? – not 'our' contemporary. In a sense, what can be meant by this 'we', is perhaps decided by these questions.

---

52. Although the point is more general, one can see in anorexia and boulimia examples of the kind of havock a non-domesticated 'it enjoys' can bring to the life of the subject (e.g. the beautiful study of Christiane BALASC, *Désir de rien. De l'anorexie à la boulimie*, s.l., Aubier, 1990).

53. 'The Paradox of Morality: An Interview with Emmanuel Levinas', in R. BERNASCONI - D. WOOD (eds.), *The Provocation of Levinas. Rethinking the Other*, London / New York, Routledge, 1988, p. 175.

CHAPTER TEN

CAN ONLY A 'YES' SAVE US NOW?
ANTI-RACISM'S FIRST WORD IN DERRIDA AND LEVINAS

In November 1983, an exhibition was opened in Paris containing paintings and sculpture by eighty-five of the world's most celebrated artists. The artworks would travel round the world until the day had come when the itinerant museum thus constituted could be "presented as a gift to the first free and democratic government of South Africa to be elected by universal suffrage"[1]. I presume that in the meantime this gift has been offered, but I don't know whether it has been accepted. And in reading over the touching piece on "Racism's last word" which was Derrida's contribution to the catalog of that travelling exhibition, I cannot but wonder whether it should have or even could have been accepted. "A memory in advance", that is how Derrida back then had called "the time given for this exhibition" (291): "if one day the exhibition wins, yes, *wins* its place in South Africa, it will keep the memory of what will never have been, at the moment of these projected, painted, assembled works, the presentation of some present" (298, italics Derrida). Will one ever be able to accept such a memory? Can one accept it without rendering loquacious the "silence" with which that exhibition "called out unconditionally"[2] as long as it did not "take place", did not take "its place" (293)? Would accepting it not suggest that we have reached that "future for which *apartheid* will be the name of something finally abolished"[3]? Would it not deflect our attention from the fact that, contrary to what we had all hoped, for us, today, *apartheid* – racism's so-called last word – is not yet a name that "resonate[s] all by itself, reduced to the state of a term in disuse"[4]? But even beyond these considerations of fact (for it is a fact, for example, that in my own country a racist party that campaigns for

1. Preface to the catalog of the Paris exhibition, quoted in the *Translator's Note* to J. DERRIDA, 'Racism's Last Word', *Critical Inquiry* 1985(12), p. 290. References to this article will be given in the text by pagination number only.
2. *Ibid.*, p. 299: "This silence calls out unconditionally; it keeps watch on that which is not, on that which is *not yet*, and on the chance of still remembering some faithful day".
3. *Ibid.*, p. 291: "the *rearview vision* of a future for which (*etc.*) ...".
4. *Ibid.*: "Confined and abandoned then to this silence of memory, the name will resonate (*etc.*)...".

a Flemish-nationalist version of *apartheid*, has been doing all too well during successive past elections), do we not have to ask whether we will ever be in a position to do justice to the "unconditional" appeal with which, according to Derrida, these paintings "gaze and call out in silence" (299)? Would the suggestion in Derrida's piece that we will indeed one day be in such a position not undermine, or at least seriously complicate, everything that he has since then and even before then, taught or published on the question of ethical justice? For example, would the fact that we feel we are in a position to inscribe this exhibition in a particular *topos*, e.g. the topos of a democratic South Africa, not suggest that we have exhausted its appeal and that we (or the South Africans) have done everything the appeal expected us (or them) to do? But then at least one gift would have been accepted and the author of *Given Time*[5] would have to remark that by the same token (indeed, by turning it into a token) it has been annulled: "as soon as the other accepts, as soon as he or she takes, there is no more gift" (GT 14). Unless of course, there never was a gift since according to the same analysis one would have to say that the exhibition stopped being a pure gift from the moment it laid down the conditions under which it could one day be received: for to say what needs to be done and how one is to become worthy of a gift, would seem, according to the author of *Given Time*, already to insert the gift into the logic of a counter-gift and to contaminate its "impossible logic" with that of an economy of the donor who by laying down the condition 'be democratic!' "right away sends [himself] back the gratifying image" of his own capacity for democracy, and thus would "recognize himself in a circular, specular fashion, in a sort of auto-recognition, self-approval, and narcissistic gratitude" (GT 23)[6].

No doubt Derrida would wish to protest against this bizarre attempt to turn the tables of his own analysis against himself. No doubt he would point out that it is precisely to avoid such misunderstanding that *Racism's last word* had stipulated repeatedly and right from the start that this exhibition "is not a presentation" (291) and that, since the time implied in its gift was

---

5. J. DERRIDA, *Given Time: I. Counterfeit Money*, Chicago / London, The University of Chicago Press, 1992. The 'Foreword' locates the origin of the ideas developed in this book in a seminar given in 1977-78 at the Ecole Normale Supérieure in Paris. (Henceforth: GT).

6. Cf. *ibid*.: "The simple intention to give, insofar as it carries the intentional meaning of the gift, suffices to make a return payment to oneself. The simple consciousness of the gift right away sends itself back the gratifying image of goodness or generosity, of the given-being who, knowing itself to be such, recognizes itself in a circular, specular fashion, in a sort of auto-recognition, self-approval, and narcissistic gratitude".

not the "future modality" of some "living present"[7], the exhibition, once arrived at its place, would therefore "keep the memory of what will never have been ... the presentation of some present" (298).

Not deriving from any present, and *hence* without a subject who gives and who receives (for in this context the term 'subject' for Derrida implies self-presence[8]), the exhibition could still be regarded as a gift, and even as a pure gift: "a gift that cannot make itself (a) present" (GT 29). And hence a gift which would continue to call out with an unconditional appeal. Such a gift would speak in silence and that silence, Derrida notes, would be "just" (299). It would be the silence of justice itself. For justice needs to be silent and the call it sends needs to be unconditional, it needs to escape or break through any horizon of expectation, it needs to retain the character of an event which comes as an "absolute surprise"[9] to those who are called upon. Indeed, justice for Derrida "is the experience of the other as other, the fact that I permit the other to be other, which presupposes a gift without exchange, without reappropriation, without jurisdiction" (DA 37). Anti-racism's first word, then, would seem to be a 'yes!' before, as the phrase goes, all opposition between yes/no (cf. DA 36), or a "Come hither" which would open what Derrida now calls a messianic space "without messianism" since it would not anticipate and hence reduce the alterity of the one "to whom 'come hither' is addressed". Only by responding with such a 'yes!' could we refrain from defining the absolute other in advance: "This absolute hospitality is offered to the outsider, the stranger, the new arrival. Absolute arrivals must not be required to begin by stating their identity; I must not insist that they say who they are, and whether they are going to integrate themselves or not; nor should I lay down any conditions for offering them hospitality, for whether or not I shall be able to 'assimilate' them into the family, the nation, or the state. With an *absolute new* arrival, I ought not to propose contracts or impose conditions. I ought not; and in any case, by definition, I cannot" (DA 32).

Of course, Derrida would be the first to admit that we do so all the time.

7. For this point, see the clarifications in J. DERRIDA, *Spectres de Marx*, Paris, Galilée, 1993, e.g. p. 110 (with regard to the similar distinction between a 'démocratie à venir' and a 'future democracy').

8. The quote in note 6 continues: "And this is produced as soon as there is a subject, as soon as donor and donee are constituted as identical, identifiable subjects ...".

9. Cf. 'The Deconstruction of Actuality. An Interview with Jacques Derrida', *Radical Philosophy*, 1994(-68), esp. pp. 32 ff. (henceforth quoted as DA); *Spectres de Marx*, pp. 110 ff.; GT 122: "There must be event ... for there to be gift .... And this event ... must remain in a certain way unforeseeable. ... [The gift] must *appear* chancy or in any case lived as such, apprehended as the intentional correlate of a perception that is *absolutely surprised* by the encounter with what it perceives ..." (last italics mine).

He certainly doesn't need to be reminded that what he is saying here about new arrivals is "politically impracticable": "There is no State-nation in the world today which would simply say: 'We throw open our doors to everyone, we put no limit on immigration'. As far as I [= J. D.] know ... every State-nation is based on the control of its frontiers, on opposition to illegal immigration, and strict limits to legal immigration and right of asylum. The concept of the frontier, no less than the frontier itself, constitutes the concept of a State-nation" (DA 34). But does this mean that the 'Come hither!' of justice is only impracticable "*as long as* politics is based ... on the idea of the identity of a body known as the State-nation" (*ibid.*)? What is the status of this "as long as"? Is a politics conceivable without the concept of a frontier? Would Derrida, unexpectedly, be willing to take the side of those who, like Habermas[10], do not want to rule out such a possibility? What is the difference between the concept of a frontier implied in the idea of a State-nation and the "organicist" "axiom of a national front" that Derrida is criticizing in Le Pen[11] in the following terms: "the front is a skin, a discriminating 'membrane': it only lets in what is homogeneous or capable of being homogenized, what is assimilable, or at most what is heterogeneous but considered 'benign': the appropriable immigrant, the proper immigrant" (DA 35)? Can there be a politics – a democratic politics – without such a skin intervening at some point and constituting a 'membrane' no matter how thin or how permeable, but never infinitely permeable? If one thinks there can not be, one can perhaps begin to appreciate the self-avowed "political impracticability" of Derrida's stance on "*absolute* new arrivals". The claim would simply be that "any politics which fails to sustain some relation to the principle of unconditional hospitality has completely lost its relation to justice" (*ibid.*). And the suggestion is that without such relation to justice there can be no democracy. It is this "come hither!" of justice, this "yes!" to the ab-solute uncontrollable event – or advent, as Merleau-Ponty might have said – of a future beyond our reach, that constitutes the difference between a frontier and a front, between an uncontrollable '*démocratie à venir*' and the attempt to set the course for a future democracy that would only be the reign of a politics without transcendence[12]. There is no democracy without the appeal of justice, and

10. J. HABERMAS, 'Citizenship and National Identity: Some Reflections on the Future of Europe', *Praxis International*, 1992(12:1), esp. p. 18: "The arrival of world citizenship is no longer merely a phantom, though we are still far from achieving it. State citizenship and world citizenship form a continuum which already shows itself, at least, in outline form".

11. Jean-Marie Le Pen: French politician of the extreme right; leader of the nationalist party *Front National*.

12. See note 7.

there is no justice without undecidability, i.e. without an element that escapes the control of what can be calculated. One will have to decide, but one will never know whether the decisions one has reached are such that they fully satisfy the appeal of justice[13]. Democracy, as Lefort would say, is an "impossible task" since it is left without the touchstone that would allow it to know that the task has been carried out correctly. Hence it is never really there, democracy is always "yet to come", and in this excess of a still outstanding future lie both its conditions of possibility and – to use one of Derrida's cherished expressions – its conditions of impossibility. Democracy is a never-ending story because it is a story that is only told once – or even because – its beginning has been lost: after the demise of the theologico-political we can no longer simply restore transcendence, nor should we seek salvation in a totalitarian or nationalist restoration of immanence[14]. Stretched between immanence and transcendence, democratic politics needs a principle to keep reminding it that whatever its results, they will have limited the unlimitable. Which is why Derrida would probably argue that a politics which fails to sustain some relation to the principle of unconditional hospitality has not only "lost its relation to justice", but will have ceased to be a democratic politics in the same movement. And since the only relation which doesn't condition this unconditional hospitality, and leaves the other his *absolute* otherness, is that of a 'yes!' before all opposition between yes/no, there can be no democracy without such a 'yes!'. Only a 'yes', it seems, 'can save us now'.

*

It is a bit late, I realize, to confess that I only went to such length in spelling out what seems to be at stake in Derrida's 'yes!' in order to change the stakes and perhaps even to change the game. But I needed to establish a context in which I could inscribe a vague worry, even an irritation with the way in which a certain notion of the democratic and a certain conception of ethics (Derrida's 'justice') are mutually articulated here. And before doing so, I felt compelled to show that there is a point to this articulation, and that behind Derrida's fashionable and – according to some – elusive vocabulary one can detect the embarrassment of a *philosophical* common sense that, if we are honest, we would probably have to admit to be very much our own. For

13. Cf. J. DERRIDA, 'Force de loi. Le "Fondement mystique de l'autorité"/Force of Law. The "Mystical Foundation of Authority"', *Cardozo Law Review*, 1990(11), pp. 962 ff., 968 ff.

14. Cf. Cl. LEFORT, 'The Permanence of the Theologico-Political?', in ID., *Democracy and Political Theory* (transl. D. Macey), Oxford, Polity Press, 1988, pp. 213-55.

after all, who among us would like to share the nationalist axiom of Le Pen; and who could deny that in rejecting such an axiom, one will have to distinguish the concept of frontier from that of front? Even Habermas, in his plea for a post-national identity, and in the accompanying attempt to delineate a notion of democratic citizenship that could "prepare the way for a condition of world citizenship", will have to explain whence comes the "impulse" for the different ways of life coexisting equally within the constitutional framework of a democratic legal system, "to open these ways of life to others"[15]. Can there be such an "impulse" without Derrida's 'yes!', a *"yes* (that) marks that there is an address to the other" and that "the other no longer lets him- or herself be produced by the same"[16]?

And yet, it is precisely this use of concepts like 'same' and 'other', which always turn up from the moment that Derrida brings up this 'yes!', that worries me. Wasn't it Derrida who first warned us about the use and provenance of such concepts? Was it not at least part of the aim of *Violence and Metaphysics*[17] to show that these Levinasian concepts could only be introduced after the prior introduction of a certain concept of God? Had the author of *Violence and Metaphysics* not tried to show how the relation between the ego and the other necessarily depended on a certain violence which could not be avoided, since to do away with it would be tantamount to either absorbing the other in the ego, or to turn him into part of the world? Was it not due to the hymen – or one could say: the membrane – between *ego* and *alter ego*, that the other could appear 'for me' without losing his alterity? Was the notion of "transcendental violence" not introduced precisely to point to the 'fact' that there had to be something of the 'other' which could not appear in order for him to appear at all? That there had to be *as it were* a moment of suppression or elision in the appearance of the other, for him to remain other, and that everything turned around the 'as it were' of this "irreducible violence of the relation to the other" which is "at the same time nonviolence, since it opens the relation to the other" (VM 128-9)? An other who would fully appear to me would not be an other; only by not-appearing while appearing can he be distinguished from me. And yet this essential withdrawal in the appearance of the other had to be noticed somehow for otherwise it would only be a condition for his appearance that would play no role at all in formulating an ethics 'of'

15. J. HABERMAS, *art. cit.*, p. 17.

16. J. DERRIDA, *Ulysse gramophone. Deux mots pour Joyce*, Paris, Galilée, 1987, p. 127.

17. J. DERRIDA, 'Violence and Metaphysics. An Essay on the Thought of Emmanuel Levinas', in ID., *Writing and Difference* (transl. A. Bass), Chicago, University of Chicago Press, 1978, pp. 79-153, and cf. our discussion in chapter 6. Derrida's essay will be quoted as VM.

alterity. It would only be 'transcendental', and not a question of 'transcendental *violence*' (VM 128 ff.). But the upshot of this analysis was that the impulse for an ethics of "original finitude" (e.g. VM 103 – but the expression abounds) derived precisely from the unavoidability of this common frontier between 'me' and 'the other': the other had to be *ego* in order to be *alter ego*. Or in other words, the alterity of the other could not be absolute: to be other, he has *to share* with me *the form* of being an *ego*. It could only appear as such by not appearing: it could only be noticed by resisting the equally necessary and unavoidable attempt at assimilation. Hence, what ultimately distinguished Derrida's position in *Violence and Metaphysics* from that of Levinas was a different appraisal of the relation between phenomenology and ethics. Whereas for Levinas, to appear already means to lose one's absolute alterity (for to appear is to appear *to someone* and hence to be forced to share his categories), and ethics as a consequence had to do with a dimension anterior to the "identifying" light of phenomenology, Derrida contended that "the phenomenon of respect [for the other] supposes the respect of phenomenality" (VM 121). To invert this order of priority, Derrida further contended, was necessarily to leave the realm of an ethics of *originary* finitude and to resort to the gesture of a classical metaphysics of the infinite which would describe the titles of the finite only by comparison (e.g. VM 104). It was the introduction of the very notion of (a) God that Derrida was at pains to avoid.

Hence my worry and my irritation: for the vocabulary and the schemes we have seen Derrida resort to in order to argue for the "come hither!" of an unconditional hospitality, seem to return to a Levinasian opposition between the 'same' and the 'other'. As does, for example, the idea of a 'pure gift' that orients the analysis of *Given Time*[18], or the attempt to characterize the 'event' in terms of an *absolute* surprise[19]. Indeed, Derrida's very conception of justice as "experience of *absolute* alterity"[20] and his insistence on its "indeconstructability" again seem to derive from what he now calls "an inheritance from Levinas" (DA 37). My aim, of course, is not to tell Derrida how he has to handle this inheritance. But since we are all in a sense inheriting from Levinas, I wanted to sketch in rather broad strokes – I know – Derrida's way of receiving this inheritance, in order to point to what perhaps could be a different way. The reason why I am interested in finding such a way is not because I wish to correct the *political* impracticability of

18. Cf. GT, e.g. 14 (ad 'phenomenality'), 15 (irreducibility of the gift to its phenomenon or its meaning), 24 (ad 'odyssey') – in all these passages the word 'gift' comes to occupy a structurally similar place as the word 'face' in Levinas.

19. For Levinas on "absolute surprise": OB 99.

20. J. DERRIDA, 'Force de loi/Force of Law', *l.c.*, p. 971.

Derrida's unconditional hospitality. It is rather that I am worried by what is perhaps its underlying assumption of *ethical practicability*. For if one makes ethics – Derrida's justice – dependent on the unconditional appeal of the other, the fact that we find ourselves constantly falling short of such an appeal will be a fact that can be ethically qualified. Levinas will call it egoism, a giving in to the temptation of Evil. Evil is an intra-ethical term. It belongs to the alternative between the 'yes' and the 'no' which is opened up by the originary 'yes' *before* all opposition between 'yes' and 'no'. It is the authority of this latter 'yes' that concerns me. In other words, I wonder whether what in the light of this 'yes' will necessarily be presented as a falling short of the appeal of the other, and thus as a move to be situated already *within* the realm of ethics, could not or should not be regarded differently if one follows if not the letter, then at least the spirit of the analysis offered in *Violence and Metaphysics*. More precisely, I wonder whether what Derrida has called in that text "originary finitude" should not lead us to consider that there is perhaps a way of not responding to the appeal of the other that does not fit into the yes/no opened up by the original 'yes'. This non-response which is not an intra-ethical no, perhaps not only escapes the realm of ethics, but may even signal that its unifying horizon has been breaking up. The choice, then, would seem to be one between a 'no' which does and a 'no' which does not bow to the authority of the 'yes' before all yes or no.

My question in this chapter ultimately aims at weighing the consequences of these two avenues for a problem – anti-racism – that I assume is our common concern. To avoid any unnecessary suspense, I will immediately announce the stakes. If anti-racism's first word is a 'yes!', it will have to argue against racism by claiming that colour for example is not important, whereas, in the absence of such a first word, the argument will have to be exactly the reverse while at the same time pointing the way to a critique of those movements (African-Americanism, nationalism) which believe colour to be important, but for the wrong reasons. It will all depend, then, on a word. Not just on the choice between the two words already mentioned, but on a choice that I suspect precedes that choice. For the first word, as Levinas reminded us, is not simply a 'yes!'. The "unconditioned 'yes' of submission" to the absolute appeal of the other is not that of "an infantile spontaneity" (OB 122), because it itself derives from another word, to which I alluded in my title and which, once mentioned, will, I hope, clarify my subtitle and explain why –notwithstanding the time and the effort it took to supply the necessary context to make the first and barely hidden quote in my subtitle accessible– the rest of this essay will have to be devoted primarily to a discussion with Levinas. For there is a second and less easily perceptible quote hidden in my subtitle and it simply says this: "The first word says the saying itself. ... [It] only says the saying itself before every being and every thought ... But if the first saying says this very saying, here the saying and the said, *cannot equal one another*. For the saying in being said at every moment breaks the definition of what it says and breaks up the totality it includes. ... This first saying is to be sure but a word. *But the word is God*" (CPP 126). Let me first explain why this quote brings together all the elements necessary to understand the uniqueness of Levinas's position in what since Kant we have come to consider as the main coordinates that define the ethical realm.

I. A SPECIAL HETERONOMY
FROM THE SACRED TO THE HOLY

The Kantian revolution in ethics is usually rendered by stating that for Kant the law no longer derives from the Good (heteronomy) but that the Good is made possible by it. Autonomy then means that the law no longer is 'given' by an instance preceding it, by what Rogozinski has called a 'Hors-la-loi' (an Out-law): "No matter how diverse, the moral philosophies of the Tradition all authorize themselves by a single gesture ... the violent gesture by which the gift of Law is torn from the hands of the Law and given to a more 'original' instance, an Out-Law that arrogates itself the power to make the Law"[21]. But if it is true that Kant is the first to render that power to the law and to let the law give itself, it is equally striking that Levinas's heteronomy does not fit well into this scheme. For the central idea of Levinas's ethics is that there is only an ethical law because the Out-Law of the Good *refuses* the power to make it. The Good is precisely Good because it abdicates and forces us to deflect our attention from it. It is, as Levinas often stresses, anarchic and hence it "does not reign" (OB 194 n4). But, as he also adds, "it would reign in its own way" (OB 194 n2) if it would only be situated at some point or in some dimension beyond our reach (from whence it could, for example, attract us). That is why it has to leave a trace: the trace of its abdication. As is well-known, that trace is the face of the other. By being in the trace of the Good – or of the Infinite, as Levinas more often calls it[22] – the face of the Other becomes not, as one may expect, the repre-

---

21. J. ROGOZINSKI, 'Vers une éthique du différend', in H. KUNNEMAN - H. DE VRIES (eds.), *Enlightenments. Encounters between Critical Theory and Contemporary French Thought*, Kampen, Kok Pharos, 1993, pp. 92-119 (my translation). For a similar analysis see the title-essay in J.-L. NANCY, *L'impératif catégorique*, Paris, Flammarion, 1983.

22. I will use the Good, the Infinite and God without further distinction, as is the case in Levinas's own texts, for reasons explained below (section 3).

sentative of the Law, nor the Law himself, but only a reminder that the Out-Law who could give the law has left and will only return when he no longer needs to give it. God becomes an ethical imperative, but he is not the one who addresses it to me. *It is only because he has given up his entitlement to be its addressor, that there is such a thing as an ethical address.* In a sense this means that for Levinas there is no ethics without God, but since it is not an ethics consisting of laws issued by God, it also means that there is no God without ethics: "revelation is made by the one that receives it" (OB 156).

Just as there could be no 'Achtung' in Kant, without the fact of reason, there can be no ethics for Levinas without God. But just as *Achtung* is for Kant not itself the fact of reason, but *Achtung for* the fact of reason, so in Levinas the face of the Other could not be what demands *Achtung* from me, were it not 'in the trace of' the Infinite. And just as Kant only introduced the fact of reason as a result of a failed deduction[23] (the law could not be deduced from freedom; freedom had to be deduced from the law), so Levinas introduces the idea of the Infinite to signal that a certain deduction will fail to capture the sense of ethics: responsibility cannot be deduced from freedom. But it is precisely at this point that he parts ways with Kant: "To distinguish formally will and understanding, will and reason, nowise serves to maintain plurality in being or the unicity of the person if one forthwith decides to consider only the will ... that decides only through respect for the universal to be a good will" (TI 217). As we know from our analysis in chapter five, for Levinas, Kantian universality has the 'fatal flaw' that it requires rendering symmetrical what is, at bottom, an asymmetrical position (obligation). Levinas's critique aims at the consequence of this move: by leaping out of the logic of obligation in an attempt to graft it onto the logic of norms, the resultant formulation of the categorical imperative cannot but obfuscate that moral responsibility is about being *more* responsible than others, being *more* obligated than them. Hence Levinas's plea for a heteronomous responsibility that singularizes its addressees and makes them incomparable to others. Such a responsibility can not only not be deduced from freedom, but it will necessarily involve nonfreedom: the absence of the freedom to choose. Responsibility is older than freedom because it has obligated us, "unbeknownst" to ourselves.

There is no contradiction here: we have been chosen by the Good, but we are not its slaves. We would have been its slaves had it manifested itself in its full splendour before us – for then we would not have had a chance to

---

23. See the brilliant commentary in D. HENRICH, 'Die Deduktion des Sittengesetzes. Über die Gründe der Dunkelheit des letzten Abschnittes von Kants 'Grundlegung der Metaphysik der Sitten'', in A. SCHWAN (ed.), *Denken im Schatten des Nihilismus*, Darmstadt, Wissenschaftliche Buchgesellschaft, 1975, pp. 55-112.

deflect our gaze. But the Good is precisely Good, i.e. *holy instead of sacred*, because it has given us this chance. It is in fact nothing but that: only an Infinite can "contract" itself, and leave next to it place for a being which, although created through this contraction, has received the "grace" of being able to ignore its Creator[24]. We cannot e-mancipate ourselves from the Good but the Good only holds us in its *mancipium*[25], in order to abolish it in the same move: it is that which *itself* has set us free. This is what Levinas means by the discretion of the 'Transcendent'. It is this "anachoresis" which separates it from the sacred and ensures it of its transcendence: "transcendence is to be distinguished from a union with the transcendent" (TI 77). But, depending on how one approaches it, a union with the transcendent could just as well mean that the finite gets absorbed in the Infinite, or that the Infinite loses its infinity through contact with the finite: "If the Infinite ... would be *in* the finite, it would be assimilated, if only by its reflection"[26]. If the Infinite is to keep its infinity and the finite its finitude, there has to be at least one taboo: on incarnation. But it is a taboo which is issued by something which declares *itself* taboo. That something can only be a somebody: God.

This distinction between the sacred and the holy (the sacred being that which results from a taboo; the holy being that which has put a taboo *on itself*) is at work in every move that Levinas makes in developing his ethics, and not in the least in that first decisive statement from the opening pages of *Totality and Infinity* in which he announces what will be his 'differend' with Kierkegaard: "It is not I who resist the system, as Kierkegaard thought; it is the Other" (TI 40). Taken by itself, and without linking it to the distinction between the sacred and the holy, this statement would at best seem a bit curious to anyone familiar with the way Kierkegaard portrayed this rupture with 'the system', for example in *Fear and Trembling*. For is not Abraham's silence, which tears him out of the ethical realm and bans him from the domain of language and the universal, a predicament in which he finds himself only because an Other has commanded him to undertake that fateful journey to Mount Moriah[27]? But for Levinas Kierkegaard did not

24. Cf. e.g. TI 58-9, 89 and 104: "Infinity is produced by withstanding the invasion of a totality, in a *contraction* that leaves a place for the separated being".

25. For this link between *mancipium* and e-mancipation, see J.-Fr. LYOTARD, 'The Grip (*la Mainmise*)', in ID., *Political Writings* (transl. B. Readings / K. Paul), Minneapolis, University of Minnesota Press, 1993, pp. 148-58.

26. E. LEVINAS, *Dieu, la Mort et le Temps*, Paris, Bernard Grasset, 1993, p. 132.

27. J. DE SILENTIO, *Fear and Trembling*, in S. KIERKEGAARD, *Fear and Trembling / Repetition* (transl. H.V. Hong & E.H. Hong), Princeton U.P., 1983, e.g. p. 93: "[Abraham's] silence would not be due to his wanting to place himself as the single individual in an absolute relation to the *universal* but to his having been placed as the single

develop his analysis far enough to really come to the height of the alterity of this 'Other'. He thinks Kierkegaard's rendering of what happens at Mount Moriah is biased, for the simple reason that it stops too soon: "In the evocation of Abraham [Kierkegaard] describes how he meets God at the point where subjectivity lifts itself to the level of the religious, that is to say above ethics. But one could argue the opposite: the *attention* paid by Abraham to the voice that brings him back to the ethical order by forbidding him a human sacrifice is the highest moment of the drama. That he has obeyed the first voice is astonishing; that he kept enough distance from this obedience to hear the second voice – *there you have the essential*"[28]. The first voice is the one that orders Abraham to sacrifice Isaac, whereas the second voice is the one that lets him slaughter the ram instead. This second voice which interrupts the first is for Levinas the moment of the ethical – of the "infinite demand that appeals to your responsibility without you having the possibility to let someone else be responsible in your stead" (*ibid.*). But Levinas's argument here is not simply that by missing the second voice Kierkegaard misses the truly ethical moment of the drama: a moment that has nothing to do with losing oneself in the general (ethics for Kierkegaard) but with a responsibility that "singularizes you, poses you as a unique individual, as I [*Moi*]" (*ibid.*). The argument reaches much further: by missing the second voice, Kierkegaard for Levinas is still under the spell of the sacred. For it is only the second voice which for Levinas will break that spell: in declaring the object of the intended sacrifice taboo and in substituting another one for it, God declares *himself* to be taboo. It is this preservation "*of difference* in the non-difference of the Good" (OB 123) which Levinas will stress in linking the Good to the holy, and in distinguishing the holy from the sacred. To be sure, the Good is not indifferent, since – like the sacred – it attracts; but what distinguishes it from the sacred is that it gives to "the desire it arouses" an "inclination" "toward responsibility for the neighbor" (*ibid.*). "It is necessary", Levinas writes elsewhere, "that the Desirable or God remain *separated* in the Desire; as desirable – near but different – Holy. This can only be if the Desirable orders me to what is the non-desirable, the undesirable par excellence – the other" (CPP 164)[29]. What the second voice denies to Abraham is therefore precisely "*a relation* with the sacred" (TI 79). It denies him a religion that would consist in anything else

individual in an absolute relation to the *absolute*".

28. E. LEVINAS, *Noms Propres*, s.l., Fata Morgana, 1976, p. 90. One can find a less literal translation in the KCR volume from which I quoted in the second section of the preceding chapter.

29. I have restored the capitals left out in the translation (*De Dieu qui vient à l'idée*, Paris, Vrin, 1992, p. 113).

than in an (ethical) *relation without relation* to the other. "A you is inserted between the I and the absolute He (*Il*). Correlation is broken" (CPP 73). It is this rupture which protects "against the folly of a direct contact with the Sacred" (DF 144). What the biblical story teaches us *in its own way*, is what it means that "the absolute [becomes] purified of the violence of the sacred" (TI 77). It tells us *in its own way* what the precondition for any ethics consists of: "The metaphysical relation, the idea of infinity, connects with the noumenon which is not a numen. This noumenon is to be distinguished from the concept of God possessed by the believers of positive religions ill disengaged from the bonds of participation, who act being immersed in a myth unbeknown to themselves" (TI 77).

Of course, this is not the way that Levinas as a philosopher will tell the story: his argument is not that there was a first correlation which has subsequently interrupted itself and thereupon generated ethics. Levinas starts the other way round: he wants to describe human relations and by focusing on their ethical structure, give new resonance to the word 'God'[30]. Since the face of the other ethically appeals to me, that is, both commands me ('Thou shall not kill') and implores me ('Help me live'), the other cannot be, like Sartre would have it, "simply another freedom" (CPP 55). The other cannot simply be other in the sense of being outside me. He must be *above* me, since otherwise I do not understand how I could get caught up in an ethical appeal. The only true exteriority is an ethical one: for the ethical appeal is an appeal to help something which exists in its own right – *kath'auto*. And such a something can only be a someone: only a personal other has enough alterity ('exteriority') to shock me in such a way that I cannot adapt the shock – if I don't help the other and even if I don't feel remorse, I will at least have noticed that I denied him something he demanded from me. Things, of course, have their own exteriority, but the point of my relation to them is that they *appear to me*, which implies that I must somehow be able to locate or to label or to recognize them, – i.e. that I must be *capable* of adapting the shock with which I received them at first. But ethics is not knowledge: I always react too late to the appeal of the other, I cannot anticipate it, it is something which catches me by surprise and does not leave me the choice of being surprised or not. Responsibility is older than freedom; it is an election, an ethical singularization: I am the one who is responsible and no one can take this responsibility over from me.

All of this is, of course, very well known. But isn't Levinas *in his turn* telling us a myth? Can he explain what ethics is about without himself resorting to a structure or an intrusion "unbeknownst to ourselves"? What is the difference and is there a difference between the "*à l'insu*" of the be-

---

30. See the lectures quoted in note 26.

lievers of positive religion "who act being immersed in a myth *unbeknownst to themselves*" and the "*à l'insu*" invoked earlier when we noted that Levinas's notion of responsibility implies "the formal structure of nonfreedom in a subjectivity which does not have time to choose the Good and thus is penetrated with its rays *unbeknownst to itself* [*à l'insu*]" (OB 11)? And why does *Totality and Infinity*, the few times the expression (*à l'insu*) comes up (e.g. TI 79), always give it the negative ring of participation, fusion, in short: of the sacred, whereas *Otherwise than Being* where the expression abounds (e.g. OB 148/189), uses it to think the structure of the holy (OB 150)? Is there a contradiction (or an 'evolution') here? I think not. For Levinas's stress on the "anachoresis" of the transcendent has rendered transcendence so discreet that it might as well not be noticed. It does not rule, but it does have to leave a trace of its abdication, "but only a trace" (OB 194 n4): "Transcendence owes it to itself to interrupt its own demonstration. Its voice has to be silent as soon as one listens for its message. It is necessary that its pretention be exposed to derision and refutation, to the point of suspecting in the 'here I am' that attests to it a cry or a slip of a sick subjectivity" (OB 152). This 'here I am' points to the structure of "inspiration" in every ethical responsibility. As "a witness that does not thematize what it bears witness of" (OB 146), one could say that it marks by an address *to* the other that there has been an address *by* the other, without letting that mark reduce in any way the alterity of that other. It is thus of the exact same structure as Derrida's 'yes!'. But let us not move too quickly.

To keep the transcendent transcendent and the finite finite any direct contact, however brief, between the two has to be avoided. Accordingly, Levinas, when speaking of the 'trace' of transcendence, will not be referring to the trace left by a presence that is now absent, but to the trace left by something that has never been present: something that always already has passed. But again, such a something can only be a someone and that someone is God: "Only a being that transcends the world, an ab-solute being, can leave a trace" (CPP 105)[31]. And "a past absolutely bygone" the "irreversible lapse" of which "is sealed in a trace", – what could that be but the time of creation? Could the other be an *absolute* other, could the appeal of his face "*absolutely* surprise" me (OB 99/126, transl. altered), if this face would not "shine" "in the trace of the other"? Could "what is presented there [in or by this face] absolv(e) itself from my life and visit me as *already ab-solute*", had not "Someone already passed" and had this face not found itself "in the trace" of "the God who passed"? Had it not stood "in the trace of illeity"? Only a page or two before Levinas declares that "the first word

---

31. Unless otherwise indicated, all the following expressions have been taken from the last pages of the chapter on 'Meaning and Sense' in Levinas's CPP.

is God" – declaration that, as announced, is the *only* thing we need to understand if we want to know what anti-racism's first word is or could be – he also writes, and I believe that we now are in a position to understand what he writes: "it is because in the proximity of being is inscribed *the trace of an absence*, or of the infinite, that there is dereliction, gravity, responsibility, obsession and I. The I, the non-interchangeable par excellence, is, *in a world without play*, what in a *permanent sacrifice* substitutes itself for others and transcends the world. *But this is the source of speaking, for it is the essence of communication*" (CPP 124). At the source of speaking, a permanent sacrifice – the infinite profusion of 'yes'? We are moving closer to what we announced would be our concern. For is it true that "every other is wholly other" ("tout autre est tout autre"), as Derrida tells us in a recent essay[32]? Would it be true if he wasn't "in the trace" of that wholly/Holy Other? Could it be true if one aims to write an ethics of *originary* finitude? We have moved closer, but in order to get a grip on these questions, we clearly need another detour. All the more so, since the distinction between the holy and the sacred which we have until now let guide our analysis, is still far from secure.

II. A RETURN OF THE SACRED?

Isaac would have been sacred had he only been a separated object – an object on which rested a taboo. He would have found himself, for example, in a position structurally similar to the mother (or to Lacan's *das Ding*[33]) on

---

32.   J. DERRIDA, *The Gift of Death* (transl. D. Wills), Chicago & London, The University of Chicago Press, 1995, p. 76-7. I will abbreviate as GD with the pagination of the French original after the solidus, when appropriate ('Donner la mort', in *L'éthique du don. Jacques Derrida et la pensée du don* (Royaumont 1990), Paris, Métailié-Transition, 1992).

33.   For Lacan, human *desire* receives its specific structure through the loss of immediacy that is the effect of being introduced in the symbolic order of language. A child only becomes a subject, an 'I', by being addressed as a 'you' and receiving a name. Before entering the symbolic order of language which makes such an address possible, the child is not a separate 'self'. It lives in 'unity' with the mother, which is all but a paradisiac state: it lacks the symbolic distance that would allow it to bear e.g. the coming and going of the mother. When the mother leaves the room, it loses as it were part of its self (or better, it is literally torn apart, since it is part of the mother, having no separate 'self'). The law of the signifier is called a law of castration since it introduces a first loss: by introducing the child into language, it loses its unity which the mother. But since this loss is the price for the child to become a separate self, the mother is an object that was never *present* for the subject who lost it: one only becomes a subject by losing it. In this context, it should be stressed that the law of castration (or of the signifier), in severing the child from the mother, is actually *helping it*, and is thus more than merely repressive. As long as one lacks the symbolic distance offered by language, the behaviour of the mother can only appear as erratic and

whom comes to rest the incest taboo which is nothing else than the co-originary effect of the introduction of the symbolic order (the law of castration, the law of the signifier). But Isaac isn't sacred. His face is 'holy' because it is "in the trace" of the Holy. As a result of which, the desire for Isaac is not the same as the desire for an object always already lost. It is not a desire to touch or to reach what cannot be touched or reached. It does not aim at 'das Ding'. The desire for Isaac is an ethical desire; its only way to express itself is *Achtung*, in its double Kantian sense: *attentio* (as in '*mind* the gap') and *reverentia* (respect).

The face of the other is not that of another freedom at the same level as my own, and hence incompatible with it, turning my possibilities into 'dead possibilities' and uncovering next to my 'pour soi' a 'pour autrui' that surprises me, but that I cannot deny to be my own and that fills me with shame[34]. The relation between me and the other is not that of an aporetic dialectics because it is not a relation at all. It is what *Totality and Infinity* calls a 'relation without relation' where the other term escapes being drawn into the relation not just because it is free, but because it has an "unimpeachable right over me" (CPP 125), and on the basis of that right can forbid me to approach it in any other way than with respect. And as in Kant, this *Achtung* has the two modalities of being both a *Erniedrigung* and a *Erhebung*[35]. For the face of the other fills me with shame – but it is the shame of a bad conscience that does not arise because of something I did not do but should have done (or did do and should not have done), but that quite simply makes me ashamed of my existence itself and gives me the sense that

whimsical (she comes and goes …). Castration as an introduction into the symbolic order of language rests on a sort of trade-off: it *gives* the child the distance of language to protect itself from the apparent lawless behaviour of the mother that hitherto held it in its grip (the child will now be able to address the mother and to interpret her behaviour), but it also *robs* it of its immediate unity with the mother. Thus the '*repressive*' power of castration *produces* subjectivity and desire at the same time: all desired objects will seek to replace an object always and irretrieveably lost, but their very failure to do so is what allows the subject to live in the *human* order of desire. However, it is also an order of *desire* since the 'original loss' that gave rise to it does not prevent 'man' from "always seeking what he has to find again, but which he will never attain" (J. LACAN, *The Ethics of Psychoanalysis* (1959-60), Tavistock/Routledge, London, 1992, p. 68). In this seminar, Lacan calls this centre around which human desire 'gravitates' (*ibid.*, pp. 58, 62 and *passim*) *das Ding*: an 'object' that has always been lost and that is only 'present' *as a trace* in and through this loss: "It is to be found at the most as something missed" (p. 52).

34. I am, of course, referring here to Sartre's famous analysis of intersubjectivity in *Being and Nothingness* (cf. chapter 11 below).

35. Cf. D. HENRICH, 'Ethik der Autonomie', in ID., *Selbstverhältnisse*, Stuttgart, Philip Reclam Jun., 1982, pp. 34 ff.

"my place in the sun is a usurpation"[36]. The object of this *Erniedrigung* is, as in Kant, sensibility itself; since by existing, I enjoy and am, without even knowing, the self-centred centre of a world. But the face of the other, commanding me in its misery, reminds me that the enjoyment is a richness that I am not entitled to: it belongs to him before it belongs to me, since – and one should stress this since, for Levinas will say it is the only way of understanding what goes on here – "his gaze (*regard*) must come to me from a dimension of the ideal (*idéal*)": "the other must be *closer to God* than I. This is certainly not a philosopher's invention, but *the first given* of moral consciousness, which could be defined as the consciousness of the privilege the other has relative to me" (CPP 56). As we said before, there would be no *Achtung* without that "first given" that fulfills in Levinas's thought the same role as the Kantian *Faktum*. But just as Kant had immense difficulties in keeping the two moments of *Achtung* together, Levinas too seems involved in a rather complicated attempt to link this *Erniedrigung* to a moment of elevation (*Erhebung*). It involves nothing less than a sort of *transfiguration of sensibility*: "a disinterestedness, an 'otherwise than being' which turns into a 'for the other', burning for the other, *consuming the bases of any position for oneself* and any substantialization which would take form in this consummation ... The reverting of the ego into a self, the de-posing or de-situating of the ego, is the very modality of dis-interestedness. It has the form of corporeal life *devoted to expression and to giving*. It is devoted, and does not devote itself: it is a self despite itself, in incarnation, where it is the very possibility of offering, suffering and trauma" (OB 50). And Levinas calls this de-posing of the ego an *Erhebung*: in it the ego reaches "its final reality" (TI 178), i.e., its true, moral, self: a self tied to and devoted to others before it is tied to and devoted to itself. An original self-absence: an endless profusion toward the other. Ethical ec-stasis, ever widening opening toward the other. "Total altruism"[37], but always keeping – *minding* – the infinite distance between (moral) self and other, *respecting* the hierarchy, self-less without desire for gratification (CPP 90 ff.), without desire to touch: "I approach the Infinite insofar as *I forget myself* for my neighbor who looks at me; I forget myself only in breaking the undephasable simultaneity of representation, in existing beyond my death. I approach the infinite by sacrificing myself. *Sacrifice is the norm and the criterion of the approach*" (CPP 72); "generosity of sacrifice ... *without calculation*, for going on to infinity" (*ibid.*).

Without calculation. A pure gift. A never-ending 'yes!'. Once again, we

---

36. See the last but one motto that OB takes from Pascal's *Pensées*: "... 'That is my place in the sun'. That is how the usurpation of the whole world began".

37. E. LEVINAS, 'Transcendence and Height', *l.c.*, p. 18.

have come close to the target. But let us not be satisfied with simply finding in these quotes one more confirmation of our suspicion that Derrida's 'yes!' seems to derive from a Levinasian inheritance. Let us also note that it is difficult to see how the price for living off the profits of this inheritance could not but entail a certain neglect of the basic problem that the author of *Violence and Metaphysics* had been pointing to. For in opposing the '*without calculation*' of ethical responsibility to the *calculus* that could serve to protect the interests of an ego, it seems that Levinas is forced to use the very opposition between the 'same' and the 'other' that Derrida in that essay had been questioning[38]. Given the *absolute* alterity of the other, ethics will have to consist of an *absolute* openness toward such an alterity, and since anything short of "*total* altruism" will merely indicate that this openness has not yet been reached, *there is nothing in ethics that could prevent its sacrifice from being total too*. And as Derrida himself observed in a (much) later essay, this consequence is not without problems: "in taking into account the absolute singularity, that is, the absolute alterity obtaining in relations between one human and another, Levinas is no longer able to distinguish between the infinite alterity of God and that of every human. His ethics is already religion" (GD 84/81, transl. corr.). As we shall see, this is an important point – not so much because it would embarrass Levinas, but because it will allow him to force Derrida to study the terms of his inheritance more closely. Indeed, Levinas in his turn may wish to question Derrida as to how he can affirm that 'every other is wholly other' without having to face the very difficulty that he himself is pointing to. But let us first try to analyse this difficulty in our own terms.

For given the pains we have been at to distinguish with Levinas between the sacred and the holy, it is in a sense utterly surprising that the sacrifice should become "the norm and the criterion" of the ethical approach. After all, had not Levinas himself, in stressing the second moment of the drama at Mount Moriah, been arguing against Kierkegaard that ethics only starts when an obscure urge to sacrifice (like Abraham's) is limited? And shouldn't one infer from this that it is not sacrifice, but the 'sacrifice of the sacrifice' – the *interruption* of that first sacrificial urge – that constitutes the

---

38. E.g.: "To what exercises would Parmenides give himself over, at the frontiers of *Totality and Infinity*, if we attempted to make him understand that *ego* equals *same*, and that the other is what it is only as the absolute *infinitely* other absolved of its relationship to the Same ... [Derrida then gives two examples of such a Parmenidan exercise, both concluding: "therefore, it is *not infinitely* other"] ... At bottom, we believe, this exercise is not just verbiage ... It would mean ... that the other cannot be *absolutely* exterior to the same without ceasing to be other [etc.]" (VM, p. 126 – I have italicized 'infinitely' and 'absolutely'. The whole of (c) starting at VM, p. 125 should be quoted here).

ethical as such? Or conversely: should not Levinas's repeated characterization of ethics as an infinite sacrifice be read as indicating that in the course of his analysis this whole laborious distinction between the sacred and the holy has somehow collapsed? What else to conclude from the fact that Levinas's ethical subject "march[es] forward without concern for itself" *without the possibility* of "deserting its post" (CPP 98), but that it has become spell-bound, or as Levinas says it himself: "obsessed" by that Other that has taken him "hostage" (OB 99 ff.)? Isn't the face of that other – *since unlike the Infinite, it does not interrupt the sacrifice for which it calls* – one more avatar of the sacred?

Let us not be too quick to jump to conclusions. For it is not certain whether this question is not fundamentally misguided. For the moment, the least one can say is that in its own way it points to the cost of assuming with Derrida that Levinas is unable to distinguish "between the infinite alterity of God and that of every human" (GD 84). For if he would indeed be unable to support that distinction, this could only mean that the 'relation' to God would risk taking on the sacrificial character of the relation to every other and that both God and the Other would resort under the sacred. It would seem, then, that there would be nothing left of Levinas's ethics unless we find a way to make sense of the category of the 'sacrifice of the sacrifice' in the relation to every other and with it to save the distinction between the sacred and the holy. And Levinas, of course, will never doubt that there is such a way and that we will come to find it from the moment we stop trying, as he would no doubt think Derrida is doing, to have the 'yes' of generosity without also having the generosity of a certain 'God', or more precisely: of a God who is neither certain nor uncertain (OB 147), a God 'beyond Being'. We will come to this in a moment. But in order to prepare for this move which will allow us to see through the parallel between Derrida's and Levinas's 'yes' which we have been pursuing perhaps a bit too eagerly, let us first address an objection that will no doubt be raised by both the readers of Derrida and of Levinas, and especially by those readers who will, in view of the obvious (?) strategic importance of this alliance, resent any attempt to drive a wedge between them, even if that wedge would only consist in an attempt to take seriously some of the warnings given by the author of *Violence and Metaphysics* himself.

Readers of Derrida will remark that in more or less accusing him of falling back, with his use of the formula "tout autre est tout autre", behind the argumentation in *Violence and Metaphysics*[39], we have made the mistake

---

39. One could confront the quote from VM in our previous note with a host of quotes from later works, as we have in a sense been doing since our introduction. Here is one more example indicating a shift at some point in Derrida's work: "when there is a *yes* ... the *other*

of only stressing the latter part of that sentence and of overlooking that it should also be read as "*every* other is wholly other". Consequently, we have truncated our analysis and left out, as readers of Levinas will remark, the whole sphere of what Levinas calls 'justice' and which consists precisely in an *interruption* of the sacrifice and should thus be taken into account before coming up with bizarre suggestions such as seeing in the face of the other a return of the sacred. Let us investigate, then, what it will take for this notion of 'justice' to save Levinas the embarrassment of this return. And let us check, in particular, whether it will suffice to state that "*every* other is wholly other" to do justice to the sort of complication that Levinas has in mind here.

III. The concern for justice

To fully appreciate the stakes and the meaning of this complication, let us first briefly recapitulate. In defining the ethical situation as a call to an "infinite sacrifice", Levinas was simply spelling out the consequences contained in his major premise that there is a radical asymmetry between me and the Other "who is closer to God than I am" (CPP 56, quoted above). Although pointing to a plot (*intrigue*) that, says Levinas, "one is tempted to call religious" (OB 147), this premise itself did "not rest on any positive theology" (*ibid.*), but simply resulted from an attempt to think through the meaning of a genuine ethical responsibility. In giving the other a "right over me" (CPP 125, quoted above) and in leaving me without the possibility, let alone the right to neglect his appeal, Levinas was trying to avoid letting the ethical law depend on my willingness to let it be a law. The ethical law has to obligate me regardless of my being in agreement with it or not. Ethics is not first of all an engagement but a being engaged, which does not originate in my freedom but derives from a source higher than me: responsibility is older than freedom – it results from "the Good choos(ing) me before I can be in a position to choose, that is, welcome its choice" (OB 122). And yet, Levinas will always be quick to distinguish this prior election by the Good which gives voice to the 'yes!' or the 'here I am' of a responsibility antecedent to freedom, from a putting into serfdom that would, of course, be contradictory with our basic intuitions about what constitutes the ethical: "subjectivity sees this nonfreedom redeemed, exceptionally, by the Good ... *if no one is good voluntarily, no one is enslaved to the Good*" (OB 11). It is to this combination of *un*freedom and *absence* of slavery that we have been referring through such formulae as the "abdication of the Good" which

no longer lets himself be produced by the *same*", *Ulysse Gramophone. Deux mots pour Joyce*, *o.c.*, p. 127 (I italicized 'other' and 'same').

"interrupts" the attraction it may exert on us and in thus breaking that spell, distinguishes itself as the "holy" from the "sacred". In letting us substitute a ram for Isaac, our unfreedom is, as it were, being used by the Good to generate a freedom to which we could not have given birth on our own – the freedom of an ethical choice. This is why one would fall short of what happened at Mount Moriah if one only saw in it the institution of a taboo on human sacrifice, instead of the *revelation* of the possibility of *murder*. Clearly, these are not the same, since for Levinas the 'sacrifice of the sacrifice' points beyond Isaac being put under taboo and hence put above the ram (a taboo implies separation, substitution and hierarchization), to the consequences of a God declaring *himself* to be taboo. Henceforth ethics, instead of being "the corrollary of religion", will become "the element where religious transcendence can have a meaning"[40]. This explains why Levinas can seemingly alternate without effort between 'God' and 'the Good' – given that for him both display the same structure of the holy: "The fact that in its goodness the Good declines the desire it arouses while inclining it toward responsibility for the neighbor, *preserves* difference in the non-indifference of the Good, which chooses me before I welcome it" (OB 123). God is only God and the Good is only Good because they 'both' *interrupt* their attraction and generate from it a responsibility that each of us will have to carry alone.

But if the transcendent, or God, or the Good *interrupts itself* and if it is due to "this difference" that it is both good and transcendent, could the same be said of that face of the Other to which the Good deflects our attention? For it is through the appeal of that face that I will be singularized in an ethical sense: there is no escape from this responsibility which is mine and turns me into a "unique" and "non-interchangeable" I that can not call on others to take over that responsibility. And as we have seen, the unicity or the singularity of this 'I' does not derive from or is not guaranteed by some 'hidden interiority' but by its exposure. Ethics does not tolerate any secrets, it burns out whatever hiding place I may seek to escape its appeal, and if Levinas sees in it a plot that one may be "tempted to call religious", it is because religion for him is the end of the private[41]. Hence the necessity of a "permanent sacrifice" (CPP 124) that will prevent the 'unique' I from keeping anything to itself but its responsibility. And thus Levinas can come to see in what Kierkegaard portrays as the extreme isolation of Abraham's 'silence' "the source of speaking itself" and "the essence of communication" (*ibid.*). Abraham's silence would have been demonic and the expression of

---

40. E. LEVINAS, *Nouvelles Lectures Talmudiques*, Paris, Minuit, 1996, p. 30. I will return to this quote a number of times in this chapter (abbreviated as NLT 30).

41. Cf. the title of our preceding chapter (and the quote I give there in note 16).

a sacred *stupor*, had it not been redirected to the 'here I am' and the endless profusion of a 'yes!' in which the 'I' which has been cornered by its responsibility paradoxically finds itself in the absolute movement of a 'permanent sacrifice'. Levinas is thinking of Abraham's plea for the just in Sodom and Gomorrah (KCR 33) when he writes in a quote that we have given before: "I approach the Infinite insofar as I *forget* myself for my neighbor who looks at me ... I approach the infinite by sacrificing myself. *Sacrifice is the norm and the criterion of the approach*" (CPP 72, quoted in § 2). It is this return of the sacrifice which is holding us up here, since it seems to rest on an asymmetry which threatens to undo the very distinction between the holy and the sacred on which we have seen Levinas's ethics rest: for if my ethical relation to the other is to be defined in terms of sacrifice, does this not indicate that the face, unlike the Good or the transcendent, cannot *interrupt itself*? And hence would side with the sacred? How else to understand that strange asymmetry at the heart of Levinas's ethics: whereas the voice of the transcendent needs to interrupt itself "as soon as it is heard" to avoid conflating it with the *numen* of the sacred, the appeal that is addressed to me by the face of the other cannot *not* be heard?

Perhaps we have reached the point at which we can finally appreciate the importance of Levinas's introduction of 'justice'. Let us note immediately that what Levinas calls 'justice' is not an alternative to ethics. For then it would become what it is usually thought to be: an attempt to weigh and bring together the interests of equal parties in a society. Justice, for Levinas, who is opposing here a whole tradition, is not about a defence of already existing rights, but about that "grace" (OB 158) by which I am given a right I was not entitled to. In other words, instead of starting from rights, Levinas is looking for a way to introduce them without, however, coming back upon his conception of the ethical: that is why he thinks of justice as *"limiting"* my infinite ethical duties toward the Other, rather than as defending my rights (like in contract-theories)[42].

If there would only be that *one* Other who appeals to me, there would be no need for justice, for the ethical relation would be restricted to what happens between me and that other. Justice only comes in from the moment that the ethical "intimacy of the face to face" (OB 160) between me and the other is, as it were, disturbed by the intrusion of what Levinas calls 'the third'. But this intrusion is not just the empirical one of another Other factually coming in and claiming in his turn for attention. Regardless of a third person being present or not in the factual sense, there will always already be such a third: "the third party (*le tiers*) looks at me in the eyes of

---

42. E. LEVINAS, *Nine Talmudic Readings* (transl. A. Aronowics), Bloomington/ Indianapolis, Indiana U.P., 1990, p.100.

the Other" (TI 213). The face of the other who appeals to me, is a *human* face: it appears to me as having the recognizable *form* of the human, and therefore already refers me to all the other Others beside this one, i.e., to the Others who are his Others, i.e., to the 'third'. It is the 'presence' of these other Others which explains why eventually I will have to divide my attention between them and the one who is presently calling on me, and why I will have to weigh and compare and, ultimately, calculate: "The Other is from the first the brother of all the other men. The neighbor that obsesses me is already a face, *both comparable and incomparable*, a unique face and in relationship with faces, which are *visible* in the concern for justice" (OB 158). But Levinas insists – and as we are about to point out: must insist – that this "comparison of incomparables" should be viewed as "an *incessant correction* of the asymmetry of ethical proximity" (*ibid.*). Since justice is a correction, it presupposes ethics and, as a result, the way the ethical 'relation' qua *ethical* relation has been defined, does not itself need to be corrected. Bringing in 'justice' may allow Levinas to explain how the ethical sacrifice can be limited, and how, since I am an other for others too, "my lot is important" (OB 161) ("there is also justice for me", OB 159) but it will never be able to shed light on the sacrificial character of ethics that it presupposes and never contests.

Let us just be satisfied to note for the moment that nothing of what is said here should be seen as calling into question what has been said before about ethics, and that therefore we have every right to remain as puzzled, if not more, as we were before. Justice is not 'the truth of' ethics, for it is only ethics that can prevent justice from becoming a defence of already existing rights. Only if I have lost all my rights to the Other can there be room for a "grace" (OB 158) by which I am given a right I was not entitled to. Note, however, that the right this grace accords me does not retroactively undo my infinite obligation toward the other. I can never call on that right to escape my responsibility. Far from the truth of ethics being found in justice, the reverse seems to be the case for Levinas: "*In no way is justice* a degradation of obsession, a degeneration of the for-the-others, a diminution, *a limitation of anarchic responsibility* ... the contemporaneousness of the multiple is tied about the diachrony of the two: justice remains justice only in a society where there is no distinction between those close and those far off, but in which there also *remains* the impossibility of passing by the closest. The equality of all is borne by my inequality, *the surplus of my duties over my rights*. The *forgetting of self* moves justice" (OB 159). This is why, for Levinas, there is a difference between a just State deriving from "a war of all against all" and one deriving from "the irreducible responsibility of the one for all" (*ibid.*). It is the difference between a State that knows of no faces and installs a regime where everyone is treated as 'third', and a State that would provide for the possibility of its laws (which in order to be 'legitimate laws' presuppose symmetry and equality between its addressors and its addressees) being perpetually "tempered" by the appeal of the absolute other that Derrida was talking about, i.e., in Derrida's vocabulary: by the infinite appeal of (ethical) justice.

In refusing to let justice become the truth of ethics, or in calling for an absolute hospitality that would not and could not propose contracts or impose conditions on the "absolutely new arrival"[43], both Levinas and Derrida seek to escape the same nightmare of a national front that would only let in (or let stay in) what can be homogenized. But it would no doubt be premature to conclude from this obvious Levinasian ring to Derrida's 'yes' permitting "the other to be the other", that there is anything deeper to this alliance than the common concern not to let politics absorb ethics. For in watching these allies move in more or less the same direction, it is difficult not to be struck by the fact that one of them, in order to keep up with the other, seems obliged to always make within that common move a move that apparently has been, up to now, of little importance to the other, but that could seriously complicate matters once the war is won and they have time to pay attention to each other. Didn't we hear Derrida *already* voice the suspicion that "Levinas is no longer able to distinguish between the infinite alterity of God and the alterity of every human" – that "his ethics is already religion"?

Levinas, of course, would not agree and apart from pointing out that there is an enormous difference between an ethics which is "already" religion and an ethics defined as "the element where religious transcedence can have a meaning" (NLT 30), he would probably resent the fact that Derrida seems not to have noticed the effort it took to keep pace with him. For the extra move Levinas is making by himself within the move he and Derrida are making, is precisely the move of justice: that which "limits my duties instead of defending my rights". In opposing to the usual defence of pre-given rights an absolute, infinite duty to the absolute other, Levinas is not just joining forces with Derrida. He is also *already* taking measures to prevent this Derridian 'yes' from leading him where he doesn't want to go. For he realizes that *for the very reasons Derrida has been indicating*, it might not suffice to state that "*every* other is *wholly* other". The infinite duties to such a wholly other should one way or another be limited to prevent that other, or for that matter, every other from becoming God, as Derrida indeed

---

43. In these and the following lines I return to the quotes from Derrida which I gave at the beginning of the introduction to this chapter.

seems unable to avoid concluding: "The trembling of the formula 'every other (one) is every (bit) other' can also be reproduced. It can do so to the extent of replacing one of the 'every others' by God: 'Every other (one) is God', or 'God is every (bit) other'. Such a substitution *in no way alters* the 'extent' of the original formulation, whatever grammatical function be assigned to the various words. In one case God is defined as infinitely other, as wholly other, every bit other. In the other case it is declared *that every other one, each of the others, is God inasmuch as he or she is, like God*, wholly other" (GD 87).

Levinas would be horrified. For in suggesting this move and in suggesting that there is nothing in Levinas to prevent that move from being made, Derrida is robbing Levinas of the means to understand why the appeal of the face, *although it cannot interrupt itself, can nonetheless be interrupted without it having to be me who interrupts it*. For only a God who is not simply "the 'first other', 'the other par excellence' or the 'absolutely other'", only a God who is "*other than the other*, other otherwise, other with an alterity *prior* to the alterity of the other, prior to the ethical bond with another", in short only a God "different from every neighbor" (CPP 165-6) can arrange for a justice which can 'correct' ethics without undoing it. As we shall see, it is ultimately by letting his 'yes' rest on the authority of this one word 'God' that Levinas can part ways with Derrida and develop an ethics that leads us 'beyond the tribal', *instead of leading us straight into it* as Levinas would not fail to comment, reading a passage like this in Derrida: "What binds me to singularities, to this one or that one, male or female, rather than that one or this one, remains finally unjustifiable (this is Abraham's hyper-ethical sacrifice), as unjustifiable as the infinite sacrifice I make at each moment. These singularities represent others, a wholly other form of alterity: one other or some other persons, *but also places, animals, languages*" (GD 71). Once places, animals and languages are considered to be wholly other, there will be – Levinas would no doubt remark – nothing left to protect us from the return of the sacred. Indeed, the fate of the whole precarious economy between ethics and justice that Levinas has so laboriously constructed in the margins of his alliance to Derrida, will then come to depend on the moaning of one cat: "How would you ever justify the fact that you sacrifice all the cats in the world to the cat that you feed at home every morning for years, whereas other cats die of hunger at every instant? Not to mention other people?" (*ibid.*). But before letting things run this far out of hand, we should perhaps make one last effort to understand why, unlike the Transcendent, the face for Levinas cannot be said to interrupt itself. And why, as a consequence of this, whereas the voice of the Transcendent is of such discretion that it can go unnoticed, one cannot fail to hear the appeal of the Other. As we shall see, Levinas has a very simple reply to this.

IV. THE STRUCTURE OF
THE INTERRUPTION OF THE SACRED

At first sight, Levinas's reply does indeed look exceedingly simple: the reason that the face does not interrupt *itself*, is that the Other – every Other – is not God, but only someone who comes "in his trace" (CPP 107). What looks like a simple reply and may even strike some as a bit simplistic given its readiness to appeal to 'God' to get out of the problem, is in fact an extremely intricate and well-wrought answer that is as uncompromising as it can be. It immediately calls into question the alternative which until now silently governed our analysis: we have been assuming all along that since the appeal, for obvious reasons, could not be interrupted by the one under appeal, it would have to be the face of the Other which somehow had to interrupt itself in order to keep it within the 'Holy' which was precisely characterized by such a self-interruption. Clearly, we have no reason to come back on the first part of this argument. For what could it mean that I would be the one to 'interrupt' the appeal of the Other? The very notion of appeal implies that I am caught up in it, prior to my decision. And if, once having received it, I would be in a position to tell at exactly what point I have either fully exhausted its meaning or done whatever I find can be legitimately asked from me, the consequence would simply be that the origin of my responsibility will be brought back once more to my freedom. Which would, as both Derrida and Levinas will tell us, amount to a misrecognition of the very meaning of responsibility: a genuine re-sponsibility is one that does not originate in my freedom but derives from a source permanently other than me. To preserve its ethical character or to fulfill its function of a 'justice' (in Derrida's sense) disrupting the closed economy of our *calculus*, the appeal not only must be something that reaches me from outside, it also must preserve this exteriority. Up to this point, Levinas and Derrida are still in agreement, and it could have been Derrida who wrote that "the infinitely exterior becomes an 'inward' voice, but a voice bearing witness to the fission of the inward secrecy" (OB 147) – for such a voice "that makes signs to another, signs of this very giving of signs" (*ibid.*), such "saying without the said" (*ibid.*) only marks an address – it says 'yes!'. But unlike for Derrida, this 'yes!' for Levinas is not there to acknowledge that "what binds me to singularities ... remains finally unjustifiable" (GD 71, quoted in full at the end of the last section). Saying 'yes!' or 'here I am' for Levinas goes beyond the recognition of an incapacity to *justify*: it is to admit my *injustice*, to realize that 'my place under the sun' is a *usurpation*[44] – which is but a consequence of the appeal for Levinas coming not just from a source permanently beyond my reach, but from a source *above me*. And this is why he will think we were fundamentally mistaken in our further assumption that in order to keep the face from a relapse into the sacred, it would have to *interrupt* itself. For if it would, its appeal could never *combat* the sacred which, as we shall see, is for Levinas precisely what binds us without us being able to justify it, or better: what keeps binding us even if we find ourselves unable to justify it, as is the case for example with the "places, animals, languages" that Derrida was referring to.

There is a difference then – a crucial difference – between what is 'unjust' and what is 'unjustifiable': my 'unjustice' goes beyond what I cannot justify in that it qualifies these attachments and thereby cuts through the ties that bind me to them: in the shame with which, according to Levinas, I react to the appeal of the other, I not only admit that I am unable to justify my existence, but also that it can no longer be mine in the sense it was before. Henceforth, it belongs to the other, I am at his 'service'. Such is the difference that Levinas wishes to make between a "true value" and that which merely dresses up as value. It is, again, the difference between the Good or the Holy, and the sacred: between "a value arousing an impulse" (the for-the-other of the ethical sacrifice) and "an impulse arousing a value" (OB 127) that I have to admit is stronger than myself and that I cannot justify. For the sacred, for Levinas, is typically what overpowers us and yet through its charm leads us to believe that it is us instead of the voice of the demonic that speaks. It produces in us an ec-stasis which robs us of our *stasis* (our 'position'), all the while giving us the semblance of a freedom that is in reality serfdom: the trace of nature in us that pretends to be human. But the threshhold of humanity is for Levinas crossed only when the unjustifiable in us is equated with the unjust and when we become *dis*-interested in that blind *conatus* that keeps us tied to being (*inter-esse*). And this rupture cannot come from suicide which submits to the unjustifiable by taking revenge on it. For the unjustifiable to appear as the unjust, one will need a negativity that does not just turn against it, but that will also change its signs and thus allow us to *transcend* it. And this transcendence is, of course, the hallmark of the holy. It is the metaphysical in man.

Man cannot rise above 'the physical' by his own force. First the ties to what binds him to himself will need to be severed. Or rather: they will have to be loosened just enough for man to be able to make the effort to lift himself out of a nature that binds him and goes deeper than his own will.

44. See note 36.

The Holy is what intervenes to loosen these ties on which I hitherto *depended* to be my 'self' and what will thus grant me an *in-dependence* in which I can become a true 'self'. Such a true 'self' presupposes the eradication of all these 'others in us' that made *us* 'participate' in them and thus only gave us the semblance of an independence. And paradoxically, the only way for the Holy to immobilize the (*sacred*) force or these 'others in me', is to penetrate me in its turn and to introduce an "other in me" (which Levinas will call 'soul' (OB 191 n3)) that fully leaves me 'me': "the *author* of what had been breathed in *unbeknownst to me*" (OB 148). By "inscribing" an order in me "which *slips into me* 'like a thief'" and yet allowing me to become the author of what I have thus "received, one knows not from where" (*ibid.*), the Holy distinguishes itself from the sacred by the generosity with which it "reconciles" (*ibid.*) heteronomy and autonomy, and lets the one "revert" (*ibid.*) into the other. It only affects us and takes us by surprise because we have already been affected and are already estranged from ourselves by the heteronomy of the sacred. Even if our lives would be as white as snow, uncontaminated by a single decision, we would already have given in to a call that is *stronger* than us (*conatus essendi*) but that we cannot but consider ours: *we* live our lives. And as Derrida remarks, our lives are never as white as that, they consist of the threads of a texture torn between such calls: "Let us not look for examples, there would be too many of them, at every step we took. By preferring my work, simply by giving it my time and attention, by preferring my activity as a citizen or as a professorial and professional philosopher, writing and speaking here in a public language, French in my case, I am perhaps fulfilling my duty. But I am sacrificing and betraying at every moment all my *other* obligations ..." (GD 69). But as long as we fail to let the realization of what we can thus not *justify* about our lives bestow on us the feeling of our *injustice*, Levinas would consider these lives to be under the spell of the sacred: torn between calls that oblige us, the shape these lives will take will be but the result of a parallelogram of forces allowing those calls which happen to be the strongest to get the upper hand. Man's life would be but dice in the hands of the gods and once he would come to realize this absurdity, he could only resign to play according to their whims or attempt to freeze like a statue, hoping they wouldn't spot him.

    Instead of leaving us helpless at the realization of what we cannot justify in us, the Holy will have to alienate us of that prior alienation and thereby set us free. And to introduce this difference which qualifies the unjustifiable as the unjust, it does not rely on a call stronger than all others. To the contrary, it is only by introducing a call *weaker* than all others, that it can make an attempt to change *the meaning of all hitherto obligation and sacrifice*. It is by not having realized the full extent of this alteration of the economy of the sacred, that we could have been surprised that the appeal of the face did not interrupt itself and still demanded a sacrifice from us. But this demand, as we now realize, is not an imposition: instead of enforcing a sacrifice by ushering a call which we cannot resist and yet are charmed into making our own, the appeal of the Other is only a faint and a weak claim uttered in the margins of all these other claims that call on me. But the one reason why I cannot fail to hear it, is that in calling on my strength it is doing something that none of the other claims can do: it introduces the difference between what I cannot justify *to myself* and yet still consider mine, and what I cannot justify *to that weaker Other than me* whose fate is not my own.

By being the voice of a weaker force, the appeal of the Other can surprise me "ab-solutely", in a sense that no Absolute could: for if it were uttered directly, I would, like Abraham in the "first moment" of the drama, have to consider the message of that voice an affair in which I participate, willingly or not. Only an Other whose affairs are in no way mine, to whom I am *not tied* by any covenant whatsoever, in thus being more *ab-solute* than the Absolute, can make the meaning of sacrifice change for me: henceforth it will not result from an imperative imposed on me, but it will function as a norm that can only be saved from becoming meaningless through my attempts to approach it. If for Levinas "revelation is only carried through by those who receive it" (OB 199), it is because the God of this revelation is a God only "accessible in justice" (TI 78).

For the sacrifice to become a "norm" and a "criterion of the approach" to the Absolute, instead of an urge in which we are overpowered by enthusiasm, it is thus essential that the Other not be God and that the difference between ethics and religion be preserved. If we have seen Levinas correct Derrida in stressing that ethics is the only "element where religious transcendence can have a meaning" (NLT 30), it is because he is afraid that outside of a relation to an Other who is not God and yet "closer" to Him than I am, transcendence would take on the form of the sacred which can never have *meaning* for the one who approaches it because it would "annihilate him on contact" or "transport him outside of himself" (TI 77). A transcendence that does not "burn the eyes" has to veil itself – to lift man onto this Height, God will have to engage him, as it were, in an oblique and indirect approach: "Ethics is the spiritual optics. ... There can be no 'knowledge' of God separated from the relationship with man" (TI 78).

Thus what we could at first consider Levinas's relatively simple, if not simplistic, reply to our puzzlement over the 'non-interrupted' appeal of the Other, begins to receive its full contours. As should now be clear, to think that this appeal should interrupt itself to preserve the symmetry with the Holy interrupting itself, would simply mean surrendering the Holy to the sacred by eclipsing the lenses that precisely allow ethics to be a *"spiritual optics"*. For without the permanent *norm* of a sacrifice inviting me to "forget myself" in my approach to the Other, I would simply start sacrificing again to the values to which I am attached by forces stronger than my own. Without the incessant appeal of an Other, permanently beyond my reach, the fire of the Holy could not purify me of the sacred in me and extinguish its sacrificial pyres.

And yet, it is as if Levinas knows of all of man's weaknesses and knows that one can expect the human drive for idolatry to be strong enough to even worship a force *weaker* than his own. That is why it must remain possible that even the appeal of the face is interrupted. But for this interruption to be such that in its wake the sacred cannot triumph over the Holy, it must be experienced as a *grace*. At this point, we meet Levinas's views on justice again. But it would seem that we are only now able to appreciate why, for him, there can be no justice without God and why he refers to 'God' as the *first word*[45] without which the "unconditioned 'yes' of submission" to the absolute appeal of the other would be that of "an infantile spontaneity" (OB 122). We are, then, but one last step from considering the chances of that word to become 'anti-racism's first word'. Before we make up our minds, let us profit from what we have found to cast one last look into its dossier.

V. From a God 'beyond Being' to a Society 'beyond the Tribal'

Although we were, then, apparently mistaken in our assumption that the face should interrupt *itself* lest it became one more avatar of the sacred, Levinas might nonetheless have sympathized with part of our concern. For he has reasons of his own to make room for the appeal of the face to be interrupted – albeit not by itself, nor, of course, by me. These reasons have to do with what looks like a serious problem at the heart of his 'theory of justice', threatening it with a flat contradiction. As one will remember, Levinas seems to want to combine the impossible: he introduces justice as a limitation of my infinite duties to the other, and yet is forced to claim with equal insistence that justice is *"in no way* ... a limitation of anarchic responsibility"* (OB 159, quoted before). How can justice be a "correction" of ethics if it leaves ethics as it is and does not affect the structure of the ethical

---

45. See the quote with which we ended the introduction to this chapter.

relation? How can it be both a limitation and not a limitation?

Levinas's solution to this 'problem' is ingenious: he will argue that this limitation is a limitation of an unlimited which by its very structure gives rise to it, all the while keeping its authority over it. The name for this 'unlimited' is, as one could expect, 'God' or 'the Infinite' or 'the transcendent': "infinity or the transcendent does not let itself be assembled. Removing itself from every memorable present, a past that was never present, it leaves a trace of its *impossible incarnation*" (OB 161).

It is because this incarnation is impossible that the other is neither God nor an "icon of God" (CPP 107). And it is because it has left a trace of its impossibility, that the Other can be "in the image of God" or "find (him)self in His trace" (*ibid.*), and thus is "closer to God" than I am. Without, however, playing "the role of a mediator" (TI 79) between me and God, a "Jacob's ladder" to be thrown away after it is climbed: "The Other is not the incarnation of God, but precisely by his face, *in which he is disincarnate*, is the manifestation of the height in which God reveals himself" (TI 79/51, transl. corr.). And, as we know, there is no other revelation in Levinas's philosophy: "The Other is the very locus of metaphysical truth, and is *indispensable* for my relation with God" (TI 78). But this holds for every Other. There is not just the appeal of *this* Other who has "an unimpeachable right over me" (CPP 125), but also the appeal and the right of the other of that other – of all other others, to whom Levinas will refer as 'the third'. All these others are 'in the trace' of God. As an ethical Other, each of these Others partakes of the interdiction on representation and is this "invisible" face to which I do violence if I try to reduce it to a form that is visible to me. But since *each* of these Others partakes in that interdiction, none of them should be allowed to monopolize, to the exclusion of all others, that "trace" in which he finds himself. Which is why that interdiction in its turn has to be interdicted and *why there must be something about the Other that prevents him from being simply unrepresentable*. As we shall see, this is why there is not only the ethical obligation to the *incomparable* Other, but also the interruption of that obligation through a justice which requires *comparison* and "contemporaneousness of representation" (OB 159). But, as we shall also see, the problem of justice would not take the shape that it does in Levinas if every other would not be the other *of the other* and thus a third who by his *equal* right to my attention can intrude in the ethical relation between that Other and me; and this equality and this genetive (other *of the others*) would lose their meaning, were it not for a God who is still "other otherwise" (CPP 165-6). To refer to this other alterity of God that *precedes* the alterity of each of these Others and makes it possible, Levinas speaks of His "illeity" or of "the Third".

There are, then, only thirds because there is *a* Third whose "trace" cannot be but plural, for as we just saw only such plurality can prevent his infinity from becoming assembled: "To go toward Him is not to follow this trace which is not a sign; it is to go toward the other*s* [plural!, R.V.] who stand in the trace of illeity" (CPP 107).

One would betray the illeity of this God beyond Being if one would use this one ethical relation to this one ethical Other, in which I am presently engaged, as an excuse not to worry about the fate of all these other others who are equally in His trace. One should not seek to replace the political moment of society by the ethical. But neither should one do the reverse: to use one's concern over the fate of the masses as an excuse to refuse to engage in an ethical relation with this one other who needs my help right here and now, is no less a betrayal of that illeity. But it would be wrong to conclude from this that since one is doomed to betray either way (evidently, one cannot combine exclusive attention to one other with attention to all the others), it is best to do nothing at all – for that cynicism, too, would be a betrayal, and perhaps the worst of all. Which is why Levinas can find, in what seems to be an aporia, the way out toward a 'solution': the problem is not to avoid the betrayal – such would be the seduction of *superbia* – but to avoid forgetting that there is always a betrayal. For as we shall see, there is something about the *structure* of this betrayal that makes it prone to a certain *forgetting*.

To understand this, let us briefly reconsider what is at stake in this "comparison of incomparables" (OB 158) that Levinas calls 'justice'. The terms are clear: every other is incomparable for he is precisely 'other', *and so am I*, for my responsibility toward each of them is mine and mine alone. And there is comparison of these incomparables, since to meet one other is to meet them all, regardless of whether they are empirically present or not. The third that "looks at me in the eyes of the Other" (TI 213) will force me to *weigh* the urgency of his needs and compare them to the needs of this Other I am presently engaged with, and thus to look at both of them as impartially as I can. And this look will take time, the time to make up *my* mind, a time which is quite literally *taken*, for it is a time spent with myself and not with the other(s). Even if the activities in which I engage during this time and which have a logic and an *objectivity* of their own, will in the end serve the well-being of these others, the time they take up and which I will need to get familiar with this logic and with all the procedures that surround it, will be a time in which I have to sustain myself. A time in which I have to sleep, for example, in order to have a 'clear mind' and not to let my 'morning temper' affect my *capacity* for justice and fairness to all these others. Be they two or more, I will need *at least the time to turn my*

head and look from the one to the other, and that time is enough, says
Levinas, to give birth to *consciousness*: "the foundation of consciousness is
justice" (OB 160), or again: "Consciousness is born as the *presence* of a third
party" (*ibid.*). But like any infant, consciousness will tend to forget about the
circumstances of its birth. It may come to forget that it was (ethical)
conscience, in its scrupulous observation of its infinite duties toward every
other, which necessitated "an event like meditation – synchronization,
comparison, thematization" (*ibid.*) and with it the entry of ethical proximity
into "the space of contiguity" where the meditating I *not only can but must*
be "together-in-a-place" (OB 157/200; transl. corrected). To carry through "the
work of justice" (OB 160) the meditating I of consciousness cannot but
"synchronize" (*ibid.*) and 'syn-topize' them in a common space and time
(e.g. the 'actual value' of the interests of future generations will have to be
calculated), and in so doing, it will have to share this space and time *with*
them, – which does not mean here that it will have to *give* it to them, but
that it will have to *take* it from each of them.

In this movement which Levinas himself calls a "*necessary interruption* of
the Infinite" (OB 160), ethical proximity will "take on a *new* meaning" (OB
157): there will be an *interruption* of my "obsession" (OB 86 ff.) by that Other
whose appeal haunts me and whom I breathlessly try to approach in the
movement of an infinite sacrifice. For a moment at least I will breathe on
my own, take in air, take place, and during that moment in which there is
a localization and a temporalization of my consciousness, it may look as if
this time and this 'place under the sun' which are the *birthmarks* of *my*
consciousness have the status of natural rights, instead of resulting from a
"usurpation". The *cogito* of meditation that needs light in order to see the
cogitata that it must compare, may become fascinated by light itself, and in
enjoying seeing for its own sake, in thus forgetting what one could call with
Derrida "the nocturnal source of all light" (VM 86), start to find its "centre of
gravitation" (OB 159) in itself. Evil for Levinas is this obstinacy with which
one resists one's true gravitation, or one could perhaps even risk saying:
one's 'natural' place: "Justice is impossible without the one that renders it
finding himself in proximity. His function is not limited to the 'function of
judgement', the subsuming of particular cases under a general rule. *The
judge is not outside the conflict, but the law is in the midst of proximity*" (*ibid.*).
It is the Evil of the *kosmotheoros* who wants to escape the *earth*'s gravitation
and become a planet on his own, which threatens the judge. Not only him,
but everyone who judges, and thus every consciousness. Born in light,
everything human will have to face this temptation which is the temptation
to stay 'outside of it' and to let in only what one can assimilate or master.
Consciousness, then, in its basic drive for *a-patheia*, in its resistance against

any affection that will affect it in an unforeseen way, would be for Levinas the first model of a *national front*, that is of a *totality* that by nestling itself in the contiguous *exteriority* of space, has already betrayed *Exteriority*. And this is a risk that all that derives from this model, all syn-chrony and syn-topy cannot but be exposed to: "being, totality, the State, politics, techniques, work are at every moment on the point of having their centre of gravitation in themselves, and weighing on their own account" (*ibid.*). But let us not forget that this risk is unavoidable – it is due to "the *necessary* interruption of the Infinite being fixed in structures, community and totality" (OB 160).

That which cannot "be assembled" and cannot be "incarnated" is nonetheless assembled and incorporated. Even necessarily so. Or perhaps one should say that it both 'is' and 'is not', for it resists what it necessitates and in thus refusing to take a place in Being (where one either 'is' or 'is not'), it grants Being its place all the while putting it under the authority of a 'beyond Being' that, as we have seen, refuses to "reign" (cf. section I of this chapter), thus putting Being before a risk *that is its very birthright*: "Illeity is the origin of the alterity of being in which the *in itself* of objectivity [i.e., comparing, weighing, ... and thus "essence as synchrony" (OB 157), R.V.] *participates, while also betraying it*" (CPP 106). Being – which is for Levinas: presence, light, consciousness, in short: phenomenality – can only come into being by betraying its origin. But this origin, by never having 'been' present, in only leaving a trace of its always already "having passed", and by dispersing the trace of this trace into a plurality of Others, pushes Being into this betrayal. Infinity makes its own interruption *necessary*. And it thus makes it *possible* that Being takes itself as its own origin, and forgets about "the origin of the origin" (OB 160), forgets that for the 'gift of Being' to 'take' 'place', the 'origin of the origin' had to be an origin that had been breaking up already before setting up camp, and that was first concerned *not to be there, so that it could make room for Being to be there*. For there to be what philosophy calls an origin – appearance (*ibid.*), presence, foundation – something had to make room first, had to "contract" (TI 104) itself. And this something is for Levinas a someone and this 'contraction' is the true sense of a *creatio ex nihilo* whereby room is made for a being – for Being – to gain its independence by forgetting its dependence. It is, says Levinas, "a great glory to the creator to have set up a being which (...) has an independent view and word" (TI 58-9). This is not creation in an onto-theological sense: this is about *Being* as such having its origin in something that refuses to be an origin, and thus refuses to *impose* itself. One will have understood why Levinas can speak here alternately of the Good, the Holy, or even of God – provided that one is prepared to hear this word in a new way – a way 'beyond Being'. Without such a God, there is no justice except a justice that gravitates in itself and that will thus end in the violent perversion of a system that mistakes means (its existence) for ends, which is, as is well known, the first law of any organization. Bringing in 'God' allows Levinas to dis-organize society without preaching anarchism: "'Thanks to God' I am another for the others. ... *The passing of God*, of whom I can speak *only* by reference to this aid or *this grace*, is precisely the reverting of the incomparable subject into a member of society" (OB 158).

There are two moments to this *grace* that Levinas is referring to here, although they both belong to one and the same 'passing of God'. For what 'this passing' really means is that both I and the Other are turned away from a 'union' with the Transcendent. The Transcendent – God, for Levinas – has not only rendered me the grace of deflecting my desire for the infinite to the non-desirable stranger instead of letting the glory of its infinity "burn (my) eyes" (TI 77). God renders me, as it were, a second grace by increasing the burden of this responsibility and turning it into a responsibility to all the others that come in his trace. However paradoxical this may sound, it is precisely the infinity of this responsibility which makes it bearable for me, since, as we have seen, it will issue in the political realm of 'the third' (the other of the other) which, while presupposing the structure of the ethical appeal, at the same time gives us not the right to but the *grace* of an interruption that neither I nor the Other could have brought about: "There is weighing, thought, objectification, and thus a decree [*arrêt* – also and better: a stop, an interruption] in which my relationship with illeity is *betrayed*, but in which it is conveyed before us. There is *betrayal* of my anarchic relationship with illeity, but also a *new* relationship with it: it is only thanks to God that, as a subject incomparable with the other, I am approached as an other by the others, that is, 'for myself' " (OB 158)[46].

That this 'betrayal' can be at the same time a *new relationship* with what is thus betrayed, is what motivates Levinas to not just link this illeity to the Good, but to God. Without this God who is, as one will remember, "accessible only in justice" (TI 78), it would seem difficult if not impossible to think that a betrayal could be more than a betrayal and even be a sort of

---

46. As this passage makes clear, thought, objectification and with it, the whole of the ontological realm, rests on a modification of a prior ethical dimension. Hence for Levinas, ethics precedes ontology and is to be considered as first philosophy. Consequently it seems that the 'second' grace we were referring to, is to be considered as truly a second 'moment' (hence: "a *new* relationship with illeity"). This is the reason why I will refer below to *two* betrayals of the Infinite. Not to make this distinction would force one to rest with the weaker claim of the equiprimordiality of the ethical and the ontological.

loyalty. Just as it would be difficult if not impossible to understand that "my lot is important" (OB 161) without that being at the same time the expression of my self-importance. In the absence of such a God, either 'my lot' would be what has to be defended against the claims of all the others, or – if one insists upon putting duties above rights, with every other becoming wholly other and there being no difference between that alterity and the alterity that Levinas distinguishes as 'God' – my lot would be the unbearable one of having to live with the thought that whatever I do, I am, as Derrida writes, "sacrificing and betraying at every moment all my other obligations: my obligations to the other others whom I know or don't know, the billions of my fellows (without mentioning the animals that are even more other others than my fellows), my fellows who are dying of starvation or sickness. I betray my fidelity or my obligations to other citizens, to those who don't speak my language and to whom I neither speak nor respond, to each of those who listen or read, and to whom I neither respond nor address myself in the proper manner, that is, in a singular manner (this for the so-called public space to which I sacrifice my so-called private space), thus also to those I love in private, my own, my family, my son, each of whom is the only son I sacrifice to the other, *every one being sacrificed to every one else* in this land of Moriah that is our habitat every second of every day" (GD 69).

But just as Abraham left Moriah and returned, never to be directly addressed by God again, as the Talmudic tradition stresses[47], so Levinas would remark to Derrida as he did to Kierkegaard that there is a land beyond Moriah. Meaning not only that there is justice beyond the sacrificial, but also that this justice harbours a lot for me that is different from the one that Derrida pictures here. For justice is not just ethics writ large and brought to the point where it can only mourn its every sacrifice as being a betrayal of all its other obligations. Justice forbids the beautiful soul the haven of its interiority and exacts from it the humility of accepting a life in institutions "where subjectivity is a citizen with all the duties and rights measured and measurable which the equilibrated ego involves, or equilibrating itself by the concourse of duties and the concurrence of rights" (OB 160). Instead of wallowing in the infinity of my betrayal, justice demands that I enter into a "new relationship" with it. Which is to say that I have to accept becoming "an other like the others" (OB 161) and that "there is also justice *for me*" (OB 159). Not to accept that "my lot is important" is just as mistaken as seeing in that importance a natural right and thus forgetting "that it is still out of my responsibility that my salvation has meaning" (OB 161). Both rest on a denial of the "passing of God" and on an incapacity to

47. A. NEHER, *L'exil de la parole. Du silence biblique au silence d'Auschwitz*, Paris, Seuil, 1970, pp. 192 ff.

accept "this aid or this grace" (OB 158) which reverts "the incomparable subject into a member of society" (*ibid.*). It is the same egoism which triumphs in the one who claims his rights to find their origin in himself, and in the one who refuses to be *given* a right and a place for himself and who prefers to stay in the epicentre of an infinite sacrifice that is at the same time an infinite betrayal where in Derrida's words "every one (is) sacrificed to every one else" (GD 69).

VI. THE TERMS OF AN INHERITANCE

Such, then, would seem to be the reason why Levinas would not simply rejoice in hearing Derrida say 'yes!', but would also urge him to hear in that 'yes!' the echo of that "first word" which keeps the economy of the 'saying' and the 'said' in balance and invites humanity to look for its true unity in that tension where "the said never equals the saying", and yet in fixing and betraying it enters into a new relationship with it. But "by only saying the saying itself" this God has only the weak force of a word "always subject to repudiation and in permanent danger of turning into a protector of *all* the egoisms" (OB 161). God is the risk that the 'beyond being' takes in giving way to 'being' – the risk of a creation that does not impose itself on its 'creatures', the "blinking light" of a "revelation" (OB 154) satisfied to be no more than "the question mark" (*ibid.*) in this 'said' in which the 'saying' becomes "fixed" as it "is written, becomes a book, law and science" (OB 159). That this God becomes "accessible only in justice" (TI 78) should not be read – as it often is – as a degradation of God to an ethical God. For in the light of the foregoing we should perhaps better read this as saying that this word 'God' is only heard – and with an entirely new ring – when we allow this question mark to tinge the rhythm of our every 'said'. That is: *when we come to experience justice – the importance of our lot – as grace.* To be sure, 'this grace' is *beyond good and evil*, it is not an ethical term – it merely signals "the goodness of the good", but it could not signal this in any other element than ethics which is, as one will remember, for Levinas "the [only] element in which *religious* transcendence can be experienced" (NLT 30). And only a humanity which has learned "to say grace for this grace"[48] can put itself above and beyond 'the tribal' bonds of a fraternity that is only the result of shared characteristics, and a common soil. But the unity of this humanity itself does not rest in a common genus underlying the differences between men. It is a unity that is "posterior to" a different kind of fraternity: the fraternity of strangers, of those who have nothing in common, i.e.,

48. On this expression, cf. Levinas's remarks in *Autrement que Savoir. Emmanuel Levinas (avec les études de Guy Petitdemange et Jacques Rolland)*, Paris, Osiris, 1988, p. 28.

ethical fraternity. The sacred spell of particularism can only be broken by a universalism that itself derives from or is fed by an ethical singularity that has nothing to do with a responsibility (or a 'duty') that could be the responsibility of all: "The moment when fraternity reaches its fullest sense, is when, in the brother himself, the stranger is recognized. The beyond the tribal"[49].

Like Derrida, Levinas would probably be the first to admit that, for the moment, this 'beyond' is "politically impracticable". But he would no doubt point out that, at this moment when Europe is, once more, set aflame by a war over *Blut und Boden*[50], it is all the more urgent to defend the ideas that lie at the source of this 'beyond'. Only God, he might want to add, could save us now. Not just a god, for *a* god never comes alone and in his wake the flames of the sacred will be ignited again by the followers of the many gods who compete with him. Not just a god, then, but the God of monotheism, for only monotheism can be "a school of xenofilia and anti-racism" (DF 178), because only monotheism can "oblige the other to enter in the discourse *(discours)* that will unite him with me" *(ibid.)*: "Monotheism, the word of the One God, is precisely the word that one cannot not hear, that one cannot not reply to. It is the word that forces one to enter discourse. It is because the monotheists have made the world listen to the word of the One God that Greek universalism can operate in humanity and slowly bring it to unison" *(ibid.)*. Parmenides had to be killed in order for his programme to grow to its full sense and maturity. Henology had to be attacked because it was planted in a soil – ontology – where it could only grow poisonous fruit. But Levinas's ethics that contested Being its first place, knows that it cannot simply take over that place. Humanity cannot be brought to unison by ethics alone. There would be no unity if ethics would be left to itself, without being interrupted in that sacrificial urge that, if pursued to its end, would let humanity explode. And there would be no *true* unity – i.e. a unity that allows for plurality – if justice would be more than such an interruption and if it would reign over ethics. Only a justice tempered by ethics can bring unity without annulling diversity: only thus will henology turn into

---

49. E.g. E. LEVINAS, 'La vocation de l'autre' in *Racismes. L'autre et son visage. Grands entretiens réalisés par Emmanuel Hirsch*, Paris, Les Editions du Cerf, 1988, p. 96.

50. For an extremely violent attack on 'rootedness' see Levinas's 'Heidegger, Gagarin and Us', in DF, pp. 231-4, e.g. 232: "One's implementation in a landscape, one's attachment to *Place*, ... is the very splitting of humanity into natives and strangers". As Derrida had already remarked in *Violence and Metaphysics* (p. 145) Levinas obstinately insists on treating the 'Place' as "an empirical Here" or "a given proximity", instead of seeing in it "a promised one", "an Illic". This prevents him from ever considering the possibility that natives could themselves be seen as strangers.

ontological pluralism. Only thus will reason be defined by peace[51]. Which is why there can only be peace if we stop betraying the 'double betrayal' that, as we have seen, the passing of God imposes on us: the first 'betrayal' is what preserves us from a union with the Transcendent, the second from a union with this particular Other who finds himself in His trace[52]. The particularism that stands in the way of peace is a betrayal of each of these two betrayals that we need to preserve the glory of the Infinite. Particularism in ethics takes on the face of egoism: it is what prematurely closes our endless opening toward the other, it is the seduction of Evil which makes the I interrupt the appeal that has called on him more than on any other (CPP 137). And particularism in politics rests on the attempt to invert, if not deny, the hierarchy between the face and the form, between ethics and justice: it is the attempt to separate humanity into those who have the right 'characteristics' and those who haven't, and to reduce the face of the latter to what Levinas would call their 'form'.

As we have seen, it is first and foremost a concern over this second type of particularism which had made Derrida seek an alliance with Levinas: his insistence on an absolute hospitality which does not propose contracts or impose conditions on the absolute new arrival, is but another way of affirming that there is and will always be the gap between what Levinas calls the face and the form. But when Derrida adds that "I ought not; and in any case, by definition, I cannot impose" any such conditions – any such 'form' – on the absolute arrival (DA 32, quoted before), he seems also to align himself with the reasoning underlying Levinas's treatment of the first type of particularism. For, of course, Derrida knows that although we cannot impose conditions on an absolute arrival without losing its very absoluteness (by definition, such conditions would *relate* the *ab-solute* event to us, and hence cancel what makes it an *event*), we do so all the time. The 'I ought not', then, is for Derrida, as it is for Levinas, more important than the 'I cannot'. Which is why Derrida, like Levinas, seems to be in need of a word "that one cannot not hear". A word that Levinas calls 'God' and of which we just heard him say that "it is the word that forces one to enter discourse". It is because of the force of this word that when Levinas speaks of what Derrida would call "a yes before all yes or no", he stresses that it is not the 'yes' of "an infantile spontaneity" (OB 122) and that he distinguishes it from the 'yes' with which I could or could not reply to the appeal of the other. This 'yes' – the word of God which I hear in the face of the Other, and which I would not hear without the word 'God' – is thus not simply my

51. *La vocation de l'autre, l.c.,* p. 94.
52. These two 'betrayals' correspond to the two moments of 'grace' discussed in the previous section.

'yes'. It is anterior to the opposition of 'yes' and 'no' because it is, as we have seen, anterior to my decision. It grounds the 'I cannot' in the 'I ought not', in that it points to what *forces* me to decide and to what is thus presupposed by my every decision, be it that of a 'yes' or a 'no'. It is not what gives voice to my acceptance of the appeal of the other, for such an acceptance would have as its logical counterpart the possibility of my rejecting it. The 'yes' which forms the linchpin that holds together the whole of Levinas's ethics and thus ultimately grounds his protest against both ethical and political particularism, does not have such a logical counterpart. For it points to the anteriority of the good to evil and to "a pact with the good" which is itself anterior to "the alternative of good and evil"[53]. And as should by now be clear, 'God' is the name in Levinas that guarantees that there is such a pact *and* that the alternative which is opened by it, is both strict and exhaustive. To erase that name and to ignore that pact is, to be sure, always possible, but the enactment of that possibility is but a further confirmation of that pact: it would be a 'no' the meaning of which has always already been determined in advance by the very structure of that pact – it would be Evil.

In view of this, one can understand better perhaps why Derrida should show himself so embarrassed by what he himself calls his "inheritance from Levinas" (DA 37). For if his thoughts on the absolute event really want to go beyond the definitional 'I cannot', if he really wants to link them to a non-neutral absolute hospitality, he seems to be in need of the 'I ought not' that Levinas could provide him with by letting the 'yes anterior to the yes / no' coincide with the 'Good anterior to good / evil'. But this would bring in God and Derrida seems hesitant to do so. The result of this 'indecision' are a series of remarks in his more recent texts where Derrida seems to express a hesitation vis-à-vis Levinas the status of which remains entirely unclear. Let me just give one example of this embarrassment before suggesting a way out of it, if not for Derrida then at least for those of his readers who, like myself, have been more than a little surprised to hear the author of *Violence and Metaphysics* declare that "before a thought like that of Levinas, I never have an objection. … I find it difficult to see [in whatever] divergence [there may be between me and Levinas] anything else than differences of 'signature', i.e., of writing [écriture], of idiom, of ways of handling things, of history, of inscriptions linked to the bio-graphical, etc. *They are not philosophical*

53. E. LEVINAS, *Nine Talmudic Readings, o.c.*, p. 43 (I have restored the French original which speaks of 'un pacte avec *le* bien': *Quatre Lectures Talmudiques*, Paris, Minuit, 1968, p. 95).

differences"[54].

The example I am thinking of is from *Politics of Friendship*, where Derrida suddenly writes after having expressed all sorts of reservations and hesitations before those who are in search of a "fraternity beyond fraternity" and typically end up being more exclusive than they had promised to be precisely because they approach the stranger as a brother (instead of, as Levinas, would say, seeing a brother in the stranger): "I add that the language of fraternity appears to me *just as* problematic when … Levinas uses it to extend humanity to the Christian"[55]. Equally problematic! But why so? For Levinas's move 'beyond the tribal', as I just reminded the reader, seems precisely to break with what Derrida calls the "andro-phratrocentric" approach to the stranger which still imposes on him or her the name of the brother (rather than the sister, etc.) and thus seems to behave entirely in accordance with Derrida's 'yes!' or 'come hither!' which, as we saw in the introduction to this paper, precisely refrains from "naming" and imposing conditions of brotherhood. To be sure, Levinas still uses the word 'fraternity', but what could be wrong with it, since he explicitly states that it is a "fraternity beyond all biology" (OB 87), "that precedes the commonness of a genus" (OB 159), and for which he coins the phrase "seeing in the [biological, etc.] brother a stranger" – a phrase which could be Derrida's own and which, it would seem, he could not dispense with, since he tells us that notwithstanding his "reticence" (PF 237) before the word 'brother', he has no intention to "denounce fraternity or fraternization" (*ibid.*)?

What is at stake in this hesitation which seems to disappear in Derrida's text as abruptly as it came up? One could, of course, say that Derrida suspects that a certain difference seems to escape even as subtle a discourse on fraternity as Levinas's. And indeed, when Levinas extends the notion of ethical fraternity up to the point where it could also come to include a

----

54. From Derrida's reply to André Jacob who is questioning him as to his difference with Levinas (in J. DERRIDA - P.J. LABARRIÈRE, *Altérités*, Paris, Osiris, 1986, pp. 74-5, my translation. In the light of this quote the virtual absence of any distantiation from Levinas in Derrida's recent *Adieu à Emmanuel Levinas* (Paris, Galilée, 1997) becomes perhaps a bit more understandable (one of the very few reservations Derrida expresses is in a footnote on the Palestinians (p. 196), but as I tried to show elsewhere, it would seem as if Derrida has by that time already accepted too much from Levinas for him still to be able to *think* that distance (cf. my ' "And Cain said to Abel: –". Filling in the blanks while moving "beyond the tribal" with Levinas and Derrida', in E. BERNS (ed.), *Derrida's 'Politics of Friendship'*, to appear from Tilburg U.P./Purdue U.P.).

55. J. DERRIDA, *Politics of Friendship* (transl. G. Collins), London/New York, Verso, 1997, p. 305. Quoted as PF.

Christian like *Abbot Pierre*[56], the difference to which the Christian refers by calling him- or herself a Christian seems to fall out of the picture. But out of what picture exactly? And why should that difference nonetheless matter? Does it not suffice to act in accordance with absolute hospitality, to welcome *Abbot Pierre* as a face – the face of a stranger who is "not required to state his identity" and on whom Levinas in his turn does not impose any identity?

I find it hard not to conclude from this that Derrida has moved himself into a position that is so close to Levinas that it has become impossible for him to state exactly what his remaining 'reticence' might amount to. And yet, instead of seeing here only a "difference in signature" as Derrida suggests, I should like to risk the hypothesis that the difficulty he experiences in articulating what is *philosophically* at stake in his hesitations is due to the fact that they cannot be articulated once one has entered the logic of the 'yes' before all yes and no, which seems to be at the core of Derrida's 'inheritance' from Levinas. As I said before, my aim is not to tell Derrida how he has to handle this inheritance, nor how he could avoid being faced with some of the costs that seem connected to it. But before *we* decide to share this inheritance with him, we might do well to consider at least for a moment the possibility that there is a cost to this 'yes' that cannot even be expressed as long as one accepts its premises. To investigate that possibility, I would like to return first to the very distinction on which we have seen the whole of Levinas's ethics rests: the distinction between 'the face' and 'the form'. As I will try to show, the analysis we have given of this distinction in chapter five, and in particular some of the critical questions which it allowed us to put to Levinas, seem entirely in line, if not with the letter, then at least with the spirit of *Violence and Metaphysics*. But I want to do more than merely repeat a point made before and then somewhat self-congratulatorily suggest that it could have been and should still be Derrida's own. My reason for inserting that earlier analysis of the face and form in the discussion between Levinas and Derrida is that after the developments of this chapter, we seem to have reached a point where we could listen to what Levinas would reply to Derrida's remark about "transcendental violence" which we had made *more or less* our own in the chapter on 'Uneuropean Desires'. More or less – but perhaps rather 'less' than 'more', as Levinas will help us realize.

56. Derrida is quoting a passage from a conversation between Levinas and Fr. Poirié, where Levinas evokes the memory of a certain Abbot Pierre whom he met in the concentration camp and who "by each of his movements restored in us the consciousness of our dignity" – an example of what Levinas calls "fraternal humanity".

VII. WHAT DOES IT COST TO SAY 'YES'?
THE 'FACE' AND THE 'FORM' REVISITED

As one will remember, the 'form' for Levinas, who is in this the heir to a whole tradition, is what gives things their visibility, and hence allows for the *reduction* of the other to the 'same'. Whereas it is the face – that of the other by which he is "in the trace of the infinite" and hence can "break through" or "divest himself" "of the form which does already manifest him" (CPP 96) – that allows Levinas to truly speak of a *reduction* here. That face is not visible. Like the Sartrean gaze (*regard*) it is what looks at me, and – Levinas would add – forces me to look down. Looking up or looking back would mean for Levinas, as it meant for Sartre, to reduce the other to his form: "The best way of encountering the Other is not even to notice the colour of his eyes"[57]. Just as for Sartre[58], there seems to be – there *must* be – a strict alternative for Levinas between the gaze and the eye, i.e., in Levinas's terms: between the face and the form. To reduce the first to the latter signals for Levinas, as it signalled for Sartre, the attempt to reduce the Other qua "hole in the world" to a part of the world, that is, to deny the other's transcendence. And only God can prevent Levinas's categories from being drawn into the Sartrean 'maelstrom', for, as we have seen, only God (and by 'God' I mean the structure that word 'God' stands for in Levinas) can preserve the hierarchy between the face and the form, or the saying and the said[59]. Only 'God' can give to the face of the other that strange absence by which it is more than just a gap in the world or another transcendence. And only 'God', by preserving the dignity and the elevation of that *ethical* hole, can also prevent it from becoming a 'black hole' that would fatally draw the rest of the universe into it. Which is why God took care that every 'invisible' would also be accompanied by a form that without "degrading, diminishing, limiting" (OB 159) the dignity attached to the invisibility of each face, would de-face (OB (158)/201: *dé-visager*) it and allow for a representation that only succeeds insofar as it remembers that it fails to capture what it supposedly represents: "the contemporaneousness of the multiple is tied about the di-

---

57. E. LEVINAS, *Ethics and Infinity. Conversations with Philippe Némo* (transl. R.A. Cohen), Pittsburgh, Duquesne U.P., 1985, p. 85.

58. J.-P. SARTRE, *Being and Nothingness. An Essay on Phenomenological Ontology* (transl. H. E. Barnes), New York, Philosophical Library, s. d., p. 258: "If I apprehend the look (*regard*), I cease to perceive the eyes". We will explore this parallel (and what is hidden by it) between Sartre and Levinas more fully in chapter 11.

59. I shall not pursue this latter distinction here. Suffice it to say that it is governed by the same hierarchy as the opposition face/form and should be deconstructed in the same way.

achrony of the two ... this necessity presupposes a hither side [*un en-deça*], a pre-original, a non-presentable, an invisible" (OB 159, 160). The synchrony of justice never exhausts the diachrony of ethics, the visible realm of Being is not supplemented by, but is itself a supplement to the Invisible of the Otherwise-than-Being.

Between the face and the form, then, a border. A frontier that must be defended at all costs if we want to leave open the possibility to tear down all (national) fronts. Politics has to keep a relation to what Derrida calls 'justice' and Levinas calls ethics, if we want to keep it on the right track. Either a frontier between ethics (the face) and politics (the form, i.e. the comparison, i.e. justice), or else the "discriminating membrane" of a front that lets in only what it can appropriate. Only a 'yes!' can save us now. Provided, as we now know Levinas would force Derrida to admit, that this 'yes' be protected from the spell of the sacred by letting its authority derive from the word of a God who 'is' beyond Being. But perhaps Derrida can escape the burden of such an inheritance which we have seen him unwilling to accept, by returning to the intuitions that guided him in his first encounter with Levinas.

For isn't there a certain violence in the assumption that the ethical dignity of the other is to be entirely situated at the side of "the face"? Isn't it exactly this violence which Derrida has taught us to detect: the violence of a metaphysics that in order to preserve the purity of (self-)presence had to posit the exterior outside of the interior? And isn't Levinas, in separating the face and the form, another heir to this violence[60]? What prevents him not only from arguing, but even from considering that the ethical dignity of the other, instead of being situated on the side of the face, would have to do with his incapacity to fully be at that side? What if the other would be dependent in his alterity on a form he cannot get rid of or simply disappear in[61]? What if his 'misery' – his nakedness – would consist in the fact that he does not have enough face, nor enough 'form' to be situated at either side? Too much form to be that face in which Levinas situates his ethical dignity; too much face to disappear into that centre or that context which could fully

60. With the proviso that far from wanting to preserve the purity of a certain presence, Levinas could be shown to have the sole aim of defending the purity of a certain absence (e.g. the absence that forbids that the form would become an *original* supplement to the face (or the said to the saying)). But a purism of absence is not different in kind and perhaps no less 'violent' than a purism of presence.

61. In the following lines I return to what I have put forward at the end of our fifth chapter and try to insert these ideas in a dialogue between VM and Levinas, as I imagine it.

cover him with their form – the 'form' of a culture, for example[62] – and protect his shivering nakedness? Isn't the ethical dignity of the other to be located in the tension *between* face and form that it is his fate to 'incarnate'? Instead of being that face which is 'signification without context', the 'misery' of the other derives from the fact(icity) of being neither pure signification, nor context, but in between them both – doomed to utter words and to speak, and although eternally engaged in revoking them, in 'undoing the said by the saying', fatally finite in this engagement: unable to have meaning except through a linguistic incarnation which is more than a mere envelope for an already constituted meaning, and hence unable to erase the (original) contamination of the saying by the said. Not having enough form to be fully dressed, and too much invested by the 'form' of an inheritance that has already obliged him before he could choose to accept it or not, the other is both not naked enough and too naked to have that poverty which he needs to be placed "in the trace of the infinite". Which is why respecting him can not simply be a matter of defending the priority of ethics to culture, as Levinas wants us to believe. To be sure, one does not respect the other if one reduces him to one more representative of an ethos. But to deny, for example, that there is something in that ethos which he tries – but always fails – to represent, is also not to respect him. To the contrary, to impose on the other as a condition for respecting his alterity, that he be that face which is without roots – would that not be violence *par excellence*? The violence in which the "pure gift" of respect would become annulled by the conditions it has imposed on those it supposedly respects? The violence of e-mancipation perhaps, which mistakes the *mancipium* of that unspeakable *in-fantia* to which the Other owes his alterity, for the absence of a speech yet to come[63]? And isn't it this violence which is inflicted on the other every

62. In 'Meaning and Sense' one will find Levinas arguing that "before culture and aesthetics, meaning is situated in the ethical, *presupposed* by all culture and meaning" (CPP 100). But, again, this argument for the priority of ethics over culture never considers that there could be a third way beyond (or better: before) the opposition between ethics/ethos (i.e. cultural form) which, depending on how one positions oneself to what we have been suggesting in the preceding chapters, may or may not have been the way Merleau-Ponty's endo-ontology in *The Visible and the Invisible* had been pointing to. Be that as it may, it is at any rate striking to witness how Levinas, in this essay which is largely devoted to Merleau-Ponty, succeeds in obliterating what was perhaps his only intuition: that to say that I am "of the world" also implies that I am "not it" and that consequently the critique of the *kosmotheoros* should be supplemented by a critique of *fusion*. Which is also to say that for Merleau-Ponty, 'incarnation' is not an alternative to 'transcendence', as Levinas is implying, but its very condition.

63. For these italicized notions which I borrow from Lyotard, see chapter 5, e.g. notes 15 and 16.

time in the name of a humanism, and even the humanism of the other man, a certain unity, and even in the name of plurality, is simply opposed to the blindness of a certain particularism? Isn't the first gesture of this violence exactly this suggestion: that the choice between universalism and particularism is that between transcendence or immanence? Between ethics and ethos? Between thought and historicism? Between truth and contextualism? Between the face and the form? And perhaps this list of choices is still incomplete. Perhaps we should add to it the choice between 'yes' and 'no', between 'good' and 'evil' and thus begin to suspect that at the root of Derrida's embarrassment with Levinas lies the latter's assumption that all of these choices belong to a strict and exhaustive alternative, an 'either / or' that as we have seen, is governed precisely by the word 'God' which for Levinas at least would be 'anti-racism's first word'.

But what about that word, and what about these alternatives, if the other would be, for example, what a certain jargon is trying to teach us to call 'an otherwise-coloured person' or a 'person of colour'? Shall we say that the colour of the other is not important, because underneath it we are all the same, as a certain humanism would like us to believe? Shall we teach people a different vocabulary and force them no longer even 'to notice differences' as some of the proponents of political correctness are trying to do[64]? Or shall we criticize both of these views in the name of a different and more subtle humanism of the other man, and say that the reason why such differences of "form" do not matter, is not that we are all equal, but that we are all brothers, in the sense that each of us is subordinated to, while responsible for, all the others who have a right over him? But is the face of the other – that gaze which calls me to order and reminds me of my infinite responsibility – simply to be opposed to its form, in this case: its colour? Couldn't the colour of the other be just one more of those 'supports' of the gaze that Sartre already mentioned? Couldn't the colour of the other function as a support of the gaze, just as the eyes, the "white farm-house at the top of a little hill" or the rustling of branches do[65]? Better still: couldn't it itself become a gaze? For as Lacan remarked, Sartre's assumption that the gaze cannot be seen, is simply false[66]. To turn this remark against Levinas: is it not the assumption that the colour of the other would only be his form which allows Levinas to think of the opposition between the face and the

64. Cf. Jerry ADLER's report 'Thought Police. Is this the new enlightenment on campus or the new McCarthyism?', *Newsweek* January 14, 1991, pp. 42-8, esp. 47.

65. *Being and Nothingness, o.c.*, pp. 257-8. We will return to what is suggested here, in our next chapter.

66. J. LACAN, *The Four Fundamental Concepts of Psycho-analysis* (transl. A. Sheridan), Harmondsworth, Penguin Books, 1979, p. 84.

form as the opposition between the invisible and the visible? But if the colour of the other would simply be another visible, then why is it so disturbing? Would there be any racism, any discrimination of the other on the basis of his colour, if it wasn't disturbing? Whence, then, that enormous curiosity, that endless enterprise to tell us by way of fiction ('The heart of darkness') or science[67] or quite simply phantasm (e.g. all the sexual jokes about blacks) what the meaning of that other colour consists of? Whence that energy, which if totalled would perhaps amount to nothing less than the energy that went into colonization itself, whence that effort at inscribing the meaning of that difference that keeps eluding us? And whence all those efforts on the side of those who had been discriminated against and now, in their turn, are trying to write the truth about the meaning of their colour[68]?

Clearly, there seems to be more 'at stake' in colour than can be captured by the remark that it is simply a diacritical difference (and hence like any other signifier), or the counter-remark which attempts to place it into the imaginary (be it that of the colonizer or the colonized). But for these 'stakes' to embarrass Levinas we need to do better than suggest that the reason why the question of colour seems not appeased by either of these two orders (symbolic; imaginary), has to do with its function as a gaze. For Levinas could in principle always reply that from the moment that a form (like 'colour') stares at us and makes us feel uneasy, it simply takes over the function of a *face* that rests in itself and escapes our attempts to appropriate it through giving it (our) meaning. In that sense, there would be nothing in the distinction face/form that excludes the differently coloured Other – indeed, such an Other would be but another example of an ethically absolute Other. In other words, Levinas need not assume that colour is simply another visible, a form that is irrelevant to the Other's face. He might even be tempted to make his own a formulation which we have borrowed in earlier chapters from Merleau-Ponty and admit that colour, apart from being a visible form, is also an 'invisible' in the latter's sense: that of the other which I *cannot* see and he *cannot* see either. For it is precisely, Levinas could remark, because the colour of the Other is not just his outer wrapping, that the Other suffers from being *reduced* to his colour (as in racist remarks). And Levinas could thus agree with Derrida's suggestion in *Violence and Metaphysics* that the question of ethics presupposes that there must be something of the other which precisely cannot appear for me in order for him to appear qua Other. But Levinas would think that Derrida is simply missing his own point about what he calls "transcendental violence" – "an

---

67. E.g. cf. chapter 7 ((ethno-)anthropology).

68. *If* I am informed correctly, African-Americanism could function here as an example (R. HUGHES, *The Culture of Complaint*, Oxford U.P., 1993, chapter 2 sections VI-VIII).

irreducible violence of the relation to the Other" (the Other cannot fully appear) which is "at the same time non-violence, since it opens the relation to the other" (VM 128-9). For to speak of transcendental *violence* seems to presuppose that the Other *suffers* from his inability to fully appear. The problem, then, is not only that the Other qua *alter ego* cannot fully appear to my *ego* without losing either what makes him an *alter* ego or what makes him an *ego*, but that he cannot fully appear *to himself*. His own meaning escapes him – he is not just *ego*, or *alter ego*, but a *face*, and that is: naked. A nakedness that derives from the fact that what is supposed to be his outer wrapping (the 'form' that covers him and which I can see), nestles as it were, inside him without ever becoming fully his own. The 'misery' of the Other could be, for example, that he cannot 'see' his colour (in the sense of fully appropriate and exhaust its meaning), whereas I can: it is precisely this asymmetry which makes the Other vulnerable. I could always choose to ignore or to suppress that the colour of the Other is more than simply a visible – I could choose not to see its gaze. But the Other cannot: his colour will always be a gaze *for him*; before staring at me, it is always already staring back at him. Which is why Levinas would not agree with Derrida's suggestion that what we are dealing with here is simply a "transcendental violence" – for either this expression forgets that the other's inability to fully appear is precisely at the source of his misery or it does a bad job in trying to acknowledge that 'misery': by suggesting that what is an "irreducible violence" is "at the same time non-violence", it introduces a time which in being common to me and the Other already ignores that part of the Other's alterity which comes before that time and to which Levinas tries to refer by stating that I always come too late for the appeal of the Other. If this 'original belatedness' would not be an essential part of the opening of the relation to the Other, that relation would be strictly neutral: it would be a relation between ego and alter ego in which nothing more would be at stake than what Derrida calls "the transcendental symmetry of two empirical asymmetries" (VM 126).

When Levinas says that the yes before all yes or no is not that of an "infantile spontaneity", he is trying to point to an asymmetry that is neither simply empirical, nor transcendental. The infantile 'yes' is a 'yes' that considers itself to be its own origin. It is the 'yes' of someone who thinks, like Job (OB 122), that he can only be held responsible for what he did not do, but should have done, or for what he did, but should not do. It is a 'yes' that ignores that there can be what Levinas calls a "responsibility without fault". It ignores the fact that responsibility is older than freedom and that it does not consist merely of a common time in which my interests and those of the other collide. It is a 'yes' that is entirely situated within 'Being'. In contrast, the 'yes' before all yes or no, the 'yes' that would not be the 'yes' of infantile spontaneity never arrives in 'Being': it orients it, but it cannot force it to abide with what it offers. God or the Good, as we know, leave a trace of their passing by, but they refuse to reign. And the trace of that trace *in me*, is precisely an affect that I cannot explain: it is a feeling of shame before the Other, to whom I did not do any wrong. This shame which overcomes me, is, as it were, an acknowledgement that I arrived too late. Even if I am punctual, the something of the Other that cannot appear for him to be Other, has precedence over my punctuality: the Other, that is, has a right over me. A right that derives from that 'yes' before all yes or no, which as we know, Levinas calls God. It is due to the priority of that first 'yes' that even my 'yes' to the appeal of the Other will never be able to make up for my delay. Which also means that the gap between my time and the time of the other, is more than a not-at-the-same-time: instead of letting us drift apart, perpetually missing each other, this gap gives meaning to the relation that it opens between us. Ethical meaning.

As one can see, it is not easy to outwit Levinas. But it is also easy to see why neither the letter of the 'first' Derrida (*Violence and Metaphysics*) nor the hesitations of the later Derrida can truly escape the intrigue that Levinas has been weaving around his version of antiracism's first word. When *Violence and Metaphysics* tried to make fun of Levinas's 'absolute alterity' and placed it before the same paradoxes with which Parmenides teased the young Socrates, it 'forgot' (?) that Levinas's 'absolute other' Other was *still related* to me through shame, and that far from being a relapse into empiricism (VM 151 ff.)[69] Levinas's description of the encounter with the Other as 'experience *par excellence*' (TI 109/196) presupposed an intricate structure of belatedness (*Nachträglichkeit*) in which something that does not *belong* to my time or to

69. Let us not miss the occasion to note that Derrida here in the final movement of his text, joins, without any apparent reservations, what has perhaps been *the* movement by which philosophy ever since Plato's *Theaetetus* has sought to close its circle: "By making the origin of language, meaning, and difference the relation to the infinitely other, Levinas is resigned to betraying his own intentions in his philosophical discourse. The latter is understood, and instructs, only by first permitting the same and Being to circulate within it. A classical schema here complicated by a metaphysics of dialogue and instruction, of a demonstration which contradicts what is demonstrated by the very rigor and truth of its development. *The thousand-times-denounced circle of historicism, psychologism, relativism, etc.* But the true name of this inclination of thought to the Other, of this resigned *acceptance of incoherent incoherence* inspired by a truth more profound than the 'logic' of philosophical discourse, the true name of this renunciation of the concept, of the a prioris and transcendental horizons of language, is *empiricism* [Derrida's italics]. For the latter, at bottom, has ever committed but one fault; the fault of presenting itself as a philosophy" (p. 151 – the reader will perhaps remember the opening pages of our introduction).

the time of the other nonetheless brings them into accordance. And, as we have seen, the later Derrida's thoughts on absolute hospitality point to a similar belatedness where my delay with respect to the event that overcomes me, for example in that figure without figure of the absolute arrival that he calls the stranger, has the non-neutral structure of an 'I cannot' that points beyond it to an 'I ought not'. Anti-racism's first word, it would seem, cannot be but a 'yes'.

That is, it must be a 'yes', unless we contest Levinas's claim that the alternative between 'yes' or 'no' is strict and exhaustive. Unless we contest that there is a common structure which holds this 'yes' and this 'no' together and hierarchically orders them as the 'yes' of the good and the 'no' of evil which can never be on a par since they point to a preceding pact with the Good. Which means for Levinas that there are only two ways to respond to the face of the Other: either with or without shame. But the shameless 'no' with which I choose to ignore the appeal, is for Levinas but a suppression of the shame which I feel nonetheless: not to respond to the appeal is already to respond, it is to flee from it and to seek refuge in what he calls "artificial paradises"[70] in which we seek to numb that sensibility that the Other has awakened in us. Shame is not an affect that one may or may not have. It is the affect that corresponds to the one word that is not a candidate for our choice since it has chosen us before we can choose it: the 'yes' which Levinas alternately calls 'God' or the 'Good'. This 'yes' sobers us up, and the only choice we have is that of staying sober or of seeking refuge in a drunkenness which already presupposes that sobriety.

What this reasoning, which is absolutely central to Levinas, clearly shows is that what he calls 'shame' is phenomenologically not motivated by his description of the face and the form. It is, more precisely, underdetermined by that description. Indeed it must be, for otherwise the empirical absence of shame in such or such a response to an appeal would be on a par with its presence. The 'no' would be as 'good' as the 'yes'. There would be no 'yes' before that alternative which orients it and imposes its structure on it. *But if one cannot 'refute' Levinas without begging his question, one could perhaps try to bypass it.* For example, when we suggested in our earlier description of 'colour' that the colour of the other is a form which starts to function as a gaze, Levinas could have replied that it is this gaze which he would call the face. But one could always reply in turn that such an assumption precisely presupposes not only that the colour of the other makes us uneasy, but also that the true name of that uneasiness is ethical shame. But is this so? Could one not also, and with equal right, claim that what produces that unease in me, is that this gaze seems both to escape my 'yes' and my 'no'? The

70. See the quote in note 40 of the preceding chapter.

'reason' the alterity of the other is so disturbing for me, would then be that I cannot even reply to it with a 'yes!'. Or to be more precise, since neither Levinas nor Derrida are suggesting that such a 'yes!' would be something I can *will* to do, and in that sense would be at my disposal: my very disturbance over it seems to derive from the fact that it confronts me with a *double* incapacity. The incapacity, first, to give that colour – that invisible – a meaning that could appease its gaze; and secondly, the incapacity to even receive from it a meaning 'for' my self, e.g. by feeling that it has a 'right over me', that it calls into question my existence, in short: by recognizing its appeal as an *ethical* one. The disturbance I feel the moment I am confronted with such an 'invisible visible' (and colour, the reader will have remarked, is only one example among many that could be shown to have the same structure)[71] may not be *directly* ethical in Levinas's sense. It could just as well point to a disruption of the ethical horizon within which the alternative between 'yes' and 'no' was assumed to be strict and exhaustive. It could point, that is, to an 'interruption' of the appeal of the other that differs from the interruptions which we have described in this chapter. An interruption which is neither mine, nor the other's, nor 'God's', but one that comes from an 'intrigue' that is spun by another candidate for infinity than the one that Levinas has presented us with. What this means is that, as the reader of the preceding chapter may have guessed by now, we will perhaps have to reconsider the titles of the 'there is' for such a position. But, for the moment, it should suffice not to close off prematurely the possibility of there being another candidate. For example, by reading once more in this apparent *interruption of the face by its form*, an appeal to our unconditional hospitality[72]. For what this interruption means is that there is perhaps no such appeal. There may be no 'yes' to hold together and to orient the alternative 'yes' or 'no': it is perhaps already too much to link the absolute arrival to such a 'yes' which already names it and imposes the condition on it that if it should not arrive, this 'not' would merely be the absence of an arrival. The non-donation of the event would then still point to donation as the more original meaning of the event. There was a time

71. One could say that the Other has a 'vague debt' to his/her colour (a *debt* since it is not without importance; a *vague* debt since it resists both his and my attempts to explicate its meaning). Colour represents without rendering present that 'Thing' at the centre of our decentrement, as do all these 'small things' we cherish in our own culture and become irritated by in another.

72. As in a number of Derrida's most recent texts to which I must confess I am totally deaf: *De l'hospitalité. Anne Dufourmantelle invite Jacques Derrida à répondre*, s.l., Calmann-Lévy, 1997 and *Cosmopolites de tous les pays, encore un effort!*, Paris, Galilée, 1997. The movement in these texts is, it seems, Levinasian and thus open to the kind of objections we are trying to make here and in the following chapters.

when Derrida questioned exactly that move in an attempt to liberate the infamous 'death of God' from a prior reference to the word (of) 'God': "The aspect of living and original speech *itself* which Levinas seeks to save is clear. Without its possibility, outside its horizon, writing is nothing. In this sense, writing will always be secondary. To liberate it from this possibility and this horizon, *from this essential secondariness*, is to deny it as writing, and to leave room for a grammar or a lexicon without language, for cybernetics or electronics. But it is only in God that speech, as presence and horizon of writing is realized without defect. *One would have to be able to show that only this reference to the speech of God* [and hence to that 'yes', the 'logic' of which we have tried to analyse here, – R.V.] distinguishes Levinas's intentions from those of Socrates in the *Phaedrus*; and that *for a thought of original finitude* this distinction *is no longer possible*. And that if writing is secondary at this point, nothing, however, has occurred before it" (VM 102-3). It is toward such a thought of original finitude that we turn in the next chapters. Not with the ambition of showing that the whole of Levinas's work rests on a distinction that for us would no longer be possible. But with the more modest and perhaps less noble aim of satisfying our curiosity and finding out what would happen if one would have the temerity to drop that distinction. It is perhaps the predicament of our age that it has been as reckless as that. We do not want to judge. We want to know where we are at.

CHAPTER ELEVEN

THE GAZE OF THE BIG OTHER
LEVINAS AND SARTRE ON RACISM

Levinas is often said to provoke. And although I am hardly in a position to deny this (how could I, since I am obviously obsessed enough by what he has to say, to keep coming back to it?), I cannot help it if the very solemnity with which one refers to the 'provocation of Levinas' makes me wonder whether it is not hiding a less solemn erotics. I cannot help it if, like Alcibiades back then with those who were attracted by Socrates's powers to provoke, I feel the urge to 'enlighten' Levinas's co-symposiasts and to warn them against his powers of seduction. For I am at war with the man, and if, again like Alcibiades, I risk insulting those who are under his spell by claiming that he is not at all what they think he is, it is in a sense because this war has become too big for me to fight alone and because I need allies. And as an abounding Levinas-literature shows, to forge such an alliance it is not enough to point to the 'provocation of Levinas'[1], for it seems as if a whole readership is precisely attracted to Levinas because he provokes or because of the sort of provocation contained in his work. As if there is something about its way of shocking people that is sufficiently soothing to make them choose its side. How else to explain that this philosophy has met with virtually no resistance and is on its way to monopolizing at the very least the intersection between phenomenology and ethics?

One need only think here of what happened to Sartre's famous analysis of the gaze[2] from the moment that people discovered that one could find in Levinas's analysis of the face of the other a sort of fire-escape from the hell that Sartre, as now became clear, confused with intersubjectivity. Levinas, without any hesitation, was immediately portrayed as the better and more promising philosopher who helped us see through Sartre's game: for the gaze of the Other, we now discovered, did not just stare at us, it also

---

1. An allusion to the title of an early collection of essays on Levinas: R. BERNASCONI - D. WOOD (eds.), *The Provocation of Levinas. Rethinking the Other*, London/New York, Routledge, 1988.

2. J.-P. SARTRE, *Being and Nothingness. An Essay on Phenomenological Ontology*, New York, Philosophical Library, s.d., pp. 252 ff. (Henceforth quoted as BN. I have preferred to render 'regard' by 'gaze' instead of 'look' as in this translation).

concerned us. And henceforth, the French *regarder* lost its Sartrean overtones and the threat once contained in "Autrui me regarde" somehow was transfigured into the promise of an ethical deliverance. Little did it matter that for the Levinasian Other to become the one whose appeal liberates us instead of the one whose gaze alienates us, as Sartre thought, we were asked to accept that that Other be put in a position of utmost transcendence, that leaves him or her with "a right over me" (CPP 125), whereas I was to find myself devoid of all rights, taken hostage by that Other whose appeal I could not escape and who contests and then sets fire to any interiority I might try to hold on to, in order to protect me from that infinite demand that obsesses me even though uttered by a voice weaker than my own. I will come back to this official portrait of Levinas as a critic of Sartre. But for the moment I only wanted to point to the astonishing fact that, notwithstanding the extreme, albeit 'ethical', violence in the language that Levinas had chosen to introduce in order to protect us from Sartre's influence, as far as I know, no one took to the defence of Sartre. As if there is nothing in the analysis of *Being and Nothingness* that could be used to question some of the basic premises in Levinas. Being desperate for allies as I am, I will later not shrink from embarking on precisely the opposite argument. But as one can already expect (for my title is by no means a compliment), this will only be a first strategic move in a more complicated battle whose first aim is to sow as much discord as possible and by any means, including joining with those whom I will later turn against.

I will not just defend Sartre, then, I will also betray him. Just as I will not engage in an attack on Levinas before I have helped him to build his defence lines as strong as possible. And knowing the contemporary interest in following war in real time, I want to make sure that, when I finally engage in a war on all fronts, no one can afford to take the comfortable position of a spectator following what is going to happen next from the cosy intellectual distance of the home-front. In short, I want to do better than CNN and implicate my readers more intimately in this battle. Hence my subtitle, which touches on something too serious to leave any of us indifferent. It is, of course, bad taste to try to set people up against Levinas by bringing up his views on racism. But I could think of no better strategy to catch in the act the effectuation of that secret desire in all of us to which Levinas's provocation seems to respond. As we shall see, it is a certain gaze which we welcome in that provocation. For it seems to protect us against another gaze that we are more afraid of and we would find less easy to bear.

I

Racism is no longer what it used to be. Since it discovered that it could do without the notion of race, it has proved itself all too willing to grant its critics their point. Better still: it took over their values and utterly confused them by missing no occasion to stress the importance of difference. In this *heterophilic* form today's neoracism could easily profile itself as radically anti-discriminatory, and thus: anti-racist! Rejecting classical racism's obsession with 'the loss of rank' and the debasement of 'superior peoples', a radical right-winger like Jean-Marie Le Pen in France has no difficulty to admit that he "loves North-Africans". But since they have a right to be different, they need to be able to live in a place where the purity of their difference does not risk becoming contaminated by another culture. And thus, it would not only be to France's benefit, but to their own, were the immigration problem to be resolved "by the peaceful, organized return of immigrants"[3]. Profiting from the relativist climate generated by anti-racism's well-meaning attacks on any idea of hierarchy between cultures, Le Pen and others are merely turning the tables on their critics when claiming to share both their concern that differences should be protected, and their suspicion that universalism is but an indifference to difference. One could, of course, contest that it is. But it is difficult to see how such a plea for a true universality would not, in one way or another, have to travel the road along which Levinas had set the beacons for his own attempt to show that it is not culture which is an alternative to reason, but ethics.

As is well-known, Levinas's argument for the priority of ethics above both culture and reason[4], follows from his description of the face of the Other. Like Sartre before him (e.g. BN 258), Levinas is struck by the difference between noticing the colour of someone's eyes and feeling his gaze rest upon you. And he is still in agreement with Sartre when he sees in the reduction of the other's gaze to his eye a denial of the transcendence of the other. As he explains to Nemo: "The best way of encountering the Other is not even to notice the colour of his eyes! When one observes the colour of the eyes one is not in social relationship with the Other. The relation with the face can surely be dominated by perception, but what is specifically the

---

3. Le Pen (cf. chapter 10 n11) quoted in the excellent analysis of Pierre-André TAGUIEFF, 'The New Cultural Racism in France', *Telos*, 1990 (nr. 83), p. 109 (cf. also in that same issue, Alain POLICAR, 'Racism and its Mirror Image', pp. 99-108).

4. On this priority see especially his 'Meaning and Sense', in CPP, pp. 75-107, e.g., p. 100: "meaning is situated in the ethical, *presupposed by all culture and all meaning*".

face is what cannot be reduced to that"[5]. As this quote makes clear, Levinas is parting ways with Sartre at the very point where they meet. For although they both agree on there being an essential difference between, on the one hand, what Sartre calls the gaze and Levinas the face, and, on the other hand, what one could call the looks of the Other, Levinas goes much further than Sartre in not only claiming that the face of the Other *cannot* be reduced to his outward appearance, but that it also *should not* be reduced to that. This is why Levinas can speak of the "best way" to encounter the Other, whereas for Sartre there simply seems to be no good way to have such an encounter. The deeper reason for this being, of course, that Sartre is operating with a model of a reversible asymmetry between me and the other, where everything turns around the basic incompatibility between the other's transcendence and my own. Either the Other looks at me and turns me into an object, or I look at him and immanentize his transcendence.

It is this reversibility which is contested by what Levinas sees as the asymmetry between me and the other. He agrees with Sartre that when I merely look at the Other, the result will be that I deny him his alterity and turn him into an object that poses no threat to my subjectivity. But when the Other looks at me, the situation is not simply reversed: for Levinas that look – and that look alone – has the status of an appeal that, far from objectifying me, is calling me to my true subjectivity. The look of the Other – his appeal – does not alienate me by handing me over to the world, but is precisely saving me from the world by calling into question that part of me that is clinging to the world and that is unable, if left to itself, to cut through the roots that bind me to this world. And these roots are, of course, the famous *conatus essendi*: the fact that, were it not for the intervention of the Other, I would persist in my being because I am the sort of being that cannot but care for its own being. Indeed, for Levinas the reason why Sartre can describe the gaze of the Other as profoundly alienating, is because he is but another heir to this deep and unquestioned legacy of the *conatus essendi* in Western thought. For what Sartre describes as alienating, is precisely the fact that through the gaze of the Other, the For-itself (*pour-soi*) is forced into the painful discovery that there is a dimension to its being that is resistant to its freedom of "being what it is not and not being what it is". As soon as there is an Other, there is an outer dimension to this freedom that it cannot recuperate and that, for this very reason, does not leave it indifferent. The For-itself is threatened in its freedom of having only itself to thank for the choices it makes and thus always retaining the possibility of coming back upon them. For this perpetual engagement now has a witness

5. E. LEVINAS, *Ethics and Infinity. Conversations with Philippe Némo* (transl. R.A. Cohen), Pittsburgh, Duquesne U.P., 1985, pp. 85-6.

who can only see it as a *being engaged*, and whose gaze thus "freezes" or "stifles" what for me, taken on my own, would have remained a perpetual possibility: an expression of my engagement and of its powers to always disengage itself. Henceforth, this engagement will have a meaning that concerns *me* and that I therefore cannot but assume: shame is for Sartre precisely the acknowledgement that there is a dimension of my being that I feel responsible for, although its meaning escapes me. Through the Other, then, I have to accept becoming a stranger to myself: apart from being a For-itself I am also a For-the-other, and thus I cannot but find myself in a wholly new dimension of my existence which Sartre calls the "unrevealed" (BN 268). Suddenly, for example, I discover that I have a "character" of which the other can give me a description, in which I will not recognize myself although I will know that "it's me"; – as Sartre writes: "I accept the responsibility for this stranger who is presented to me, but he does not cease to be a stranger .... for I *am* this me but I am not this nothingness which separates me from myself" (BN 274). And, as is well-known, the whole of Sartre's dialectic of intersubjective relations is going to be drawn into this "conflict" between the nothingness that I am and the nothingness that I am not and that separates me from myself. This latter nothingness, which Sartre presents as the transcendence of the Other, will either have to be annihilated or seduced so that it might render its secret to me. But both are, of course, equally impossible and for the same reason: for it does not matter whether the Other succumbs to my violence or to my seduction, since it is in vain that I am trying to make his gaze my own. The place of the Other will forever elude my grasp since it is defined as the place from which I cannot see myself. The For-itself will remain forever unable to absorb the For-the-other into itself. This "alienation" is the price of inter-subjectivity. Man is a being whose being is broken into two irreconcilable dimensions.

Of course, Levinas will be far from satisfied with Sartre's elaborations. For he will disagree with its premise which is, as I already pointed out, but a camouflaged *conatus essendi*. Indeed, when Sartre claims that the other's gaze confronts me with a dimension of my being that does not leave me indifferent, he is simply reinforcing a previous point that he had been making about the For-itself, which *Being and Nothingness* had introduced as a being that had to be its lack of being. With this cumbersome description Sartre was simply reiterating Heidegger's dictum that 'man's' essence lies in his existence, and the famous Sartrean opposition between the In-itself (*en-soi*) which is what it is and the For-itself (*pour-soi*) which is not what it is and is what it is not, was but a way of underscoring that man is first and foremost a being-in-the-world. But for Sartre man *suffers* from the rift of this ec-stasis, without which however he would merely be a thing and without world. Hence the For-itself is engaged in a "useless passion", for although it would like to undo the lack of being that prevents it from falling together with itself, it cannot, for without this lack, it wouldn't be a For-itself and it would lose its humanity. Perpetually chasing what it is at the same time running from, the For-itself is already before the appearance of the other deeply involved (*conatus*) in the pursuit of a being (*essendi*) which through being denied to it, keeps it on the move. Although this ideal of combining its For-itself with an In-itself is a silly dream, it is this divine desire to become a *causa sui* (where indeed For-itself and In-itself are one and the same) that keeps man living. And it is because he is already dreaming this dream, that the confrontation with the Other constitutes such a painful awakening. For the Other by becoming a witness to my trivial pursuit is both confronting me with the impossibility of what I try to achieve and incorporating it in a new way. Henceforth it will not only be the In-itself that will escape me, but also my For-the-other. A new leak, as it were, is introduced into my being, but if this leak affects me in the way it does, it is because it is reinforcing a leak from which I suffered already. But this amplification produces such noise that I risk losing contact with that meaningless aim which, as long as it attracts me, brings meaning into my life. If I am to save my life, then, I will have to save my dream and thus I will have to look for ways to implicate the other in it. But since this is in principle impossible, in the long run my fall out of paradise (BN 263) will turn out to be a direct route to hell.

It is this picture of a being which is fooled into being and forever being fooled by the very structure of its being, that Levinas is going to contest in Sartre. But he can only do so by paying a price that not all of the readers who welcomed him as a critic of Sartre, seem to have been aware of. For it is, of course, not sufficient to sing the praise of the ethical asymmetry of the Other and to pretend as if it would suffice to plant some ethics into the Sartrean universe to make it inhabitable.

In order to turn the gaze of the Other into the face of the Other and to distinguish between the effect of that face on me and the effect of my gaze on him, one will have to come up with an explanation of how the call or the appeal in the face of the Other can reach me without me experiencing it as merely another threat or another ruse on the part of the Other to rob me of my transcendence. And the only way to do this, is to contest that my "final essence" or my "final reality" – these are Levinas's own words![6] – would lie

6. TI 178: "as responsible I am brought to my final reality"; 178-9: "When I seek my final reality, I find that my existence as a 'thing in itself' begins with the presence in me of the idea of Infinity"; 179: "... my final essence, ... my responsibility"; 253: "in my religious being, I am *in truth*." (Levinas's italics). All of these quotes should be read together with

in my *conatus essendi*. There must be, then, another dimension to my being (as *Totality and Infinity* would still put it) or a dimension 'otherwise than being' with which I am nonetheless *familiar*[7], if I am to undergo a fundamental conversion by being confronted with the appeal of the Other. If this appeal can *interrupt* my being, without that interruption becoming simply a violent traumatic intrusion from without, it must, as it were, ring a bell in me so that I can at least recognize in it a possibility of my own. Or in other words: as Levinas seems to be more candidly aware of than some of his readers, the alterity of the Other cannot be so absolute that it leaves me without a connection – it is not for nothing that ethics is described as a *relation*-without-relation! It is precisely this characterization of ethics as a relation-without-relation which distinguishes it from the without-relation that there is 'between' me and 'my' death and in general 'between' me and all the avatars of the *il y a*. As we have seen in chapter nine, 'death' is precisely described by Levinas as a prototype of the *il y a* because it stands for an alterity that is the end of all 'between' and that is of such an absoluteness that not only can I have no relation with it, but that I am crushed by it (TO 74, 79). And no matter how violent a picture Levinas sometimes sketches of the intrusion of the Other, he will always take care to explain that this violence is a "*good* violence" (e.g. OB 43), that it does not stifle me but *awaken* me, and that it does not alienate, but *liberate*. Of course, I will experience this intrusion of the Other as violent in some sense, for this Other, by being a face, already uproots the familiarity of my world by piercing through the forms in which I habitually bring to rest whatever is unfamiliar to me. But although the alterity of the Other is unfamiliar to me and hence makes me feel ill at ease, it is not so unfamiliar that it would throw me into a panic or an anxiety that fully takes control over me. *My response to the alterity of the Other is not panic but shame*. And whereas in panic I am no longer myself and on the point of losing myself, in shame, on the contrary, I am fully singularized. As Levinas never tires of stressing, only in ethical responsibility do I become a fully singular 'I'[8].

passages such as "And yet the Other does not purely and simply negate the I; total negation, of which murder is the temptation and the attempt, refers to an antecedent relation" (TI 194) that Levinas calls fraternity and by which he means "a pre-original not resting on oneself" (OB 75).

7. OB 177: "One has to find for man another kinship than that which ties him to being". And cf. OB 137: "The antecedent familiarity with being is not prior to the approach. The sense of the approach is goodness without knowledge or blindness, beyond essence".

8. This is a repeated claim in *Otherwise than Being*, and in its turn repeated by Levinas's commentators (e.g. A. Lingis's Introduction to OB, xxx) – but it leaves one wondering how Levinas can make it without coming into flat contradiction with his own analysis of enjoyment which was introduced in *Totality and Infinity* as "the very pulsation of the I" (TI

The very popularity of this formula should not make one lose sight of the difficulty here and of the audacity with which Levinas solves it. In defining responsibility as a situation characterized by "the impossibility of evading, without any field of initiative" (OB 109), Levinas is boldly attributing it just those traits that he had always been using to describe the 'il y a': a situation with no exit, no escape in which I am left without the possibility to react and where, in being exposed to this terror that doesn't let go of me, I am forced to become a paralysed witness to my own disappearance. But although there is no escape from the appeal of the Other, this appeal will only "paralyse" me – an expression that crops up time and again – in order to push me into my true movement: that of an infinite sacrifice, in which I am no longer tied to myself, but to the Other. What this means is that the *il y a* is, as it were, turned against itself: for what is paralysed is in truth that *conatus* that didn't let go of me and held me in its grip. The appeal of the Other precisely by being other, i.e. something that I cannot draw into my world, resists that grip that has tied *me* to my world and to my being: "the I loses its hold"[9], and instead of being de-subjectivized, I become *for the first time* a truly unique, irreplaceable and singular I that is 'for the other' and no longer 'for itself' (OB 52).

One cannot but admire the elegance of the way in which Levinas seems to be taking the sting out of Sartre's dramatic descriptions of the encounter with the Other. Sartre was right, he is telling us, in seeing in the Other "a pure hole in the world"[10], "but he stopped his analysis too soon" since he missed the distinction between the paralysing force of the face – which subjectivizes me – and the paralysing force of the gaze which by turning me into an object, robs me of my subjectivity. "The encounter with the Other in Sartre threatens my freedom, and is equivalent to the fall of my freedom under the gaze of another freedom" (TI 303), because Sartre has both too low

---

113), and thus also as a dimension in which the subject already has a singularity of his own! E.g. OB 73: "Beyond the multiplication of the visible in images, enjoyment is *the singularization of the ego* in its coiling back upon itself. Winding of a skein, it is the very movement of egoism. [etc.]". Notwithstanding Levinas's repeated suggestions to the contrary (e.g. OB 123: "the *uniqueness* of the responsible ego is *possible only in being obsessed by another* [etc.]"), the difference between responsibility and the pre-ethical life of the subject cannot lie in the singularizing effect of the former. It must have to do with a difference between *degrees* of singularization: hence my use of the expression "a *fully* singular 'I'". But it would seem that this analysis itself already presupposes the claims I pointed to in notes 6 and 7.

9. 'Transcendence and Height', *loc. cit.*, p. 17.

10. 'The Trace of the Other', in M.C. TAYLOR (ed.), *Deconstruction in Context: Literature and Philosophy*, Chicago/London, The University of Chicago Press, 1986, p. 354; and cf. CPP 103.

a view of my freedom and of the Other. When he defines man as being "condemned to freedom" (e.g. BN 485), this very formula betrays its origins, for this freedom is nothing more than a passion and not even the uselessness of that passion can allow man to escape from the meaningless vortex into which he is driven. This freedom which is still *conatus* (a being driven by forces behind one's back) is still under the spell of the *il y a* – which by some silly whim has given man the leeway in which he can be tossed around. And nor is this all, for what further prevents Sartre from seeing that man, instead of being *doomed* to freedom, is "liberated to serve"[11] is that for him inter-subjectivity is merely a relation between two identically constituted subjects: the Other will then be simply defined as "another freedom"[12]. And the relation between these freedoms will be one of conflict, in which again the malignant force of the *il y a* has its finest hour. To put an end to this conflict and to this triumph of a "bad infinite" (TI 158-9), one will need to point to a different force. And it is to this force of the Good – to this *good infinity* – that Levinas is directing us when he refuses to define the Other as "transcendent because he would be free as I am", and insists that "his freedom is a superiority that comes from his very transcendence" (TI 87). And at this point Levinas can no longer avoid the word that some of his readers would have preferred him not to use: "the Other measures me with a gaze incomparable to the gaze by which I discover him" (TI 86), because he is "closer *to God* than I" am (CPP 56).

Without this 'God' – a word that, needless to say, is entirely unacceptable to Sartre for whom 'God' stands for *causa sui* and hence for a mirage and a 'contradictory idea' (BN 615) – Levinas would not be able to *stabilize* and *orient* the asymmetry between me and the Other and thus prevent it from becoming the perfectly reversible seesaw that it is in Sartre's universe. But as we shall see, once this word is introduced, inter-subjectivity becomes a *ménage à trois* in which God, by being differently related to me and the Other, assures the possibility of there being a hyphen between us which, by keeping us apart, at the same time keeps us together. And as one can suspect, the reason why Levinas will refuse the alternative between reason and culture, between universalism and particularism is that it is but the effect of the erasure of that hyphen. To understand this, we will have to

11. I take this expression from an interview Johan Goud had with Levinas and which was published in Dutch as 'Wat men van zichzelf eist, eist men van een heilige', in J. GOUD, *God als Raadsel. Peilingen in het spoor van Levinas*, Kampen/Kapellen, Kok Agora – DNB/Pelckmans, 1992, p. 165. Levinas himself is opposing his view on freedom here to Sartre's.

12. E. LEVINAS, *En Découvrant l'Existence avec Husserl et Heidegger*, Paris, Vrin, 1988, p. 173.

follow him once more in his carefully balanced construction of this 'intrigue' between God, me and the Other which is merely another name for what we have heard him call before the 'good infinite'. But now that things are getting more serious and that it looks like we are going to have a good battle, we might do well to temper our enthusiasm and start preparing for secret negotiations with the enemy. For it could be that Sartre's world is not that uninhabitable after all – who knows what richness lies concealed beneath this rather bleak picture that Levinas paints for us?

II

Before we engage in any further manoeuvres, let us make sure that we know what is at stake in the oncoming battle. There can be no doubt that what we have just heard is the sound of the preliminary skirmishes for a bigger confrontation since we have seen Levinas and Sartre come up with different answers to the same problem. What they both would like to understand is in what sense the Other makes a difference, that is: how the Other not only reveals to me what I already was, but how he "establishes me in a new type of being which can support new qualifications" (BN 222). Indeed, if the encounter with the Other would only be the actualization of pre-given potential that I already carry within, it would not really be an encounter with *the Other*, but rather *through* him a better way of meeting myself. It is no coincidence, then, that both Sartre and Levinas take *shame* as their main paradigm for such an encounter. For in shame I am not just meeting myself *through* the Other, I am also confronted with the ineliminable alterity of the Other: "shame is shame *of oneself before the Other*" (*ibid.*). There are two structures here – the *For-itself* and the *For-the-Other* – and there is a tension between them that Sartre insists on calling an alienation; thus stressing that for him this becoming grafted of the For-the-Other upon the For-itself is nothing less than a "loss of mastery", of control, autonomy. In short: for the For-itself the For-the-Other means an enforced entrance into a condition of "slavery" (BN 267): "all of a sudden I am conscious of myself as escaping myself, not in that I am the foundation of my own nothingness but in that *I have my foundation outside myself*. I am for myself only as I am a pure reference to the Other" (BN 260). If one is to understand this correctly, one should not forget that when Sartre is talking about shame, he is not primarily referring to that state in which I become conscious of my wrongdoings. The famous example of being caught in front of a keyhole is in that sense profoundly misleading. For it suffices that I am sitting on a chair and that someone comes in and sees me sitting, for there to be 'shame' in Sartre's sense, which is strictly ontological and refers to my loss of transcendence: "Pure shame is not a feeling of being this or that guilty object but in general of being *an* object; that is, of recognizing myself in this degraded, fixed, and dependent being which I am for the Other" (BN 288). And perhaps Sartre is less pessimistic than he seems when he goes on to conclude from this that "shame is the feeling of an *original fall*, not because of the fact that I may have committed this or that particular fault but simply that I have 'fallen' into the world in the midst of things and that *I need the mediation of the Other in order to be what I am*" (BN 288-9).

Levinas's irritation with Sartre goes back, of course, to this ontological recuperation of the Biblical fall. It is this arrogance with which ontology takes precedence over ethics – and as we shall see: over religion – which according to him has prevented Sartre from seeing in shame something more than an alienation. For Levinas to become conscious of oneself as "having one's foundation outside of oneself" (BN 260, quoted above) is exactly the contrary: it is a liberation. Heteronomy and freedom are not opposed, as Sartre thinks, for the one gives birth to the other. And although Levinas agrees that the appearance of the Other introduces a new dimension into my being, he will firmly disagree that this is just a dimension added on to the existing one. The For-itself is not just placed in tension with a For-the-Other, but is undergoing a profound transformation which is not a fall but a lifting up, an elevation: out of nature into humanity. Far from forcing me into slavery, the Other gives me the chance to escape it – humanism of the other man is a verb: it means that it is the Other who humanizes me by "introducing into me what was not in me" (TI 203). For it is the Other who puts me under the Law and being under the Law, being called to one's responsibility is not a condition of slavery but a condition for true freedom. Without the Other my freedom is not free enough because it presupposes me and therefore cannot truly liberate. To be sure, this freedom is a freedom of choice, but since whatever I choose depends on me making the difference, I remain outside of this choice whose consequences always return to me and are but a loop in which I keep meeting myself. No wonder, then, that there are moments when this loop reveals itself to be a cage in which I have to pass my time, and lie bored like an animal, profoundly indifferent to all of these choices which are unable to make a difference. The Law, however, puts me before a choice that truly makes a difference for it is one that not only affects me but the Other also. There is a difference between a boredom where I no longer care whether it will be fish or meat that is to be served to me, and a boredom where my indifference, and even to my own death, will make a difference to the Other who needs me to assist him or to console, to raise or to educate her. Being under the Law is supreme freedom and supreme choice – it is a state in which my own indifference is not enough to do away with difference. In missing this point, Sartre's existentialism is all but a humanism. It is a celebration of nature in man.

It would seem, then, that although they are dealing with the same problem, Levinas and Sartre could not be farther apart in their answers. Indeed, if one looks at what Sartre calls 'slavery' – "I am a slave in so far as I am the object of values which come to qualify me without my being able to act on this qualification" (BN 267) – one is presented with a description of the very situation that according to Levinas gives rise to freedom. For man cannot give freedom unto himself. He can only become free by feeling the weight upon him of values which come to qualify him without him being able to act on that qualification: "Value in its original radiation renders 'pure' or 'impure' before any intentional movement, without there being a free attitude toward value that could be taken up" (OB 198n.28). Values hold because they "'weigh' on the subject" (*ibid.*). They are "valid before freedom" (OB 197n.27), and point to "a susceptibility which cannot assume what it receives, but which, in spite of itself, becomes responsible for it" (OB 198n.28). Responsibility is not a choice or an engagement, it involves a 'being chosen' and a 'being engaged' that goes farther back than what I can remember and yet is "otherwise" 'weighing' on me than "the way a cause weighs on an effect" (*ibid.*).

With this "otherwise" we have, of course, once again reached that point where Levinas's ethics finds itself inextricably knotted to his metaphysics, his phenomenology and his religion. Everything else starts from here and leads back to it, including as we shall shortly see, his position on racism. Perhaps it is time, then, to take a closer look at this position and let it enliven and deformalize what I am afraid until now may have struck you as yet another of these sterile discussions between intellectuals specialized in talking past one another. I would like to show, to the contrary, how there is something deeply problematic in this position on racism which will lead us back into the heat of Levinas's debate with Sartre, but this time not as spectators, but as participants who in order to survive must find a way to escape not only the Sartrean Minotaur that Levinas is trying to outwit but also the labyrinth of the intrigue of the infinite which he constructed in order to break its spell.

III

Levinas's understanding and condemnation of racism follow seamlessly from the position we have seen him defend against Sartre. For racism consists in the attempt to deny to the Other his invisibility; it reduces his "invisible" face (cf. OB 88, 89ff., 157) to a visible form that I can know, inspect, measure and pass judgement on. The Other thus is forced to appear and to become nothing but a phenomenon. But this light into which I drag him is not neutral; it is for Levinas violence *par excellence* and a deep profanation of the mystery of the Other – of that in him which cannot appear and be brought on the surface. The mistake in this – literally – superficial approach of the Other is that his alterity is taken to result from his difference. As if his otherness would only be a matter of different attributes, a differently coloured skin for example, or a different place and time of birth, a different race or a different culture. And this 'mistake' is far from innocent: because of it the Other will be forced into his difference, forced to have roots in that context that I associate him with. By mistaking the order of priority between the Other's alterity and his differences, I expose him to the powers of an Origin and think of his alterity as a result of something in that Origin taking *possession* of him. Such a culturalization or contextualization of the Other denies him the right to an otherness still different from and not absorbable by that culture, or that context or the meaning I attribute to that physiognomy. Hence, for Levinas this *sacralization* of the Other is an injustice that hands him over to *Powers* stronger than him: his Race, his Culture, his History, his Facticity. It is to deny what is *holy* in the Other: the unbridgeable gap between his face and his form, in which Levinas wants us to recognize his destitution, his nakedness and his misery. The Other, he seems to suggest, suffers from the fact that his alterity does not result from or does not fall together with the attributes that make him different: "Stripped of its very form, a face is frozen in its nudity. It is a distress" (CPP 96). To treat the Other as if he is clothed, fully dressed by his "cultural ornaments" (*ibid.*) is to misrecognize that he is a stranger, not just to us, but to himself. For the Other is always more than his outer appearance, and since Levinas insists on seeing in this 'more' not just his richness, but his very misery and the reason why even under the load of these characteristics which make him different, he is still shivering, one can only conclude that the Other as a stranger *is first and foremost a stranger to himself, and only subsequently to us.*

Let us note in passing that what Sartre called alienation – the effect of the gaze of the Other on me – seems thus to be transplanted onto the Other himself, but without this being the sole effect of my gaze on him. For the rift between the visible form and the 'invisible face' of the Other, the gap between what Sartre called the *For-the-Other* and the *For-itself*, is presented by Levinas as the very alterity and the destitution of the Other. Perhaps racism is so shameless because it is insensitive to this shame of the Other; or rather: perhaps racism is so cruel because it sees through this shame of the Other and then denies it to him by denying him the *For-itself* and forcing him into the *For-the-Other*. Racism, then, would deny the Other his dignity and his misery at one and the same time. Its aim is to make the Other suffer by treating him as someone who, or rather: as *something that* does not suffer.

It is tempting to pursue this analysis of racism by raising the by now obvious question: but what if I am suffering likewise from the rift between my For-myself and my For-the-Other? Couldn't racism be analysed as an attempt to anaesthetize that suffering in me and wouldn't we then need to point to an ethics where the 'solution' to the problem of suffering would not just lie in a suffering-for-the-Other, but in my own attempt to hold out and differently relate to the suffering in me? No doubt this sort of approach would be much closer to the spirit, if not to the letter of Sartre's programme than it would be to Levinas's ethics. For as we know, Levinas's whole strategy was to stabilize Sartre's asymmetric intersubjectivity and to put the Other unambiguously above me. As a result, the face of the Other is not just associated with his destitution, but also with his glory and his height: its *inability to disappear into its form*, is not just presented as the Other's misery but also as his dignity: "The Other who manifests himself in a face as it were *breaks through* his own plastic essence, like a being who opens the window on which its own visage was already taking form ... this manifestation is a *surplus* over the inevitable paralysis of manifestation" (CPP 96). A surplus, and not just a lack. A "piercing through" (TI 198), a "breaking up" (*ibid.*), and a "divesting itself of the form which does already manifest him" (CPP 96): "For a face is the *unique* openness in which the signifyingness of the trans-cendent does not nullify the transcendence and make it enter into an immanent order" (CPP 103).

How are we, then, to understand that the misery of the Other is but the reverse side of his dignity and that this *absence* of form which makes the face "freeze in its nudity" (CPP 96, quoted above), that this, its very "hunger" for a form, a role, a context which would put an end to its condition of being a home-less stranger, an ex-patriate, is at the same time its pride and its glory, its richness and its height which turn its manifestation into a "visitation" and an "epiphany" where it is "alive" instead of becoming captive and stifled like a phenomenon that is "already, in whatever respect, an image, a captive manifestation of its plastic and mute form" (CPP 95)? The difficulty is, of course, not solved — and perhaps not even noticed — by simply repeating what Levinas has written about the appeal of the Other which comes *both* from above and from below. For the question is: what is the status of this 'both'? And there must be an answer to this, for if Levinas would leave the Other to his hunger, if he would be satisfied to see in him only the suffering of a For-itself that is longing to absorb its For-the-Other and beyond that, its In-itself, he would have defined the Other as Sartre defined man in general: as an impossible project to become a *causa sui* and thus as a useless passion. And, of course, Levinas cannot leave it at this. The passion that he recognizes in the Other is much closer to – surprisingly as this may sound both to him and his readers – the Passion of Christ, in Gethsemane for example[13]. For the Other is dis-figured by God: instead of letting the chalice pass, God puts the Other in His trace, thus providing him not only with the infinity but also with the pain that prevents his face from coming to rest in his form. In other words: when Levinas says that the Other is "in the trace of God", he is commenting in another register on the result of his phenomenological distinction between the face of the Other and the form – or: the figure – of the Other. Racism, as a consequence, then becomes a kind of inverted idolatry: by reducing the Other to his 'form' or his 'context' or his 'role', it is refusing to take notice of the gap in the Other that prevents him from being only a figure. Racism is a figuration of the Other that misrecognizes his initial dis-figuration. However paradoxical it may sound, one would still be within Levinas's own logic, if one would see in racism but the mirror-side of the divinization of the Other that is so popular in our culture. For to say that the Other is *in the trace of* God, is to state that he is not God, and that God is "other than the Other" (CPP 165).

13. Although Levinas has on different occasions pointed to the importance of the Christian idea of *kenosis* and presented it as some sort of middle ground on which the Jewish and Christian traditions could meet, it would seem to me that he would refuse to put the accent where Christianity has put it: God 'incarnates' and becomes human in Christ perhaps most clearly at the point where the Son asks his Father "to let that chalice pass". In this weakness and this anxiety of Christ, incarnation gets its deepest kenotic significance and already points to the Cross. In contrast, Levinas stresses what in the *kenotic* emptying out of God resembles the ethical haemorrhage of a proximity in which I bleed for the Other. My point would rather be, as I explain in what follows, that if there is to be a parallel at all with *kenosis*, it should be sought *in the misery of the Other*, who *suffers* from his "incarnation": like Christ, every Other is but the son of God, and not God himself, and therefore the face of the Other that bursts through the form, at the same time announces the glory of a Height and the misery of a nakedness. If read in this – paradoxically more "Christian" way – certain passages in *Otherwise than Being* could perhaps be turned against a criticism of Levinas that I have formulated elsewhere in this volume – e.g. OB, p. 90 on the "ambiguity" of the face, which later brings Levinas to the following question: "And yet as a destitution, a trace or shadow of itself and an accusation, a face makes itself an apparition and *an epiphany*; it shows itself to a cognition as though the plane of the known were all the same ultimate, and cognition all-inclusive. Does a face abide *both* in representation and in proximity; is it community and difference? What meaning can community take on in difference without reducing difference? (…) Have we eliminated from signification *the idea of lack and want of presence? Have we removed from the idea of enigma, where infinity comes to pass, the idea of uncertainty?*". One should no doubt, in reading Levinas, avoid giving too quick an answer to this crucial question. Which means that *one must hear it first*.

And perhaps Levinas is one of those very few contemporary philosophers who still realize that in order to think intersubjectivity to its end, one does not need two, but three terms – and thus a *ménage à trois*.

For it is evident that this new register is not just an arbitrary redescription of the difference between the face and the form of the Other. However embarrassing and even superfluous the use of the word 'God' in this context may seem to some of Levinas's readers, it is absolutely central to his preoccupations. For if the Other would not be in the trace of God and if I would not hear, as Levinas repeatedly stresses, "the word *of God* in the face of the Other"[14], I would not be able to hear the Other in his absolute otherness at all. His appeal, instead of reaching me and of not being able to miss me, would never arrive. Or if it did, it would be so ab-solute, so other that the sheer weight of its alterity would crush me. In other words, what I am stressing here is that the introduction of the word 'God' is Levinas's *metaphysical* answer to a problem that cannot be fully resolved or even understood as long as one stays at the *ethical-phenomenological* level of the description of the face of the Other. In *Time and the Other,* for example, he could only point to this problem, but not really resolve it: "How can a being enter into relation with the other without allowing its very self to be crushed by the other?" (TO 77); or again near the end of that early piece: "How, in the alterity of a you, can I remain I, without being absorbed or losing myself in that you? How can the ego that I am remain myself in a you, without being nonetheless the ego that I am in my present – that is to say, an ego that inevitably returns to itself? How can the ego become other to itself?" (TO 91). As Levinas increasingly came to realize, 'paternity' is not a good enough answer to these questions. It is perhaps not an answer at all, and certainly an unattractive one, opening the gates to just those evil spirits that he was trying to ban. Let me briefly insist on this point for it will take us into the heart of the structure that Levinas is referring to when linking racism to a tribalism that can only be superseded when "in the brother himself, the stranger is recognized"[15].

This move 'beyond the tribal' is also, if not first and foremost, a move beyond or better: 'before' paternity. For 'paternity' as it was introduced in *Time and the Other* and as it is in a sense still operative in *Totality and Infinity* (but significantly, now in a part entitled '*beyond* the face'), involves a relation between the father and the son and thus always risks returning to a particularism at odds with Levinas's project of finding access to a true universality. To be sure, Levinas will later qualify this analysis and state that

14. E. LEVINAS, *Altérité et Transcendance*, s.l., Fata Morgana, 1995, p. 114.

15. 'La vocation de l'autre', in *Racismes: l'Autre et son visage. Grands entretiens réalisés par Emmanuel Hirsch*, Paris, Les Éditions du Cerf, 1988, p. 96.

every other can be in the position of my son, but it is not clear whether this is a convincing move to make. For, as one will remember, the son in *Time and the Other* was precisely put in the position of that "you" that allowed me, *as a father*, "to remain I without being absorbed or losing myself in that you" (TO 91, quoted above). He was the figure of that stranger "who, entirely while being Other, *is myself*" (*ibid.*). More or differently other than my "work", not a "property" which I have since "I am in some way my child", and yet more than an "alter ego" and thus the bearer of a structure which will prevent my ego from "returning to itself" and let it escape from the loop in which, as we have seen, its incomplete victory over the *il y a* has kept it running in circles. In the relation-without-relation between the father and the son, a perspective perpendicular to the *conatus essendi* was opened and thus an intimation of a fuller "freedom" (TO 91) was announced: "In fecundity the I transcends the world of light – not to dissolve into the anonymity of the *il y a*, but in order to go further than the light, to go *elsewhere*" (TI 268, Levinas's italics). But this "elsewhere" in which Levinas sees "the tedium of repetition cease" (*ibid.*) and wishes to recognize "the transcendence of trans-substantion" in which "the I is, in the child, an other" (TI 267), is still the elsewhere of the one whom I can call *my* child. And one need only think of the difference between my biological children and my intellectual children – those springing forth from what the German optimistically calls my position as a *Doktor-Vater* (a 'supervisor' as the English more brutally puts it) – to realize that it is perhaps no coincidence that Levinas should be downplaying here the importance of this possessive pronoun which points to *what is beyond the symbolic in paternity*. No matter how other my children may turn out to be, even if they have become so other that I can in no way recognize even the slightest trait of myself in them, I can and will still find *consolation* in the thought that they are my own, *my flesh and blood* and that they bear *my name*. And I cannot find this consolation in a teacher to student relation where the fact that I am a promoter will at best only be noted in a preface and where no matter how strong my imprint or my influence on this work may have been, its success in some sense depends on its ingratitude and perhaps even on its erasing that minimum of symbolic recognition of my being credited here or there in a footnote. This Other is more absolutely other than my son, and more is asked of me here. In a sense an absolute gratuity is presupposed by this structure which has no longer anything in it to console me with. And for that very reason, the "tedium of repetition" is also interrupted at a deeper level than it could ever be within the bounds of a physiological-cum-symbolic fecundity.

Levinas's tendency to present the biological as of no significance whatsoever for a philosophical analysis of paternity, also explains the optimism with which for a while he believed he had found in paternity an answer to the problem he had posed himself since *Time and the Other*. But this optimism does not stand up under analysis: the consolation that this Other, my son, however other he may be, is still my flesh and bones has at its reverse-side the possible continuation of the terror of the *il y a* which is all but defeated in the relation between the father and the son. Indeed, as any father will recognize and perhaps forgive Levinas for not mentioning, it is not always gratifying to our narcissism when we are suddenly struck by a certain likeness between our children and us: for what is thus repeated in the child is not always the best of ourselves, it could be that in us which we have fought against all our lives and which indifferent to this fight, now atavistically returns in this or that character trait of the son who isn't even aware of it. Belittling all our efforts to interrupt the repetition of the chain of being, we meet what we hated in our fathers, in their grand-children and in the *nausea* of existence which overcomes us at such moments, the *il y a* which Levinas himself has not for nothing called the *etcetera*[16], would take over from us and drown us, were it not that in such moments our position as fathers in the symbolic order can function as both a life- and a safety-belt: no matter how great my nausea, I am still a father and this symbolic designation can help to make me bear that pain that I would not have been able to *anaesthetize* myself.

It is, of course, no coincidence that this is the second time this word comes up in the midst of my exposition of Levinas. But it shouldn't surprise those who remember that I shamelessly promised to court the enemy that I was later going to turn against. All the better, then, if my Sartre will make some of my readers think of Lacan, as long as they have the patience to realize that it is still too soon to put all the cards on the table. What we learned from this brief excursus into paternity at this point only serves to clarify what Levinas has in mind with going 'beyond the tribal' and explicitly commenting on this by the Biblical reference to a God in which we all can recognize ourselves as his "children": "Filiality of the transcendence. The superior form of piety, above all tribal link: to address oneself to God as to the Father"[17] – sentences uttered in the course of an interview on racism! But as I am trying to show, these 'religious' sentences are not without a counterpart in the metaphysics motivated by and underlying Levinas's ethics. For it is not just a figure of speech or the intrusion of

16. 'Emmanuel Lévinas: visage et violence première (phénoménologie de l'éthique). Une interview', in A. MÜNSTER (ed.), *La différence comme non-indifférence. Ethique et altérité chez Emmanuel Lévinas*, Paris, Editions Kimé, 1995, p. 138.

17. 'La vocation de l'autre', *l.c.*, p. 96.

an alien vocabulary into his philosophy, when Levinas states that in the face of the Other I hear "the word of God". Indeed, racism in its very denial of a face to the Other, in its *figuration* of the Other, is a refusal to hear this word, and thus an attempt to close itself to this voice which in the appeal of the Other I cannot not hear.

Perhaps we should start here: with this strange fact that, whatever will be my response to the appeal of the Other, I cannot not hear it. And with the even stranger fact that this has nothing to do with the Other, but with the very structure of my being or if one prefers, with the trace in it of a familiarity with an otherwise than being. For I am a creature and it is to this "creature status" (OB 92/117: *créaturialité*) that Levinas is referring when he likens the structure of responsibility to "a sound" that becomes "audible only in its echo" (OB 106). Responsibility as the echo of something preceding it and that never shows up as such, is the *belated* effect of the word of God in me: "The order that orders me to the Other *does not show itself to me*, save through the trace of its reclusion, as a face of a neighbour. There is the trace of a withdrawal which no actuality had preceded, and *which becomes present only in my own voice*, already obedient" (OB 140). It is this situation of finding myself already responsible, "despite-me, for-another" (OB 11), already "ordered toward the face of the other" (*ibid.*), that Levinas is trying to do justice to by linking it to the concept of *creatio ex nihilo* which is already underpinning the metaphysical depth structure of *Totality and Infinity*. The problem to be solved is that on the one hand responsibility involves a "response" which "answers, before any understanding, for a debt contracted before any freedom" (OB 12) since my obligation to the other does not follow from a signed contract between him and me, nor from any other contract at which I was present as a signatory; but on the other hand, this "debt *before* any freedom" cannot just put me in the position of an effect that follows the course set for it by its cause, because then it could not give rise to my freedom and the appeal of the other would be but a physical stimulus that profits from an already established stimulus-response pattern to get from me what it wants. And yet, as I kept insisting, this appeal will somehow have to ring a bell in me for otherwise it would not even be noticed: "Something already concluded appears in my relation with another. It is there that I run up against the immemorial"[18]. And Levinas's solution is to treat the appeal of the Other as the echo-chamber, as it were, in which the sound of a bell which was ringing in me all along, not only becomes audible for the first time *but also finds its one and only meaning* which is, of course, ethical.

Were it not for the Other who comes, as it were, between me and God, my status as a created being would first and foremost, if not only, involve a

18. E. LEVINAS, *Of God Who Comes to Mind*, Stanford U.P., 1998, p. 96.

relation between me and my creator. I would discover myself as dependent and finite, but it would be difficult to see how this dependence would not "absorb" the dependent being, and how it could "*at the same time*" maintain its "independence" (TI 88). The concept of creation *ex nihilo* is introduced to elucidate the structure of this 'at the same time': it "leaves to the creature a trace of dependence, but it is an unparalleled dependence: the dependent being draws from this exceptional dependence, from this relationship, its very independence ... its separation with regard to the Infinite" (TI 104-5). Independence and separation mean rupture with participation and thus with what Levinas calls 'the sacred': instead of taking possession of His creatures, this God allows them to remain ignorant of their Creator, i.e. in Levinas's vocabulary: to be atheists. Instead of revealing Himself to them, "burning" them with the "numinous" impression of His revelation, He has the humility to withdraw "in a contraction that leaves a place for the separated being" (TI 104). But this also means that Man is put into a position from which he can "redeem creation" (*ibid.*) – not by engaging in a direct relation with God, but in a social relationship with the Others who come in His trace. For it is the ethical responsibility toward each and every one of these Others in which I find, that is, discover, myself, which is the trace of the unparalleled dependence that Levinas was talking about: in this dependence I am free to act as a responsible, independent being for whom "learning that it is created" amounts to "putting itself in question" (TI 89): "The *miracle* of creation lies in creating a moral being". And, as Levinas concludes, "this implies precisely atheism, but at the same time, beyond atheism, shame for the arbitrariness of the freedom that constitutes it" (*ibid.*).

From this one can infer what the absence of shame in racism really amounts to for Levinas: it is an attempt to take the appeal of the face of the Other at its face-*value* by cutting it off and disconnecting it from the sound that was to find in it its echo. And thus he would think of racism as an atheism of a different sort: one that not just ignores its Creator, but that chooses to remain ignorant by refusing to take the opportunity to enter into man's "true condition" which Levinas, – as one could by now have guessed – calls his "religious being" (cf. TI 253, quoted in note 6). For a religious being is a being that does not "weigh on (its) own account" (OB 159). It is a being which is under the Law which since time immemorial has "bound" it (OB 76) with others and "destined" it[19] to others before connecting it to itself. Therefore, the only way for the religious being to live its true condition is to engage in the intrigue that the Infinite has plotted for it, i.e.,

---

19. *Ibid.*, p. 165; the French original has 'voué' which could also be translated as 'devoted': *De Dieu qui vient à l'idée*, Paris, Vrin, 1992, p. 249.

the ethical relationship with the Other. Only in this condition where as a responsible being I lose all my rights and owe everything to the Other – to all the Others – can I experience *the grace* of receiving a place next to them[20]. For grace, which is a religious term, seems only to have meaning for Levinas "within the realm of ethics"[21]: it is the unexpected result that befalls me through an exacerbation of the infinite sacrifice implied by the ethical relationship. For I owe not just everything to this one other but to all the others and since they are all in the trace of the same God, they are all in an equally asymmetric position toward me. And at this point of my extremest confusion, as I turn my head from one to the other, not knowing where to go first, in this very turn of my head, in that second in which I am neither with the one nor with the other, the grace of light touches me and allows me a moment for myself: while turning my head, I can start thinking, comparing and calculating. In short, I can be with myself. The *cogito* and the subject of liberal rights, indeed the infamous subject of 'metaphysics' as such, result from a hypertrophy of ethics. But since the reason which is born here is a reason that does not gravitate in itself, Athens will need Jerusalem to remind it of the true meaning of its orphanage.

It should come as no surprise, then, that this point in our history where we are witness to an unprecedented explosion of instrumental rationality, should also be marked by a return to tribalism. For Levinas both are but the reverse side of each other: symptoms of Reason and Culture finding their weight in themselves and engaged in a pointless joust in which each of them tries to carry more weight than the other. Racism is but a symptom of the religious crisis in the West and if it takes on the at first sight contradictory features of atheism and idolatry, of a denial of God and of a return of the sacred, this is because the God who is dying here is not just the God of metaphysics and ontotheology, but a God otherwise than Being, whose contraction has put him "in permanent danger of turning into a protector of all the egoisms" (OB 161).

IV

With this last salvo the war is over. Which is not the same as won. For we still have to count the casualties. And on all sides. Things have, of course, been going a bit quickly, as is the case with our modern wars that as Bau-

---

20. I am commenting here on the notoriously difficult third paragraph of OB 158 where Levinas is using the word "grace".

21. Cf. *Nouvelles Lectures Talmudiques*, Paris, Minuit, 1996, p. 30: "L'éthique n'est pas le corollaire du religieux. Il est, de soi, l'élément où la transcendance religieuse peut avoir un sens". On this quote, cf. chapter 10 above.

drillard says, 'do not take place'. So we should perhaps replay to find out what exactly has happened. And as we wait for the tape to rewind, I cannot resist the temptation to reveal who has been my secret addressee here – for there must be someone in the position of *Agathon* given that I have associated myself with Alcibiades and placed Levinas in the position of Socrates. I do not mean this disrespectfully, all the less so since there is clearly something 'Alcibiadic' about the sort of questions with which the author I am going to put here in the position of Agathon, had been disturbing himself – and could it be a coincidence? – one of the many Symposia around Levinas. I am thinking, of course, of Robert Bernasconi, one of Levinas's readers and commentators of the first hour, and in particular of a question he put at such a Symposium and which is worth quoting here in full since it gives voice to an objection that I cannot imagine not to have crossed the reader's mind as he or she was watching that formidable display of forces with which Levinas was trying to impress Sartre: "is Levinas's account of the encounter with the Other as a stranger", Bernasconi asked, "sufficiently nuanced as to be able to welcome the Other in his or her ethnic identity beyond the prejudices that divide ethnic groups?"[22] (QGWT 22). This was a good and important question to pose and with the advantage of hindsight, one can only wonder why it came to be raised so relatively late in the Levinas-reception, especially if one takes account of the impressive amount of quotations from Levinas Bernasconi was able to refer to in order to show that he was not inventing this question out of thin air. Let me just point here to one very central quote that is by no means a *hapax legomenon* since Levinas kept repeating this same sentence in different interviews: "I always say – but in private – that the Greeks and the Bible are all that is serious in humanity. Everything else is dancing" (quoted in QGWT 14)[23]. One can understand why sentences like these prompted Bernasconi to his question and made him become skeptical vis-à-

---

22. R. BERNASCONI, 'Who is my neighbor? Who is the Other? Questioning "the Generosity of Western Thought" ', in *Ethics and Responsibility in the Phenomenological Tradition. The ninth Annual Symposium of the Simon Silverman Phenomenology Center*, Pittsburgh, Duquesne University, 1992, p. 22. Henceforth quoted as QGWT. I owe a lot to this article which helped me to raise some of the questions that I try to formulate here.

23. Cf. apart from the references in Bernasconi, similar passages e.g. in E. LEVINAS, *Beyond the Verse. Talmudic Readings and Lectures*, London, The Athlone Press, 1994, p. 198 ('Everything else is local colour'); 'Entretiens avec Emmanuel Lévinas', in Fr. POIRIÉ, *Emmanuel Lévinas*, Besançon, La Manufacture, 1992, p. 103: "Je dis parfois: l'homme c'est l'Europe et la Bible, *et tout le reste peut s'y traduire*" – which is a thought that one finds expressed in various ways throughout Levinas's Talmudic writings. In this context, see also: DF, p. 137: "And it is not always the idylls that have been destroyed by Europe's penetration of the world".

vis "the generosity of Western thought" (CPP 101) to which Levinas was referring in the very same pages in which he developed his attack on culturalism and relativism most strongly and pleaded for a priority of ethics over both culture and reason. And yet, I cannot but firmly disagree with Bernasconi's attempt at the end of that paper to split the differences and to see in Levinas on the one hand the unfortunate victim of a long-standing "idea of the West (that) seems to be what protects him from an encounter between cultures at the level of alterity" (QGWT 25) all the while, on the other hand, refusing "to deny the resources his thought offers for breaking through the dominant schema of Western dogmatism" (QGWT 26). It is this hesitation which is not just Bernasconi's but that of a whole generation of 'deconstructivist' Levinas-readers (I am not using this expression as a sneer, but as a rough sociological category), that made me decide with all due apologies, to place him metonymically in the position of Agathon here, i.e. of the one whom I would most like to corrupt.

For I think that in the terms of the battle that I have been staging here, there can be little doubt that this "idea of the West", this conjunction of Athens and Jerusalem and the accompanying neglect of all "the rest", is by far more central to Levinas's philosophy than Bernasconi is willing to admit. In other words, it would seem that it is this very central idea of a conjunction between the Greek and the Judaic traditions rather than the slightly peripheral idea of the West which, for Levinas, would make it not just difficult to acknowledge, but even to take seriously the kind of objections that Bernasconi and I would like to address to him. Indeed, everything in that idea and all the ramifications of which I have shown it to be quilting point in Levinas's thought, would seem to oppose him to the intuition that guides these questions which I repeat, I share with Bernasconi. For what difference could it make to speak of the ethnically different Other and how can one even suggest that to take account of this difference, Levinas's thought would need to be further developed or opened to other resources contained in it but suppressed by a relic of Eurocentrism? As we have seen, for Levinas the Other's alterity does not follow from his, in this case: ethnic difference but precedes it just as ethics precedes culture. To suggest that the Other's difference and, for example, the colour of his or her skin should make a difference to this alterity would mean for Levinas that one has already conceded to racism the very ground from which it springs: to respect the Other not as an Other "without any cultural adornment" (CPP 96) but as an ethnic Other, would be to contextualize him again and to expose him to the sacred absorptive powers by which his ethnic group or his culture or his context try to take possession of him. Just as to suggest that it could make a difference whether someone's face is black or white, would already be enough for Levinas to suspect that the whole edifice on which the distinction between the face and the form of the Other, between his gaze and the colour of his eyes, is kept in careful balance, would be in danger of collapsing.

And perhaps it is. For it is evident that the reason why these objections cannot be heard by Levinas *in the way* they are meant, is because they do not fit in the economy of the visible and the invisible that governs *the whole of his thought*, and that is ultimately the economy between 'being' and 'Otherwise than being', underlying all the further oppositions between the *visible* form and the *invisible* face, between the said and the saying, between context (form or role) and signification without context (face), between totality and infinity. It is oppositions such as these which block the entrance to the question that is truly at stake here and that cannot leave us indifferent for it concerns the misery of the Other. For the Other that Bernasconi and I are talking about, is an Other who is – in my words – '*not without* context', '*not without* form', '*not without* culture', etc.: not just a colourless face, but neither that colourful form in which his face has disappeared; not just an abstract man, but neither a mere sample of his culture. And this is why it is important for him that he should not just be recognized in his humanity, as an "abstract man" (CPP 101, in the etymological sense of dis-engaged), as a face without context, but as different from this abstract humanity, as a black who cannot be reduced to his blackness, but who would also feel reduced if told that his colour doesn't matter. And the examples can be multiplied. But their general point would seem to be that people want to be recognized neither because of a difference that precedes their alterity nor because of an alterity that precedes their difference. They want to be recognized because there is a difference that is not indifferent to their alterity and from which they cannot let the latter be abstracted. But they also refuse to let themselves be reduced to this difference because that reduction would imply that such difference is not only not indifferent to them, but that they also know why, – which they don't: a black does not know what it means to be black and that is why he is angry not just with those who discriminate against him because of his colour, or with those who respect him notwithstanding his colour, but also with those whose respect would somehow be based on the suggestion that he – the person who respects – can understand why the other's colour means so much to that other[24]. For neither of us understands the meaning of our colour, or of our culture or of anything else which we find hard to eidetically variate without losing our singularity. Neither of

---

24. Hence the well-known experience of all those white anti-racists, male feminists, etc. who after displaying for years model behaviour, suddenly find themselves accused, and apparently for no reason at all, of anti-black feelings, sexism, etc.

these is indifferent to us; indeed many of them would be a breaking point, and yet we do not know why. Any other who suggests he does and implies that we do, however tolerant he may think himself to be, will meet with a more acrimonious resistance than those who discriminate us openly or those who do so indirectly by respecting us for the wrong reasons. For, as Sartre would have said, such an Other is doing more than holding back our un-revealed from us, *he is suggesting that it is as revealed to us as it is to him*.

And yet, to be entirely consistent with the full picture of the battle between Sartre and Levinas that I have sketched before, this rehabilitation of Sartre which I am announcing here, can only be momentary. For in truth, Sartre would not have approved of what I just said. Indeed, he could not without belying the very premise on which his whole analysis rests. As one will remember, for Sartre the non-revealed was a non-revealed *for me*, but a revealed for the other. Without the gaze of that Other, there would be no such non-revealed, but only a For-itself. As a result, Sartre has to blame the Other for *imposing* this non-revealed on me, and there is nothing in his analysis which can stop the For-itself from correctly inferring from that premise that the Other is the *cause* of my alienation and thus from plotting ways in which to rid me of that obstacle. The problem with my facticity, with the colour of my skin for example, comes from the Other who invests it with *a meaning* that escapes me. Were it not for this Other, I could choose to invest it with a *meaning* of my own: all facticity, which for Sartre is but the contingent form that the necessity of our contingence (of our not being *causa sui*) takes, is thus presented as compatible with the freedom of the For-itself to give it the meaning it *chooses* to give it (BN 328, 523 ff.). Sartre would be right to protest, then, against my using his language for implying an entirely different structure: that of an un-revealed that is not only not a revealed to us, but also not to the Other. To be sure, we would not be confronted with it, were it not for the Other, but the truth or the meaning of what we are thus confronted with, does not rest in the Other. Indeed, the problem seems to be that we are confronted here with something about us – something in which we recognize our singularity – that does not leave us indifferent but not because its meaning is kept from us by the Other, but because we feel indebted to it, without us knowing what that debt amounts to. Nor do we suspect that the Other knows – indeed, what we find most irritating is an Other who implies that he knows what we know. For we do not know, and yet we suffer. We suffer because we are alone with this debt and because it does not tell us what it wants from us. We don't know what it means to be white, but we feel that we wouldn't be the same if we were black and *vice versa*. And even though we can choose to give a meaning to this our colour, we know that that choice will never be enough to satisfy that law which has left its mark on us but which was cruel enough not to tell us its meaning. *Man is a being*, I am suggesting, *whose being consists in caring for something that does not care for it*. This mark which has marked my being to the point of singularizing it, does not speak. It is "weighing" upon me, but not as a cause on its effect. For between this effect which is me, in my irreplaceable singularity, and that cause, there is a hiatus, a gap or a rift which I cannot close, nor can anyone else. I am a split subject, carrying an other in me that I have to distrust and yet cannot betray even though I do not know what it means to be loyal to it.

As the reader no doubt noticed, in using the expression "weighing but not as a cause on its effect" I shamelessly availed myself of Levinas's vocabulary to turn my back to Sartre, – as one does with allies who are no longer of any use. But if I slaughtered Sartre with a Levinasian knife, I was profaning it at the same time and putting it to a use of which Levinas would not approve. Indeed, how could he without allowing me to disconnect what he had taken himself such pains to connect? I am referring, of course, to Levinas's attempt to interpret both the misery and the dignity of the Other as the effect of the same dis-figuring rift that is opened up, though in different ways, not just in the Other, but also in me by the passage of a God who has always already passed. The introduction of this God who – as Levinas says in a rarely quoted, but very central passage – "sees the invisible and *sees without being seen*" (TI 244), allowed Levinas to project onto a point, both outside me and outside the other, the cause for the trouble between us in the Sartrean universe, where as one will remember both I and the Other were trying to occupy for good that place where one *would see without being seen*. By putting God on that place and reserving it for Him alone, Levinas could silence Sartre by beating him on his own terrain. Levinas keeps the place that was occupied in Sartre's analysis by the *personal* gaze of the intersubjective other (to whom the meaning that escapes me – my non-revealed – was supposed to be revealed), but he expels the intersubjective other from it and puts God in his stead. But he does not contest to Sartre that there is a *personal* gaze and thus a meaning and a deeper 'truth' to subjectivity. He only locates that gaze differently. Indeed, what Levinas calls 'God' is the name for that meaning and that deeper truth that escape me, but the secret of which is not revealed to the ethical Other. As a consequence, that Other cannot be blamed (as the other is in Sartre) for keeping a secret from me. He is, to the contrary, related to me, because there is a meaning with which he is invested and through which he can make me escape myself. This 'ethical' meaning which does not originate in the Other, nor, of course, in me, is a Meaning that orients and de-neutralizes the space between me and the Other and turns it into an ethical *proximity* in which

I am *for the Other*. 'God' is Levinas's name for this 'curvature' of intersubjective space (TI 291). And ethics, consequently, becomes that realm in which the 'to be seen without seeing' which created such havock in Sartre, instead of effecting an alienation that crushes the subject, imposes on it a metanoia that thoroughly alters it. Ethics would not or could not be that realm if there were only (as in Sartre) me and the other, and if there was not a Third who could, as it were, take the blame for 'seeing without being seen' upon Him. In other words, because Levinas locates what one could call with Lacan the gaze of the big Other outside of the relation between me and the other, the violence which Sartre made endemic to intersubjectivity (by letting the gaze of the intersubjective other *coincide* with the gaze of the big Other) can be siphoned out of it, and the gaze of the intersubjective other can become that of a face in need.

In thus putting peace *before* war, ethics can become, for Levinas, that realm in which peace is given a chance. 'God' is the name for the move that guarantees *that chance* – He is not a guarantor of peace, but of the *possibility* of peace. 'War', conversely, is, for Levinas, the name for what happens when transcendence becomes immanentized: war breaks out as soon as what we called the gaze of the *big* Other becomes incarnated in the gaze of a 'small', intersubjective other (it is thus the result of not 'distinguishing' between the alterity of God and that of the face that comes only in His trace)[25]. 'Meaning' will then inevitably lose its transcendence and degrade to the status of a secret that is kept from me – i.e. from an 'I' that believes that it could be without secrets and in full possession of itself (even if that self is the self of a For-itself that is what it is not and is not what it is, i.e. a pure openness without 'attachment') were it not for *this* other whose very otherness reveals to him what is not revealed to me. 'God', by contrast, is the name for a dispossession which does not result from the introduction of another subject supposed to possess what it holds from me, but 'God' by being Other than the other, by taking the place of the gaze of the 'big Other', and by being Other than me, opens the realm of intersubjectivity as such and gives it an orientation that interconnects in a non-neutral 'asymmetry' both me and the other. Having slipped in me "like a thief", "unbeknowst to me" (OB 148), (what Levinas calls) 'God' thus allows for the possibility of a *metanoia* that Sartre had been unable to think: the *conversion* in which I am "trans-figured" (TI 246), however painful that process may be, is a purification in which I reach my "last reality": "Responsibility in fact is not a simple attribute of subjectivity, as if the latter already existed in itself, before the ethical relationship. Subjectivity is not for itself; it is, once again,

25. See above, chapter 10.

initially for another"[26]. Without the concept of a creator *ex nihilo* who left in me a "trace" of an "unparalleled dependence" (TI 104, quoted above), Levinas would not be able to think the 'initiality' of this 'initially for another'. 'God' is the name *or the structure* that allows him to state that "paradoxically it is qua *alienus* – foreigner and other – that man is *not alienated*" (OB 59). Just as it is the Goodness of this God that has "chosen me before I have chosen it" (OB 11) that allows Levinas to repeat time and again, that it "reabsorbs, or redeems the violence of non-freedom" (OB 123) by which it has come to weigh on me. Without this violence I would never have come to find myself responsible and thus, 'for the first time' says Levinas, *without ever explaining the firstness of this first time*[27], a truly unique and irreplaceable, for responsible subject.

But perhaps it is no accident that Levinas never explains the firstness of this first time. For he cannot do so without thereby pointing to the weak spot underlying his whole argument. I am referring to the fact that if Levinas would allow me to already be a fully singular subject before ethics comes in, the whole process of ethical redescription that he is explicitly introducing with the appeal of the Other 'that I cannot not hear' should be rethought. As I tried to explain, the word 'God' and the accompanying idea of *creatio ex nihilo* served to clarify the structure of this double 'not' on a metaphysical level; it is Levinas's answer to the problem of how an absolute alterity can reach me, without crushing me and doing away with my independence. Thus, although I cannot but hear the Other's appeal, I am still free to take it up or not. But if I don't, this neglect will be ethically qualified: it will be Evil, resulting from my *decision* to side with the *conatus essendi* in me. And this is the central operation underlying what I just referred to as ethical redescription: the pretension that 'the light of ethics' can catch everything preceding that light in me. Before the Other humanized me, I was 'nature' driven by the force of the *conatus essendi*; in this 'aesthetic stage' I was egocentric but not in a moral sense. I could not but involuntarily relate everything else to me. But this egocentrism will shift to egoism as soon as I am put before the choice between being for me and giving in to my *conatus* or being for the Other. And Levinas can only suggest that these are the terms of the choice, because he thinks that I am "initially for the other". Giving up being for myself, will then mean to give up finding my point of gravitation in myself and to reach contact as it were with my *true* gravitational point, my "final reality" which is to be for the other. 'God' is still a personal gaze in as much as by giving weight to the gaze of the other, it is in the last instance the trace of God in both me and the other that

26. E. LEVINAS, *Ethics and Infinity, o.c.*, p. 96.
27. See note 8 above.

prevents the gaze of the other from confronting me with the kind of alienation that Bernasconi and I are explicitly – in my case – or implicitly – as should be the case in Bernasconi if his doubts are to carry any weight – supposing.

This alienation has to do with the fact that we believe that *already before ethics man is a being whose being consists in caring for something that does not care for him*. And this something can take various shapes, it can hide in the colour of our skin for example, but it points to a general structure: man is singularized by a mark which he cannot read – and this dyslexia inspires terror in him, which is why he tries to turn away from it and to associate with others in common symbolic circuits of recognition which provide him with tentative answers to the problem he has to face: how to deal with a vague debt that obliges him from within, but at the same time from without since this debt by being vague and refusing to tell us how we have to pay it off, as it were breaks open our intimacy, constitutes an outside in our inside, and turns us into decentred beings that are already gravitating around a centre from which they cannot get away but to which they at the same time cannot find access. The gaze of the other, according to this reasoning, does not so much provoke shame in us as it makes us uncertain, and brings us to the point of panic for it confronts us with something *in* us that we had to look away from in order not to be lamed by its terror. For in the wake of this gaze it would seem as if *another* gaze is awakened: the gaze of the ex-timate in our intimacy, the gaze that reminds us of the vagueness of the debt which singularizes each of us.

It is this second gaze which is awakened in us by the gaze of the other, which I would call *the impersonal gaze*, and which I believe to undermine the structure of and the assumptions behind Levinas's 'ethicization': for if this gaze sets me in panic, it is because it is not something that is meant to be felt. Rather it comes from a point that we all try to look away from and protect ourselves against – indeed, the self or the ego could be shown to be already such a defence-structure. In Levinas's terms this would mean that what he calls the hypostasis (the erection of the subject) is not just formed *against* the *il y a* but as it were 'around it', in an attempt to isolate – or better: 'to bind' – it. And if one thinks of the example of the 'it wakes' that Levinas gives[28], I believe one can see that I am merely taking seriously these early analyses, when I introduce an 'it sees' and link it to the problem of racism on phenomenological grounds. Indeed, what I said about the fate of the tolerant anti-racist who will sooner or later be confronted out of the blue with the incrimination that he is still a racist, can only be taken seriously if one takes seriously the thought that my skin, by 'looking' at the other, as it

28. See above, chapter 9.

were unloosens a gaze 'in' him, a gaze that splits him and is looking at him via the colour of his skin. That colour is not nothing, without it the other would be a different human being. It is thus part of his singularity, but it does not tell him what it stands for and it thus confronts him with the fact that in his being he has to care for something that interferes with his being but that refuses to be satisfied with being just a visible part in it.

This second 'gaze' is neither good or bad. It comes before the Good that vows me to the other before being vowed to myself. For what my colour does to him, his is doing to me, and without the word 'God' and the structure that it stands for, the gaze which I awaken in him and the one he awakens in me are neither interconnected nor hierarchisized – if my panic were shame, as Levinas does and must presuppose, these two gazes would meet: the misery of the other who 'suffers' from not being able to see his own colour and from being exposed to its impersonal gaze, would be an appeal through which both myself and my relation to him are personalized. And however demanding that appeal would be for me, it would still bring with it the unexpected comfort of an even fuller singularity[29] than the one I had before. The gaze behind the gaze of the other, the gaze of the big Other from which that gaze derives its authority over me and without which it could not strike me with the weak force of an appeal, is thus basically a good gaze. It is the gaze of the Good through which the personal triumphs over the impersonal. Its role in Levinas's philosophy is to fend off the danger not of an impersonal that triumphs over the personal, but of an impersonal that more intimately belongs to it. If one contests this role, as I think one should, and introduces into Levinas's philosophy the hypothesis of an impersonal gaze that is not opposed to, but part of my – decentred – singularity, one can expect to see the foundering of the hierarchy between good and evil that Levinas not only is, but cannot avoid relying on. As we shall have to ask ourselves in the conclusion to this volume, it could be that what such a gaze is suggesting is that there is not just the Being of Heidegger that Levinas is confronting with the Otherwise than Being of the Good and the *epekeina*, but that there is also an Otherwise than Being that is still otherwise than this Otherwise we find in Levinas. Levinas, as we know from chapter nine, would call it 'transdescendence' – but he has perhaps not given it all the care that it deserved.

But, then again, neither did we. All we know until now is that if man is a being that has to care for something that does not care for it, to care for that something cannot simply mean – that much is clear – to look it, as it were, straight in the face. How could it, since I suggested that to be confronted with it, somehow brings an unrest and even a panic over us? We

29. Again, see note 8 above.

will, then, need to 'anaesthesize' it somehow. Or to turn our back to it. But, as the present chapter suggested, this is exactly what racism does: in ascribing (imaginary) meaning to the colours of the other, in locating it in the mythical hierarchy of race (etc.), racism attempts to get a grip on the impersonal gaze – not just the gaze of the Other, but the gaze in itself. As we shall see in the next chapter, liberalism too can be seen as such an attempt to anaesthetisize a certain something that does not care for us, and that we nonetheless could not (and would not be prepared to) simply leave behind. Which is why the choice we are facing, cannot simply be either for or against 'anaesthetics'. There may be types of 'visibility' – of symbolic structures – that allow us better (!?) than others to cope with the fact that for man the source of his dignity is also the source of his misery.

CHAPTER TWELVE

LOSING FACE
RICHARD RORTY'S LAST WORDS

I recently overheard the announcer of one of those multi-cultural radio programmes reading between the musical interludes excerpts from a book in which she found a variety of amusing anecdotes on the subject of kissing as it is encountered in the four corners of our planet. I vaguely remember from her presentation that the phenomenon was to be found more or less everywhere, although not always in the same fashion or between the same people or with the same meaning. The entire matter was presented with that light mixture of amazement and irony which we often recognize in ourselves when we stop for a moment to reflect on the colourful variety which distinguishes us from the rest of humanity without at the same time making us feel in any way separate from them. What tends to stimulate our sense of 'belonging' at such moments – like a patch 'belongs' in a patchwork quilt – appears to be the realization that the very differences in question do not stand in the way of our solidarity with the rest of humanity but constitute, rather, a sign of solidarity and perhaps even a prerequisite thereof. We suddenly begin to reflect on the ways and times (and, of course, people) we ourselves are in the habit of kissing and something of the tenderness with which we gazed on that colourful collection of slightly differing customs from around the globe begins to reflect on us too. As if the innocent contingency which is at work in such diversity, also casts a particular glow on it, the rays of which somehow manage to bring us closer to one another. For a moment we are under the spell of I don't know what magic which enables us not just to accept others as they are, but also to accept ourselves all the while giving up our usual urge to see in the apparent difference between 'us' and 'them' a problem that can only be solved by forcing 'them' to adapt to 'us' or by 'us' making an effort to adapt to 'them'. In discovering *contingency* we react with the gentle sense of *irony* of a person who feels himself or herself moved to *solidarity*[1].

1. *Contingency, Irony, and Solidarity* is, of course, the title of Richard Rorty's book (Cambridge, Cambridge U.P., 1989) with which I try to discuss in the present chapter. I will refer to it as CIS. Other abbreviations for Rorty: *Essays on Heidegger and Others*. Cambridge U.P., 1991 (= EH); *Objectivity, Relativism, and Truth*. Cambridge U.P., 1991 (= ORT).

Such irony has nothing to do with the well-known and supposedly typical 'ironic' attempt to step back from oneself and to adopt the detached position of the person for whom everything is possible because nothing is really engaging. We are not, therefore, dealing here with the kind of irony Kierkegaard attacked when he characterized the ironist as someone who is driven by an 'interior infinitude' and who through the continuous endeavour to liberate herself from every finite relationship with the self while constantly searching for something new, ends up as an eternal and empty 'I' for whom no given reality is adequate[2]. The attempt to escape one's personal finitude by constantly trying to be somewhere other than where one actually is, distinguishes this type of Kierkegaardian irony from the irony we have been discussing. Indeed, the very gentleness of that feeling which spontaneously engulfs us when we are reminded of the almost folk-loristic variety which characterizes the humanity of which we are a part, is itself, if not the cause, then at least the indication of the fact that at such moments we encounter an aspect of our finitude, in the face of which we feel no particular urge to take our leave. Instead of planning our escape and leaving behind us our finite selves, it seems as if here something of the hurriedness with which we are constantly in search of ourselves is silenced, and as if that uncertainty with respect to ourselves and our ultimate meaning against which the irony described by Kierkegaard tries to protect us, suddenly gives way to a sense of security and acceptance. Although apparently insignificant in itself, the realization that other people do not kiss as we do has the unusual result that we suddenly not only find ourselves willing to accept the differences in question (perhaps unsurprisingly so, for after all they are hardly objectionable) but also – and this is the surprising part – to respond to them in a manner quite *disproportionate to what we actually found* concerning ourselves and others. The gentleness which takes us over and the relative tenderness with which we look at ourselves and others appears to lead momentarily to a sense of solidarity which cannot be but regarded as exceedingly generous by anyone limiting him- or herself to the objective content of that experience of contingency which for no apparent *reason* seems to have the strange power to elicit such feelings of solidarity in us.

As I have already pointed out, we are dealing here with a rather innocent and almost trivial experience of diversity and it would be wrong at this point to lose sight of that innocence and to treat it without further argument as a model for the experience of diversity as such. Obviously, there are less innocent and more demanding encounters with 'the other'. There is, for

2. S. KIERKEGAARD, *The Concept of Irony with Continual Reference to Socrates* (transl. H.V. Hong & E.H. Hong), Princeton 1989, p. 283. Cited in the text as CI.

instance, the contact with an alterity which challenges us because it confronts us with a way of being human which may be interesting and accessible enough to present us with what we could come to regard as a valid way in itself or even as a potential alternative to our way. It suffices that fate places before us such an alternative which, given our enculturation or personal history, we might not otherwise have imagined, to make it seem worthy of consideration and we sometimes might find it even so charming and promising that we may be inclined to give up what we already have or at the very least to make that alternative partly our own. Here, of course what draws us to the other and in so doing changes our relationship with our selves, is far from that innocent difference through which we correspond with one another without being the same as one another and whereby we appear in some strange way to have reconciled ourselves with our own finitude and the finitude of others. For now we meet an other who is not innocently different from us. Indeed, his very otherness benignly reminds us that the project of our own existence is richer in possibilities than we had hitherto imagined. Instead of crudely confronting us with our limitation in time and space, this other, precisely by being finite *as we are*, seems to be inviting us to treat him as one of 'us' and to let us reduce his difference to no more than him having realized things which *in principle* we could have realized ourselves. Although the realizations in question *de facto* are not our realizations, we take this otherness to be more benign than possessive and hence are led to consider them ours *de jure*. Challenging as such a contact with alterity may be, it is also lucrative since there is apparently nothing to it which prevents us from treating it as an alterity *for* us. In short, what comes into existence in such contact with the 'interesting' other is a sort of solidarity of 'project developers'[3]. And just like that mildly ironic solidarity we discussed before, this solidarity too seems to have the capacity to reconcile us with ourselves, as if our finitude, through a strange kind of alchemy, is mixed with the finitude of the other, and in that process somehow becomes less finite.

Of course, other scenarios are still possible, and it is in fact one of these other scripts that brings someone like Rorty to approach the relationship between contingency, irony and solidarity in a manner completely different from anything we have done up to now and to draw conclusions which appear to be incompatible with the intuition which we have allowed to direct us hitherto. What is interesting in Rorty's approach and could provide us with a healthy contrast is that his admirable efforts to draw a line between the logic of ethnocentrism and the logic of (a certain form of) irony

---

3. Cf. my 'Transcultural Vibrations', *Ethical Perspectives*, 1994 (1:2), pp. 89-100.

seem to result in a notion of solidarity which seems less than persuasive[4]. Let me focus on this aspect of Rorty's work for a moment before confronting him with the consequences of having neglected the at first sight trivially different type of irony which we have signalled at the beginning of this essay.

I. Irony versus solidarity

The ironist so feared by Rorty seems to be somewhat similar to the ironist described by Kierkegaard who, like a child, runs headlong from one possibility to the other without ever letting himself be determined by one or other of such possibilities. Like Rorty, Kierkegaard distrusts the bulimic bingeing of one context after another without ever finding a context 'appropriate' to oneself: it betrays the vanity of those who can only maintain themselves by pointing out the vanity of everything else. But whereas Kierkegaard sees in irony the attitude of a subject that takes itself too seriously, Rorty relates the irony in question with an inability on the part of the subject to take itself seriously. This is why Rorty, in contrast to Kierkegaard (CI 257), does not oppose irony to doubt, but rather attempts to define it via an excessive, almost pathological doubt: for Rorty the ironist is someone who "spends her time worrying about the possibility that she has been initiated in the wrong tribe, taught to play the wrong language game" (CIS 75). But this simply means that the ironist is drawing the wrong conclusions from her own finitude. Not that she does not recognize that finitude, for she is aware of the fact that for all of us there will ultimately be a string of 'final words' (a 'final vocabulary') to which we will revert in order to justify our actions or our convictions or our lives (consider, for example, those final and always rather vague words which crop up during discussions between conflicting value systems). The ironist is also aware that there is not only more than one such 'final vocabulary' but that we lack, moreover, a noncircular criterion to enable us to choose between vocabularies and deem one 'more correct' or 'better' or 'truer' than the other. Nevertheless, although she has absolutely no reason to think that the 'final vocabulary' on which she depends might be 'wrong', the ironist is still confronted with "radical and continuing doubts" concerning the vocabulary in question precisely

---

4. As I argued elsewhere there is a considerable confusion in both Rorty himself and his readers as to who is the "true heroine" (as Rorty puts it somewhere) of CIS: the ethnocentrist or the ironist; a confusion which I believe to be the symptom of a certain undecidedness in CIS which I am trying to further interpret in this chapter (see my ' "Hold the Being." How to split Rorty between irony and finitude', *Philosophy & Social Criticism*, 1999 (25:2), pp. 27-45).

because she is "impressed by other vocabularies" (CIS 73). She will be tempted, therefore, to abandon her own final vocabulary and to try out one new vocabulary after another without ever setting her doubts at rest. The ironist suffers, in fact, from her inability to belong 'somewhere' and to allow that 'somewhere' to determine her. At the same time, however, she longs for that 'somewhere' and is very unhappy that 'the affairs' of her tribe continually appear to elude her. What she really wants is to be seized by such 'affairs'. Using Kierkegaard's terminology: the ironist wants to avoid at all costs "reaching beyond the object" (according to Kierkegaard, the fundamental attitude of irony). On the contrary, she wishes to "penetrate the object" (according to Kierkegaard, the frustrated ambition of doubt).

Rorty finds such a desire unhealthy and insists that we should be in a position "to recognize the contingency of the vocabulary with which (we) state (our) highest hopes" while remaining "committed" to it nevertheless (CIS 46). Personal commitment is perfectly combinable with a sensitivity for the finitude or the contingency of the 'horizon' within which or through which such commitment is made possible in the first place. Given that a final vocabulary is not ultimately groundable it would be wrong to conclude that any action performed with reference to such a string of 'final' words would have no meaning. It is precisely the attempt to avoid this error which turns Rorty into an advocate of *ethnocentrism*. For what defines ethnocentrists is that, instead of being "ashamed" of their finitude (CIS 103), they decide to "steer the course" permitted by their vocabulary. Although they consider themselves to be "contingent through and through" they do not experience "any particular doubts about the contingencies they happened to be" (CIS 87). They refuse, for example, to "leap outside their Western social democratic skins" whenever they encounter another culture (ORT 212). From the perspective of the ethnocentrist, then, irony is an illness: it leads to the cheap relativism Rorty refers to as "wet liberalism" – a relativism which has made us "so open-minded that our brains have fallen out" (ORT 203). Such open-mindedness, such relativistic, liberal respect for the otherness of others only leads to seeming solidarity. What actually happens is that the ironist clings like one drowning to every 'other' who happens to be passing by. Instead of seeing in that other someone just as finite and dependent on 'final words' as herself, someone who is equally adrift, the ironist turns the other into a point of anchor and obliges the other to help her escape her finitude. Irony definitely does not lead to solidarity.

But how then could ethnocentrism possibly lead to solidarity? For what distinguishes the ethnocentrist from the ironist is precisely the fact that there is a limit to his openness and to his readiness to place himself in question. The ethnocentrist is really an anti-anti-ethnocentrist, who thinks that he "has to start from where (he) is" and is aware "that this means that there are lots of views which (he) *simply cannot take seriously*" (ORT 29) because they imply beliefs, for example, which cannot in any way be intertwined with his own beliefs. What prevents him being dragged along by ironic self-doubt is the fact that he finds that "the limits of sanity are set by what *we* [i.e. those who share the same final vocabulary] can take seriously" (ORT 187-8). How can one be in solidarity, however, with those who fall out with such boundaries, those we simply take for 'mad'? If *contingency* does not lead to *irony* but to ethnocentrism, does *solidarity* not end up being threatened with extinction?

II. ETHNOCENTRISM VERSUS SOLIDARITY (LEVINAS, HABERMAS)

One has to admit that this is a serious issue, one with which Rorty is not alone in the struggle. The solutions appear to be limited. One might, for example, abandon contingency – and with it the notion of a final vocabulary – and try to salvage solidarity at the cost of finitude. One way or another, then, one will have to propose a vocabulary which has the capacity to decide between the various competing final vocabularies and to provide them with that absolute orientation which they themselves lack by definition. At the very least one would have to provide for a procedure which would allow the conflicting convictions generated by such vocabularies to clash with one other in such a way that the likelihood of arriving at a set of norms equally convincing and therefore binding for all the parties concerned is not *a priori* out of the question. Here one can recognize the respected courses taken by Levinas and Habermas. For someone like Rorty, however, the negotiation of both courses would inevitably be at the cost of those for whom they were originally contrived. Both Levinas and Habermas will propose a procedure, the negotiation of which will oblige one henceforward to follow that new course and no other. A toll will have to be paid for such a procedure, however, one which will force those who follow it to cut into the very flesh of their finitude. Levinas: ethics is a discussion into which one cannot not enter; precondition: in order to provide ethics with such inescapability it will have to "precede" all forms of culture (CPP 100 ff.); premise: the ethical value of the other is to be found in his or her face, i.e. in his or her 'infinity' – that 'surplus' which is too great for the 'form' or the 'context' and which makes the other into an *ab-solute*: someone who, as an ethical other, is "*disengaged* from all culture" (*ibid.* 101). But what if the misery of the other is due precisely to the fact that he or she is *neither* detached from a [cultural] final vocabulary *nor fully contextualized* *by it*⁵? The same problem arises with Habermas: by speaking I already oblige myself to stand up when requested for the claims to validity I make in doing so. I cannot extract myself from such responsibility without a 'performative self-contradiction'; premise: although claims to validity take place within a concrete context, they are not dependent on that context and in fact they *break* that context *open* (same metaphor as Levinas for the relationship face / form [face / context]). If this were not the case then, according to Habermas, the idea of practical or theoretical truth (infinity) would be sacrificed on 'the altar' of context (finitude)⁶. What, however, if there is no truth outside of discourse, outside of that relationship with final vocabularies which Rorty is so wont to emphasize? Hasn't Habermas ma-noeuvred himself into a position where he cannot possibly take seriously the *factum* that we are simply unable to take every conviction seriously? Does Rorty's ethnocentrism, with its norms for 'sanity', not point to a fundamental finitude which expresses itself, for example, in the fact that we are not prepared to sit down with everyone in order to weigh up the various claims to validity because that would already presume that we were at least able to 'hear' what those other people had to say? Does the idea of a final vocabulary, to which we are 'attached' in every sense of the word, not perhaps suggest that there is precisely an inability to hear the other (in the sense of 'take the other seriously') which cannot simply be reduced to the absence of a *readiness* to listen, i.e. to my unwillingness to hear? We can also turn the whole thing around: if our convictions are indeed related to 'final words' as Rorty claims, is it not an outrageous illusion to think that people should be prepared to adjust their convictions in function of the better argument, given that the ground of such argumentation itself escapes argumentation? Do we not then unintentionally inoculate them in this way with the bacteria which destroy the ironist?

One can understand Rorty's opposition to these proposals – in seeing what they would cost us, he is a much better 'economist' and consequently a much 'deeper' thinker (for there can be no depth to a thought which spends ideas as if in Wonderland) than some of his critics would have us believe. Nevertheless, a different solution had to be found and in choosing that solution Rorty had to pay a price for the water-tight distinction he wanted to establish between irony and ethnocentrism.

5. For this line of questioning: chapters 5, 9 and 11 of the present volume.
6. Cf. chapter 3 above.

III. ETHNOCENTRISM AND
LIBERAL SOLIDARITY (RORTY)

The suggestion rings familiar in our ears: in the private sphere everyone does whatever he or she wants; one can even play the ironist if one considers it necessary as long as one does not imagine that one's search for that ideal vocabulary which would be most aptly to one's 'self' should also have any consequences for the public arena. On the contrary, those who enter the public arena are expected to be able to work up the necessary 'mental acrobatics'[7] to turn themselves into ethnocentric liberals, i.e. into people who, in spite of all their private doubts with respect to the final vocabulary in which they were raised, can nevertheless muster the necessary loyalty not to simply toss overboard the common vocabulary of the society in which they accidentally find themselves. At the same time, they are expected to muster *the additional tolerance necessary* to leave alone those people who find themselves in such a society but remain dependent on a different vocabulary (e.g. minorities who do not comply with the standard of 'mental sanity' which the majority maintain 'in spite of themselves') as long as they keep the operation of that final vocabulary within their own private sphere. Accordingly, the ethnocentrist is liberal for two reasons. First, because he sees that "the best way to cause people long-lasting pain is to humiliate them by making the things that seemed most important to them [e.g. 'final words', R. V.] look futile, obsolete and powerless" (CIS 89). Secondly, because he desires a public space which is *neutral* enough to oppose such humiliation. In other words, he desires to afford everyone the *freedom* and *equality* to maintain himself or herself within his or her own final vocabulary, but he thinks that the only kind of *fraternity* that would make such *freedom* and *equality* possible is one which has to be shielded from the sustained consequences – be they ironic or otherwise – of their private 'attachments'. Fraternity (solidarity) is of the essence: negative freedom.

Two problems present themselves here, however, and both are classics. First, it may not be so difficult to believe that real ironists can return to the private sphere with relative ease, albeit it at the cost of their participation in the public arena (cf. the current de-politicization problematic). But it is less clear how the non-ironic ethnocentrist will be able to muster the 'mental acrobatics' necessary to look his or her contingency in the face, find no difficulties therein nor allow it to affect his or her 'commitment', while at

---

7. I owe this expression to a discussion with my colleague André Van de Putte who pointed to a similar problem in his 'Rawls's Political Liberalism. Foundations and Principles', *Ethical Perspectives*, 1995 (2:3), pp. 107-29.

the same time, as soon as he walks out the door and goes for a stroll around the *agora,* leaving behind those contingent beliefs which he happens to possess and is unable *and unwilling* to give up because they define the limits of *what he 'is able' to take seriously.* A second and related problem is the following: if people are indeed 'vulnerable' in the 'final words' or 'things' (or 'values') to which they are 'attached' and which have meaning for them although they cannot completely 'penetrate' that meaning (in which case one would be able to engage in careful argumentation which would ulti-mately provide one with reasonable grounds to choose a particular final vocabulary, all of which runs contrary to the very notion of *final* vocabulary as such), is it not perfectly normal that they would not want to be 'left alone' with those words and things? Is it not more likely that they will attempt to seek – especially 'public' – recognition for the actions they perform with reference to their 'final words' or in honour of their 'final' things? Is a freedom which *only* wants to be left undisturbed not too scanty and too hollow to constitute an 'element' for a game of recognition that should enable people to put up with the uncertainty which overcomes them because of the ultimate obscurity of the 'attachments' for which they did not choose but to which they "devote" (CIS 37) their lives? Where is that uncertainty the greatest, where is that ultimate obscurity most evident if not precisely in our contact with those who *are not able* to take us seriously? And what could be more humiliating and destructive than to be allowed to 'sing along' in a choir whose conductor requests that we don't make a sound in the interests of the 'public' good? What kind of acrobatics would one need to be able to continue one's private way together with other 'eccentrics' in the full knowledge that there are public standards which declare what we are 'allowed' to do behind closed doors to be mentally insane[8]? Does Rorty, in choosing ethnocentrism above irony, not make irony *unavoidable*? Is he not making us out to be sicker than we actually are? Is he not trying to establish solidarity on the wrong ground because the actual relationship between 'contingency, irony and solidarity' has escaped him? There may be some truth in this, given the fact that he later admits to have overlooked the difference "between ethnocentrism as 'an inescapable condition' – roughly synonymous with 'human finitude' – and as a reference to a particular *ethnos*" (ORT 15) such as "we, postmodernist bourgeois liberals" or "we, the rich North Atlantic democracies".

---

8. As explained at the beginning of this section, Rorty seems to make the norms of mental health depend on something like an 'average vocabulary'. It is unclear to me how he arrives at this average, and who is the 'we' that is contained therein.

IV. TWO FORMS OF ETHNOCENTRISM:
THE SUCCESS OF NEGATIVE FREEDOM

Isn't it precisely because Rorty forgets about the distinction between these two forms of ethnocentrism that he could so easily be seduced by the classical ideal of negative freedom? This freedom seems less attractive as soon as one distinguishes the always particular content of ethnocentrism (Rorty's second type in the quotation above) from the structure of being "ethno-centred" (Rorty's first type, which he admits to assimilating with the second) – when, in other words, one does not conflate the "what" and the "that" of ethnocentrism. The link between ethnocentrism and finitude seems to be not merely a question of the always finite content of a particular ethnocentrism, but more a matter of our always being, one way or another, centred on 'a' content or 'an' *ethnos* or 'a' final vocabulary. The ironist against whom Rorty fulminates seems to be someone who does not make this distinction, or at least someone who misses its point: by flitting between as many contents as possible and never staying anywhere, the ironist is in fact fleeing from finitude; as if by always being somewhere *else*, he tries to forget that, whatever he does, he is always *somewhere*. In search of the True Content that continually eludes him, the ironist appears to be the victim of his own impossible attempt to replace 'somewhere' with 'nowhere'[9]. What is so disturbing about finitude, and the reason why people flee from it, has not so much to do with the 'what' (*ethno*centrism) or with the 'that' (ethno*centrism*), but rather with the fact that this 'that' is always the 'that' of a 'what'. It is this complex structure that makes people uncertain and vulnerable, and this also explains why they are in search of another form of recognition than the one negative freedom can offer them. Because the 'that' is always the 'that' of a 'what', it seems not to be enough by itself: it seems as if the centredness of finitude might be softened by a different 'what', one that has more appeal and makes life easier to bear. Yet it is not only this doubt that gnaws at people's hearts, there is also a *doubt about this doubt* which makes them long for recognition of the 'what' of their 'that', a

---

9. The ironist thus seems an example of what Heidegger in *Being and Time* points to as the 'they's' tendency to be "everywhere and nowhere" (§ 36). But Heidegger's point is not the one that I am going to make. *Dasein*'s "pure 'that it is' " (BT § 29) confronts it with the 'fact' that every 'what' is the 'what' of a 'that'. Which is not the same as saying that every 'that' is the 'that' of a 'what'. The distinction may appear Byzantine, but, as I try to show elsewhere, it implies at least a reconsideration of what BT does with (or to) "facticity" (cf. my 'In Respectful Contempt. Heidegger, Appropriation, Facticity', to appear in J. FAULCONER - M. WRATHALL (eds.), *Appropriating Heidegger* (proceedings of the May 1999 Park City (Utah) Conference), Cambridge U.P.).

recognition that assures them that whatever it is they live for – and which could always have been otherwise – is worth it.

Because they overlook this complex structure of human freedom, proponents of negative freedom such as Rorty base their argument on a premise which it is in their interest to leave unexplained. Rorty's confusion of the two forms of ethnocentrism, for example, leads him to simply oppose the ironist's pathological doubt to the ethnocentrist's healthy self-confidence, and to no longer see what the two have in common. Ultimately, though, when one thinks about it, both the ironist and the ethnocentrist are equally sick: the ironist is someone for whom no 'what' can offer sufficient footing since it is always too thin for his 'that'; the ethnocentrist on the other hand is someone for whom the accidental 'what' completely coincides with his 'that'. For the ironist, the 'that' wins over the 'what'; for the ethnocentrist, it is just the opposite, but this reversal also appears to be a flight from finitude – a finitude that seems precisely to consist of the 'that' and the 'what' always being off balance. While the ironist cannot bear this idea and flees from it, the ethnocentrist covers it up: he clings to the particular contents of *his* ethnos and thereby spares himself not only the ironist's doubt, but also what I just called 'the doubt about the doubt'. For the ethnocentrist, the doubt about the doubt is something like a double negation, hence a certainty: the certainty that his 'what' provides him with what he no longer has to look for. And because there is then no longer anything that can throw him off balance, for the ethnocentrist the problem of recognition is actually beside the point. He knows that he is already recognized and supported by the structures of the ethnos to which he has conformed. Hence his inflexibility and the foundation of his intolerance: the ethnocentrist is indeed unable to be open for others – for then, as Rorty himself notes, his brains might just fall out, and this means, in our terms, that the doubt about the doubt might just surface once again, and with it the question whether the recognition of like-minded people is indeed sufficient.

By promoting the ethnocentrist as a model, Rorty is conveniently able to avoid this question, and in his model for an 'open' society he can work from the assumption that the members of this society will be able to find satisfaction, in what really concerns them, by withdrawing into the comfort of their "private clubs" and by deriving enjoyment from a neutral public sphere that Rorty compares to a market (more specifically: an Arab "bazaar") where one should behave as if one were at any ordinary market: it is not a matter of recognition, but of haggling to get the best deal[10]. But do

10. ORT 209: "you smile a lot, make the best deals you can, and, after a hard day's haggling, retreat to your private club. There you will be comforted by the compassionship of your moral equals."

people really want to be left alone with 'their own thing' inside the familiar walls of their private club? Doesn't negative freedom leave them alone precisely in that dimension of their existence where, admittedly, trust in their commitment triumphs over irony, but there still remains that gnawing feeling of the 'doubt about the doubt' – a gnawing that draws people out of themselves and out of their "tribe", and leads them to seek the recognition and appreciation of other clubs, rather than remaining satisfied with the recognition of their own club? One's 'own thing' – one's own 'what' of the 'that' – might be precisely that in a person's life with which he does not under any circumstances want to be left alone. It is that within a person that drives him outwards, into the *agora* for instance – i.e., into a sphere where, in one way or another, a form is given to the transcendence that does not so much surpass a person as drive him outside of himself. By its own rules and its own demarcation, the public sphere, as it were, puts a stop to that endless desire that prevents a person from staying with himself, with 'his own thing'. The *agora* civilizes this desire, or at least attempts to do so.

Viewed in this way, negative freedom cannot give people what they really desire. It must disappoint them and, in the long term, can only lead to a disinvestment of the political (a 'depoliticization' with deeper roots than is most often assumed). The concept's theoretical prestige seems to be exclusively determined by the fact that neither the defenders nor the critics of negative freedom make a distinction between the 'that' and the 'what' of finitude, and as a result only understand the need for a specifically public sphere on the basis of what Rorty calls "ethnocentrism as reference to a particular *ethnos*". That there exists more than one such reference point in our modern, 'fragmented' societies is then grist for the mill of the proponents of negative freedom: for how could the public sphere withstand all the pressure exerted on it by all those requests for recognition, if not by declaring itself incompetent in such matters? Those requests are simply out of place here: they are the expression of a desire that belongs in the private sphere (clubs of like-minded members). Responding to that desire would be a fatal mistake. It is precisely by not responding to it that the public sphere can preserve the neutrality that distinguishes it from the private sphere. Ethnocentrism belongs indoors, within the walls of one's own *ethnos*. If one wants to venture outside, then something will have to be given up. Without "mental acrobatics", one will never get there. The modern political sphere can no longer sanctify the uncertainty about whether that to which "we devote our lives" (CIS 37) is really worth the effort.

It will have become clear that, while negative freedom may be disappointing, it is not so easy to get rid of. But neither would it be sensible to become discouraged by the impasse at which we apparently find ourselves. Let us turn, then, to examine the origin of the impression that we are indeed confronted here with an aporia.

It is beyond question that the modern political sphere can no longer sanctify the uncertainty about whether that to which we devote our lives is really worth the effort. But to conclude from this that the political sphere actually resembles, or ought to resemble, a market rather than a club, seems to be a needless contribution to the purely negative image that people still have of the political – as if it were only a necessary evil, or less harshly: as if neutrality and negative freedom, just like democracy according to Churchill, would not be in any sense good solutions, but only the least bad and, for this reason, inevitable. Such a purely negative assessment of the political seems to me to overlook the logic specific to the political sphere to which Hannah Arendt already drew attention: as public sphere *par excellence*, the political sphere makes free because it makes visible. It seems to me that, on the basis of what we have just said, Arendt's argument can be made stronger than she in fact formulated it. Indeed, it needs to be, since Arendt's idea that one would come 'among the people' in order to escape the suffocation and unfreedom of the *oikos*, and to breathe in the free air of the *agora*[11], would make little impression on someone like Rorty. We are, he would no doubt object, no longer in Greece. Speaking among the free and equal – that *praxis* which, according to Arendt, is free and the highest human activity, since its end is not external but internal – can nowadays also take place indoors: either in the *oikos*, where the woman is no longer spoken of in the same breath with the household furniture and the slaves; or else in the congenial debates of Rorty's private clubs. The attraction of such clubs – our entire associative life – seems to lie precisely in their ability to slip in between the private and the public about which Arendt speaks, thereby apparently offering us both the freedom of the *agora* and the security of the private sphere. As a result, the disinvestment of the political sphere appears inevitable, since this development seems to sever the link between freedom and the public sphere and thus to disable the very argument with which Arendt had attempted to defend the specificity of the political as the only realm in which man would be free. Yet perhaps this is a mistaken impression.

V. LOSS OF FACE: ARENDT UPDATED

Let us return for a moment to the gentle sense of irony that I described in the opening lines of this article. Although this irony is easy to recognize, still

---

11. H. ARENDT, *Qu'est-ce que la politique*, Paris, Seuil, 1995, pp. 54 ff. And, of course, *The Human Condition*, Chicago/London, The University of Chicago Press, 1958.

it seems somewhat too fleeting and especially too innocent and beautiful to provide a real solution to our problem. Either it is a matter of grace, in which case it does not lend itself to instrumentalization, or else one tries to cultivate this attitude, but then it seems that one will run up against the classical drawbacks linked with the 'aesthetic attitude'. For such an attitude would seem to be inappropriate the moment it goes and gets involved with, say, the problem of recognition. For the Other wants to be taken seriously in the 'what' of his 'that', and this requires more than mere aesthetic emotion regarding the irreducible plurality of all that is human. The Other is ill served by such emotion, at least as long as it remains within the 'aesthetic sphere' and only on that basis lets itself become concerned with ethics. But what is the alternative?

The answer seems to be that the emotion provoked by the fact that the relation between the 'that' and the 'what' in human life is permanently out of balance is precisely the affect that makes possible the transition from ethics to politics. For let us not forget, ethics, too, is no longer able to sanctify the uncertainty about that to which we devote our lives. As far as their objective content is concerned, the others' attachments and the things they cherish are always trivial, laughable and disappointing for someone who is not gripped by them. And the problem for ethics is that the other nevertheless wants us to recognize him in those attachments, and not only because he suffers from them, for recognizing him in his 'that' alone would only perpetuate his suffering. What the other wants is for us to remove his uncertainty about the 'what' of his 'that'. But how could we possibly do this? It is precisely another 'what' of our 'that', precisely another 'attachment' that prevents us from taking his attachment seriously!

Ethics, then, confronts us (at this level) with an aporia: either we cling to our own attachments and become indifferent to the appeal of the other, or else we respond to that appeal, but this can only happen if we cut away everything in us that prevented us from taking the other seriously. Either his attachments or our own must be sacrificed. Rorty opts unambiguously for the former ("let's work by our own lights", ORT 213); Levinas, for the latter, as I have shown in the preceding chapters. Yet the problem seems to be that both choices are equally unpleasant since they are equally violent: neither the other's attachments nor my own are something that he or I possess, and which we might distance ourselves from, albeit with pain in our hearts. Rather, such attachments possess us, just like the "last words" of Rorty's final vocabulary possess people: it is on the basis of these last words that we can be who we are and have the leeway to lead a life that seems good and worthy to us. And it is this leeway that would disappear if we were asked to give up these words, or if we were pushed with our backs to them, as Rorty himself realized. People are vulnerable in their last words, they are laid open to humiliation and ridicule, precisely because these are words out of which other words become available for them. To be pushed with one's back to these words is to have one's back against the wall, to have no way out, to be cut off from all other words – in short, to be rendered speechless. It is in such a situation that a person is deprived of his humanity, not only because he feels that he has been robbed of speech, but especially because he then begins to feel something against which he can no longer offer resistance: someone rendered speechless quite literally loses face – his face loses all its familar features in being "occupied" (like a city is occupied) by passions that well up somewhere inside and that are stronger than himself.

It would seem that not only is ethics not the sphere in which the 'doubt about the doubt' and hence the desire to be recognized in the 'what' of the 'that' might be silenced, but also that a solution must be found in order to prevent that sphere from collapsing under a dynamic that it cannot control. The core of this dynamic has to do with what I would call the 'terror of the invisible': that through which an attachment is attached, is not itself visible, does not let itself be pinned down, escapes every enumeration of its concrete characteristics and, precisely because of this, such an attachment holds me or the other in a grip that we cannot explain to each other. 'Something' about the attachment affects us, and it is just because we cannot ourselves arrive at any knowledge of what exactly this 'something' consists in, that we do not want to be left alone with it, and that we are not satisfied by the mere recognition of like-minded people, and that we seek recognition among those who are not affected by this 'something' and who, despite themselves – because they are not so affected, and due to an indifference that they have not chosen either – cannot give us the recognition we want. Were the disappointment over this 'refusal' not mitigated by that gentle irony for which we are seeking a function here, then that terror that inhabits people and drives them outwards would inevitably break out and wreak havoc in the world. But at the same time, this 'refusal' would find the mitigation I am speaking about irrelevant, if it did not see a link in this irony that can connect ethics with another sphere.

That other sphere is politics. But it is a politics whose logic must be related to the predicament of ethics, not a politics of a merely negative freedom about which Rorty speaks. Instead of that necessary evil that we cannot avoid and that we must maintain in order to be left as much as possible in peace, it seems that politics – precisely because of its eminently public character – offers an 'element' in which that intimate terror that threatens to overwhelm ethics can be taken up in such a way that the situation does not immediately escalate. Because politics is a *public* sphere, it can impose a *regime of visibility* on its participants by expecting them to enter public discussion in such a manner that the chance of any party losing face is minimized. This is the reason why compromise is rightly called the art of the political: politics is not directly concerned with recognition, but only laterally – it avoids the core of the issue and deals with what is feasible. Rather than bluntly refusing the recognition that others ask of us, thus putting their backs against the wall of that 'something' for whose sake they are prepared to shed blood, politics offers them the possibility of losing *something*. By allowing them to speak, politics pulls them out of a situation in which they have *nothing* more to lose since even words elude them, and engages them in a discussion where they do not have to betray their attachments, but where it is precisely those attachments that force them to address concrete problems having their own recalcitrant character and which – if only because of this technicity and complexity – form a dam against an all too immediate contact with their attachments. The participants in such a political sphere are compelled to visibility: they must wear the *masks* of their political role, not in order to mislead others about their real intentions, but as a kind of 'detour' *for themselves* that would make the 'traffic' with their attachments both *possible* and *bearable*. These masks protect them, first and foremost, from themselves: from that in themselves that is also private *for themselves*, from those attachments that make them who they are but which they do not possess, which rather possess them. One might also say: these masks set us free – following Arendt – but not because they place public freedom against private unfreedom, but because they protect against the private *in* the private, against those passions *inside* us that are stronger than ourselves and that nonetheless seem to have something to do with that *about* us – with our attachments – from which we derive our 'selves'. Not that these masks can entirely nip all passions in the bud: they cannot remove tragedy and drama from our lives. But they form our second skin, and even if we feel how the skin under that skin is pricked by angst or anger, they can spare us the public shame of losing face, like the protagonist in Kobo Abe's novel[12]. As this character discovers, it requires "courage" to fraternize with other people – perhaps the "courage" Arendt refers to in her essay on freedom, where she said that it is the primary political virtue[13], a

---

12. K. ABE, *Das Gesicht des Anderen* (transl. from the Japanese by Oscar Benl), Frankfurt a.M., Eichborn, 1992. The reference is to a chemist who damages his face irreparably in a laboratory experiment. He designs a mask giving him "the face of another" (hence the book's title) and tries in his new form to seduce his wife who, he wrongly assumes, no longer recognizes him.

13. H. ARENDT, 'What is freedom?', in ID., *Between Past and Future. Eight Exercices in Political Thought*, Harmondsworth, Penguin Books, 1993, p. 156.

courage that might have to do primarily with getting rid of the idea that underneath those masks there is something else that is more valuable than the masks themselves, and that should be capable of being exhibited as such, to ourselves first of all. It is this suspicion, I believe, that we must set aside, not with the courage of despair, but with the courage that arises by itself from the gentle irony that formed the point of departure for these reflections. By allowing the second skin of the masks to grow into our first skin, we inscribe the rhythm of this irony in what is henceforth private and invisible in each of us. But this growth is never finished, and we will continue to feel that pain within us. We will have to bear it and withstand it, at least if we want to achieve a real tolerance that is based on more than an ironic or relativistic indifference.

Tolerance does not ask that we pretend to be impressed when we hear in a public space all of the trivial things that were spoken in those salons that fascinated us, like the narrator of Proust's *Recherche*, only as long as we were denied entrance to them. But the fact that one cannot 'hear' the other – cannot take him seriously – does not yet mean that one need not listen when the other takes the floor and demands recognition for the things he considers important. Admittedly, the other is asking there for a recognition that we, despite ourselves, cannot grant, because of that 'deafness' that is not of our choosing. Yet the solidarity that a society can still maintain after the demise of the theologico-political (Lefort)[14] demands that we subjugate the stiffness which has attacked our knees (Hegel) with a genuflection: if one cannot listen to the words of the other, then one must listen to one's own deafness resounding in that word and have the good grace to know that this deafness – that silence in us that refers to a loneliness not of this world, nor of the next – nevertheless calls us to yield and to make room in the acrobatics of some kind of 'contraction' for something that according to the rules of the game (cf. political debate) will in turn make room for us. Without the gentle irony of someone who is struck by his or her own 'deafness', the solidarity of politics will become the solidarity of an economy in which people simply wait their turn and politely draw in their elbows in order to avoid being prodded in the ribs themselves. To be sure, the modern political sphere can no longer sanctify the uncertainty about whether that to which we devote our lives is really worth the effort. But it is perhaps the only remaining sphere where those who can no longer kneel might still go down on their knees without running the risk of losing their balance[15].

But in order to keep this balance, we will need to find new words that will help us to understand what in fact we already knew all along: that

14. Cf. Cl. LEFORT, *Essais sur le politique: XIXième-XXième siècle*, Paris, Seuil, 1986.
15. The presence of this risk defines *ethics*.

human existence – where in a certain sense we are never alone – contains a silence which shows that not being alone is not the same as being with or for others. If there still is something like metaphysics, then it seems to me that its primary task is to prevent this silence from being drowned out by the chatter of intersubjectivity. Perhaps the reason why, at the end of this somewhat bizarre journey through 'contemporary' philosophy, I am still not rid of the word 'dissociation' is that it is not a contemporary word. If one listens to it closely – if, that is, one listens in a different way than those of our contemporaries who only see it as an inability to really listen to others – it will remind us that there is a solitude within us that is not of this life nor of the next, and that true finitude is precisely a staying in touch with that silence in us that is no longer from anywhere.

CONCLUSION

STILL OTHERWISE...?

BETWEEN FOUCAULT AND LEVINAS

Upon rereading the preceding pages, I am struck by the fact that, notwithstanding my effort to 'take Foucault into phenomenology' and thus in a sense to dissolve what I learned from him in a new element, there remains an insight that is decidedly Foucaultian which resists this current and, in reversing it, seems to draw phenomenology into Foucault. It can be summarized in one word: dissociation. By 'dissociation' I mean something quite simple which nonetheless might explain a great deal of the fascination that Foucault's early work exercised on my generation: it is the dissociation between understanding in the sense of comprehension and understanding in the sense of sympathy. What Foucault calls "discourse" gives rise to such a dissociation: between different epochs of our culture, but also, between different cultures or within one single culture between, for example, social classes or generations or even – and I will come back to this – between individuals. Discourse works as a kind of filter through which certain things or statements literally can be seen or heard, but not others. Before the truth of a proposition can be decided, for instance, it must first be heard (it must be able to appear, Heidegger would say) and taken seriously. As I have suggested in my introduction, what is at stake here is a different sort of relativism than the one which people usually try to discredit by invoking the 'self-refuting argument' which has been used from Plato to Habermas ("performative contradiction") to supposedly settle the matter. As one can learn from the smile which appears involuntarily on our lips, or the strange unease which comes over us when we are confronted with differently structured discourses (like those Foucault describes in *The Order of Things*), the 'self' that is supposed to synthesize without contradiction the content of its statement with the fact of stating it, is too finite to carry that weight. If this synthesis fails, this is because the ability to take something seriously belongs to the constitution of our subjectivity without itself having been constituted by us. Though we might well understand how another culture or another discourse is structured (for instance, by examining, like Foucault, the rules underlying its coherence), such understanding does not automatically mean that we *show* understanding for it, that we sympathize with it. Our finite ability to take something seriously, to attach importance to it, shows that we are already occupied by something, gripped by something, tied to something, and that it is this past which has never been present which is responsible for the gap between the subject's 'saying' and its 'said' – a gap which one only begins to notice through contact with true others, or with the true other. In such an experience of the other, something about us is revealed to us which we cannot completely appropriate: we feel ill at ease, we laugh – nervously or a bit too uproariously – at the strangeness of that other, but this laugh is not like the other kind of laugh where we let ourselves go. It is more a laugh with which we protect ourselves from something, and it is because we feel this protection that it remains strange to us. There is in us something strange that nevertheless makes us who we are, and that resonates within us and for us whenever another stranger passes by. Even before we know it, we are assaulted by an affect which, in a certain sense, itself takes the initiative to protect us but, in so doing, also confronts us with or exposes us to something in ourselves which is older than we are. We are not only dissociated from the other; we are dissociated *within* ourselves. I say *within* ourselves rather than 'from' ourselves (and certainly not from our 'self') because such a dissociation does not mean the death of the subject, but gives the subject its very structure: the dissociated subject may be a split subject, but it is clearly still a subject, albeit one that is 'decentred'.

This decentring of the subject is obviously a term deriving from (post)structuralism, but I have been giving it in this volume a kind of existential spin by not only linking it with discourse, cultures, structures, etc. – in short, with a field which articulates the subject – but also by using it to indicate the structure of our singularity as such. A kind of *existentialization of Foucault*, then. And why not? If one defines discourse as what establishes the difference between what in principle might have been said and what in fact was said[1], then what prevents us from using the same or a similar definition to refer to what is singular about each one of us? The difference between the possibilities offered us by language and the use which each subject makes of them, or the difference between opening one's ears and what one hears, or the difference between one's ability to understand others (an ability which seems unrestricted) and one's ability to sympathize with them – would it be an exaggeration to extend this decentring of the subject with regard to a discourse which he has not instituted toward the subject himself, and to find in it the structure of a singularity which he does not give to himself, but which gives him to himself, which he does not institute, but

1. As we have seen Foucault do in his 'Réponse à une question', *Esprit*, 1968(36:5), p. 863 (cf. chapter 2).

which singularizes him?

It is this 'existentialization' of Foucault which at first gave me the impression that Levinas's work was the place for me to look for a further clarification of the structure of a subjectivity decentred in that sense. Indeed, his texts abound with terms such as "absolute past", "passivity older than the opposition between activity and passivity", "singularization", "separation" all of which seem to share the same intuition about the structure of a subject's constitution as the one that had led me to conclude unexpectedly from the work of Foucault, and against Foucault's own conclusions, that post-structuralism was anything but the announcement of the death of the subject. But as I was soon to find out, Levinas for me could be no more than the name of a corpus of texts into which I could introduce some of these ideas as one introduces a contrast injection in medicine the better to read X-ray photographs. And it is easy to see why. For all these terms which looked so promising to me are linked by Levinas exclusively with ethics and responsibility and not, for example, with truth. In contrast to the lessons I had drawn from Foucault or the later Heidegger, truth for Levinas means simply the attainment of a universality, of a knowledge which can be shared by everyone. This left me not only with the impression that the point of 'discourse relativism' had been overlooked in no less brutal a way than with Habermas, but also that the matter did not end there. For instance, Levinas greatly stresses that it is ethical responsibility alone which singularizes me ("unique and irreplaceable I"). I found that a rather strange claim, not only then, for the reasons I just mentioned above, but also now, for reasons which I have found to be internal to his argument.

In what follows, I will limit myself to these internal reasons. But since they are not unrelated to the prehistory I just brought to mind, I would first like to briefly recall that relation. It has to do with the notion of 'rootedness' which, as I have shown repeatedly, is central in Levinas, but which he interprets in a way that I think is far too restrictive without ever justifying this restriction: it simply refers to the *Blut und Boden* of a subject who jealously guards and circumscribes its particularity, excluding all others. However one looks at it, then, rootedness, for Levinas, betrays egoism. This is so even in those texts where Levinas describes it in a more subtle way as something of which the subject is not the proud possessor, but which takes possession of the subject: a claim made on the subject by the sacred powers. But as we know from our analysis in chapters nine and eleven, this claim too becomes egoistic from the moment the appeal of the Other offers the subject a chance to escape and tear himself away from what is still natural within himself. For Levinas, the subject is always rooted before it comes into contact with the Other: at the very least it is rooted in Being, and it is no coincidence that he describes this rootedness as a *conatus essendi*, a kind of law of inertia that determines the being's being in Being, without the law being noticed by the subject (in this sense, it is the structure of a nature of which it is unaware: the 'ess*a*nce' of a subject which is busy being – 'essance' in the Heideggerian sense, against which *Otherwise than Being* reacts from the very beginning). Indeed, it is not insignificant that Spinoza remarks in the proof of *Ethics III,6* ("everything in so far as it is in itself endeavours to persist in its being") that "a thing cannot have anything within itself whereby it can be destroyed" – I will return to this later. What should at least be clear by now is that what I called above the subject's decentrement points to an attachment that does not simply coincide with the rootedness Levinas speaks about. Certainly not in the primary meaning (since it is not an attachment where the subject possessively glues itself to the ground of its own particularity). And not in the secondary meaning either, unless one specifies precisely what is meant by "possession".

Interestingly, for Levinas this term always carried a negative connotation. Possession is a movement toward a fusion or a participation in which the subject would lose its independence and, as a result, would cease to be a subject. The sacred is numinous, burning or digesting whoever comes into contact with it; this is why it is opposed to the Holy, which does not impose itself but turns away, thus allowing the subject to deepen its independence by offering it something – ethics – in which the Holy is no longer directly operative, but only as a "trace". As I have tried to show in chapter five, this opposition between the sacred and the Holy delimits Levinas's position from that of a Lyotard or a Lacan. But I have also tried to argue how Levinas's commitment to that opposition results in his having to ignore what I called the "true distress" of the Other. Let me briefly recall this argument in order to show in what sense the decentred or attached subject implied by Foucault's 'discourse' or Rorty's 'final vocabulary' (chapter 11)[2], at least in my existentializing reading of them, would make a difference to this immensely influential view of ethics.

I. LEVINAS ON THE "DISTRESS" OF THE OTHER

Let us start by taking a fresh look at that quote which, in chapter five, became the point of resistance around which my reading of Levinas in that and later chapters became organized. Levinas there refers to the Other as a face that is "naked" and that "stripped of its very form, is frozen in its

---

2. As the reader will not have failed to notice, although these notions are not identical, what attracts me in Foucault and Rorty is precisely the decentrement of the subject implied by both the notion of 'discourse' and of 'final vocabulary'.

nudity"[3]. This nakedness is not simply a metonymy where one sort of human helplessness, the lack of clothing, stands for all the others. Of course it means this as well, but Levinas also gives it metaphysical resonance by specifying that it is not a matter of a nakedness caused by lack of clothing in the ordinary sense. Even a well-dressed Other is naked, since he is stripped of his form. Even such an Other is other than the exterior or interior which I am able to see. The Other is more than a phenomenon; he is a "face". Although this word has become so familiar to us that we no longer even pause to think what precisely it refers to, it is still worthwhile to make an effort not to confuse our intuitive recognition with our conceptual mastery. Everyone spontaneously recognizes the distinction between the face and the form of the Other, but it is sufficient to note that Sartre, as one will remember from the analysis in chapter eleven, also made that distinction in order to realize that there is in this case something like an underdetermination of the theory by reality, and that it is of greatest importance to arrive at some understanding of what Levinas means exactly by his conceptual distinction between face and form. And one of the most exact passages is precisely this one where the face is said to be "naked" because it has been "stripped of its form".

To understand what is meant there, it is helpful to bear in mind that Levinas sometimes mentions "context" or "role" instead of "form". To reduce the Other to his role or context means not treating him as Other. The waiter who serves me is merely a pair of hands supporting the serving tray which could easily be replaced by different hands. Or to give a further example: to call this African with such and such a name 'a black', or to treat him as such, is to transform him into a substitutable exemplar of a sort. Of course, Levinas has nothing against the existence of roles and contexts, and he would shudder at the idea of interpreting his ethics as a recommendation to go and build a 'personal' relationship with everyone, including the waiter for example. What he means is that the ethical dignity of the Other has to do with something in the Other that falls outside that role or context and is not absorbed by it. For a waiter to fall outside his role, it is sufficient that he literally falls and hurts himself: then he becomes the face of a person in need. This non-absorption of the face by the form or role or context is also called its infinity, to indicate that it is not simply a lack but also a dignity which obligates me, a surplus or excess of the face over the form, not simply a distress but also a beseeching which commands me and which has rights – but no power – over me. The appeal of the Other, as we heard Levinas say repeatedly, comes both from above and below.

3. CPP, p. 96 (as I mentioned before, I prefer "frozen" to "paralyzed" for rendering "*transi dans sa nudité*").

Intuitively, it is quite clear why Levinas is putting such great stress on what is technically termed the "alternance" of the face. If the appeal would only come from above, it would have too much force to allow for my *responsibility*; if it would come only from below, it would not have enough force. The appeal must have just enough force not to leave me indifferent – and this is why Levinas stresses that I cannot not hear it – but it also has to leave me free to choose whether and how to respond to it. But, as I stressed time and again – and it is a point the implications of which I should like to further pursue here – even a non-response will be a response and will for Levinas be qualified in the terms of the horizon opened up by the appeal: ignoring the appeal will be Evil, following it up will be Good. The face of the Other has thus a *weak* force because it is bereft of the means to enforce its appeal on me; but this weak force is a *force* because it brings an orientation into Being which Being does not have on its own. Being for Levinas is a realm of indifference; only through the face of the Other can there be introduced into this realm something that is not (ultimately) indifferent. This idea that Being is oriented by something outside of or above Being is what lies behind Levinas's dissatisfaction with the anti–Platonism that for him represented all that was shallow in the spirit of his time – as he provocatively put it in an enormously influential essay entitled "Meaning and Sense", where he opened his attack on all sorts of culturalisms, contextualisms and relativisms, and which by far constitutes the best introduction to his thought: "The saraband of innumerable and equivalent cultures, each justifying itself in its own context, creates a world which is, to be sure, de-occidentalized, but also disoriented. To catch sight, in meaning, of a situation that precedes culture, to envision language out of the revelation of the other (which is at the same time the birth of morality) in the gaze of man aiming at a man precisely as *abstract man, disengaged from all culture*, in the nakedness of his face, is to return to Platonism in a new way. It is also to find oneself able to judge civilizations on the basis of ethics" (CPP 101).

Although one may well agree with Levinas about the sort of danger he seeks to avoid, a much less convincing consequence of this "return to Platonism" is that it completely detaches human dignity from form or context. For ethics "to precede culture" the Other in his of her ethical dignity needs to be thought of as an ab-stract or ab-solute Other in the etymological sense of the word: "The Other who manifests himself in a face as it were breaks through his own plastic essence (...) His presence consists in *divesting* himself of the form which does already manifest him (...) The nudity of a face is a bareness without any cultural ornament, an absolution, a detachment from its form in the midst of the production of its form" (CPP

96). If the Other would be attached to a (cultural) context, he would be 'rooted' and hence, Levinas seems to reason, be completely absorbed by or fully immanentized into that context. But since such a contextualization of the Other would clearly do him violence, there must be something about his alterity which resists – not in a physical, but in an ethical sense – that violence. As we have seen, it is this "weak resistance" of what Levinas calls the face of the Other which turns that Other into a person *to whom I am linked and to whom I am obligated, in spite of* and *before* all culture. To respect the Other qua Other, I must treat him as an Other detached from his culture and not, for instance, as 'a black' – in Levinas's words, "to be in relation with the face means that upon seeing a black, one does not notice the colour of his skin, nor the colour of his eyes, but that one speaks to him and through the word takes responsibility for him (...) 'To see the face' is nothing but the possibility to address the black and be his brother"[4].

Does this alliance and this specific form of ethical brotherhood really do justice, however, to the distress of the Other? Does it not already exclude a form of distress (or at least remain insensitive to it)? If the face indeed shivers from the cold because it is "stripped" of its form or context, does that not indicate that it actually needs that form or context? The reason why I attach such importance to these questions which I have raised before, is that I suspect – and perhaps this suspiscion could profit from being made more explicit here – that for Levinas to recognize that need, would mean to accept a form of rootedness which he cannot accept without thereby jeopardizing another essential ingredient of his argumentation concerning the *conatus essendi*. Indeed, as I shall explain, the rootedness which I link with the true distress of the Other shows that it is perhaps too simple to define a person as *conatus essendi*. And, as I hope to be able to show, this has enormous consequences, since if one admits that, then the fundamental thrust of Levinas's ethics threatens to become stalled. In what follows, I will work this out step by step, beginning with a reconsideration of the distress of the Other.

II. AN ALTERNATIVE APPROACH
TO THE "DISTRESS" OF THE OTHER

It would seem that, in the light of what I have developed until now, there is an obvious question that must be raised: what prevents Levinas from

4. My translation from the Dutch text of an authorized interview with Levinas published as 'Wat men van zichzelf eist, eist men van een heilige', in J. GOUD, *God als Raadsel. Peilingen in het spoor van Levinas*, Kampen/Kapellen, Kok Agora-DNB/Pelckmans, 1992, p. 165.

linking the distress of the Other with what I have called the decentring of the subject? The Other would then be – just like me – a subject who is tied to or attached to something to which it is denied access and from which it cannot break free. And, precisely *because of these two characteristics together*, the Other would *suffer* from this attachment. To make this suffering and this distress somewhat more clear, I could say that this attachment which singularizes the subject (which is therefore 'older' than the subject, and has 'marked' it before the subject was even aware of it) has the structure of a *vague debt*: because the debt is vague, the debtor does not know *what* he must do in order to repay it (he is 'denied access' to it); and because it is a debt – something which obligates the subject – he cannot give up the debt (break free of it) without losing himself or, more precisely, without losing what singularizes him and thereby losing his own singularity. The 'that' without the 'what' of this debt is not nothing, but nevertheless the debt does not lend itself to determination. One is never finished with it; there is no end to this distress; every assistance falls short in advance (which does not mean that this distress should leave us indifferent – I will come back to this).

In order to make this rather abstract train of thought more concrete I should like to return once more to the example of skin colour. It is perhaps strange at first sight to claim that someone might have a 'vague debt' with regard to their skin colour. And I must admit, the example is not perfect, since it would be easy to misconstrue as claiming that our skin colour should be important to each of us. But my intention is not to decree what should be the case; rather, I want to analyse what under certain circumstances – our own circumstances: think of the resurgence of racism – is in fact the case. As I explained at length in chapter eleven, Levinas would see racism as one more attempt to deprive the Other of his alterity, to reduce him to his "form" – the colour of his skin, the physiognomy of his face, etc. The alterity of the Other would be reduced to certain characteristics which make him different from us and, in this way, the Other would be robbed of his mystery or his enigma – a mystery which consists precisely in the fact that the Other's alterity is not the consequence or the sum of his other "qualities", but *precedes* them, is independent of them, as the face is independent of form, or ethics independent of culture. This is why Levinas says, in the quote I cited earlier, that to be in relation to the face of the Other means not taking account of skin colour but rather speaking to the Other. The Other's ethical dignity is precisely something which cannot be grasped or controlled in any form; the face does not lend itself to be known. The Other is not so much unknown as unknowable: his alterity is an excess or surplus which splits or breaks open the form, rather than lets itself be trapped in it. Form is coagulation, death, mask; the face is living presence, "signification without context". To reduce the Other to his form, to his role, to his context, to contextualize him within his culture is tantamount to murdering him, depriving him of his unique dignity, reducing him to an exemplar of a sort, taking from him that which makes him a singular person – in short, misrecognizing his face. This face has no colour and no gender: it is of no importance who or what the Other is, or what he or she looks like. The Other is first and foremost a person.

What Levinas is actually saying here is that it should have no importance *for me* – the face is in this sense a relational term: it is that about the Other which disturbs me, unsettles me and resists (ethically) my attempts to reduce it to what is familiar. With something that can be grasped within a form, I am not in a relation that would call me into question. Not so with the face: here I am put in a relation without relation which upsets me, if only because it calls my "rights" into question. But what exactly is involved in Levinas's determination of the alterity of the Other? For the face is not exclusively a relational term: to determine the alterity of the Other as a face which has always already withdrawn from the "form", and to call the Other, for that reason, a stranger – is that not to say something about that Other himself? And even if one accepts that the Other's skin colour should be unimportant to me – *concesso non dato* – does that also mean that it should be unimportant to the Other? I suspect not: the Other would not be very pleased if I were to say that I help him because I respect the person he is, irrespective of his origins, his gender, his culture, his skin colour – in short, the ab-stract Other, "detached" from all form or context. To say that the Other is "not absorbed by" his form or his culture or his context does not necessarily imply that he is detached from it. A black person will undoubtedly be aggravated if I reduce him to his blackness, but this leaves open the question whether he would appreciate being treated as a brother with whom I might begin to converse, regardless of his skin colour. What the Other wants is for me to recognize him as a *singular* Other, not because of his characteristics (which he always shares with others, thus making him replaceable), but not detached from his characteristics either (for that too makes him replaceable). In Levinas's vocabulary, this would mean that, at least for the Other himself, the determination of his alterity in terms of an opposition between alterity and characteristics would have to be re-examined. It is true that the Other's alterity is not a consequence of his characteristics, but it seems a mistake to make alterity precede these characteristics and detach it from them (as Levinas does explicitly)[5]. Instead

5. See chapters 5 and 11 above which precisely tried to call into question the alternative with which Levinas is constantly operating, as in the following quote from an interview on racism: "Other, not at all because he would have other attributes or would be born in

of saying that the Other is a face and therefore meaning without context, etc., it seems one should rather say that the Other is 'not without' form, 'not without' context, etc., and that he is a stranger not because he is *without* form or *without* context, but because he is 'not without'. The Other's characteristics do not leave him indifferent; his alterity is stuck to them without being able to be reduced to them. The tragedy or distress of the Other lies in his not knowing how they are stuck, in *being attached* to a form or context which he cannot get rid of without losing (a part of) his singularity, but which he cannot be absorbed into either, in which he cannot lose himself. A white man does not know what it means to be white, and yet *under certain circumstances* he may notice his whiteness, it will isolate him, he will be confronted with his own whiteness as with a skin which cannot be peeled away, which burns him and turns against him without him knowing what he must do to soothe it. The skin which at that moment singularizes him also strikes him with panic, since it confronts him with the structure of every singularization: that about us which makes us irreplaceable (which we cannot think away without thinking ourselves away), without our having chosen it (so it is not a choice we could revise) does not tell us what we must do in order to live with it. It does not lend itself to being grasped in a meaning, and yet it has marked us. It counts for us, and yet it does not let itself be counted. It confuses us, and yet if we untangle this confusion then *we* no longer count.

Attachment, decentring, vague debt: these are all words which I have used in this volume to indicate the terror dwelling in people's hearts, a terror which is not intimate, since it is never familiar, but ex-timate[6], a strangeness which lives with us but not according to our house rules. Man is a being who must take account of something that takes no account of him: of a guest who is there from the same moment we are there, and who presents a bill, an IOU which, to our amazement, bears our signature and yet remains illegible – like in the story with which Benjamin begins one of his

---

another place or another time, or because he would be of a different race. ... *It is not at all the difference that makes the alterity; it is the alterity that makes the difference*" (my transl. from 'La vocation de l'autre', *l.c.*, p. 92).

6.   A term I borrow from Lacan; cf. J.-A. MILLER, 'Extimité', in M. BRACHER e.a. (eds.), *Lacanian Theory of Discourse: Subject, Structure and Society*, New York/London, New York U.P., 1994, pp. 74-87 (article in English). In these and the following lines I feel very close to the appropriation of Lacan that one can find in Lyotard's *The Inhuman. Reflections on Time* (transl. G. Bennington & R. Bowlby), Cambridge, Polity, 1991.

Kafka studies[7]. The signature is our initial inscription, but strangely enough our hand itself grew out of this writing which is as obscure as the name which it re-'presents'.

I am white or I am black, man or woman – but what does that mean? If I question my body, if I examine it, if I look at what sort of secondary sexual characteristics it might have, it does not answer. It tells me nothing about what it means to be a man or a woman[8]. These days, of course, I can change my gender, but even then something remains silent. I can enlarge my breasts, I can make them smaller, but the breasts of the ideal woman are like the circumference of a circle. My body changes, I begin menstruating, I become a woman, but that is merely blood, it is too fluid to become writing, I cannot read it. Something has changed, but this menstruation which has made me a woman does not tell me what it means to be a woman. Just as that name which I have been given, and which refers to me as a singular human being, does not tell me what it means to be this singular person. I am that name, but it goes out on its own, it is there when I am not around, as it will still be there when I am gone. I have it but I do not possess it, it is neither my property nor even my usufruct – it is rather a servitude imposed on me by language, yet it is never clear exactly what this servitude consists in. What does it mean to honour one's name, or another's name? Or all those other names which, in one way or another attach themselves to us – Flanders, Belgium, Europe – and which can only be made into uniquely determining descriptions through violent means (the violence of nationalism is the revenge of the name against those who think they know its secret, who pride themselves on being the only ones to have escaped the *vagueness* of the debt, who drag others with them because they have heard the Voice telling them what that debt means).

On this view, racism and nationalism are attempts to evade this terror within us. Anaesthetics. Fictions: to renounce the vagueness of the debt, a legend is concocted which is then passed off as the authentic text. This legend offers protection, which is why it is so dangerous, why it is so readily believed, why it is so successful – because it tries to close the gap between what Levinas calls the face and the form. But, as I point out in the next section, the meaning of these terms has shifted in the course of our argument.

---

7. W. BENJAMIN, 'Franz Kafka, zur zehnten Wiederkehr seines Todestages', in H. SCHWEPPENHÄUSER (ed.), *Benjamin über Kafka*, Frankfurt a.M., Suhrkamp, 1981, pp. 9ff.

8. On this question, see Darian LEADER's wonderful *Why do women write more letters than they post?*, London/Boston, Faber and Faber, 1996.

III. RECONSIDERING THE FACE AND THE FORM

Perhaps it will help to clarify matters if I summarize the foregoing sections in a simple diagram:

Levinas:
face	"breaks through"	form
		context
(living)		(coagulation)
ethical dignity		ontology
Infinity		Totality
Otherwise than Being		Being

versus:
face	tension	form
	"not without"	
	ethical dignity	

Contrary to Levinas, I suggest that one should situate the ethical dignity of the Other neither on the side of what he calls the face nor on the side of the form. The Other's misery is that he cannot simply disappear into his form, but neither is he merely a face which is released from form through its surplus. I think the reason the Other shivers from the cold is that he misses his form, he longs for it, but can find no access to it (the sign that marks us refuses to become signifying). Because of this misery of singularity, this desire to read the unreadable, he is not a face that can break through the form unscathed. The misery of the Other is that he cannot be the face of which Levinas speaks: he is too much 'attached' to his 'form' to withdraw from it the way the face does, but not so much that he disappears into it.

I wrote 'form' in quotation marks just now by way of suggesting that something is not quite right with this form: it is not the form which Levinas places in opposition to the face, and it is not the form and the visibility which he ascribes to the phenomenon. Everything about my skin colour or my name or my sex is visible. And yet, someone else who simply looks and sees all there is to be seen cannot see that 'more' *or that 'less'* by which I am attached to it, by which I feel obligated to it. The misery of my attachment cannot be seen, it seems utterly unreasonable or even ridiculous as soon as it begins to shine on certain objects, words or places, which for me constitute a breaking point (holy words or names, *Rorty's "last words"*, the chador, the family grave – and even: the earth which I took with me before I was exiled, over which I pray but also weep[9]). There is something about such objects which makes them different from the objects of ontology, something which resists the grip of *logos*: they are irreplaceable and their irreplaceability is indescribable, but it is not simply the indescribability of too massive a presence like that of *haecceitas*. These 'objects' (words, names, things, certain customs) have a rigidity, a kind of inelasticity which has nothing to do with their concrete qualities, but rather with the fact that they come in the place of a certain structure which leaves its trace in them without ever being grasped by them. Such objects are the kind that people would die for (the whole problem of multiculturalism is ultimately centred on this rigidity which we cannot understand in each other)[10]. In Rorty's vocabulary, we could say that in such objects "the blind impress all our behavings bear" has come to "crystallize" (CIS 37). And, as he remarks himself, "any seemingly random constellation of such things" can serve as a candidate here and "set up an unconditional commandment to whose service a life may be devoted" (*ibid.*). Although Rorty does not explain how we should read this "setting up" of a commandment, he does add importantly that it is "no less unconditional because it may be intelligible to, at most, only one person" (*ibid.*). But if one goes all this way, why not go further? Why not think of such objects not in terms of what *sets up* an unconditional commandment, but as what receives the imprint of a commandment already there, and tries to keep it at bay by localizing it, by inscribing it in *these* objects rather than in others? Perhaps the very rigidity of these objects which for the people concerned cannot be simply replaced by others, has to do with the fact that they already form a first defence structure, a first attempt to inscribe a vague debt that cannot be inscribed and yet must be inscribed if its terror is not to annihilate us. For some *contingent* (as in CIS) reason, these objects, I suggest, have become the bandages that have had to staunch a bleeding which could have been much worse, from which we might have bled to death. Which is why, as I argued against Rorty's liberalism, we do not like to be left on our own with them and why we reach out to others in the hope that their recognition and their respect for these objects can be interpreted as a sign that what we happen to devote our lives to is worth our devotion

9. I am thinking here of some of the examples that Michael Ignatieff gives in his thoughtful *Blood and Belonging: Journeys into the New Nationalism*, London, BBC-Books/Chatto & Windus, 1993.

10. Cf. my 'Levinas, le Multiculturalisme et Nous', in A.M. DILLENS e.a., *Questions au libéralisme*, Brussels, F.U.S.L., 1998, pp. 47-59, in which I compare Levinas's views to those of a sophisticated liberal opponent like W. Kymlicka who seems to leave more room for such 'rigidities' (an English translation of this article will appear in *Ethical Perspectives*, Sept. 1999).

to it. *Man is a being who is driven outward toward the others by something 'within himself'.*

This is ultimately why I do not follow Levinas when he leaves it to ethics to interrupt my *conatus essendi*. For it seems to me, recalling *Ethics III.6*, that as a result of the singularizing structure described above it is far from obvious that one can say of a person that there is nothing *"in him* by which he might be destroyed" and that he persists in his Being unless hindered by an influence from outside. And although, as I suggested at the end of chapter nine, with the category of the *il y a*, Levinas had all the resources he needed to protest against such an assumption, it is striking that he never did. One could show this systematically by examining how the category of the *il y a*, from *Totality and Infinity* on, was presented more as a threat from the outside than as the threat of an outside *within* the interior of the subject. That would not be too difficult a task, but I will postpone this partly exegetical question for another occasion, restricting myself here to simply underlining what is at stake. Indeed, on closer examination, it is absolutely not surprising that this sort of slippage has taken place. Levinas has no other option but to determine the person as *conatus*, and in this determination to implicitly accept the proof from *Ethics III.6*, for otherwise the basic move of his ethics would come under threat.

IV. RECONSIDERING THE BASIC MOVE
THAT ALLOWS FOR LEVINAS'S ETHICS

The core of Levinas's argument can be summarized as follows: through the appeal of the Other, my existence suddenly appears in a way that it could not have done without the Other, and in so appearing it changes irrevocably its character – something irreversible takes place which Levinas designates as humanization. Let me briefly clarify this.

Before the appeal of the Other, the subject lives in the mode of enjoyment, where everything is *inadvertently* referred to the subject. Such a 'freedom' is in fact still nature, precisely because of the involuntary self-centredness. Of course, the subject has the possibility of making choices (between, for example, meat or fish), but the subject itself always escapes these choices since they always already presuppose it. Whatever I do, whatever I choose, the choice never liberates me from myself, it is *ultimately* always indifferent because it ultimately refers back to me. Since I am the ground and the measure for the different weight which those alternative choices have for me, the choices can never really affect me, their value ultimately depends on the value that I give to them, and so they lose their value the moment I give up that position. That is why such a freedom can always lapse into boredom and deep indifference to the possibilities it offers. The limit of a freedom which only makes a difference to me is my own indifference.

True freedom, according to Levinas, presupposes that the circle in which the subject only encounters itself is broken. True freedom presupposes a true choice and such a choice only occurs when the result of that choice not only makes a difference to me but also to an other. It is such a choice that the appeal of the Other confronts me with: any indifference I might display regarding my own existence and the possibilities it offers me do not affect that choice, because I am now in a situation where my indifference still makes a difference for someone else. This not only implies that I no longer have control of my own existence (my suicide, for instance, would deprive the Other who needs me), but also that this life can no longer be lived as it used to be lived. My involuntary self-involvement can no longer remain what it was because the Other's presence makes me realize that what I had, until now, involuntarily referred to myself – even the air that I breathe and the bread that I eat – is henceforth something which *I* refer to *my* self, thus depriving some Other. What used to be natural and involuntary then becomes arbitrary: it loses its obviousness. And it is this fall from what was still natural in me (the *conatus essendi*) which leads Levinas to see in the appeal of the Other the institution of my true freedom and the last hurdle which I must pass in order to by truly human. One could almost say that ethics completes the Creation, and there is a clear Kantian resonance (transition from the hypothetical to the categorical) when Levinas here emphasizes the orientational power of the appeal of the Other and thus also of the Good. The idea of Creation accordingly acquires an *almost* exclusively ethical connotation[11]: it is the insertion of what really makes a difference into a (dis)order that always threatens to revert to indifference. In this new "ethical" phase, the previous "aesthetic" phase is *completely* redescribed: what was originally involuntary self-involvement, *conatus* in which we were entangled, is now confronted with the choice between holding onto that *conatus* and self-involvement or giving it up (in whole or in part) for the benefit of someone else. One is responsible and, therefore, fully human only when one is forced into answering. This, for Levinas, is the reason why responsibility precedes the freedom of the aesthetic phase and institutes another, different freedom (of the ethical).

This whole operation stands or falls on the assumption that the process

---

11. On this "almost" and on Levinas's idea of creation *ex nihilo* in general, see my contribution to the volume of essays that J. Bloechl is preparing for Fordham University Press (*The Face of the Other and the Trace of God: Between Ethics and Religion in the Philosophy of Levinas*).

by which the pre-ethical phase of *conatus essendi* gets redescribed in ethical terms cannot simply be reduced to the violence of a new order imposing its own categories upon another order which it then subdues. Levinas consequently always stresses that the violence of the Good is a "good violence"(OB 43): "No one is good voluntarily. We can see the formal structure of nonfreedom in a subjectivity which does not have time to choose the Good and thus is penetrated with its rays unbeknownst to itself. *But subjectivity sees this nonfreedom redeemed, exceptionally, by the goodness of the Good*" (OB 11). This 'making good' consists of nothing other than what I have just been describing: the Good liberates, institutes a new freedom, and gives people a fixed point or point of orientation around which they can gravitate. Furthermore, this point is not just another gravitational point different than the one around which their existence revolved until now, it is "better", especially in the sense that only this point is the true gravitation point around which a truly *human* existence revolves. One comes into one's *true* element, then, only through the appeal of the Other – which is why Levinas considers that appeal not just as an alienation, but as an alienation of the alienation (which still held one within nature: the not-yet-completed aspect of Creation), and hence as a *purification* which brings one into contact with one's "final reality" (TI 178).

V. SOME CONSEQUENCES
OF THIS RESISTANCE TO LEVINAS

If one agrees with this characterization of what I have called Levinas's basic move (and my aim was simply to recapitulate what, according to me, Levinas is saying; the aim was not critical but hermeneutic), and if one is also prepared to admit that the suggestions I have made concerning the subject's singularity are not unreasonable (that they must be further developed, is equally obvious), then it seems to me one can no longer deny that a very interesting and difficult problem is taking shape, one which I think represents very clearly the true background of our contemporary ethical *debacle*. This problem has to do with the fact that there may be some very good reasons for believing that the 'ethical redescription', which I am claiming is Levinas's basic move, overlooks an important complication. If it is indeed the case that the subject is already singularized before ethics, and if this singularization is carried out according to the procedure I described above, then this 'ethical redescription' seems to run up against an important obstacle. As we have seen, Levinas assumes that, through the intervention of the Good by way of the Other's appeal, the subject is enabled to get rid of the old gravitation point and, despite the accompanying pain, is provided with a new one which "better" conforms to the *human* condition. This is why the subject's involuntary egocentrism can be given the following choice, *without remainder*: either admit its arbitrariness (egoism) or else renounce itself (extirpation of *conatus*). Ethics can then be summarized as being placed before the alternative: either *pour soi* or *pour autrui*. Choosing the former is an unambiguous choice for Evil, since Levinas takes it for granted that one is "initially for the other"[12], though one only discovers this fact in and through the appeal of the Other. But what would happen if, before the subject is moved by that appeal, it cannot be determined simply as a *conatus essendi*? What if every human is a being who already bears within himself something which threatens to destroy him from the inside? And what if one cannot simply get rid of that something without ceasing thereby to be human and reverting to nature? What if it is this 'something' that already determines the difference between the human and the natural (perhaps not *all* the difference, but at least an essential part of it)? What if man is indeed a being who must take account of something that takes no account of him?

The answer is obvious: if it is indeed possible to define someone in these terms, then no ethical redescription without remainder can occur through the appeal of the Other. The appeal does not simply relieve me of the involuntariness of my self-involvement, my egocentrism, it touches me more deeply: it confronts me with my decentredness, with that vague debt inside me which I had diverted toward the others in an attempt to somehow remain faithful to it without being obliterated by it. Indeed, as I stated above, it is precisely the vagueness of the debt that drives me outside, making me seek out the already present symbolic frameworks (or "final vocabularies") of the community of which I am coincidentally a part. Not that those frameworks can provide any definite answer to the question of how I should repay the debt. But they at least allow me to take some distance from it, and to muddle along (think, for example, of how the proper name is always constrained by a set of rules determining how and with what consequences it can circulate). Because of these frameworks, I am no longer completely alone with those marks that singularize me; *not that I am with the others, but I am not without them either*. My *mitsein* is that moment of my Being by which I am protected from the rigidity of an absolute singularity. However imprecise this notion of 'protection' may be, it is nevertheless sufficient as an indication that the 'self' which it permits me to become involved with can only maintain itself in a complicated choreography of back and forth movements between the vague debt and its symbolic articulation. (The Heideggerian problematic of authenticity and

12. E. LEVINAS, *Ethics and Infinity. Conversations with Philippe Némo* (transl. R.A. Cohen), Pittsburgh, Duquesne U.P., 1985, p. 96.

inauthenticity returns here in a different guise: to remain alone with the vague debt leads to rigidity; to completely disappear into *mitsein* leads to a fusion in which all singularity disappears. It is not my penis that will tell me what it means to be a man; yet to be *this* man cannot be resolved by my conforming to the ideal of 'being a man' as it is symbolically articulated within 'my' community). The appeal of the Other throws this choreography out of balance, at least when it is related to one's full humanity, and to what I earlier called the 'distress of the Other', an Other who is a stranger precisely because he is, *like me*, attached to something and suffers from that attachment because he does not know what it stands for, nor can he simply give it up since that is not within his power. Such an Other – a *true* Other, a stranger – cannot but disturb me and make me ill at ease, without this unease being translatable into shame, since shame for Levinas means shame for the nature which I was and which forever ceases to be nature through the appeal: an egocentrism which, if it could be maintained, would now be nothing but egoism.

But everything I have said above would seem to suggest that there is within the ego a 'moment' which cannot be given up and ethically reconfigured because (as O'Brien in Orwell's *1984* realizes when torturing Wilson) *giving it up would amount to self-destruction*: for what is at stake is a 'self' which provides protection from the terror of the vague debt. In what Levinas calls the involuntary self-involvement of enjoyment, I do not just gravitate around myself; I gravitate according to the structure just described in a gravitational field with two poles: the vague debt and its symbolic articulation. So it is not my nature, but that whole field as well as my precarious position within it which is revealed when I come into contact with the misery of a 'true' Other. And since every Other is singular, every Other can in principle be such a true Other, and he becomes one – forming a *threat* to me – as soon as the singularity of his attachment draws my attention to the structure of the vague debt within him, but also within myself. This is clearly the case, for instance, with those others whom we find strange because they try to live with their attachments in *different* symbolic articulations than ours. The *otherness* of those articulations shatters the obviousness of my own, which only then become noticeable *as* symbolic *articulations* with all their essential limitations, i.e., in their essential inability to establish once and for all what that vague debt means *exactly*. Hence my unease, my anxiety, possibly even my panic: instead of helping me to 'look away' from my vague debt, like familiar others would do (those who share more or less the same symbolic articulation), the true others force my gaze onto that vague debt, unintentionally of course but no less painfully for that. And the whole problem is what happens to me then – racism, for example, seems to be an extreme reaction that can only be explained by the inability to deal with such a confrontation. But can one in fact ever deal with it, (as I said above, the vague debt has something rigidifying about it) except indirectly, with a sidelong glance? To tackle this question, which I cannot do here, would mean extending the whole field of the ethical problematic: there is not just the appeal of the Other's face, but also something like my appealability, and this does not depend on me alone, but also on the extent to which the morals (*Sitten*) of my community (its symbolic articulations) have prepared me for their own precariousness and for my having been allocated to them.

It seems to me that there is no place in Levinas's ethics for this appealability to arise as an ethical *problem*. Admittedly, his entire ethics refers to a metaphysics which I have not discussed here, but whose internal coherence I have tried to demonstrate in some of the chapters above. Although this metaphysics indeed takes my appealability – my having been created – as its major theme, and although one can hardly accuse Levinas of taking this appealability for granted, it is striking that he can find only a single word for its failure to appear: Evil. Perhaps my opposition to Levinas could be summarized by stating that I think he introduces this word *too early*, thereby not only underestimating the complexity of the crisis in ethics, but also excessively narrowing the field of ethics. This is not to reproach Levinas, whose eminence is not in doubt, and it is perhaps not even a proper argument. It is a hesitation framed within a debate where what is at stake transcends philosophy. The reality within which we live is, I fear, already Levinasian, for it seems that this entire ethics leads *not just to a naturalization of the one appealed to* (as *conatus essendi*) *but also to a naturalization of the one who appeals*. The "misery" which is given a place here seems to be the only one in which we can still recognize ourselves in our end of the century unease. As Alain Finkielkraut writes, "humanitarian action means real progress until the day when it gained a monopoly on morals and behaviour. Henceforth, it is misery without clemency. The other side of its concern for suffering is its disdain for everything in life which cannot be reduced to Life in the biological sense, an Olympian indifference to 'peasant' humanity (*la paysanne humanité*)"[13].

True, Levinas would reply as he always did, that "humanity is not a forest" (DF 23) and that this attachment "to the Place" which Finkielkraut is defending when he remarks that "man without his inscription into a world ... is nothing more than the anonymous and organic Life pulsating in him"[14], is but a giving in to the forces of the sacred and to the possession of

---

13. A. FINKIELKRAUT, *Comment peut-on être Croate?*, Paris, Gallimard, 1992, p. 88.
14. *Ibid.*

the soil: "The Sacred filtering into the world ... is the very splitting of humanity into natives and strangers" (DF 232). Autochthony which is defined in *Totality and Infinity* as being "enrooted in what one is not" all the while being "within this enrootedness" "independent and separated" (TI 143) is for Levinas what prevents us "from perceiving men outside the situation in which they are placed", i.e., as human faces "shining" in their "nudity" (DF 233). And thus "autochthony", the solitary enjoyment of an I will have to be "put in question", accused by the appeal of the Other who is a stranger and lacks the enrootedness which I took for granted. But what if it is not just me but also the Other who is "enrooted in what he is not"? What if this Other is, like me, not a stranger because he is without any roots at all, but because he is a stranger to his 'roots', indebted without knowing what the debt consists in? What if this Other is *for example*, and it is only an example, 'ethnically different' (Bernasconi's question) and what if his problem is that he finds it, like me, equally impossible to separate his alterity from this difference, or to let this difference become the Meaning of his alterity (as in any ethnic nationalism for example)? What would it mean to approach this Other 'independently' of this his predicament? Doesn't one then risk finding oneself in the position of the doctor whom Finkielkraut describes in another terrible phrase as "too occupied in filling with rice the mouth that is hungry to still listen to the mouth that is speaking"[15]? And perhaps the tragedy of Levinas who is of course right to see in the doctor "an a priori principle of human mortality" (TI 234), is that what is perhaps most important to him in this philosophy to which we owe so much, also leaves it without the means to resist becoming fatefully attracted to that humanitarian plight: "of course", we heard him say in the course of an interview with Johan Goud, who confronts him with what looks like a similar objection, "it can be difficult to see the face in all these visages that all are of a different colour. But 'to see the face' is nothing else than the possibility to speak with the black and to be his brother"[16].

But isn't there a brotherhood where the untiring willingness to speak and to address us can become a way to impose the discipline of the family on us and a refusal to recognize that there is a part of us and a history that cannot be said in that vernacular? One cannot but wonder whether Levinas's continuous insistence on the difference between the said and the saying and his repeated attempt to show that the saying, although it will always "freeze" into a said, can never be "*absorbed*" by it (OB 45 ff.) and that *like the face with the form*, the saying too keeps piercing, breaking through and breaking up

---

15. A. FINKIELKRAUT, *L'Humanité perdue. Essai sur le XXe siècle*, Paris, Seuil, 1996, p. 128.

16. Levinas in his conversation with J. Goud (cf. note 4), p. 176.

the said into which it inevitably gets paralysed, – one cannot but wonder whether this stress on the power of the saying to "un-say" (*dédire*) the said, has not rendered him totally deaf to this sort of question. And yet questions like this cannot be easily ignored. Not just by those who find themselves a bit disappointed by what Levinas has to offer them for their intellectual struggle against racism, but by anyone interested in coming to terms with this philosophy. For one does not come to terms with a philosophy by discreetly ignoring its unthought. An unthought which is, as is well-known, not outside of or *the* outside of a thought, but as it were its inner rhythm which has allowed it to take the high flight that it has. And 'unthought' may indeed be the proper term here, for it seems as if Levinas could not have even started to think, had he not been totally deaf to the sort of question to which I have been pointing. It is not just his thought, then, which has rendered him deaf to them, but it is this deafness which has given rise to this thought. And with it a said which in the way it has come to him, left him in a position where his saying, *instead of permanently undoing that said*, found itself time and again drawn to it.

Such is, no doubt, the mark of a great philosophy: a web of words where the saying of a philosopher at last has found the said that it wanted to say and then is doomed to endlessly repeat it and to outlive itself. Which is perhaps why the philosophical dialogue is not just the brotherhood of man that Levinas might wish to recognize in it, but rather the experience of a *dissociation* that has its bearings outside of philosophy as well, and for ex- ample in ethics – though not just there – since it seems to complicate that proximity which Levinas has tried to present as the ethical *par excellence*. For there is not just a proximity between me and the Other, but also a distance that refuses to become part of the ethical distance implied in proximity: there is a gap between me and the Other that we cannot cross or let work for ethics, every time our saying or his fail to come across or to reach that other side, drawn back as it were by a said which it could not completely unsay. In other words, what I am suggesting is that just like we found the face to be 'not without' form, the saying is perhaps 'not without' said. Just like there is a 'form' which is more than a form since something in it cannot be known and remains un-revealed, there seems to be also, for each of us, a said which is more than a said for we keep saying it as if by repeating it we would somehow come to know it. And when the saying of the Other confronts us with these our "last words", or when our saying con- fronts him with his, it is not certain whether that fundamental ethical conversion which Levinas presents as the elevation of man out of nature, can take place without our thus giving up our point of "gravitation" (TI 236, 239, 244) implying at the same time the loss of what is already more than nature, not just to us but also to the Other. For it is not certain whether it is only in ethics that we become a singular object *for the first time* and *if, before ethics, we would already be more than a simple* conatus essendi, *then it is not certain whether the violence of the Good is as purifying and harmless – without alienation and irritation – as Levinas suggests.* Just at it is not certain whether one can keep thinking of the ethical crisis in terms of an opposition between closedness and openness and interpret the absence of such openness as a refusal descending from the "Luciferian lie" of "Evil" claiming to be the contemporary, the equal, the twin of the Good" (CPP 138).

Perhaps "modern anti-humanism" was more right or at any rate, more sober than Levinas suggests when it refused to find "in man, lost in history and in order, the trace of this pre-historical and an-archical saying" (CPP 139) that Levinas has been trying to unearth. Perhaps it realized that a proximity which doesn't retreat before its own silence could be just as dangerous – or just as violent – as the silence of a Thrasymachus (TI 201) who stubbornly refused to give way to proximity. Perhaps it suspected that behind this philosophy which in a sense is still too confident in the sublative powers of ethics, there is a metaphysics that is too keen "to die for the invisible" (TI 35) and that lost its trust in the visible too soon. When saintliness is forced to leave its traditional place amongst the acts of supererogation and is turned into the paradigm of the ethical, a world risks crumbling and with it, the symbolical frameworks and the ethical life of institutions which are there to provide us with the *masks* that help each of us forget and anaesthetize the wounds that turn us into a singular subject not just before, but also beyond and apart from *ethical* intersubjectivity. Which means perhaps that Levinas not only seems too confident in ethics, but also – and in a different sense of ethics – not confident enough. To work out that 'different sense' implied in the question of singularity that I have been pointing to, would be to engage from a different angle in all the dimensions – phenomenological, ethical, metaphysical, religious – knotted together in the Levinasian intrigue of the infinite. It would be to untie that knot and to tie another one –not that of Being but of a still Otherwise than Otherwise than Being.

*

Otherwise than Otherwise – the labouriousness of this expression is meant to convey more than a double negation: this 'something which is not a thing' which has been haunting these pages, points toward a mè-ontology which does not need to hide behind the Good for it to defend a sense of transcendence that has perhaps been underestimated by those who would have preferred transascendence to be its only legitimate heir. The idea of a closure which is not the closing of a more primordial openness – an absurdity toward which we have found ourselves drawn from the very first pages of this book – becomes perhaps a bit more acceptable if one sees in it, instead of a denial of the Good, a defence of its true frailty. Transdescendence is not the refusal of transascendence. In these pages at least, it has been put forward as its complication. The argument from despair or the notion of the demonic ("the violent one does not leave himself") overlook this complication. As we hope to have shown, the risk in employing these strategies is that they threaten to turn what is tragic about man into a farce, where at the highest point of the drama one triumphantly uncovers what one had hidden before. But it is not blindness not to find anything underneath this cloth. It is all the gravity of our condition.

ACKNOWLEDGEMENTS

All of the chapters in this book were written with the support of the Fund for Scientific Research (Flanders). I should like to thank the Fund for the rare academic freedom this research position gave me and I am deeply obliged to the presidents of the Institute of Philosophy (K.U.Leuven), professors U. Dhondt and C. Steel, for inviting me on their staff and encouraging me to teach this material in a yearly 'Continental Philosophy'-seminar at the English section of the Institute and in a number of other lecture-courses.

Although I have benefited from the attention of many academic audiences, at home and abroad, my greatest debt is to my students and to the philosophical community at Leuven. Apart from Rudolf Bernet's, the voice of many others somehow resonates in this material: special thanks to Roland Breeur, Herman De Dijn, William Desmond, Urbain Dhondt, Sam IJsseling, Paul Moyaert, Bart Raymaekers, Ignace Verhack and Philippe Van Haute for the attention they gave to one or more of these texts and to Arnold Burms for reading all of this material in at least one version and often saving it from the paper-shredder. Finally, I should not forget to thank Jeff Bloechl and Dale Kidd for years of attempting to make the language in which I write more akin to English; and Chris Gemerchak and Vince Wargo for their editorial work. My typist, Ms. Ariane Titeca, surprised me with one more talent of hers by tending to the lay-out of this book. I am much obliged to Ms. Ingrid Lombaerts for her technical advice and to Steven Spileers and Jan Maeyaert for their advice on the index. It was a pleasure to cooperate with Ms. Maja de Keijzer at Kluwer's Humanities.

Chapters 8, 9, 10 and the Introduction are unpublished. All the other chapters have been to a greater or lesser extent revised. I gratefully acknowledge permission to reprint the following material:

Chapter 1 first appeared in *Research in Phenomenology*, 1994 (24). Published here with permission of Humanities Press, Inc., Boston MA.
Chapter 2 was first published in Dutch in *Tijdschrift voor Filosofie*, 1991 (53:3). It was subsequently reworked on the basis of an English draft by David Bowen and Greg Renner for *Research in Phenomenology*, 1991 (21). Same copyright owner as chapter 1.

Chapter 3 first appeared in *Radical Philosophy*, summer 1991 (61).

Chapter 4 first appeared in P. BURKE - J. VAN DER VEKEN (eds.), *Merleau-Ponty in Contemporary Perspectives* (Phaenomenologica 129), Dordrecht/Boston/London, Kluwer, 1993.

Chapter 5 was first published in Dutch in *Tijdschrift voor Filosofie*, 1995 (57:4). It was reworked on the basis of a translation by Dale Kidd for *Man and World*, 1996 (29), copyright Kluwer.

Chapter 6 was translated by Dale Kidd for *Epoché. A Journal for the History of Philosophy*, 1996 (2:1). Copyright by the author.

Chapter 7 was first published in the same journal, 1994 (4:2), copyright by the author.

Chapter 11 first appeared in the Proceedings of the Fifteenth Annual Symposium of The Simon Silverman Phenomenology Center, 1998.

Portions of chapter 12 and of the Conclusion go back to first English publications in *Ethical Perspectives. Journal for the European Ethics Network*, resp. 1996 (3:2) and 1997 (4:3).

I should like to thank all the editors of these first publications, and especially Bart Pattyn, editor of *Ethical Perspectives*, and Dale Kidd, for their help in making my work accessible in English. Finally, I owe a debt of gratitude to Len Lawlor and Fred Evans for releasing chapter 8 which was originally intended for a volume on Merleau-Ponty which they are editing for SUNY.

INDEX

This index is not an analytic table of contents. It is composed in view of supplying the reader with entries into the book that are not immediately evident from its table of contents. Which is why the entries for the main authors discussed in this volume are kept to a strict minimum.

Phaenomenologica

66. D. Cairns: *Conversations with Husserl and Fink*. Edited by the Husserl-Archives in Louvain. With a foreword by R.M. Zaner. 1975   ISBN 90-247-1793-0
67. G. Hoyos Vásquez: *Intentionalität als Verantwortung*. Geschichtsteleologie und Teleologie der Intentionalität bei Husserl. 1976   ISBN 90-247-1794-9
68. J. Patočka: *Le monde naturel comme problème philosophique*. 1976
                                                                    ISBN 90-247-1795-7
69. W.W. Fuchs: *Phenomenology and the Metaphysics of Presence*. An Essay in the Philosophy of Edmund Husserl. 1976   ISBN 90-247-1822-8
70. S. Cunningham: *Language and the Phenomenological Reductions of Edmund Husserl*. 1976   ISBN 90-247-1823-6
71. G.C. Moneta: *On Identity*. A Study in Genetic Phenomenology. 1976
                                                                    ISBN 90-247-1860-0
72. W. Biemel und das Husserl-Archiv zu Löwen (eds.): *Die Welt des Menschen - Die Welt der Philosophie*. Festschrift für Jan Patočka. 1976   ISBN 90-247-1899-6
73. M. Richir: *Au-delà du renversement copernicien*. La question de la phénoménologie et son fondement. 1976   ISBN 90-247-1903-8
74. H. Mongis: *Heidegger et la critique de la notion de valeur*. La destruction de la fondation métaphysique. Lettre-préface de Martin Heidegger. 1976
                                                                    ISBN 90-247-1904-6
75. J. Taminiaux: *Le regard et l'excédent*. 1977   ISBN 90-247-2028-1
76. Th. de Boer: *The Development of Husserl's Thought*. 1978
                            ISBN Hb: 90-247-2039-7; Pb: 90-247-2124-5
77. R.R. Cox: *Schutz's Theory of Relevance*. A Phenomenological Critique. 1978
                                                                    ISBN 90-247-2041-9
78. S. Strasser: *Jenseits von Sein und Zeit*. Eine Einführung in Emmanuel Levinas' Philosophie. 1978   ISBN 90-247-2068-0
79. R.T. Murphy: *Hume and Husserl*. Towards Radical Subjectivism. 1980
                                                                    ISBN 90-247-2172-5
80. H. Spiegelberg: *The Context of the Phenomenological Movement*. 1981
                                                                    ISBN 90-247-2392-2
81. J.R. Mensch: *The Question of Being in Husserl's* Logical Investigations. 1981
                                                                    ISBN 90-247-2413-9
82. J. Loscerbo: *Being and Technology*. A Study in the Philosophy of Martin Heidegger. 1981   ISBN 90-247-2411-2
83. R. Boehm: *Vom Gesichtspunkt der Phänomenologie II*. Studien zur Phänomenologie der Epoché. 1981   ISBN 90-247-2415-5
84. H. Spiegelberg and E. Avé-Lallemant (eds.): *Pfänder-Studien*. 1982
                                                                    ISBN 90-247-2490-2
85. S. Valdinoci: *Les fondements de la phénoménologie husserlienne*. 1982
                                                                    ISBN 90-247-2504-6
86. I. Yamaguchi: *Passive Synthesis und Intersubjektivität bei Edmund Husserl*. 1982
                                                                    ISBN 90-247-2505-4
87. J. Libertson: *Proximity*. Levinas, Blanchot, Bataille and Communication. 1982
                                                                    ISBN 90-247-2506-2

Phaenomenologica

88. D. Welton: *The Origins of Meaning*. A Critical Study of the Thresholds of Husserlian Phenomenology. 1983   ISBN 90-247-2618-2
89. W.R. McKenna: *Husserl's 'Introductions to Phenomenology'*. Interpretation and Critique. 1982   ISBN 90-247-2665-4
90. J.P. Miller: *Numbers in Presence and Absence*. A Study of Husserl's Philosophy of Mathematics. 1982   ISBN 90-247-2709-X
91. U. Melle: *Das Wahrnehmungsproblem und seine Verwandlung in phänomenologischer Einstellung*. Untersuchungen zu den phänomenologischen Wahrnehmungstheorien von Husserl, Gurwitsch und Merleau-Ponty. 1983

ISBN 90-247-2761-8
92. W.S. Hamrick (ed.): *Phenomenology in Practice and Theory*. Essays for Herbert Spiegelberg. 1984   ISBN 90-247-2926-2
93. H. Reiner: *Duty and Inclination*. The Fundamentals of Morality Discussed and Redefined with Special Regard to Kant and Schiller. 1983   ISBN 90-247-2818-6
94. M. J. Harney: *Intentionality, Sense and the Mind*. 1984   ISBN 90-247-2891-6
95. Kah Kyung Cho (ed.): *Philosophy and Science in Phenomenological Perspective*. 1984   ISBN 90-247-2922-X
96. A. Lingis: *Phenomenological Explanations*. 1986

ISBN Hb: 90-247-3332-4; Pb: 90-247-3333-2
97. N. Rotenstreich: *Reflection and Action*. 1985

ISBN Hb: 90-247-2969-6; Pb: 90-247-3128-3
98. J.N. Mohanty: *The Possibility of Transcendental Philosophy*. 1985

ISBN Hb: 90-247-2991-2; Pb: 90-247-3146-1
99. J.J. Kockelmans: *Heidegger on Art and Art Works*. 1985   ISBN 90-247-3102-X
100. E. Lévinas: *Collected Philosophical Papers*. 1987

ISBN Hb: 90-247-3272-7; Pb: 90-247-3395-2
101. R. Regvald: *Heidegger et le problème du néant*. 1986   ISBN 90-247-3388-X
102. J.A. Barash: *Martin Heidegger and the Problem of Historical Meaning*. 1987

ISBN 90-247-3493-2
103 J.J. Kockelmans (ed.): *Phenomenological Psychology*. The Dutch School. 1987

ISBN 90-247-3501-7
104. W.S. Hamrick: *An Existential Phenomenology of Law: Maurice Merleau-Ponty*. 1987

ISBN 90-247-3520-3
105. J.C. Sallis, G. Moneta and J. Taminiaux (eds.): *The Collegium Phaenomenologicum*. *The First Ten Years*. 1988   ISBN 90-247-3709-5
106. D. Carr: *Interpreting Husserl*. Critical and Comparative Studies. 1987.

ISBN 90-247-3505-X
107. G. Heffernan: *Isagoge in die phänomenologische Apophantik*. Eine Einführung in die phänomenologische Urteilslogik durch die Auslegung des Textes der *Formalen und transzendenten Logik* von Edmund Husserl. 1989   ISBN 90-247-3710-9
108. F. Volpi, J.-F. Mattéi, Th. Sheenan, J.-F. Courtine, J. Taminiaux, J. Sallis, D. Janicaud, A.L. Kelkel, R. Bernet, R. Brisart, K. Held, M. Haar et S. IJsseling: *Heidegger et l'idée de la phénoménologie*. 1988   ISBN 90-247-3586-6
109. C. Singevin: *Dramaturgie de l'esprit*. 1988   ISBN 90-247-3557-2

Phaenomenologica

110. J. Patočka: *Le monde naturel et le mouvement de l'existence humaine.* 1988
ISBN 90-247-3577-7
111. K.-H. Lembeck: *Gegenstand Geschichte.* Geschichtswissenschaft in Husserls Phänomenologie. 1988   ISBN 90-247-3635-8
112. J.K. Cooper-Wiele: *The Totalizing Act.* Key to Husserl's Early Philosophy. 1989
ISBN 0-7923-0077-7
113. S. Valdinoci: *Le principe d'existence.* Un devenir psychiatrique de la phéno-ménologie. 1989   ISBN 0-7923-0125-0
114. D. Lohmar: *Phänomenologie der Mathematik.* 1989   ISBN 0-7923-0187-0
115. S. IJsseling (Hrsgb.): *Husserl-Ausgabe und Husserl-Forschung.* 1990
ISBN 0-7923-0372-5
116. R. Cobb-Stevens: *Husserl and Analytic Philosophy.* 1990   ISBN 0-7923-0467-5
117. R. Klockenbusch: *Husserl und Cohn.* Widerspruch, Reflexion und Telos in Phänomenologie und Dialektik. 1989   ISBN 0-7923-0515-9
118. S. Vaitkus: *How is Society Possible?* Intersubjectivity and the Fiduciary Attitude as Problems of the Social Group in Mead, Gurwitsch, and Schutz. 1991
ISBN 0-7923-0820-4
119. C. Macann: *Presence and Coincidence.* The Transformation of Transcendental into Ontological Phenomenology. 1991   ISBN 0-7923-0923-5
120. G. Shpet: *Appearance and Sense.* Phenomenology as the Fundamental Science and Its Problems. Translated from Russian by Th. Nemeth. 1991   ISBN 0-7923-1098-5
121. B. Stevens: *L'apprentissage des signes.* Lecture de Paul Ricœur. 1991
ISBN 0-7923-1244-9
122. G. Soffer: *Husserl and the Question of Relativism.* 1991   ISBN 0-7923-1291-0
123. G. Römpp: *Husserls Phänomenologie der Intersubjektivität.* Und Ihre Bedeutung für eine Theorie intersubjektiver Objektivität und die Konzeption einer phänomeno-logischen Philosophie. 1991   ISBN 0-7923-1361-5
124. S. Strasser: *Welt im Widerspruch.* Gedanken zu einer Phänomenologie als ethischer Fundamentalphilosophie. 1991   ISBN Hb: 0-7923-1404-2; Pb: 0-7923-1551-0
125. R. P. Buckley: *Husserl, Heidegger and the Crisis of Philosophical Responsibility.* 1992   ISBN 0-7923-1633-9
126. J. G. Hart: *The Person and the Common Life.* Studies in a Husserlian Social Ethics. 1992   ISBN 0-7923-1724-6
127. P. van Tongeren, P. Sars, C. Bremmers and K. Boey (eds.): *Eros and Eris.* Contribu-tions to a Hermeneutical Phenomenology. Liber Amicorum for Adriaan Peperzak. 1992   ISBN 0-7923-1917-6
128. Nam-In Lee: *Edmund Husserls Phänomenologie der Instinkte.* 1993
ISBN 0-7923-2041-7
129. P. Burke and J. Van der Veken (eds.): *Merleau-Ponty in Contemporary Perspective.* 1993   ISBN 0-7923-2142-1
130. G. Haefliger: *Über Existenz: Die Ontologie Roman Ingardens.* 1994
ISBN 0-7923-2227-4
131. J. Lampert: *Synthesis and Backward Reference in Husserl's* Logical Investigations. 1995   ISBN 0-7923-3105-2
132. J.M. DuBois: *Judgment and Sachverhalt.* An Introduction to Adolf Reinach's Phenom-enological Realism. 1995   ISBN 0-7923-3519-8

Phaenomenologica

Previous volumes are still available

Further information about *Phenomenology* publications are available on request

Kluwer Academic Publishers – Dordrecht / Boston / London